THE TRIBES AND CASTES OF BOMBAY

THE TRIBES AND CASTES OF BOMBAY

R.E.ENTHOVEN

IN THREE VOLS.

VOLUME 3

LOW PRICE PUBLICATIONS
DELHI-110052

Published by
Low Price Publications
A-6, Nimri Commercial Centre,
Near Ashok Vihar Phase-IV,
Delhi-110052
Phones: 011-27302453
e-mail: info@Lppindia.com
url: www.Lppindia.com

First Published 1922
Reprinted in **LPP** 1997, 2008
ISBN 978-81-7536-449-3 (Set)

Printed at
D K Fine Art Press P Ltd.
Delhi-110052

PRINTED IN INDIA

TRIBES AND CASTES OF BOMBAY.

MANGAN.—A sub-division of Bháts ; a synonym for Cháran.

MANGELA.—A synonym for Máng.

MANGELAS, also known as Dhivars or Tándels, numbering 11,538 (1901), including 5,815 males and 5,723 females, are residents of the Thána district, a few families being found in the adjacent districts of Broach and Surat and in Jawhár and Surat Agency. The word Mángela is said to be derived from *mág* a fishing net, or from *mangheri* a sailing vessel. Name and origin.

The Mángelás are fishermen and coasting traders and labourers. They speak Maráthi, but indistinctly and with the use of many Gujaráti words. Thus for 'Where did you go?' they say '*Kain gela hotas,*' instead of *kothe gela hotás ;* for 'come' they say '*áilo*' instead of '*álo*' and for school *shádi* instead of *shála*.

There are no endogamous divisions of the caste. The exogamous divisions, which are identical with the surnames or *kuls*, are : Kinhi, Nijak, Dhanu, Máre, Somti, Paghar, Náik, Chodhre, Damanmere, Raut, etc. Marriage is forbidden between members of one *kul* ; it is not affected by the *devak* being the same. Divisions

Marriage with a maternal uncle's daughter, mothers' sister's daughter and father's sister's daughter is not allowed. Marriage with a wife's younger sister is allowed during her life-time or after the wife's death. Two brothers may marry two sisters. Girls are married between eight and fifteen, and boys between twenty and twenty five. If an unmarried girl commits sexual indiscretions with a man of her caste, he is compelled to marry her, though, if she be already betrothed, the intended husband has the option of marrying her. Sexual indiscretions with a man of a higher or lower caste are punished by expulsion. Polygamy is permitted, but polyandry is unknown.

The offer of marriage comes from the boy's father. The father of the boy pays to the girl's father a sum of Rs. 20 known as *dej*. The time for the celebration of marriage is sunset. A Palshe Bráhman fixes an auspicious date for the marriage and also conducts the service. The principal ceremonies in connection with marriage are *ghau bharne, medh pujne, varni nene,* marriage celebration and *varát*. Marriage ceremonies.

The *ghau bharne* ceremony consists in pounding rice and wheat in a bamboo basket, and rubbing the bride and bridegroom with turmeric paste. They then worship a post of the marriage booth, *medh pujne*. The bridegroom's father takes plantains to the bride's house and distributes them to the bride's party, *varni nene*. The bride is then taken to the bridegroom's house for the marriage celebration. The leaves of the *Ficus glomerata* and the mango are worshipped as their *devak*. Feasts given by the bride's and bridegroom's father bring the marriage ceremony to a close. The seven steps *saptapadi* ceremony is supposed to be the binding portion of the marriage.

Widow remarriage is allowed. A widow cannot marry her mother's sister's son, father's sister's son or maternal uncle's son. She may marry, if she likes, the younger brother of her deceased husband. A respectable person of the caste or the widow's parents bring about a remarriage. The months of *Jeshtha*, *Bhádrapad* and *Paush* are supposed to be inauspicious for a widow remarriage. It must take place under a mango tree. A widow remarriage is generally celebrated on a Tuesday or Sunday. The caste priest leads the bride and bridegroom to the worship of Varuna and Ganpati, and the widow's brow having been marked with red powder, the hems of their garments are tied into a knot. The last ceremony is the essential part. A bachelor wishing to marry a widow is first married to a *shami* or a *rui* tree.

Divorce is not practised. A woman charged with adultery with a man of her caste is allowed to remain in her caste after paying a fine. But when she is guilty of misconduct with a man of a higher or lower caste, she is excommunicated.

Religion. Mángelás follow the Hindu law of inheritance and belong to the Hindu religion. They worship both Shiva and Vishnu and minor deities, such as Khandoba, Bahiroba, Cheda, Narsha and Gangud. They are Smárts, and do not keep images of their gods in their houses. They sacrifice a goat for the propitiation of the minor deities in the month of *Jeshtha* on any day except Saturday and Monday. They observe all Hindu fasts and feasts. They go on pilgrimages to Pandharpur, Násik, Trimbak, Dwarka, Benares, etc. In the time of epidemics they ignite sacrificial fires and occasionally sacrifice goats and fowls. Their priests are Palshe Bráhmans.

Death ceremonies Mángelás burn their dead. Persons dying of leprosy and small-pox are buried. Small children who have not cut their teeth are also buried. The deceased is laid in the grave on his back and the head is turned towards the south. The ashes and bones of the dead are thrown into the sea. On the 10th day the son and grandson of the deceased shave their head and mustache, while the other mourners shave only the head. They keep themselves impure for ten days. On the 11th day, eleven balls of rice, one being larger than the rest, are prepared and offered to the departed spirit. Three cows known as *kin dhenu, vaitarna dhenu* and *moksha dhenu* are offered to a Bráhman. Some money is received for the first two but the third is given free. On the 12th day a ceremony known as *sapindi* is performed. On the 11th and 12th days 11 and 12 men respectively are fed. They observe the *shráddha* ceremony.

Mángelás eat the flesh of goats, sheep, fowls and fish. They drink liquor. They drink water at the hands of Kolis, Várlis and Dublás. No higher caste will receive anything at the hands of men of this caste. **Food.**

MANG GADDERU.—A sub-division of Mángs.

MANG GADIGER.—A sub-division of Mángs.

MANG GARUDI.—A sub-division of Mángs.

MANG RAUT.—A sub division of Mángs.

MANNU.—A sub-division of Ods.

MANSORORARIA.—A sub-division of Kolis.

MANWAT.—A sub-division of Holayás.

MANYAR.—*Sec* under Minor Musalmán Castes.

MAPARA,—*See* under Minor Musalmán Castes.

MARATHAS, according to the census of 1901, numbered 3,650,504. In 1911 the figures were given as 3,279,496. The statistics, however, are quite unreliable. It is difficult to secure a correct record of :— **Name and origin.**

(1) Maráthás Proper,

(2) Marátha Kunbis,

(3) Marátha allied castes.

The term Marátha, as is explained below, is used with various significations. A careful scrutiny of the details recorded at the census of 1891 and 1901 appears to justify the following rough estimate of Maráthás Proper and Marátha Kunbis for these enumerations :—

	Maráthás Proper.	Marátha Kunbis.
1891	2,122,576	2,421,611
1901	1,733,027	1,917,477

The 1911 statistics are clearly so confused as to throw no reliable light on the distribution between the upper class Marátha and the Marátha Kunbi. Marátha allied castes are dealt with under their separate names, *viz.*, Nhávi, Parit, Sutár, Teli, etc.

Three theories hold the field regarding the derivation of the term Marátha. These are briefly :—

(1) that it is derived from Maháráshtra, the name originally applied by Sanskrit writers in Northern India to the great Deccan plain ;

(2) that it is a compound of Mahá = great and Ráshtrika = either a Sanskrit form of Ratta or a term applied generally to petty chiefs ruling in the Deccan;

(3) that it is a compound of Mahá great, and Rátha a chariot rider or warrior, corresponding to the ancient Persian caste of Rathaishtar or chariot riders.

The first of these three derivations is favoured by Dr. J. F. Fleet and Dr. Bhagvánlál Indraji.(1)

History.

The earliest known mention of Maráthás is found in an inscription of about 100 B.C. over a statue in the rest chamber at the top of the Nána pass, leading from the Konkan into the north of Poona district. The term used here is *Maharáthágranikoviro* which probably means the hero leader of the Mahárátháş. In the Bedsa caves in the same locality there is a reference to a queen described as the Mahárâthini, dated in the first century A.D. Other similar references are found in the Bhája and Kárle caves. It is not easy to decide whether the terms Mahárátha and Mahárâthini indicate residents of Mahárâshtra or designate the individuals by their racial name, the early form of Marátha. The first theory is most probable, for a few centuries later we read in a Cingalese chronicle, the Mahávanso (A.D. 480), of the country of Maháráttha, and in A.D. 634 the Chinese pilgrim Hiwen Thsang (629—645) refers to the **Kingdom of Mo-ho-lo-cha**, presumably Maháráttha, and its

(1) Fleet's Kanarese Dynasties, p. 3.

warlike inhabitants.(1) In the middle of the seventh century an inscription at Aihole near Badámi in Bijápur district, the dominions of the Rattas and Chálukyas, relates how a king of the latter dynasty, Pulikeshin II, gained the sovereignty of the three Maháráshtras with their 99,000 villages. It will be seen that these references are all consistent with either the Maráthás deriving their name from Maháráshtra, or the home of the Maráthás having been styled Maháráshtra as a Sanskrit form of "the country of the Mahárátha". On the other hand, it is to be observed that, previous to any of the references described above, there is an inscription of 245 B.C. at Girnár, stating that the Emperor Asoka sent ministers of religion (*i.e.*, Buddhist priests) to the Ráshtikas, Petenikars and Aparántas. It is known that Petenikar refers to Paithan on the Godávari river, while Aparánta is the old name for the northern Konkan. Ráshtikas therefore indicates some people resident in the Deccan, possibly the Rattas. We know that a Bhoja dynasty became in time the Mahá-Bhojas. It is natural to suggest, as Sir R. G. Bhandarkar does, that the Rattas similarly became the Mahá Rattas, *i.e.*, Mahá-ráthás. In alternative, the reference may be to *Ráshtrikas*, *i.e.*, local chiefs, who bore this name in the Deccan as rulers over *ráshtras* or territorial divisions. Mr. D. R. Bhandarkar favours this theory. Between this and the first theory it is not easy to select. Both are probable. Neither is entirely convincing.

A third theory, which is plausible, though equally lacking in confirmation from contemporary evidence, is mentioned by Campbell in the account of Maráthás given in the Ratnágiri volume of the

(1) The Chinese pilgrim Hiwen Thsang (629—645) describes the kingdom or Moholocha, apparently Maháráttha or Maháráshtra, as nearly six thousand *lis* of twelve hundred miles in circuit. The capital, which was towards the west near a large river, had a circumference of thirty *lis* or six miles. Hiwen Thsang describes the people apparently the warlike Marátha tribe, as tall, boastful and proud. "Whoever does them a service" he says, "may count on their gratitude, but no one who offends them will escape their vengeance. If any one insults them, they will risk their lives to wipe out the affront. If any one in trouble applies to them, forgetful of themselves they will hasten to help him. When they have an injury to avenge they never fail to warn their enemy; after the warning each puts on his cuirass and grasps his spear. In battle they pursue fugitives but do not slay those who give themselves up. When a general has lost a battle, instead of punishing him corporally they make him wear women's clothes, and so force him to sacrifice his life. The state maintains several hundred dauntless champions, who every time they prepare for combat, make themselves drunk with wine; and then one of them, spear in hand, will defy ten thousand enemies. If they kill a man whom they meet on the road, the law does not punish them. Whenever the army goes on a campaign, these braves march in front to the sound of the drum. They also intoxicate many hundreds of naturally fierce elephants. At the time of coming to blows they drink strong liquor. They run in a body, trampling everything under their feet. No enemy can stand before them; and the king, proud of possessing these men and elephants, despises and slights the neighbouring kingdoms."

Bombay Gazetteer. It is suggested that the Maráthás took their name from the *rath* or war chariot in which they once fought, *Ráthas* being the riders in chariots (*rath*). It is interesting in this connection to note that the ancient Persians had a warrior caste known as Ratha-ishta or riders in chariots (*see* PARSI). The plains of the Deccan would be suitable country for fighting in chariots, and the Maráthás have always been a warlike people. It is quite possible that the earliest known lords of the Deccan went to battle in chariots, and thence derived their name.

About 1020 the Arab geographer Al Biruni mentions Marhat Des as a country to the south of the Narbada. In 1320 the French friar Jordanus refers to " the kingdom of Marátha " as very great. In 1340 the African traveller Ibn Batuta notices that the people of Daulatábád or Devgiri were Marháthás, whose nobles were Bráhmans. From the beginning to the end of his Deccan history (1290—1600) the historian Ferishta often mentions the Maráthás. In his account of the Musalmán Turk conquest under Alá-ud-din Khilji and his generals, Ferishta refers to the Maráthás as the people of the province of Mhárát or Mherat, dependent on Daulatábád and apparently considered to centre in Paithan or, as it is written, Mheropatan. In 1318 Harapál, the son-in-law of the Devgiri Chief, rebelled and forced the Musalmáns to give up several districts of Maráth. In 1370 Jádhav Marátha, the chief of the Náiks, revolted in Daulatábád, persuaded its Musalmán governor to join him, raised the Ráthod chief of Báglán and other local leaders, and collected a great army in Paithan. Till the end of the Bahmani supremacy (1490) some Marátha chiefs, among them the Rájás of Gálna and Báglán in Násik, were practically independent, paying no tribute for years at a time. After the close of the Bahmani supremacy (1490), under the Ahmednagar, and to a less extent under the Bijápur kings, one or two Marátha chiefs remained nearly indepenpent. Others were continued in their estates on condition of supplying troops, and others took service with their Musalmán rulers and were granted estates and the Hindu titles of Deshmukh, Sar Deshmukh, Náik, Ráo, and Rája. In several cases the daughters of leading Maráthás were raised to be the wives of Musalmán kings. Of the lower ranks of Maráthás many were employed as mercenary troops, most of them as cavalry, but some also as infantry. On one occasion (1507) the bulk of the people between Paithan and Chákan in Poona are spoken of as rebellious Maráthás.

Besides their correct name, the Maráthás are often called Bargis, word of uncertain origin. Shakespeare seems to derive it from the

Sanskrit Vargya as if it originally meant a man of a class (*varg*) or faction. Grant Duff describes it as a word of unknown origin, apparently a slang term of contempt used of the local levies by the regular foreign cavalry. In another passage Grant Duff states that all the troops officered by Maráthás were formerly called Bargis and that when he wrote (1826) in many parts of India the Maráthás were still known by that name. The following are the leading instances of the use of the term Bargi by the Musalmán historians. In the fifteenth century, according to the author of the Mirát-i-Ahmadi (1760) the Marátha chiefs of Báglán in North Násik had for generations borne the title of the Baharji or Bargi chiefs. The word Bargi is applied to the Marátha cavalry under Bijápur in 1549 and again in 1560. It is frequently applied to Telugu troops and estate holders under the Kanarese kingdom of Vijayanagar (1336—1565), and to the Bijápur troops after Bijápur (1570) had extended its power over much of the territory formerly held by Vijayanagar. In 1613 the Emperor Jahángir in his autobiography calls the Marátha skirmishers of Ahmednagar Bargiyán. In 1616 the Bargis of Ahmednagar are described as a very hardy race, and Jádhav Rái, apparently Shiváji's maternal grandfather, is called Bargi. These quotations show that the Musalmán historians applied the term Bargi both to Telugu and to Marátha cavalry. This double use of Bargi has been taken as evidence that the origin of the word is the Támil Vaduga, that is, northern, a term which in the Támil country is commonly used of the people of Telingana. It is also used of Kanarese immigrants to the Nilgiri hills, and might, with equal correctness, be used of the people of Maháráshtra.*

The Maráthás came into prominence with the rise of Shiváji Bhosle (1627—1680) whose successful rebellion against the Bijápur Kingdom founded the Marátha Empire, and led to his coronation at Ráigad as ruler of a great part of the Deccan and Konkan in 1668. He was then solemnly invested with the sacred thread as a Kshatriya, and documents were procured from Udaipur connecting the Bhosles with the Sisode Rajputs. The value of this evidence has since been disputed. Maráthás, however, continue to claim a twice born status, and to follow many of the Kshatriya practices to this day. It is clear that the fighting classes and large landowners gained considerably

---

**Bom. Gaz.*, Vol. XXIV, pp. 81—85. Bargi is, however, either a corruption of the Persian word '*bargir*' meaning a mounted soldier for whom horses and equipment are provided free in contrast to the '*Silledar*' who provides his own or else the Maráthi word *barge*, which is given in Molesw[illegible] as the equivalent of lawless or licentious, *i.e.*, a not unsuitable description of Ma[illegible]a horsemen, who were notorious plunderers.

in social precedence owing to the rise of the Marátha confederacy with its five centres at Poona, Nágpur, Indore, Gwálior and Baroda. For want of a more distinctive title these must be styled Maráthás Proper.

The word Marátha covers three classes that were probably one in origin but are now distinct. These are :—

(1) Maráthás Proper, the chiefs, landowners and fighting Maráthás of the Deccan and Konkan, claiming Kshatriya rank, eschewing widow re-marriage and socially superior to the cultivating classes, from whom, however, in places they will take girls in marriage.

(2) Marátha Kunbis or cultivators, also known as Kulvádi.

(3) Marátha occupational castes such as the following :—

1. Bhandári	7. Nhávi
2. Chitrakathi	8. Parit
3. Gavandi	9. Sutár
4. Kumbhár	10. Takar
5. Lohár	11. Táru
6. Máli	12. Teli

These would be classed as Maráthás when found in other parts of India, and have certain features of special significance in common with the first two groups.

It has already been noted that Maráthás Proper claim to be Kshatriyas, the second of the fourfold divisions of Manu. As proofs in support of this claim they state that they belong to the four ancient Kshatriya royal *vanshas* or branches, *viz.*, Suryavansha, Somavansha, Brahmavansha and Sheshavansha, that they have the ninety-six mythological Kshatriya families, or *kuls*, that many of their *kul* or family names are common clan names of Rajputs (who are supposed to be the modern representatives of the ancient Kshatriya race), that there is historical evidence to show that marriage connections were formed between royal Rajput houses and the ruling Marátha families, that like the Rajputs they observe *purdah*, wear the sacred thread and prohibit widow re-marriage, that they have bards or Bháts like Rajputs, and that, as among Rajputs, the Nhávi or barber performs the function of serving water at their feasts, although he is considered comparatively unclean by the surrounding population in the Deccan. But against the above it can be said that when a caste or a portion of a caste rises in the social scale on account of wordly prosperity, it adopts a mythological pedigree like the four *vanshas* from which the Maráthás claim descent; that, as shown later on, there is a great difference of opinion as to the names of the ninety-six *kuls* claimed by the Maráthás (in fact the number far exceeds ninety-six), that the Rajputs have formed marriage connections even with Koli and Bhil chiefs who have not the least pretensions to Kshatriya blood; and that it is the universal practice among the lower castes, when they wish to rise in the social scale, to imitate the higher by prohibiting widow marriage, wearing the sacred thread and adopting other similar customs. Admitting the similarity of clan names, this is by no means necessarily a proof of similarity of descent. The *purdah* system, the employment of family genealogists or Bháts, etc., can very easily be adopted by a caste ambitious to be classed as Kshatriyas and imitating with that view Rajput manners and customs.

The common belief in Maháráshtra regarding the origin of Maráthás is that there is little or no difference, so far as caste is concerned, between Maráthás and Kunbis. Some indeed, among whom are Maráthás themselves, are of opinion that the two classes are one and the same. The line of demarcation between the two communities is not a hard and fast one as inter-marriages between well-to-do Kunbi families and the lower sections of Maráthás are not infrequent. Such inter-marriages usually take the form of a Marátha boy being married to a Kunbi or Kulvádi girl. Such marriages are common in remote parts of the Presidency. On the other hand, Marátha girls would not be given in marriage to Kunbi boys. Thus the Maráthás Proper assert their social supremacy, and though akin to Kunbis, they must be considered distinct. Kunbis prefer the designation Marátha to that of Kunbi, as more honourable. The Kunbis however do not lay any pretensions to Kshatriya origin. They are as a rule connected with field work, while the Maráthás, though they may be mere cultivators, more often follow other avocations and regard cultivation as a secondary profession on which they may fall back if they are unsuccessful in other lines. Hence it would appear that Kunbis and Maráthás are differentiated rather by wealth and social status than by any hard and fast caste distinction. Socially the Marátha is the superior of the Kunbi, and this is evinced by the facts that while Kunbi widows remarry, Marátha widows do not, that while Marátha ladies of recognised rank observe *purdah*, Kunbi women do not observe it, and that while Marátha ladies insist on gold in preference to silver ornaments, Kunbi women are content with any that they can get.

It is not possible in these pages to deal finally with the controversy that exists regarding the origin of Maráthás Proper, and their relation to the other Marátha divisions in the Presidency. But in the course of the Survey some important evidence has been collected dealing with the social structure of Maráthás of all three classes, and indicating reasons for assuming that they had a common origin.

Devaks and balis. A reference to the articles on certain Dravidian castes in the Presidency, *e.g.*, Halepaiks, Halvakki Vakkals, Mukris, Mogers, etc., will show that their social structure is based on a survival of totemism, each exogamous group being named after some well known animal, fish, bird, tree, fruit or flower. These are known as *balis*. In the case of the three classes of Maráthás above referred to, the exogamous groups possess *devaks* or marriage guardians, which seem in origin to have been exactly the equivalent of the Kanarese *balis*. In some instances they are identical with them. The object represented by the *bali* is not only worshipped by the section named after it, but is also protected from injury according to rules laid down for the purpose. Although the *devaks* among Maráthás and the allied castes are not so highly revered, still among many of them sameness of *devak* is a bar to intermarriage, and some of the exogamous sections or *kuls* of the Maráthás are named after their *devaks, e.g.*, More after *mor* and Sálunke after *Sálunki*. The *devak* is usually some common tree such as the *Bel* (Ægle marmelos), *Pipal* (Ficus religiosa), *Vad* (banyan) or the *Shami* (Prosopis spicigera). In its commonest form it is the leaves of five trees, of which one, as the original *devak* of the section, is held specially sacred. It is worshipped specially at the time of marriage, which suggests its former close connection with marriages. It is also worshipped at the time of entering a new house, and when preparing a threshing floor at harvest time. The installation of the *devak* is an important part of the marriage ceremony in Marátha marriages. The following tables give lists of the *balis* and *devaks* that have been identified in the course of the Survey. Against the *devaks* which are common to Maráthás Proper and Marátha Kunbis are shown the names of certain castes of the Deccan in which they have also been found. These are by no means exhaustive, that is to say, these other castes possess many *devaks*, not yet recorded, besides those against which they have been shown.

List of devaks *found among Maráthás Proper and Marátha Kunbis with other castes from which reported.*

1	2	3
(1) Aghháda	.. Achyranthes aspera.	
(2) Amba	.. Mango	.. Bhoi. Chitrakathi. Mahár. Nhávi. Gondhali. Parit. Sutár. Gábit. Otári, Rával.
(3) Anjana	.. Hardwickia binata	.. Teli. Kumbhar.
(4) Apta	.. Bauhinia racemosa	.. Bhoi. Teli.
(5) Arai	.. Mimosa rubricaulis	.. Bhoi. Pinjári.
(6) Aráti	.. Mimosa hamata	.. Bhoi. Mahár.
(6a) Avala	.. Phyllanthus emblica	.. Támbat.
(7) Bábul or Dhamak	.. Acacia arabica	.. Mahár. Bhoi.
(7a) Beheda	.. Terminalia belerica	.. Támbat. Machhi.
(8) Bel	.. Ægle marmelos	.. Mahár. Machhi. Phudgi.
(9) Bhárdavájácha pankh	Crow pheasant's wing.	
(10) Bor or Boráti	.. Zizyphus jujuba	.. Bhoi. Mahár. Otári. Pinjári.
(11) Chat	.. Spinning wheel whirler	.. Holaya.
(12) Chinch	.. Tamarind	.. Parit.
(13) Davana	.. Artemesia phalleris.	
(14) Devnal	.. Phragmitis communis	.. Máli.
(15) Dive (tinshesáth)	.. 360 Lights.	
(15a) Dukar	.. Pig	.. Burud.
(16) Garudácha pankh	.. Eagle's wing	.. Chámbhár.
(17) Garud vel or gul vel.	Tinospora cordifolia	.. Nhávi.
(18) Ghoda	.. Horse	.. Nhávi.
(19) Halad	.. Turmeric	.. Nhávi.
(20) Harina	.. Mouse deer	.. Mahár.
(21) Haryáli or Arkhe	.. Cynodon dactylon	.. Chámbhár. Kharde Váni.
(22) Hastidant	.. Ivory.	
(22a) Hivar	.. Acacia leucophlœa	.. Ahir. Kumbhár.
(23) Jámbhul	.. Eugenia jambolana	.. Bhámta. Bhoi. Dhor Sutár.
(24) Jowári	.. Sorghum vulgare	.. Bhámta. Parit.

1	2	3
(25) Kadamb or Kalamb	.. Anthocephalus cadamba	.. Bhandári. Rámoshi. Chámbhár. Nhávi. Váni. Parit. Sutár. Teli. Takar.
(26) Kamal	.. Lotus	.. Dhangar.
(27) Kándyánchi Mál	.. A garland of onions.	
(28) Kásav	.. Tortoise	.. Mahár.
(29) Ketak or Kegad	.. Screw pine. Pandanus odoratissimus.	
(29a) Khair	.. Acacia catechu	.. Burud.
(30) Knife	.. ....	.. Bhámta. Chitrakathi.
(31) Kocha	.. Turmeric bulb	.. Sutár. Kumbhár. Váni.
32) Kohala	.. Pumpkin	.. Chitrakathi. Bhil.
(33) Koya	.. A bird. Cacomantis passerinus.	Chámbhár.
(34) Kumbhár Kukde	.. Crow pheasant.	
(35) Kunda	.. Andropogon intermedius.	Máli.
(36) Kurhád	.. Axe	.. Bhámta. Bhoi. Holaya. Dhor. Parit. Sutár. Nhávi. Vaidu.
(37) Mandaráche phul	.. Flowers of the Rui tree.	
(38) Maryádvel	.. Ipomœa biloba	.. Táru. Dhor. Máli.
(39) Mhas	.. Buffalo	.. Mahár.
(40) Mor Moráche pis	.. Peacock & feathers	.. Bhoi. Táru. Chitrakathi. Mahár. Chámbhár. Bhil. Máli. Burud.
(41) Nág	.. Cobra	.. Mahár. Váni. Parit.
(42) Nágchámpa	.. Mesua ferrea	.. Mahár. Parit. Sutár.
(43) Nágvel or Támbul	.. Piper betel	.. Mahár. Vanjári.
(44) Nandruk	.. Ficus retusa	.. Mahár.
(45) Náral	.. Cocoanut	.. Bhámta.
(46) Nim	.. Melia azadirachta	.. Nhávi. Kharote. Váni.
(47) Nirgundi	.. Vitex negundo.	
(48) Pair	.. Ficus rumphii	.. Támbat.
(49) Pála	.. Ehretia buxifolia	.. Chitrakathi.
(50) Palas	.. Butea frondosa	.. Gondhali. Shimpi. Sutár. Gábit.
(51) Pánch pálvi	.. Leaves of five trees	.. All castes that have *devak.*
(52) Pangára	.. Erythrina indica	.. Gábit.

	2	3
(53) Pánkanis	.. Reed Mace Typha angustata.	Mahár Rámoshi. Nhávi. Máli.
(54) Paratinicha pankh	.. Pied wagtail's wing.	
(55) Phanas	.. Jack fruit. Artocarpus integrifolia	Nhávi.
(56) Pipal	.. Ficus religiosa	.. Bhandári. Bhil. Gábit Nhávi. Machhi. Burud.
(57) Pipri	.. Ficus tsiela	.. Bágdi.
(58) Pithiche bávle	.. A doll made of flour.	Mahár.
(59) Rájahansa	.. Swan or Goose	.. Chámbhár.
(60) Ruchkin	.. Calotropis gigantea (?)	.. Bhoi. Mahár.
(61) Rudrákshánchi Mál	.. Elœoccarpus ganitrus	.. Mahár,
(62) Rui	.. Calotropis gigantea	.. Gondhali. Otári. Rával Burud.
(62a) Sag	.. Tectona grandis	.. Nhávi. Shimpi.
(63) Sálunkicha pankh	.. Wing of a bird, gracula religiosa.	Chitrakathi. Máli. Vanjári.
(64) Sávar	.. Bombax malabaricum	.. Takar.
(65) Shami	.. Prosopis spicigera	.. Chitrakathi. Gondhali. Otári. Machhi. Rával.
(66) Shankh	.. Conch Shell.	
(67) Sheli	.. Goat.	
(68) Shishechi gol	.. A leaden ball.	
(69) Sone	.. Gold	.. Thákur.
(70) Súrvad	.. Rosha grass. Andropogon schenanthus.	
(71) Surya phul	.. Sunflower	.. Táru. Takar. Nhávi. Parit Mahár. Holaya. Parit. Thákur. Dhangar. Máli.
(72) Tad	.. Palm tree. Borassus flabellifer.	.. Mahár. Bhil.
(73) Támba	.. Copper	.. Mahár.
(73a) Tarvad	.. Cassia auriculata	.. Burud.
(74) Tarvárichi dhár	.. Sword blade	.. Nhávi. Thákur.
(75) Umbar	.. Ficus glomerata	.. Bhandári. Mahár. Chámbhár. Nhávi. Dhor. Takar. Gábit. Machhi. Váni.
(76) Unta Kantari	.. Globe thistle Echinops Bhoi. Echinatus.	
(77) Vad	.. Ficus bengalensis	.. Bhandári. Mahár. Chámbhár. Burud. Nhávi. Takar. Gábit. Otári. Phudgi.
(78) Vásanvel	.. Cocculus villosus	.. Chámbhár. Teli. Máli Rámoshi.
(79) Velu	.. Bamboo	.. Nhávi.
(80) Vet	.. Cane.	

List of balis *found among Kanarese castes with the castes from which reported.*

1	2	3
(1) Ajjana	.. Upas tree. Antiaris toxicaria.	Ager, Gám-Vakkal, Halepaik Halvakki Vakkal, Kumbhár, Moger, Nádor, Sappalig.
(2) Ammana	.. ....	Uppár.
(3) Ane	.. Elephant	.. Agig, Ambig, Gám-Vakkal, Halepáik, Haslár, Kumbhár, Moger, Mukri, Nádor.
(4) Ala	.. Banyan. Ficus bengalensis.	Gám-Vakkal, Halvakki Vakkal.
(5) Arashina	.. Turmeric	.. Gám-Vakkal, Halepaik, Kare-Vakkal, Moger.
(6) Argal	..	Halvakki Vakkal.
(7) Baler	.. Plantain	.. Halvakki Vakkal, Moger.
(8) Balina, bale	.. A fish	.. Halvakki Vakkal, Moger.
(9) Bangar	.. Gold	.. Halepaik, Moger.
(10) Bargal	.. Hog deer	.. Halvakki Vakkal, Moger.
(11) Betta	.. Cane	.. Gám-Vakkal, Halepaik, Halvakki Vakkal, Moger.
(12) Bhatta duddi	.. ....	.. Desh Bhandári.
(13) Bhairana	.. ....	.. Halepaik, Halvakki Vakkal.
(14) Chendi	.. Cerbera odollum	.. Gám-Vakkal, Halepaik, Halvakki Vakkal, Harkantra, Kare Vakkal, Kumbhár, Moger.
(15) Chinna	.. Grewia umbellifera	.. Halepaik, Halvakki Vakkal, Moger.
(16) Depnig	..	Shilangi.
(17) Devana	.. Artemesia phalleris	.. Halepaik, Halvakki Vakkal Gám-Vakkal, Moger.
(18) Devatar. Devdari ? ..	Cedrela tuna	.. Gám-Vakkal, Halepaik, Kumbhár, Sappalig.
(19) Devi	.. ....	.. Ambig, Halepaik, Halvkki Vakkal, Moger, Mukri.
(20) Dyavana	.. Tortoise	.. Ager, Gám-Vakkal, Halepaik, Halvakki Vakkal, Moger, Mukri, Sappalig, Uppár.
(21) Ekramati	.. ....	.. Gám Vakkal.
(22) Gurumargi. Gudmurki.	Dolichandrone falcata	.. Desh Bhandári.

1	2	3
(23) Ganga	.. The Gangávali river.	.. Amber, Halepaik, Moger, Nádor, Sappalig (Devdig), Uppár.
(24) Gangadhar	....	.. Moger.
(25) Godkan	.. *See* 46 ?	.. Halvakki Vakkal.
(26) Guravina Gorvi	.. Iohnocarpus frutescens	.. Ager, Halepaik, Halvakki Vakkal, Moger.
(27) Hálu	.. Chonemorpha malabarica	Moger.
(28) Handi	.. Pig	.. Halepaik, Moger, Mukri.
(29) Hebbal, Hebbalsina	.. Artocarpus hirsuta	.. Mukri, Moger.
(30) Hire	.. Luffa acuntangula	.. Gám-Vakkal.
(31) Hole	.. ....	.. Halepaik, Halvakki Vakkal
(32) Hongar	.. Erythrea indica	.. Moger, Nádor.
(33) Honna	.. Calophyllum inophyllum.	Haslár.
(34) Honne	.. Pterocarpus marsupium.	Gám-Vakkal, Halepaik., Kare Vakkal, Moger. Nádor, Sappalig (Devdig).
(35) Hulyana or Huli	.. Phyllanthus reticulatus	.. Moger.
(36) Jertin	.. ....	.. Kare Vakkal, Moger.
(37) Jetti	.. ....	.. Moger.
(38) Kambli, Kumbal	.. *See* 46	.. Desh Bhandári.
(39) Kadvina	.. Elk	.. Halvakki Vakkal, Moger, Mukri.
(40) Kane	.. Kadamb, Stephegyne parvifolia	.. Gám-Vakkal, Halvakki Vakkal.
(41) Kanne	.. A virgin ?	.. Halepaik, Harkantra, Moger Mukri.
(42) Kavdechi	.. Acacia speciosa or Godachi, Zizyhus xylopyra ?	Moger, Mukri.
(43) Kedagi	.. Screwpine, Pandanus odoratissimus.	Halvakki Vakkal, Moger.
(44) Kendi Kand ?	.. Prosopis spicigera ?	.. Halepaik, Moger.
(45) Kodchan or Kodsan	.. Mappia oblonga	.. Halvakki Vakkal.
(46) Kodkal	.. Monkey	.. Halvakki Vakkal.
(47) Kodkan	.. Gnetum scandens	.. Halvakki Vakkal, Moger.
(48) Kojjale	.. ....	.. Kare Vakkal.
(49) Kugal Kuggini ?	.. Ipomœa campanulata	.. Gám-Vakkal, Halvakki Vakkal.

1	2	3
(50) Kunte Kunti ?	.. Murraya exotica ?	.. Halvakki Vakkal.
(51) Macholi	.. Axe	.. Halvakki Vakkal.
(52) Mahár. Mhád ?	.. Palm tree. Caryota urens. ?	Halepaik.
(53) Majkal	.. ....	.. Halvakki Vakkal.
(54) Majkin	.. ....	.. Shilangi.
(55) Manal	.. ....	.. Halepaik Halvakki Vakkal.
(56) Manjal	.. ....	.. Halvakki Vakkal, Moger.
(57) Manjana	.. ....	.. Halvakki Vakkal, Moger.
(58) Mandri	.. ....	.. Desh Bhandári.
(59) Megan	.. Chital ?	.. Halvakki Vakkal, Kare Vakkal, Moger, Mukri.
(60) Miggi	.. ....	.. Halvakki Vakkal.
(61) Muskin	.. ....	.. Halvakki Vakkal.
(62) Nág	.. Cobra	.. Halepaik, Halvakki Vakkal, Moger.
(63) Nágchámpa	.. Mesua ferrea	.. Moger.
(64) Neralu	.. Jámbal. Eugenia jambolana.	.. Gám-Vakkal.
(65) Putte	.. White ant heap	.. Ambig.
(66) Salyan	.. Porcupine	.. Halepaik, Nádor. Sappaling (Devdig).
(67) Sarpan	.. A snake	.. Halepaik, Mukri.
(68) Saryan	..	
(69) Shalya	.. Porcupine	.. Halvakki Vakkal, Moger.
(70) Shendi	.. Toddy palm. Phoenix sylvestris.	.. Moger, Haslár.
(71) Shetti	.. A fish ?	.. Ambig, Gám-Vakkal, Halepaik, Kare Vakkal, Kumbhár, Moger, Mukri, Nádor, Sappling (Devdig), Uppár.
(72) Shige	.. Soapnut. Acacia concinna	Gám-Vakkal, Halepaik, Halvakki Vakkal, Kannada Madeval, Moger. Nádor.
(73) Shire	.. Gynandropsis pentaphylla	.. Ager, Gám-Vakkal, Halepaik, Halvakki Vakkal, Kare Vakkal, Kumbhár, Moger, Mukri, Nádor, Sapplig (Devdig).

1	2	3
(74) Shivin or Shivana	.. Gmelina asiatica	.. Gám Vakkal, Halepaik, Moger.
(75) Shiv-matan	.. ....	.. Desh Bhandári.
(76) Tolana	.. Wolf	.. Devdig, Halepaik, Harkantra, Mukri, Nádor Sappaling, Uppár.
(77) Tatti	..	.. Gám Vákkal.
(78) Ugri	.. Argyreia pilosa	.. Gám Vakkal.
(79) Vadkan	.	.. Kare Vakkal, Moger.
(80) Vajra	.. Myrabolam	.. Gám Vakkal.
(81) Vali	.. A creeper	.. Halepaik, Moger.
(82) Varle	.. White ant heap	.. Kumbhár.

It has not yet been possible to find the English equivalents of many of these *bali* names. They are mostly the names of trees or creepers common in Kanara and Mysore. It is noticeable that the following are found among both the *devaks* and the *balis* :—

1. The screwpine.
2. The Jámbhul tree.
3. The banyan tree.
4. The hog or mouse deer.
5. The axe.
6. Gold.
7. The tortoise.
8. The cane.
9. Turmeric.
10. The Nágchampa tree.
11. The cobra.
12. The pig.

The *Rui* and the *Shami*, which are so common in the Deccan, but are not commonly met with in Kanara, do not appear among the *balis*. It is specially significant that the Kanarese castes do not possess the composite totem or leaves of five trees known in the Deccan as the Pánchpálvi. It is a common process of evolution for tribes and castes to rise in the social scale by discarding totemistic divisions for *kuls* or family stocks, which are later replaced by the Brahmanic *gotra.*(1) With the Maráthás the process seems to have passed through a stage where the *devak* became a combination of five separate *devaks*, and is known as *pánch pálvi* (*vide* List No. 51). These are worshipped very much as the *vansh* or images of five ancestors are worshipped in remote parts of the Presidency to the present day. Finally the *kul* or family stock took the place of the totemistic division ; but the

(1) Compare Risley, Tribes and Castes of Bengal, pp. XLII *et seq.* where it is shown that totems are succeeded by eponymous divisions, *i.e., kuls* and that these in time gave place to divisions based on *gotras*.

sanctity of the totem either individually or in the fivefold form has been generally preserved. It is clear that the *devak* is a survival. It may therefore be held to be a valuable indication of racial origin.

Appearance. Most Maráthás are middle sized, regular-featured and well made; a few are handsome and warlike. But except that they are fairer and better mannered, they cannot be distinguished from Kunbis. The women are often fairer and slenderer than Kunbi women.

Dress and ornaments. The men cut the hair of the head close and wear moustaches and whiskers, but not beards. Some keep the topknot and earknots and shave the rest of the head, leaving a clean shaven passage between the knots, gradually narrowing from the brow to the centre and again growing wider till it reaches the back of the head above the neck. In many heads this passage is wholly or partly blocked by the bunch of hair on the crown of the head. The women dress their hair with much care, either tying it in a back knot or *buchada* or plaiting it in a braid which they wear in an open circle at the back of the head. They use false hair and are fond of decking their hair with flowers. The men dress in a turban, a coat, a shoulder cloth and a waistcloth, trousers or short drawers called *cholnás*. Instead of the turban they often wear a headscarf called *rumál* of about three to four yards or a *patka* of ten to fifteen yards length. The Marátha coat fits very closely, especially the arms and chest. The sleeves are generally longer than the arms, the extra forming numberless small plaits or folds over the lower arm between the elbow and the wrist. The coat is tied in front below the right shoulder and in the centre of the chest, part of the right chest being left open, especially by those who pride themselves on their depth of chest. From the chest the coat falls in long full folds to the knee and sometimes a few inches below the knee. A Maráthá's holiday coat is of silk or cloth of gold. It is not so tight as the every-day white coat, and sleeves have fewer puckers. Maráthás have begun to wear English-shaped coats, shirts, jackets, and boots. The Marátha waistcloth is shorter than the Bráhman waistcloth and the puckers in front and behind are fewer, the ends hanging and fluttering loose. The Marátha shoe, which is finely decorated with silk and gold borders, is stained a deep red and differs from the Bráhman shoe by leaving open the whole except the toes and an inch of the upper part of the foot, and having its small round heel as hard as stone. Formerly a sword was part of the regular Marátha dress. Now a walking stick has taken the place of the sword. They also draw a shawl over their shoulders when they attend the court or *darbár*.

Except that they do not pass the skirt back between the feet and that they draw one end of the robe over the head, Marátha women wear the same indoor dress as Bráhman women. They mark their brows with vermilion and tattoo a small crescent or *chandra* between the eyebrows, and a small dot on the chin and on each cheek, and figures of *Tulsi* and lotuses representing the goddess Lakshmi, the words *Shrirám Jayrám* in *Bálbodh*, and pictures of Krishna and his beloved Rádha on their forearms.

Language. The home tongue of Maráthás is Maráthi, which they speak almost as correctly as Bráhmans. The names in common use among men of good class are Chandraráo, Jánojiráo, Mánájiráo, Pratápráo, Sambháji, Santáji, Sayáji, Shiváji, Suryáji, Udáji, etc., and among women Ambábái, Báyajábái, Chimnábái, Hansábái, Jamnábái, Jijábái, Lálubái, Pritábái, Rájasbái, Revubái, Sakvárbái, Soyarábái, etc. Many men affect Rajput names such as Jasising, Rámsing, Fattesing, etc.

Divisions. Maráthás proper have three divisions. They consist of three social groups, (1) Assal or Kulin, that is, pure, (2) Lenkávale, Shinde or Kharchi, that is, illegitimates, and (3) mixed Maráthás, who go by no particular name. The first are those who can trace their descent to some ancient respectable family, who have not spoilt their purity by connections with any but such families, who prohibit widow marriage, wear the sacred thread and observe the *purdah*. The Lenkávales are the illegitimate offspring born of Marátha parents, while the mixed Maráthás consist of the progeny of a Marátha father and a woman of another caste or *vice versa*. These latter are known as Akarmáse in some places, but an Akarmáse or bastard division is to be found in many castes, and so an Akarmáse does not necessarily denote a bastard born of a Marátha parent. The Assal Maráthás are very particular in forming marriage connections with Assal Marátha families only. The Lenkávales and Akarmáses marry with one another, and may take brides from the Akarmáse divisions of other castes as well. They closely resemble Marátha Kunbis in their ceremonies and customs. The Assal Maráthás differ from them in some details. This article deals with them only.

Assal Maráthás claim to belong to four main branches or *vanshas* each containing twenty-four *kuls* or families. They are :—

(1) Brahmavansha or the Brahma branch.

(2) Sheshavansha or the Serpent branch.

(3) Somavansha or the Moon branch.

(4) Suryavansha or the Sun branch.

This classification has evidently been adopted from the mythological divisions of the Kshatriya race in support of their claim to Kshatriya origin. But it has not been found possible to assign definitely to each branch the twenty-four families attributed to it, neither are the names of the ninety-six families or *kuls* the same in all places. In fact, if all the names of the ninety-six *kuls* are compiled in one list, the total far exceeds ninety-six and many of the names disclose identity with the Kunbis, whom the aristocratic Maráthás consider to be distinct from them.

A list of the ninety-six *kuls* taken from a Maráthi pamphlet called *Kshátravansh ságar*, published by a Marátha of high birth, is given below with the *devaks** of each given against the name of each, where known :—

Ahirráo or Ráo ..	25, 75.
Angre ..	51.
Bábar ..	75 or 79.
Bhágvat ..	51.
Bhálerráo ..	Unknown.
Bhise ..	
Bhoite ..	51.
Bhosle or Sisode ..	51.
Bhováre ..	Unknown.
Chálke ..	66 or 75.
Chinge ..	Unknown.
Dabháde ..	25.
Dalvi ..	1.
Daphale ..	Unknown.
Darekar ..	
Devmáne ..	
Devráo. ..	
Dhamdhere ..	
Dhavle ..	19, 25, 69.
Dháyavar ..	40.
Dhone ..	74.
Dhuap ..	
Dhulmál ..	19 or 29.
Gáikvád ..	51.
Gálád ..	Unknown.
Gauli ..	
Gavene ..	19, 25, 69.

* These are shown by numbers in the list of *devaks* given above.

Ghátge .. .. 51.
Ghorpade or Bhosle .. 62.
Gole .. .. Unknown.
Gujar or Pavár .. 25, 74.
Harphale .. ..
Hirve .. ..
Ichára .. .. } Unknown.
Ingale .. .. 26.
Jagdále .. .. 25 or 29.
Jádhav .. .. 75.
Jagdhane .. .. Unknown.
Jagtáp .. .. 25, 56, 75.
Jávle .. .. Unknown.
Kadam .. .. 19, 29, 69.
Kákade .. .. Unknown.
Kále .. .. 19, 25, 29, 69.
Kánade .. ..
Kesarkar .. .. } Unknown.
Khadtare .. .. 75.
Khandágle or Ráthod .. 38 or 66.
Khándekar .. .. Unknown.
Khánvilkar or Ráne .. 71.
Kharate .. .. Unknown.
Kokáte .. .. 66.
Kshiraságar .. .. 51.
Mahádik or Hande .. 56.
Mahipál .. .. Unknown.
Malke .. .. 71.
Málusare .. .. 51.
Máne .. .. 16 or 17.
Mánkar .. ..
Mhávar .. .. } Unknown.
Mohite or Chaván .. 19, 62, 69, 78.
More .. .. 15 or 40
Nalavde, Náikváde or Nánekar. 42.
Nimbálkar .. ..
Nisál .. .. 75 or 79.
Pánsare .. .. 19, 25 or 69.
Pátankar .. .. Unknown.

Páthare	..	.. 75.
Phadtare	..	.. 19, 25, 29, 69.
Phálke	..	.. Unknown.
Pingle	..	.. Unknown.
Pisál	..	.. Unknown.
Rájmáne	..	.. Unknown.
Rannavare	..	.. Unknown.
Rasál	..	.. 51.
Ráut	..	.. 51.
Renuse	..	.. 74.
Sálunkhe	..	.. 26 or 63.
Sámbáre	..	.. 19, 25 or 69.
Sávant	..	.. 26 or 61.
Shankhpál	..	.. 66.
Shelár	..	.. 26.
Shelke	..	.. Unknown.
Shinde	..	.. 1.
Shirke or Tuvar		.. 75.
Shitole	..	.. Unknown.
Suryavanshi, Sur or Surve.		51.
Tavse	..	.. 19, 62, 69, 78.
Teje	..	. 19, 25, 69.
Tekle	..	.. Unknown.
Thorát	..	.. Unknown.
Thote	..	.. Unknown.
Vágh	..	.. Unknown.
Válke	..	.. Unknown.
Visáte	..	.. Unknown.
Yádav	..	.. 75.

According to the publisher of this book, which is not authenticated by any historical evidence, a king of the Lunar race, by name Somasharma, had six sons, Chaván, More, Iavár, Ráshtrakunda, Dhámapála and Anaga (or Ahir Jádhav) each of whom founded a group of families and became the eponymous hero of a family within the group. Thus, Chaván founded a group consisting of the fifteen families named Bhávkar, Chaván, Dalapate, Dhadam, Dure, Gavháne, Khádekar. Kalbhar, Lád, Mohite, Randive, Takare, Támbe, Vákade and Várange. These families have certain symbols and rites in common, and marriages are decided upon after a consideration of the *gotra* group connection. Again, another king of Solar race had seven sons Dhitak, Kadam, Kálamukhi, Nikam, Pratihár, Prokat and Shelár, of whom the first six also founded similiar family groups, Prokat being lumped in with

Pratihár and having no separate group of his name. The numbers assigned to these two groups vary, but the total comes to over two hundred families. But this is not all. Mr. Pátankar (the publisher of the book) next proceeds to exhibit the ramifications of the Brahmavansha and Sheshavansha stems, and in this way adds about hundred families more. The leading branch of the former stem he makes the Chálukya, now represented by the Dubal, Indalkar, Ingale, Ingamale, Phadtare, Pisál, Rannavare, Sálunkhe and Sávant and other families. To the Brahmavansha stem are also assigned Bhoite, Dábháde, Damále, Devkar, Garud, Gauli, Ghorpade, Gujar, Káte, Máne, Nalavde, Ráutráo, Sitole and others, to the Sheshavansha are assigned Dhone, Dhumále, Jagtáp, Kadu, Kathar, Khaláte, Lád, Nágtilke, Shelamkar, Shelke, Shinde, Upáse and others. Whatever the value of this enumeration, it would seem to be seriously discounted by the fact of the author giving a list of the ninety-six *kuls*, at the close of which he mentions casually yet another method of division, that by *Sapta kuls* or family groups of seven. He names the components of the chief *Sapta kuls* as follows :—

(1) Ahirráo *alias* Ráo.

(2) Bhosle *alias* Sisode. (1)

(3) Gujar *alias* Pavár.

(4) Khánvelkar *alias* Hande.

(5) Mohite *alias* Chaván.

(7) Shirke *alias* Tuwar.

He gives no explanation to account for the aliases, nor does he seek to reconcile these ninety-six traditional *kuls* with the two hundred families which he himself has deduced from the Lunar and Solar Kings, or with those of the two other stems.

Other authorities state that not only are there *Sapta Kuls* but also *Panch Kuls* and that the groups of seven may even be extended to eight. According to them the basis of grouping is intermarriage and (in the case of the true *Sapta Kuls*) an alleged descent from Kshatriya ancestors.

The list of the ninety-six *Kuls* as given by Mr. Pátankar differs considerably from those obtained from other sources. For instance,

---

(1) The attempt made here to connect the Bhosle family with the Sisode Rajputs of Udaipur is in accordance with claims advanced by Sivaji. But the avidence on which the claim rests is not convincing. The whole of this lists of *Sapta Kuls* may be taken as a mere attempt to show a Rajput origin for certain Marátha families.

one list does not give the following names included in Mr. Pátankar's list :—

Chinage.	Mahipál.
Daphale.	Mánkar.
Devráo.	Mhávar.
Dhamdhere.	Mise.
Dhulap.	Nimbálkar.
Gátád.	Pátankar.
Gauli.	Rájmáne.
Gole.	Rananavare.
Hirve.	Shelke.
Ichháre.	Shetake.
Jávale.	Tavase.
Kánade.	Tekale.
Kesarkar.	Vágh.
Khándekar.	Válke.
Kharáte.	Visáte.

On the other hand, the following names in the list referred to above are not in Mr. Pátankar's list :—

Angane.	Málap.
Bágwe.	Nikam.
Bhogale.	Pálande.
Darbáre.	Palve.
Dewkante.	Pándhare.
Dhavale.	Parate.
Dhenkane.	Phánkade.
Dude.	Phátak.
Gángnáik.	Sálav.
Gavase.	Tavade.
Ghumál.	Thákur.
Khair.	Turvar.
Lád.	Wághale.
Madhure.	Vande.

Also Mr. Pátankar gives Gujar as the alias of Pavár, Ráo as that of Ahirráo, Hande of Mahádik, Bhosle of Sisode, Tuvar of Shirke, Chaván of Mohite and Ráne of Khánvelkar. Lastly, it is curious to note that Nikam, one of the names in the list referred to above, omitted by Mr. Pátankar, is the name assigned by him previously to one of the sons of the Solar King. Similarly, Lád is connected by him with the Chaván group, but omitted from the list of ninety-six *kuls*. Darbáre is connected with the More group, Dhavale and Sálve with the Pavár, and Phátak with the Kálamukhi group. But these do not occur in his list of the ninety-six *kuls*.

The above remarks are made by way of showing that the claim of the Maráthás to belong to the ancient ninety-six families of the Kshatriya race has no foundation in fact, but must have been advanced after they rose to power. Enquiries conducted on this point show that there are at present only fifty-four families of pure or Assal Maráthás, which are as follows :—

Ahır.	Ingale.*
Angane.*	Jagdále.
Bábar.	Jagtáp.
Bágne.	Kadam.
Bagráo.	Kále.
Bhogale.*	Kánkade.
Bhoite.	Khair.*
Bhonsle.	Lád.
Chaván.	Málap.*
Chálukya (Chálke).	Máne.
Dábháde.	Mahádik.
Dalvi.	Mohite.
Dhamále.	More.
Dháyabar.	Nalavde.
Dhekane.*	Nikam.*
Gavane.*	Pálande.*
Ghátge.	Pándhare.*
Ghorpade.	Pánsare.*
Hande.	Pavár.
Phadtare.	Sankhapál.
Phálke.	Shinde.
Pingle.	Shirke.
Pisál.	Shitole.
Ráne.	Surve.
Renuse.*	Thorát.
Ráut.	Yádav.
Sávant.	

Some of these again, being tainted by the presence of Kunbi representatives, have been marked with asterisks.

Maráthás have numerous surnames, the chief of which are as follows :— Surnames.

A'dkáre, A'dsul, A'gláve, Ahererav, Alpáte, Antrále, Anvále, A'rchale, A'sve, Avalkar, Avtáde, Bábar, Bád, Badad, Bádal, Bágal,

Bakar, Bande, Barage, Barangule, Bate, Bavchikar, Bavdhankar, Bávle, Bedge, Belánde, Bhádirge, Bhagat,Bhákad, Bháme, Bhápkar, Bhátmáre, Bhiláre, Bhingári, Bhiungde, Bhuikar, Bhogay, Bhoite, Bhoj, Bhonsle, Bhor, Bhujbal, Bhujvar, Bieháre, Bichukle, Binikar, Birámne, Bitle, Bode, Bogar, Bokde, Boráde, Bote, Burse; Chálkhe, Chapte, Chaudhare, Chávat, Chavhán, Chende, Chhatre, Chikhle, Chitruk; Dábháde, Dádhmode, Dáingde, Dalvi, Damde, Dandvate, Daphle, Dasále, Dengde, Devkar, Dhave, Dháigunde, Dhamdhere, Dhanavde, Dhapupse, Dhátav, Dhaugde, Dhemre, Dhenkne, Dhere, Dhopre, Dhulap, Dhumál, Dinde, Divthankar, Dodphade, Dongre, Dubal, Dumbre; Gáikvád, Gájre, Garad, Garje, Gavas, Gavli, Gavsekar, Gele, Ghadshi, Gháil, Ghárge, Ghátge,Ghodke, Gholap, Ghongáne, Ghonge, Ghorpade, Ghugre, Ghule, Ghure, Ghutugde, Gidde, Gije, Gojáre, Gore, Gujál, Gujar, Gunjál; Hagvane, Hajáre, Hánde, Himme, Hinge, Hitápe, Hotále; Ichu, Igrálkar, Indulkar, Ingle, Ingvale, Ipáre; Jádhav, Jagdale, Jagtáp, Jamdáde, Jamedár, Jartare, Jatapate, Jhámbre, Jinjurte, Jitvadekar, Joshi, Jugdár, Juvekar; Kabáde, Kachre, Kadam, Kákde, Kále, Kámble, Kámekar, Kamte, Kándar, Kándvi, Kank, Kánsare, Kanse, Karle, Karpe, Karvalkar, Káshid, Káte, Káthkar, Káthvate, Kavde, Kembde, Kesarkar, Kesre, Khabkar, Kháde, Khair, Khákre, Khale, Khálvate, Khandágle, Khándekar, Khánvilkar, Kharáde, Khardekar, Khare, Khedar, Khirságar, Khodke, Khokde, Khole, Khopkar, Khule, Kirát, Kirdatta, Kirtekar, Kodag, Kodge, Kokáte, Kolse, Kolte, Kore; Lád, Lagháte, Lágvankar,Lahre, Lakde, Lánde, Lándge, Látvade, Lávand, Laváte, Lombte, Londhe, Lugde, Lungse; Magar, Mahádik, Mahángure, Málusre, Mándavkar, Mándgule, Mandlik, Mandvekar, Máne, Manve, Marde, Márekari, Margale, Maske, Methe, Misál, Mohite, Morbále, More, Mudade, Mulik, Mundekar; Nádke, Nágtilak, Náik, Nalávde, Nalge, Nálhe, Nan-navre, Nátle, Navár, Nigvekar, Nikam, Nimbálkar, Niprul, Nitavde, Nogdand; Páchundkar, Padalkar, Padiyár, Padvale, Págham, Pálav, Pálkar, Pámbre, Pándhre, Pandit, Panhále, Parab, Pátáde, Pátankar, Patháde, Paule, Pavár, Páygan, Pendhári, Phadtare, Phákde, Pháráte, Phasalkar, Phávde, Pimpre, Pingle, Pisál, Pol, Pote, Povle, Punugad; Radtonde, Rájgire, Rájmáne, Rakte, Randive, Ráne, Rannavre, Ransing, Rasál, Ráut, Ravalde, Ravde, Ráyjop, Redekar, Rendálkar, Rote; Sáble, Salgar, Sálim, Sálonkhe, Sálvi, Sángle, Sanmukh, Sánthe, Sárang, Satál, Satále, Sátpute, Sávant, Savâshe, Seráde, Shankar, Shatphale, Sheds, Shelár, Shelke, Shevále, Shinde, Shipalkar, Shirasvade, Shirke, Shitole, Siste, Sole, Somáse, Sonmule, Sonugde, Supál, Supekar, Survasi, Surya; Tadsare, Takekar. Tákvadekar, Támbde, Tanpure, Táte, Tátugde, Távre,

Telvekar, Thamke, Thánekar, Thombre, Thopar, Thorát, Thorbole, Thorvat, Tikáde, Tikhe, Timgre, Tipye, Tivte, Todkar, Toraskar, Tore; Uduge, Ukshikar, Undre, Upalkar, Upár; Vádinge, Vádkar, Vágh, Vághmare, Vagre, Váimde, Válekar, Vánáre, Vánkde, Várange, Velvankar, Vicháre, Vir; Yádav, Yekre, Yevle.

The above list is interesting because it includes the names (in some cases apparently in the true or unsanskritised forms) of many early Deccan Hindu dynasties, of whom all traces have passed away. Some are identical with Rajput clan names, and this is one of the grounds on which the Maráthás claim to be Kshatriyas. But similarity of surnames by no means implies similarity of race. In this connection it may be observed that the protégés often take the surnames of the patrons. Thus there are Chaváns, Cholkes, Mores, Pavárs, Shelárs and Yádavs among Kolis, Dhangars, Mahárs, Mális, Rámoshis, Mángs and several wandering tribes which seem to be but slightly connected. In a Lamáni settlement the servants used to take the surnames of the head of the settlement. There are two or three historical instances where even Bráhmans have assumed the surnames of their Marátha patrons, *e.g.*, the Ghorpades of Inchalkaranji, the Dhamdheres of Poona, etc., The Bivalkars are known as Angres in Bombay. It is said that the highland clans of Gordons and Campbells have derived their surnames in the same way. A list of surnames of the above description is given below :—

Abhire.	More.
Anang.	Pavár.
Chálke.	Parihár.
Chándel.	Pisál.
Chaván.	Sálunkhe.
Chávre.	Shelár.
Dhámpál.	Shinde.
Gore.	Shisode.
Gujar.	Surve.
Kadam or Kalamb.	Tuvar.
Kalchure.	Yádav or Jádhav.
Lád.	

Besides *kuls* and surnames, Maráthás also claim to have *gotras* like Bráhmans. The *gotras* commonly found among them are :—

Agasti.	Kaundinya.
Angira.	Kaushik.
Atri.	Mályavant.

Bháradwája.	Paráshar.
Dálabhya.	Shándilya.
Garga.	Vairunya.
Gautam.	Vashishtha.
Jamadagni.	Veda.
Kapil.	Vishvámitra.
Káshyap.	

The majority of the caste do not know to which *gotra* they belong, their guides in this respect being the caste priests and printed books. And even among these authorities there is great confusion in the matter of assignment of *kuls* to *gotras*. Thus, according to one account, the Mores belong to the Gautam *gotra* while another account assigns them to the Bháradwája *gotra*. So also the Chaváns are stated to belong to the Kapil *gotra* by some and to the Vashishtha *gotra* by others, the Pavárs to the Vashishtha and Gagra *gotra*, and so on. Sameness of *gotra* is not necessarily a bar to intermarriage, the chief restrictions in this respect still being sameness of *kul* and *devak*. This would seem to suggest that the *gotras*, like the four *vanshas* and *kuls*, were adopted by the tribe after they rose in social dignity.

As stated above, marriages are prohibited between members belonging to the same *kul* or *devak*. Marriage with a father's sister's or mother's sister's daughter is not allowed. A Marátha may marry his maternal uncle's daughter. Marriage with a deceased wife's sister is allowed and brothers are allowed to marry sisters. Boys are generally married between twelve and twenty-five and girls before they come of age, though attainment of puberty is no bar to a girl's marriage. Jághirdárs and ruling chiefs sometimes keep their daughters unmarried for a considerably longer period than ordinary Assal Maráthás if they do not get suitable husbands for them. Polygamy is allowed and practised, but polyandry is unknown. Widow remarriage and divorce are strictly prohibited.

Birth. A girl goes for her first confinement to her parents, where a poor Marátha midwife waits on her. At the time of delivery the midwife cuts the navel-cord, bathes the mother and child, and lays them on a cot. When a son is born the joyful news is carried to friends and kinsfolk and packets of sugar are distributed to them. The priest, who is asked to repeat *shántipátha* or soothing verses every evening from the first to the tenth day, repeats them over a pinch of ashes and rice, and hands the ashes to the midwife to be rubbed on the brows of the mother and child. A light is kept burning the whole night for the [first] ten days. A few days after the birth the *játakarma* or birth ceremony is performed, when the priest and friends and kinsfolk are asked to the house, musicians are engaged to play their instruments, betel is served to men guests, and packets of vermilion and turmeric are distributed among the women, and a feast to the guests ends the ceremony. At the present day only a few keep up this practice. But as a rule all Maráthás are particular about the fifth or sixth day worship, as those days are believed to be full of danger to the new-born child. Maráthás share the common belief that convulsive seizures and most other forms of disease are the work of spirits. They think that only by worshipping "Mother's Fifth" and "Sixth" can the child be saved from the attacks of evil spirits which are said to hover about the lying-in-room lying in wait. The reason may possibly be that, owing to the sloughing of the navel cord, the child is at that time liable to tetanus and convulsions. Elderly matrons in the house take the utmost care to keep a light always burning in the lying-in-room day and night, especially from the fifth to the tenth day, and during that time never leave the mother alone in her room. On the fifth day a few friends and relations are asked to dine at the house. In the lying-in-room a betelnut and a sword or sickle are set on a low stool, and flowers, sandal-paste, burnt frankincense, and food are laid before the low stool in the name of Mother Fifth or Pánchvi. The mother bows before the goddess with the child in her arms and prays Mother Fifth to save the child from the attacks of evil spirits. The guests are treated to a dinner, and men guests pass the whole night singing ballads or *lavnis* while women guests watch by turns in the lying-in-room. Mother Sixth or Satvái is worshipped on the sixth day with the same details as Mother Fifth, and a few friends are feasted. The mother is held impure for ten days and no one except the midwife touches her. The midwife rubs the mother and the child with oil and bathes them. Then she bathes, takes her food, and waits upon the mother. During the first ten days the midwife eats nothing unless she has bathed from head to foot both morning and evening. The family are held impure for ten days in consequence of a child birth. During this time they are allowed to touch others, though they cannot worship the house gods. On the eleventh the clothes of the mother are washed, the room is cowdunged and the family are purified by drinking water which is given them by the family priest. On the eleventh the men renew their sacred threads and lay sandal, flowers, burnt frankincense, and sweetmeats before the house gods. On the evening of the twelfth a few women are asked to the house, musicians play, and the child is cradled. The women dress the babe in a child's hood or *kunchi*, and name it saying, 'Cut off ties and chains and join the umbrella and palanquin'. The anniversary of the child's birthday is kept by a feast to friends and kinsfolk, and on that day the ceremony called *chaul karma* or hairclipping is performed by the well-to-do Maráthás, especially the families of chiefs; and *sardárs* or nobles gird their boys with the sacred thread between ten and twelve with nearly the same ritual as at a Bráhman thread-girding.*

Marriage ceremonies. The negotiations for marriage commence with the girl's father. Of late the formalities observed in former times have gone out of use. When the parties come to terms, an agreement in writing is made to that effect.

The horoscopes of the boy and the girl are cast, and if they agree, it is well and good; but even if they do not agree, the marriage contract is entered into, if the parties are anxious for the match. After a marriage has been settled, a lucky day for the marriage and the turmeric-rubbing is fixed in consultation with an astrologer, as also the names of the women who are to rub the turmeric paste.

The marriage consists of the following ceremonies:—

(1) *Sákharpuda or Sákhar-Sádi.*—A party from the boy's house goes with music to the girl's house. The girl and her father seat themselves on two low wooden stools, the latter to the right of the former. Ganpati and Varuna are worshipped. The boy's father or other elderly male member on his side applies red powder to the girl's forehead, presents her with articles of dress and ornaments, and puts sugar into her mouth. Betelnut and betel-leaves are distributed, and the ceremony is over.

(2) *Tila.*—A party from the girl's house goes to the boy's. The boy's father worships Ganpati and Varuna; a dress is presented to the boy by the girl's father; *pánsupári* is distributed, and the ceremony ends.

These two ceremonies constitute the betrothal.

(3) *Patrika-pujan.*—Each of the priests of the bride and the bridegroom writes on a piece of paper the auspicious moments for the marriage and the turmeric rubbing, as well as the names of the bride and the bridegroom. Ganpati is worshipped and the bride's priest hands over the paper written by him to the bridegroom's father with a blessing, and *vice versa*.

(4) *Akshat.*—Is the invitation procession. First, rice grains are placed before the image of the family-god in the house asking him to

**Bombay Gazetteer*, Vol. XXIV. pp. 72-73.

be present at the wedding. Next, the procession moves through the streets and local friends and kinsfolk are called to the marriage.

(5) *Ghána.*—This ceremony is performed in the marriage pandals of both the bride and bridegroom. A turmeric root, some wheat, and a betel-nut are tied in a piece of new cloth, which is tied to the handle of the handmill. by married unwidowed women. Next the women grind some wheat by the hand-mill, singing songs. Two wooden pestles are then tied together with a piece of new cloth containing a turmeric root, a betel-nut and a little wheat. Some wheat is put into a bamboo basket, and pounded with these pestles. The provisions for the marriage are to be prepared after this ceremony has been performed, but in practice this rule is not observed.

(6) *Halad and Telvan.*—A party of married unwidowed women from the boy's house go with music to the girl's house taking turmeric paste, articles of dress, etc. The girl is sprinkled over with oil by a washer-woman, and then the women selected for the turmeric rubbing rubher with turmeric paste, and she is bathed. Next the girl is presented with a new yellow robe and bodice and ornaments which she puts on. What remains of the turmeric is taken with music to the bridegroom's. The boy is rubbed with it by the same women who rubbed the girl and he is bathed. A yellow dress is then presented to him by the girl's father, which he has to wear when he starts for the marriage. Red and turmeric powder are distributed among the women, and the ceremony ends with a feast at the houses of both the boy and the girl.

(7) *Mandap-pratishtha and Devakapratishtha.*—This ceremony is performed at the houses of both the boy and the girl. It consists of—(1) *Ganpatipujan* (*worship of Ganpati*), (2) *Punyáhavachan*, (3) *Nándi-Shráddha* and (4) *Grikhamakha*. Of these, the *Grikamakha* is performed even after the marriage ceremony is over. A spot in the marriage booth is cow-dunged and decorated with drawings of quartz powder; three wooden stools are placed on the spot and they are covered with a rich velvet or woollen carpet. The bride or bridegroom, and the parents of the party, bathe, dress in rich clothes, and seat themselves on the stools facing east. Next, if any ceremonies to be performed on the boy or the girl have not been performed on them, they are made to undergo a *práyaschitta* (penance), and the father of the boy or the girl says "I am going to marry my son (daughter) named *** in order to be free from the debt to gods and ancestors, and to continue the performance of righteous deeds, and to propagate

offspring fit to perform the deeds" The ceremonies of *Ganpati pujan, Punyáhavachan and Nándishraddha* are then performed.

It is enjoined that the marriage booth should be erected on an auspicious day. In fulfilment of this a post is planted in the marriage booth (which has been already erected) and a piece of cloth with turmeric root and a betelnut is tied to the post. The *devak* is next installed. The article representing the *devak* is placed in a winnowing fan along with betelnuts which represent the family gods. The winnowing fan is placed near the house gods and worshipped. Five unwidowed women wash a grindstone and lay sandal, flowers and sweetmeats before it, and a family washerwoman worships a stone slab *páta*, and a feast to friends and relations completes the guardian or *devak* worship. The *devak* is installed first at the girl's house and then at the boy's. After it has been installed, articles of dress are presented to the parents of the bride and bridegroom; first by members of their families, and then by other relations and friends.

(8) *Vir.*—This ceremony is performed by these only in whose families one or more celebrated warriors have lost their lives on the battle-field. An elderly male member belonging to a *kul* different from that of the party to be married is made to take the part of the *Vir* (warrior). He is taken with music to the bank of a river. The seven *Asras* (water nymphs) are worshipped, and the *Vir* is also worshipped and presented with a dress. The *Vir* puts on the dress and holds a sword in his hand. He is then brought back to the house accompanied by music. On his way back, red powder is constantly thrown on his body. At the entrance to the house, rice mixed with curds and a cocoanut are waved near the person of the *Vir*. Next, the sword in his hand is taken and placed near the house-gods. The *Vir* has to remain in the house till the end of the marriage ceremonies.

(9) *Anusthán.*—In order that the marriage may pass of without any inauspicious occurence, prayers in propitiation of Ganpati, the family deity, Mrutyunjaya, and the ill-favoured stars of the party are held through the medium of Bráhmans. These prayers commence on the day of the installation of the *devak* and continue till the end of the marriage. Sometimes the prayers are offered before the commencement of the marriage.

(10) *Vágdán.*—This ceremony takes place in the pandal at the girl's house. The boy's father accompanied by a party of males and females goes with music to the girl's house. After they are seated, the girl, dressed in rich clothes and ornaments, is brought, and seated on a low wooden stool. The boy's father gives into her hand a

cocoanut and a betel-leat packet and says thrice to her father, "I shall accept your daughter in marriage for my son". The girl's father says thrice to him "Accept". Both of them then worship each other, and the ceremony is over.

(11) *Gadagner or Kelvan.*—This ceremony takes place both at the boy's and at the girl's house. It consists of offering cooked food to the family-god and then feasting relations and friends. After dinner is over, the boy and the girl are presented with articles of dress by their respective family members.

(12) *Varadhava.*—When the time for marriage draws near, the bridegroom is dressed in the yellow dress presented to him by the girl's father at the time of the turmeric-rubbing ceremony. His brow is decked with the marriage coronet or *báshing* and a dagger is put into his hand, with which he must not part till the marriage is over. He is then seated in an *ambári*, on the back of an elephant or on a horse. Musicians walk in front, and behind them walk all the men of the party, followed by the bridegroom. Behind the bride-groom walks his sister closely veiled with a *shela* (gold scarf) holding the *shakundiva* or lucky lamp laid in a dish, and another veiled woman follows her with a metal or earthen pot called *shenskara* holding rice, betelnut and water, and covered with a mango branch and a cocoanut set on a heap of rice in a bamboo basket. The women walk between cloths which are held round them by women servants, or ride in closed palanquins. The party halt at the place (generally a temple) fixed upon for performing the *Simantpujan*. A male relative of the boy is then sent on horse-back with music to the girl's house. He is called *Varadhava.* (1) He is treated to a dinner and presented with a dress by the girl's father. Next, the *varadhava* goes back with the girl's party to where the boy has stopped. The boy is worshipped by the girl's father (*Simantpujan*) and the combined party starts for the girl's house for the marriage. On reaching the bride's house, one or two unwidowed women pour water on the feet of the animal on which the bridegroom has come. The bride-groom then dismounts, the priest throws cumin seed or *jiri* on the booth. The bride's mother meets him at the booth door with a dish holding two wheat flour lamps, waves small rice balls and wheat

(1) Of late either the bride's party goes to the bridegroom's village or town for the marriage or *vice versa.* Formerly it was not so. The marriage was celebrated as a rule at the bride's village. The bridegroom's party left their village and halted at a house in the girl's village prepared for them by the girl's father. This was called *janosghar.* When the boy's party arrived at the boundary of the girl's village, the *varadhava* was sent to inform the girl's father of their arrival. Although the necessity for a *varadhava* has now ceased, the custom is preserved.

flour lamps round the bridegroom, throws the rice balls to one side and lays the wheat flour lamps at the bridegroom's feet; another unwidowed woman of the bride's house pours a dish full of water mixed with lime and turmeric on his feet. The bridegroom presents the woman with a robe and bodice, the boy's father hands the bridegroom a cocoanut, and leads him by the hand to a place prepared for him near the marriage altar. The men guests are seated on carpets in the marriage hall. The women alight from their palanquins hidden by curtains held round them by their women servants, and are welcomed to their seats in a hall only separated from the men's hall by a cloth partition near the marriage altar or *bahule.* Dancing girls amuse the guests in the marriage hall and the servants load their muskets and hold themselves ready to anounce the lucky moment by firing their guns.

(13) *Ghatikásthápan.*—This takes place at the girl's house. At the exact moment when half the orb of the sun is visible above the horizon, a *ghatikápátra* (a cup at the bottom of which a hole is made of such a size as to sink the cup in exactly one *ghatika*, that is, 24 minutes) is floated in a pot filled with water by the family priest. By this *ghatikápátra* the auspicious time for the marriage is determined. Before the ceremony, Ganpati and Varuna are worshipped. The priest receives a present of clothing in return for this service

(14) *Gauriharpuja.*—A *páta* (stone slab) and a *varavanta* (curry stone) are placed near the house gods, pictures of Gauri and Hara are drawn over the slab with turmeric powder, and a cotton thread is passed round it. A dish filled with rice grains is placed near by to represent Indráni. The girl bathes, puts on a new robe and bodice, worships the Gaurihar and Indráni, and sits there till the wedding time.

(15) *Viváha* (*marriage*).—Shortly before the lucky moment arrives, the girl's father worships the paper on which the lucky moment for the marriage has been written. Next, two small heaps of rice grains are made near the marriage altar by the priest, and a cloth with a central cross mark is held between the heaps. The bridegroom stands on one heap facing west, and the bride is brought and made to stand on the other heap facing east. A mixture of rice grains *jiri* (cumin seed) and sugar is given into the hands of both. The maternal uncles of the bride and bridegroom stand behind them with naked swords crossed over their heads. The priests stand on either side of the curtain and tell the pair to look at the lucky cross and pray to their family gods. The priests repeat lucky verses and throw red rice at the pair. One of the priests hands red rice to the guests, which they throw over the pair at the end

of each lucky verse. When the auspicious moment arrives, the astrologer claps his hands, the horn-blower or *shingi* blows his horn, the guns are fired and the musicians play. The priests draw aside the curtain, and the bride and bridegroom throw a little of the mixture of the rice grains, etc., over each other's heads. Next some *mantras* are repeated and the pair again throw rice over each other's heads thrice or five times.

(16) *Madhuparka.*—Next, the bride's father and mother sit on two low wooden stools in front of the bridegroom face to face ; the father washes the feet of the boy and the mother pours water over them. The father then worships the bridegroom and pours *madhuparka* (honey and curds mixed together) over his hands. The bridegroom throws to the four points of the compass a few drops of the *madhuparka* and also sips a little of it. If the girl's father has former sons-in-law, the *madhuparka* is performed first on them and then on the bridegroom.

(17) *Kanyádán.*—Next, the hands of the bride and bridegroom are joined by the girl's father, a pot of bell metal is held under them by the priest, and the girl's mother pours water with some coins in it over their clasped hands. This completes the *Kanyádán* or girl-giving. The bride's father then presents the bridegroom with clothes, ornaments, vessels, land, animals, conveyances, etc. Next the priest sprinkles water over the pair, repeating *mantras*, and the bride and bridegroom throw grains of rice over each other and put garlands round each other's necks. Married unwidowed women on the girl's side then seat the pair facing east, and the girl is given a robe, a bodice, an upper garment, and a lucky necklace, which she puts on. The boy ties another lucky necklace round her neck and puts ornaments on her person. Ganpati is worshipped and money is distributed to Bráhmans by both parties. The priest then worships five betelnuts and ties them into the upper garments of the bride and bridegroom. These betelnuts are thus kept separate till the marriage is over. The hems of their garments are then tied into a knot by the priest, blessings are invoked upon them by elderly persons on both sides, and the pair worship Lakshmi, Indráni and Párvati.

The guests in the hall are presented with betelnut and betel-leaves, flowers, and fragrant cotton sticks called *pháyás* and take leave soon after the *Kanyádán* is over.

(18) *Viváhahoma and Saptapadi.*—The *Viváhahoma* or marriage sacrifice is next performed on the marriage altar. The altar is a square, the length of its sides being four, five, or seven times the span of the girl's

hand. Its height is one cubit from the ground. It has steps and over it is raised a small canopy. It is decorated with plantain trees, flowers, leaves, etc. The bride and bridegroom are seated on two low wooden stools set on the altar, the bride on the bridegroom's left. The bride's father stands near them, holding parched grains of rice, sesame seed, etc. The sacrificial fire is lit and fed with parched grains of rice, clarified butter, sesame seed, cotton sticks and *palas* (Butea frondosa), or other sacred wood with the same rites as amongst Bráhmans. The bride's brother squeezes the bridegroom's ear and is presented with a garment. The pair then leave their seats, walk seven times from right to the left round the sacred fire, and the *Saptapadi* is over.

Kankans or marriage wristlets are then tied to the wrists of the pair, the knot of their garments untied, and they are shown the *Dhruva* or Pole star. Next they bow before the family gods and the day's proceedings are over. From this day to the home-taking or *Varát* the bridegroom stays at the bride's and is feasted.

(19) *Ambavan and Rukhavat.*—On the following morning, women from the boy's house take *ámbavan* (leavings of food, vegetables and roots mixed in water which is generally given to cattle) to the girl's house, and give it to the girl's mother as a jest. Then women from the girl's house take *rukhavat* or sweetmeats with music to the boy's house. The *rukhavat* consists of two kinds of dishes, one for show and one for use. The show-dishes and sugar-coated betelnuts and almond balls are as large as or larger than unhusked cocoanuts, the dishes for use are of ordinary size and are prepared with great care. The *rukhavat* is sometimes taken to the boy's house at the time of his starting for the marriage. He is seated on a low stool set in a wheat square, and the sweet dishes are arranged in rows about the stool. The bridegroom is presented with a turban, his brow is marked with vermilion to which grain is stuck, lights are waved about him by unwidowed women, and he is told to help himself to the dishes.

On the morning following the marriage, the bride and bridegroom play at the betelnut hunt and rub each other with turmeric. The boy is seated on the altar and the girl stands behind with turmeric powder in her hand and tries to force some of it into his mouth. The boy keeps his mouth closed tight and tries to prevent her, and if she succeeds forcing some into his mouth, he is laughed at and asked if he is hungry. Then the boy stands behind the girl and tries with his left hand to force turmeric into her mouth. Next, the boy holds a betelnut in his hand and asks the girl to take it from him. They struggle and the girl manages to snatch it away. Then the girl holds a betelnut in her closed fist and asks the boy to take it. If the boy fails he has to beg it of her, and is laughed at. Lastly the pair bathe, and change their clothes, and a feast is held. The above games are played at the boy's house also after return with his bride.

(20) *Sunmukhadarshan.*—In the evening the boy's mother performs the ceremony of seeing the daughter-in-law's face or *Sunmukhadarshan.* The bride's mother, accompanied by music and her women friends, asks the bridegroom's mother to her house, whereupon, accompanied by her own kinswomen and friends, the family priest and music, the bridegroom's mother returns the call, taking bamboo baskets, sesame seed, gram balls, betelnuts, cocoanut kernels, dates, a robe, a bodice, ornaments, sweetmeats and fruit. On the way she feigns anger and tries to return home, when the girl's mother presents her with a robe and bodice, the washerwoman spreads sheets of cloth on the way, and the bridegroom's mother and her friends go walking over them to the bride's house with music. At the girl's the priest worships the betelnut Ganpati and the waterpot Varuna, and the boy's mother dresses the girl in the clothes she has brought and sweetens her mouth with sugar.

(21) *Airani or Zál.*—Is a ceremony of presenting *airani* to the boy's mother by the girl's father. A piece of cloth is spread in a big bamboo basket, and 16 dry dates, 18 cocoanut kernels, 16 turmeric lamps (a big one surrounded by 15 smaller ones), 16 betelnuts, cooked food, fruits, coins and 2 jars filled with water with gold in them, are set upon the cloth. This is called *airani.* The girl's father worships, first the boy's parents and his kinsfolk, and then *Umámaheshwar* who is supposed to be present in the *airani.* Next, he presents the *airani* to the boy's mother by pouring water on her hand.

The *airani* is then set on the heads of the nearest male and female relations of the boy and they are presented with articles of dress. When this is over, the girl is seated on the laps of the boy's parents and of his relations and friends. On this day the girl's parents have to fast till this ceremony is over.

(22) *Varát.*—After the *airani* is over, the bride and bridegroom go into the god-room, bow to the gods and to their parents, and start in procession for the boy's house. On reaching there, an image of Lakshmi made of wheat flour is worshipped, milk is offered to the goddess and the bridegroom's mother first makes the boy drink some of the milk and then the girl. The girl is then given a new name, which is told to the party assembled, sugar, betelnut, betel-leaves are distributed and

the party disperses. Next, the boy and the girl and the boy's mother are served food on one plate from which they feed one another, and the ceremoney ends.

(23) *Rájbheti and Rásnáhani.*—In an open space women from the boy's and the girl's house stand on two sides under the leadership of the mothers of the bride and the bridegroom. A curtain is held between the two parties. Both parties walk slowly towards each other, and as soon as they meet, the curtain between them is drawn aside. Each party then tries to win over the other, that is, to drag them on to their side. There is great merriment and the parties pelt one another with *gulál* or red powder. The ceremony is called *Rájbheti* because it is an imitation of the meeting (*bheti*) on battlefield of two kings (*rájás*). Then comes the *Rásnáhani* or festive bathing. The girl's mother, accompanied by women and music, goes to the boy's house to invite his mother to her own. A large square frame is made and covered on all sides with cloth. This is held around the women to hide them from public gaze. Thus veiled, the boy's mother is taken in great pomp to the girl's house. On the way water is poured from time to time on her feet, and all the women in the party throw *gulál* or red powder at one another. At intervals the boy's mother halts, and whenever she stops, a dress is presented to her by the girl's mother. On reaching the girl's house, the boy's mother is seated in a *makhar* (a gaily made up frame of wood) painted green with drawings of the *kárli* creeper (Momordica charantia) or some other plant. She is then bathed to the accompaniment of music, and presented with a green dress and green bangles, which she puts on. She is also presented with false ornaments jokingly. A feast to the party assembled ends the ceremony. Some women make it a vow not to eat a particular plant, until they are bathed in a *makhar* painted with representations of it at the time of their son's marriage.

(24) *Devakotthápan* or the unshrining of the *d. vak*, is the closing rite of the marriage. It is performed on the 2nd, 4th, 5th, 7th, 8th or 10th day of the marriage. The details are the same as are observed in installing the *devak*. When it is over, the priest and other Bráhmans are worshipped, feasted and presented with articles of dress and money.

Maráthás give two sorts of dinners to their marriage guests, *godi* or sweet and *khatti* or sour. The *godi* feast (a feast of sweet-dishes without any flesh) is given before and the *khatti* (which chiefly consists of flesh dishes) after the *Devakotthápan* ceremony.

Even though the bride is of age, the marriage consummation does not form part of the marriage ceremony. The consummation ceremony is put off till the bride's first monthly sickness after the marriage. In performing the age-coming ceremony, the girl is seated in a gaily decked wooden frame or *makhar* with arches on each side in a specially prepared hall. Plantain stems decked with tinsel and coloured paper are set at each corner of the frame. The girl is dressed in a rich yellow robe and bodice, and her brow is marked with vermilion on which rice grains are stuck. Her head is hung with a network of flowers and garlands are tied round her neck and lines of vermilion drawn on her feet. The news is handed round among friends and kinsfolk, and sugar packets and cocoanuts are distributed at every house in the neighbourhood. Women are engaged to play at the house while the ceremony lasts. The girl is unclean for three days. On the fourth she is rubbed with oil and turmeric and bathed, and a lucky day, between the fourth and the sixteenth, is named for the puberty ceremony. On the morning of the lucky day the pair are rubbed with turmeric and fragrant oil and bathed while music plays. Friends and kinfolk are asked, and the pair are seated on low stools, the girl to the right of the boy. The priest attends and lights the sacred fire as at the Bráhman puberty ceremony. The pair bow before the gods and elders and the ritual is complete. A grand feast is given to women friends and neighbours at noon and in the evening the ceremony called *otibharan* or lapfilling is performed. The pair are seated on two low stools set in a wheat or rice square, the girl to the left of the boy, and the brows of both the boy and the girl are marked with vermilion. Rice grains are stuck on the vermilion, and married women fill the girl's lap with a bodice cloth, wheat, cocoanut, fruit, packets of vermilion and betelnuts. Their fathers-in-law present the boy and girl with clothes and ornaments, and the girl's father presents the pair with bedding, lamps, metal waterpots, and betel cases. The rest of the ceremony is the same as the Bráhman puberty ceremony. During a girl's first pregnancy in the third, fifth and seventh months, while music plays, five unwidowed women fill her lap with wheat, a bodice cloth, a cocoanut and fruit. She is asked to dine by women friends and relations during the seventh and the eighth months and is presented with robes and bodices. She is taken with women friends and relations to some garden where a longing feast or *dohalejevan* is given her.* **Puberty ceremonies.**

Maráthás worship by preference Shiva and his consort Párvati **Religion.**

---

* *Bom. Gaz.*, Vol. XXIV, pp. 79-80.

or Devi. They worship Shiva in his various forms such as Khandoba, Bhairav, Ravloba, Rokdoba, etc., and Párvati in her incarnations as Amba, Bhaváni, Durga, Shitala, Lakshmi, Jogai, Bolai, etc. They also worship all other Bráhmanic, local and boundary gods, keep the usual fasts and feasts, and visit the places of Hindu pilgrimage. Their priests are Deshasth Brahmans, who conduct their ceremonies and perform the daily worship of the house gods of the well-to-do.

Death ceremonies.

When a Marátha dies the body is bathed and dressed in a white sheet, laid on a bier and tied fast to the bier with strings. Betel-leaves, flowers and powder are thrown on it, and sometimes half a dozen gold or silver flowers are strewn over the bier. The well-to-do Marátha dead are carried in a palanquin to the burning ground, which is generally on the bank of some stream or river, accompanied by kinsmen and proceeded by Holár or Mahár pipe-players. The body is bathed in water, the pyre built and the dead laid on it and burnt with nearly the same rites as at a Bráhman funeral. When the body is nearly consumed, the party bathe in the river and return home. On the second, third or fourth day, the ashes are gathered, and, except a few bones which are buried somewhere near the burning ground, they are taken to some holy place or river and are thrown into the water. The rest of the funeral ceremony is performed on the third, fifth, seventh, or ninth at the latest. On the tenth, rice or wheat flour balls are offered to the dead. On the eleventh the family, which since the death has been impure, is cleansed by eating the five products of the cow. They then distribute to Bráhmans clothes, pots, umbrellas, shoes, cows and cash in the name of the dead. On the twelfth, balls or *pindas* are offered to the dead and his ancestors, and on the thirteenth the *shráddha* is performed in the name of the dead, and friends and kinsfolk are treated to a dinner. On the fourteenth the mouth-sweeteening or *god-tond karne* is performed, when relations meet, and treat the chief mourner to a sweet dinner. At the end of every fortnight, month and year from the date of decease, uncooked provisions are given to Bráhmans in the deceased's name, and the anniversary of his death is kept by a *shráddha*, when friends and relations are asked to dine at the house. The deceased is remembered every year in *Mahálaya-paksha*, the dark half of the *Bhádrapad* (approximately August-September) on a day corresponding to the day of decease. The chief mourners for one full year avoid gay colours and sweet dishes and do not attend marriage or other festive parties.*

* *Bom. Gaz.*, Vol. XXIV, p. 80.

Maráthás are mainly grant-holders, landowners, soldiers and husbandmen. A few are ruling chiefs. For the most part the pátils, or village headmen, in the Central Deccan belong to this caste. Some are traders, and many are in the army or in other branches of Government service. Occupation.

As a class Maráthás are simple, frank, independent, and liberal, courteous, and when kindly treated, trusting. They are a manly and intelligent race, proud of their former greatness, fond of show, and careful to hide poverty. The Marátha is proverbially *dauli* or fond of show. A Marátha though almost starving will raise a copper's worth of clarified butter and rub his moustache and hands with it, and sit washing his hands and face in front of his house, that passers by may think he has had a rich dinner. A Marátha may dress in a rag at home but he has always a spare dress which he himself washes, keeps with great care, and puts on when he goes to pay a visit. He hires a boy to attend him with a lantern at night, or to take care of his shoes when he goes into his friend's house and hold them before him when he comes out. They say that war is their calling, and few Maráthás of good family, however well educated, willingly take service as clerks. As a rule a well-to-do Marátha has in his service a Bráhman clerk called *divánji* or minister, who often takes advantage of his master's want of education to defraud him and sometimes ends by making his master his debtor.*

The staple food of well-to-do Maráthás is wheat cakes, rice, split pulse, clarified butter, and vegetables and condiments; middle class families on ordinary days eat *jowári*, rice, *bájari*, bread, *sámbháre* or liquid pulse seasoned with chillies, spices and salt, and vegetables; the daily food of the poor is millet bread, chopped chillies, and pulse sauce. All eat flesh and fish. The well-to-do eat mutton or fowls daily. Middle class families use them about once a week, while the poor use them only occasionally on *Dasara* in September-October and *Shimga* in March, and during marriages. Maráthás seldom use liquor, though no caste rule forbids either liquor or narcotics. They do not eat beef or pork. At the houses of the well-to-do the food is cooked and served generally by servants called *sovalekaris* or "persons ceremonially clean", but in the middle class and poor families the women are the cooks and servers as usual. Food.

MARATHA.—A sub-division of Gondhalis, Gopáls, Kalávants, Murlis, Kolhátis, Bhois, Gavandis, Bhadbhunjás, Vanjáris, Bhávsárs

* *Bom. Gaz.*, Vol. XXIV, pp. 70-71.

Nhávis, Shimpis, Dhangars, Sális, Mális, Vánis, Khatris, Kumbhárs, Telis, Kunbis, Lohárs, Sonárs, Mángs, Kolis, Vaidus, Son Kátkaris, Gavlis.

MARENAVA.—A synonym for Kunchi Vakkal.

MARI.—A sub-division of Darjis.

MARU.—A sub-division of Rávals, Dhedas, Chárans, Sonis, Kansárás, Audich Bráhmans. A territorial name meaning those from Márwár.

MARVADI.—A sub-division of Kachhis, Dhedas, Meghváls, Hajáms, Sutárs, Vághris. A territorial name meaning those from Márwár.

MARVI.—A sub-division of Kolis.

MARWARI.—*See* Marvadi.

MASHAIK.—A synonym for Sayad.

MASHAL.—A sub-division of Kabbaligars.

MASHALJI.—A synonym for Khándeshi Nhávi.

MASTAN.—A synonym for Rasulsháhi.

MASUNDE.—A sub-division of Bhois.

MASURIA.—A synonym for Matko Hajám.

MA-THAKUR.—A sub-division of Thákurs.

MATHAPATI.—A sub-division of Jangams.

MATHKAMBLE.—A sub-division of Mahárs.

MATHUR.—A sub-division of Káyasths.

MATHURA.—A sub-division of Vanjáris.

MATHURAJIN.—A synonym for Máthura.

MATHVADI.—A sub-division of Bhils.

MATI.—A sub-division of Ods.

MATIA.—A sub-division of Kanbis.

MATKO.—A sub-division of Hajáms.

MAUMIN.—A synonym for Meman.

MAVCHI.—A sub-division of Bhils.

MES, numbering 66 (1901), including 33 males and 33 females, are found principally in Cutch. They are half Hindu, half Musalmán by religion. They make their living by hunting and weaving leaf mats. A Me eats food cooked by a Musalmán, but a Musalmán will not eat food cooked by a Me.

MEDAR.—*See* Burud or Medar.

MEDATVAL.—A sub-division of Shrigaud Bráhmans.

MEDERA.—A synonym for Medora.

MEDORA.—A sub-division of Vániás.

MEGHVALS, (1) numbering 33,697 (1901), including 17,035 males and 16,662 females, are found entirely in the State of Cutch. The Meghváls are also known as Ganeshia, Rishia, Rikhia or Rákhia, and are sometimes styled Dhedha or Dheda. Name and synonyms

According to some, the caste is called Meghvál after their common ancestor Megha Rishi. Another account gives the following story in explanation of the origin of the term Meghvál.

Long ago in the reign of one of the Hindu kings of Junágad, probably Ra Navagana, their *guru*, Mátang,(2) came to a pond near the capital. He desired to make ablutions, but he was prevented from doing so by the men who were on guard there. On his asking why the waters were so carefully guarded, he was told that the Bráhmans had predicted that there would be a famine for twelve years. Upon this, he told them that there would be plenty of rain that year, and that the king should not thus deny them, the Meghváls, the use of the water. He was laughed at, and he went away saying that he would stay till the rainy season, on the top of the Girnár hill, and that they might go and tell the king that that year the rains would not stop till the waters touched his beard, as he sat there. That year the rains came in such a deluge that they continued for days till the city was in danger of being submerged. The king became anxious, and then learnt how a certain Mátang, a Meghvál, had predicted the flood and declared that it would not stop till his beard was drenched with rain water as he sat on the top of the Girnár hill. Upon this, the king went to him in person and requested him to stop the rains. He replied that his beard must first be drenched with rain water and the rain would then stop. Some rain water was brought in a gold plate and his beard drenched therein. The rains then stopped. Because Mátang stopped the rains, he and his caste-fellows came to be known by the name 'Meghvál'; the word *megha* meaning rain and *vál* meaning to ward off, the whole meaning 'one who wards off rain'.

---

(1) This article is complied from materials supplied by Mr. M. K. Mehta.

(2) Mátang has now become a generic term for all those who are descended from their first *guru*, Mátang.

The synonym Ganeshia has its origin in Ganesh, the favourite god of the caste. The term Rishia or Rikhia is derived from the word *rishi*, as the caste believe themselves to be descendants of a Rishi. They are called Dheda or Dhedha, because they drag away dead animals, the word being derived from the Gujaráti word *dhayadavun*, to drag.

The titles of respect by which the castemen are addressed are Metar, Mátang, and Matia. Metar is an official title given to a member of the caste who acts as a mediator between the caste and the Government in matters of disputes, taxes and tolls. They are called Mátang and Matia after the names of their *gurus*: several families directly descended from them being commonly known among them by those names.

The large settlement of Meghváls in Cutch may be attributed to Cutch being primarily and in ancient times a country of herdsmen like Rabáris, Chárans, Káthis, Ahirs and such other tribes owning large herds of cattle, camels, goats and sheep; for, to these tribes, Meghváls were indispensable, to dispose of the carcasses of dead animals by eating the flesh, preparing and tanning the skins, and by weaving wool into blankets and other cloth; and so it is that the various endogamous divisions of the Meghvál community are found attached to the fortunes of various pastoral and agricultural communities. Máheshri Meghváls, for instance, as coming from Sind, say that they are the followers of the Jádejás and the Chárans. There appears to be much truth in this, since there is little difference between the dress worn by a Tumbal Cháran woman and that by a Máheshri Meghvál woman. Márwáda Meghváls believe that they came with the Káthis and Ahirs. Gojra Meghváls appear to have come with the Kanbis, the great agricultural class that came from Gujarát. Chárania Meghváls are, in fact, the bondsmen of Kachhela Chárans. They were weavers, shoe-makers, leather-workers, making well-buckets, saddles, harnesses, and other sundries necessary for cultivators and cart-drivers, and all round servants, cutting wood and grass, acting as guides and performing sundry other duties, too numerous to mention.

Status. The Meghváls are an impure caste. Their touch is defiling. They are not allowed to draw water from the village well. They are obliged to live beyond the outskirts of villages. The village barber will not shave them. The village washerman will not wash their clothes. They are not allowed to enter recognised Hindu temples and to take part in orthodox Hindu ceremonies. In former times they could not wear even a turban, but had to put on a roll of yarn instead They could not spit on the ground, but had to spit into a horn or a small earthern pot, which they had to carry fastened round their necks. Their foot-prints, as they walked, were considered so unholy that it was believed that those who walked into them were in danger of contracting leprosy, and consequently they were obliged to go with a number of prickly shrubs fastened to their garment as a trail, which might obliterate their prints as they walked. The same penalties were imposed upon the Mahárs of the Deccan as recently as the reign of the Peshwás.

Regarding the origin of the Meghváls, the *Bombay Gazetteer* says :—

" The Meghs, probably the Magians of Timur, are a large part of the population of Riyási Jammu and Aknur, a pure race of low caste, apparently outcaste in other places. They are perhaps the Mekei of the Aryans and to them belong the Mekhowál (Makvánás). They claim to be Sárasvat Bráhmans.(1) Burnes speaks (2) of the Megvárs of South Thar as an aboriginal or Ját race. They are probably connected with the Mehárs of Lower Sind and the Megháris of Baluchistan, and are, perhaps, Pliny's Megari or Megallae and the Mokars of the Rajput chronicles. Burton speaks (3) of the Sind Meghávars as Dheds or Meghváls, tanners, shoe-makers and weavers, found in many parts of Sind. The Umarkot Meghávars were very well-to-do, with priests, *guravs*, and sacred books, *pothis*, of their own. They were said to come from Málwa. " **Origin.**

Máheshri Meghváls are probably Burnes' Meghvárs of South Thar, an aboriginal or Ját race. They may also have been connected with the Mehárs of Lower Sind and the Megháris of Baluchistan, for there is little doubt that they have come to Cutch from Sind with the Sammás ; for, to this day, the Ráo of Cutch, when he is installed on the throne, gets his forehead marked with the blood from the little finger of a member of that caste, called Mátang, a lineal descendant of that Mátang, who, according to them, won for the Jádejás the kingdom of Cutch. Besides, the tombs of their *guru* Mátang and his son and grandson Lunád and Mámai are in Sind ; that of Mátang at Makali near Nagar-Thátta, that of Lunád at Bhagrani, a village in Sind and that of Mámai at Rayma Bazár in Lower Sind. They may also have been connected with the Mehárs of Lower Sind and the Megháris of Baluchistan, for they have a curious legend about the birth of their *guru* Mátang. They believe him to be an incarnation

(1) Cunningham, Arch. Rep., II, 13, (2) Royal Geog. Soc., IV, 93, (3) Burton (Sind, 323).

of a local Musalmán prophet (the name that they give is Murtaja Ali), born of Hindu or Rishi parents. The story is an illustration of the crude notions of this backward race attempting to magnify the importance of their *guru*.

"When the Muhammadan prophet died", says the story-teller, "he assured his disciples that when they returned after burying him, a camel laden with a box would issue from a neighbouring hill, and in that box would be their spiritual guide, but that they should not look behind. The men could not resist their curiosity and looked behind and discovered the camel laden with a box; but as they looked, the camel disappeared and the box fell into the river (the Ganges). Now it so happened that three Rishi girls, one of them a daughter of Gautama, were on the bank of the Ganges fetching water, and the box came floating to them. The daughter of Gautama, whose name was Jasbái, claimed to know what the box contained, while another girl said that she should, in that case, have the box. The box, on being opened, was found to contain a baby, who entered the body of the daughter of Gautama, and she became pregnant. Gautama thought that the baby was an incarnation, and he asked Mátra Rishi to accept her in marriage. Mátra Rishi married her, and wishing to delay the birth closed her womb by a belt, but the birth took place in the form of a tear. The child was therefore called Mátang, because his mother, *ma*, had used a belt, *tang*". The story arises out of a pun on the word Mátang. Another version of the story simply says that Mátang was the son of Mátra Rishi and grandson of Gautama Rishi, and that he was a Pokharna (Pushkarna) Bráhman by caste, but that afterwards he became degraded by marrying a Meghvál woman.

Endogamous divisions. Meghváls have four endogamous divisions, who eat together but do not intermarry. They are as follows:—

1. Máheshri or Kachhi Meghváls.
2. Márwáda Meghváls.
3. Gojra Meghváls.
4. Chárania Meghváls.

Máheshri Meghváls were probably the first to come to Cutch, and they are perhaps named after some goddess (Mahesh *lit.*, great god Shiva, and Maheshri may be the goddess Párvati, the consort of Shiva), like Máheshri Vániás, who also like them, have come to Cutch from Sind. Márwáda Meghváls are so called because they have come from Márwár, their original home. Gojra Meghváls derive their name from Gujarát, their original home whence they have come into Cutch. Chárania Meghváls are very probably an offshoot of the Márwáda Meghváls and they came to be called Chárania when they became associated with Káchhela Cháranş.

The exogamous sub-divisions of the caste are as follows :— Exogamous divisions

Máheshri Meghváls.

Ayadio
Bhio or Bhaiyo.
Bhumia.
Bharcha.
Bochia.
Chande.
Dungarkia.
Dagara.
Dhuo.
Danicho.
Dheda.
Dora.
Fofal.
Fulia.
Juad.
Kopal.
Kanad.
Khankhála.
Lálan.
Lohio.
Mátang.
Mothária.
Nángsi Potra.
Pingol.
Pária.
Pátária.
Rolo.
Ronsia.
Sincha.
Suyadio.
Sanjot.
Sodham.
Sondhara.
Singrakhia.
Siju.
Vinjoda.
Vighoro.
Visaria.
Vádo.
Vársángio.

Márwáda Meghváls.

Asár.
Bochia.
Bhátia.
Badia.
Bhadru.
Bokha.
Badga.
Chhuret.
Dugia.
Gudár.
Gudiia.
Hingda.
Jepa.
Jugu.
Kháret.
Katua.
Kudeja.
Locha.
Masánia.
Punvár.
Padgudud.
Parmár.
Padiár.
Sundhera.
Siju.
Sunjot.
Vánia.
Varendh.
Varsur.
Vághela.

Gojra Meghváls.

Anthu.
Bámbhania.
Bochia.
Chavda.
Dáfda.
Gohel.
Jhinjhuvádia.
Jádev.
Lovár.
Locha.
Monyátra.
Makvána.
Parmar.
Ráthod.
Shekheswa.
Sarvaria.
Solanki.
Thámbhu.
Tundia.
Vághela.
Vighora.
Vinjhoda.

Chárania Meghváls.

Bhátia.	Gogia.	Kádi.
Chaván.	Hetnia.	Mádhad.
Dhavad.	Hágatia or Ságatia.	Parmár.
Dharda.	Jhánkhad.	Padáiya.
Fafal.	Khimsuria.	Vádhaiya.
Fáfda.	Khetarnia.	Vijuda.

Language. Máheshri Meghváls speak Cutchi. Márwádás and Gojrás speak a kind of mixed dialect resembling Gujaráti in the main. Chárania Meghváls' dialect is like that of the Kachhela Chárans. The names in common use among Máheshri Meghvál men are Aja, Vela, Námori, Hemo, Versi, Sejpál and Páncha; and among women Válbái, Tejbái, Kánbái, Kesarbái and Rámái. The common names of males among the Márwádi Meghváls are Mándan, Petho, Lála, Budha, Pabu and Málo and among women Ratanbái, Dhanbái, Sajanábái, Premábái and Mulbái. The principal names of the Gojra Meghvál males are Hamir, Ruda, China, Ranmal and Bháno, and of females Dáhi, Gomi, Lálu, Bháni, Lakháman. The typical names of Chárania Meghvál men are Mánsur, Khimráj, Devo, Jivan, Válo, and of women Gangái, Láchha, Ráma and Jiván.

Marriage. Marriages are prohibited between members of the same sub-division. The members of the Mátang section take wives from the other sections, but do not give their daughters in marriage to them. This is due to the founder of the section, Mátang, being the spiritual guide of the caste. Intermarriages take place between the Máheshri Meghváls and the Máheshri Meghvál Bráhmans. The practice began when Mátang gave his daughter in marriage to a Máheshri Meghvál Bráhman. A Meghvál can marry a woman of his mother's, maternal grandmother's or paternal grandmother's section. But intermarriage on the mother's side is allowed only when the relationship is removed two or three generations. It is not customary for two men to exchange daughters, but it is not prohibited. A Meghvál may marry his wife's sister during the wife's life-time as well as after her death. Two brothers may marry two sisters.

Marriage is generally adult, the marriageable age ranging from twelve to sixteen. If an unmarried girl becomes pregnant, her fault is condoned by marrying her by the widow remarriage ceremony. If she has been betrothed, the betrothed man has the option of marrying her or not. In the case of the betrothed not marrying her, she is married to her seducer or to any other person. The seducer is fined from Rs. 12 to Rs. 40 by the caste, of which about Rs. 3 go to the State. Polygamy is allowed and practised, but polyandry is unknown.

The offer of marriage comes from the boy's parents through the medium of a priest, who is paid about one anna for the trouble. The Máheshri Meghváls have no custom of paying a bride-price or dowry. In the case of others, the boy's parents have to pay to the girl's parents a sum of money, varying from Rs. 25 to Rs. 50. Among the Máheshris, the service is conducted by a Mátang; among the others, by a Bráhman priest.

Among the Máheshri Meghváls the marriage is not celebrated in the usual Hindu form. Neither the *chori* or marriage altar is built, nor the sacrificial fire enkindled. The marriage ceremony is performed before a *Bára Mati Panth* figure drawn with flour on the floor, with twelve compartments to represent twelve different forms of religion or doctrine, as they say. Red powder is sprinkled near the figure and a light fed with *ghi* is lighted in a brass lamp of peculiar size, having twelve knobs. The bride and bridegroom are seated near this figure of *Bára Mati Panth*, and those that are present sit round with their heads uncovered. A Mátang conducts the service, reciting *mantras* in a dialect, half Cutchi half Gujaráti.

Among the Márwáda and other classes of Meghváls a *chori* or mariage altar is erected, with four pillars of earthen vessels placed on its four sides; but instead of the sacrificial fire, there is a light fed with *ghi* or cocoanut oil with an installation of nine planets (*Navagriha-sthapana*) represented by nine betelnuts, corn and red powder. The bride and bridegroom, with the ends of their garments tied into a knot, are made to walk four times round the light and their hands are joined. The rest of the ceremony resembles that of local castes of similar standing.

The remarriage of widows is permitted. Among the Máheshri Meghváls, the widow is expected to marry her late husband's younger brother, but is not compelled to do so. She is free to marry any man of her choice. Among the other three divisions, it is a rule that a widow must marry her deceased husband's younger brother. A widow remarriage is celebrated on a Sunday. The service is conducted by a Meghvál Bráhman or a Mátang. The ceremony is very simple. Sweet balls are offered to Ganesh, and the heads of the pair are brought into close contact, which completes the ceremony.

A husband can divorce a wife on the ground of her infidelity. A wife can divorce a husband if he is cruel or impotent, or is suffering from some similar disability. If the wife be in fault her parents are fined, and if the husband be the guilty person he is fined. A divorced woman is allowed to marry by the widow remarriage form. In the case of such a marriage, the woman has to pay to her first husband a sum of Rs. 12 to Rs. 25. Adultery is settled by a fine. The caste follow the Hindu law of inheritance. An extra share, generally in the form of a house, is given to the youngest son.

Religion. The Meghváls profess Hinduism. They may be said to belong to the Máta Panthi sect in general. Máheshri Meghváls however do not worship Máta in particular. All the Meghváls worship by preference the god Ganesh. No Meghvál locality is found without the Ganesh *otto* or open verandah shrine of the god Ganesh. Máta is worshipped by Márwáda, Gojra and Chárania Meghváls under the name of Bhagvati. Meghváls also worship Yakshas, the goddess Shitala (small-pox goddess) and Kshetrapáls (snake gods). At many of the shrines of these gods Meghváls or their Bráhmans are the recognised worshippers and they have a share in the offerings, made to them. Máheshri Meghváls hold in great reverence also the tombs of their *gurus* Mátang, Lunád, Mámai and Matia ; of these the last is held in special veneration by the Meghváls of Kánthi (South Cutch). Just as there are families known by the designation of Matang, so there are families known by the name of Matia. Máheshri Megváls often go on pilgrimage to these places.

Márwáda and Gojra Meghváls hold in great estimation a saint called Rámdev Pir, whom they consider their patron saint. The chief shrine of this saint is at Runáje in Pokarna in Márwár. He was a Rajput of the Tunvar tribe, and is said to have flourished in the 13th or 14th century. He became deified by the performance of miraculous deeds. Even to this day there are in Cutch direct descendants of the Rámdev family called Rámdev Potra (*lit.*, sons of Rámdev) after him, living in the village of Farádi. These descendants of Rámdev had a certain poll-tax, a kind of slavery tax, on the Meghváls, but of late they get through the State a fourth part of the income which accumulates through fines, etc., from the Meghvál caste instead.

The priests of Máheshri Meghváls are Máheshri Meghvál Bráhmans, those of Márwáda Meghváls, Márwáda Meghvál Bráhmans, and so with the rest. The Máheshri Meghváls and their priests eat together and intermarry. The other three divisions interdine only with their priests, who form one caste. Some of the Meghvál Bráhmans have Shrimáli, Dave, Someshvar and such other high class

Bráhman surnames. This supports the belief that the Meghvál Bráhmans are a community converted from other Bráhmans by Mátang, the first *guru* of the Meghváls. The status of these Bráhmans is as low as that of Meghváls. Among the Máheshri Meghváls, their Bráhmans play a subordinate part to their Mátangs, who generally officiate at important ceremonies.

The dead are generally buried in a lying position with head to the north. The Máheshri Meghváls sometimes burn their dead, in which case they have to give twelve dinners to the caste. The Márwáda and other Meghváls say that they bury their dead after applying fire to the toe. The period of mourning ranges from twelve days to two months. For the propitiation of ancestors in general crows are fed on the Diváli day. A certain make believe of the *Shráddha* ceremony is also performed on the eleventh day after death in the case of females and on the twelfth day in the case of males. Death ceremonies.

The Meghváls believe weaving, hewing wood, skinning dead animals and tanning to be their original occupations. Their present occupations are also the same. Meghvál Bráhmans, as a rule, do not do skinning and tanning business. The majority of Márwáda Meghváls are weavers, while the Gojra Meghváls are mainly skinners and tanners. Máheshri Meghváls do all the work referred to above. Occupation.

Chárania Meghváls, owing to their association with Káchhela Chárans, do not do the skinning and tanning business themselves, but get it done by others. At one time their occupation was exclusively that of driving the pack-bullocks of their masters, the Chárans, and otherwise serving them. Even now many Meghvál families are attached to Cháran families, whom they serve at the time of marriage and on other important occasions. The demand for pack-bullocks having ceased on account of the opening of railways, Chárania Meghváls have lost this work, and the ties between them and their Cháran masters are loosening. They have taken to the occupations of their brethren.

A few Meghváls are agriculturists, holding State land on service tenure, in lieu of service which they render as *bhomiyas* or guides. In almost every village there is a family of *bhomiyas*.

Meghváls eat fish and flesh and also the carcasses of cows, sheep, goats, and buffaloes. They abstain from eating monkeys, pork, the flesh of uncloven-footed animals, fowls, crocodiles, lizards, jackals, rats, etc. They eat the leavings of other people and drink liquor. They eat *kachhi* and *pakki*, drink and smoke with Musalmáns. They Food.

do not eat from the hands of Kolis, Párdhis, Mes, Bhangiás, Dátaniás, Turis, Dhádhis, Lámghás and Musalmán Hajáms. No Hindu caste will eat, drink or smoke with the Meghváls.

MEGHVAN.—A sub-division of Dhedás.

MEHARIA.—A synonym for Bhoi.

MEHDAVI.—*See* under Minor Musalmán Castes.

MEHTAR.—A title applied to several caste headmen.

MEHURUNA.—A sub-division of Vanjáris.

MELA.—A synonym for Bhangi.

MEL SONI.—A sub-division of Sonis.

Name. **MEMANS,** also called Maumins or Believers, numbering 97,114 (1901), including 45,641 males and 51,473 females, are found principally in Gujarát districts and States and in small numbers in all large towns in the Presidency. Beyond the Presidency they have spread as traders and merchants, and formed settlements in Calcutta, Madras, the Malabár Coast, South Burma, Siam, Singapore and Java, in the ports of the Arabian peninsula except Maskat, in Mozambique, Zanzibar and the East African coast.

Divisions. Memans have five divisions as follows :—

1. Cutchi from Sind and Cutch.
2. Halai from Halar in Káthiáwár.
3. Dhokas from Dholka in Ahmedabad.
4. Dhoraji Bhávnagri from Bhávnagar in Káthiáwár.
5. Verávadas from Verával in Káthiáwár.

Of the above, the Cutchis and Halais are the descendants of the converts of the market gardening Kácchiás of Káthiáwár and the trading Lohánás of Sind. The Dhokas, Bhávnagris and Verávadas are offshoots of the Halais.

History. The history of the origin of the Memans is as follows :—

Mauláná Abdul Kadir Muhi-yud-din Giláni, the Saint of Saints, died at Baghdad in A.D. 1165 (H. 561). On his death-bed he ordered one of his sons Táj-ud-din to settle in India and display to its people the light of Islám. In A.D. 1421 (H. 838) Sayad Yusuf-ud-din Kadiri, fifth in descent from Táj-ud-din, was in a miraculous dream ordered to set sail for Sind and guide its people into the right way of Islám. When Sayad Yusuf-ud-din reached Sind, its capital was Nagar-Thatha and its ruler was a chief of the Samma dynasty

(A.D. 1351—1521) with the title of Markab Khán [probably Jam Rai Dan (A.D. 1454)], who received Sayad Yusuf-ud-din with honour and entertained him as his guest. At this time Mánekji, the head of the eighty-four *nukhs* or divisions of the Lohána community, was in favour at the court of Markab Khán. Markab Khán became a follower of the Sayad, and Mánekji with two of his three sons and 700 Lohána families followed their ruler's example. Of the two sons of Mánekji who became converts, Rávji was called Ahmed and Rávji's sons Sundarji and Hansráj were named Adam and Táj Muhammad. On their conversion the saint changed the name of the community from Mota and Lohána to Maumin or Believer, and, investing Adam with a dress of honour, appointed him hereditary head of the new community with his seat at Wara near Thatha. The Hindu relatives of the converted Lohánás called on their spiritual guides to pray to Darya Pir, the Indus spirit, to remove the saint. The Indus spirit heard this prayer. The saint refused a grant of land, and after receiving his followers' assurance that they would continue to support his descendants as their religious heads Yusuf-ud-din retired by sea to Irak. Before leaving he blessed his people, a blessing to which the Memans trace their fruitfulness and their success in trade. Pir Buzurg Ali Kadiri of Mundra in South Cutch, who died in A.D. 1896, was eighteenth in descent from Sayad Yusuf-ud-din. According to this account, at the invitation of the Jádeja Ráo Khengar (A.D. 1548—1584) under Kannawa, a descendant of Adam Sháh, the Memans moved from Thatha to Bhuj; and, under the favour of Ráo Khengar who honoured Kannawa with the title of Seth, founded the Meman ward of that city. At an uncertain date the Lohána or Cutchi Memans passed from Cutch south through Káthiáwár to Gujarát. They are said to have been strong and wealthy in Surat during the period of its prosperity (A.D. 1580—1680). As Surat sank, the Cutchi Memans moved to Bombay, the settlement receiving a large increase in consequence of the sufferings caused in North Gujarát and Cutch by the A.D. 1813 famine. As Káthiáwár did not suffer less than Cutch from the famine of A.D. 1813, many Káthiáwár Memans from Halár and Bhávnagar migrated to different parts of Gujarát, chiefly to the North Gujarát States and Ahmedabad and also to Surat and Bombay.

Memans, both Cutchis and Haláis, are Sunnis of the Hanafi school, to which most of the Indian and Turkish Musalmáns belong. As a class Memans are religious, though some of them, especially the Cutchis, keep to early non-Muslim social usages. The most notable of these non-Islámic customs is their refusal, like their ancestors the Lohánás, to allow their daughters and widows any inheritance. So Religion careful are the Memans to perform the pilgrimage to Mecca that about forty per cent. of their number have the honourable prefix of Háji or pilgrim. As soon as he has laid by money enough, a Meman takes his wife and sometimes very young children, and, undaunted by the dangers of the voyage, for He who cares for him at home will guard him on the way to His House, starts for Mecca and, if he can afford it, Medina. If he has wealth and leisure, the Meman pilgrim visits Baghdad to worship at the shrine of his patron saint Maulána Abdul Kádir Gilàni. For those who have not made or are unable to make the great pilgrimage several Indian shrines are usually visited, in Gujarát the shrine of Shah Alam at Ahmedabad and the spirit-scaring tomb of Miran Sayad Ali Dátár at Unja about fifty-six miles north of Ahmedabad. Since the opening of the Rajputána Railway, the Meman from Gujarát and Bombay has become a constant visitor at the death-day fairs or *uras* of Khájah Muin-ud-din Chishti of Ajmer. Like other Sunnis, the Meman's belief in magic and sorcery centres in the traditional maxim " Magic is true, but he who practises magic is an infidel." To the practice of white magic, soothsaying (*fal kholna*), and the procuring of luck-charms and amulets they have like other Musalmáns no objection. They also believe in astrology and consult astrologers, a practice condemned by the Prophet. Their advisers in soothsaying and witchcraft are poor Sayads.

The religious head of Cutchi Memans lives at Mundra, about forty miles east of Mándvi, in Cutch. He pays his followers a yearly or two-yearly visit, when a money subscription called *kheda*, from Rs. 2 to Rs. 200, is gathered from every Meman family and paid to the Pir. Memans also honour the Bukhári Sayads of Ahmedabad. Besides a high priest living usually at Sarhind in the Punjab and visiting his Gujarát followers about once every five years the Halais have a provincial head or *mukhi* who lives in Dhoráji in Káthiáwár. This man has powers to hear and pass orders in petty marriage and divorce and sometimes in inheritance cases.

Occupation. Except a small body of craftsmen, Memans are traders, merchants, dealers or shopkeepers in any branch of commerce except intoxicants and other traffic which is forbidden to the followers of Islám.

Food. In food and drink they resemble the general body of Musalmáns.

MENDALE.—A sub-division of Kolis.

MENDAR.—A sub-division of Jogis.

MENDHE.—A sub-division of Dhangars.

MENDJOGI.—A sub-division of Bharádis.

MERS, numbering 24,137 (1901), including 12,474 males and 11,663 females, are found chiefly in Káthiáwár. They are probably the same as the Mheds, Mers or Mánds, who were the most powerful tribe in Lower Sind at the time of the Arab conquest(1) (A.D. 712). The legend of their origin is that when Ráma built the bridge between Hindustán and Ceylon, and crossed over it with his army of monkeys, he created a man from a hair from the back of his neck, and left him to guard the bridge. He called him Keshvála Mer, *kesh* hair. When he returned from Ceylon he married this Mer to a *Rákshas* or demon whom he had brought back with him. Their descendants married into Rajput families and were the origin of the tribe. Walker says they were called Mer from their being on terms of friendship *mher* with the Jethvás. The Mers themselves call themselves Rajputs, and claim a Rajput origin, stating that they are descended from one Randhirji, a Jethva who held twenty-four villages in the Barda district. Their claim is not admitted by the Jethva Rajputs, though they are attached to them from time immemorial. They are a kind of feudal militia, liable to military service. They hold their land on a service tenure, and, in common with the Rabáris, are allowed many privileges and immunities. They do not pay rent for their lands but a hearth tax, and, if they cultivate, they pay a small sum as plough tax. They also pay a quit-rent or *sukhadi*, for the village assigned for their maintenance. If they breed horses or camels they are bound to give the males to the Rána. Their military service has now ceased, but in former times they were the great stand-by of the State. They could turn out three or four thousand strong and, though they obeyed the Rána generally, they served under leaders chosen by themselves from among their own numbers. For every Mer slain in action the Rána paid his heirs Rs. 100 and some additional income. Mers, though frugal, hospitable, simple and kindly, are not free from thievish propensities, and many of them joined the Vághers during the revolt of that clan, with which they have many sympathies. They are divided into four clans, (1) the Keshválás, (2) Rájsukhás, (3) Gohils, and (4) Adidrás (descendants of a Sumra Rajput). They intermarry and allow widow marriage, but in other respects conform to Rajput customs.(2) Name and origin.

MERAI.—A synonym for Darji.

MESHRI.—Religious distinction, generally returned as a caste name by Vaishnav Vánis in contradistinction to Shrávak or Jain Vánis.

---

(1) Elliot and Dawson, I, 128. (2) *Bom. Gaz.*, Vol. VIII, pp. 138-9.

META.—A sub-division of Kolis.

METARIYA.—A synonym for Bhangi.

METHKARI.—A synonym for Barge.

METRI.—A synonym for Kotegar.

METWAL.—A synonym for Medatwál.

MEVADA.—A sub-division of Dhedas, Vániás, Sutárs, Bráhmans.

MHAISBHADRE.—A synonym for Máng Gárudi.

MHALI.—A synonym for Nhávi.

MHAR.—A synonym for Mahár.

MHASKE.—A sub-divison of Dhangars.

MHETRE.—A synonym for Mahár.

MINAHIDIYO.—A sub-division of Kilikets.

MINIGADIK.—A sub-division of Kudavakkals.

MINI MADIG.—A sub-division of Mángs.

MIR.—*See* under Minor Musalmán Castes; also a sub-division of Párdhis.

MIRASI.—A synonym for Mahár.

MIRDHA.—*See* under Minor Musalmán Castes.

MIRJU-MALI.—A sub-division of Vaidus.

MISKIN.—A sub-division of Devángs.

MISTRI.—A synonym for Sutár.

MITH.—A sub-division of Lonáris.

MITH AGRI.—A synonym for Sudh Agri.

MITH GAVADA.—A sub-division of Gávadás.

MITHOBA.—A sub-division of Alkaris.

MITNA.—A sub-division of Machhis.

MOCHI.—A sub-division of Mángs.

Name and origin.

MOCHIS, numbering 128,272 (1901), including 64,902 males and 63,370 females, are found all over Gujarát, chiefly in towns and large villages. They claim descent from Rajputs living near Chámpáner who are said to have been given their present name because one of them made a pair of stockings or *moju* out of a tiger's skin; but no proof in support of this tradition is forthcoming. Their origin is evidently functional.

Mochis have three main endogamous divisions of a territorial type, (1) Ahmedábádis, (2) Khambhátis, and (3) Suratis, who eat together and intermarry. They are further divided into many sections according to their occupation. The chief of these craft sections are as follows :— Endogamous divisions

1. Angigarás or makers of idol ornaments, including Krishna's peacock and feather caps and the talc tablets or *gokhs* of the goddess Bahucharáji.
2. Bakhtargarás or armour makers.
3. Chándlágarás or makers of lac spangles.
4. Chitárás or painters.
5. Dhálgars or shield makers.
6. Jingars or saddlers.
7. Munágarás or workers in enamel.
8. Mochis or shoemakers.
9. Netragarás or makers of idols' eyes.
10. Pákhariás or makers of ornamental horse trappings.
11. Pánágarás or gold and silver foil makers.
10. Rasaniás or electroplaters.

Formerly these different sections ate together and intermarried. Of late in some places the Chándlágarás, Chitárás and Rasaniás have crystallized into distinct castes. Their taking to cleaner callings has so raised them in social position that, though they do not touch a Mochi, high class Hindus treat them as they treat bricklayers, carpenters, masons and other artisans.

Mochis have several surnames in common with Rajputs, all of which are exogamous. The chief of them are :— Exogamous divisions.

Chohán	Gohil	Makvána	Ráthod
Chudásama	Jethva	Máru	Solanki
Dabhi	Jhála	Parmár	Vághela

A Mochi is not allowed to marry his father's sister's, mother's sister's or mother's brother's daughter. Girls are generally married before ten and boys after eight. A man may take a second wife with the consent of the first if the latter is barren. Divorce is granted, but in some parts of South Gujarát to the husband alone. Widow re-marriage is allowed, and in some places the widow marries the younger brother of her deceased husband.

Mochis worship images in their houses. The followers of Swáminaráyan are regular in visiting their temples.

Religion. Except a few in Cutch and the Panch Mahále, Mochis believe in exorcism, witchcraft and omens. Holding them to be spells contrived by an enemy for their undoing, they are seriously alarmed if they find near their homes a lemon with red lead in it, or five beans of *adad* (Phaseolus mungo), or an ivory image daubed with lampblack. They keep the regular Hindu fasts and feasts, and visit the usual places of Hindu pilgrimage. Some of them take to religious lives and make a name as *bhagats* or holy men. In all their ceremonies they employ Bráhman priests, who are called Mochi Gors and are despised by other Bráhmans. No ceremonies are performed on the day of a birth. On the night of the sixth day the goddess Chhathi is worshipped, when the wall of the lying-in room is marked with red powder and on a footstool is laid, besides a reed pen and a water jar, a sword or scimitar wrapped in cloth and set upright. Female relations worship these articles, and the child is made to peep at them. In some places, instead of the jar and sword, an earthen cake is laid on the house-roof. The child is named on the twelfth day. After childbirth, the woman keeps herself aloof for ten or fifteen days. When the ceremony of giving the child its first cooked food is performed, the child is given a few mouthfuls of coarse wheat flour mixed with sugar and butter and some brass cups are distributed to friends and relations. A few Cutch Mochis wear the Bráhmanic thread, but without any thread-girding ceremonies. Except that in the Panch Mahále some *guvár* (Cyamopsis psoraloides) beans are scattered on the bridegoom before he enters the bride's house, their marriage ceremonies, though less detailed, are in the main those performed by Kanbis.

Death ceremonies. They burn their dead. Four cocoanuts are kept hanging from the bier, one at each corner, and are thrown to the four quarters of the heavens at the halting place midway between the house and the burning ground. In Cutch, when the dead body is laid on the pile, the lighting begins from the toe of the left foot. When the body is burnt, a heap of wheat flour in the shape of Shiva's *linga* is made on the burning ground and handfuls of a mixture of water, milk, curds and cow's urine are poured one hunhred and eight times on the wheat flour *linga* out of an earthen jar. The jar is covered with cotton thread and its mouth is closed by a lid bored in four places. A sweet-ball is laid on the lid and the jar is set near the *linga*. For three days a second earthen jar full of milk and water is placed on the house-roof. The nearest male relations of the deceased have their heads, chins and upper lips shaved on the tenth day. A *shráddha* ceremony is performed for three days from the eleventh to the thirteenth day after death. Castepeople are feasted for one or two days. When they cannot get a Bráhman on the death days, they lay wheat cakes and milk on the roof.

Occupation.

As the names of the different sub-divisions show, the Mochi is a man of varied callings, working in leather, painting, electroplating, enamelling, and making tin, gold and silver foil. Mochis also work as gold and silver carvers, as embroiderers on wool and silk, as diamond polishers and setters, and as bricklayers. Besides making saddles, bridles, shields, scabards, hunting-whips and bags, the Mochi's chief employment as a leather-worker is shoemaking. He occasionally works in cotton mills and other factories. preparing leather belting, etc., etc. He buys the hides of cows, oxen, sheep, goats and buffaloes from Musalmán hide merchants and occasionally from Dhedás and Bhangiás who dispose of dead cattle. As a rule a Mochi neither tans hides nor cobbles shoes.

Food

Mochis eat fish and the flesh of sheep, goats and fowls, and drink liquor. Of late years, through many Mochis becoming followers of Swáminaráyan, the use of flesh and liquor has grown less and in some places has ceased.

The Mochi holds a low position in the social scale, and though he does not touch Khálpás, Dheds, or other depressed classes, a high caste Hindu considers the touch of a Mochi a pollution

MOCHIGAR.—A synonym for Mochi Máng.

MOCHIGOR.—A sub-division of Audich Bráhmans.

MOCHI-MOMNA.—A sub-division of Khojáhs.

MODH.—A sub-division of Vániás, Bráhmans, Ghánchis.

MODI.—A sub-division of Koravas.

MODIA.—A sub-division of Vániás.

MODIKAR.—A synonym for Gárudi.

Name and origin.

MOGERS, numbering 4,502 (1901), including 2,550 males and 1,952 females, are found in the Honávar and Kumta *tálukás* of the Kanara district. The occupation of the caste was originally fishing, but the branch now settled in Kumta have discarded this for a higher calling, and attempt to disclaim connection with the remainder by endeavouring to copy the customs of the Gaud Sárasvat Bráhmans. It is stated that the Mogers were once foot soldiers in the service of the kings of Banvási, but no historical confirmation of this statement is forthcoming. Mogers consist of three endogamous divisions, the Aliyasantána, Makalasantána, and Randesantána, *i.e.*, those who inherit through females, those who inherit through males, and the descendants of widows who remarry Their exogamous sub-divisions, known as *balis*, are as follows :—

(1) Shetti bali	..	Shetti = a fish.
(2) Ḍeva bali	..	Deva = god.
(3) Honne bali	..	Honne = a tree (*Pterocarpus Marsupium*).
(4) Dyavana bali	..	Dyava = a tortoise.
(5) Kendi bali	..	Kendi = a tree.
(6) Chendi bali	..	Chendi = a tree (*Cerbera odollam*).
(7) Gangádhar bali	..	Unknown.
(8) Hole bali	..	Unknown.
(9) Balin bali	..	Bali = a sea fish.
(10) Ane bali	..	Ane = an elephant.
(11) Shirin bali	..	Sher or sherkul = a tree (*Gynandropsis pentaphylla*).
(12) Tolana bali	..	Tola = a wolf.
(13) Shendi bali	.	Shendi = the toddy palm.

Members of each *bali* show reverence to, and abstain from injuring, the object after which it is named. The *bali* is traced through females. In cases of adoption, the members of the *bali* from which the adoption is made cannot marry with the members of the adopting *bali* for seven generations.

The Mogers speak Kanarese at home, but most of them know Konkani. The names in common use among men are, Manjayya, Bájiráo, Timmappa, Subráyya, Dása, Venkappa, Jettayya, Annappa, Kántappa, Ráma and Sidappa; and among women, Parmeshri, Subadri, Padmávati, Mahálakshmi, Ganpi, Devamma, Shivamma and Venkamma. They had originally no surnames, but names formerly used to distinguish families from one another by means of the situation of their houses and professions have come to be treated as surnames. Examples of these are: Mápári meaning salt-weighers, Hádimani or roadside house, Kadimani or last house, and Táribagla or ferry gate.

The Mogers have an hereditary headman called *budvant* who has power to call caste meetings and settle minor disputes. Important cases are settled by the religious head of the caste, the Swámi of Paratgali. Outsiders are not admitted into this caste.

Girls are married before they come of age, boys from the age of ten to thirty. A member of the caste can marry his maternal uncle's daughter, but not his mother's sister's daughter. A man may marry his deceased wife's sister. Brothers cannot marry sisters. Polygamy is allowed and practised, but polyandry is unknown. The remarriage of widows is allowed, but is said to be seldom practised. The offer of betrothal generally comes from the girl's family. Formerly the marriages of Mogers were celebrated after the fashion of the Ambigs, but of late they have adopted the marriage ceremonies of the Gaud Sárasvat Bráhmans. The essential portions consist in the mutual exchange of garlands by the bride and bridegroom, the *dháre* ceremony and the *homa* or marriage sacrifice. Divorce is not allowed. The main body of the caste follow the Makalasantána or succession through males. The Aliyasantána or succession through females is only practised by the minority. **Marriage.**

They belong to the Hindu religion and are followers of the Vaishnava sect. Their spiritual guide is the head of the Vaishnava monastery at Paratgali in Goa. They pay him contributions and in return are branded with hot metal seals bearing the conchshell, discus, mace, and lotus of Vishnu. They reverence all Bráhman and village gods, especially Vithoba and Venkataráma, whose images they keep in their houses. They have also a great regard for Jatgas, to whom offerings of goats and fowls are made. They have great faith in sorcery, soothsaying and in the spirits of the dead. They observe all the Hindu holidays. Their priests are Havik Bráhmans. **Religion.**

They burn their dead, burying those who die of cholera, small-pox and leprosy, and children who have not cut their teeth. Formerly their funeral rites were like those of the Ambigs, but of late they have adopted the Bráhmanical ritual.

The hereditary occupation of the caste is catching fish. Most of them have abandoned this occupation, although Mogers are still to be found at Honávar who follow the traditional calling. The Kumta Mogers have taken to trade in cotton, rice and betelnuts. They also serve as clerks and brokers. Some of them are cultivators and domestic servants. **Occupation.**

The staple food of the caste is *rági*, rice and fish. They eat flesh and drink liquor, though the Kumta Mogers profess that they now **Food.**

abstain from both. They take *kacchi* and *pakki* from Bráhmans only.

MOGHA.—A synonym for Rabári.

MOLAVAR.—A sub-division of Khálpas.

MOLESALAM.—*See* under Minor Musalmán castes.

Name. **MOMINS** * or Believers, also called Momnás in some parts of Gujarát, numbering 21,568 (1901), including 11,086 males and 10,482 females, are found in small numbers in all parts of the Presidency. They are divided into two territorial groups—Gujarátis and Deccanis or those found in the Deccan and Karnátak. They are described below separately.

GUJARAT MOMINS are the descendants of Hindus of many castes, converted to the Shiáh form of faith by different members of the family of Ismália Sayads, of whom Imámsháh (A.D. 1449) of Pirána is the most distinguished. Of their conversion two stories are told—one, that Imámsháh by bringing rain after two seasons of scarcity converted a large number of Hindu cultivators. The other, that a band of pilgrims were passing Pirána on their way to Benáres. Imámsháh offered to take them there. They agreed and in a trice were in the holy city. They paid their vows, bathed in the Ganges, and awoke to find themselves in Pirána.

Gujarát Momins have two divisions—Ahmedabadis and the rest. Most of them shave the head and wear the beard; but the Ahmedabadis spare the Hindu topknot and shave the face except the upper lip. Ahmedabadis wear the Vánia turban and in every part of their dress copy the Hindus. Other men wear a three-cornered Muhammadan turban and coat and either the Hindu waistcloth or trousers so loose as to give them the name of *Ghágaria* or petticoated Bohorás. The women, except a few in Surat, dress like Hindus.

Except the Ahmedabadi sect, all Momins intermarry, the Kázi of ordinary Musalmáns performing the ceremony. They are Shiáhs in faith. Except the Ahmedabad sect, they read Kutb-ud-din's Gujaráti *Kurán*, and as a prayer repeat their saint's name. The Ahmedabad sect, instead of the *Kurán*, read Imámsháh's book of religious rules and some of them are said stealthily to worship Hindu gods. Many Momins who are Shiáhs at heart profess to be Sunnis. But there would seem to be in Surat a small body of Momins who

* Momins must not be confounded with Momnas, a half Hindu half Muhammadan caste of cultivators found mainly in Cutch, although probably originally both may have formed one community as the story of their origin is identical.

really belong to the orthodox faith. These have lately separated though they still intermarry with their Shiáh connections. All practise circumcision and bury the dead. In other matters the customs of the Ahmedabad sect differ considerably from those of regular Muslims. Hindu names are common in North Gujarát though rare in the south, and while with ordinary Momins marriages take place according to the Musalmán rules, the Ahmedabad sect, in addition to the Musalmán marriage, call in a Bráhman and go through a Hindu ceremony. In North Gujarát, among all Momins, marriages take place at a very early age, sometimes before the children are weaned, and they follow the Hindu practice of holding a high festival when the bride comes of age and goes to live with her husband. At deaths, like Hindus, the women wail and beat the breast.

Gujarát Momins are silk and cotton weavers, dyers, cloth-dealers and husbandmen. In Kaira and other parts of North Gujarát many of them are said to have once been husbandmen. The women weave and prepare thread.

Almost all Gujarát Momins eat flesh, but for fear of offending the Hindus, whose wishes their position as weavers forces them to humour, they do not use it at their public dinners.

DECCANI MOMINS are said to be the descendants of Hindu converts of the Koshti or Sáli caste. They are said to have been brought to Islám by the persuasion of the Arab missionary Khwája Sayad Hussain Guisudaráj of Gulburga who lived early in the fifteenth century, and of Husham Pir Gujaráti of Bijápur who lived about the close of the sixteenth century.

The hereditary occupation of Deccani Momins is weaving. They marry only among themselves, and as the women are as hardworking as the men, some of them have two or even three wives.

Their manners and customs differ little from those of other Musalmáns. In religion they are Sunnis of the Hanafi school, and most of the old men are said to be religious and careful to say their prayers. Their spiritual head is the representative of Khwája Sayad Hussain, the saint who converted them. He visits them yearly or once every second or third year, when they give him presents of cash and cloth. The spiritual guide, on making a new disciple, teaches him the creed and gives advice about conduct. Besides the religious and moral teaching the guide gives each of the disciples a list of his forefathers back to saint Khwája. The disciple treats this list with the highest respect. He keeps it and values it as dearly as his life, and sometimes has it buried with him in the belief that the holy names will satisfy the angels and prevent them from torturing him in the grave. Some of them practise Hindu customs by keeping the usual Bráhmanic and local festivals and offering vows to Bráhmanic and local gods.

MOMNA.—A sub-division of Kanbis; a synonym for Momin.

MORI.—A sub-division of Vághris.

MOSAL.—A sub-division of Kabbaligars.

MOSALGAR.—A sub-division of Kabbaligars.

MOTA.—A sub-division of Chodhrás.

MOTALA.—A sub-dsivision of Bráhmans.

MOTINATH.—A sub-division of Audich Bráhmans.

MUDALI.—A synonym for Mudliár.

MUDLIARS or Mudalis, numbering 837 (1901), including 424 males and 413 females, are found in Poona, Belgaum, Bijápur and Dhárwár. They are immigrants from Madras and belong to the Vellálás, the great cultivating caste of the Támil country.(1)

Names. **MUGHALS**, numbering 27,682 (1901), including 14,804 males and 12,878 females, are found in all parts of the Presidency. They include two distinct classes—the Persian and the Indian or Chughadda Mughals.*

Persian Mughals are found chiefly in Cambay and Surat. They are the descendants of Persian political refugees and merchants. They always place the title *Mirza* 'born of a great man,' before their names, and add *Beg*, lord, as Mirza Muhammad Beg; the women add *Khánam* to their names, as Husaini Khánam. The distinctive features of the race are middle size, rather inclined to stoutness, light skins, hooked noses and clear features. Some have blue or grey eyes, and most have a humorous and intelligent expression. They are mostly Shiáhs in religion and have a name for carefully keeping the rules of their faith. Some of them are traders and the rest are in Government service. As they form a distinct community with their own places of worship, and as they generally marry among themselves, the Persian Mughals have fewer Hindu customs than most other Musalmáns.

Indian Mughals are found in small numbers in all parts of the Presidency. They appear to be the descendants of the Mughal conquerors of India, who penetrated into Gujarát and the Deccan, and have left many descendants where they once ruled. Like the Persian Mughals, the men always place the title *Mirza* before their names and

(1) Castes and Tribes of Southern India, Vol. V., p. 84.

* So called after the son of Changiz Khan.

add *Beg*, and the women add *Khánam* to their names. Except that they are fairer in complexion, they do not differ in appearance from ordinary Musalmáns. They are Sunnis of the Hanafi school, differing in no way from the great body of the Sunni Musamláns. Most of them earn their living as Government servants, messengers and police.

MUJPHADIA.—A sub-division of Gandhariás.

MUKRIS, numbering 5,082 (1901) including 2,486 males and 2,596 females, are found entirely in the district of Kanara. They are sometimes called Hebbe-gaudas or old Gaudas, the latter being a synonym of the Halvakki Vakkals. The precise meaning of this synonym is obscure, though it would seem to suggest some former connection between the Halvakki Vakkals and the Mukris. **Name and origin.**

There are no endogamous divisions of the caste. Their exogamous sub-divisions, known as *balis*, are as follows :— **Divisions.**

1. Kanne bali .. Kanne = virgin.
2. Tolana bali .. Tola = a wolf.
3. Shendi bali .. Shendi = Toddy palm.
4. Kavdchi bali .. A tree = Acacia speciosa.
5. Ane bali .. Ane = elephant.
6. Shirin bali .. A tree = Gynandropsis pentaphylla.
7. Shetti bali .. Shetli or Shetti = a fish.
8. Dyavana bali .. Dyava = tortoise.
9. Handi bali .. Handi = pig.
10. Hebbali bali .. A tree = Artocarpus hirsata.

The members of the Shendi *bali* will not touch toddy nor go beneath the shade of the toddy tree, and similarly with the Shirin *bali*, the tree is avoided and never injured. Members of the elephant division will not wear ivory ornaments. Descent of the *balis* is traced only through males. The fourth and last of these divisions seems peculiar to the Mukri and Moger castes. Others are common among Dravidian castes of Kanara.

The Mukris speak Kanarese. The names in common use among men are Bolla, Jetti, Bira, Maru, Durgu, Lingu and Nágu ; and among women, Mari, Kanni, Jethi, Shivi, Yenki and Lingi. They have no stock names or surnames, but they add the word *Halli* or *Mukri* to their names.

The Mukris are a well-organized communities and have group-heads or *bárkas* and village-heads or *budvants*, each of whom has an **Organization.**

attendant or *kolkár*. Their settlements are divided into forty groups and the groups into four divisions. The four divisions are Hebbankeri in Honávar with eighteen groups ; Hegde in Kumta with six groups : Kumta with seven groups ; and Gokarn with nine. The village-heads or *budvants*, who are subject to the group-heads or *bárkas*, have power to call and preside over councils, to enquire into breaches of caste rules, and to punish offenders in accordance with the opinion of the majority of the members. The decisions are enforced on pain of loss of caste. The greatest social offence is to beat a casteman with a sandal, or to incur a sandal beating from a man of another caste. The punishment for beating or being beaten is a fine varying from Re. 1 to Rs. 16. Of this amount three-quarters are spent on a caste feast. The remaining quarter is paid to the manager of Hanumant's temple, who keeps four annas for himself and places the rest to the credit of the temple funds. When he receives his share of the fine, the priest gives the culprit a little of the water in which the idol has been bathed. The offender, whether the beater or the person who is beaten, is taken to a river, and after bathing is given some holy water, part of which he drinks and part he rubs on his body. The caste is then feasted with palm-beer, rice, curry and sweet gruel. A Mukri who eats with a person of lower caste, or a Mukri widow who becomes pregnant, is turned out of caste. The widow' s paramour has to pay a fine and to undergo special purification. On paying the fine, which is spent in the same way as the fine levied on a man who has been beaten with a slipper, the offender, with one or more castemen, goes to Gokarn, where his head and face, including top-knot and moustaches, are shaved by a casteman. He is then bathed in the sea, and led to the temple of Mahábaleshvar where, for the use of the priest, he lays on a plantain leaf two pounds of rice, a cocoanut and a copper coin. On returning to the village he again bathes in the presence of two caste people and passes through seven temporary *cadjan* huts, which are burnt as soon as he passes through them. When the huts are completely burnt, the offender drinks water brought from Hanumán's temple and joins some castemen in a dinner. Adultery by married women is punished by severe beating at the hands either of the husband or the next-of-kin. Insult to a headman or improper conduct at a public meeting is punished with fine up to Re. 1, the amount being spent in the same way as the fine levied in a sandal-beating or widow-pregnancy case. Once in two or three years the caste meets at Honjikatta near Chandávar in Honávar. Every man has to take with him four annas, six to eighteen pounds of rice and a cocoanut. The meeting lasts three to ten days according to the business to be settled. At these meetings offenders against social discipline are tried, and important matters touching the welfare of the community are discussed. The Mukris do not admit outsiders into the caste.

Marriage

Girls are married either before or after they come of age. Widow marriage and polygamy are allowed and practised, but polyandry is unknown. The offer of betrothal generally comes from the boy's family. The boy's father with four or five castemen, goes to the girl's father and makes a proposal for the marriage. On the girl's father consenting to the proposal, the *tera* or bride-price, which is never less than Rs. 20, is settled, toddy is served, and a dinner of rice and cocoanut milk is given to the assembly. On the day before the ceremonies begin, a Havig priest is asked to fix the lucky moment for the marriage, and he is paid six pounds of rice, five cocoanuts and four annas in cash. The marriage ceremonies last four days. On the first day the bridegroom's party go to the girl's house and deck her with ornaments and flowers. Early next morning, from the bride's and bridegroom's, messengers are sent to ask the caste people to the wedding. When the guests come, they are seated on mats spread on the ground in the marriage booth. Special respect is shown to the headmen of the caste by seating them by themselves in a raised part of the booth with an attendant standing behind them. When the guests have come, the bridegroom is dressed in a narrow waistcloth, a shoulder cloth and a head-scarf. He takes in his hand a couple of betel leaves, and, holding a cocoanut in his hand, bows to the family god, which is an unhusked cocoanut, and to the sweet basil plant, and breaks a cocoanut before each of them. When this ceremony is over, all present go in procession with the bridegroom to the house of the bride. On reaching the bride's, her parents lead the bridgeroom into the marriage booth where he crawls under the low arched branch of a fig tree, and, while women sing Kanarese songs, he is bathed with water from two large earthen pots placed on either-side of the arch. When the bathing is over, the bridegroom is seated on a low wooden stool. Cooked rice, fish curry, vegetables and sweet gruel are served. In the evening a large quantity of toddy is set before the guests, and both men and women drink freely and dance, moving in a circle to the sound of pipe and drum. When the liquor is finished and the dancers are worn out, the headman ties the ends of the bride's and bridegroom's garments, joins their hands, and pours water over them. After this the bride and bridegroom retire for the night. Next day the pair go to the bridegroom's house, where they are feasted with palm-juice and sweet gruel, rice and fish curry. On the fourth day the bridal party return to the bride's house, where a feast is given. This ends the ceremony.

The headman or *budvant* is given two pounds of rice and half a cocoanut.

The marriage of widows is permitted. The pair to be married must first obtain the permission of the caste people by paying a sum of Rs. 10. The ceremony consists in the presentation to the widow by her new husband of a robe, which she puts on. A feast is then given to the caste people.

A husband may divorce his wife on account of her misconduct. A divorced woman cannot marry again during the life-time of her husband.

Religion. The members of the caste follow the Hindu law of inheritance. They belong to the Hindu religion. Their chief god is Virabhadra, whose shrine is at Hegde in Kumta, where, in January, the whole cast meets at the yearly festival of the god. They also worship Jatkás, Mhastis, Ammás and the other village gods. Next to Virabhadra, they honour Venkataráma and Hanumán of Chandávar in Honávar. They call Hanumant *gurudevaru*, the divine teacher. Each Mukri family pays 1 to $1\frac{1}{3}$ annas to Virabhadra and Hanumán regularly every year through their headman, and they keep wooden images of Virabhadra and Venkataráma in every pot or hollow pillar of sweet basil. The images are bathed and daubed with yellow clay or *gopichandan* every day before meals. After bathing the gods, the worshipper walks several times round the sweet basil plant, bowing to it as well as to the sun. After this they pluck a leaf of the plant, and dip it in a metal water pot set at the feet of the image of Virabhadra, and let the water drop from the leaf into their mouths. Their leading holidays are *Makarsankránti*, *Shimga*, *Yágudi*, *Diváli*, *Bhandihabha*, local hook-swinging festivals and the *Teru* or car festivals. They make pilgrimages to Chandávar in Honávar and to Tirupati near Madras. Those who go to Tirupati are called *dásas* or slaves of the god, and are treated with much respect. All lay by small sums of money as offerings to Venkataráma, and either take or send the amount. They have no religious teachers.

They do not employ Bráhmans for religious or ceremonial purposes. All their ceremonies are conducted by the *budvants* of the caste.

Death ceremonies. They bury the dead and mourn three days. On the third day after the death all adult male neighbours come to the house of mourning. The chief mourner cooks a small quantity of rice, without salt, strains it dry, dissolves a little tamarind in the water, bakes three rice cakes, and brings some palm-beer. Then, with the guests, he goes to the grave, taking with him some of the food, and lays it near the grave, as an offering, and stays there till the cakes are eaten by crows. When the men start for the grave, the women begin to cowdung the floor of the house and finish the work before the men return. On returning, the mourners and the guests bathe in cold water, take a little of the cakes and other eatables, and go to their houses. On the eleventh day all the caste people in the village are invited; those who are relations bring with them different kinds of eatables. The people of the house cook dry rice, fish curry and sweet gruel, and lay in a stock of palm juice. Portions of everything cooked in the house, as well as of what has been brought by relations, are spread on a plantain leaf and given to a cow. After this all the guests and house people dine together and drink palm-beer. On every new-moon a cow is fed with rice, curry and sweet gruel to please the dead.

The Mukris are hard-working and well-behaved, but thriftless. **Occupation.** They are field-labourers and makers of shell lime. Most of them are employed by Havig Bráhmans in their spice gardens, and are bound to labour for a term of years, for life, or for several generations, in return for money advanced to meet marriage expenses; some also work as labourers and take contracts to dig wells and reclaim or level lands. When money is borrowed from the landlord, a man generally binds himself by a written agreement to pay interest at ten or fifteen per cent. If he is unable to pay, he generally works a certain number of years for the landlord in return for the money and interest. They earn only enough for their bare maintenance, many depending on the higher classes of Hindus, especially on Havig Bráhmans, for funds to meet the expenses of their marriage ceremonies, in return for which they have to serve their creditors for long periods. In such cases they are required to work during the rainy season, when tilling operations are carried on, and receive from their employers rice for their maintenance and a suit of clothes. During the fair months they are free to work on their own account.

They eat the flesh of tortoises, fish and all kinds of four-footed **Food.** animals except cows, buffaloes, tigers, lizards, monkeys, jackals, snakes, etc. They are very fond of drinking toddy and liquor.

MULTANI.—A sub-division of Khojáhs.

MUNAGAR.—A sub-division of Mochis.

MUNHCHIRA.—A synonym for Rafái.

MUNHPHODA.—A synonym for Rafái.

MUNI.—A synonym for Mánbháv.

MURAD.—A sub-division of Jogis.

MURDE.—A sub-division of Várlis.

MURLI.—A sub-division of Mahárs.

Name and origin. **MURLIS** and **VAGHES** numbering 229 (1901), including 106 males and 123 females, are found in small numbers all over the Deccan. The figures are obviously misleading, since members of this and similar castes recruited by dedication are apt to describe themselves by their parent caste name. When a man has no children or his children are short-lived, he vows that if Khandoba blesses him with a child, he will set it apart to worship and attend upon the god. Girls offered to Khandoba in this way are called Murlis, and boys Vájhes. Sometimes married women also become Murlis, leaving their husbands and even their children, saying that they have made a vow to Khandoba or that they are warned in a dream that they should be the wives of Khandoba, and not of men. Middle and low class Hindus respect and bow before the true Murli who is wedded to the god as a girl. They look down upon women who leave their husbands and children to become Murlis. This custom of dedicating boys and girls to Khandoba as Vághyás and Murlis prevails chiefly among Kunbis and other Hindu castes of similar standing.

Divisions. There are three divisions of Murlis and Vághes, *viz.*, Marátha, Dhangar and Mahár, of whom the Maráthás and Dhangars eat together. None of these divisions will intermarry.

Initiation ceremonies. Murlis are married to the god Khandoba between one and twelve and always before they come of age. When a Murli is to be married to Khandoba, her parents take her to Jejuri in Poona sometime in *Chaitra*. They bring turmeric, dry cocoa-kernel, flower garlands, nosegays, a robe and bodice, a sash, a turban, milk, curds, sugar, butter, honey and flowers, and, with a Gurav priest and a band of Vághya musicians, go to the temple. At the temple the girl is bathed, the god is rubbed with turmeric, and the rest of the turmeric is rubbed on the girl. The girl is dressed in a new robe and bodice, green glass bangles are put round her wrists, and flower marriage ornaments or *mundávals* are tied to her brow. The god is worshipped, the turban and sash are presented to him, and the Gurav, taking in his hands a necklace or *gátha* of nine cowrie shells, fastens it round the girl's neck. This is called *gátha phodne* or breaking the cowrie necklace, and the Gurav is paid Rs. 1¼ as the price of the necklace. The girl is made to stand to the left of the god, and the guests throw turmeric over the god-bridegroom and the bride, crying out twice *Elkot ghe*, *Elkot he*, *i.e.*,

Take, Elkot ; take, Elkot ! Her parents pay the Gurav who acts as priest Rs. 5, and each Vághe and Murli who is present receives a copper coin. The bride and her parents retire, and at their house give a feast to Murlis and Vághes.

When a Murli comes of age she finds a patron, who pays her a sum of from Rs. 25 to Rs. 100. If the sum is Rs. 50 or more, half the money goes to the Vághe-Murli community, who spend it in caste vessels and in feasts. With the balance the girl buys a robe and a bodice for herself, and some bedding. She sets up a bamboo frame, puts green bangles on her wrists, and, dressing in the new clothes, sits in the frame and has her lap filled by Murlis ; or, if there are no Murlis, by married women. She is taken to the village Máruti with Murlis, Vághes, and music, presents the god with a copper coin and betel packet, returns home, and feasts her caste fellows. She then lives with her patron.

Vághes generally marry into their father's caste, but there is no objection to the intermarriage of a Vághe boy and a Vághe girl. Their children are Vághes and marry with their father's caste.

A Vághe is always dedicated in Khandoba's temple at Jejuri in Poona on any day in the month of *Chaitra*. When parents have to dedicate a boy to Khandoba they go to Jejuri, stay at a Gurav's house, and tell him the object of their visit. The boy's father buys turmeric, dry cocoa-kernel, a cocoanut, some milk, curds, honey, sugar, a flower garland and a nosegay, some sandal paste, and a turban and sash. Then taking the boy, the Gurav, Vághes and Murlis go in procession with music to Khandoba's temple. At the temple the Gurav bathes and worships the god, offering him the turban and sash and Rs. 1-10-0 in cash. He then marks the boy's brow with turmeric, throws turmeric over his head, fastens round his neck a deer or tiger skin wallet hung from a black woollen string, and thrice throws turmeric and dry cocoakernel over the god, twice repeating the words *Elkot ghe*, that is, Take, Elkot ! All who are present in turn throw turmeric on the god and the ceremony is over. The Gurav is paid Rs. 5 as his fee and Rs. 1¼ as the price of the wallet, and each of the Vághe and Murli guests is presented with a copper coin. When the parents return home, cooked food is offered to the house Khandoba and a feast is held.

Vághes are considered Khandoba's disciples, and Maráthás and other middle and low class Hindus bow down to them. They have to go to Jejuri once every three years.

Except in the initiation ceremonies described above, the Murlis and Vághes do not differ from Marátha Kunbis in religion and customs.

Their favourite gods are Khandoba, Bahiroba, Bhaváni, Jotiba and Satvái.

Occupation. Murlis are prostitutes and beggars. In addition to the dress worn by Kunbi women, they mark their brows with turmeric powder and wear a necklace of nine cowrie shells. They generally go a-begging with two or three Vághes who beat small drums or *dafris*. The Vághes dance and the Murli sings songs, generally indecent, in praise of Khandoba. Some Murlis reside at Jejuri, while the rest wander over the Deccan in bands of three or four men and women, begging, singing songs, and playing on bells or *ghols*.

MUSALE.—A sub-division of Kolis.

MUSALMAN (1) numbering 4,567,295 (1901), including 2,430,184 males and 2,137,111 females, are found throughout the Presidency. Many are immigrants or their descendants who came to the country as Muhammadans, from the eighth century onwards; others are converted Hindus who either joined Islám from conviction in response to the teaching of missionaries or responded to pressure applied by zealous Moslem rulers such as Mahmud Begada, Aurangzeb, and latterly the Mysore despots Hyder and Tipu.

The most important missionaries were :—

(1) Abdulláh, who founded the sect of Shiah Bohorás of Gujarát (A.D. 1067).

(2) Khájáh Muin-ud-din Chisti (A.D. 1165), who finally settled at Ajmere, where he made many converts and died in A.D. 1235.

(3) Sayad Muhammad Jaunpuri who came to Gujarát in A.D. 1509, claiming to be the Imám Mendi.

(4) Sháh Alam, the ornament of Mahmud Begada's reign (A.D. 1459—1513).

(5) Táhir the preceptor of Muzaffar II (A.D. 1513—1526).

(6) Imám Sháh of Piráná.

(7) Pir Mahabir Khandáyat, an Arab preacher, who came as a missionary to the Deccan about the beginning of the fourteenth century (H. 704 A.D. 1305) and is bured in the Ark Killa or citadel at Bijápur.

(8) Khwája Khunmir Husaini (1520).

(1) This article is based on K. B. Fazullah Latifullah's account in Bom. Gaz., Vol. IX, Part II.

(9) Sayad Muhammad Sádik Surmast Hasaoni (1568); and

(10) the Arab missionary Khwája Sayad Husein Gaisudaraz, better known as Khwája Mukdám Gesudaráz of Gulbarga, who, according to a Hindu tale, converted in the thirteenth century a large body of Momins or cotton weavers. The learned men were mostly invited by the Muhammadan rulers of Gujarát, notably by Muzaffar in A.D. 1395 and Mahmud Begada in A.D. 1471.

The proximity of the Bombay Presidency to Persia, Mesopotamia and Arabia has led to successive immigrations, which commenced with the Arabs many years before the birth of Muhammad (570 A.D.). The conquest of Northern India in the 12th century brought Musalmán power into Khándesh and Gujarát, while their capture of Daulatábád, the ancient Devgiri in the Deccan, leading to the establishment of the kingdoms at Ahmednagar, Bijapur, Golconda and the fall of the Vijayanagar Empire spread their dominion over the remainder of the Presidency, including the Konkan.

Thus for a time a religion differing sharply from Hinduism in its attitude towards caste distinctions was the faith of the ruling dynasties throughout the Presidency. Immigrants and their descendants under the name of Sayads, Shaikhs, Mughals and Patháns formed one community, and though Sayads claim social precedence over the other three and prefer to marry with Sayads, there is no sort of prohibition, either by religion or custom, of intermarriage.

The position of converted Hindus, with regard to intermarriage is more difficult to define. Once converted, their religion permitted intermarriage freely; but custom has been slow to follow suit. Of all the castes in which a Musalmán section is found it would seem that the following only are disposed to marry freely with all Musalmáns :—

1. Atár .. .. Perfumers.
2. Barutgar .. .. Firework makers.
3. Bedar .. .. Fighting men.
4. Bhisti .. .. Water carriers.
5. Dalál .. .. Horse dealers.
6. Darzi .. .. Tailors.
7. Goniväla .. .. Grain dealers.
8. Hakim .. .. Healers.
9. Kágzi .. .. Paper makers.

10. Kalaigar	.. ..	Tinsmiths.
11. Kapshgar	.. ..	Shoe makers.
12. Maháwat	.. ..	Elephant drivers.
13. Maniár	.. ..	Bangle makers and hardware dealers.
14. Náikvári	.. ..	Fighting men.
15. Nálband	.. ..	Farriers.
16. Patvegar	.. ..	Tassel makers.
17. Rafugár	.. ..	Cloth darners.
18. Rangrezi	.. ..	Dyers.
19. Sárbán	.. ..	Camel drivers.
20. Saikalgar	.. ..	Armourers.

It is interesting to note that these castes represent almost entirely occupations that would be required by the camp followers of an army on the march, *e.g.*, elephant and camel drivers, farriers, water carriers, armourers, horse dealers, gunpowder makers and tinsmiths. Bedars, of course, are a well known fighting tribe, which with their northern branch or Rámoshis, would be well represented in any military camp. It may be that the close relations thus established between members of these castes and other Musalmáns helped to remove the prejudice against intermarriage on the part of these converts. In the table given below (p. 99) a selection from Kázi's records affords evidence of these intermarriages and would seem to show that the custom is spreading to certain other castes that do not admit such intermarriages being permissible.

Thus among Musalmáns we have three well defined groups :—

(1) Immigrants and their descendants known as Sayads, Shaikhs, Mughals, Patháns, Bohorás, Memons and Khojáhs.

(2) Hindu converts marrying freely with other Muhammadans.

(3) Hindu converts retaining their former prohibition of marriage outside the caste.

The first will be found described under separate articles (*see* Sayad, Shaikh, etc.).

They came first from Arabia as sailors, merchants and soldiers to the ports of the Konkan in great numbers. From the accounts of Sulaimán (A.D. 851) the earliest Arab traveller, it would seem that about the middle of the ninth century, the Balhára, that is, the Ráshtrakuta (A.D. 752—873) of Malkhed in the Deccan, then sovereign of the Konkan and Gujarát, was very partial to Arabs.[1] Al Masudi (A.D. 916) found Islám honoured and protected. "On all sides", he says, "rise chapels and splendid mosques where the daily five prayers can be prayed."[2] At Saimur, probably Cheul about thirty miles south of Bombay, were 10,000 Musalmáns chiefly from the Persian Gulf. Ibn-i-Haṅkal (A.D. 943) found mosques at Anhilaváda, Cambay and Sindán; and Al-Idrisi (A.D. 1070—1100) says Nahrwála (Anhilaváda) was frequented by large numbers of Musalmán traders.[3] These traders, who came mostly from the Persian Gulf, established themselves in considerable numbers in the chief Gujarát cities. Encouraged to settle by the Rajput kings of Anhilwáda, they were treated with much consideration and allowed to manage their affairs, to practise their religion and to build mosques.[4] During the fourteenth, fifteenth and sixteenth centuries, when much of the Konkan was in the possession of the Bahmani and Bijapur kings, a fresh impulse was given to immigration, both from the increased importance of places of trade, and from the demand for Arab and Persian soldiers. As late as the Maráthás the services of Arab seamen were still in demand.[5] The Konkani Musalmáns of Bombay, generally known among Musalmáns by the term Kufis, seem, as the name shows, to have come to India from the Euphrates valley, and to belong to the same wave of Arab settlers who are known as Naváyats. The tradition of the people and the accounts of many Musalmán historians agree that the bulk of them fled to India from the Euphrates valley about the year 700 (82 A.H.) to escape massacre at the hands of the fierce governor Hajjáj bin Yusuf.[6]

The foreign elements mentioned above were further augmented by Musalmán invaders from the north of the eleventh and twelfth centuries and by foreign Musalmán soldiers, traders, refugees and slaves who kept flocking into Gujarát both by land and sea from the end of the

---

(1) Elliot's History, 1—4.

(2) Meynard's Prairies d'Or, 1—382.

(3) Elliot's History, 1, 5, 24, 27,34, 38, 88, and Reinaud's Memoire sur l' Inde, 220.

(4) Bom. Gaz., Vol. IX, Part II, p. 2, footnote 1.

(5) In 1683 the Company's merchantman President was, off Sangameshawar, attacked by two ships and four grabs. The crew were Arabs who said they were in Sambhaji's pay. Orme's His. Frag., 120.

(6) Bom. Gaz.. Vol., X, p. 133, footnote I.

thirteenth century.[1] Most of them came singly and were absorbed into the general Musalmán population. In mordern times three events have, on a somewhat larger scale, added to the foreign element of the Musalmán population. These are, towards the close of the eleventh century, the arrival from Yaman in Arabia, with a band of followers, of the religious head of the Shiáh trading Bohorás; about the middle of the seventeenth century the establishment at Surat of the Janjira Sidis as admirals of the Mughal fleet; and during the eighteenth century the influx of Arab missionaries and of several bands of Persian political refugees. [2]

Hindu converts of the second class are described shortly under MINOR MUSALMAN CASTES. Others will be found referred to under the article dealing with the parent Hindu caste. It may be observed here that it is almost impossible to secure accurate statistics of these Musalmán divisions at the time of a census. Many caste members will simply style themselves Musalmán. Others will return themselves under the general term of Shaikh, which is used to denote any Hindu convert, and thus totally to obscure the fact that they belong to a caste such as Atár, Nálband, etc. Where figures are given therefore, for the minor Musalmán castes this must be taken as every little evidence of the real extent of the Sub-division. Musalmán pregnancy, birth, betrothal, marriage and death rites are given below.

Pregnancy. ***The exorcist Amil.***

The Urdu proverb *Margae mardud, na fatiha na darud:* Here lies the wretch eternally damned without the *Fatiha* or the *Darud* [3] shows the horror felt by the Musalmán at the prospect of leaving no issue to perform these ceremonies on his behalf. His desire for the immortality given by children, especially by male children, is much akin to the Hindu hankering after issue to save him from the hell of oblivion by performing his *shráddha* or mind feast. After a year or two of married life, if their union is not blessed by issue, some Musalmán women resort to remedies to obtain children. Saints, living or dead, are appealed to, the former to bless by giving charms or medicines to the wife who yearns to be a mother. The law doctors or exorcists also give charms, written on a piece of paper to wash in rose-water and drink.

Some *Amils* or exorcists give their applicants cardamoms or cloves or pieces of candied sugar on which the mystic and powerful names of God have been blown. These are supposed to possess the virtue of casting out the spirit of barrenness, since as a rule barrenness

(1) Bom. Gaz., Vol. IX, Part II, p. 3, footnote 1.
(2) Bom. Gaz., Vol. IX, Part II, p. 3, footnote 2.
(3) *Fatiha* is the opening chapter of the Kurán in praise of God: *Darud* the calling down of blessings on the Prophet.

is believed to be due to spirit-possession. Others direct strands of thread to be worn round the abdomen or the neck; others again simply write or trace some name or charm of words with the tip of the finger over the womb of the woman or the loins of the man. The exorcist or *Amil* has also to help after conception to secure that the issue may be male. He gives charms to be washed and drunk every month or some written charm to be washed in water for a monthly bath. Some dead saints have a reputation as child-givers. To tie knots on bits of string or ribbon with one end attached to a post or pillar supporting a canopy over a saint's grave or to a trellis or balustrade around a shrine is considered by barren women one of the surest means of obtaining issue. Blochmann (Ain-i-Akbari, 267, note 1, paragraph 3) notices that the tomb of Shaikh Salim-i-Chishti at Fatehpur Sikhri, in whose house the Emperor Jehángir (A.D. 1605—1627) was born, is up to the present day visited by childless Hindu and Musalmán women. A tree in the compound of the saint Sháh-i-Alam of Ahmedábád yields a peculiar acorn-like fruit which is sought after far and wide by issue-seekers and carried away and given to their wives, who eat the fruit, and from the moment the fruit is eaten, conceive. If the birth of a child follows the eating of the acorn, the man or woman who took the acorn should for a certain number of years come at every anniversary of the saint and nourish the tree with a supply of milk. The leaves of the tree near the grave of the Mirán Sáheb of Unjha are also said to favour conception. In addition to these, jasmin and rose bushes at the shrines of certain saints are supposed to possess issue-giving properties. To draw virtue from the saint's jasmin, the woman who yearns for a child bathes and purifies herself and goes to the shrine and seats herself under or near the jasmin bush with her skirt spread out. As many flowers as fall into her lap so many children will she have. In north Gujarát, if after the birth of a child no male issue follows, or being born does not live, the first-born child is believed to be the cause of the evil. The first-born is looked on as possessed by some malignant spirit who destroys the young lives of the new-born brothers and sisters. So at the mother's next confinement molasses and sesame seed are passed seven or nine times over the new-born infant from head to foot, and the elder boy or girl is given these to eat. The molasses represent the life of the young one given to the spirit who possesses the first-born. Children born deformed or with one or two teeth are supposed to exercise a baneful influence over their parents and near relatives. A child born with teeth is believed to exercise so malignant an influence that the early death of one of the parents is almost certain.

If the treatment of the live, or the relics of the dead, saint result in pregnancy the greatest care is taken that no baneful influences interfere with a safe delivery. The lady is made to wear a number of charms and always to carry a knife or other piece of iron. She must not go out of doors, especially on new-moons and Thursdays, and on all days at sunset must avoid groves and the sea and river side. Charmed silk threads called *bhárdori*, literally the spirit-laden cord, are worn round her waist and abdomen, and, especially if any portion of the period of her pregnancy falls on or about the days of *Diváli*, which is considered an evil spirit-time, she requires the greatest care. She is not allowed to go under the *mándwa* or alcove built before a house on marriage or other festive occasions. She must avoid marriage or death ceremonies, must not pass under the city gates, and must cross no river or sea. During eclipses of the sun and the moon particular care must be taken that neither she nor her husband, nor even the relatives of her husband, eat or drink or smoke or cut or clip or break anything. If any of them eat a *pán* or betel-leaf or even fold a *pán* the child is sure to be born with ears folded like a '*pán*' leaf: if the relation cuts or clips anything the child is sure to have a deformed finger or a hare-lip.

The *bhárdori* or weight that is the spirit-laden cord, in the sense of the ill-luck imprisoning cord, is regarded as a preservation of the child from conception to delivery. It is a seven-braided piece of silk upon which the Mulla or exorcist spends time and trouble, repeating over it verses of the Kurán or charms and tying a knot at each repetition, making the number of knots correspond with the number of pregnancy months and giving the silk to be wound round the womb. The braids are particoloured white, red, green, black and fine variations of these leading colours. This silk cord is a guard against miscarriage and all the evils, spiritual as well as physical, that cause miscarriage. At the end or beginning of the ninth month the braid is unwound and some incense is burned under it and together with some flowers it is thrown into an unused well, or, if no well is at hand, into a river or a lake or other water. During the period of pregnancy the woman may not wear new clothes, jewels, even bangles, the symbol of married life which the married woman holds most sacred. All the usual adornments of the person otherwise considered necessary are during pregnancy laid aside and looked upon as forbidden. No eyelid is darkened with antimony, no finger or toe-tip, no palm or sole is reddened with henna, no tooth is blackened with *missi*, and certain kinds of food are forbidden. The pregnant lady is not to touch a cocoa-kernel, nor to taste any underground root except the exotic potato. The ban against ornaments lasts till the *satmása* or seventh month celebration.

After the last pregnancy ceremony the wife goes to her father's house and stays there till her confinement is over. Among the rich and middle classes the servant who first brings his master news of the birth of a child gets a present of Re. 1 to Rs. 2. Soon bands of musicians and the hated *hijdas* or eunuchs (1) crowd round the house on the lookout for gifts. Some peculiar customs are observed at the birth of a child. No sooner does the stranger appear than the midwife or *dai* announces its sex. If a boy she says, nominally to save the mother a shock of happy surprise, but at heart to deceive the evil spirits of jealousy, "It is only a girl blind of one eye." If a girl is born, the fact is stated since the birth of a girl can cause no jealousy. Boy or girl, the new born child is laid in a bamboo *supla* or winnowing-fan while the more pressing needs of its mother are being ministered to. A piece of new red cloth is wound rather tightly round the little one's head and the young one is ready to hear the *takbir* or call to prayer. That its Creater's name may be the first word it hears, the father, as soon as the child is bathed, repeats in its ear the call to prayer, *azán*, beginning with the words Alláh-o-Akbar God is great.(2) As soon as the first bath is over pieces of black-thread are wound rather tightly round the child's wrists and ankles as its first armour against the evil eye. Its eyes or rather eyelids are stained with soot made of *ghi* and lampblack, its eyebrows are pencilled with soot, dots of lampblack are made on its little cheeks, palms and sole and a lock of its hair is gummed or waxed so that any one with an evil eye feeling them or looking at them may not meet an even glossy surface. Every morning and evening frankincense and the *rái-ispand*, corruptly termed *rai-band*, that is mustard (3) and henna seed, is passed seven or nine times over the mother and the child from head to foot, and thrown into the fireplace and burned. Often red Birth.

---

(1) The eunuchs beat a drum and sing, while one of their numbers, with the help of a pad or pillow, acts the part of a woman with child, in child-birth, and nursing. At Ahmedábád not only the *Hijdás* but some of the *Bhawayyás* or Hindu strolling players claim presents on the birth of a boy with a pertinacity that is not satisfied till the whole of their demand is paid. The person claiming the gift is generally the clown or fool of the troop. He does not dance or sing, but by his obstreperous sallies of coarse abuse tries to make his stay so annoying that to get rid of him no expense is thought too great. To avoid the nuisance some people satisfy his demands at his house by sending him a present of eight annas or a rupee.

(2) Occasionally at the time of birth a Bráhman is called and told to draw up a horoscope. He chooses certain letters, with one of which the child's name should begin. The paper is kept by the parents of the child and referred to on great occasions. The Bráhman is paid Rs. 5 to Rs. 20.

(3) In his Urdu Dictionary Forbes says the seed of the henna plant is burnt at marriages to drive away evil spirits. Henna seed mixed with mustard seed is also burnt after a child is born, particularly at the door, to prevent demons from entering.

chilly seeds are thrown into the fire, especially to judge whether an ailment of the child is physical or spirit-caused. If the burning of the chillies creates no pungent vapour, a spirit is surely the cause of the disease. If the burning chilly has its proper pungent smell the ailment is natural. Sometimes a piece of alum is burned with the mustard-seed, the burning alum swelling into fantastic forms which to the wise show the sex of the person who owns the evil eye. During the five days before the *chatti* or sixth-day celebration no fire or salt or water is to be given to any one from the house in which a woman is confined. To accustom the child to noise a copper or brass dish is struck at his ear before the father repeats to him the *takbir* or call to prayer. To harden the child cold water is sprinkled over him before his bath.

Naming. Early in the morning of the sixth-day the child is named. The father, grandfather or other male relative opens the Kurán at a venture, and the first letter of the first word of the third line is the initial of the child's name.(1) Sometimes a name is chosen because it had

(1) The class of names recommended by the Prophet are the slave or servant of Alláh or servant of the most Merciful, Abd-ulláh or Abd-ur-Rehman. Among Sayads, boys' names generally end in Ali, as *Ahmad-ali, Akbar-ali, Mumtaz-ali*, or in *Husain* as *Fazl Husain*, and sometimes though rarely in *Sháh*, as *Muhammad Sháh* and *Taj-Sháh*. Among *Shaikhs*, boys are called *Umar Usmán, Muhammad, Mahmud, Husain, Ghulám-husain, Ghulám-ali, Gulmám-ahmed*. These names are common in all families. The following are used almost solely in families of good position: *Shams-ud-din, Moin-ud-din, Saadullah, Fazlullah*, and the like. The names of Shaikhs are preceded either by the word *Muhammad* or *Shaikh* as *Muhammad Asadullah* or *Shaikh Ghulam Ali*. Among Mughals, boys are called *Amir, Muhammad, Hasán, Husain* and *Ali*, the word *Mirza* always preceding and *Beg* following the name. Pathán boys have the same names as Mughal boys, only there is no *Mirza* and *Khán* is added instead of *Beg*. The commonest names for women are for all classes and grades, taken from the Kurán, such as *Fatimáh, Khadijáh*, or *Aishah*. Among the higher Musalmán families such Arabic phrases as best of women *Khair-un-nisa*, Noblest of women *Amir-un-nisa*, or Moon of women *Badra-un-nisa* are commonly used. Among Sayads a woman's name is followed by *Begam*; among *Shaikhs* by *Bibi*; among Mughals by *Khanam*; and among Pathans by *Khán*. Besides these parents who have lost children or whose children do not live give curious names showing deformity or the most abject humility. *Naththu*, literally nose-bored, is a name which accompanies the actual boring of the nose of the new born child on the principle of deforming the child and so making it less liable to spirit attacks. Another name is *Punju* or *Kachra*, that is, refuse. Sometimes when a child is born after the death of several children the child is thrown into a grain-winnowing fan *supla* with a lot of dirt or refuse and the fan is dragged outside the door with the child in it and made over to some other member of the family as whose property the child re-enters the house. After his ride in the winnowing-fan the child is named, Ghasita, that is, The Dragged. If he is a Pathán this becomes Ghasitkhán, if a Sayad or Shaikh Mir or Shaikh Ghassu or Bhisu, names which occur among all ranks of Muslim and Hindu society in Gujarát. These old naming practices have their root in the belief that untimely births or the death of the new-born are due to the anger or jealousy of uneasy family ghosts, chiefly of women who have died in child-birth with the main object of life unfulfilled. To this belief there attaches the further experience that the unfriendly ghost is easily outwitted. The ghost or other spirit on the lookout for the soul or life of the new-born hears the child is deformed or worthless and so turns its mind to some more gainful mischief. Further the ill will of the ghost is not towards the child but to the child's father or mother. The ghost's aim is to harm the child of the father or the mother; against the aunt's child the ghost has no manner or grudge. This is similar to the Jewish custom according to which the infant Joseph was supposed to steal a sash of one of his aunt's, which being found on his person he was according to patriarchal law claimed by his aunt for a certain number of years. *See* Sale's Translation of the Kurán, Chapter XII, 196, note (O).

been borne by one of the child's forefathers or because the giver thinks it lucky. In the evening of the same day the husband's kindred bringing gold or silver anklets or necklaces, money or clothes, go to the wife's father's house. Sweet cakes are distributed, and, after sunset, the husband gives a dinner to the wife's relations. In the women's rooms the child and its mother are dressed in their best and the midwife makes a six cornered lamp of flour with as many wicks as corners. This is lighted, fed with clarified butter, and kept in a plate along with parched rice or millet *jowári*, and fruit. The presents brought by the husband's friends are now offered and a few small silver coins are given to the midwife. The young mother is then led to a casement and made to counts even stars. When this is over, the husband's people return to their homes. The sixth-day ceremony includes another propitiation of the female relatives that have died in child-birth. Food untouched by unclean persons is cooked and the *Fatiha* repeated for the souls of women who have thus died, and the food is distributed to the poor. The value of the presents made by the husband's friends would, in the case of a rich family, vary from Rs. 20 to Rs. 50, and from Rs. 10 to Rs. 20 in the case of a middle class family. Among the poor, silver necklaces *hansli*, or anklets *kadián*, and a pair or so of ornamented shirts worth Rs. 5 to Rs. 10 are sometimes given.

On the seventh, fourteenth or twenty-first day after birth comes the purely Muhammadan and by all classes carefully kept rite of sacrifice *akika*. In this rite there are two parts, the shaving of the child's head and the killing of one or two goats. If the child is a girl, one goat, and if the child is a boy, two goats, are bought. Some friends are asked and a barber is called. When all is ready the father of the child, or some one specially named by him, at a given sign, as the barber passes the razor along the head of the child, draws a knife across the goat's throat saying, "I sacrifice this animal or animals for the child named *Wali*, blood for blood, skin for skin, flesh for flesh, hair for hair." When the shaving is over, the child's hair and nails are laid on a flat half-baked cake and carried away to be thrown into a river. The barber goes round among the men guests and each drops a small coin into his cup. Before they leave, the guests are entertained at dinner.(1) Sacrifice

(1) In preparing the goat for cooking none of its bones may be broken. The bones must be seperated from the flesh and buried. The flesh and skin are divided into three shares. One share is given in charity, a second is distributed among friends, and the rest, except that the child's father and mother may not join, is eaten by relations.

Fortieth day. On the fortieth day, in honour of the mother's recovery, *náos* or grass boats of the same kind as those made by the water-carrier for the seventh-month pregnancy ceremonies, are with music taken to the nearest water, a lamp is lighted, and the boat set adrift as a thank-offering to Khája Khizr or Elias.(1) The father of the child's mother presents her with clothes and the child with some small quilts and a cradle.

Salt Tasting When the child is four and a half months old and able to take food stronger than milk, comes the ceremony of mutton sucking *botan*, or, as the Persians call it, salt-tasting *namak-chashi.* Friends bring the child presents of clothes worth Re. 1 to Rs. 5. In the evening dressed in his best, the child is offered by his father's sisters some rice and milk *khir*, on a rupee,(2) and after the rice and milk is given a piece of flesh to suck.

Birth day. The child's first birthday *sálgiráh* is the next time for merry-making.(3) As a rule only female relations are asked. These come and in the women's quarters pass the day in feasting and the night, except in some strict higher class families, in playing the drum *dhol*, and singing. Sometimes men also are asked, given a dinner, and afterwards entertained by professional musicians. Before they leave each of the guests gives the child Re. 1 to Rs. 5. This birthday feast is given only by the rich and by some of the middle class. Poor families do not give it.

Initiation. When a child, whether a boy or a girl, has reached the age of four years four months and four days comes *bismilláh*, the taking the Name of God, a ceremony no Muhammadan neglects. On this day a rich man will feast from a hundred to two hundred guests. In the evening after the dinner is over, the child, covered by a skilfully woven flower-sheet called *sehra* is taken to the men's room, where the priest *mulla*, the guests, and a band of young children are waiting, The child is seated on a rich cushion or *masnad*, sweetmeats are laid before it, and of these, two covered with gold-paper are given to it, and after the priest, the child repeats the opening chapter of the Kurán.

---

(1) Khája Khizr is the water genius, the Patriarch Elias, skilled in divination who discovered and drank the water of life.

(2) Though from this time he takes other food besides milk, the child is not weaned till he is twenty-one months old. This is according to a precept from Kurán: From bearing to weaning let thirty months pass

(3) The word *salgiráh* or yearly knot owes its origin among Indian Musalmáns to the Mughal practice of the emperor's mother keeping a silken string in the *harem* and adding a knot for each year of the emperor's life. Blochmann's Ain-i Akbari, 262. note l.

When this is done, the priest chants some Hindustári verses in praise of the child's parents, invoking blessings on the child's head, and at every pause the young band of choristers shout a loud Amen. When the children are eating the sweetmeats a procession is formed and the child is taken to kiss the tomb or *dargáh* of the family guardian saint. As soon as the procession returns, presents are made to the child, silver or gold coins rolled in paper with the name of the giver written on it. As the child passes into the women's quarters the women guests crowd round it, each striving to be the first to take on herself the child's sorrows. After this is over and the child has put off its flower-robe, the women guests amuse themselves listening to the women players or *domnis*.

Circumcision. At the age of six or seven comes circumcision or *khatna*. Friends send presents of sugarcandy, clarified butter, and sweetmeats, and, though this is commoner among the middle than among the higher classes, the recovery of the child is celebrated with great rejoicing. Among north Gujarát Musalmáns circumcision is neglected till an age bordering on puberty, when it is performed with a pomp and circumstance almost equalling those at a marriage, and all the preliminary rites like the *birat* or arranging the pots of clay, a remnant of the pot rites, are observed. In north Gujarát circumcision is styled a *shádi* or joy-time, a word applied in south Gujarát only to marriages.

The First Ramzan Fast. After circumcision come rejoicings and a dinner in honour of a boy or girl keeping their first *Ramzán* fast. This is chiefly celebrated by people belonging to the upper and middle classes. It is said that the merit of a boy's or girl's first fast passes to their parents. At its seventh or eighth year, a child, if strong enough to bear the privation, is made to fast one day in the *Ramzán*, and that day is marked by a dinner to which a choice party of friends and relations is called.

The Present Hadya. Soon after the first *Ramzán* fast, when its Kurán lessons come to an end, the child's parents give its teacher a present *hadya*. A small party is asked, and, before them, the child repeats the beautiful Chapter LV from the holy book styled *Surah Ar-Rehmán*, that is, The Most Compassionate, being a description of the bounties Alláh has showered on man. Except the teacher's present of clothes and money worth Re. 1 to Rs. 50, a suit of clothes for the child, and parched rice, almonds and walnuts distributed among children costing Rs. 1¼ to Rs. 5 there are no expenses. (1)

(1) Bom. Gaz., Vol. IX, Part II, pp. 147—162.

Marriage rules

Marriage is prohibited to the ordinary near relations, but not between first cousins. A man cannot marry his foster-mother or foster-sister, unless the foster brother and sister were nursed by the same women at intervals widely separated. A man may not marry his wife's sister during his wife's life-time unless she has been divorced. A Muhammadan cannot marry a polytheist, but he may marry a Jewess or a Christian. Polygamy is permitted to the number of four wives, but is rare in practice. Divorce is at the option of the husband, but is rare among the gentler classes, both the parties to it being looked upon with opprobrium. A divorcer finds it hard to marry a second time, and a woman once divorced tries as far as she can to shun matrimony for the rest of her life on the grounds of the homely Zenánáh proverb : by changing the bed, fate cannot be altered. The dislike, almost loathing, with which an Indian Musalmán looks upon divorce is so great that one of the strongest of his oaths is : May she who has given me birth be thrice divorced if I do so.

Of the three forms of divorce two are easily recalled ; but in the third, which is called the severer *báyin*, when the word divorce is repeated three several times it is final until the wife has married and is again free. After divorce a woman cannot marry for three months called the *iddat* or term during which the husband is bound to maintain her.

Marriage ceremonies.

Boys are generally married between sixteen and twenty-two and girls between ten and eighteen. When their sons reach manhood, parents generally consult professional matchmakers or go betweens, women free to enter the houses even of the strictest. Some girl likely to make a good match is before long chosen, and the women of the lad's family pay a visit at the girl's home. After seeing her and talking together, the guests are offered a glass of sugared water. This they drink if they think well of the girl, but if they think she will not suit, they decline. After drinking, in sign that they ask her in marriage, they drop some sugarcandy into the girl's mouth. Then they talk of ornaments and fix the day for the betrothal. On the bethrothal day, both at the boy's and girl's houses, there is a meeting of kindred. In the evening at the boy's house ornaments and sweetmeats are laid out on neatly covered trays and are generally sent to the girl's house with music. With the presents go the women of the bridegroom's family and a gay procession of children of their relations and friends. On reaching the bride's house the men and children who formed the procession sit in a booth outside of the house, or, if there is no booth, in some part of the house prepared for their reception. Here *sherbat* sugared water is handed round, the person serving it, generally a relation or a near friend of the wife's family stating that it is in honour of the betrothal. Each person on putting down his cup drops, for the good of the man who has served it, annas 2 to Rs. 2 into the saucer. Meanwhile the women guests going into the house deck the bride with ornaments, put the troth ring on her finger, and cover her with a scarf *dupatta*. Then after drinking sugared-water and coffee and getting flowers and rosewater they leave, taking with them trays filled with fresh presents, a handkerchief, a ring, a gold turban or *mandil*, and sweetmeats. Except when things are hurried and the betrothal and marriage take place at the same time, the betrothal lasts for at least a year. During this time on every holiday gifts pass between the betrothed couple.

Some months before the marriage day the bride's female relations meet at her house and make ready the smaller articles of dress. Every night when their work is over, for about a fortnight before the marriage day, the women sing together to the accompaniment of the drum or *dhol*. Eight days before the marriage the bride keeps to one room, and both she and the bridegroom are made to wear yellow clothes. Two or three days before the marriage, both at the house of the bridegroom and of the bride, a store of earthen pots is laid in. If the women observe the *pardáh* or veiling, the pots are arranged in the inner apartments, but if the women are not *pardáh*, they are arranged in a temporary booth or alcove in front of the house. That the object of arranging these pots is to house and so please ancestral spirits is known and admitted. Food is laid on the pots, and the opening chapter of the Kurán or *Fátiha* is repeated. After the pots have been arranged both at the bride's and the bridegroom's the women of the family, while female musicians sing songs, rub the bride or bridegroom with gram flour mixed with oil and perfumes called *ubatna*. The chief ingredients in this cosmetic are the flour of washed wheat and *mung* (Phasoleus munga) turmeric and sesame oil. As this cosmetic has to ward off all the evil influences which hover round the bride and bridegroom, every care must be taken that no element of evil enters into the guardian *ubatna*. To stop the approach of evil the hand-mill in which the grain is ground has its handle smeared with sandal paint, and a *midhal* (Vangueiria spinosa) nut and some *pán* or betel-leaves and betelnuts wrapped in a piece of new red cloth are tied to it. Then seven *suhágans*, that is married women whose husbands are alive, sit to grind the grain and into the flour pour clarified butter or sesame or jasmin oil. When the *ubatna* is ready henna leaves are ground in the same way. A square diagram is traced on the floor with rice and a stool is set in the square. The bride or bridegroom in a suit of her or his oldest clothes dyed yellow is led forth and seated on the stool. The *ubatna*, amidst the songs of women either the relations of the family or hired female musicians, is rubbed all over the body and henna is applied to the hands and feet. In rubbing on the cosmetic each of the seven matrons takes her turn. She puts a piece of candied sugar into the bridegroom's mouth, throws a handful of rice over the bride or bridegroom's head, passes the mustard seed seven times over the bride or bridegroom's body, and takes on herself the ill-luck or *balás* of the bride or bridegroom by cracking the joints of her fingers across her temples. Finally she passes a pice or more over the bride or bridegroom, hands the coin to the musicians if hired or lays it at the foot of the stool to be given in charity and retires. When all seven matrons have performed their task, a knife, dagger or other sharp iron instrument and a lemon are handed to the bride or bridegroom which she or he is to be careful to keep till the bath on the marriage day. During these days, to keep off the evil eye, a bracelet or a garland of gold must also be worn. Seven songs called *tonas* or charms sung by *domnis* or hired female singers before the *julwah* or unveiling of the bride in the presence of the bridegroom, which form a portion of the marriage ceremony, are said to possess special anti-magic and spirit-power. If the bride be spirit possessed to the slightest extent the sound of the *tonas* makes the spirit instantly declare itself. When the bridegroom comes songs are again sung and has height is measured by an odd number of red and white braids. These braids are woven into a thick cord which is used by the bride in her trouser string. The bride and bridegroom's houses are put is order, painted or whitewashed, and outside of each house is built a booth or hall, sometimes very splendid with gilt pillars, friezes and cornices and hung with glass-lamps and pictures. The first post of the booth is driven into the ground after the point has been rubbed with sandal oil and enveloped with a piece of new red muslin in which are wrapped betelnuts, betel-leaves and the lucky wedding *midhal* nut Vanguieria spinosa. A cocoanut is broken and the kernel distributed among the workmen who built the booth and the members of the family. As the whole house is given over to the women this hall is for the time the men's room. For some days before the marriage, musicians are hired to play in front of the house. This is a time of great merry-making. One day, outside of the house for men and inside for women, earthen vessels are filled with the red and yellow colours used in dyeing cloth. In the evening the men among themselves and the women among themselves each with a little jar full of colour, chasing and waylaying, cover one another with the dye.

At such times from Rs. 5 to Rs. 20 or at most Rs. 30 of colour is used One amusement for the women during the days before a marriage is the twisting, knotting and tying of silver rings into silk and gold thread wristbands *kangna*. Of these one is given to the bride and the other to the bridegroom, and after marriage each has to unravel the knots and twists in the other's bracelet. On the evening of the marriage day, the bridegroom's party send to the bride's with a procession of children in carriages and on horseback with music and led horses, a band of hired women and servants carrying as many as two hundred or more earthen pots painted in gold and green filled with sweetmeats and dried fruits, and trays with dresses.(1) On arrival the children are seated in the marriage hall or shed with the men and are treated to *sherbat*, each of the little guests dropping silver coins the smallest of which is a two-anna piece into the cup or saucer in aknowledgment of the trouble of the server, who is often either a poor or juvenile relation of the bride. In her room the bride is bathed by the women of her family, clothed in new robes, and decked in some of the jewels. Then with trays refilled with clothes for the bridegroom, with henna *mendhi* and with the wife's chattels *jahez*,(2) the company goes back to the bridegroom's. On their return the bridegroom is dressed in his wedding clothes, and the furniture of what is to be his room is set in order. At nightfall, an occasion of much merriment, the sister of the bride comes to apply henna to the bridegroom's hand. On one side of a screen or partition sits the lady and on the other the bridegroom and some of his friends. Only the bridegroom's hand should be passed under the screen. But instead of this, many hands are thrust through, and the lady has to trust to her wit to choose the hand she should punish by pinching and the hand she should adorn with henna. Her mistakes are greeted with much laughter, and when in the end she paints the bridegroom's little finger with henna she receives a present of Rs. 5 to Rs. 10. When this play is over, the bridegroom's guests sit listening to dancing girls and buffoons *bhánds* or to a company of Arab Nativity hymn-singers called *Mauludiás*. *Mauluds*, that is, Muhammad-mas carols, are gradually displacing dancing girls and buffoons. At the close of the *maulud* coffee, warm sweet-milk in small coffee cups, and sweets or sugar-cakes called *batáshás* are distributed to singers and hearers.

---

(1) This procession is called the *cari* or *sáchak*, that is, the present.

(2) *Jahez* or paraphernalia includes clothes, jewels, furniture and ornaments for a lady's sitting room and bedroom and a set of cooking vessels. This continues to be the wife's property, and has to be returned to her in case of divorce.

About ten, the time comes for the bridegroom to fetch the bride. The bridegroom is clothed in a *sehra* or flower-sheet fastened round his head by a string which the father ties with thankful heart that to him has been granted the wish of every Indian Musalmán; May I live to tie my son's *sehra* knot. Then the father or some other male relation lifts the bridegroom on a horse, and with music and followed by all his friends he starts for the bride's. (1) As he passes under her window the bride lets fall on the bridegroom some grains of rice. He is led before the door of the house, and is handed a cup of sugared-water by his brother-in-law, to whom in return he gives Rs. 5 to Rs. 10. The women of the bridegroom's family and the wives of his chief friends follow the procession in closed carriages. On their arrival at the bride's they retire to the ladies' quarters, where, till the bridegoom is called in to see the bride, they are entertained by women singers *domnis*. When the bridegroom comes, those who do not appear before him, retire. The men of the bridegroom's party when they arrive, seat themselves in the brightly lighted marriage hall, the bridegroom's party ranged on one side and the bride's on the other. In the space between are three seats; one in front of his party for the bridegroom, one in front of the bride's party for her agents and the third between the two for the registrar, the *Kázi* or his deputy. The bridegroom, if very young, is carried, or, if grown, is led to his seat and the bride's agents find their way to theirs. Then the registrar, seating himself, asks the bride's agents whether she, with a certain portion or *meher* (2) accepts so and so as her husband. If told she will have him, he takes the declaration of two other witnesses. He then making the bridegroom repeat the creed, puts to him the same question. The proceedings are recorded, and the guests, raising their hands, offer the marriage thanksgiving. When the ceremony is over, the registrar receives a shawl and Rs. 5 his fee, and leaves the house taking his share of the marriage sugarcandy, trayfuls of which are distributed among all present. The hired musicians, who so far have been silent owing to the presence of the representative of the law of

(1) Both in south and north Gujarát, among the rich, before the bridegroom's horse is carried a miniature garden *bádi*, a three sided frame-work of coloured paper with bowers and leaves cut in tinsel or talc. Though some of these models are very elaborate, costing Rs. 50 to Rs. 200, they are made only to amuse the crowd, one of whom before the procession reaches the bride's house, generally manages to seize the frame, and the rest scrambling for bits of it tear the whole to shreds.

(2) Though the rich sometimes give more, the portion of *meher* is generally fixed at Rs. 17 the dower of Fátimáh the Prophet's favourite daughter, or at Rs. 750, the dower of the Prophet's wife Aishah. Among the rich and the middle class the marriage portion of a girl is what is legally termed the *meheri misl* or the portion of her peers, that is, the girl's grandmother, aunts and sisters.

Islám, strike up a loud discordant peal. [1] Then, till the bridegroom is called to receive his bride, the men pass their time in listening to hired dancers and singers. When the husband is called,[2] a dancing girl, stepping backwards, singing and keeping time by beating him with flower twigs, slowly leads the bridegroom into the ladies' quarters. Here she hands him over to the *domnis* or female musicians, who in the same way lead him to a seat. On his way to his seat the bridegroom is jealously guarded by his sisters or other near relatives from the onslaughts of the younger sisters or relatives of the bride who hang about unobserved, and if they get an opportunity, dart on the bridegroom and if his female relatives are not on the alert wring his ears unmercifully. Soon the bride, veiled and arrayed in her wedding garment, is carried in by one of her relations and seated before the bridegroom, and a set of ceremonies,[3] in which the rest of the night passes, are begun. At dawn the bridegroom is for the first time shown his wife's face in a mirror, and from a Kurán placed between them the chapter of Peace is read. This is the sign that the time has come for the bride to leave her father's house.

After the marriage the husband with his wife and family pass some days in a garden-house, spending their time in amusements and singing.

On each of the first four Fridays or *chár jumágis* after marriage the bride and bridegroom are asked to dine at the bride's father's house. On the first and perhaps the second Friday some of the bridegroom's friends and relations, both men and women, are asked. In north Gujarát the young couple stay from the evening of a Thursday to the following evening. In the south they go on the Friday evening and generally leave next morning. Much is thought of these Friday dinners, and if they are not given, a man seldom visits his father-in-law's house. So too, after marriage, the relatives of the bridegroom and the bride do not visit each other till each party has once formally invited the other. [4]

---

(1) With the fee is also charged a mosque-fee of Re. 1¼, which goes to the person who serves as the warden of the mosque in the street where the bride lives.

(2) In north Gujarát the husband walks alone, and this at five or six in the morning instead of about three or four in the afternoon.

(3) These seem to be the humorous survival of the eating together form of marriage. The bride, who should not voluntarily move a muscle, is by one of the musicians made to take in her hand a piece of sugarcandy, some pounded sweet-bread, or a dry date, then her hand is stretched out to her husband's mouth, and as he tries to secure the morsel her hand is drawn away. This in different forms with much merriment goes on for a long time.

(4) Bom. Gaz., Vol. IX, Part II. pp. 162—167.

Religion. Sunnis and Shiáhs.

Both the leading forms of the Musalmán faith, the Sunni and Shiáh, are found in the Bombay Presidency, the former being more common than the latter. Except some of the Sayads, and Mughals of Gujarát, the trading Bohorás, the Táis and some of the Momnás who are Shiáhs, all are Sunnis.

Points of difference.

The original question in dispute between Sunnis and Shiáhs, whether as the Sunnis hold, Abubakur, Umar and Uthmán were the lawful successors of the Prophet, or were, as the Shiáhs contend, usurpers, defrauding Ali of his right to the Khiláfat, has given rise to several differences in belief and practice. The chief of the differences are that the Shiáhs leave out of the Kurán certain passages which they say were written by Uthmán; they add a chapter in praise of Ali which they say Uthmán kept back; and to other parts they give a different meaning from that accepted by the Sunnis. The Shiáhs do not believe in saints, and follow the precepts of the twelve instead of the four Imáms. (1) They claim for their head doctors in Persia, the *mujtahids* or religious superiors, the power of altering the spiritual and temporal law; the Sunnis say that the time for change ceased with the four Imáms Sháfai, Abu Hanifah, Malik and Hambal. (2) In practice some sects of Shiáhs differ from Sunnis, chiefly by counting the month from the fading of the old moon and not as the Sunnis do, from the shining of the new moon. They pray thrice instead of five times a day, and in praying hold their hands open by their sides instead of folding them below the breast. (3) Except these and a few other particulars, the belief and customs of the rival sects are the same.

Belief.

Belief in the unity of God; in his angels; in his books, the Jewish Christian and Muhammadan scriptures; in his prophets; in his government of the world; in good and evil as coming from Him; and in the day of resurrection, are the chief articles of a Musalmán's faith. A

---

(1) The twelve Shiáh Imáms are: (1) Murtuza Ali (date of birth not known) died at Kufa, A.D. 660; (2) Imám Hasan, born A.D. 625; (3) Imám Husain, A.D. 626; (4) Zain-ul-Abidin, A.D. 653; (5) Muhammad Bákir, A.D. 675; (6) Jafar Sádik, A.D. 698; (7) Musi Kázim, A.D. 745; (8) Musi Raza, A.D. 770; (9) Taki Abu Jaáfar, A.D. 810; (10) Abdul Hasan Askari, A.D. 829; (11) Abu Muhammad Askari, A.D. 845; (12) Al-mehdi, A.D. 971. The four Sunni Imáms are: Sháfai, A.D. 767—819, Abu Hanifah, A.D. 700—733, Malik (A.D. 708—713, died A.D. 735), and Hamba (born A.D. 780, date of death not known).

(2) The four Sunni Imáms have given rise to the four schools, the Hanafi, Sháfai, Maliki, and Hambali. Except the Arabs who belong to the Sháfai school, Gujarát Sunni Musalmáns are Hanafis.

(3) When praying with a *jammat* of the Sunnis the Shiáh deports himself according to the orthodox part of the company in obedience to the Shiáh doctrine of *takiyyah* literally fear or caution. Where the Shiáhs are in a minority they practise this doctrine and while acting upon they even vilify their own sect if their personal safety requires. Blochman's Ain-i-Akbari, 338, note 2.

Muslim should pray [1] five or three times a day, give a part of his goods to the poor, [2] fast in the month of *Ramazán*, and make a pilgrimage to Mecca and if a Shiáh, to Karbala and Sháh Najaf if he has no debt and is rich enough. Muslim worship consists of a number of bows and prostrations accompanied with prayers and verses from the Kurán. [3] Each of the five daily prayers has its separate form, and on Fridays and on the days of the *Ramazán* and *Bakr* festivals, the reading of prayers is accompanied by a sermon. The funeral prayer is simply repeating several times the words *Alláh-o-Akbar*, God is great.

Practice.

Though as a body not very zealous, Musalmáns are on the whole careful to observe the chief rules of their faith. Few of them go to the daily public prayers. But the Friday service is well attended; and crowds join with fervour in the long night prayers *taráwih* of the *Ramazán*. Though among Sunnis it is chiefly a time of noisy merriment, to Shiáhs, both men and women, the *Muharram* is a season of the keenest grief and real self-denial. Almost all observe the month of fasting and attend services on the *Ramazán* and *Bakr Id* feasts. All who can afford it give alms freely, and few, except those of Hindu origin, lend money at interest or drink spirits. They reverence the name of the Prophet and the Kurán and accept the doctrines of their faith. The irregular classes of Shiáhs and most of the Sunnis become *murids* or disciples, the former to their *mullás* and the latter to some religious person called their *pirzádah* or *murshid*. Among the women, a few, chiefly unmarried daughters of Sayads and some Shaikhs, and many of the trading Bohorás, both Sunnis and Shiáhs, are well taught in the Kurán and other religious books. Many are pious, and, though not allowed to appear at places of public worship, are careful to repeat their daily prayers and to keep fasts and other religious observances.

---

(1) The Sunni prays five times : before sunrise *fajr*, at noon *zuhr*, between four and sunset *asar*, at sunset *maghrib*, and from 8 to 12 p.m. *isha*. Some very religious Sunnis say a sixth prayer *tahajjud* at midnight, and a seventh called *ishrak* two hours after the morning prayers. The Shiáh prays three times : before sunrise *fajr*, at noon, when he repeats both the *zuhr* and the *asar* prayers, and at sunset, when he says the *maghrib* and *isha* prayers. Some of them say also the midnight *tahajjud* prayers.

(2) The poor tax *zakat*, literally purification, is 2½ per cent. on all incomes over a hundred rupees a year, and from the poor seven and a quarter pounds of wheat a head to be paid in the *Ramazán* month.

(3) The body of he person praying as well as the place of prayer must be free from anything causing legal uncleanness. The prayer must always be preceded by ablution *wuzu*, unless nothing that constitutes legal defilement has taken place since the former ablutions. Praying in company at a mosque is considered more meritorious than saying prayers at home.

Vows. The vowing of vows is older than Islám and is not opposed to the law of the Prophet. The sacred Kurán represents the prophet Zakariyah (Zacharias) vowing a vow of abstinence from speech for a certain number of days in return for the promise of a son. The Virgin Mary when advised to betake herself to an unfrequented spot for the birth of her son is asked to give forth as a reason for her isolation from the society of her people the fact that 'she had vowed to heaven a fast not to speak unto men for the day' (Kurán Chap. XVI). In Islámic times the Prophet advised his daughter the Lady Fátimah and her husband Ali to vow a fast of three days for the recovery from illness of their sons Hasan and Husain. Vows to fast, to repeat a certain number of prayers, to give in charity a certain sum of money, to feed a certain number of poor, or to found some religious or charitable building or institution are vows strictly in accordance with the letters and spirit of the law of Islám. Such vows are offered only by the strictly pious. On the other hand vows admitting the instrumentality of any person living or dead, whether prophet or saint, are regarded by the religious as idolatrous. The Wahábis are bitter against such practices, denouncing the makers of such vows as little better than heretics. The Hindu instincts and ways of thought of the Indian Musalmán have brought into existence a number of beliefs among which the efficacy of vows offered to dead saints and even to the *Zaris* and *Táziáhs* or the miniature shrines of the martyrs of Karbala better known as *tábuts* and to *Dulás* people inspired by the martyrs have the first place. Such vows are of three classes : Vows made to saints ; vows made to *táziáhs*, *zaris* or *tábuts* or other institutions of the Muharram ; and vows made to genii or fairies or spirits. (1)

Musalmáns have strong faith also in spirits, in magic, in the power of the evil eye and in omens.

Holy days. Except the *Muharram*, the *Ramazán* and the *Bakr* festivals which are common to both the Sunnis and Shiáhs, the two sects keep different holy days. They are as follows :—

On the tenth of *Safar* the second month, Shiáhs repeat dirges and offer prayers for the souls of Hasan and Husain.

On the thirteenth of the same month come the *Tera* or *Talan Tezi.* Sunnis keep this day in honour of the Prophet's recovery from a severe sickness. In the morning in north Gujarát prayers are offered for the Prophet, and parched gram and molasses are eaten.

---

(1) Bom. Gaz., Vol. IX, Part II, pp. 125—128.

On the last Wednesday of the same month, a day known as the *Akhari-chárshambah*, Sunni [1] townspeople fry sweetmeats and eat them in the fields and gardens outside of the city in memory of a recovery of the Prophet from a dangerous illness.

The twelfth of *Rabi-ul-awwal* the third month, the *Wafát* or day of the Prophet's death, is among Sunnis the greatest day in the year next to the *ids.* In the evening, rice and milk *khir*, a dish of which the Prophet was fond, is cooked and prayers are offered for the Prophet's soul.[2] In the evening, private services are held at the mosques with sermons and chants. After the service is over the stone-footprint, hair, or other relic of the Prophet which may be treasured in the mosque is shown.

On the seventeenth of the third month Gujarát Musalmáns mark the *Maulud* or birthday of the Prophet by feasting and giving presents.

On the eleventh of *Rabi-us-sáni* the fourth month, Sunnis celebrate the birth of Sayad Abdul-Kádir Jiláni, commonly known as the Pirán-Pir or Saint of Saints of Baghdád. On this day the poor light eleven or twenty-two lamps, and, in the houses of the rich and well-to-do small leafless trees or green-bordered frames, called *mehdi*, are hung with eleven lamps and covered with presents of fruit and sweets for children. At night powdered sugared-bread or *malidah* is eaten.

On the eleven first nights of *Rajab*, the sixth or nativity month in honour of the Prophet's birth, among Sunnis sermons or *wázes* are preached and *mauluds* chanted. Great numbers attend, and on the eleventh many charitable people in Ahmedábád and some in Surat and Broach, give a morsel of sacred food called *tabarruk* to every one present. At Ahmedábád the heads of the Rafáis, followers of Sayad Ahmed Kabir, a nephew of the Pirán-Pir, march about carrying green banners, playing kettle-drums, and brandishing and beating their bodies with a chained mace *gurz*, with a pointed handle. They are generally asked by more than one person to share the sacred food or *tabarruk* which is served to them in small dishes.

On the fourteenth evening of *Shábán*, the eighth month, comes the night of record *Shab-i-barát*. On this night the fates of unborn souls

(1) The festival is common both to Shiáhs and Sunnis. Shiáhs say that, as Safar is the unluckiest of months, its last day is passed in feasting out of the city, that evil may remain outside and not find its way into their homes.

(2) These customs are observed from the first to the twelfth of Rabi-ul-awwal. the twelfth day being held most sacred. The Shiáhs fix this festival on the 28th of the same month.

are registered in heaven. Among Sunnis requiems are sung, sweets and sweet-bread are eaten and sent as presents to friends, and fire-works are let off or sent to relatives, especially to those to whom a son or daughter of the house is betrothed.

The nineteenth and twenty-first days of the ninth month *Ramazán* termed *Katli Imám Ali* and *Hazrat Ali* are kept holy by Shiáhs, the nineteenth as the day on which Ali was wounded and the twenty-first as the day on which he died. On both days they give beggars food and pray for Ali's soul and mourn.

At the end of the *Ramazán* fast, that is on the first day of *Shawwál*, the tenth month, comes the fast-breaking festival *Id-ul-Fitr* commonly known as the *Ramazán Id.*(1) This feast is one of the two greatest Musalmán festivals. Sunnis and Shiáhs of all ages and of both sexes bathe, put on new clothes and perfume themselves. They give alms in money or grain, mostly wheat, this form of charity being called '*fitrah,*' for without alms their fast is vain, and take a light meal of vermicelli, milk, clarified-butter, sugar and dates. Between eight and twelve the men form a procession and escort the *kázi* or other Musalmán of high position to the *Idgáh,* that is, the place for the special Id prayers, most of them repeating mentally the glorification of the name of Alláh in the following words: *Alláh-o-Akbar. Alláh-o-Akbar. La-Iláha illalláho Alláh-o-Akbar Alláh-o-Akbar wa lilláhil hamd.* Great is Alláh, Great is Alláh: there is none as great as Alláh: great is Alláh, unto Him be all praise. The prayers at the Idgáh, together with an Arabic sermon, in an old stereotyped form in praise of the Id, read by the Kázi standing on the pulpit, wooden staff in hand in imitation of the Prophet, last for about an hour and a half, and when the prayers and sermon are over, the people go home and spend the rest of the day in feasting, making presents and paying and receiving visits.

On the tenth day of *Zilhajj*, the twelfth month, the day after the chief pilgrimage day at Mecca comes the second great feast, the festival of sacrifice *Id-uz-zuha*, also called the *Bakr* or Cow-Id in commemoration of the offering of Ismael by Abraham.(2) Early in the morning religious beggars and others crowd round the dwellings of Musalmáns, begging for alms. On this Id as on the Ramazán Id all, except those who are mourning the loss of a near relative, wash, put on their best clothes and perfume themselves according to the

(1) Shiáhs differ from Sunnis in keeping the Ramazán Id a day sooner and in not going to the Idgáh.

(2) Musalmáns hold that Ismael, not Isaac, was the son offered by Abraham.

behest and the practice of the Prophet. The whole body of Sunni Musalmáns go riding or driving in procession to the Idgáh and after prayers return home, and, if they can afford it, sacrifice goats and send presents of the flesh to relations and friends. The rest of the day is spent in visiting. Alms [1] are generally given about the time of the *Bakr* festival, either in cash, in grain or in cloth.

On the eighteenth of *Zilhajj*, the twelfth month, a great Shiáh holiday called the lake holiday *Id-i-ghadir* is held. On this day the Prophet seated by a lake proclaimed in a joyous moment that Ali was his own flesh and body.

On the twenty-eighth of *Zilhajj* comes the festival of Baba Shuja-ud-din Abu Lulu, a fire worshipping convert to Islám, who, on this day, murdered the Khalifah Umar. On this account Shiáhs hold the day sacred and rejoice for three days.[2]

The officers entrusted with religious duties are (1) the beadle *mujáwar*, (2) the mosque guardian *mutawalla*, (3) the priest *mulla*. (4) the preacher *khatib*, (5) among the Shiáhs the singer of elegies *marsiahkhan*, (6) the law professor and doctor of divinity *maulavi*. and (7) the civil judge *kázi*.

That death may not attack him unawares, or in a foreign land, is the wish of every Muhammadan. To one on the point of death the chapter of the Kurán, telling of death and the glorious future of the true believer, is read, the creed and prayer for forgiveness are repeated, and a few drops of honey are dropped into the mouth.[3] After death the eyes and mouth are closed, the body is laid on a wooden platform, carefully washed [4] and perfumed, and covered with a scented shroud of white cloth. For a woman to die in the evening is a hopeful sign of her future forgiveness. She has lived within the veil and within the veil she goes to her Maker. It is well to die on a Thursday or a Friday or any day in the month of Ramazán and on any other holiday. Death on a Wednesday is unlucky. Four deaths take place in the family which loses one of its members on a Wednesday. Death

(1) Alms (*zakát* or purification) should be given of five things, money, cattle, grain, fruit, and merchandise. The amount varies, though in general it is said to be one-twentieth of a year's income. Alms should be given to pilgrims, beggars, debtors, religious champions, travellers, and proselytes.

(2) Bom. Gaz., Vol. IX, Part II, pp. 139—142.

(3) The death agony is supposed to be the final temptation of the arch-fiend, who greets the thirsty soul as it leaves the body with the luring sight of a cup of sweets. If the soul falls into the snare the cup is dashed away and the tempter disappears.

(4) The Sunnis, unlike the Shiáhs, use warm water to wash the dead. In this water *bor* or *jujube* leaves are boiled.

If the death happens at night the body is not taken away till dawn. Otherwise, so soon as it is shrouded and the friends have taken their last look,(1) among the wails of the women,(2) all of whom stay behind, the body is laid on the bier,(3) lifted on the bearers'(4) shoulders, and borne away, the company of men raising the cry *Lailáha illalláh* There is no God but Alláh, and trained singers chanting solemn hymns. Over the bier four bearers carry a piece of brocade called the canopy *shámiánah.*(5) Upon the bier is a shawl, green or other dark colour for men and red for women. The grave is either where the deceased has asked to be buried or in the family burial ground. At the mosque the bier is set down in the outer court, the mourners wash, and, standing in a row, repeat the funeral prayer *Alláho-Akbar* God is great. They move to the ready dug grave,(6) laying the body in it, the head to the north and leaning on the right side so that the face turns towards Mecca. They lay clods of consecrated earth (7) close to the body, and the mourners fill the grave repeating the verse of the Kurán, "Of earth We made you, to earth We return you, and from earth will raise you on the resurrection day." They retire to the house of mourning and standing at the door repeat a prayer for the soul of the dead, and all but near relatives and friends who stay to dine, go to their homes. The duty of helping at funerals and of praying for the souls of the dead is solemnly enjoined on all Musalmáns and is carefully observed by them. Though a *farz*, that is, a divine behest, it is also a *farz-i-kifáyah* or duty which if attended to by a sufficient number of the faithful does not demand the presence of all. Among the rich the clothes of the dead are given in charity

---

(1) When the deceased is the head of a family his widow is brought in, dressed in her richest robes, to take a last look at her lord. A husband is not allowed to look at his dead wife.

(2) The wailing of women is against the order of the Prophet. In Surat and Broach it is practised only among the poor. In north Gujarát it is common among all classes except Arabs.

(3) Biers or *janázahs* are used only in south Gujarát; in the north the body is laid on a cot. It is unusual to lay the body in a coffin.

(4) The bearers are never hired men, always the nearest relations and friends. An exception is made at the funeral of a married woman, when, unless he means never again to marry, the husband is not allowed to join in carrying the bier.

(5) A burial of this kind takes place only in the case of the rich and a few of the middle class.

(6) The grave may be in one of three forms. The most common is a pit where the body is placed and earth thrown in. The other is a hollow formed by planks placed aslant. The third is a hole of soft yielding mud into which the body is gently left to sink. Coffins also are used, but only by the very rich.

(7) This earth is consecrated by reading and breathing over it some of the last chapters of the Kurán.

and grain is distributed.[1] Till the third day no food is cooked in the house of mourning. At Ahmedábád the friends and relations of the deceased send ready-cooked dinners. In south Gujarát dinners called *bháthi* are cooked at the house of mourning at the expense of near relations. On the morning of the third day after a death a feast called *Ziárat* is held. A large company of relations, friends and others meet in the mosque, where each of them, reading from small books a chapter of the Kurán, finish with a prayer that the merit of the act may pass to the soul of the deceased. A sermon *waáz* is then preached by a Maulvi. After the sermon a tray full of flowers and a vessel with a sweet-smelling mixture and oil in a small metal or porcelain cup is passed among the guests. Each guest as the tray passes picks a flower and drops it into the vessel and the whole is poured over the grave. Sweetmeats or *batáshás* are distributed and the friends present shawls to the son or sons of the deceased ; and before leaving the mosque and again on arrival before the house of the deceased, prayers are offered for his soul. After this, among the rich and some of the middle class a dinner is given on as grand a scale as a wedding dinner. A man may without disgrace avoid this third day feast.[2] But on the fortieth day, the fourth month, the sixth month, the ninth month, and the last day of the first year he must give choice dinners.[3]

The only form of mourning laid down by Muhammadan law is in the case of the death of the head of a house, the strict seclusion of his widow. This lasts for four months and ten days and during that time the widow, unless she is forced to do so, never leaves the house. Besides this strictly Muhammadan observance, other customs have been adopted from the Hindus. As soon as life is gone, the mother and the widow of the dead break their bangles. The mother may get new bangles but except when they are of gold or silver the widow, unless she marries, never again wears bracelets or a nosering. In south Gujarát the women of the poorer classes, and in the north all except those of Arab families or of families entertaining strict religious opinions wail in Hindu fashion. In the north, too, when a woman first visits the widow, on seating herself she bursts into a wail. The chief mourner joins in the cry, keeping it up until she is soothed

(1) North of the Mahi the grain is distributed at the house of mourning, and in the south at the mosque.

(2) At Ahmedábád the great dinner is given on the fortieth day. On the third day a smaller number of friends and beggars only are fed.

(3) This is no modern failing. Ovington (A.D. 1689) says the Mughals are very profuse in their funeral expenses, lavishing away, at immoderate cost, to their friends memory enough to sink a rich fortune, Voyage to Surat, 245.

by her friend. This custom is known as the *munh dhánkna* or face-hiding. The shortest term of mourning is six months. For the first forty days the rooms are stripped of their furniture, cots, cushions and pillows are put out of sight, and all members of the household sleep on the bare ground and no food is cooked in the house. During the whole six months no holiday is observed, no gaieties attended, and no music heard. At the end comes the *sog uthána* or grief-lifting, when some friend asks the family to visit him. For his nearest relations a man for about a year wears a white turban.(1) If young, a widow wears some dark coloured dress ; if old, she wears white but never either yellow or red.(2)

Food. An animal only becomes lawful food for Muhammadans if it is killed by cutting the throat and repeating at the time the words *Bismilláh Alláho Akbar* or 'in the name of God, God is great.' But in shooting wild animals, if the invocation is repeated at the time of discharging the arrow or firing the gun, the carcass becomes lawful food. This last rule of Sunni law is, however, not known to or not observed by, many Muhammadans, who do not eat an animal unless its throat is cut before death. Fish and locusts may be eaten without being killed in this manner. The animal so killed by *Zabh* is lawful food when slain by a Moslem, Jew or Christian, but not if slaughtered by an idolator or an apostate from Islám. Cloven-footed animals, birds that pick up food with their bills, and fish with scales are lawful but not birds or beasts of prey. It is doubtful whether the horse is lawful. Elephants, mules, asses, alligators, turtles, crabs, snakes and frogs are unlawful, and swine's flesh is especially prohibited. Muhammadans eat freely of mutton and fish when they can afford it, but some of them abstain from chickens in imitation of the Hindus. Their favourite drink is sherbat, or sugar and water with cream or the juice of some fruit. Wine is forbidden in the Korán, and the prohibition is held to include intoxicating drugs, but this latter rule is by no means observed. According to his religion a Muhammadan need have no objection to eat with a Christian if the food eaten is of a lawful kind; but he should not eat with Hindus as they are idolators. In practice, however, many Muhammadans have adopted the Hindu rule against eating food touched by Christians, while owing to long association together they will partake of it when cooked by Hindus.

---

(1) In Surat this rule is not always kept.

(2) Bom. Gaz., Vol. IX, Part II, pp. 168—170.

MINOR MUSALMAN CASTES.

These include a large number of converted Hindus who come under the general term Musalmán, but have their own pseudocaste divisions, *e.g.*, Abdáli, Bágbán, Dudhvála, Kákar, Kasái, Nálband, Tái, and vary very greatly in the extent to which they conform to the tenets of Islám. In some cases, members of these divisions so far adhere to the old Hindu caste notion that they will only marry inside their division. In other cases, where the influence of Islám is more fully felt, they will marry with any other Musalmán though the tendency is to contract unions only with other Hindu converts of a similar social standing.

A list of such cross-unions, collected from the Kázi's marriage registers in various districts of the Presidency, is given below, exemplifying the practice in vogue :—

List showing intermarriages between Musalmán sub-divisions.

Name of District.	Caste of Bridegroom.	Caste of Bride.
Ahmedabad ..	Kasái ..	Sipâhi.
Do. ..	Sayad ..	Bágbán.
Broach ..	Shaikh ..	Tái.
Kaira ..	Khokhar ..	Sikhligar.
Panch Mahâls ..	Belim ..	Vághela.
Surat ..	Malek ..	Pathán.
Kolába ..	Atár ..	Khatib.
Ratnagiri ..	Kázi ..	Shaikh.
Ahmednagar ..	Maniár ..	Atár.
Do. ..	Támbat ..	Atár.
Do. ..	Sikligar ..	Dáruvála
Poona ..	Maniár ..	Sikalgar.
Do. ..	Támboli ..	Atár
Do. ..	Sikalgar ..	Atár.
Do. ..	Sutár ..	Maniár.
Do. ..	Patvegar. ..	Támboli.
Sátára ..	Atár ..	Patvegar.
Belgaum ..	Atár ..	Sikalgar.
Do. ..	Pinjára ..	Bágbán.

The names of these divisions are in many instances occupational as, for instance, Nálband, a farrier, Kasái, a butcher, Dudhvála; a

milkman. The original Hindu name has been abandoned on conversion, *e.g.*, Kunbis converted are named Bágbán.

A brief description of the minor Musalmán castes of this nature is given in this article, the castes, being shown in alphabetical order. The larger castes such as Bohorás, Memons, Khojáhs, etc., will be found treated in separate articles. It is only possible to hazard a guess why in some cases the groups are endogamous and in others marry with members of other Musalmán divisions. The desire to cling to the original caste exclusiveness is probably an indication of the strength locally of Hindu influence. Where Musalmán ideas have greater weight, the prejudice against intermarriage breaks down.

In the case of certain of these minor sub-divisions it is the practice to invite both a Bráhman priest and a Mulla to perform the wedding ceremony. Beef is commonly eschewed by such converts and many Hindu rites and holy days are observed. India presents numerous opportunities of studying the effect on caste divisions of conversion to a casteless religion ; and the reader will find an instructive parallel to the inconsistencies of these minor Musalmán social units in the sub-divisions of Lingáyats treated under the article LINGAYAT.

Finally, we come to a class of Musalmán converts who still bear the name of the original Hindu caste from which they were converted and of which they form a numerically insignificant division to the present day. These Musalmán sections of well-known castes have been briefly described under the caste article for Hindus. It will be readily understood that census statistics are of small value for the divisions of Musalmáns since the majority are content to return themselves merely as ' Musalmán, ' without referring to their division whether an endogamous group or not.

ABDALIS, numbering 240 at the Census of 1891, and not recorded separately at the Census of 1901, are found in small numbers all over Gujarát. They are also called Dafális or Fadális, players on the tambourine. They belong to the lawful *básharra* order of beggars and beg in the name of God, beating the one-end drum *danka*, and singing religious songs. Their chief employment is to chant the wild spirit and genii hymns that are required by exorcists as an accompaniment to the practice of their rites. They are not very religious and have little organization. Abdális have a fixed due or tax upon the houses of Musalmáns in towns and villages.

BAGBANS OR BAGVANS, literally gardeners and fruiterers, numbering 780 (1901), including 371 males and 409 females, are found in small numbers all over the Deccan, Karnátak and the Southern Marátha Country. They are descended from Kunbis and Mális said to have been converted during the time of Aurangzeb (A.D. 1686—1707). Even now when Kunbis are converted to Islám they are styled Bágváns. They usually marry among themselves, and form a separate community with a well-organized union, settling their social disputes at meetings under a *chaudhari* or headman, who is chosen from the richest and oldest members of the community. Bágbáns have strong Hindu leanings, eschew beef, keep Hindu festivals and offer vows to Hindu gods. Though Sunnis of the Hanafi school in name, they seldom pray or keep Musalmán customs except that they circumcise their sons. They respect and obey the Kázi and employ him to register their marriages. They deal in fruit and vegetables.

BARUTGARS, or Firework-makers, are mixed Hindu converts, converted according to their own account by Aurangzeb. They marry either among themselves or with any of the regular Musalmán communities. They are Sunnis of the Hanafi school, and do not differ from other regular Musalmáns in their religious and social customs.

BELIMS are converted Rajputs of the Belim tribe. They have now ceased to form a separate division, and marry freely with Musalmáns of any section. The term Belim is now little more than a surname.

BENAWAS, the Penniless, also called Alifsháis from wearing a black Alif-like line down the brow and nose, are found in small numbers all over Gujarát. They belong to the order of lawless *básharra* beggars They move about in bands of from five to ten begging in the name of God. In each town they have a headman called treasurer, *bhandári*, chosen from among their number. To him each of the community pays his earnings, and except what is given back for expenses, the treasurer forwards the amount to the *murshid* or spiritual head of the order. Out of the funds in the *murshid's* hands, when a new member joins, a dinner is given. Of late years their number has fallen.

BHATYARAS, or Cooks, numbered 357 at the Census of 1901, including 171 males and 186 females, and were returned in some of the Gujarát Districts and States. Many must have been returned as Musalmáns unspecified, as they are found also in the Deccan and Karnátak. They are said to be descended from mixed Hindu castes, and trace their conversion to Aurangzeb. They marry only among themselves, but have no special organization and no headman, except the Kázi who settles their social disputes and registers their marriages. They are

Sunnis of the Hanafi school, but are seldom religious or careful to say their prayers.

BOJGARS, or Millet-beer Brewers, local converts of mixed Hindu origin, notably of Bhois, are found in small numbers in Belgaum and Sholápur. They marry amongst themselves, and form a distinct community with a headman of their own. They are liquor-sellers, labourers, fishers and palanquin-bearers.

CHATLAS are a wandering tribe occasionally found in north Gujarát. Of their origin nothing has been traced. They are wood-cutters, bringing in firewood from the forests and acting as carriers. They are Musalmáns only in name, and know nothing of their religion. They believe that the dead become saints *pirs*. Every year, on the anniversary of the Pir's death, the family calls the tribe to the tomb, and gives a feast of wine, mutton and pork. They bury the dead standing, building a raised tomb two feet square and in the centre a square altar half a foot higher. They feed even on carcasses.

CHHARAS, also called Ghágariás or Petticoat People, are occasionally found in small numbers all over Gujarát. They are supposed to be converted Hindus, but of their origin nothing certain is known. During the rains they meet in one place, holding their marriage and other family ceremonies, and settling their disputes. At the beginning of the fair season they break up into bands, moving about with Brinjári dogs and donkeys, begging, stealing and passing counterfeit coin. They are Musalmáns only in name, and know nothing of their religion. They have a union and headman called *náik*.

CHUDIWALAS, Bracelet-makers, are found in all parts of Gujarát. They make and sell bracelets of glass and lac or tin, some of the tin being ornamented with borders of gold and brass leaf. They are Sunnis in religion, some knowing the Kurán and saying their prayers. They marry with other Musalmáns. They form a well-ordered body, but have no headman.

CHUNDADIGIRAS, Silk-knot-Printers, are found all over Gujarát. They claim to be of Arab descent, and to have come into Gujarát through Sind ; but most of them are probably of Hindu origin. They form a distinct community marrying only among themselves. Both men and women make patterns in cloth by gathering the silk in puckers and rosettes and knotting it. In Surat, they also dye. Some are in Government service as messengers and constables. Sunnis in faith; they are zealous for their religion, some, both men and women, knowing the Kurán. They have a union but no headman.

DALALS, or Brokers, are found in small numbers in Ahmednagar city. They were originally *sipáhis* or soldiers from the Nizám's country. They marry either among themselves or with any of the regular Musalmán classes. They act as brokers only in horse sales. They are Hanafi Sunnis, but seldom say their prayers.

DALDIS or fishermen, found chiefly in the Ratnágiri *táluka* of the Ratnágiri district and the Janjira State have the tradition that their forefathers came in ships from across the seas. Their appearance and position among the local Musalmáns would seem to make it probable that they are partly converted Hindus, probably Kolis, and partly the descendants of immigrant Musalmáns and slave girls. According to Major Jervis (1) they are a race of people descended from the Arabian colonists who settled on the western coast in the seventh or eighth century and correspond with the Moplás of Malabár. They marry only among themselves or with other poor Konkani families. Their manners and customs do not differ for those of Jamátis. They are Sunnis of the Sháfai school but few of them are religious or careful to say their prayers. Some are sailors and cultivators and some go to Bombay in search of work. Others make and sell nets and rope of all sorts, and most of those in Ratnágiri are fishermen differing little from Hindus in their way of fishing.

DARVESHIS, literally religious beggars, seem to be converts, perhaps of the Shikári caste. They are a class of wandering bear and tiger showmen. They marry either among themselves or with any other religious beggars, and form a separate community and settle social disputes at meetings of the men under a headman or *Sargiro*, who has the power of fining any one who breaks their caste rules. They are Sunnis of the Hanafi school, but are not religious. Their only connection with the Kázi is that they employ him as marriage registrar.

DHAVADS, or Iron-smelters, numbering 388 (1901), including 183 males and 255 females, are chiefly found in the Mahábleshwar hills in the Sátára district. They are said to represent local Kolis converted by Aurangzeb. They marry among themselves and form a separate community, and have a well-managed body under their elective headman or *pátil*, who settles their social disputes with the consent of the castemen, and punishes those who break the caste rules with fines which generally take the form of caste feasts. They smelt the iron which is found in laterite or iron clay hills. But partly from

(1) Statistics of Western India, pp. 14-15.

the growing scarcity of fuel and partly from the cheapness of foreign iron and hardware goods, their iron smelting has nearly ceased. They live by cutting and selling grass, gathering honey, and making and selling iron nails, tongs and frying pans. Except that they call themselves Hanafi Sunnis, circumcise their sons, and ask the Kázi to register their marriages, they have few Musalmán customs. They keep Hindu feasts, eschew beef, and worship Hindu gods.

DHULDHOYAS, Dust-washers, are found in considerable numbers all over Gujarát, but chiefly in Nadiád and Mehamadábád. They numbered 444 at the Census of 1891, but were not recorded separately at the Census of 1901. They are said to be converted Hindus of the Khatri caste. They have a story that once, when their earnings as weavers were low, they were blessed by a beggar and told that in future they would find gold in dust. The men buy dust and other rubbish from the houses of goldsmiths, wash and sift it, and carefully pick out the particles of gold or silver found in the refuse. They marry only among themselves, and form a separate body with a headman of their own. Sunnis in faith, they are, as a class, religious, knowing the Kurán and saying their prayers.

DUDHVALAS, Milkmen, also called Gádits or Cartmen, and from their former castes Sábaliás and Gavlis, are found in all parts of Gujarát, especially in Ahmedabad and Baroda. They are said to be converted Hindus chiefly of the Sábalia and the Gavli castes. They marry only among themselves and form a separate community with a headman. They sell milk and hire out carts. They are Sunnis in name, but are not religious. As among Hindus, the women join in the marriage procession, singing Gujaráti songs, and at deaths wailing and beating the breast.

GAMETIS, Holders of a village or *gám*, are found in Gujarát. Except in the size of their estates, they do not differ from Kasbátis, with whom they intermarry.

GHERMEHDIS, Disbelievers in Mehdi or the coming Imám, are found in small numbers in most parts of Gujarát, in Bombay, Ahmednagar, Sholápur and Belgaum. They consider the name Ghermehdi abusive and delight in calling themselves Mehdevis. Their chief settlements, which are known as *dairah*, are in Pálanpur, Ahmednagar and Hyderabad (Deccan) where they live apart from other Musalmáns. The Pálanpur Mehdevis call themselves Sayads and Pirzádáhs.

Ghermehdis are converted Hindus and foreign Musalmáns, the followers of a certain Muhammad Meḥdi, a descendant of Ḥusain the grandson of the Prophet, born in A.D. 1443 (H. 847) in Jaunpur, a town near Benares. Muhammad at the age of forty began to act as a saint *wali*, and both at Jaunpur and afterwards at Mecca, drew around him a large body of followers. On his return to India, at Ahmedabad in A.D. 1497 (H. 903) and at Pattan in A.D. 1499 (H. 905), he openly laid claim to be the looked for Mehdi. Throughout his career he is said to have performed many miracles. He travelled much, accompanied by two companions, and died in Farah, a city of Khurasan, in A.D. 1504 (H. 910), maintaining to the last that he was the promised Mehdi. After his death his disciples dispersed, part returning to Gujarát under Sayad Khodmir. For a time his followers in Gujarát remained unmolested, but later on they were persecuted and their leader put to death, and during the time of Aurangzeb they were greatly repressed.

Though free to profess their opinions, the Mehdevis still practise caution *takiyah* and are anxious to pass as orthodox Musalmáns. They hold that Muhammad their saint was the last Imám, the expected Mehdi. They marry only among themselves. In Gujarát they have no headman, but form circles *dairahs* governed by rules of their own. In Ahmednagar, they have a distinct organization under a headman named *Murshid* or instructor, who registers marriages, and punishes breaches of caste rules. By occupation they are constables, messengers, servants and husbandmen.

GORKHODIAS, Grave-diggers, found in small numbers in all parts of Gujarát, are of mixed origin, partly foreign, partly Hindu. They hold a very low position, marry among themselves, and have no union or headman. Sunnis in religion, some of them learn the Kurán but are not regular in saying their prayers.

HAKIMS or Practitioners, also called Pahelwáns or Wrestlers, are found in small numbers in Bijápur. They call themselves Shaikhs. The men practise medicine without any training or learning, and the women act as midwives and songstresses in marriage and other ceremonies. They do not form an organized body and are only a nominal community marrying among the general classes of Musalmáns and differing little from them in customs and manners.

HUSAINI BRAHMANS (1) call themselves followers of the Atharwa Veda. They take their title from Husain, the grandson of

(1) In the Deccan there is a caste named Hussaini Bráhmans or Sahadev Joshis, who are astrologers and beggars by profession and Hindu by religion.

the Prophet, in whose name they ask alms. They are not converts to Islám, but adopt such of its doctrines as are not contrary to the Hindu faith. Their head-quarters are at Ajmir, and they are found in Baroda and Ahmedabad. They are of the lawless *besharra* group of beggars. Except beef, they eat secretly the ordinary kinds of animal food. Besides by begging, they earn a living by practising astrology and palmistry. They believe in the Saint Khajah Muin-ud-din Chishti of Ajmir, and consult both Muhammadan and Hindu omens. Except that they wear the Hindu browmark *tila*, that they often give their children Hindu names, that they do not circumcise, that a priest of their own class marries them, and that their dead are buried sitting, their customs, even to observing the *Ramzán* fast, are Muhammadan.

JAMA'TIS or members of the community, the leading branch of Konkani Musalmáns, are chiefly Shaikhs. Some families call themselves Kháns, but it seems probable that they are not of Afghán descent, but are the representatives of successful soldiers who won the title of Khán. They are found chiefly in the Kolába and Ratnágiri districts. Their home speech is Konkani Maráthi with a slightly peculiar pronunciation and a mixture of Urdu, Persian and Arab words. As a rule the men do not prefix Shaikh to their names, but add a surname taken either from their calling, as Khot, Kázi or Chogale, or from the dwelling place, as Tamrolkar and Tungekar. Their women add Bibi to their names. They generally marry among relations and in their own community. It is thought degrading to marry with any other class of Musalmáns. In religion all are Sunnis of the Sháfai school, but few are religious or careful to say their prayers. Some are land holders holding estates granted them as *kázis* or as preachers and others have villages which they originally took in farm. Some trade with Bombay in rice and timber and some in salt; others hold posts as forest inspectors and police chief constables. Some are sailors. The majority of the poorer families work as husbandmen and field labourers. Except that at marriages a dough lamp, filled with clarified butter lit is, by the women, carried to a river, pond or well, and left there, and that for five Thursdays after a death dinners are given to relations and friends, their ceremonies do not differ from those of other Musalmáns.

KAFSHGARS, or Shoe-makers, are found in small numbers in the cities and cantonments of Poona and Sholápur. They are said to be descended from strangers from Kabul who came to the Deccan during Musalmán rule. They make the yellow or red broadcloth shoes which are generally worn by Musalmán married women. They marry either among themselves or take wives from any of the regular Musalmán communities. They are Sunnis of the Hanafi school, and obey the Kázi, but are not careful to say their prayers.

KAGZIS, Paper-markers, numbering 544 (1901), including 283 males and 261 females, are found chiefly in north Gujarát, and scattered in small numbers in some parts of the Deccan. They make and sell the strong coarse country paper for which Ahmedabad has long been famous. They marry only among themselves and, under their spiritual guide, form a distinct body. Sunnis by religion, they believe in Sháh-Gharif-un-nawáz of Nandurbár in Khándesh, and those in Gujarát are followers of the Chishtis of Ahmedabad.

KAKARS, numbering 122 at the Census of 1891, and not recorded separately at the Census of 1901, are found chiefly in Belgaum, Dhárwár, and Bijápur. They originally belonged to the Kákarzáhi tribe of the Afgháns. According to their own story, about the middle of the eighteenth century they came to India as mercenaries of Ahmad Sháh Abdáli, and in 1758, on the defeat of the Abdáli governor of Sirhind by Raghunáthráo, wandered in bands through Malwa, the United Provinces and Gujarát, leading the life of outlaws. At last, hearing of the rise of Hyder Ali's power in Mysore, they joined him, and remained in his service in a mounted battery till the fall of Tipu in 1799. They marry only among themselves and are a well-organized community with a headman styled *Jamádár*. They are Sunnis of the Hanafi school, and some of them are religious and careful to attend prayers at the mosque. The men are servants, messengers and grooms, and the women sell poultry and head-loads of fuel.

KALAIGARS, or Tinsmiths, are found in small numbers throughout the Deccan and Karnátak. They call themselves Shaikhs. They marry either among themselves or with any of the regular classes of Musalmáns, and are a well-organized community under an elective headman called *Chaudhari*. They are Hanafi Sunnis in religion, and many of them are religious and careful to say their prayers. They tin copper and brass vessels, and are chiefly employed by Musalmáns and Christians.

KALANDARS, or Monks, are found in small numbers all over Gujarát. They wander over the country begging, and are very sturdy and troublesome in their demands. They are Sunnis of the lawless *besharra* order. They shave the whole body, the shearing of the eyebrows being one of the most important initiatory rites.

KAMLIAS, the perfect, were recorded as numbering 4 in Ahmedabad and Mahi Kántha at the Census of 1901. They are sprung from Kanoja Bráhman worshippers of Bahucheráji, who were converted by the Musalmán emperor Ala-ud-din (A.D. 1297). Their name is derived from *Kamál* or perfect, the title given to their headman when converted to Islám. When they go to Bahucheráji they beg in the name of the goddess. They do not circumcise, and except that they brand a dead man's breast and bury him, their ceremonies are Hindu. Some of them are said to be married and have children, others are said to earn a living as eunuchs.

KARALIAS, Potters, are found in Ahmedabad city. They are descendants of Hindus of the Kumbhár or potter caste. They are Sunnis in name, paying little attention to religion. They marry among themselves and with the Kathiárás or wood-cutters. With the Kathiárás they form one body *jamát*, and have a headman to settle disputes. They have a class-lodge *vádi* in Ahmedabad, where during the mango season they hold feasts, enforcing attendance by fine.

KASAIS, or Butchers, also called Kasábs, Khátiks and Sultánis numbering 13,170 (1901), including 6,686 males and 6,484 females, are found all over the Presidency except the Ratnágiri and Thána districts. The name Sultáni is in use only in the Karnátak, and is said to have been given to them because they were converted by Tipu Sultán. Kasáis have two divisions, Gao Kasáb or Gái Kasáb, that is, beef-butchers, and Bakar Kasáb or Lád Kasáb, that is, mutton-butchers, who neither eat together nor intermarry. The Bakar Kasábs look down upon the Gao Kasábs, whose touch they hold impure. Both divisions marry among themselves only, and are well-organized communities with a headman or *Choudhari* chosen from the most respected members. Both are Sunnis of the Hanafi school, but in name only. They respect the Kázi and employ him to register their marriages. The Bakar Kasábs have a strong Hindu feeling and eschew beef, worship and offer vows to Hindu gods, and keep Hindu festivals.

KASBATIS, owners of towns or *kasbás*, found in many parts of north Gujarát, are some of them descended from Baluch or Pathán mercenaries and others from Rajput converts. They hold large grants of land, and are quarrelsome and litigious. Sunnis in faith, they are not a religious people ; only a few know the Kurán or say their prayers. Occasionally, but of late much more rarely than formerly, they marry Hindu wives, Rajputs and sometimes Kolis. At such marriages the bride's friends occasionally call in a Bráhman; in either case the ceremony is entirely Musalmán. They give their daughters only to Musalmáns. They have no headman and do not form a distinct community.

KATHIARAS, Fuel-sellers, are found in Gujarát. They marry with Karáliás and do not differ from them in religion and customs.

KHOKHARS, converted Rajputs of the Khokhár tribe, are found in small numbers in north Gujarát and Káthiáwár. They are said to derive their name from *koh* mountain and *gir* taker, because they once took an impregnable mountain fortress. They are mentioned in the A in-i-Akbari [1] as a tribe of some importance in Pind Dadan Khán in the Punjab. They claim Afghán extraction, and state that they are still represented by a Khel (tribe) of this name. As far as possible they intermarry among themselves, but do not object to matrimonial connections with the Bábis, Lohánis and other Patháns. They are landholders in Pattan and also perform military service. Some are peasants, labourers and messengers.

LAKARHARAS, or Wood-sellers, are found in small numbers in all parts of the Deccan. In most places they are a mixed population of Shaikhs and a few Sayads. During the reign of Aurangzeb they were joined by a large number of Hindu converts who were either wood-sellers when they were Hindus or took to wood-selling when they became Musalmáns. They sell wood both for building and for fuel. They are Sunnis in name, but are not careful to say their prayers. They form a separate community with one of their number as head, who has power to settle disputes by small fines which go to meet the expenses of the nearest mosque.

MAHAWATS, or Elephant-drivers are said to be Rajput converts. They call themselves Shaikhs. As the demand for elephant-drivers has nearly ceased, they have taken to different callings, working as servants, messengers or constables. They have no special class organization and no headman, and marry with any one of the regular classes of Musalmáns. Most of the men and almost all of the women eschew beef, and have a leaning to Hindu customs, inclining to keep Hindu festivals and believing in Hindu gods. They are Sunnis of the Hanafi school, but few are religious or careful to say their prayers. They respect and obey the Kázi and employ him to register their marriages and settle social disputes.

---

(1) Blochman's edition, p. 465, note 2.

MAKWANAS, converts from the Makwána tribe of Rajputs or Kolis, are found over many parts of north Gujarát. Their sons marry either into Musalmán, Makwána or Koli families; their daughters into Musalmán families of the Makwána, Bábi or Dholka Pathán tribes. They employ a Bráhman priest at their weddings. They are Sunnis in faith, but as a rule care little for their religion. They earn their living as petty landlords, peasants, messengers and constables.

MALIKS (Lords) are converted Hindus and found all over Gujarát. They are landlords and peasants and are employed in Government service as messengers and constables. The women spin, but do not work in the field. They are Sunnis in name but are not religious, few of them knowing the Kurán or caring to say their prayers. In their marriage and other customs they do not differ from other converted Rajputs.

MANYARS or Glass bangle makers, also known as Shishgars, numbering 1,815 (1901) including 904 males and 911 females, are found all over Gujarát and the Deccan and parts of the north Konkan and Karnátak. They are of mixed Hindu origin, and are said to have been converted by Aurangzeb. They marry either among themselves or with any of the regular Musalmáns. They have two divisions, Proper and Bangarharás, who eat together and intermarry. The hereditary occupation of the caste is making bangles of glass, wax and ivory. Chinese and European competition have forced them to give up their old craft, and they have become petty shopkeepers and dealers in hardware and miscellaneous articles. They have no special organization and no headman except the Kázi who settles their social disputes. They are Sunnis of the Hanafi school, but are not religious or careful to say their prayers. Those in Gujarát revere Sháh Alam, the well-known Ahmedabad saint.

MAPARAS, Corn-weighers, are found in all parts of Gujarát. They closely resemble the Manyárs.

MIRS, Nobles or MIRASIS, Landlords, also called Langhás or singers, Dholis or drum-players, and Doms after the tribe of that name, are found all over Gujarát, Káthiawár, Cutch, Pálanpur and Mahikántha. At the census of 1901 they numbered 3,624 including 1,867 males and 1,757 females. They were originally of two classes, one descendants of Gujarát Bháts or bards, the other from northern India partly of Bhát descent and partly connected with the Doms. They marry only among themselves. Some own land, and in the rainy season many work as cultivators. In the fair season the men move about either alone or in twos or threes, begging, singing and telling tales, both Hindu and Musalmán, and playing on the drum, the fiddle, the guitar and the tambourine. The women stay at home and under the name of Domnis or Langhis, at marriage and other feasts, attend at Muhammadan houses and play and sing before the women. The Mirs are zealous followers of Dáda Mián, an Ahmedabad Sayad, paying him yearly Re. 1 head-money or forty pounds (one *man*) of wheat. They are a well-managed community with the Sayad as their head.

MIRDHAS, originally spies, are found in very small numbers in north Gujarát. They are said to be of part-foreign part-Rajput origin. Under the Gujarát Sultáns they served as spies. They are now employed as messengers and constables.

MOLESALAMS, found chiefly in Broach and in the Rewa Kántha, are half converts to Islám made from among Rajputs, chiefly in the reign of Mahmud Begada (A.D. 1459—1513). The Molesalám Thákors of Amod and Kerwáda in Broach claim descent from Jádav Rajputs who were converted by Mahmud Begada in A.D. 1486.

Molesalám Thákors and chiefs, while employing Kázis, Sayads and Maulavis, maintain the descendants of their old Bráhman family priests and support their Bháts and Chárans, whom the rich engage to wile away their leisure hours by reciting poetry, and the poor to serve as priests at marriages. A Molesalám will marry his daughter to a Sayad, a Shaikh, a Mughal or Bábi, but not, as a rule, to a Musalmán of the lower order. The son of a chief may get a Rajput girl in marriage. But other Molesaláms marry either among their own people or the poorer classes of Musalmáns. Molesaláms dine with other Musalmáns, but except that they sometimes take flesh, they eat and drink like Hindus.

MUSA SUHAGS, followers of Musa with the married woman's dress, are to be found singly all over Gujarát. Their patron saint Musa, who lived at the close of the fifteenth century, according to one account, dressed in woman's clothes as a symbol that he was devoted to god as a wife to her husband. According to another account, Musa was so pressed and worried by the crowd that to hide himself he used to go about dressed as a woman. In memory of their leader's disguise most of the beggars of this order, though they do not shave the beard, dress like married women in a red scarf *dupatta*, a gown and trousers. They also put on bracelets, bell-anklets and other ornaments. They go singly, blessing the people without music or other show. As the dress and vow of celibacy are disliked, the Musa

Suhágs gain few disciples, and as they have no children their numbers are falling.

NAGARJIS or NAKARCHIS, Kettle Drummers, are found in small numbers in Sátára and Bijápur. They marry among themselves only and form a separate community under an elective headman or *chaudhari*. They are employed both by Hindus and Musalmáns at marriages, and on festive occasions at local temples and the shrines of Musalmán saints. Some have taken to tillage. Though in name Sunnis of the Hanafi school, they have strong Hindu leanings, keeping Hindu feasts, eschewing beef, and worshipping Hindu gods. They respect and obey the Kázi and employ him to register their marriages.

NAGORIS, numbering 1,408, including 695 males and 713 females, were recorded at the Census of 1901 in Pálanpur, Mahikántha and Káthiáwár, but they are also found in Ahmedabad, Viramgam, Bhávnagar, Baroda and Broach. They derive their name from Nágor in Malwa, their original home. In Pálanpur they call themselves Kháns from having given up their original occupation of cart-driving and taken to that of arms. They appear to be recruited from many classes from their surnames such as Kázi, Mughal and Shaikh. They marry only among themselves, and form a separate community with a union and a headman chosen by the people. They are Sunnis in name, but as a class the men are not religious. Most of them are cart-drivers. Before railway times they brought goods and people from Malwa to Ahmedabad. Now they go only short distances. The women work as labourers and sell milk.

NAIKWARIS are found in large numbers in Násik, Khándesh and Ahmednagar, and thinly scattered over the other Deccan districts. They are said to be Marátha Kunbis whose forefathers were converted to Islám by Tipu's father Hyder Naik, from whom they take their name. After the fall of Seringapatam they passed north as soldiers of fortune under the Peshwás, and many of them settled at Násik. Náikwáris are generally soldiers, messengers, and constables, and a few are husbandmen. In Ahmednagar and Poona, some of them find employment with bankers as watchmen. Some are Sunnis and some who live in outlying parts keep many Hindu customs, calling a Bráhman as well as a *Mulla* to their weddings. A few are Wáhábis. They have a well organized community with their most intelligent and respected member as the head.

NAKSHBANDS, Mark-makers, belong to the law-abiding *básharra* order of beggars. They are found in small numbers all over Gujarát. They are followers of a saint named Khájah Bahá-ud-din

Nakshband. Holding in their hand a stout-wicked flaming unshaded brass lamp, which neither rain nor wind can put out, they move about singly chanting their saint's praises. The Nakshband reverence for fire is said to be a trace of the attempted revival of Magiat element worship in Persia and Tartary about A. D. 946 (H. 383), the period of Shiah ascendancy at the court of the Khalifahs of Baghdád during the supremacy of the Persian house of Buwaih or the Bowides. Children are fond of the Nakshband, and go out in numbers to give him money. In return, as his name shows, he marks them on the brow with oil from his lamp. Nakshbands are Sunnis in religion, and as they live only in ones and twos they have little organization.

NALBANDS, or Farriers, are found in small numbers all over Gujarát, the Deccan and Karnátak. They are of mixed Hindu origin, converted by Aurangzeb, and call themselves Shaikhs. They make their living as farriers, messengers and servants. They shoe horses and bullocks. They marry either among themselves or with any of the general classes of Musalmáns. They obey the Kázi and through him settle social disputes. They are Sunnis of the Hanafi school, but are not religious or careful to say their prayers.

NAVAYATS, or Shipmen, numbering 1,273 (1901), including 548 males and 725 females, are found only in the Kanara district. They are also known as Saudágars or traders. They are said to represent Persian merchants who, in the seventh and eighth centuries, left their home on account of the persecutions of the fierce governor Hajaj-bin-Usaf, and came and settled on the Malabar and Kanara coasts. They marry only among themselves and form a separate community, but have no special organization nor headman. They are Sunnis of the Hanafi school, and are very religious and careful to say their prayers. They deal in piece-goods and were formesly well-to-do. They suffered heavily during the 1876—1887 famine when some of them were forced to give up trade and take to husbandry.

PANJNIGARS, or Cotton-thread Starchers, are found all over Gujarát and in Sholápur. They have a division named Hir Pánjnigárs Silk Starchers, with whom they intermarry. Sunnis in name, they are not a religous class. They marry only among themselves and have a well-managed union with a headman.

PIRZADAS are a class of Sayads found in Násik only. They are descended from the saint Sayad Sháh Muhammad Sádik Sarmast Husaini, who, about the close of the tenth century of the Hijra (A. D. 1568), came from Medina, and having travelled over a greater part of Western India, settled at Násik. Many of them are landholders.

Some deal in hay, grain or fuel, some are municipal contractors, and some are money-lenders. They are Sunnis in faith and do not form a separate community.

RAFAIS, that is, exalted, also called Faceslashers *Munhphodás* or *Munhchirás,* occur in considerable numbers over the whole of Gujarat. They are a class of the lawless *besharra* order of beggars. They are followers of Sayad Ahmad Kabir. Holding in the right hand a twelve-inch iron spike called *gurz*, sharp-pointed and having near the top many small iron chains, the beggar rattles the chains, and, if people are slow in giving him money, strikes at his cheek or eye with the sharp iron point and seems to cause no wound. They beg in the name of God, and are very persistent and troublesome. They are Sunnis in religion.

RAFUGARS, or Cloth Darners, are converts of mixed Hindu origin and ascribe their conversion to Aurangzeb. They have no special class organization nor any headman except the regular Kázi, who acts both as marriage registrar and as judge in settling social disputes. They are Sunnis of the Hanafi school and are said to be careful to say their prayers. Besides darners many are soldiers, constables and servants.

RASULSHAHIS, followers of the Prophet, also called Mastáns or Madmen, are found in small numbers all over Gujarát. They are Sunnis of the lawless *besharra* order, without wives or settled homes. They carry a large wooden club and beg for money to pay for drink. They are very dissipated and troublesome. They are a very small body with a religious head but no organised community.

RATHORS, converts from the Ráthor tribe of Rajputs, numbering 221 (1901), including 119 males and 102 females, were recorded only in Mahi Kántha, but are to be found in small numbers in different parts of north of Gujarát. They are Sunnis in name, but are not religious, neither learning the Kurán nor saying their prayers. A few of them have Swáminaráyan pictures in their houses and reverence them. Their ceremonies are in many respects Hindu. At marriages the larger landlords keep to the Rajput custom of sending a sword to the bride's house and bringing her back for the ceremony to the bridegroom's village. When the bride is a Hindu, both Bráhman and Musalmán ceremonies are preformed. At deaths the women wail and beat the breast. Except that they marry only among Rajputs and Kolis, either Hindu or Musalmán, they do not form a separate community and have no headman. They earn their living as landlords, peasant and messengers.

SAIKALGARS, Sikalgars, or Sikligars, that is, Armourers, numbering 1,957 (1901), including 1,075 males and 882 females, are found in small numbers all over the Deccan and Karnátak. They are said to represent Hindu Ghisádis and Lohárs converted during the time of Aurangzeb. They marry either among themselves or with Manyárs, Atárs and Patvegárs. They have a headman, called Mukadam in some places and Mehtar in others, who has power to fine any one who breaks their caste rules. They are Sunnis of the Hanafi school in name only. They eschew beef, offer vows to Hindu gods, and keep Hindu festivals. They employ the Kázi to register their marriages, but do not show him much respect. They furbish and polish weapons and tools and make razors, knives, pack needles, carpenters' tools, and all sorts of cutlery.

SALTANGARS, Saltánkars or Tanners, are found in small numbers in Poona and Sholápur. They are said to be descended from Hindus of the Chámbhár and Mochi castes, and trace their conversion to Aurangzeb. They marry among themselves only, and have a well-managed union under a headman chosen from the oldest and richest members of the community. Though Sunnis of the Hanafi school, they seldom say their prayers, and have strong Hindu leanings, eschewing beef, offering vows to Hindu gods, and keeping Hindu festivals. They respect and obey the Kázi, but their purely Musalman custom is circumcision. They buy sheep and goat skins from butchers, tan them and sell them to shoemakers. Their trade has lately suffered much owing to the competition of Mehmans and Labhes from Bombay and Madras.

SARBANS, or Camel Drivers represent converts of several Hindu castes, notably Rajputs. The demand for camel drivers having ceased, they have taken to new pursuits, some earning their living as servants and messengers and others as husbandmen. They marry either among themselves or with any of the ordinary Musalmáns. They are Sunnis of the Hanafi school, but are not religious. Some eschew beef and worship Hindu gods. They obey and respect the Kázi in all matters.

SHAIKHDAS or Shaikhs, found chiefly in Broach and Ahmedabad, are one of the classes of devotees who worship at the shrine of Bála Muhammad Sháh, one of the minor Pirána saints. In their ways they differ little from the Mátia Kanbis. They bury their dead, but except for this observance and for their name, their customs are Hindu. They are not circumcised, and do not eat with Musalmáns, but wear forehead marks *tilás* and many of them belong to the sect of the Swáminaráyans. At the time of marriage both a Musalmán and a Hindu priest attend. The Musalmán ceremony is performed by a Fakir, and the Hindu rite of *chori* or altar-worship by a Brahman.

SIPAHIS, soldiers, numbering 18,175 (1901), including 9,303 males and 8,872 females, were recorded only in Káthiáwár, but are found in considerable numbers in all parts of Gujarát. They seem to be of mixed origin, partly descendants of immigrants and partly of Rajput converts, as their surnames Chohán, Ráthor and Parmár show. They marry with other Musalmáns, but have a union and a headman. They are husbandmen and labourers, and are employed in Government service as soldiers, constables and messengers. Sunnis in faith, some of them know the Kurán, say their prayers and pay respect to a spiritual guide.

SOLANKIS, converts from the Solanki tribe of Rajputs, are found in small numbers in different parts of north Gujarát. They intermarry with the Ráthors and other converted Rajputs, and do not differ from them in religion and customs.

TAIS, Silk Weavers, numbering 4,787 (1901), including 2,258 males and 2,529 females, are found in all parts of Gujarát. They claim to take their name from Tái, a city between Turkey and Arabia, and to have been taught weaving and sewing by the Prophet Idris. They claim descent from Hatïm of Tái, the famous Arab hero, who flourished immediately before the birth of the Prophet and whose name is proverbial for generosity in Arabia. In Gujarát they are a mixed class, some of them foreigners, who seem to have come from Sind about a thousand years ago, and others are converted Gujarát Hindus. They marry among themselves and form a separate union with a headman of their own. Except in Bulsár, where some families do business as bankers and money-lenders, all weave cotton ropes and turbans. They are Sunnis in faith, and, especially in Ahmedabad and Surat, are a religious class, going to the mosque five times a day.

WARRAKS, or Paper-makers, are found in small numbers in Ahmednagar. They are a branch of Shaikhs, and marry with any of the regular classes of Musalmáns. Most of them are servants and messengers.

MUSA SUHAG.—See under Minor Musalmán Castes.

MUSKIN MALLAVA.—A sub-division of Mallavas.

MUSTIGAR.—A synonym for Khetri.

MUWALLAD.—A sub-division of Sidis.

MYASA.—A synonym for Jas Berad.

NADAF.—A synonym for Musalmán Pinjári.

NADE.—A sub-division of Mángs.

NADIA.—A sub-division of Machhis and Khálpás.

NADIG.—Kanarese term for Hajám or barber.

NADORS, numbering 6,005 (1901), including 3,394 males and 2,611 females, are found in the Kumta, Ankola and Honávar *tálukás* of the Kanara district. Little is known regarding their origin, and the derivation given in the Bombay Gazetteer for their name, *viz.*, *nádu*, a village, throws no light on it. There is a tradition in the caste that their ancestors came from Cochin to escape the persecution of the Moplás, about four centuries ago. **Name and origin.**

The caste consists of two endogamous divisions. (1) Torke Nádors, (2) Uppu Nádors. The former consider themselves socially superior to the latter, from whom, however they do not differ in appearance, speech, food, dress or character. It seems probable that the division in the caste occurred owing to the Uppu Nádors at one time manufacturing salt (*uppu* = salt) and thus falling below the rest of the caste, who were cultivators. **Endogamous divisions.**

The caste contains the following exogamous divisions or *balis* :— **Exogamous divisions.**

1. Ajjana bali .. Ajja = fruit of the upas tree (*antiaris toxicaria*).
2. Ane bali .. Ane = the elephant.
3. Chendi bali .. Chendi = a tree (*Cerbera odollam*).
4. Ganga bali .. Ganga = the river Gangávali.
5. Hole bali .. Hole = a field (?)
6. Honne bali .. Honne = a tree (*Pterocarpus marsupium*).
7. Nág bali .. Nágchampa = a tree (*Mesua ferrea*).
8. Salyan bali .. Saler = a porcupine.
9. Shetti bali .. Shetti = a fish.
10. Shige bali .. Shige = a tree (*Acacia concinna*).
11. Shire bali .. Shire = a tree (*Gyandropsis pentaphylla*).
12. Tolana bali .. Tola = a wolf.

The *bali* is traced through females—an indication of a former system of polyandry now extinct. Members of each *bali* refrain from injuring, and show reverence to, the tree or animal from which it takes its name. Thus the members of the *Nág bali* will not wear the flowers of the Nágchampa (*Mesua ferrea*) in their hair, and those of the *Ane bali* worship the elephant with offerings of cocoanuts.

The Nádors closely resemble the Halvakki Vakkals in their costume, speech, daily life, and style of living. Outsiders are not admitted into this caste.

Marriage ceremonies.

Girls are married from the age of five to twelve ; boys from ten and upwards. Sexual license before marriage is not allowed. Polygamy is permitted if the first wife is barren, quarrelsome, or suffering from an incurable disease. Polyandry is unknown. The offer of marriage comes from the boy's father. When a match is settled, the betrothal ceremony, known as *huga mudisavadu* (from *hu*, flower, and *mudisavadu*, decorating) is performed, in which the boy's father accompanied by relations and friends visits the girl's house, taking sweetmeats and flowers, decorates the girl with the flowers, and gives her the sweetmeats. The party is then treated to a feast by the girl's father. If the girl's father is poor, the boy's father pays him from Rs. 10 to Rs. 50 for the marriage expenses. The day for the marriage is fixed by the caste priest, a Havig Bráhman. On the marriage day, a few hours before the marriage takes place, a ceremony known as *valemuhurta* is performed, when split black gram is taken to the girl's house by the boy's party and ground in a grinding mill by the bride and other women. The party then return home and start for the girl's house with the bridegroom. They are received midway by the girl's party. When the whole party reach the girl's house the bride is brought out and seated opposite the bridegroom, a cloth is held between them, marriage verses are repeated, and grains of sacred rice are thrown on the couple—this being the essential portion of the ceremony. On the second day the bridegroom returns to his house with the bride, and on the third day they go again to the girl's father's house. The festivities end on the fourth day when the ceremony of *teratalgi* is performed. This consists in the boy's party taking to the girl's house a *tali*, *i.e.*, a plate with Rs. 20, rice grains, a cocoanut, flowers and a burning lamp. These things are presented to the girl. If the girl's father is poor he retains the Rs. 20, if well-to-do, he returns the amount to the boy's father. The girl is then handed over.

The re-marriage of widows is permitted, but is not much in vogue. A widow cannot marry her late husband's younger or elder brother or a member of his *bali*. A widow marriage can be celebrated at any time during the year. It takes place always at night and no priest is present. Married women on the boy's side are present. The widow's new husband has to present her with a robe and nose-ring, the putting on of which completes the ceremony. A bachelor is not allowed to marry a widow.

A husband may divorce his wife on the ground of her misconduct. A wife may leave her husband, but she is not allowed to marry in his lifetime. A woman guilty of adultery is turned out of the caste.

The Hindu law of inheritance is followed.

Nádors are Hindus. Their family god is Venkatráma of Tirupati, to whom they perform pilgrimages. They observe almost all the Hindu holidays. Their religious teacher is the head of the monastery at Shringeri. They worship Golibir, Shántapa, Kengal, the Shaktis, and other village gods. The *tulas*, *pipal* and the Indian fig tree are also worshipped. The plough and weapons are worshipped on the Dasara day. Every year when the rainy season sets in, and whenever an epidemic breaks out, cocks and goats are offered to the Shaktis. A portion of the offerings is received by the officiating priests, who are Kumbhárs, and the remainder is eaten by the offerers. The priests of the caste are Havig Bráhmans. **Religion.**

The dead are burnt. Children having no teeth and persons dying of small-pox are buried with head to the north. The bones and ashes are thrown into a river or carried to Gokarn and thrown into the sea. If a man meets a violent death and his corpse is not found, an image of grass is made and burnt in his name. The mourning for the burnt lasts for twelve days and for the buried forty-five days. For one year after death a *shráddha* is performed every month, and after that once a year. **Death ceremonies.**

Nádors are agriculturists. Many are occupancy rayats and pay assessment to Government on their own holdings. Some are tenants of superior holders. Some are landless day labourers. A few have taken to Government service.

The caste has an organization similar to that of the Halvakki Vakkals for the settlement of caste questions.

They eat goats, fowl and fish only. They do not drink liquor. They eat from the hands of Bráhmans only. The highest well-known caste who eat with them is the Halvakki Vakkal caste. **Food.**

NAG.—A sub-division of Devángs.

NAGAR.—A sub-division of Bráhmans and Vániás.

NAGARI.—A synonym for Shaiva Gurav ; a sub-division of Bháts.

NAGARIA.—A sub-division of Vánjhá.

NAGARJI.—*See* under Minor Musalmán Castes.

NAGARKAR.—A sub-division of Gavlis.

NAGHORI.—A synonym for Nágori ; a sub-division of Didu Vániás.

NAGLIK.—A sub-division of Shimpis and Lingáyats.

NAGORI.—A sub-division of Vániás ; *see* also under Minor Musalmán castes.

NAGOSHI.—A sub-division of Bohorás.

NAGRI.—A synonym for Nágori Vánia.

NAHAL.—A sub-division of Bhils.

NAIDUS, [1] numbering 767 (1901), including 395 males and 372 females, are found in small numbers in Poona and Belgaum. They are immigrants from Madras. Most of them are writers.

NAIK.—A title applied to Rámoshis, Berads, Kumbhárs, etc.; also used by Bráhman and other high caste bankers in the Deccan and Karnátak. A synonym for Devli and Náikda.

Name and origin.

NAIKDAS, numbering 59,161 (1901), including 29,322 males and 29,839 females, are found chiefly in the Panch Mahál̈s, in Surat district, and the Rewa Kántha and Surat Agencies. They are also known as Naiks. The name 'Naikda' or 'Little Naik' is probably due to their being considered inferior to the Broach Talabadás, who were formerly known as Naiks. Of their origin as a separate class two stories are told. One that their ancestors were grooms to the Musalmán nobles and merchants of Chámpáner who took to the woods when on the fall of that city (A.D. 1550—1573) their employment was lost. A second account states that they are descended from an escort sent into western Gujarát by the Rája of Chámpáner. There seems little doubt that they were largely employed in Chámpáner in some menial capacity. In 1818, when they first came under British rule, the Naikdas had the worst possible name for savage cruelty. In 1826 they were said to "exceed the Bhils in their predatory and lawless habits, in their cruelty, blood thirstiness, and life of independence, and in the total disregard of all the customs and usages of social

(1) Castes and Tribes of Southern India, Vol. V, p. 138.

life their chief used to organize forays and engage Sindis and Makránis to help them. Numbers of cattle were collected and kept in the hills until ransomed. The proceeds of the raid were then distributed among all who had taken part in it. In 1838 their depredations became so daring that a force had to be sent against them. For some years they were more orderly ; but in 1854 they were still a savage and predatory class, living in the most remote and impervious forests. In 1857 certain Gujarát mutineers tried to raise them to revolt. The attempt was to some extent successful but was delayed till too late to cause much mischief. In 1868 they were stirred up to rebellion by one of their holy men or *bhagats*. Since then the tribe has remained quiet. The habits of all are not settled. Some wander from one place to another in search of employment during the fair weather. In the rainy season they settle down and perform agricultural labour. Their dwelling is a hut, the frame of rough timber, the walls of reeds and bamboo generally plastered with cowdung and clay, the roof peaked and thatched with grass and dried teak or palm leaves. Among the Naikdas authority is centred in four chiefs, Of these, one resides at Sivrajpur in Halol, a second at Gondola in the Chota Udaipur State, a third at Sagtala in the Baria State, and a fourth at Poili in the hills above Dandiapura under Jambughoda. According to the *Bombay Gazetteer* these men could between them raise the whole tribe of Naikdas at a moment's notice. Naikdas are degraded Kolis. They are undoubtedly of a primitive stock, much mixed from various sources. They admit persons of higher castes, such as Kolis, Bhils, etc., into their caste. The convert has to treat the the Naikdas to liquor. The Naikdas profess not to marry with any other caste. But if a Koli woman lives with a Naikda, or a a Koli with a Naikda woman, the couple can be admitted into the Naikda caste.

Divisions. There are no strictly endogamous or exogamous divisions of the caste. The commonest surnames among them are Dámara, Tadwala, Anása, Bámna, Rathwa, and Dhanka. Dámra, Rathwa and Dhanka Naikdas seem to be partly Bhil. Marriages are performed when the two parties are removed from the common ancestor from two to seven generations. The Dámra, Rathwa, Pattia, and Bamna divisions consider themselves superior to the other Naikdas and usually refrain from intermarrying. If a member of one of these divisions marries a girl from the remaining Naikdas, he is fined from ten to twelve rupees, and has to treat his caste-men to liquor. The Bámnas possess two divisions, namely, Ujwália (bright) and Andhária (dark) Bámnas, of which the latter division is inferior to the former. An Ujwália Bámna may marry a girl from the Andhária division, but a girl of the Ujwália division may not be married to a boy of the inferior or Andhária stock, under penalty of a fine if this rule is infringed. Marriage with a mother's sister's son, father's sister's son, and maternal uncle's son is not allowed. Marriage with wife's sister is allowed. Two brothers may marry two sisters.

Marriage. Boys and girls are married between fifteen and twenty-five. In many cases they do not perform any marriage ceremony. If a girl reaches the age of sixteen and her parents have not betrothed her, she may go and live with any man she chooses, and if he agrees to pay her parents seventeen rupees, no objection is raised. If a girl commits sexual indiscretions with a man of her caste before marriage, the girl is married to the man involved. In this connection a very strange custom prevails. If the man involved declines to marry the girl, some four or five respectable persons of the caste are summoned, the man takes the girl on his lap in their presence, and repeats the word 'mother' seven times. The male culprit is then suckled by the girl, and is allowed to regard her as his mother. He is then fined five or seven rupees and is released from the obligation to marry her. If a girl commits sexual indiscretions with a man of a lower caste, she is turned out of her caste. Polygamy is permitted. Marrying several wives is considered to be a source of honour and importance, and consequently a Naikda in good circumstances marries from two or four, or sometimes seven, wives. Polyandry is unknown.

The offer of marriage comes from the boy's father. Before a marriage is settled, the bride and the bridegroom are given the option of choosing each other. Four or five persons of the caste act as mediators in the settlement of marriage. They are given liquor for their services. The boy's father pays to the girl's father from ten to thirty rupees. He uses this sum in treating his guests to liquor and to defray the marriage costs. Some, instead of paying money, give a *kalshi* (a measure of corn) or sixteen maunds of grain. Four or five persons of the caste fix the marriage day. Marriages are celebrated on Mondays, Wednesdays, Thursdays, or Fridays. Naikdas do not count their week days in the usual fashion. They have peculiar marks, such as the *Rajpurnohat* (the market day at Rajpur), the *Gujrinohat* (the market day at Guji), *Chandanohat* and so forth, for the days of the week. The ceremony of marriage is conducted by two old men, one from each family, who for the time are called priests or *pujáris*, or by a person having knowledge of ghosts and goblins, and who can avert evil influences, who is styled *Badro*. The bride and bridegroom are termed among them *ladi* and *lada* respectively. On reaching the bride's village, the wedding party eat cakes which they bring with them. The bridegroom goes to the bride's home in a procession. A *toran* or bough is prepared with raw thread and mango leaves, and leaves of the *aso* tree (*Saraca indica*) are applied to it. The bridegroom while entering has to pull off a mango leaf carefully between his two fingers, namely, the middle and the fore-finger, without breaking the thread. If he is unable to do so he is beaten, and he is only honoured if he succeed in pulling off the leaf. Then the mother of the bride receives the bridegroom, and he is led into the marriage booth. The bride is then brought from the house. A woman takes the bride on her shoulder and a man the bridegroom, and dancing is commenced to the sound of drums. After this, the bride and bridegroom are seated face to face in a square or *chori*. Fire is kindled. and the couple are asked to take four rounds. The bride and bridegroom feed each otherfive times with *kansár* or some kind of sweetmeat or rice. These are the binding portions of the ceremony. They then worship Ganpati and sprinkle red powder over the image and the marriage is over.

Widow remarriage is allowed. A widow cannot marry her mother's sister's son, father's sister's son, or maternal uncle's son. She may marry the younger brother or any other relative of her deceased husband, except his elder brother. A widow remarriage is brought about either by the parents of the widow or by the widow herself. When a remarriage is brought about by the parents of a widow, they take from the bridegroom five to ten rupees. Sometimes a widow remarriage ceremony is not observed at all. A widow may go to live in the house of any man whom she selects. But in such cases the widow is said to have "entered the house of a man"—a status less recognized than widow remarriage. Widow remarriage is performed among the Naikdas who live in the vicinity of big cities on Tuesdays and Sundays. Those who live in forest tracts perform it on any day. At the time of remarriage, four or five men known as wise men are present. The widow is given new clothes to wear. The widow and her new husband sit together and a lamp of clarified butter is lighted. The couple sprinkle water mixed with red powder over it and tie marriage threads to the wrists of each other. This is the binding portion of the ceremony. In some parts a wise man of the tribe places the hand of the widow in that of her new husband, and the ceremony is over. The husband then takes her away with him. Widow remarriage is performed at night, for it is the common belief that if a widow is married in the day time the village will be burnt.

Both husband and wife can ask for a divorce. The husband divorces his wife in the case of infidelity on her part. When a woman "enters the house" of another man and lives with him, the original husband gets a refund of the marriage expenses. A husband and wife, in the presence of two men of the caste, tell each other that they have become separated. The wife tears off a piece of her garment, throwing it on the husband's body, and the husband tears off a small piece of his garment and throws it on his wife's body. This act of divorce is known as *chhuta chheda karva*. A woman divorced for adultery with a man of her caste or with a man of a higher caste is allowed to marry a second time. Her marriage is conducted in the form of a widow remarriage. A woman divorced for adultery with a man of a lower caste is turned out of her caste.

Religion.

Naikdas follow the Hindu law of inheritance, and are animistic in religion. They have a preference for the worship of goddesses and adore Kálika, Ambámáta and Mahákáli. They sometimes pour oil over Hanumán. Though they are not allowed to enter her temple, they worship the Máta or mother, on Páwágad hill, and at other local fairs their objects of worship are spirits and ghosts. They respect the tiger and swear by its name. They think that if they swear falsely they would at once be killed by the tiger. They worship the *Shami* (Prosopis Spicigera) tree and their bows and arrows. On the *Kalichodas* day in *Ashwin* (October-November) they make offerings to goddesses. Their leading holidays are *Holi* in February-March, *Akhatri* in April-May, *Diváso* in August-September, and *Diváli* in October. They worship their dead ancestors, in whose honour they fix teak posts in the ground, roughly hacking them at the top into something like a human face. These are termed *khatris*. Offerings to them are made on *Kalichodas* day in *Ashwin* (October-November). They show no respect for the Muhammadan religion, and neither worship nor make offerings at Muhammadan shrines. When cholera and small-pox are raging they worship Máta and Kákábalia. Naikdas show no respect for Bráhmans, and care little for Bráhmanic rites, fasts, or feasts. A common local belief is that they hold the killing of a Bráhman to be an act of merit. Referring to the feast on the thirteenth day after death their proverb says, "By the death of one *tilvani* or brow-mark *tilak* wearer, a hundred are fed."

Death ceremonies.

They burn their dead usually at a place about four miles from their village. Children under two years of age are buried. The ashes and bones are either thrown into a river or left if there is no river near. When life is extinct, the corpse, wrapped in cloth, is laid on a bamboo bier and carried by men of the tribe, or taken in a cart, to the burning ground (*sivdi*). When the pyre is ready, it is kindled by the deceased's nearest male relation. Nine days after the burning of the body, the nearest relations go to the burning place and collect the ashes into a heap, and on the heap place an earthen jar full of water. On their return home the relations of the deceased shave their heads and faces. On the same day the person who lighted the funeral pyre cooks rice or panic *kodra* at his house. He lays the cooked grain on a plate made of four leaves of the *khakhra* (*Butea frondosa*) tree, pours a little butter over it and sets fire to it. Some more of the grain, placed on five leaf plates, is sprinkled with butter and given to five children to eat. On the twelfth day the family of the deceased prepare rice or panic *kodra*, and pulse, with, if they can afford it, a little butter, and invite those who were at the funeral, or if they are rich enough, the whole village. The guests do not all meet. They come when they like, and, receiving their share of the food, either eat it on the spot or take it with them to their homes. They perform no memorial or *shráddha* ceremonies.

Occupation. The Naikdas are labourers and wood cutters. Only a few own bullocks and ploughs and till fixed fields. Most are content with rough hillside tillage, burning brushwood to sow coarse grain among the ashes. Besides cultivating, they are employed in picking the flowers and berries of the *mahua* tree, some medicinal roots and barks, and in collecting gum, lac, leaves for cigarette making, honey and wax. As wood cutters they are either hired by forest officers or by large landholders, or themselves cut timber and take it to market for sale. In almost every part of their work their women help them; and they seldom leave the district in search of employment.

Food. Except the ass, crow and snake, they eat any kind of flesh, including the flesh of the cow, large black ants, squirrels, monkeys whom they jokingly call tree sheep, and even dead animals. They are much given to *mahua* spirit, and at their festivals drink to excess. Bhils drink water at the hands of Naikdas. No higher caste will eat at the hands of this caste. From the Bombay Gazetteer it appears that the Naikdas eat with Musalmáns, and that a Naikda guilty of taking his meals with a Dhed, Chamár or Bhangia would be readmitted into his caste by giving a dinner to his castemen. They therefore rank very little above the impure castes. They show little sign of progress.

NAIKIN.—A synonym for Bhávin.

NAIKLOK.—A synonym for Rámoshi.

NAIKMAKKALU.—A sub-division of Berads,

NAIKWADI.—A synonym for Berad.

NAIKWARI.—*See* under Minor Musalmán Castes.

NAKARCHI.—A synonym for Nagárji.

NAKHVA.—A title applied to the sea-faring Kolis of Thána.

NAKSHBAND.—*See* under Minor Musalmán Castes.

NAKSHE.—A sub-division of Kattais.

NAKUL.—A sub-division of Devángs.

NALBAND.—*See* under Minor Musalmán Castes.

NAMADA.—A sub-division of Raddis and Uppárs.

NAMAL.—A sub-division of Bráhmans.

NAMDASE.—A sub-division of Holayás.

NAMDEV.—A sub-division of Shimpis.

NANA.—A sub-division of Chodhrás.

NANDIKOLA.—A sub-division of Jangams.

NANDIWALES, a class of wandering beggars, numbering 218 (1901), including 105 males and 113 females, were recorded at Ahmednagar, Khándesh, Poona and Sátára. They take their name from *Nandi* a bull, as they beg from house to house taking with them bulls dressed in smart cloths with fringes of jingling bells and bell necklaces

NANDODRA.—A synonym for Nandora.

NANDORA.—A sub-division of Bráhmans and Vániás.

NANDRAINA.—A synonym for Nandrána.

NANDRANA.—A sub-division of Bráhmans.

NANDVANA.—A sub-division of Bráhmans.

NAPAL.—A sub-division of Bráhmans.

NAPIT.—A synonym for Nhávi.

NARBHARI.—A sub-division of Kachhis.

NARDA.—A sub-division of Dublás.

NARDIK.—A sub-division of Bráhmans.

NARODA.—A caste of cultivators in Cutch.

NARSINGPURA.—A sub-division of Bráhmans.

NARSIPURA.—A sub-division of Vániás; a synonym for Narsingpura.

NARVANKAR.—A sub-division of Gaud Sárasvat Bráhmans.

NATS, numbering 584 (1901), including 279 males and 305 females, are found chiefly in Gujarát. They are a wandering tribe of tumblers and acrobats from Márwár. They are Hindus and worship Metri Máta. They allow widow marriage and bury their dead.

NATH.—A synonym for Bharthari and Jogi.

NATRAVALA.—A sub-division of Brahma Kshatris.

NAVA.—A sub-division of Shrigaud Bráhmans.

NAVABHAI.—A sub-division of Ods.

NAVAYAT.—*See* under Minor Musalmán Castes.

NAVE MARATHA.—A synonym for Urap Agri.

NAYERS, numbering 65 (1901), including 44 males and 21 females, are found in small numbers only in Kanara. They are immigrants from Madras. They are mostly husbandmen.

NEGAR.—A synonym for Deváng.

NEHRE.—A sub-division of Kolis.

NEKAR.—A synonym for Deváng.

NEMA.—A sub-division of Vániás.

NEMADI.—A sub-divis on of Báris.

NESAK.—A sub-division of Ahirs.

NETRAGARA.—A sub-division of Mochis.

NEVE.—A sub-division of Vánis.

NEYAKAR.—A synonym for Jád.

NHAVIS or HAJAMS, the barber caste of the Presidency, numbering 224,761 (1901), including 115,338 males, and 109,423 females, are found in all parts of the Presidency. The religious distribution is (1901) :—

Hindu	188,086
Lingáyat	24,621
Musalmán	12,054

Nhávis are also known as Nadigs, Váriks, Kshauraks, Nápits Kárágirs, Sanmukhs, Valands, Gháijos, Matkos, Kelásis Mhalis and Vavdichaskis. The name Hajám is in use all over the Presidency except in Kanara. Nadig is the Kanarese term for a Nhávi or barber. Nhávi is the corrupted form of the Sanskrit Nápit a barber, and is in use all over the Presidency except in Gujarát. Hajám is derived from the Arabic *hajám* to cup. The name Várik, which means time-keeper, is in use only in Sholápur. Kshaurak, derived from the Sanskrit *kshaura* shaving, and Kelási are names by which the caste is known in Kanara. The name Sanmukh is met with only in Sátára. Nápit is the Sanskrit term for a barber. The term Kárágir means an artisan, and thus the Nhávis are addressed by the lower castes of the Deccan out of respect for them. The remaining names are in use in the Gujarát districts and States. The term Váland is derived from *vál* hair, Gáijo from *gha* a wound, from the barber's occupation of Name and origin.

healing wounds, and Matko from an earthen pot *matku* on which barber boys are taught to shave. Of the origin of the name Vavdichaski or well-movers, the story is that a company of barbers held a picnic outside their town. They stopped near a well or *vávdi*, and after the picnic they found that the water made such excellent *bháng* or hemp-liquor, that they determined to carry off the well, so, binding one of their turbans round the parapet, they pulled at it till the fumes of the liquor passed away.

The Nhávis of the Deccan state that the founder of the caste was the serpent Shesha who encircled Shiva's neck and was told to take human form at the time of the thread ceremony of the god Brahma. For this reason they hold themselves superior to Bráhmans and other castes, even to the god Vishnu. They say it was not Brahma who created the universe, but Shiva, for, before the creation of the universe, Shiva and the serpent Shesha were in existence. Some, playing upon their name, say that they are born from Mahádev's navel or *nábhi*. The Gujarát Hajáms claim to be the descendants of Kshatriyas who, during Parshurám's persecution, assumed disguises, and changed the sword for the lancet and the art of killing for that of healing.

The above traditions are obviously an attempt on the part of the caste to raise themselves in the social scale. In the Deccan, at least, this attempt was hardly necessary, since the names, surnames, social organization, religion and customs of the Marátha Nhávis are identical with those of the Maráthás. In some places, even to this day, among the higher Marátha families, Nhávis are required to serve water at dinners, and in Násik and Khándesh, they are also employed as cooks. These facts seem to suggest that the Maráthás and the Marátha Nhávis originally belonged to one tribe ; and indeed there is much evidence to suggest that many similar functional castes in the Deccan were originally Maráthás. (*See* MARATHA.)

Occupation.

The hereditary occupation of the Nhávi is shaving, hair-dressing and nail-paring. He is an indispensable member of the village community, and formerly enjoyed *inám* or rent-free lands for his services. Village barbers are not paid in cash, but in grain at harvest time. Their services are required at many social and religious functions such as hair-cutting, marriage, death, etc. At *Diváli* the barber rubs his patron's body with oil and holds a mirror to his face, and is rewarded with money or a bodicecloth. In Gujarát, among Rajputs and Kunbis, the Hajám is the go-between in marriage arrangements, and among most Hindus he carries to the father the news of the birth of a male child. Among Central Gujarát Pátidárs, the burden of the arrangements both at weddings and at funerals falls on the Hajám. Among Musalmáns of the Bohora community, he invites the guests to public feasts. He is also a torch-bearer, and, in well-to-do families, often serves as a house servant, sweeping the house, preparing the beds, cleaning and lighting lamps, escorting the men and women of the family, and shampooing his master. Some are also employed as *pharás* or lamp-lighters in the Courts of Native Chiefs and in British Courts of justice. The Dholis or drumbeaters in Gujarát, who at marriages beat drums from three to eight days at the house of the bride and bridegroom, who walk before the bridegroom in the marriage procession, and who by the sound of their drums proclaim the joining of the hands of the bride and bridegroom, are barbers of the Mataka class. In Kaira, the Dholis are Rávaliás by caste, and in the Rewa Kántha, Dhánkás or Bhils. In addition to the functions mentioned above, the barber practices surgery, opening boils and abscesses, and bleeds by applying leeches.

Some women of the Masuria or Matko Hajáms in Surat and the Panch Mahâls shave widows and young boys. Some serve as servants in Kunbi and Rajput families. Most of the Hajám women, both Marátha and Gujaráti, act as midwives.

All the Gujarát Hajáms bear torches. In the Deccan, the Khándesh Hajáms only are torch-bearers, and they are on that account considered degraded. Many of the Marátha Hajáms are musicians, and play at weddings and on other festive occasions. On the occasion of marriages Nhávis are as a rule umbrella-bearers.

In most large Káthiáwár towns, nearly every caste has its own barber. Even in Zanzibar and Arabia the Káthiáwár merchants are careful to provide themselves with barbers from their native country. In other parts of the province, the barber has generally fixed customers of different castes. Except in Cambay, where they are called *parekhs* or shopmen, few barbers have regular shops.

Marátha Nhávis do not shave Buruds, Jingars and other degraded Hindus, Europeans, Native Christians and Musalmáns. The Junari Nhávis have no such scruples, and they are therefore lowered in social estimation.

The Nhávis of the Bombay Presidency have three territorial divisions, who have nothing in common except their occupation. Besides these there are also found Telangi Nhávis, Madrási Nhávis.

Márwári Nhávis, and Pardeshi Nhávis, who are immigrants from other provinces.

MARATHA NHAVIS have two territorial divisions, Maráthás or those living in the Deccan, and Konkanis or those living in the Konkan. These divisions neither eat together nor intermarry. In the Thána district, where members of both divisions are found, the Konkanis consider themselves superior and do not eat from the Maráthás, who eat food cooked by the Konkanis.

The Maráthás have the following divisions :–

1. Gangátirkar or Godávari, *i.e.*, those living on the banks of the Godávari.
2. Ghátis or those living on the Sahyádri Gháts.
3. Junari or Pardeshi, or Nhávis from Junnar in the Poona district.
4. Kunbis or cultivators.
5. Khándeshi or those living in Khándesh, also called Mashálji from their occupation of bearing *masháls* or torches.
6. Váideshi or Nhávis from Vái in Sátára.
7. Vájantri or musicians.
8. Yelmár.

Of these divisions Kunbis and Ghátis eat together, but none intermarry. The Váideshis stand highest in the social scale, and the Junaris the lowest, because they have no scruples against shaving Europeans, Musalmáns, Jingars, etc.

The Marátha Nhávis resemble the Maráthás in dress, food, speech, social organization, religion and customs ; so much so that their *kuls* and *devaks* also are identical. In former days the Nhávi used to attend every feast at Kunbis', Mális' and Maráthás' houses, and pour water on the hands of the guests, both when they began and when they ended eating. In some places, he also served the food. Besides this, he also accompanied married girls when they first went to their husbands' houses. This custom has now almost died out ; but in Násik and Khándesh, Marátha Nhávis are still found preparing and serving food in high caste Marátha families.

KONKANI NHAVIS have two divisions, Proper and Shindes or bastards. In the Ratnágiri district, the Shindes can be purified and allowed to dine in the same row with the Nhávis Proper, such members being known as *Pankti-pávan kelele* Nhávis, *i.e.*, Nhávis purified for dinner purposes only. In the southern part of Ratnágiri and in the Sávantvádi State, there is a third division who circumcise, and on that account are considered inferior and called Bandes or illegitimates.

The Konkani Nhávis have Marátha surnames similar to their brethren in the Deccan, and like them their exogamous divisions are based on *devaks*, marriages being prohibited between members having the same *devak*. The *devaks* discovered so far are as follows :—

Name of *kul*.	*Devak*.
1. Bágkar ..	.. *Pánkanis* (Reed-mace).
2. Bhágvat ..	.. *Pánchpálvi*.
3. Bide ..	.. Mango and the axe.
4. Chaván ..	.. *Gulvel* (Tinospora cordifolia).
5. Gáikvád ..	.. Leaves of the *ság* (teak), *umbar* (Ficus glomerata), mango, *jámbhul* (Eugenia jambolana), *pipal* (Ficus religiosa).
6. Jádhav ..	.. *Pánkanis* (Reed-mace).
7. Kadam ..	.. *Kalamb* (Anthocephalus cadamba)
8. Korde ..	.. *Pánchpálvi*.
9. Lád ..	.. *Umbar* (Ficus glomerata).
10. Pavár ..	.. Sword-blade.
11. Ráut ..	.. Horse and *umbar* (Ficus glomerata).
12. Shinde ..	.. *Velu* (bamboo)
13. Vágh ..	.. Sun-flower.
14. Vághchavare	.. *Pánchpálvi*.

In the Sávantvádi State, the *devaks* commonly found are the *Kalamb*, *Umbar* (Ficus glomerata), *Vad* (banyan tree), mango, *Phanas* (the jack tree) and *Pipal*. These *devaks* are totemistic as the objects representing them are not touched, cut, or otherwise used. They are worshipped at the time of marriage. The *devak* is put in a new winnowing-fan or on a piece of new cloth strewn with rice, and is installed near the house gods, where a lamp is kept burning till the end of the marriage.

The Konkani Nhávis do not differ from Bhandáris in their religious and social customs. Their widow remarriage ceremony, which differs in some particulars from that of the Bhandáris, is as follows :—

If the widow's father is poor, her intended husband has to pay him Rs. 10 to Rs. 25 to defray the expenses of the marriage. This payment is called *vida*. If the widow's father is well-to-do, he not only does not receive the *vida*, but on the contrary pays some money to the widow's intended husband. A sum of Rs. 5 to Rs. 10 is paid to the caste *panch* who sanction the marriage. The bridegroom goes to the bride's father's house at night, accompanied by a Ghádi, a Rául, a Kásár, a Mahár, the caste *panch* and two or more widows. There is no music. He presents the widow with a robe, a bodice, a lucky necklace, some ornaments and three black silk tassels. Dressed in these the widow comes out and the pair are seated side by side on two low wooden stools. Next, three widows perform the *shensa* ceremony, *i.e.*, apply rice grains to the widow's forehead. A plantain leaf is then placed in front of the pair, it is strewn with rice grains, a metal drinking water-pot filled with milk or cocoanut fluid is set thereon, and a mango twig is put into the water-pot. This is called *Ghat*. It is worshipped with an offering of a cocoanut, new bangles are put on the widow's wrist by the Kásár, and red powder is applied to her forehead by one of the widows present. The *shensa* ceremony is again performed, the bridegroom takes off his turban and puts it on his knee, and a widow applies red powder and rice grains to the knee. One of the widows then fills the lap of the bride, which is the binding portion of the ceremony. Next, a feast of cock's flesh is given to the castemen assembled.

On the same night before daybreak, the widow's new husband with his wife and party start for home, the wife holding a cock under her arm. At the same time a casteman leaves for the widow's deceased husband's house taking with him a cocoanut, some fruit, rice grains, and Re. 1. When he reaches there, he places these things either in the house or in the courtyard unseen by anybody. When the procession of the remarried couple reaches the boundary of the widow's village, the cock under the widow's arm is immolated and a cocoanut is broken. The body of the cock and the cocoanut are given to a *virakti* (worshipper of a village deity). Next, another cock is placed under the widow's arm and the procession proceeds on its way. When they reach the boundary of the bridegroom's village, another cocoanut is broken and the cock under the widow's arm is killed by a *virakti*, and the head of the cock together with a hair from the widow's head and a bit of her robe are buried under a rock. The body of the cock is taken away and eaten by the *virakti*, who is also paid some money for his services by the bridegroom. All these efforts are directed to preventing the spirit of the widow's deceased husband from troubling the second husband. When the party reach home, a jar filled with water is placed on the threshold of the door. The widow takes it on her head and enters the house, thus ending the ceremony.

KHANDESH NHAVIS have two divisions, Ahirs and Táyades who eat together but do not intermarry. They do not differ in their religious and social customs from other Khándesh castes of similar standing, except that the Ahirs have a totemistic social organization, some of the totems being as follows :—

Name of *kul*.	Totem.
1. Báviskar ..	.. *Ghondhan* (Cordia Rothii).
2. Borsa ..	.. *Nim* (Melia azadirachta).
3. Chitie ..	.. *Shami* (Prosopis spicigera).
4. Nikumbh ..	.. *Nim* (Melia azadirachta).
5. Phulpagar ..	.. *Pachna* (Capparis grandis).
6. Sonnis ..	.. *Nim* (Melia azadirachta).
7. Thákare ..	.. *Halad* (turmeric).

KANARA NHAVIS or Kelásis have the following exogamous divisions :—

Name of Division.	Family god.
1. Amdallikár ..	.. Bantdev.
2. Relekerikár ..	.. Bantdev.

Marriages are prohibited between members of the same division. Children of brothers and sisters cannot marry, but a brother's daughter can be given to a sister's son, or a sister's daughter to a brother's son. In the latter case, a double chain is given to the bride as she has to return to the family from which her mother came. Polygamy is allowed and practised, but polyandry is unknown. Widow remarriage is allowed, but seldom practised. Divorce is not allowed. Marriage is generally infant, the ceremonies being of the standard type. The essential portion is the mutual garlanding of the bride and bridegroom. The Kanara Kelásis worship village and Bráhman gods and keep all local holidays. Their family god is Venkataráma of Tirupati. They have strong faith in soothsaying and witchcraft. Their priests are Havig Bráhmans and their religious teacher is the head of the Kekkár monastery in Honávar. The well-to-do burn their dead and the poor bury. Their staple food is rice, *rági* and fish, but they eat flesh except beef and pork and drink liquor.

GUJARAT HAJAMS have five main divisions as follows :—

1. Babars or Márvádis
2. Bhátiás
3. Limbachiás
4. Malu
5. Matko or Masuriás

Of these divisions the Limbachiás rank highest. They allow Bhátia Hajáms to smoke out of their pipes. But they will not eat with any other division. None of the divisions intermarry, nor do they eat together except that all will eat food cooked by a Limbachia. The Limbachiás claim descent from a band of Rajputs who after some defeat fled for protection to their goddess Limach in Patan. The goddess saved their life ; and in acknowledgment they took her name.

Gujarát Hajáms perform no ceremony on the day of a birth. On the sixth day the goddess Chhatti is worshipped, and among the Surat Masuriás, along with rice and red powder, a razor is laid before the goddess. In the family of a Pálanpur Limbachia, when four or five girls are to be married, the marriage day is fixed after consulting the horoscope of the oldest girl, and the other girls are married on the day found lucky in her case. With this exception the marriage customs of Hajáms do not differ from those of Kanbis. Divorce and widow marriage are allowed. The levirate is permitted. By religion they are Bijpanthis, Kabirpanthis, Rámánandis, Shaivas, Vallabhách-áris, and in the Panch Mahâls, some are followers of Kuberdás. Some of them worship in their houses the images of Ganpati, Hanumán, Krishna, Mahádev and Rám. They keep the usual Hindu fasts and feasts. In the Panch Mahâls, besides observing the regular Hindu holidays, they fast on the second of every Hindu month and do not eat till they have worshipped the new-moon. They visit the ordinary places of Hindu pilgrimage. The Limbachiás are careful to visit the shrine of their goddess Limach in Patan. They believe in witchcraft, sorcery, the evil eye and the ordinary omens. Their priests belong to many divisions of Bráhmans, Audich, Borsadia, Modh, Ráyakvál, and Shrigaud who, though they officiate at their ceremonies, think it rather disgraceful to be called barber's priests or Hajámgors. The dead are burnt. In some parts of Káthiáwár, while taking the dead body to the burning ground, five men bathe and put on the Bráhmanic thread. Of the five, four carry the dead body and the fifth the earthen vessel with live coal. In other parts of the province, the mode of carrying the dead body is the same as among Kanbis. Some Hajáms, on the twelfth day after a death, raise a pile of six or twelve earthen jars near the house of the deceased, and wrap a cotton thread round them. The potter is called and unrolls the thread, cuts it in pieces and takes the jars. Among other Hajáms, on the night of the twelfth day, the chief mourner worships the stars by throwing into the sky flowers dipped in sandal wood dust. With this difference the death ceremonies are the same as among Kanbis. Except the Masuriás of South Gujarát who eat goat's flesh and drink liquor, Hajáms eat the ordinary food grains.

Though Limbachia Hajáms allow Bhátia Hajáms to smoke out of their pipes, high caste Hindus will not, at least in Central Gujarát, drink water brought by à Bhátia Hajám. Socially Hajáms have a low position, though they do not shave people of the unclean classes. They eat food cooked by high caste Hindus and by Kanbis ; but except the Matkos they do not eat food cooked by Kolis or others below them in rank. Neither Limbachia nor Bhátia Hajáms eat food cooked by Cutch Bhátiás because Bhátiás formerly ate fish. On the other hand, some of the unclean classes do not eat food cooked even by Limbachiás.

NIHIR.—A sub-division of Várlis.

NILARIS are known also as Rangáris and Nilgars. The word 'Nilári' is occasionally transposed into 'Niráli' and means an indigo dyer. In 1901 the Nilári caste, excluding Musalmán Niláris, who are dealt with separately, numbered 16,151, including 8,269 males and 7,882 females, of which total only 368 were returned as Nilgars, or Kanarese Niláris, who are Lingáyats. The figures for the Nilgars are vitiated, however, by the fact that many Nilgars may have been included in 'Lingáyats unspecified', while a few may have been wrongly included under Nilári. The caste is found scattered throughout Khándesh, the Deccan, and Southern Marátha Country. Nearly one-third are residents of Khándesh, and it seems possible that the original Niláris were immigrants from the north. It would appear, at any rate, that the Nilgars or Kanarese section, who are Lingáyats, have penetrated the Southern Marátha Country from the Marátha speaking districts, for they are still divided into exogamous divisions bearing the names of some of those in the parent stock, thus :— Name and origin.

Exogamous divisions of Niláris.	Exogamous divisions of Nilgars.
Misal	Misal
Mehetar	Mehetar
Chitrakar	Chitrakar
Kadge	Kadar
Kalaskar	Kharnar
Kadarkaı	Mohal
Nakil	Yengi

The Niláris claim to have once been Kshatris, a caste of dyers in Northern India. The caste tradition relates that their ancestors, who were twin brothers, on being pursued by Parashurám, hid in a temple belonging to the goddess Ambábai and sought the goddess' protection. The goddess gave one brother a piece of thread and a needle, and the other a paint which she spat at him and told the one to sew and the other to dye. Meanwhile Parashurám begged the goddess to make over to him the two Kshatris, but she denied all knowledge of them, and Parashurám went back disappointed. From that time the sewer became a Shimpi and the dyer a Rangári. From this story it would appear that the Shimpis and Niláris were originally closely connected, and it is not improbable that they gradually differentiated as their numbers increased. Traces of their once belonging to the same caste remain in the Niláris of Kolhápur, who are stated to belong to the Shimpi caste, and do not differ from the Shimpis in religious and social customs. The caste also style themselves Námdev, after the fashion of the Shimpis. According to another account, the traditional founder of the caste was Prakásh, who was the son of a Kukut mother and an Ahir father. There is probably a large Ahir element in the Khándesh Niláris. In appearance and customs they resemble Marátha Kunbis.

Divisions. There are two main endogamous divisions of the caste : Hindu and Lingáyat, who neither eat together nor intermarry. Of these the Hindu Niláris have a division of Kadu Nilári for those who have lost caste on account of infringing caste rules. They will eat with these, but not marry. The exogamous sub-divisions are identical with surnames. The common surnames are Lokhande, Patange, Phutáne, Bágare, Bhumkar, Kadarkar, Kaláskar, Nakil, Misal, Pátaskar, Bagade, Basme, Nadári, Kunthe, and Pingre. They have also *gotras* but these appear to be a recent innovation, as they do not stand in the way of intermarriages. The names of these *gotras* are Káshyap, Gángawa and Vashishtha. Persons bearing the same surname cannot intermarry. Sameness of *devak* is also a bar to intermarriage. Every section has a separate *devak*. The chief *devaks* are the beam of a pair of scales, weaving implements, and the *pánchpálvi*.

Marriage. A member of the caste cannot marry his father's sister's or mother's sister's daughter. He may marry his mother's brother's daughter. A man may marry two sisters and two brothers may marry two sisters. Polygamy is allowed and practiced, but polyandry is unknown. Girls are generally married from five to twelve, and in the case of poor people, even after puberty. Boys are married up to the age of twenty-five. Maidens committing sexual indiscretions are excommunicated. The offer of marriage comes from either side. The marriage ceremonies of Niláris resemble those of the Marátha Kunbis in all details.

The remarriage of widows is permitted. A widow cannot marry her father's sister's, mothers' sister's, or mother's brother's son, or a member of her late husband's section. A widow remarriage is celebrated at night in an isolated place beyond the village boundary. The service is conducted by a Bráhman priest or a Jangam. The widow is seated on a low wooden stool, her new husband on a bullock's pack-saddle. The hems of the pair's garments are tied into a knot, and a lucky necklace is fastened round the widow's neck, which completes the ceremony. The remarried pair are not allowed to enter the village for two days after the marriage. Should a bachelor desire to marry a widow, he is first married to a *shami* bush. Divorce is allowed if the husband and wife do not agree, or the wife's conduct is bad. The party who wants the divorce has to pay the marriage expenses incurred by the other party. A divorced woman can marry again by the widow remarriage form, if the cause of divorce be not adultery on her part, for which offence she is excommunicated. The caste follow the Hindu law of inheritance.

Religion. Niláris are Hindus of the Smárt sect. Some are followers of the Várkari sect. They worship all the Hindu gods and goddesses and observe all the Hindu holidays. Their family deities are Bahiroba of Sonári in Ahmednagar, Bhaváni of Tuljápur in the Nizam's country, Kálkádevi of Ahmednagar, and Khandoba of Jejuri in Poona. They make pilgrimages to Alandi, Jejuri, Pandharpur, Gokarn and Benares. They believe in sorcery, witchcraft, and lucky and unlucky days, and consult oracles. Their *guru* or spiritual teacher is a man of their own caste, who is called Nágnáth. Their priests are Deshasth Bráhmans. The widow remarriage ceremony is sometimes conducted by a Jangam. The death ceremonies are conducted by the caste elders.

Death ceremonies. The dead are either burnt or buried. At burial the corpse is seated with face to the east. The body is carried either slung in a cloth or on a bier. The death ceremonies of Niláris resemble those of the Marátha Kunbis. They mourn ten days and feast caste fellows on the thirteenth. The *shráddha* and *mahálaya* are performed for the propitiation of the deceased ancestors.

The hereditary occupation of the caste is dyeing cloth and yarn. Many of them also weave robes and shoulder cloths. Their business is brisk in the fair season. Those who dye are specially busy during the great Hindu and Musalmán festivals. A few own lands.

Food. They eat fish and the flesh of goats, sheep, hares, deer, and domestic fowls, and drink liquor.

The Nilgars or Lingáyat Niláris are found chiefly in Belgaum, Dhárwár, Bijápur, and the Southern Marátha Country. Their head-quarters are in Indi and Bijápur. They are non-Panchamsáli Lingáyats entitled to the *ashtavarna* rites. They resemble the Panchamsáli Lingáyats in their ceremonies and customs. Their religious teacher is a Jangam who lives at Shidgeri in Kolhápur. They eat from Nágliks and Koshtis, but not from Raddis, Kumbhárs, and Kudvakkalgars. As shown at the commencement of this article, they appear to be an off-shoot of the Marátha speaking Niláris who have penetrated south and adopted Lingáyatism.

NILGAR.—A synonym for Nilári.

NILKANT.—A sub-division of Jáds.

NILKANTH GURAV.—A synonym for Shaiva Gurav.

NIMA.—A synonym for Nema.

NIRALE.—A sub-division of Mahárs.

NIRALI.—A synonym for Nilári.

NIRDHI.—A sub-division of Bhils.

NIR MALLAVA.—A sub-division of Mallavas.

Name. **ODS,** VADDAS or BELDARS, numbering 94,096 (1901), including 48,090 males and 46,006 females, are found all over the Presidency including Sind, the bulk of the tribe being residents of the Karnátak. Of this number 97 were shown as Musalmáns in the census of 1901. The name of the tribe is also spelt Odde, Wodde, Waddár, Vadár, and Orh, and appears to be in some way connected with Od-desh or Orissa. The tribe is found in large numbers throughout India, their occupation being working in earth and stone. The term Od or Vadda is commonly said to be derived from the Kanarese *oddu* to join from the occupation of joining stones in building. The term Beldár is derived from the Persian *bel* a pickaxe.

Origin. The Ods claim a Kshatriya origin, and state that they are descendants of Bhagirath, son of Sagar. According to the Rás Mála [(1)] Sidhráj sent for a number of Ods from Málwa to dig the Sahasraling lake at Pátan. He fell in love with one of their number Jasma, and

(1) Vol. I, p. 177.

wished to take her to his palace. She declined, and endeavoured to make her escape. He pursued her and, in overtaking her, slew several of the Ods. Jasma, in committing suicide, cursed the king, and declared that his lake should never hold water. The curse was removed by the sacrifice of Mayo, a Dheda. Jasma further declared at the time of her suicide that no Od woman should thereafter be good-looking, and warned her race against ever oiling the hair or anointing the eyes. It may be admitted that an Od woman is not comely, and that she strictly avoids the use of oil and collyrium; but this can scarcely be taken as a confirmation of the tradition related above.

According to another account, the first ancestors of the Ods were two brothers by name Jasalo and Kasalo who lived in Márwár. They are said to have migrated into Gujarát in the time of the king Sidhráj Jesing. At that time the Jasdan prince had two daughters, one of whom, Jehman, the prince gave in marriage to Kasalo. She became a *sati*. Of the ninety-nine tanks dug in the time of that prince, those dug through the agency of Jehman produced a gold brick for every cubit hand of earth taken out. These gold bricks were given to Jehman, who fed the labourers from the proceeds. These labourers became the Od tribe. These traditions regarding their origin, with slight variations, are current all over India except in the south, their original home. The stories seem to have been invented to give the tribe a better status than they would have been entitled to as immigrants from Dravidian countries; but it is quite possible that some admixture with local outcastes has occurred in the case of the northern sections. The skill of Ods in earth work and masonry has led to a demand for their labour in all parts of India. The divisions still found in both the Deccan and Karnátak of Gádi or Bhandi, Mannu or Máti, and Kalu or Dagad, clearly show the movement of the tribe from the south northwards, the more northern section being described as Pardeshi. The Bhoja or Uru Vaddás may possibly have settled in villages in the days of the Bhoja dynasty, and thus preserved the name of the Bhoja dynasty of the Deccan.

In the course of its migrations the tribe appears to have been recruited from members of many other castes. The Ods of Kanara still admit members from higher castes such as Lingáyats, Kurubs, Kammárs, etc. If the applicant for admission be a male, his head and mustaches are shaved, the tip of his tongue is branded with a burning stick of the *nim* tree (Melia azadirachta) and he is required to put on a new dress and to drink the *tirth* or holy water of a Jangam. In the case of a female, the same initiation is required except the shaving, but in addition, she is stripped of her bodice and the glass bangles are removed from her right wrist. This ceremony obtains amongst the Bhandi Ods only. Amongst the Mannu Ods and Kalu Ods the same ceremony is performed, with the difference that the tip of the tongue is branded with red-hot gold and the *tirth* used is that of the family god. Amongst the Uru Ods, the candidate for admission is shaved and seated in a small hut. The hut is then set on fire and the neophyte makes a hurried escape. The burning of the hut is presumably intended to represent the completion of the candidate's former existence as member of another caste. He is then given the *tirth* to drink. The same ceremony is performed in the case of females, except that they are not shaved and that they are stripped of their bodices.

There are four main territorial groups of the Bombay Ods as follows :—

1. Marátha and Kanarese. 3. Sind.
2. Gujaráti. 4. Pardeshi.

Pardeshis are Ods who have travelled to the north. The remaining three groups differ much in their religious and social customs.

MARATHA and KANARESE ODS form the bulk of the tribe in this Presidency, are dark, tall and regular-featured, with high noses, thin lips and long necks. The dress of the men consists of breeches, a headscarf, a shouldercloth, and sometimes a jacket. They wear sandals and forbid shoes so strictly that any member wearing shoes is put out of caste and is not allowed to rejoin. Their women wear the robe, but not the bodice. Men wear brass ear and finger-rings, and women brass ear and nose-rings and necklaces. They wear glass bangles only on their left wrists and do not wear flowers in their hair or mark their brows with red powder.

Language. Marátha and Kanarese Ods speak Telugu at home. They also speak a broken Maráthi and Kanarese in the Maráthi and Kanarese speaking districts respectively. The names in common use among men are Gidda, Hanma, Nága, Tima, Bálya, Ráma, Shetya, Parshya, Bashya, Bábu, Chima, Hanmant, Piráji and Topáji and among women, Báyaja, Chaodi, Durgava, Hanmákka, Hulgava, Nágamma, Ramákka, Sataya, Shetti, Timi, Vasari, Yama and Yelli.

Endogamous divisions. Marátha and Kanarese Ods have four endogamous divisions as follows :—

Marátha.	Kanarese.
1. Bhoja or Uru.	1. Bhoja or Uru.
2. Máti.	2. Mannu (= Máti).

Maratha.	Kanarese.
3. Dagad or Páthrat.	3. Kalu (= Dagad).
4. Gáda, Ját or Jánti.	4. Bhandi (= Gáda) or Báil.

All these divisions are found in Mysore and are noticed by Mr. Rice.[1]

Bhoja or Uru Ods take their name from the Bhoja dynasty of the Deccan, and the Kanarese *Uru* a village. They are found only in the Karnátak. They make and sell charcoal and cement. Máti and Mannu Ods take their names respectively from the Maráthi Máti and Kanarese Mannu, meaning earth. They are so called because they work in earth. The terms Dagad and Kalu mean a stone. Dagad Ods are stone workers. Bhandi Ods derive their name from the Kanarese Bhandi a cart, the synonym Bail meaning a bullock. Their Maráthi name Gáda means a cart. They are cart-drivers. They also make *Jántis*, or stone handmills for grinding corn, in the Marátha districts, which has led them to be called Jánti Ods. Bhoja Ods do not intermarry or interdine with the other divisions. The other three divisions eat together, but do not intermarry.

Kanarese Ods have exogamous divisions known as *bedagus*, the chief of which are as follows :—

Alákuntlor.	Kiátánor.	Rápánor.
Bantanglor.	Kunchápor.	Sátálor.
Bayamatkor.	Naidplor.	Uppatálor.
Dandaglor.	Pallápor.	Vallapor.
Dyáranglor.	Pitlor.	

In the Deccan their exogamous sub-divisions are identical with surnames. The commonest surnames are as follows :—

Alkute.	Gunjál.	Pavár.
Chaugule.	Jádhav.	Pitekar.
Chaván.	Kusmand.	Shelár.
Dandavat.	Máhárnavare.	Shelavade.
Dukare.	Madage.	Shinde.
Dhotre.	Mándkar.	Thorat.
Gáikvád.	Mohite.	

Many of these are common Marátha surnames.

Marriages are prohibited between persons having the same surname or *bedagu*. A member of the tribe may marry his father's sister's or mother's brother's daughter. A man may marry two sisters and Marriage.

(1) Mysore, Vol. I., p. 337.

brothers may marry sisters. If a maiden is seduced by a casteman, he is compelled to marry her. If a girl commits sexual indiscretions with a man of a lower caste, or if she has a child by him, she is turned out of the caste. If the offence is committed with a member of a higher caste, she is allowed to remain in the caste, and may marry by the widow remarriage ritual. Polygamy is allowed and practised. As the Od women are useful workers, well-to-do Ods have two to eight wives whom they buy from people of their own caste. Polyandry is unknown.

The offer of marriage comes from the boy's father, who has to pay a bride-price of from Rs. 5 to Rs. 32 to the girl's father. The day for the marriage is fixed by the headman of the tribe, or by the boy's father in consultation with a Bráhman. As a rule Od marriages take place at sunset on Thursdays, Sundays or Mondays provided these are not full or new moon days. The service is conducted by the caste elders. It is to be noted that, in the marriages of Ods, music, turmeric, the *mangalsutra* or lucky necklace and the *báshing* or marriage coronet are not used in most places.

The marriage ceremonies of Ods vary in some details in different localities. They may be described as follows :—

In Ahmednagar, a blanket tent is pitched at the house of the girl's father. The day before the marriage the girl's father with some castemen goes to the boy's house, and brings him and his party to his house. They halt in the tent. The family gods are worshipped, and the boy's brow is marked, once with sandal-wood paste and five times with turmeric. The girl's brow is similarly marked, and the pair are bathed in warm water by married unwidowed women of the girl's house. The bridegroom is dressed and seated in the tent, and the bride goes into the house. Next the bridegroom steps into the house and returns to the tent, leading the bride by the hand. The couple stand facing the east, married unwidowed women sing lucky marriage songs, reddened grains of rice are thrown over the pair by all assembled, and they are seated on a blanket side by side. Next, the pair bow before the family gods and elders and a feast takes place. On the second or third day a ceremony known as *phal* is performed, in which the pair pour milk five times over each other's hands (the *dháre* ceremony), and play hide and seek with betelnuts. Relations present the pair with articles of dress, and the bridegroom presents the bride with a suit of clothes and ornaments. A caste feast with meat and liquor ends the ceremony.

In Poona, marriage booths are erected at the houses of both the boy and the girl. A branch of the *umbar* (Ficus glomerata) is tied to one of the posts and worshipped by the *karvali* or the sister either of the bride or the bridegroom. *Kankans* or marriage wristlets are tied to the wrists of the boy and the girl at their houses, the boy is rubbed with turmeric paste, and a portion of the paste is sent with music to be rubbed on the girl. Next, the bridegroom is taken in procession to the temple of Máruti in the girl's village. From Máruti's temple his brother is sent to the bride's and brings back a suit of clothes for the bridegroom. The boy is then brought to the bride's booth, a piece of bread is waved round him and thrown away in order to propitiate the evil spirits. The bridegroom passes into the booth. The rest of the ceremony resembles that performed by the Ods of Ahmednagar, with this difference that copper coins are waved round the bride and bridegroom after grains of rice have been thrown over their heads, and the *kankans* on each other's wrists are untied by the bride and bridegroom before the latter returns to his house with his bride. In some parts of the Deccan, they have a *devak* which consists of a mango or *umbar* (Ficus glomerata) and is fixed to the pillars of the marriage booth. A piece of cloth containing a little red rice, a packet of betelnuts and leaves, a turmeric root, and *shami* (Prosopis spicigera) leaves, are added as part of the *devak*.

In Belgaum, at the time of marriage, the bride and bridegroom are seated on a blanket in front of the girl's house, and two pieces of turmeric root with betel leaves are wrapped in a cloth and tied to the right wrist of both the boy and the girl. The girl wears a glass bangle on her left wrist, and the boy ties a black bead necklace round her neck with a piece of white thread. Friends and relations throw rice on their heads, and they are husband and wife. On the next day they are thrice rubbed with turmeric and the marriage ceremony is over.

In Dhárwár and Bijápur, the turmeric-rubbing ceremony takes place on the day before the marriage. In Dhárwár, on the same day, the bride and bridegroom are made to sleep at nightfall in a blanket booth with a girl of eight or nine years old lying between them. In Bijápur, on their way to the bridegroom's, after the marriage has been performed, the pair call at the houses of five Ods and bow to the heads of the families, each of whom drops from five to ten copper coins into the laps of the bride and bridegroom.

In Kanara, the betrothal known as *hirevilla* takes place on the morning of the marriage day. It is followed by a ceremony called *airáni*. Five unwidowed women, each taking an earthen jar, go to a well or tank. An image is made in the name of the Ganges, and worshipped. Next, each of the women ties a *kankan* (a packet of betel leaves) to the jar taken by her, and one to her right wrist. The jars are then filled with water and taken to the girl's house, where two *páls* (blanket tents) are erected, one for the males and the other for the females. One of these jars is placed in the men's *pál*, one in the women's *pál*, and the other three are put near the household gods. A turmeric root fastened to a woollen thread is kept hanging in each of the jars in the *páls*. The bride and bridegroom are rubbed with turmeric paste in their respective *páls*. Next comes the *halagamb* ceremony, in which a wooden post, to which are tied leaves of the *umbar* (Ficus glomerata) and the *nim* (Melia azadirachta) is planted in the ground; and two persons, taking the boy and the girl on their shoulders, walk five times round the post. Next, the girl stands in front of the post and the boy fastens a lucky necklace round her neck. This is the binding portion of the ceremony. A feast to the caste people terminates the marriage.

The remarriage of widows is permitted. A widow cannot marry her father's sister's or mother's sister's son, or a member of her late husband's section. She may marry her maternal uncle's son. A widow remarriage can take place in the dark fortnight of any month except *Ashádh*, *Bhádrapad* and *Paush*. In Kanara, it is celebrated only on a Thursday or Sunday. The ceremony consists either in tying the pair's garments together, or in filling the widow's lap after she has put on new clothes presented by her new husband. The faces of the remarried pair should not be seen for three days after the marriage. In some places, a bachelor is not allowed to marry a widow. In others, he can do so after he has married a *rui* tree.

Divorce is allowed if the husband and wife do not agree or the wife's conduct is bad. A divorced woman may marry again by the widow remarriage form. A woman taken in adultery with a casteman or a member of a higher caste is allowed to remain in the caste if she pay a fine or give a dinner to the castepeople. If the offence is committed with a member of a lower caste, she is excommunicated. The caste follow the Hindu law of inheritance.

Religion. Maráthа and Kanarese Ods belong to the Hindu religion. Those in Kanara are followers of the Vaishnava sect. They worship all Bráhmanic gods. Their family deities are Venkatráma of Giri or Tirupati in North Arcot, Narsoba, Mahádeva, Máruti, Jánái, Satvái, Murgava, Nágamma and Yellamma. They are specially devoted to Venkatráma, in whose honour they hold a feast every third or fourth year. On lucky days a stone image of Venkatráma is carried in procession from the village and set on the edge of a pond or on the bank of a stream.

A Bráhman priest washes the image, marks it with sandal paste, presses grains of rice on the paste, and puts flowers on the image. The Ods then make an offering of cooked rice, *polis* or sugar rolly-polies, and husked wheat boiled in milk and sugar. The Bráhman priest is given Rs. 1 to 10 and undressed food. After the priest has gone, the party feast, and, in the evening, throw the idol into water and return home. The Ods do not eat animal food on Fridays, Mondays and Saturdays, in honour of their gods Narsoba, Venkatesh and Máruti. Images of deceased ancestors are made and worshipped. They offer liquor and flesh to their gods on the *Dasara* day, which they partake of themselves. They make pilgrimages to Pandharpur, Tuljápur, and Venkatgiri in North Arcot. They believe in soothsaying, witchcraft and evil spirits, and stand in great fear of exorcists. To prevent the family dead from bringing sickness into the house, they worship the dead every year. A little spot in the house is cowdunged and a robe, a bodice or a waistcloth is worshipped on it with an offering of a sweet fried dish. The Poona Ods say that they are not troubled by ghosts, as the pork which they eat and keep in their houses scares ghosts. The religious teachers of Ods are men of their own caste. They occasionally visit their dwellings and levy yearly tributes in money from their followers. They settle social disputes, but do not give religious or moral teaching. The religious teacher of the Kanara Ods is the head of the Shrivaishnava Bráhmans, whose monastery is at Shriranga on the banks of the Káveri near Trichinopoly. They generally wear the marks of Vishnu. Their favourite deities are Vishnu and the goddess Yellamma, whose chief shrine is in Belgaum district. They carry with them an image of Yellamma in the form of a woman and in her honour hold a yearly feast which lasts for three days. The ceremonies are performed by a man of their own caste. The offerings consist of cocks, goats, fruits, spirits and flowers, and the ceremony ends with a general feast to the whole community. All the ceremonies of the Ods are conducted by the caste elders.

Death ceremonies.

The dead are either burnt or buried, burying being more common. On the third day after death a fowl is killed, its flesh and some rice are cooked separately, taken to the burial ground with an earthen pot filled with water, and set on the grave as an offering to the deceased. The person who carries these articles must not look behind him on his return. In some places, millet cakes are offered instead of flesh and rice. In the evening the corpse bearers are feasted. The Ods observe mourning for twelve days, and feast castepeople on any day after the third and before the fifteenth day after death. For the propitiation of the deceased ancestors, offerings of new clothes and goats and fowls are made on the Hindu new year's day, one of the *Navrátra* days, or on any other auspicious day. They do not perform the *Shráddha*.

Occupation. The hereditary occupation of the bulk of the tribe is working in earth and stones. The Bhoja Ods make and sell charcoal and cement. The Máti Ods dig ponds and wells and make field embankments. The Dagad Ods cut and make grind-stones and quarry, and work as masons. They also make stone images of gods and animals. The Gáda Ods carry building stone either in low solid-wheeled carts or on donkeys. The Ods are one of the hardest working classes in the Deccan and Karnátak, working in gangs, generally by the piece. Their services are indispensable for irrigation and railway works in the Deccan and Karnátak. Some of the Ods work as field labourers and often make contracts with the owner of a field to finish a certain work for a certain sum of money in a given time. When the bargain is made, men, women and children fall on the work and take little rest till it is finished. A few of the Bhoja Ods hold land under the *rayatvári* system.

Food. Ods eat the flesh of goats, sheep, fowls, hogs, rats—of which they are specially fond—monkeys, jackals, bears, tigers, and almost all other kind of flesh except beef. They drink liquor to excess. They rank below the cultivating classes and above the impure castes, whom they do not touch.

GUJARAT ODS state that they are emigrants from the Deccan, which seems probable from the fact that they use the *pánchpálavi* at the time of marriage, and that some of them are followers of the Rámdási sect. They have two endogamous divisions, Proper and Návábhái or new comers (residing in Pachhegam in Káthiáwár), who eat together but do not intermarry. The Návábháis admit into their fold Kolis and members from other castes of a similar status. The Gujarát Ods have a few exogamous sections which point to a Rajput connection. In all probability each section represents the stone-masons attached to the Rajput clan of which they bear the name. Instances of such sections are, Bhattis, Chuháns, Solankis, etc. A Gujarát Od cannot marry his father's sister's, mother's sister's, or mother's brother's daughter. Two sisters may be married to one man at the same time or the younger of the two sisters after the death of the elder. Two brothers may marry two sisters. Polygamy is permitted only if the first wife is barren. Polyandry is unknown. Girls are generally married between fourteen and eighteen, boys between twenty and twenty-five. Betrothals take place at a very early age. Cases of misconduct before marriage are rare. If any occur, the caste *panch* has the power to force the guilty parties to marry or to impose a fine on the parents of the girl if their connivance is proved, and may outcaste the parents and the girl altogether.

The offer of marriage comes from the boy's father. The marriage dower is fixed by the caste at Rs. 120. When accepting the offer, the girl's father demands a sum varying from Rs. 16 to Rs. 60, which in deducted from the *des* (dower) at the time of marriage. In other respects the marriage ceremonies of the Gujarát Ods resemble those of local castes of similar standing, except that a *toran* or string of five kinds of leaves (*pánchpálavi*) is hung over the entrance to the marriage booth.

The marriage of widows is permitted. The levirate or *dewartun* is compulsory in Káthiáwár, but is not observed in Gujarát. In the case of a widow refusing to marry her husband's younger brother, she has to give a dinner to the tribesmen.

Divorce is allowed. The ceremony consists in calling the wife publicly mother or sister, which frees the husband.* In such cases, if the wife remarries, she pays no fine. If on the other hand, the wife divorces the husband (by calling him brother or father), and remarries, the new husband has to pay a fine of Rs. 200 to the former husband, a part of which is spent on treating the tribesmen to a sumptuous dinner. The tribe is governed by Hindu law with slight modifications.

The Gujarát Ods follow the Hindu religion. They are followers of the Swámináráyan, Kabir and Rámdási sects. They worship by preference the god Shiva. They make pilgrimages to Tulshi Shyáma or Prachi and Dwárka. A few go to Benares. Their religious teacher is Báwá Goraknáth. Their priests are the village Bráhmans (*gámots*) who do not eat with them. They enjoy the same status as other members of their caste. The dead are buried in a lying position with head to the north. To propitiate the unmarried and childless dead the ceremony of *nil parnávavi* or a mock marriage of a male and a female calf is performed.

Gujarát Ods eat the flesh of goats, sheep, deer, and scaly and scaleless fish, and drink liquor.

---

* In connection with this ceremony, see a very curious custom among the NAIKDAS, p. 122 supra, in case of irregular connections between men and women of the tribe.

SIND ODS have six exogamous sections, all of which are common among Rajputs. They are :—

Bhatti.	Parmár.	Solanki.
Chaván.	Ráthor.	Tunvar.

Marriages with maternal relations within seven degrees and with near agnates are prohibited. There is no strict rule regarding the marriageable age of boys and girls. Sexual license before marriage is said to be neither recognised not tolerated. Polygamy is strictly prohibited unless the first wife is barren, insane or subject to an incurable disease. In such cases the consent of the caste *panch* is necessary. The marriage ceremony is of the standard type. The remarriage of widows is permitted. The first claimant to a widow's hand is her late husband's elder brother, the next claimant being the younger brother. If, when one of these is available, a widow marries an outsider, she and her new husband are put out of caste. The form of widow marriage is generally the same as that of a first marriage. But the Umarkot Ods have adopted the following form which is observed by the Kirárs, otherwise called Bhábhrás or Mahesari Vániás :—

According to this form, marriage with a deceased husband's brother is prohibited. On the day fixed for the marriage the widow's intended husband goes to her house. The widow puts on the garments and ivory bangles sent to her by him on the day previous, and the skirts of the pair's garments are united. Next, the pair proceed to the new husband's house, the widow taking on her head a jar filled with water. The jar is taken down by the husband, the pair enter the house, and the widow grinds a little corn, and thus completes the marriage. Divorce is not allowed. The tribe follow the Hindu law of inheritance.

The Sind Ods worship by preference the goddess Hingláj. Some worship Rámdev, supposed to be an incarnation of Krishna in Márwár. Those who worship Rámdev do not make sacrifices. Others offer goats or sheep in the month of *Chaitra* and during the *navarátra* days in *Ashvin.* The flesh of the offerings is distributed among those present, whether they be Ods or not, who do not abstain from flesh. The priests of the Sind Ods are either Sárasvat or Pushkarna Bráhmans, who are received on terms of equality by the other Bráhmans, as they do not partake of meals prepared by the Ods.

The Sind Ods bury their dead, stating that the custom is due to their first ancestor Sagar having been buried in the earth in his attempt to find water. Formerly they performed a death ceremony known as *Sankhadál* (from *sankh* a shell) for the propitiation of the deceased ancestors. The ceremony is thus described :—

A piece of cloth measuring $1\frac{1}{4}$ cubits is spread over a newly cow-dunged floor and covered with another piece of a red cloth. Over this a circle is made with seven small heaps of rice grains. On each heap are placed a betelnut, a pice, a dry date, a cardamom and a clove. In the centre is laid a small metal jar filled with water with Rs. $1\frac{1}{4}$ in it, and its mouth is covered with a cocoanut. A lamp fed with ghi is kept burning hard by. An image of wheat flour is made, representing the deceased, and placed in a large flat metal dish, which also contains cow's urine and sandalwood powder. A shell is filled with water contained in the jar placed on the red cloth, and poured 108 times over the image by each member of the deceased's family, also 5 to 10 times by the tribesmen present. Next, under instructions from the *gosáin* (priest) two or more members of the deceased's family are brought to him and the *gosáin* gives them *upadesh* (religious instruction). *Sukha* (a preparation of *bháng*) and eatables are then distributed among those present, and the night is passed in singing hymns. Next morning before daybreak, the image and the water contained in the dish are thrown into a river.

The above custom, though alleged to be in vogue in Márwár, seems to have been abandoned by the Ods residing in the desert of Sind, who have adopted the standard funeral rites of local castes.

The Sind Ods eat the flesh of goats, sheep, deer, antelopes, pigs, black partridges and fish of almost every kind, and drink liquor. They have no scruples against eating the leavings of their caste fellows, but they will not eat the leavings of others.

PARDESHI ODS profess to have come from Northern India in the time of Aurangzeb. They have the following *gotras* :—

1. Bagewara.	9. Katona.	17. Ratoya.
2. Baghaya.	10. Kunbyathop.	18. Ravancharia.
3. Bilewara.	11. Mahengaya.	19. Savipagar.
4. Chaukya.	12. Mundela.	20. Shirmorya.
5. Gavhar.	13. Nigoya.	21. Sultanya.
6. Ismorya.	14. Pakharmar.	22. Tarvarya.
7. Janva.	15. Pandya.	
8. Kahorya.	16. Purbhaya.	

ODDE.—A synonym for Od.

OJHA.—A synonym for Kumbhár.

OLGANA.—A synonym for Bhangi.

OLPADIA.—A sub-division of Dublás.

ORH.—A synonym for Od.

OSVAL,—A sub-division of Bráhmans and Vániás.

Name and origin. **OTARIS** or metal casters, from the Maráthi *ot* to cast, numbering 1,290, including 650 males and 640 females, are found in small numbers scattered all over the Deccan and the Konkan. The caste is Hindu, and it seems probable that 18 males returned as Musalmán in the Census of 1901, are wrongly classified.

Divisions. There are no endogamous divisions of the caste. There appear to be no exogamous sub-divisions above families bearing the same surname. The commonest surnames are Kandore, Khedvan, Sátpute, Vandar, Kalasáit, Sávan, Chápe, Tarál, etc.

Marriage. A member of the caste cannot marry his father's sister's or mother's sister's daughter. He may marry his maternal uncle's daughter. A man may marry two sisters, and two brothers may marry two sisters. Girls are generally married between the age of five and twelve and boys between fifteen and twenty. Misconduct on the part of a girl before marriage is not uncommon, and if brought to light, is punished with a fine or by a dinner given to the caste people. If the man involved be a member of the caste, he is similarly punished ; but if he be of a lower caste such as a Mahár or Máng, the girl is turned out of the caste. Polygamy is allowed and practised, but polyandry is unknown. The offer of marriage is made by the boy's father. The settlement of the marriage day and the ceremony itself are entrusted to a Bráhman priest. The principal ceremonies are *Soyarik* in which the boy's father presents to the girl a new robe and bodice, a rupee, and a packet of sugar ; *Laginghada, i. e.*, fixing the marriage day ; *Halad* or rubbing the boy and the girl with turmeric paste ; *Belmáthan*, the fixing of the post of the marriage booth ; *Telan*, the sprinkling of oil on the bride and the bridegroom by married women ; *Lagna*, the marriage, in which the boy and the girl are seated opposite to each other, a cloth is held between them, sacred verses are repeated by the Bráhman priest, after which the boy takes hold of the girl's hands and the priest fastens round their necks nine stringed garlands ; *Hátola*, the giving away of the bride to the bridegroom ; *Lájáhom*, the marriage sacrifice ; *Kasára*, mutual feeding of the bride and bride-groom with raw sugar and ghi ; and *Mangalvedha*, walking thrice round the sacrificial fire, the last being the essential portion of the ceremony.

The *devaks* or marriage guardians of the caste consist of the leaves of the mango tree, of the *shami* (Prosopis spicigera), the Indian fig tree, *bor* (Jujube) tree, and *rui*. In addition, some worship the *pardi* or pair of scales as a *devak*.

The remarriage of widows is permitted. A widow can marry her father's sister's or mother's brother's son. She is not allowed to marry her mother's sister's son or a member of her late husband's section. A widow's marriage must be celebrated at night on a Sunday, Friday or Tuesday from the eighth to the last day of the dark fortnight of a month. The caste *panch*, a Bráhman priest, and the relations and friends are present on the occasion. The widow's new husband gives her a sum of money for purchasing clothes and ornaments. The ceremony consists in seating the widow and her new husband side by side on low wooden stools, applying red powder to the widow's forehead, and the bringing together of the heads of bride and bridegroom by the Bráhman priest. A bachelor is not allowed to marry a widow. Divorce is allowed with the sanction of the caste *panch*. The caste follow the Hindu law of inheritance

Religion.

Otáris belong to the Hindu religion. Their family gods are Kálkádevi of Paithan, Ambábái of Aundh, Jotiba of Ratnágiri, Khandoba of Jejuri and Sidhoba of Mhasvad. They have house images and worship Bahiroba, Bahiráji, Bhaváni, Dhanái, Janái, Khandoba, Máruti and Nágji. Images of persons who have died a violent death are installed among the house-hold gods. Offerings of domestic fowls and goats are made to the village gods on any day except Mondays and *Ekádashis*. Otáris worship the implements of their work such as scales and saws on the last day of *Ashádh* and *Fálgun*. Vows and offerings are sometimes made to Musalmán Pirs. The Indian fig tree, the banyan tree and the *pipal* are worshipped. Otáris go on pilgrimage to Saptashringi, Alandi, Jejuri, Pandharpur, Benares, Násik and Tuljápur. Their priests are Deshasth Bráhmans. They observe all the Hindu holidays.

Death ceremonies.

The dead are either burnt or buried. The ordinary funeral rites are observed and a feast is given to the caste people on the eleventh day after death. On this occasion one of the nearest relations of the chief mourner presents him with a new turban. He puts it on, goes to a village temple, bows to the god, and returns home. For the propitiation of dead ancestors *Shráddha* is performed every year.

Occupation.

The main occupation of the caste is casting metal. They make molten images of Hindu gods, platters, jingling bells and *jodvis* or toe-rings. The women assist by preparing earthen moulds, blowing the bellows, and hawking the toe-rings.

Food. They eat fish and the flesh of sheep, goats, hares, deer and domestic fowls. They drink liquor.

PADAMROTI.—A sub-division of Rávals.

PADAM SALI.—A sub-division of Sális.

PADE.—A sub-division of Mális.

PADHARIAS are found in small numbers in almost every village bordering on the *Nal* or large fen which lies between the Dholka and Viramgám *tálukás* of the Ahmedábád district and Káthiáwár. They are said to be Kolis who were put out of caste for eating dead animals and retired to the borders of the *Nal*. Their chief occupation is cutting grass and digging out the *bir*, the root of which is the common food of the Nalkantha side every hot weather, for sale to other villages. The men also fish and snare duck, which they eat or sell. Their condition is poorer even than that of the ordinary Vághri. They are Hindus and worship Hingláj Máta. The bridegroom has to pay a bride-price of Rs. 50 to the girl's father. If a widow cannot pay this amount to the relations of her deceased husband, she must marry his brother or other near relation.

PADIARS numbering 302 (1901), including 145 males and 157 females, are found entirely in the Kanara district. The word Padiár is a modification of the Támil *padiwál*, *i.e.*, a hired servant paid in grain. It is derived from *padi* a measure of corn. They are a class of prostitutes recruited from women taken in adultery. They have no subdivisions. The girls are usually prostitutes. The *shes* or knife-marriage ceremony is performed when a girl is over ten years of age. Girls are also said to be married to the god Mahábaleshwar at Gokarn. They are Hindus, their family god being Venkataráma of Tirupati. Their religious teacher is the Havik Swámi of Rámchandrapur in Mysore. The dead are burnt. Many of the women are singers and dancers. The men act as musicians. Some of the men and women, like Devlis, do menial work in temples and some cultivate land. They eat fish and flesh except beef and pork, and drink liquor.

PADMA SALI.—A sub-division of Sális.

PAD SALI.—A sub-division of Sális.

Name. **PADTIS** numbering 3,510 (1901), including 1,804 males and 1,706 females, are found in the *tálukás* of Kárwár, Ankola, Kumta, Honávar, Sirsi and Yellápur in the Kanara district and in Goa territory.

They have two endogamous divisions, Kanarese and Konkani, who neither eat together nor intermarry, although they do not differ in religious and social customs. There are nine exogamous sections named after various villages as follows :— Divisions.

Kanarese Padtis.

	Name.		Family god.
1.	Kotárkar	..	Rámnáth.
			Betál.
2.	Tálekar	..	Mallikárjun.
3.	Nagekar	..	Bhumidevata.
4.	Gainkar	..	Betál.
5.	Chinchonkar	..	Rámnáth.
6.	Gáondi	..	Bhumidevata.

Konkani Padtis.

7.	Nágekar	..	Bhumidevata.
8.	Májálkar	..	Betál.
9.	Kánkonkar	..	Mallikárjun.

Marriages cannot take place in the same section. Marriages among brother's and sister's children are prohibited, but a brother's son or daughter can marry a sister's daughter or son. A member of the caste is allowed to marry two sisters, and two brothers may marry two sisters. The caste appears to have come into Kanara from Goa about six or seven generations ago; but owing to its having taken to manufacturing salt, a profession followed by a very low caste in Kanara, the parent stock stopped all intercourse, and has since been a separate community. Outsiders are not admitted into the caste. Girls are generally married between nine and thirteen, and boys between fourteen and eighteen. Polygamy is allowed, but rarely practised unless the first wife is barren. Polyandry is unknown.

Marriage ceremonies.

The offer of marriage is made by the boy's father. The settlement of the marriage day and the ceremony itself are entrusted to the village *joshi*. When a match is approved of by the parents of the bride and bridegroom, the betrothal takes place, in which the girl's hair is decked with flowers presented by the boy's parents. On the morning of the marriage day the boy and the girl are rubbed with turmeric and oil. The boy then goes in procession to the girl's house, where a cloth is held between him and the bride, and they garland one another. Next, their hands are joined and water is poured on them. This is known as *dháre*, and is the essential and binding portion of the ceremony. On the following evening a ceremony called *gavan* is performed at the bride's house, in which the bride and bridegroom are seated on a cot, grains of rice are thrown on their heads, and cash presents from annas two to a rupee are made to them by relations and friends; and they are made to play a game with a copper ring and a betelnut in a pan filled with water. The caste is then feasted. On the third day the pair go to the bridegroom's house, the ceremony of *gavan* is again gone through, castemen are feasted, and the marriage garlands are removed from the heads of the bride and bridegroom. On the day following, the pair go again to the girl's house and return to the boy's house after five days, when the marriage ceremonies end. The remarriage of widows is allowed. A widow can marry any man except her maternal uncle's son or a member of her late husband's family. The sanction of the *budvant* of the caste must be obtained before celebrating a widow-marriage, which may only take place on days not suitable for first marriages. A few old men and remarried widows are present on the occasion. On the day appointed, at night-fall, the widow goes to her new husband's house, bathes, and stands with her hair unbound. The glass bangles on her wrist are broken by one of the old men present, and the ornaments and clothes given to her by her first husband are sent to his relations, together with Rs. 4 to Rs. 6 paid by her second husband. Next, the widow puts on new clothes, ornaments, and bangles presented by her second husband; the pair are seated on the threshold of the house, and vermilion and grains of cooked rice (dried) are applied to the widow's forehead by one of the widows present. This ends the ceremony. A remarried widow is not allowed to take part in any auspicious ceremony, not even in the celebration of her daughter's marriage. But if she has a son, she is considered purified on her giving a feast to the caste-people, and is thus raised again to the rank of unwidowed women. A bachelor is not allowed to marry a widow. Divorce is not allowed. The caste follow the Hindu law of inheritance.

Religion.

They are Hindus and worship the ordinary Bráhman and village gods. Their family deities are Rámnáth, Vetál, Mallikárjuna and Bhumidevata. Some of them also worship *purushas*, that is, dead ancestors, to whom small temples are dedicated. They have great faith in sooth-saying and sorcery and in the powers of spirits. They observe all the local holidays including *bhánds* and *játrás*. They make pilgrimages to Gokarn, Pandharpur, and Tirupati. When cholera or small-pox breaks out, offerings of cocks and goats, and sometimes even of buffaloes, are made to the Mariamma goddess of Sirsi. The priests of the local village temples are also consulted, and offerings of cocoanuts, flowers, vermilion, eye salve, robes, bodice cloths and plantains are made to the deities, and patients are made to drink *thirthprasád*, *i.e.*, water in which their idols have been bathed. On certain occasions vows are made to Musalmán Pirs, and if they are fulfilled, camphor, frankincense, and raw sugar are offered to them. On the Dasara day they worship their implements of husbandry and offer fowls to them. Fowls, sheep and goats are also offered to the village deities at the hookswinging festival. The priests of the caste are *joshis*, a class of Dravid Bráhmans, who are not received on terms of equality by the other Bráhmans.

Death ceremonies. They either burn or bury the dead. At burial the corpse is laid with the head turned to the north. For the propitiation of dead ancestors they perform the *mahálaya* every year on the ninth day of the bright half of *Ashvin*.

They believe their original occupation to have been the cultivation of salt-marsh lands. Most of them are permanent or half-share tenants or tenants-at-will; a few make salt; the rest are day labourers and are paid in cash.

They occasionally hunt hares, deer, and wild boars, and catch fish for their own use. They eat fowls, mutton, venison, fish and wild boars; and drink toddy and liquor.

Food. They eat *kacchi* and *pakki* from the hands of Bráhmans, Vánis, Konkan Maráthás, and Gámvakkals; and *pakki* only from Bhandáris and Komárpaiks. They take neither *kacchi* nor *pakki* from Sonárs.

PAGIS numbering 127 (1901), including 37 males and 90 females, are found only in the Kárwár *táluka* in the Kanara district, living on the bank of the Káli Nadi in small isolated settlements. They derive their name from the Konkani word *pag* to fish, and appear to have come from Goa, where there are shrines of their family deities Málkárjun, Guru pardeshi, and Mahámái. They are said to be a branch of the Khárvis of Goa. They have no sub-divisions. Girls are married before they come of age. Polygamy and widow marriage are allowed and practised, but polyandry is unknown. They worship all local gods and goddesses and observe all the Hindu holidays. The special object of their devotion is Mahámáya, who has a shrine at Kadra, which they visit every year during the annual festival between October and November. They then offer blood sacrifices of fowls and sheep to the goddess. Their family priests are Karnátak

Bráhmans and their spiritual teacher is the head of the Smárt Monastery at Shringeri. They believe in soothsaying, witchcraft and ghosts. Their ceremonies resemble those of the Harkantras. Their hereditary calling is fishing, but they now seldom catch fish, being mostly engaged in plying ferry boats across the Káli Nadi, cultivating lands, and working as unskilled labourers. They eat fish and flesh except beef and tame pork and drink liquor. They rank with Khárvis and other fishermen.

PAGI.—A synonym for Thákarda.

PAHELWAN.—A synonym for Hakim.

PAKALGHAT.—A sub-division of Lohárs.

PAKHALI.—A synonym for Bhisti.

PAKHARIA.—A sub-division of Mochis.

PAKNAK.—A sub-division of Gollas.

PAL.—A sub-division of Kolhátis.

PALAI.—A sub-division of Rávals.

PALEVAL.—A synonym for Palivál.

PALIA.—A sub-division of Dublas.

PALIMANGA.—A sub-division of Bháts.

PALIVAL.—A sub-division of Vániás and Bráhmans.

PALSHE.—A synonym for Palshikar.

PALSHIKAR.—A sub-division of Bráhmans.

PALVADA KOTWALIA.—A synonym for Vitolána.

PAN.—A sub-division of Mahárs ; a synonym for Malhár Koli.

PAN AGARA.—A sub-division of Mochis.

PAN AGLE.—A synonym for Sudh Agri.

PANBHARI.—A synonym for Malhár Koli.

PANCHACHARI.—A sub-division of Lingáyats.

PANCHAL.—A sub-division of Lohárs and Sutárs.

Name and origin.

PANCHALS numbering 60,489 (1901), including 31,273 males and 29,216 females, are found in the Karnátak and adjacent parts of the Deccan. They are numerous in Mysore and Madras. Pánchâls are also known as Vishva Bráhmans, or Acháris. They claim to be identical with the Rathakar, Actash, Kavi Madhavi, Suhasta Sour and Narashansha castes in Vedic references. In Madras they are styled Kammálans.[1] The name Paththár or Pattár is shared by them with the Sonárs. The latter, as well as Sutárs, Lohárs, Támbats and Pátharvats, are inclined to describe themselves as Pánchals, on the ground that they follow an occupation common to them and one of the Pánchál divisions. The census figures are thus very unreliable.

The caste presents no little difficulty.

It is not easy to decide whether a guild of artizans working in the five materials of gold, iron, brass, wood and stone has become a caste of Bráhmanic status, or whether, on the contrary, Bráhmans, having taken to work in these materials, have become an artizan caste while retaining their superior position. The fact that the skill required for working in either metal, wood, or stone, does not differ greatly, would explain to some extent both an affinity between castes working in the different materials, and the fact that a caste taking to the handicrafts could adopt all these methods of earning a living. It is on the whole more probable that the caste had its origin in a Bráhman group becoming artizans than in an industrial guild assuming Bráhmanic rites and privileges, and that the fact is an illustration of the stage of social development in India when status ceased to depend on occupation and became hereditary. The wealthy position held by workers in precious metals may have enabled the Pánchals to uphold their claims to Bráhmanic rites and status over a long period of time in face of the strong opposition which has at times been evinced towards them by Bráhmans of a more orthodox occupation, notably during the rule of the Peshwás. Care must be taken to distinguish between Pánchals properly so called and the distinct castes of Sonár, Kánsár, Sutár, Lohár and Pátharvat, which in many cases have established Pánchál sub-divisions and are disposed to adopt the traditional origin of the Pánchals. They are, however, entirely different in origin, and the fact is emphasized by there being five distinct endogamous groups, not interdining, nor have they the close resemblance in rites and appearance to Bráhmans that the Pánchals possess. There is no small risk at the time of a census of confusing the so-called Pánchál sub-division of these five castes with the Pánchál caste proper.

According to some, the term Pánchál is derived from *pánch* five and *al* to melt, because Pánchals melt gold, silver, copper, brass and zinc. According to others, they are so called because they have only

(1) Castes and Tribes of Southern India, Thurston, Vol. III, p. 106.

five *gotras*, *viz.*, Ahabhuvan, Pratna, Sánag, Sanátan and Suparna, while some maintain that the name Pánchál is the result of the community containing five classes—Sonárs or Aksális (goldsmiths), Sutárs or Bádigs (carpenters), Kásárs, Támbats or Baligars (coppersmiths), Lohárs or Kamárs (blacksmiths) and Pátharvats or Kallukutigs (stone masons). Of the above derivations, the first is the most probable, as the Páncháls form one caste, the members of which follow the occupations of the five artizan castes referred to above, this difference of occupation being no bar to intermarriage.[1] Taking advantage of this five-fold occupation of the Páncháls, and of the fact that the Pánchals hold a comparatively higher status, the five artizan castes mentioned above also call themselves Pánchals, and some appear to have evolved a Pánchál division which does not marry with the rest of the caste. Enquiries on this point clearly shew that the Pánchals are a distinct caste, differing considerably in religion and customs from the five artizan castes. Thus, the five artizan castes eat fish and flesh while the Pánchals are strict vegetarians. Sonárs and the other artizan castes eat food cooked by Bráhmans, but the Pánchals object to doing so, considering themselves superior to Bráhmans. According to Sir W. Elliot,[2] Pánchals are a relic of the Buddhists. If this were correct, their name might be a variant of Pánchsil, the followers of the five rules, an old name for Buddhists ; but the theory is quite devoid of confirmation. The caste claim descent from Manu, Maya, Twashta, Shilpi and Daivadnya, the five sons of Vishvakarma, the divine architect. It is to be noted that this mythological origin for the name Pánchál is also claimed by the five separate artizan castes mentioned above. Pánchals claim to be Bráhmans. They follow the Bráhmanic *sanskárs* or sacraments, and perform their ceremonies according to Vedic rites. Their claim to Bráhman rank has never been allowed in recent times. On the contrary, they were often persecuted for performing Vedic rites, and, during the rule of the Peshwás, were not allowed to tuck the *dhotar* or waistcloth up between the legs and in at the waist, a mark of Bráhmanic rank. In 1909 an old man described how he witnessed a Pánchál branded on the buttocks by the Chief of Nargund in Dhárwár for wearing his *dhotar* in the prohibited fashion. It is, however, worthy of note that whenever religious disputes between Pánchals and Bráhmans were referred to the religious heads for decision they refused to

(1) In Molesworth's Maráthi Dictionary the term is thus defined :—Pánchál, a common term for five castes, Sonár, Sutár, Lohár, Kánsár, Pátharvat. These all wear the *jánve* sacred thread.

(2) *Jour. Ethn. Soc.*, London, New Series, I, III.

support the Bráhmans and admitted the claim of the Pánchâls to Vedic rites.

Pánchâls have five *gotras*, which are exogamous. They are Ahabhuvan, Pratna, Sánag, Sanátan and Suparna. The Támbats or Kásárs belong to the Ahabhuvan *gotra*, the Pátharvats to the Pratna *gotra*, the Lohárs to the Sánag *gotra*, the Sutárs to the Sanátan *gotra* and the Sonárs to the Suparna *gotra*. Marriages are prohibited between members of the same *gotra* and *pravar* and within seven degrees of relationship both on the father's and mother's side. **Exogamous divisions.**

A Pánchál is not allowed to marry his father's sister's or mother's sister's daughter. He may marry his wife's sister during the wife's life-time as well as after her death. Brothers are not allowed to marry sisters. As among Rigvedi Deshasth Bráhmans, it is common for a man to marry his sister's daughter. Girls are married before they come of age, boys at any age after the performance of the thread ceremony, which generally takes place between the age of seven and ten. Widows are not allowed to re-marry, and, as among Bráhmans, their heads are shaved. Divorce is not permitted. **Marriage.**

Pánchâls are followers of the Rigved and mostly belong to the Smárt sect. They worship by preference Shiva, Vishnu, Ganpati, Devi and the sun. They also worship minor gods such as Khandoba, Bahiroba, etc. The tutelary goddess of the caste is Kálika or Kálamma, whose shrine is at Shirsangi in the Belgaum district. They worship daily the chief implements of their work. As stated above, their priests belong to their own caste. There are many among them who can recite the *vedas*. There are also several hereditary astrologers and physicians and *agnihotris*. They have their own monasteries called *Mathasinhásans* or religious lion thrones presided over by *Dharmagurus* or religious preceptors who settle caste disputes in consultation with the caste *panch*. They profess not to recognise the Shankaráchárya. They observe all the Bráhmanic *sanskárs* and all their ceremonies are performed according to the Vedic rites as laid down in the scriptures. **Religion.**

Pánchâls are vegetarians and do not eat food cooked by members of any caste but their own. **Food.**

PANCHAM.—A sub-division of Shimpis, Gavlis, Kumbhárs, Telis and Gánigs.

PANCHKALSHIS[1] are spread over numerous portions of the Town and Island of Bombay, but their strongholds are Sálsette and **Name and origin.**

(1) From materials supplied by Mr. Vasantrav S. Ravut and Prof. Nilkant S. Takakhav, M.A., and the Secretary of the S. K. Hitechhu Mandali.

the coastland northward upto Daman and southward down to Revdanda in the Alibág *táluka*. The total population of the caste can, with difficulty, be ascertained from Census Reports. The difficulty is occasioned by the fact that the members go under very different names; under the name Sutár and Vádval they may be numbered with other castes. The population of the Sáshtikar sub-division of the caste may be put down approximately at about 6,000 and that of the Ashtágarkar sub-division at about 2,000. A census of the Vádval division was taken by an independent agency in 1901, and the number then returned was 7,916, and about 8,000 may be taken to denote the correct figure now.

Pánchkalshis are also known by the name Somvanshi Kshatriya Páthare, which is the racial or tribal name; but their sub-divisions are called by different names, such as Sutárs and Vádvals. These two names indicate the occupation of the larger number of the castemen, and are descriptive names. The name Pánchkalshi may be considered generic, embracing all the divisions. The name Sutár is given by outsiders to that sub-division of the caste which originally resided in the island of Sálsette. The name Vádval is the title of the sub-division particularly found in the Bassein, Máhim and Dahánu *tálukás* of the Thána district formerly known as the Feringana and literally means the managers of *wádis* or orchards, *viz.*, of cocoanut and palm groves. The origin of the name Pánchkalshi is a matter for speculation,[(1)] but the explanation usually given is that this name arises from an old custom of the caste, by which at the marriage ceremony the bridegroom sat upon a chair of state or *sinhásan* decked with five *kalashas* or little cupolas. Others advance an equally plausible derivation of this name from the pile of five *kalashas* or earthen water-pots which are placed at either side of the main entrance from the verandah or *mandap* on the occasion of marriage.

Pánchkalshis have the same tradition[(2)] about their origin as the Pátáne or Páthare Prabhus of Bombay. They claim to have come[(3)] to these parts of Bombay, Sálsette, Kelva-Máhim, the Ashtágar sea-coast villages of Alibág *táluka* and the adjoining districts, with Rája Bimba or Bhima, about the end of the thirteenth century, from Paithan on the Godávari south of Devgiri. Hence their Kshatriya origin.[(4)] There is another theory that king Bimba, though descended from the royal family of Devgiri, had a principality at Anhilváda Pátan

(1) *Vide* Gazetteer of Bombay City and Island, Vol. I, p. 236.

(2) *Vide* Edwardes' "The Rise of Bombay," page 31.

(3) *Vide* Transactions of the Bombay Geographical Society, Vol. I, 1844, pages 132-33.

(4) *Vide* Edwardes' "The Rise of Bombay," pages 22-23.

in Gujarát proper, whence he migrated on the overthrow of the Hindu principalities by the Muhammadans. This immigration was synchronous with the Muhammadan occupation of the Deccan and of Gujarát, *i.e.*, during the regime of the Khiljis. Rája Bimba is said to have made Máhim or Mahikávati in the Island of Bombay his capital.[1] Subsequently the kingdom of the descendants of Rája Bimba was itself overthrown by the Muhammadans. Under the Portuguese, who succeeded the Muhammadans, there was much persecution,[2] and this is said to have forced many members of the caste to fly to the outlying parts of the Southern Konkan and join those who were already settled in the Ashtágar. Many were then converted to Roman Catholicism by force[2] and their descendants may still be traced at Bassein and Sálsette. They rendered material help to the Maráthás during the siege of Bassein and the acquisition of adjoining country in 1739-40. In consequence of this help the Naik family of Anjore, among others, obtained the title of *Sarpátil* and received *Inám* lands from the Peshwa's Court.[2] To the siege of Bassein and other events of the great Maráthá-Portuguese struggle are traced back the patelships of many families of the Vádval division.

Pánchkalshis contain the following divisions :— Divisions.

1. Ashtágarkar—
   (1) Proper.
   (2) Janjira.
   (3) Malekar, Máli or Cheulkar.
2. Sáshtikar.
3. Vádval.

At a caste meeting in 1779 a resolution was passed against marriage between Sáshtikars and Ashtágarkars. However, intermarriages between these two divisions, though not frequent, are not rare. Pánchkalshis in the Janjira State, described on p. 412 of Bombay Gazetteer, Vol. XI, do not marry or dine with the rest of the caste. The Mális, found in the Mala division of Chaul, separated about a hundred years ago, on account of their women selling flowers and fruit in the open market, which led to the other members of the caste refusing to marry or dine with them. The Vádvals are said to have separated some time in the fourteenth century. There is a disposition to challenge their claim to be Pánchkalshis ; but a careful examination of various documents including letters from the Shankaráchárya in 1836 and 1852 A.D. and a resolution of the Palshikar Bráhmans of the Bassein *táluka* in 1855 seems to leave little doubt that the

(1) *Vide* Edwardes' "The Rise of Bombay," pages 22-23.
(2) *Vide* Edwardes' "Gazetteer of the City of Bombay." Vol. I, p. 237.

Vádvals are entitled to style themselves Pánchkalshis. The split between Vádvals and the rest of the caste is reputed to be due to the admission of a Koli into the caste. Both the Vádvals and the Sáshtikars allege that the Koli was admitted to the sub-division to which they do not belong. The fact remains that for some such reason Vádvals became a separate endogamous sub-division several centuries ago.

Exogamous divisions.

All the divisions of Pánchkalshis claim that they have *gotras* or exogamous sub-divisions, the chief of which are Bháradwáj, Bhárgav, Gárgya, Gautam, Harit, Jámadagni, Káshyap, Kaushik, Kaundanya, Nágrishi, Padmáksha, Shándilya, Trimbak, Vairákshya, Vasishtha and Vishwámitra.(1) These *gotras* do not indicate descent from a common ancestor, but discipleship to a common religious preceptor or *guru*.

Marriage rules.

Marriages are prohibited between members belonging to the same *gotra*. A man cannot marry any of his ascendants in the paternal or maternal line. He cannot marry the daughter of his father's sister, but there is no prohibition against marrying the daughter of the maternal uncle or of the maternal aunt (mother's sister). Such marriages are common, though they are not sanctioned by Yajurvedic ritual. There are several instances of a man marrying his deceased wife's sister, nor is there any bar to his marrying the sister of a living wife. Such alliances are however very rare. A man can marry the sister of his brother's wife even in the life-time of the latter. The marriage age for boys out of Bombay is from fourteen to twenty, and for girls from eight to eleven. In the City of Bombay the marriage age for boys is from sixteen to twenty-five and for girls from twelve to eighteen. Both among the rich and poor, especially in the City of Bombay, it is now becoming very common to postpone the marriage of girls till they have attained the age of puberty. The bride is always younger than the bridegroom, and the difference in their ages is generally from four to eight years; formerly, in the days of child marriages, it sometimes used to be as low as one year. An unmarried girl who has reached puberty is not allowed illicit intercourse with any man, nor would such conduct escape punishment if detected. Polygamy is allowed, but polyandry was never known in the caste. Polygamy is falling into disuse, and recourse is had to a second wife in the life-time of the first, generally when the first wife has proved barren or when relations between the husband and wife have become strained by irreconcilable differences. Owing to the spread of education, polygamy is now out of favour. Divorce is not allowed on any account. If a woman is

(1) *Vide* Raghunath Pootalaji Rane's "Bimbákhiáh", 1877, pages 156-57.

discovered misbehaving herself she will be ejected from her husband's house and often put out of caste. A wife so renounced cannot marry again. In case of proved cruelty on the part of the husband or his people, she may live apart and claim maintenance or alimony.

Marriage ceremonies.

Generally among the Pánchkalshis the bride's father or relations approach the bridegroom's parents, and this is usually done by sending their daughter's horoscope for comparison with the boy's. The opposite is the case in the Vádval division. Among them the bridegroom's parents or relations approach the bride's parents and request them to send their daughter's horoscope for comparison. This does not however mean that girls are at a premium compared with boys in the matrimonial market. Among all Pánchkalshis the parents of a girl find a difficulty in securing a good match. The family priest generally negotiates and arranges these matches, but at times they are arranged by friends and well-wishers of the family, especially elderly women. No special *dakshina* is prescribed to the priest for the match-making, though the bride's father is sure to remember him at the marriage ceremony. The custom of *hunda* or compulsory dowry in cash does not exist among any section of this caste, though some years ago in the Sáshtikar sub-division attempts used to be made in that direction by the bridegroom's people insisting on the presentation of valuable jewellery and other things, and the innovations had to be forbidden, more or less successfully, by caste resolutions. Certain presents in jewellery to the bride by her parents such as a nose-ring, ear-ring, five copper pots, etc., varying in value according to the means, are considered indispensable as also a finger-ring or two to the bridegroom, worth one *tola* of gold. The priests fix the day and hour for the auspicious event, and it is the priest belonging to the bride's family who officiates with his assistance. All the usual ceremonies which obtain among other high Hindu castes are gone through, *e.g.*, *Vágnischaya*, *Simántpujan*, *Madhupark*, *Antarpát*, *Sutravereshtán* and *Pánigrahan*, *Lájáhom*, *Saptapadi*, etc., and occasionally *Airinipradán*. It is the *Saptapadi* rite, as usual, which makes the marriage union indisoluble. While the *Antarpát* ceremony is going on, it is a custom to hold aloft an instrument such as a sword or dagger piercing the canopy above the heads of the bridal pair. This seems to be a survival of olden times, a reminiscence of the old Kshatriya custom. At the same time, eight married persons (who must not be such as have married widows) are made to stand near the bride and groom who are reckoned as witnesses to the ceremony and are called *ashtavargas*.

Widow remarriage is permitted, but it is not so common as among the backward classes. A widow can perform the *pát* or remarriage ceremony with the son of her father's sister or of her mother's sister, but not of her mother's brother. Nor can she remarry with any one from the *gotra* of her deceased husband. Persons interested in the widow or widower's family generally bring about such remarriages. No permission is necessary from the caste *pancháyat* but in certain sections it is usual for the intention of such a marriage to be declared before a council of elders. The *pát* ceremony does not require particular auspicious stars, but days generally regarded inauspicious by the Hindu calendar such as new-moon day, etc., are not chosen. Only those who have gone through the *pát* ceremony themselves (both males and females) can be present at such a marriage. The *pát* ceremony is not performed with the publicity of an ordinary marriage. The chief ceremonies are as follows :—*Ganpatipujan*, *Panyáhavachan*, *Otibharan*, *Mangalsutrabandhan* and *Arti*. The whole ceremony is gone through at night after about 9 p.m. generally under a mango tree, and takes about an hour. The *Mangalsutrabandhan* is the essential part, the completion of which solemnizes the marriage. None but a person who has already been once married in the ordinary way is allowed by caste rules to marry a widow. In most cases a widow having a child will not care to remarry ; in the exceptional case when she wishes to remarry, having children, no particular rule can be followed with regard to the disposal of children. It will depend on the circumstances of the case. Generally widows who have passed the age of thirty do not care to remarry. One who has once married a widow is incapable of again marrying a virgin. All ornaments received from the family of the deceased husband are surrendered to the representatives of that family, and from the date of remarriage the widow bride severs all existing relations with that family. The members of the deceased husband's family keep aloof from her and her second husband on all public occasions.

Religion.

Pánchkalshis follow the Hindu law of succession of the Mayukh and Mitákshara schools. They profess the Hindu religion. They may be described both as Shaivas and Vaishnavas as they worship Shiva as well as Vishnu in his chief incarnations, and other deities such as Dattátraya, Ganpati and Vithoba. Among minor gods, Khandoba, who is considered an incarnation of Shiva, has a few votaries in certain families, but there is no special day or month dedicated to his worship. Every family has some *kuladevata* or tutelary goddess, but her worship only takes place on solemn occasions like marriages and on the annual *jatra* or fair days of the respective goddesses. The principal tutelary goddesses are Mahálakshmi, Ekvira, Vajreshwari, Jogeshwari, etc. They do not worship any animal or plant except such as are considered holy by the whole mass of the Hindu community. Among these the cow, the *tulsi* (sweet basil) and *shami* (Prosopis spicigera) plants, the *pipal* (Ficus religiosa), the *vad* (banyan tree) and the *umbar* (Ficus glomerata) may be reckoned. Among books, special reverence is paid to the Bhagavat Gita. Ordinary offerings of flowers and sweets are the rule; except that in some families, after some great event in the house, a cock or goat is sacrificed as an offering to Khandoba or some tutelary goddess. The custom which now generally prevails is to let loose a goat or a cock in the temple yard of the god or goddess, which is generally taken by the Bhopi or Gurav, *i.e.*, the temple priest. In the few cases when a goat or fowl is sacrificed, the sacrificing person himself eats it in company with his relatives and friends. In cases of small-pox, Shitaládevi goddess is worshipped. In cases of cholera and other epidemics, the tuterlary gods of the village or district are propitiated by a ceremony called *santhik* or the expiatory rite. This ceremony requires the sacrifice of a goat and the offering of a large quantity of boiled rice sprinkled with *gulál* or red powder in which a blazing torch is inserted. The sacrificed goat is partaken of by the worshippers. This ceremony has now become almost obsolete. Pánchkalshis make pilgrimages to the principal places of Hindu pilgrimage, and observe all the great Hindu fasts and feasts. They believe in astrology and witchcraft, but cannot be described as demon-worshippers. The sorcerers and witches generally belong to the Marátha and similar communities; on rare occasions a Muhammadan Pir is consulted. Mahár sorcerers are not in favour, being considered to be too vindictive. At all devotional ceremonies such as the thread ceremonies, weddings, funerals, anniversary rites, etc., the officiating priests are the Palshikar Bráhmans. In certain villages of the Ashtágar, owing to the absence of Palshikars, other Bráhmans such as Deshasthas and Konkanasthas are brought in to officiate as priests.

Death ceremonies.

Pánchkalshis, whether rich or poor, burn their dead. Infants who have not cut their teeth and those who have died of small-pox or leprosy are buried. The bones and ashes of the dead are generally thrown into the sea or a river, and sometimes a part of the bones is kept preserved to be consigned to the waters of a sacred river like the Ganges. When a person is about to die he is removed from his bed or cot to the ground. Holy water is sprinkled on him and a wreath of *tulsi* leaves is put round his neck. When a death takes place in a family, the chief mourner has to undergo a purificatory bath, while the priest chants some *mantras*. If the deceased is an ascendant, the chief mourner and the other mourners of the same degree shave their heads (except the top-knot) and mustaches. Having done this, he offers oblations of rice (*pinda*) in honour of the dead. The corpse is bathed and wrapped up in a new *dhotar* or *lugda* according as the dead person is male or female. If the deceased is female, with her husband living, she is arrayed in a yellow cloth and decked with some of the ornaments in her customary use and handfuls of flowers, almonds, walnuts, betel-nuts, etc., are heaped into a skirt of her dress (*oti*). All the relations present, men and women, salute the dead. Finally the corpse is put upon a bier of bamboo and plaited cocoanut leaves called *závalies*, and borne by four persons on their shoulders to the cremation ground, the priest and the chief mourner (who holds the sacred fire for burning the dead body) preceding the bier. All the persons attending the procession are bare headed. Women do not accompany the funeral procession. Half way to the cremation ground the oblations of rice are repeated, and they are offered a third time on reaching the cremation ground. The corpse is then laid on the pyre, and a fourth oblation takes place before it is ignited. Immediately after the body is burnt the *asthhisinchan shráddha* is performed, which is supposed to mark the final stage in the cremation, and the mourners return home. Funeral obsequies and purificatory rites continue to be performed during the following thirteen days; during the first ten of which all persons belonging to the *gotra* of the deceased observe mourning (*sutak*) and other persons will not have contact with them, on the penalty of being forced to undergo a purificatory bath. During these days, visits of condolence are paid to the mourners either in the morning or in the evening except on a Saturday, Wednesday or new-moon day. From the ninth to the thirteenth day offerings of all kinds, according to the means of the family, are made to the Bráhmans, and religious rites are performed. On the evening of the thirteenth day the caste people come together to the house of the deceased and solemnly put an end to the mourning by taking the chief and other mourners out in a procession to some temple close by. This is generally followed by a caste dinner in honour of the memory of the deceased. In case of the death of any of the ascendants or elder collaterals on the paternal side, a change of head-dress becomes imperative for the chief mourners from the moment of the thirteenth day procession for about a year; and the honour of presenting such a head-dress, in token of mourning, which is usually of a sombre colour, belongs to the fathers-in-law of the respective mourners or other near relatives.

Funeral oblations or *shráddhas* are also performed on the twenty-seventh day and sometimes thereafter on the day of the death once in every month for a year, of which the six-monthly and the *bharni* oblations (*i.e.*, the *shráddha* performed on the fifth of the dark half of the month of *Bhádrapad*) are essential; and after a year has elapsed, the oblations of the first anniversary day are celebrated with great solemnity. The annual *shráddha* is performed on the day corresponding to the day of death in the latter half of the month of *Bhádrapad*. Where the deceased's family can afford it, a *shráddha* is also performed on the anniversary day, which is known as *kshaya-tithi*. In performing the *shráddha* for one's deceased father, offerings are also made to other ancestors and to deceased collaterals. Women dying in the life-time of their husbands have special oblations offered to them during their husband's life-time. This takes place on the ninth day of the *pitrapaksha*, and is called the *avidhava navami* day.

A special ceremony called *Náráyan bali* is performed for those that have died of accident; but in case of one dying childless, no departure from the ordinary rites takes place.

Occupation.

The caste believes that they were originally warriors. In consequence of the political revolutions that transferred the supreme power from the Hindus to the Muhammadans and from the Muhammadans to the Portuguese, they seem to have taken to agriculture and day labour. Under the Portuguese many of them became skilled mechanics and carpenters (house and boat builders), which is still the avocation of a large number of the Sáshtikar section, but the majority of the Vádval and Asthágarkar sections are still farmers. Most of the Pánchkalshis in Bombay are clerks and mechanics. There are a few who follow the learned professions, and their number is increasing. There are very few tradesmen.

The Sáshtikars, some thirty years ago, were mostly proprietors of the land in the different villages of Sálsette, but owing to the tempting prices of land which prevailed during the last fifteen years, many of them have sold off their estates. But even now there are some among them who still retain their lands and follow the old agricultural pursuits. Most of the Ashtágarkar and Vádval sections hold proprietary lands under the Rayatwári system, which are generally cultivated by themselves. There are a few families that hold *inám* lands. Persons holding police patilships enjoy some concessions as to paying revenue to Government. There are very few among them who work as farm labourers on the wages system, but the general practice is to cultivate the lands belonging to other persons of the community on the *khand* system, *i.e.*, by fixing a percentage of the produce as the reward of the cultivator's services. In this case the working farmer supplies his own farm cattle and workmen.

Food. Pánchkalshis partake of the flesh of the he-goat, sheep, wild boar, hare and deer, if procurable, and also of the she-goat and female sheep, though with some reluctance. They also eat fish of nearly all sorts, and fowls. They drink liquor, both country and foreign. They do not partake of anything from a dish tasted by another. They, as a rule, will not eat or drink with any other caste except Bráhmans. They eat general refreshments prepared by Maráthás and others. They smoke country *biddees* with others, but not from each other's mouth, neither do they use the country pipe or *gudgudi*. Castes like those of the Maráthás, Kunbis, etc., will partake of food and drink prepared by them. They do not drink water with Maráthás, but the male members generally have no objection to using water carried by Maráthás. In the City of Bombay, owing to social contact with various communities and creeds and the present trend of thought, restrictions as to food and drink are not so stringent on the younger generation as in the mofussil.

PANCHOLI.—A sub-division Ghánchis and Sutárs.

PANCHOLIS are a small caste of cultivators found in Káthiáwár.

PANCH SINHASANASTHA.—A sub-division of Jangams.

PANGORA.—A synonym for Panjora.

PANGULS or cripples, a class of wandering beggars, numbering 510 (1901), including 252 males and 258 females, are found mainly in Ahmednagar, Khándesh and Násik. They are said to be descendants of a lame man or *pángala* whose parents devoted him to the service of the god Shankar, because the god blessed them with children after the usual time for child-bearing had passed. In religion and customs they follow Marátha Kunbis.

PANJNA.—A sub-division of Khándesh Kunbis.

PANJNIGAR.—*See* under Minor Musalmán Castes.

PANJORA.—A sub-division of Bráhmans.

PANWALE.—A synonym for Bári.

PANYA.—A synonym for Pán Mahár.

PARAJIA.—A synonym for Káchhela.

PARAMAHANSA.—A synonym for Mánbháv.

PARASAR.—A synonym for Parjia.

PARATGI.—A sub-division of Bhois.

PARBHU.—A synonym for Prabhu.

PARDESHI.—A sub-division of Kachhis, Bhadbhunjás, Nhávis, Kumbhárs, Sonárs, Telis. A term generally applied to men coming from the United Provinces; has also become a caste name for the illegitimate children of upper India men and local women.

PARDESHI ALITKAR.—A synonym for Alitkar.

PARDESHI CHAMBHAR.—A synonym for Kattai.

PARDESHI MOCHI.—A synonym for Kattai.

PARDESHVARI.—A sub-division of Audich Bráhmans.

PARDHIS, or Shikáris (hunters), number 12,214 (1901), including 6,320 males and 5,894 females. Their occupation as game hunters takes them in small wandering bands to all parts of the Presidency; but nearly half (5,150) were found in Khándesh district at the time of the 1901 Census; and the only places in which they were elsewhere numerous were: the Cutch State, the Násik, Sholápur and Bijápur districts. In Cutch they are snake charmers and catch snakes. The word 'Párdhi' is derived from *páradh*, hunting. The tribe is also known by the name of Phánse Párdhi and Adivichanchar. *Phánse* means a noose, and this implement is much used by the Párdhis in catching game. Adivichanchar is derived from *atavi* (Kan. *adivi*), meaning forest, and *sanchar*, meaning wanderer, the name, like Phánse Párdhi, being descriptive of the life of the tribe. **Name and origin.**

As a collection of wandering bands of hunters and game snarers, the tribe has always offered an asylum to individual outcastes or broken fragments of other tribes or castes. It is therefore a somewhat heterogeneous collection, and bears evidence of having been recruited at times from Rajputs, Kolis, Vághris, Dhangars, Kabbligars, and Korchars. It is obvious that the new-comers not immediately absorbed into the tribe constitute social divisions which tend to lose their identity in course of time. The social customs peculiar to the tribe therefore tend to vary from time to time and from place to place more than would be the case with more homogeneous entities.

Endogamous divisions.

The endogamous divisions are said at the present time to be—

(1) Párdhi proper.
(2) Phánse Párdhi, or noose hunters.
(3) Haran Párdhi. (1)
(4) Mir.
(5) Korchar.
(6) Vághri.

But it is probable that the occupational distinctions are the most permanent, *viz.*, Párdhis snaring birds with the noose, Párdhis hunting antelope, and those who live by basket-weaving or other means. They mostly speak Gujaráti, indicating their northern origin; but in the Southern Maráṭha districts they talk Kanarese.

Exogamous divisions.

The tribe claims to have once been Rajput. This may be taken to mean that they have at times received Rajput recruits; and this is suggested by the existence among them of five clans or exogamous divisions known as Dábháde, Chaván, Powár, Solanki, and Sonávani. The bulk of the tribe, however, are divided into totemistic divisions worshipping different *devaks*, of which the principal are:—

(1) Thorns of the *arai* shrub (Mimosa rubricaulis).
(2) Thorns of the *bor* tree (Zisyphus jujuba).
(3) Leaves of the *shami* tree (Prosopis spicigera).
(4) Mango.
(5) Jámbhul (Eugenia jambolana).
(6) Umbar (Ficus glomerata).

The sameness of *devak* is a bar to intermarriage. Except in Cutch, a member of the tribe may marry his father's sister, mother's sister's or mother's brother's daughter. A man is allowed to marry two sisters. The Koli custom of a widow being passed on, at the death of her husband, to the next younger brother of the deceased survives in the tribe and indicates its connection with the primitive tribes of Gujarát; as does also the fact that the family god of one of their divisions is found at Pávágad. Two brothers may marry two sisters, the elder brother being married to the elder sister and the younger to the younger. Polygamy is allowed and practised, but polyandry in unknown.

Girls are married up to the age of fifteen or sixteen; boys up to twenty-five. In the case of well-to-do people, baby marriages are

(1) Haran Pardhi means hunters of *haran, i.e.,* black buck. The Kanarese equivalent is Chigri Betkar, *chigri* being the Kanarese for black buck.

also in vogue. If a girl is seduced by a caste-man, he is compelled to marry her after she has been purified by a Bráhman, and he and the girl's father are fined and made to give a dinner to the caste-people. If the seducer belong to another caste, the girl is allowed to remain in the caste after being purified, and may marry any caste-man. If the offence is committed several times, the girl is excommunicated.

Marriage ceremonies.

The offer of marriage comes from the boy's father, who has to pay a bride-price of Rs. 33 to the girl's father. If he cannot pay the amount, the bridegroom may serve in his father-in-law's house for a period agreed upon. The day for the marriage is fixed by a Bráhman who conducts the service. The principal ceremonies of marriage are : *kunku lávane* or *sagái*, that is, the betrothal, which takes place some days before the marriage ; *halad*, or rubbing the boy and the girl with turmeric paste ; *rukhavat*, or carrying sweetmeats to the boy's house by women from the girl's ; *shiravanti*, or reception of the bridegroom in a temple by the girl's party ; and *lagna*, or the marriage proper, in which a cloth is held between the bride and bridegroom, marriage verses are repeated, and sacred grains of rice are thrown over the pair, this being the binding portion. The ceremony of *zál* is next performed, and the bridegroom returns to his house with his bride.

The remarriage of widows is permitted. A widow cannot marry her father's sister's, mother's sister's, or mother's brother's son. She may marry a younger brother of her deceased husband, provided she is more than two years older. If a widow has no children by her deceased husband, her intended husband has to pay her a sum up to Rs. 60. If the intended husband be her deceased husband's brother, he has to entertain the caste-people to a dinner and pay them Rs. 2 to Rs. 4 in cash. A widow remarriage is celebrated on a dark night. Persons on both sides, a barber, a Bráhman and the caste *panch* are present on the occasion. The widow and her new husband are seated on two low wooden stools side by side, and the ends of their garments are tied into a knot by the Bráhman priest. Next, the pair feed each other with two or three mouthfuls of food, which completes the ceremony.

A husband can divorce a wife if he cannot agree with her, or her conduct is bad. A wife can divorce a husband if he is impotent, or is suffering from an incurable disease like leprosy. In both cases the sanction of the caste *panch* is required. A divorced woman can marry again by the widow remarriage form after paying a fine to the caste *panch*. The caste follow the Hindu law of inheritance.

Religion.

Párdhis belong to the Hindu religion, though a few (30) were recorded at the 1901 census as Musalmáns. Their favourite deities are Amba Bhaváni, Jarimari, and Khandoba. Those residing in the Belgaum district chiefly worship Lakshmi, Durgava and Dyámava. In Cutch they worship Gátrád máta. The family goddess of the Chaván clan is the *devi* of the famous Pávágad hill in Gujarát, that of the other four clans being the Chatarshingi at Saptashring. They also worship all village gods. Musalmán saints are venerated. When an epidemic breaks out, the gods are propitiated with blood sacrifices. The chief holidays of the Párdhis are the *Shimga* and *Dasara.* They do not go on pilgrimages and have no spiritual head. All their ceremonies, except the funeral rites, are conducted by Bráhmans, who are received on terms of equality by other Bráhmans. The death ceremonies are conducted by the caste elders.

Death ceremonies.

The dead are buried in a lying position with head to the south. In Cutch before burial the great toe of the right foot is burnt. Women who die in child-birth and persons who have visited the shrines of their family goddesses are burnt. The bones and ashes of the burnt are consigned to water. On the tenth day after death, rice balls are offered to the deceased, and caste-men are feasted. For the propitiation of the deceased ancestors the *mahálaya* is performed in the dark half of *Bhádrapad* on the corresponding death-day or the new-moon day of that month.

During the fair weather Párdhis wander from place to place in bands of three to six families. The men walk ahead carrying nets and baskets, followed by the women with the wooden cots and mat huts, and children carrying earthen pots and pans. Occasionally they own a bullock or buffalo, on which are loaded blankets, baskets, bamboo sticks, nets, and mats. The long rack-like frames in which they fit the delicate horse-hair nooses are most skilfully made, and do great damage to the game. While on the move, they live outside of villages under bamboo frames covered with matting, or under the shade of trees. Their huts are seven feet by four and five feet high, with walls and slanting roofs of straw matting, which they roll up and carry off in a few moments. If overtaken by rain, they take shelter in the nearest village. They have a social organization with a head-man called *náik* or leader, and settle social disputes at caste meetings. A person accused of adultery or other grievous sin has to pick a copper coin out of a jar of boiling oil. If he picks the coin out without harming his hand, he is declared innocent. If he refuses to put his hand into the jar, or if in putting it in his hand is burnt, he is turned out of the caste.

Occupation. Párdhis are very skilful in making horse-hair nooses. They catch pig, antelope, peafowl, partridges, rock-quail, and parrots. Some of them fret stone for grinding grain. A few are husbandmen and *jáglias* or village watchmen. Some are day-labourers and some beg. Though they have taken to comparatively peaceful habits, they have not got rid of their thieving propensities. When in towns and villages selling game, they try to find a suitable place for robbery. They commit burglaries, rob fields, and steal when the chance offers.

Food. They eat the flesh of goats, sheep, deer, fowls, hogs, peacocks, partridges, and quails, and almost all feathered game and fish, and drink liquor. In Cutch, hogs, fowl, and feathered game, except partridges, are prohibited.

PHANSE PARDHIS differ from the bulk of the Párdhis in some of their social and religious customs. They marry their girls at any age. On the marriage day the bride and bridegroom are decked with chaplets of *pipal* leaves, a tassel of thread hanging over each temple. The skirts of the bride's and bridegroom's robes are knotted together seven times, the guests throw red rice over the pair's heads, and the marriage is complete. Polygamy and widow marriage are allowed and practised, but polyandry is unknown.

They belong to the Hindu religion. The special objects of their worship are Yellamma, Tuljá-Bhaváni, and Venkatesh, whose images are kept tied in cloth and are taken out once a year on *Márnavami* in *Ashvin*, and worshipped with an offering of milk. They do not observe any of the Hindu holidays and make no pilgrimages. They believe in witchcraft and soothsaying. Those who can afford it burn the dead, the rest bury. The corpse is carried to the grave by three men, one holding the head, a second the feet, and a third the waist. On the third day a little molasses and a little clarified butter are laid on the grave. This is the only funeral rite. No other ceremonies are performed to propitiate the deceased ancestors.

Though ostensibly snarers and hunters, they make their living mainly by committing robberies. They openly rob the standing crops. The landlords stand in such awe of them that they secure their goodwill by submitting to a regular system of blackmail. If they refuse to let the ears be taken, they would run a good chance of losing the whole crop when it was gathered in the thrashing floor. Some of the Phánse Párdhis make and sell baskets. A division of them called Jogires in Dhárwár make black-stone vessels of various sizes which are used in keeping pickles and sometimes in cooking. In addition to the flesh eaten by the Párdhis, cows are said to be eaten by the Phánse Párdhis. They drink liquor to excess.

PARDHI.—A synonym for Takári.

PARIT.—A sub-division of Mángs.

Name and origin. **PARITS,** also called Dhobis, numbering 14,962 (1901), including 7,307 males and 7,655 females, are found in small numbers scattered all over the Deccan and the Konkan. The occupation of the caste is washing clothes. The term Parit, meaning simply a washerman, includes naturally groups that have little in common beyond their occupation. Thus there are Marátha, Lingáyat, Kámáthi and Telangi Parits. Lingáyat Parits are separately described under the name of Agasa. The Kámáthi and Telangi Parits, being foreigners, do not come within the scope of the survey. Another name for Marátha Parits is Kunbi Parits. The following particulars apply to Marátha Parits only.

Divisions. The Marátha Parits state that they were originally Maráthás,[1] but were severed from the community on account of their having taken to washing clothes. They are divided into two territorial groups, Deshi and Konkani, the former residing in the Deccan, the latter in the Konkan. The Konkani Parits are also known as Madvals. The two divisions neither eat together nor intermarry. The Deshis are divided into two divisions, the Proper and Kadus or bastards. They speak Maráthi like the Kunbis. The surnames and names of both men and women are the same as those of the Maráthás. The Bombay Gazetteer (Vol. XVII, page 147) states that persons bearing the same surname cannot intermarry; but recent enquiries point to the conclusion that, among the Deshi Parits, marriages are prohibited between persons having the same *devak* or marriage guardian, sameness of surnames being no bar to intermarriage. The information regarding the *devaks* of the caste collected so far is as follows :—

Name of *kul.*		Name of *devak.*
Pawár	..	The sun-flower.
Gáikwád	..	Do.
Surve	..	Leaves of *Champa* (Mesua ferrea).
Dalve	..	Do. do.

(1) See article on MARATHAS. It is extremely probable that this tradition is correct and that Parits, like many occupational castes in the Deccan, were originally Maráthás.

Name of *kul.*		Name of *devak.*
Kále	..	Leaves of the tamarind tree.
Sálunke	..	Do. do.
Vágh	..	Do. mango tree.
Kadam	..	Do. do.

The Bombay Gazetteer states that their *devaks* consist of five kinds of leaves or *pánchpálvi,* a mango branch, the leaves of the *rui* bush, an Indian millet stalk, flowers or twigs of the *kalamb* (Anthocephalus cadamba), and of the *purtak* creeper. According to one account the *devak* of all the Konkani Parits is the same, *viz.*, the *kalamb,* but it is more plausibly asserted that every *kul* or section has a separate *devak.* Thus, the *devak* of the Chaváns is the *nág* or cobra, of the Dalvis an axe, and of the Mhádiks the *kalamb.* Marriages are prohibited between members having the same *devak*, and within five degrees of relationship. A man may marry his father's sister's or mother's brother's daughter. He cannot marry his mother's sister's daughter. Amongst the Deshi Parits a man may marry his deceased wife's sister. A Konkani Parit can marry his wife's sister during her life-time. Amongst the former, two brothers are not allowed to marry two sisters; amongst the latter they can do so. Polygamy is allowed and practised, but polyandry is unknown.

Boys are generally married from twelve to thirty, girls from ten to fourteen and even after the age of puberty. Sexual license before marriage is not tolerated. Amongst the Deshi Parits, if a girl commits sexual indiscretions with a man of a higher caste she is retained in the caste on her father paying a fine of Rs. 5 to Rs. 25 to the caste *panch* and on his giving a dinner to the caste people. If the offence is committed with a casteman, the man is similarly punished and compelled to marry the girl. If the man involved belong to a lower caste the girl is excommunicated. Amongst the Konkani Parits, girls committing such offences are turned out of the caste in all cases. Marriage

The offer of marriage comes from the boy's father, who has to pay a sum of money to the girl's father if he is poor. The day for the marriage is fixed by a Bráhman, who conducts the service. The marriage ceremonies of Parits do not differ from those of the Kunbis.

The remarriage of widows is permitted. A widow may not marry a member of her deceased husband's section; but amongst the Deshi Parits instances are known of widows having married their late husband's brothers. Amongst them, a widow remarriage can be celebrated on any dark night in the latter half of any month except

Chaitra and *Bhádrapad*. The ceremony takes place in a lonely locality and is attended only by a few persons. It consists in tying into a knot the ends of the couple's garments. As soon as this is done the party attending the ceremony return home. It is considered unlucky to look on the faces of the pair till the following morning.

Amongst the Konkani Parits widow remarriage can be celebrated on any day. Elderly male members of the caste, a Kásár, a Bhagat, a Ghádi and a widow are present on the occasion. The widow and her new husband are bathed and taken beyond the village boundary. There the widow removes from her person the clothes and ornaments given to her by her deceased husband, and puts on those presented by the new one. The Kásár puts glass bangles on her wrists and toe rings on her toes. Next, the pair are seated on a blanket, a turban is placed on the knee of the widow's new husband, and the widow of the party applies red powder to their foreheads, to which she applies grains of rice. Then the widow's new husband takes the turban on his knee and puts it on his head; red powder and rice grains are then applied to the foreheads of the bride and bridegroom by all the party. Two water pots containing water and a copper coin in each, with their mouths closed with mango twigs and cocoanuts, are brought into close contact with their heads by the Kásár. Next, in order to appease the spirit of the widow's deceased husband, a rupee is tied in a piece of cloth and buried on the village boundary. Liquor is then served, the skirts of the pair's garments are tied into a knot, the widow takes a cock under her arm and the party start to return to the house of the widow's new husband. When they reach the courtyard, the Ghádi waves another cock round their heads and goes away taking the cock as a perquisite. The Bhagat cuts a little of the widow's hair and a piece of her robe, and carries away the cock held by her under her arm. The pair then enter the house, wash their hands and feet and treat the party to a dinner. Every year a cock is offered to propitiate the spirit of the widow's deceased husband. A bachelor is not allowed to marry a widow.

A husband can divorce a wife on the ground of her infidelity. The divorce is effected by performing funeral rites in the name of the wife. A divorced woman can marry again after the fashion of the widow remarriage ceremony.

Religion. The caste follow the Hindu law of inheritance and belong to the Hindu religion. Some of them are followers of the Várkari and the Kabir sect. Their favourite deities are Bahiroba, Khandoba, Mhasoba and Bhaváni. They also worship the village gods and goddesses.

The *pipal*, *shami*, *umbar* (Banyan), weapons and implements are worshipped. The Musalmán saints are reverenced. Parits make pilgrimages to Jejuri, Tuljápur, Pandharpur, Alandi, and also to Benares if means permit. Their spiritual guide is the head of the Shringeri manastery. The priests of the caste are the local Bráhmans.

When cholera breaks out a wooden image of the cholera goddess is made and carried in procession in a small wooden cart made for the purpose, round the whole village, and placed on a spot beyond the village boundary. The image is then worshipped with an offering of rice mixed with curds and the party disperse. This ceremony is not peculiar to Parits. People of all castes take part in it, and it is believed that the epidemic leaves the place with the image and enters the village where it is left. The inhabitants of the latter place sometimes carry it to the next village to avert the danger thus brought on them, and so on, until the image is ultimately thrown into a river or the sea.

The dead are either burnt or buried. The ordinary funeral rites are observed. For the propitiation of deceased's ancestors uncooked articles of food are given to Bráhmans on those days of the latter half of *Bhádrapad* which represent the death days, and castemen are feasted. The well-to-do perform the *shráddha*. Death ceremonies.

The hereditary occupation of the caste is washing clothes. They belong to the class of *balutedárs* or village servants. Village Parits, as a rule, are not paid in cash but in grain. Some of them hold lands and some are labourers. Occupation.

They eat the flesh of goats, sheep, fowls, hares, deer, tortoises and fish and drink liquor. They rank very low in the social scale almost next above the impure classes. Food.

PARJA.—A sub-division of Bráhmans.

PARJIA.—A sub-division of Sonis and Lohárs.

PARSHA.—A sub-division of Holayás.

PARSIS, (1) numbering 78,880 (1901), including 40,500 males and 38,380 females, (2) are found chiefly in the Town and Island of Bombay and in considerable numbers in the Gujarát districts and

(1) Contributed by Shams-ul-ulma Jivanji Jamshedji Modi, B.A., Ph.D., C.I.E.

(2) The figures recorded at the last three Censuses were :—

	Males.	Females.	Total.
1891	39,051	37,405	76,456
1901	40,500	38,380	78,880
1911	42,803	40,762	83,565

States and in Thána and Poona. Some are residents of Karáchi, while a few are scattered over all the principal trade centres and cantonments in India. At one time, Gujarát, and especially Surat in Gujarát, was the headquarters of the laymen. Naosári was, and still is, the headquarters of the priesthood. On the acquisition of Bombay by the British in 1661 they began to settle in Bombay, which is now their headquarters.

Name. The Community speaks of itself as the Pársis. They are, as said by Burnouf, " the noble debris of one of the most heroic and grandest people of antiquity ".(1) They derive their name from the country of Pars (or Fars), the Persia proper, from which their ancestors, who emigrated to India, derived their origin. It was the country of Pars which *gave to the whole country its name of* Persia.

Darius, the great Achæmenian Emperor who invaded India, spoke of their country as Pársa,(2) and of himself as a Parsi (adam Parsa, *i.e.*, I am a Parsi or Persian).(3) Under this great King, both Parthia (Parthva)(4) and Persia proper (Parsa)(5) were included in the great Persian Empire.

King Darius also speaks of himself as an Arya of the Aryan race or an Iráni of the Iránis (Ariya Ariya chithra,(6) lit. an Arian, of descent from the Aryans). The ancient Medes were closely connected with the ancient Persians, and so we often hear " the Medes and the Persians " spoken of together. We find a form of this name Irán in Erin, the ancient name of Ireland. The word Ire in Ireland also points to the old word Arya.

The modern Persians speak of the country as Irán, a word derived from Avestaic Airyana,(7) Pahl. Airán, Pers. Irán. Just as the Hindus, the Indian A ryas, speak of India as A′ryávarta, the Pársis, the Persian Aryas, spoke of Persia as Airyana-vaéja (Iránvej),

---

(1) " Les nobles débris d'un des peuples les plus héroiques at les plus grands de l' antiquité," (Papiers d' Eugène Burnouf, conservés à la Bibliothèque Nationale. Catalogue dressé par M. Léon Feerr, p. 127).

(2) Behistan Inscriptions I, 1; III, 1. Inscriptions of Persepolis, Dr. H. C. Tolman's Guide to the Old Persian Inscriptions, pp. 54, 63 and 77. For various references *vide* Dr. Tolman's Cuneiform Supplement. Index Verborum, p. 34.

(3) Darius's Inscription on the ancient Suez Canal. *Ibid* Tolman, Text p. 75. Translation, p. 141. *Vide* " La Stèle de Chalouf " by M. Menant. *Vide* my Paper on " The Ancient History of the Suez Canal." (Journal B. B. R. A. Society, Vol. XXIV, pp. 163—84 ; *vide* my " Asiatic Papers," Part II, pp. 174—195).

(4) Tolman, *Ibid.* Text, Transliteration, p. 62.

(5) *Ibid.* Text, p. 54.

(6) Tolman, Inscription of Naksh-i Rustam. Transliterated Text, p. 79 l. 9. Translation, p. 146.

(7) Yt. XVIII, 5, Vend I, 3.

i.e., the seed (vaéja or vij) of the Arians.[1] So, the Indian Pársis speak of their co-religionists, who have recently come from Persia, as Iránis.

The Ancient Greeks spoke of the ancient country of the Pársis as Persis and of the people as Persoi. Herodotus also speaks of the people as Aryans. He says of the Medes that " these Medes were called anciently by all people Arians." [2]

In the Old Testament, it is known by a similar name. According to Mr. M'Curdy, Elam, which formed a part of the great Persian Empire, stood, in some parts, of the Old Testament (Isaiah XXI, 2, Ezekiel XXVII, 10, XXXVIII, 5) for Persia, into which it was incorporated.[3] " The kingdom (*i.e.*, the Persian Kingdom), as such, was founded by Cyrus, its inhabitants having been anciently called Elamites from their ancestor Elam, the son of Shem, and in later times Parthians. " [4] It seems that this name Elam is the same as Eran or Iran, its founder Elam being the same as Firdousi's Erach, whose name is connected with Iran.

The ancient Hindus spoke of them as Pársika. The Vishnu Purána [5] gives a detailed list of different people, and, in that list, among what it calls " ferocious and uncivilized races " includes Pársikás.[6] Wilson says that they are known both as Pársikás or Pártakas. " The first is not a common form in the Puránas, although it is in poetical writings, denoting, no doubt, the Persians or people of Pars or Fars : the latter also read as Páradas, may imply the same as beyond (pára) the Indus." [7] It may be noted in this connection that the Pahlavas or Pallavas or Pahnavas [8] (the Parthians) are spoken of separately in the Vishnu Purána. [9]

Wilson speaks of them as " a northern or north-western nation often mentioned in Hindu writings, in Manu, the Rámáyana, the Puránas, etc. They were not a Hindu people, and may have been some

---

(1) Vend. 1, 3.

(2) Bk. VII, 62. Rawlinson's Herodotus, Vol., IV, p. 61. *Vide* Rawlinson's Essay on the Medians. *Ibid* Vol. I, p. 40. Appendix III to Bk. I.

(3) Rev. Dr. Hastings' Dictionary of the Bible, p. 701. *Vide* the word Persia.

(4) Beeton's small Bible Dictionary. *Vide* the word Persia.

(5) Bk. III, Chap. II. The Vishnu Purana, a system of Hindu Mythology and Tradition, translated from the original Sanskrit by H. H. Wilson (1840). p. 194.

(6) *Ibid*, p. 194.

(7) *Ibid*, n. 149.

(8) *Ibid*, pp. 189, 195.

(9) According to Wilson, the form Pahnavas is more usual in the text. *Ibid* p. 195, n. 158.

of the tribes between India and Persia."[1] Kálidás, in his Raghuvança, also speaks of the ancient Pársis as Pársika.[2]

The ancient Pársis, the ancestors of the modern Pársis, and their country of ancient Persia are said to have been referred to even in the Rigveda. The Parsis (Parshawa) referred to in the Rigveda (I, 105-8) are supposed to be the ancient Persians or Pársis.[3] The country of Parsu (Parháva) referred to in the Rigveda (VIII, 6-46) is supposed to be a part of ancient Persia.[4] Here, a person boasts of having looted from a foreign tribe in the country of Parsu one hundred cattle.[5] In one place, even the Parthians, an offshoot of the ancient Persians, who ruled in Persia after Alexander, are supposed to have been mentioned with the ancient Persians or Parsis. Both of them are referred to as Purthu-Parshavo (Rigveda VII, 83-1). Vishtáspa, the patron-king of Zoroaster, is identified with the Ishtásva of the Rigveda.[6] Many well-known personages of ancient Persia referred to in the Avesta have been identified with personages mentioned in the Rigveda.[7]

Some Portuguese writers of India have spoken of them as Paricos.[8] Some speak of them as Esparcis. Garcia da Orta, a Portuguese

(1) *Ibid* p. 189, n. 61.

(2) The Raghuvança of Kálidás with the commentary of Mallinátha, edited by Káshináth Pándurang Paraba, 2nd ed. (1882), p. 89. Fourth Canto, couplet 60.

"......'Gainst the Persians next.
He through the desert marched as holy men
By Sacred Learning smite their inbred foes.
The senses."

The Raghuvança translated by P. De Lacy Johnstone (1902), p. 33. Canto IV, 11, 159-61). This particular portion of the Raghuvança is supposed to be an allusion to the Persian navy (Journal, Bengal Asiatic Society, Vol. IV, No. 6 of June 1908, p. 332).

(3) "Key to interpret the Veda" by Profs. Bhágvat and Apte.

(4) *Ibid.*

(5) This inroad upon the cattle-farms of the Persians reminds us of a statement by a Persian, in his Articles of Faith (Yaçna XII, 2), where he declares his determination to defend the cattle-farms from such inroads (Us géúsh stuyé táyáatchá hazanghatchá).

(6) Ervad Sheriarji Dadabhoy Bharucha, in his article entitled "The date of Zoroaster" in the K. R. Cama Memorial Volume, edited by me, p. 8.

(7) "Zarathushtra and his Contemporaries in the Rigveda," by Shapurji Kavasji Hodiwala, B.A. (1913).

(8) *Vide* the Anglo-Lusitano of 13th and 27th December 1902, and 3rd, 10th and 24th January 1903, wherein are published some Portuguese documents referring to the Pársis, received by me from Nárgol. For a translation of these documents *vide* "The Parsi" Vol. I, No. 7 of July 1905. For a translation of the second and third batches of these documents *vide* "The Zarthoshti" Vol. IV, Nos. I and II.

medical man, who had landed at Goa on 12th March 1534, and had visited a good part of India, speaks of the Pársis as Coaris or Esparcis.(1) Anthony Monserrate, a Portuguese Father, who was at the Court of Akbar (1580—1582), also speaks of the Pársis as Coaris.(2) This word Coaris is a corrupted form of Gauars or Guebres used by Muhammadans for Fire-worshippers. He also speaks of them as Jazenese (*i.e.*, Yazadis) from the town of Jaze (Yezd) in Persia, because later on the Pársis (now spoken of by the Pársis of India as Iránis) had come from Yezd. Even now, most of the Persian Zoroastrians that come to India come from Yezd and Kerman.

Old Muhammadan writers spoke of them as Gabrs or Gaurs in the sense of infidels, a term, which they applied, at times, generally to all who were not Muhammadans, including the Hindus, (3) but especially to the Pársis. This word " Gabr " is variously derived, but it is probably the same as Pers. *kur*, *i.e.*, blind, which word can be read *gaur* and which was changed into Gabr. They called them " blind " because they thought they were blind to the religion of Muhammad. (4) Some Muhammadan authors speak of them as Zardushtis ; (5) some as Majusis,(6) and others as Pársis.(7) From the fact that they held fire in reverence, they are spoken of by some Muhammadan writers as Atash-paraçtan (8) or Azar paraçtan (9)

(1) " Colloquies on the Simples and Drugs of India," by Garcia da Orta, translated by Sir Clements Markham (1913), p. 445.

(2) Mongolicae Legationis Commentarius (*Vide* Journal, Bengal Asiastic Society, New Series, Vol. VIII (1912), p. 186).

(3) For an application of the word to Hindus, *vide* Amir Khoshro's poem Ashkiyé (Elliot's History of India, III, p. 549).

(4) *Vide* my "Anthropological Papers " Part I, p. 137 ; Journal of the Anthropoligical Society of Bombay, Vol. V, No. 7, Paper on " An Avesta Amulet for contracting friendship."

(5) The Dabistan, Bombay edition of 1277 A.H., p. 266. The 10th Taalim, 2nd Nazar. Shea and Troyer's translation, Vol. III, p. 95.

(6) Farhang-i-Jehangiri. *Vide* the word Barsam. Quoted by Blochmann in the Journal of the Asiastic Society of Bengal, Vol. XXXVII, Part I, No. 1 (1868), p. 14.

(7) Farhang-i-Jehangiri. *Vide* the word Azar, Lucknow Lithographed edition of 1293 Hijri (1876 A.D.), p. 56. *Vide* Blochmann's translation in the above Journal.

(8) (*a*) Badáoni, in his Muntakhab-al-Tawárikh. Capt. Lees and Ahmad Ali's Calcutta Text, Vol. II (1865), p. 261 1·7. For Blochmann's translation of this passage, *vide* his translation of Abu Fazl's Ain-i-Akbari, Vol. I, p. 184. (*b*) The Dabistán (Bombay edition of A. H. 1277, p. 266). Shea and Troyer's translation, Vol. III, p. 95.

(9) Abu Fazl's Ain-i-Akbari. Blochmann's Text, Vol. I, p. 43, 18th *áin*. *Vide* Blochmann's translation, Vol. I, p. 48. Azar is an old form of Atash.

i.e., Fire-worshippers. Emperor Akbar, through his Prime Minister and historian, Abu Fazal, had justified their form of worship.[1]

Origin. The ancestors of the present Pársi Community of India came from Persia, with which India had relations from very early times. According to Ferishta, who has based his history on the works of various Muhammadan authors, these relations commenced in the time of the ancient kings of the Peshdádian dynasty. The Avesta, the Scriptures of the Pársis, refers to India as Hapta-Hindu.[2] Darius the Great had conquered a large part of northern India, and both the Parthian and Sassanian kings had relations with India. Thus, when the Sassanian Empire fell before the onslaught of the Arabs, and the ancestors of the modern Pársis came to India, they came to a country, not unknown to them, at least by name and fame.

The frequent wars of the Sassanian Persians with the Romans had so weakened both powers that they could not stand against the growing power of the Arabs, some of whom were at one time subject to Persia. Again, a number of weak monarchs had undermined the power of Persia. Though Yazdazard, the last of the Sassanian kings, was a comparatively strong and good ruler, he could not stand against the growing power of the Arabs, inflamed with vigour and energy by the teachings of the new religion of Muhammad. Yazdazard was defeated at the battles of Kadesia (A.D. 636) and Nehavend (A.D. 641). During his flight and stay at Khorasan, with a view to recoup, if possible, his military strength and to make a stand against the Arabs, he was murdered at the house of a miller, at the instigation of a disloyal general, Mahoui Souri. With his death (A.D. 651), the Zoroastrian Empire of Persia ended. A number of Iranians turned Muhammadan under pressure. Thousands fled to mountain retreats. Some of the fugitive bands went to the mountainous district (Kohistan) of Khorasan. This part of Persia being further east, and thus, to a certain extent, free from severe molestation, the fugitives lived there for nearly 100 years. It seems that some part of the country was still ruled over by Zoroastrian rulers, called the Sipahbuds, *i.e.*, commanders of soldiers.

The regions of Tabaristán, Gilán, Mazenderán and the adjoining country formed the above-named country of Kohistán. It was in 749 A.D., nearly 100 years after the overthrow and death of the last

(1) *Ibid.*

(2) *Vide* my Paper on "India in the Avesta of the Pársis" (Journal, Bengal Asiatic Society, New Series, Vol. IX, pp. 427—36).

Zoroastrian King Yazdazard, that Kohistán was successfully invaded by the Caliph. Ab-Alkhaçyb, who invaded Kohistan, was assisted as a guide by one Omar B. Ala'lla, who having lived for some time under the protection of one of the Zoroastrian Sipáhbuds of the district "was well acquainted with all the roads and mountain tracks." (1) On this invasion of Kohistan a large number of Zoroastrians turned Muhammadan.

According to ancient tradition, as recorded in a poem, the Kisseh-i-Sanján (2) (*i.e.*, the story or history of Sanján), written in Persian verse in 1600 A.D. by Dastur Bahman Kaikobad, the Pársis emigrated to India in about 766 A.D. The history of their emigration to India and of their dispersion in the different parts of the country, according to the Kisseh, is as follows (3) :— **Traditional History according to the Kisseh-i-Sanján.**

Zoroaster lived and promulgated his religion in the time of King Gushtásp. His religion thrice met with decline. The first occasion was at the time of Sikandar (Alexander) who burnt the sacred books. Thus 300 years after Zoroaster, the religion was destroyed. Ardeshir (Bábakán, the founder of the Sassanian dynasty) brought about a revival assisted by Ardái Viráf. There was again a decline, and King Shápur again brought about a revival. Dastur Adarbád Márespand had a hand in this revival. Then the third decline came in the time of Yazdazard, when a Jud-din (a king of another faith) occupied the throne of Persia. From that time, Irán was broken. Both the laymen and the Dasturs had to conceal themselves to observe their religion. Some retired to Kohistán (in Khorásán) for 100 years. Thence they had to retire to the city of Ormuz where they lived for 15 years.

The first Pársis who came to India after the Arab conquest, came from this Kohistán, to which on the final overthrow and death of Yazdazard in 651 A.D. their forefathers of two or three previous generations had fled, and where they remained for about 100 years (about 751 A.D.). To avoid religious persecution, they left the country and went to Ormuz, from whence they sailed to India. The date of this event, *viz.*, about 751 A.D., as determined from the Pársi poem. corresponds closely with the date (749 A.D.) of the Arab

(1) Prof. Rehatsek's article on "The Baw and Gaobarah Sepahbuds along the southern Caspian shores (Journal, B. B. R. A. Society, Vol. XII, pp. 410—45).

(2) For an English translation of this poem, *vide* Journal, B. B. R. A. Society, Vol. I, pp. 167—191. *Vide* Anquetil Du Perron's Zend Avesta, Tome I. Partie I. pp. 18—123. *Vide* for extracts, my Paper entitled "A few events in the early history of the Párseos with their dates." *Vide* the Kisseh-i-Sanján, edited by Mr. R. B. Paymaster for text and translation, *vide* Mr. M. R. Unwala's lithograped text of the Persian Rivayat, Vol. II, p. 344, *et. seq.*

(3) *Vide* my book, Dastur Bahman Kaikobad and the Kisseh-i-Sanján (1917) pp. 8-9.

invasion under Omar B. Ala'lla, arrived at by Prof. Rehatsek, on the authority of the Muhammadan historians of Tabaristán.

After staying at Ormuz for 15 years, they thought it advisable to withdraw from that place also and to sail to India, where they landed at Diu in Káthiáwár and remained for 19 years. Embarking again at that port, they were overtaken by a storm, when they prayed to God for safety, and declared, that if they landed in safety they would found a Fire-Temple. Their prayer was answered and they landed at Sanján, where ruled a king named Jádi-Rána. Their leader, a Dastur, went before the king and prayed for quarters. The subjects of the king were willing to receive them; but the king, seeing them armed, became alarmed. He sought information from them regarding their religion, manners and customs, and then gave them quarters on certain conditions.

The principal conditions on which the Pársis were allowed to land and found a colony, were, according to the Kisseh-i-Sanján, the following :—

1. To explain at first the principal customs of their religion.
2. To give up the language of their mother-land of Persia and to adopt in its stead that of the new country of India.
3. Their women to adopt the dress of Indian women.
4. To disband themselves, and not to use arms.
5. To perform the marriage ceremony in the evening (Shámgeh).

The Rája seems to have been afraid at first of the armed immigrants, and to have desired to take precautions before giving them an asylum in his country.

The Dastur re-assured the Rája, saying: "Do not be afraid of us. No harm will come through us to this country. We shall be the friends of the whole of India (Hamé Hindustánrá yár báshim). We will destroy your enemies." Then he thus explained the principal customs which they observed: They were worshippers of God (Yazdánparast), held the sun and moon in reverence, held fire, water and the cow in esteem, and looked with respect on all creatures of God. They wore, as a religious symbol, the *Kusti* (Sacred thread) with 72 threads. The women in their sickness remained secluded, not looking at the sun, the sky or the moon, and avoiding contact with fire and water, which are believed to contain in themselves the essence of light (*nur*). The period of sickness being over, they washed and were then free of pollution. Similar abstinence was observed for 40 days after child-birth.(1)

On receiving this account of the religious customs of the Pársis, which were not unlike those of the people of his own country, the Rája gave them quarters on his land. The Kisseh-i-Sanjan speaks thus of the founding of the new colony :

" A place in the desert was accepted. The ground was excellent and they made it the place of their abode. The place was acceptable to all persons. A city was created where there was formerly a desert. It was an uncultivated and unpopulated desert. All the young and the old landed there. When the Dastur saw the good place, he found it to be a suitable place for abode. The Dastur gave it the name of Sanján, and it was made prosperous like the country of Irán."

Five years afterwards they consecrated there their fire and founded a Fire-temple, the first of its kind to be founded by the immigrants. It appears that, when they founded the Fire-temple, they sent to Khorásán in Persia for the sacred articles (*álát*) required for the ceremonial consecration of the sacred fire. Thus, the Zoroastrians in Khorásán came to know that a band of their co-religionists had settled well in India. Thereupon, a number of other Zoroastrians whom we may call a second band of refugees or emigrants, came to India, perhaps with the very party who brought the sacred requisites to India.

For about 300 years most of them seem to have remained at Sanján, though a few dispersed in various directions, going to Vankaner, Broach, Variâv, Anklesar, Cambay and Naosári. In another 200 years the dispersion seems to have been complete. As the Kisseh says : " By that time, (only) some houses of Dasturs remained in the city of

(1) There exist certain Shlokas, sixteen in number, which are believed to have been composed by a learned Pársi Dastur, to explain the beliefs and customs of his people to the Rája and his Hindu courtiers. (*Vide* the Indian Antiquary of 5th June 1872, Vol. I, p. 214, for an English translation of these Shlokas, and Dastur Aspandyarji Kamdin's " Kadim tárikh Pario ni Kasar " for a Gujaráti translation. *Vide* Dr. Drummond's " Grammatical Parts of the Guzarattee, Mahrattee and English Languages (1808). *Vide* Mr. Shapurji Kavasji Hodiwalla's article entitled " The Seventeen Sanskrit Shlokas, recited before king Jádi Rána " in the Dastur Dr. Hoshang Jamasp Memorial Volume pp. 70 *et. seq.*)

It appears that since their very first arrival, the Pársis have been anxious to explain to their Hindu brethern of their adopted country, the tenets of their religion and their manners and customs. With this view in mind, the early Pársis not only composed the above Shlokas but also translated some of their books into Sanskrit. The Trustees of the Pársi Pancháyat have had the Texts of these translations and compositions, prepared at the hands of the late Ervad Sheriarji Dadabhoy Bharucha. The texts are to be published in seven parts, four of which were already published in the life time of the learned author. The other three parts will be published shortly All these are published under the title of " the Collected Sanskrit Writings of the Pársis "

Sanján." Among those that remained was a priest named Khushmast who lived there with his son Khujaste.(1)

About 1490 A.D. a catastrophe fell upon those who remained at Sanján. The King of Gujarát, Sultán Mahmud, (2) acting upon

(1) The Kisseh-i-Sanjan is silent as to what became of the other priests. But another Persian account, written in verse in 1765 A.D. by Dastur Shapurji Manockjee Sanjána (1735—1805) under the title of Kisseh-i-Zarthushtián-i-Hindustán, *i.e.*, the Story of the Zoroastrians of India, says that the priests also had dispersed with the laymen to different parts of Gujarát. In order to avoid differences in future, they amicably fixed territorial limits within which different priests were to carry on their sacerdotal work.

These territorial divisions which were five in number were and are still known as Panthaks. The five divisions are as follows :—

1. Sanjan from the river Dantur (Dantora) to the river Pár, which has given its name to Párdi (Pár-nadi) near Udwáda. The Mobeds or priests practising their profession within these limits were known as Sanjána Mobeds.

2. From the river Pár to the river of Bariáv. These priests were Naosárians, *i.e.*, Naosári Mobeds.

3. From Bariáv to Anklesar. Those priests are known as Godárians (now known as Godavrás).

4. From Anklesar to Khambáyat (Cambay). These were Broach Mobeds.

5. Khambáyat. These priests were known as Khambátás.

This division of Panthaks seems to have taken place in about 1290 A.D.

(2) As to who this Sultán Mahmud was, Pársi tradition says that it was Mahmud Begada, who reigned in Gujarát from 1459 to 1513 A.D. This tradition is recorded in the writings of Pársi Dasturs like Moola Feeroz (1808, in his manuscript History of the Pársis), Aspandiárji Kámdim (1826, Kadim tárikh, pp. 199-200) and Frámji Aspandiárji Rabádi (1831, Hádisha námeh, p. 122) and accepted by European scholars, like Anquetil Du Perron (1771, Zend Avesta Tome I, Partie I, p. 321, marginal note), Dr. Drummond (1808. The Grammatical Parts of the Guzerattee, Mahratta and English languages, *vide* the word Parsi), Dr. Wilson (1842, Journal, B. B. R. A. S., Vol. I, p. 182 n.) and Mr. Ramsay (1872 Indian Antiquary, Vol. I, p. 213). But, latterly, Sir James Campbell, the learned writer of the Bombay Gazetteer. doubted that it was Mahmud Begada. and thought that it was Aláudin Khilji. Campbell seems to have been misled by a faulty translation of the Kisseh-i-Sanján and by Elliot's translation of a few lines from Amir Khosru's Ashakiye. Elliot, while speaking of the "Conquest of Gujarát, Chitor, Málwa, Siwana" says : "The poet passes to the conquests of Aláu-d-din in Hindustán. Ulugh Khán sent against the Rai of Gujarát, "where the shores of the sea were filled to the brim with the blood of the Gabrs." (Elliot, Vol. III, p. 549). Sir J. Campbell, not having looked into the original Persian of Amir Khosru, was misled by the word 'gabrs,' and, though he knew that the word was, at times applied even to the Hindus, thought that it referred to the Pársis, and so identified the massacre of about 1,400 Pársis, referred to in the Kisseh-i-Sanjan, with this massacre referred to by Amir Khosru. But, when we refer to the original Persian, we at once see very clearly that it is the Hindus who are referred to here as the *gabrs*. The lines which follow those quoted by Elliot and which misled Campbell, say : "He (Aláu-d-din) spread destruction in Somnáth in such a way that the chariot of the idol temple was frightened, &c." Here, we find that it is a clear allusion to the conquest of the city where stood the holy temple of Somnáth, so often invaded by Mahomed Guznavi, and that the massacre of the Gabrs, here referred to, is the massacre of the Hindus of the holy city. Thus we see that, had Campbell had before him a few more lines from Amir Khoshru than those translated by Elliot, he would not have doubted the tradition which said that the Mahmud of the Kisseh-i-Sanján was Mahmud Begada. Again, Eastwick, whose translation of the Kisseh-i-Sanján he followed, misread and mistook a proper name (Chángá-sháh) for a common name, and so led him to some doubts.

some information about Sanján and its ruler (by this time, Chámpáner had passed into the hands of the Muhammadans) ordered his prime minister, Alafkhán, to conquer Sanjan. The Hindu king of Sanján, hearing of this, sent for the leaders of the Pársi colony, and, reminding them of the help they had received from the hands of his predecessors when they first landed at Sanján, asked their help to repel the invasion. The Pársis fought for their Rája, under the leadership of Ardeshir. At first, they, in company with the army of their Hindu king, succeeded in repelling the attack; but subsequently, when Alafkhán renewed his onslaught with a larger army, they were defeated, and Ardeshir was killed. The Hindu Prince (Ráe-zádah, Sháh Zádah) was also killed, and Sanjan fell into the hands of the Muhammadans. Most of the surviving Pársis fled with their Sacred Fire to the adjoining hill of Báhrut, where they remained for 12 years. They then came down with the Sacred Fire and settled at Bánsda or Wánsda, the Pársis of which place welcomed them. The Sacred Fire remained at Bánsda for 14 years.

At this time there lived at Naosári a religious minded and charitable Pársi Chánga bin Asa (Chángásháh). He was a leader of the Naosári Pársis and a great friend of the poor of his community. One year, he, with certain others, went to Bánsda to pray before the Sacred Fire on the Adargán festival. Some time after his return, he represented to his people at Naosári (which then seemed to have a larger Pársi population than that at Bánsda), that it would be better if the Iránsháh Fire were brought to Naosári. The Naosári people agreeing, he arranged with the Sanjan priests who attended on the Sacred Fire at Bánsda to bring it to Naosári. Three priests of Sanján with their families also went to Naosári with the Sacred Fire. They were Nágan Rám, Dastur Khorshed Kámdin (Qiamuddin) and Dastur Chayán (or Jánián) bin Sáhiar (or Sáyar).

From Naosári, owing to some quarrel between the local priests and the Sanjan priests in attendance on the fire, it was removed first to Bulsár and then to Udwára, where it is still burning.

The Kisseh-i-Sanján, which gives an account of the emigration and dispersion of Pársis in Gujarát, does not give the exact dates of the several events, but simply says that such an event happened so many years after such another event, and that event so many years after another. It begins with the downfall of the rule of Yazdazard, and then says that 100 years after the event, the ancestors of the Indian Pársis remained as fugitives in Khorásán, and then went to Ormuz, where they remained for 15 years, and then went to Diu in Káthiáwár in India, where they stayed for 19 years, and so on. There is thus scope for difference of opinion as to the exact date of the above events.

But in this history of the Pársis in India, there is one important event which is connected with an incident in the history of India, of which the date is fixed on the authority of several Muhammadan historians. Taking this as a starting point, we are in position to test and fix approximately the dates given by the Persian poem.

This incident in the history of India is the conquest of the fortress of Chámpáner in Gujarát by Mahmud Begada, the king of Gujarát (1459 to 1513). According to the Mirát-i-Sikandari, the Tabakát-i-Akbari, the Tárikh-i-Fireshta, etc., the date of this event of the conquest of the fort of Chámpáner was 1484. Now this important event in the history of India is referred to in the Kisseh-i-Sanján, as having occurred previous to the time when Sultán Mahmud captured Sanján and forced the Pársis to leave it.

Thus, relying on the authority on the date of this conquest of Chámpáner by Mahmud Begada of Gujarát, and weaving round this date the events mentioned in the Kisseh-i-Sanján, we arrive at approximate dates for the several events in the history of the community. These are shown in the following table. The dates of events other than those referred to in Kisseh-i-Sanján are given on the authority of other writings.

Events.	Date in A.D.
The fall of the Persian Empire on the death of Yazdazard	651
Arrival at Ormuz after a stay of 100 years in the mountainous district of Khorásán ..	751
Arrival at Diu after a stay of 15 years at Ormuz ..	766
Arrival at Sanján after a stay of 19 years at Diu ..	785
Foundation of the Fire-temple at Sanján ..	790
The Dispersion begins	1090
The Division of the Pársi centres into *panthaks* ..	1290
The conquest of Sanján by the Muhammadans and the consequent flight to the mountain of Báhrut.	1490
Arrival at Bánsda with the Sacred Fire	1502
Arrival at Naosári with the Sacred Fire	1516
Arrival at Bulsár with the Sacred Fire	1741
Arrival at Udwáda with the Sacred Fire	1742 [1]

(1) Anquetil Du Perron gives the date of arrival at Bulsár as 1744, and that the arrival at Udwáda as 1751.

The above account covers the origin and history of the community as a whole. The priests of the community trace their descent in India from one Neryosang Dhaval and his cousins. This Neryosang Dhaval seems to have lived in or about the 12th century A.D.

Having brought down the traditional history, on the authority of the Kisseh-i-Sanján, to the time of the removal of the Sacred Fire, named Irán Sháh, to Udwáda, let us follow the history of the Community to the time, when, after the acquisition of Bombay from the Portuguese by the British, they settled in large numbers in Bombay. Their growth in the principal Pársi centres referred to in the Kisseh will be described. It is not proposed in this article to refer to the Pársis in the Punjáb and Sind, who seem to be the descendants of some other bands that came to India at or about the time when the ancestors of the Gujarát Pársis came and settled at Sanján. All trace of these is now lost. They appear to have changed their religion and become absorbed in the population of northern India. Reference will be made to the above centres in the order in which they are named in the Kisseh, which order, let it be noted, is not chronological.

The first place mentioned in the Kisseh-i-Sanján as one of the towns to which the Pársis went from Sanján is Vánkáner. We know nothing of the Pársis who went there. It is possible that the writer referred not to Vánkáner in Káthiáwár but to a small place in the Surat District with a similar name.

Anklesar and Broach, both situated on the banks of the Narbudda, which are mentioned in the Kisseh-i-Sanján, seem by the middle of the thirteenth century to have largely increased in population. It seems that the Pársis of Broach built a brick Tower of Silence to meet the growing wants of their city in or before the thirteenth century. In 1309 they had built a second Tower. It is to these towers that Jordanus refers in 1322 in his Mirabilia.(1) In most of the Riváyats which contain the replies from the Zoroastrians of Persia to the religious questions sent to them by the Gujarát Pársis, Anklesar and Broach are mentioned with Khambáyet (Cambay), Surat and Naosári. These Riváyats begin in the year 1478 and continue for about three centuries.

Variáv near Surat is the next place mentioned in the Kisseh-i-Sanján as a town to which the Pársis went from Sanján and settled. But very little is known of the Pársis of that place. Tradition

(1) Mirabilia of Jordanus, p. 21, quoted by the Bombay Gazetteer.

says that they were massacred there in large numbers. It is said, that the local Rája demanded a large tribute, and, when they refused to pay, sent troops to enforce the payment which were driven off. One day, when the males were all engaged in a festivity, the Rája again attacked them and massacred the women and children without mercy. The day was, and to a certain extent, is still observed by some Pársis of Surat, who perform the usual religious ceremonies in honour of those who died at Variáv.*

Anklesar developed a flourishing Pársi population; and in 1517 a Tower of Silence and a Fire-temple were built there. In 1616, the Pársis of Swally (Sumari), then increasing in importance, and, later the scene of numerous naval encounters between European rivals for Indian trade, sent for priests from this town. Similarly in 1659, the Pársis of Tána near Surat sent for a priest.

A Muhammadan [(1)] writer who lived in Delhi about 1211 A.D. represents the Pársis as living at Cambay at the end of the eleventh Century and as having some influence with the Hindus there. The writer, whose work is spoken of as a "Romance in History" and as possessing "no real value in point of authenticity," [(2)] represents them as conspiring with the Hindus and being mischievous to the Muhammadans there. Lieutenant. H. Robinson represents them as being mischievous to the Hindus there.[(3)] Without discussing the truth of these statements, it may be assumed from these writers' remarks that between the 11th and 13th centuries the Pársis at Cambay had increased both in numbers and influence. A few families are still to be found there, but owing to the loss of their liquor business, live in poverty.

The Pársi centre demanding greater attention is Naosári, because, at the same time that it grew in population, it became the head-quarters of the Pársi priest-hood and the seat of some literary activity. By 1142 the Pársi population there must have greatly increased, because, in that year, they sent for a priest from Sanján. Kámdin Zarthosht was the first priest to go to Naosári.[(4)] The Pársi popula-

---

* *Vide The Parsi manuscript on the ritual of Bajs*, written about 160 years ago.

(1) Maulana N'uru-d-din Muhammad Ufi. His work is named, "Jawami'ul-Hikáyát wa Lawámi'ul-Riwayat (*i.e.*, Collections of Stories and Illustrations of Histories). *Vide* Elliot's History of India, Vol. II, pp. 162—64.

(2) Brigg's Ferishta, Vol. I, p. 212 n.

(3) "Historical Narrative of the City of Cambay" as given in the Selections from the records of the Bombay Government (No. XXVI, New Series) compiled by R. Hughes Thomas. *Vide* my "Few Events in the Early History of the Parsis, pp. 19—21 for some further particulars."

4) Khan Bahadur B. B. Patel's Pársi Prakásh, Vol. I, p. 2.

tion there having increased, a Pársi lady Málanbái, wife of Behrám, had built at her own expense, a Tower of Silence and a Fire temple for the performance of religious ceremonies.(1) The Pársis of Naosári still commemorate her name in their *Dhup-nirang* prayer. Her date is not known; but it would appear to be not later than the 14th or 15th century. The ruins of the brick Tower by this lady are still visible. In 1533, another tower of stone was built by Máneck, the son of Chánga Asa (Chángasha) referred to in the Kisseh-i-Sanján.

With the growth of the Pársi population, Naosári became the headquarters of the Pársi priest-hood and has so continued to the present day. The first Pársi priest who settled in Naosári in 1142 A.D. was Kámdin Jarthosht. Some 73 years later, *i.e.*, in 1215 A.D. his two sons Rana Kamdin and Mobed Kamdin sent for more priests from Sanján, from which it may be inferred that by that time the Pársi population must have considerably increased. It is said that, in response to this call, there went to Naosári from Sanján Hom Bahmanyár with his son Faredun and his family. On the death of Hom Bahmanyár and Faredun, the latter's three sons Asa, Máhiyár and Chánda carried on the sacerdotal work. It is from these three sons and from the two sons Rána and Mobad of the first comer, that all the present Pársi priests of Naosári, derive their descent. From Naosári, with its growing priestly population, the Pársis of other towns and villages sent for priests,—Bulsar in 1414 A.D. and Diu in 1590 A.D.

Having become the headquarters of the Pársi priesthood, Naosári developed a certain literary activity. Thus, the Persian Viráf-námeh known as Viráf-i-Kausi, was written in 1533 by one Kaus Faribourz from Persia at the instance of a son and grandson of Chánga Sháh. Then followed the work of Dastur Bahman Kaikobád who recorded in Persian verse in 1600 A.D. under the title of Kisseh-i-Sanján, the traditional account of the emigration of the Pársis from Persia to India and of their settlement in various parts of the country which has been quoted above. This account was admitted by the author to be based on older accounts.

By this time, the Pársis of Naosári and Surat seem to have attracted considerable attention from the other communities among whom they lived. Abu Fazl refers to the Pársis of Rander near Surat. Akbar, when he took Surat, being desirous to know something

---

(1) *Ibid* p. 7.

more about them, sent for Dastur Meherji Ràna from Naosári and had an interview with him at Kánkra Khári near Surat (1573). Later, when he held assemblies of the learned clergy of different faiths (1576–79), he sent for this Dastur to take part in the discussions. It was in recognition of his services, that Akbar gave the Dastur a grant of land at Naosári, and it was in appraciation of these services to their community that the Pársis of Naosári formally appointed Dastur Meherji Rana their Dastur or Head priest, and gave him ecclesiastical power over other priests. Thus, this Dastur founded at Naosári the Meherji Ràna family of Dasturs who still rule as Dasturs there.(1)

It was the same interest in Old Pársi subjects that seems to have led Akbar to send for a Pársi Dastur, Dastur Ardeshir, from Persia, to help his lexicographer with Iranian lore in compiling his Persian Dictionary—the Farhang-i-Jehangiri ; and it was the same interest that seems to have drawn him to Dastur Azar Kaiván, the author of the Mukáshefát-i-Azar Kaiván, a learned Pársi of sophistic doctrines and views, who had come from Persia, with a few disciples and subsequently died at Patna at the ripe old age of 85, in 1614 A.D.

When the Pársis settled in different towns and began to prosper, they developed a special interest in the origin of their religious customs and observances, and sent special messengers to Persia, where their co-religionists lived in large numbers in Yezd and Kerman to pursue inquiries further. Many such messengers went to Persia between 1478 and 1768 A.D., bearing interrogatories from Naosári, Surat, Broach and Anklesar. The replies are known as Riváyats and are appealed to for guidance in all religious controversies.

The city of Surat is not mentioned in the Kisseh-i-Sanján among those cities to which the Pársis went from Sanján to settle. It appears that the growth of Surat as a commercial town is of more recent times. Rander on the opposite banks of the Tápti has an older history than Surat. Surat had its own trade formerly ; but it was only with the advent of the European Powers in India, that it grew into importance. The Portuguese first came there in the beginning of the sixteenth century. The Pársis seem to have settled there in the fifteenth century. In the first Riváyat of Nariman Hoshang (1478), there is mention of Pársis at Surat. They had no Tower of Silence there until the sixteenth century. On occasions they carried the dead bodies to the Towers of Silence at Naosári and Broach. A Tower was built there by Nánábhoy Poojiájee who died in 1667 A.D. The Marátha depredations in the eighteenth century, when

(1) *Vide* my "The Pársis at the Court of Akbar and Dastur Meherji Rána"

Naosári had no sufficient protection against their inroads, drove many Pársis to settle in Surat. Even the Sacred Fire (Irán Sháh), which, as related above, was brought there from Wánsda, had to be removed once (1733 to 1736) from Naosári to Surat. The second and third Towers were built in 1725 and 1742 A.D. It is said that in the eighteenth century there were about 20,000 Parsi families at Surat.[1] Other Towers were built there in 1734, 1771, 1827 (for the Pársis living in the suburb of the Rustampura), 1828 (at Kánkra Khádi), 1883 (for the Bhagarsath Mobeds from Naosári). Surat has by this time two Fire-temples of the first grade (Atash Behrám) and twelve Fire-temples of the second grade (Atash Adarán). Before Bombay, Surat was the headquarters of the Pársis. Many Pársi families of Bombay trace their descent from Surat. With the increase in European factories, many families grew in wealth, power and influence. Some of these factories had Pársis as their brokers, and one of them seems to have had a hand in hastening the capture of Broach by the English.[2]

It seems that at the time when they began to disperse from Sanjan and to settle in the north in the various parts of Gujarát, and, even earlier, some of them began to go to the south. From the Pahlavi inscriptions[3] at the Kanheri caves in the Salsette, about 20 miles from Bombay, we find, that some Pársis who, from their names seem to be fresh arrivals from Persia, visited the caves first in 999 and then in 1021. Some time before 1322, Pársis seem to have settled at Thána about 15 miles from Bombay. Jordanus,[4] a French monk-traveller, who travelled from Thána to Broach in 1322, speaks of Pársis in the country through which he travelled. Odoric of Prodenone, an Italian monk-traveller refers to Pársis at Thána in 1323 A.D.[5] They seem to have been very numerous until about 1533 A.D. when the Portuguese conquered Salsette and with it Thána also. Tradition, as related by Mr. B. B. Patel,[6] says that the Portuguese, who are known to have been very intolerant in India in the matter

(1) I describe some of the above events on the authority of "The History of Surat" (in Gujaráti 1890), by Mr. Edalji Burjorji Patel.

(2) *Vide* my paper before the B. B. R. A. Society entitled, "A few Notes on Broach from an Antiquarian Point of View" (Journal B. B. R. A. Society Vol. XXII, pp. 229—323). *Vide* my Asiatic Papers, Part II, pp. 43-68).

(3) *Vide* the late Mr. K. R. Cama's Jarthoshti Abhyás, *i.e.*, Zoroastrian Studies Nos. 2, 3 and 4 for their decipherment and translation in Gujaráti.

(4) Jules Jordanus Mirablia, p. 21 quoted in the Bombay Gazetteer. (Vol. IX' Part II, Gujarat Parsis).

(5) "Cathay and the Way thither" by Yule, revised by Dr. H. Cordier (1913). Vol. II, p. 117.

(6) Pársi Prakásh I, p. 51 n.

of religion, attempted to convert them by force.[1] To avoid such a fate they invited the leading Portuguese officers to a feast and treated them to an orgy of strong drink, whereupon, taking their wives and children, they left Thána in a body, and settled at Kalyán, where a Pársi Tower of Silence is said to have been built in 1533 A.D. A number of Pársis still live at Kalyán which has a Fire-temple and more than one Tower of Silence. A Pársi of Bombay, visiting Kalyán about 50 years ago, distinguished a difference of tone and style in the Gujaráti which the Pársis of that town spoke. Later a large number of Pársis again settled in Thána. This was when Cowasji Rustomji Patel, the grandson of Dorabji Nanabhoy, the first Parsi settler and Patel of Bombay, was given by the British Government the Patelship of Thána and a number of other adjoining villages. This was in about 1774 A. D. when this part of Salsette came into the hands of the British, under a treaty with the Marátha Chief Raghunathráo Dádásáheb. At this time, Cowasji Patel and his brother Dorabji helped and encouraged the Pársis to settle at Thána, where they have now a Fire-temple and Towers of Silence. In 1775, the above-named Cowasji Patel was honoured by the Government with a Dress of Honour for the successful Patelship in Bombay.

The history of the Pársis in Bombay is a long one. A summary of the leading incidents from their first arrival up to the end of the eighteenth century will be found in Appendix A at the end of this volume.

Admission. The Pársis do not admit outsiders into their community. As a body they do not ordinarily intermarry with members of other communities. Formerly some Pársis had children by irregular marriages or by cohabitation with women of other communities. Such connections have always been disapproved ; but the children so born were up to a few years ago, under exceptional circumstances, admitted into the fold with the special permission of the Pársi Puncháyet, who registered Pársi marriages. Of late, since the work of registration has passed into the hands of the Registrar of Pársi Marriages, under the Pársi Marriage and Divorce Act (Act No. XV of 1865), the Pársi Puncháyet has ceased to exercise any control over such admissions, and cases have occurred wherein the children born of such irregular unions were indiscriminately admitted.

Recently, when the question of intermarriage with aliens or members of other communities was discussed, the community considered

(1) For Evidence of Portuguese intolerance *see* Kháfi Khán in Elliot's History of India, Vol. VII, pp. 344-345, "The Apostles of India" by Dr. J. N. Ogilvie. p. 437, and my "Few Events in the Early History of the Pársis, pp. 23—26.

the question of children born of irregular unions. The community, as a body, assembled at a public meeting at the Allbless Baug on 16th April 1905, to receive the Report of a Committee appointed for the purpose, resolved to disallow thereafter the admission of such children. The Resolutions passed at the meeting on both the subjects, *viz.*, (1) Marriage with women of other religions and the admission of them and all aliens into the fold and (2) the admission of the children of irregular unions, were as follows :—

The First Resolution.

" That this meeting of the Anjuman (Community) acknowledges the receipt of the report dated the 2nd of March 1905, of the Committee appointed by the Zoroastrian Anjuman (Community) on the 2nd of August 1903 for the purpose of inquiring into the matter of the question of admitting persons of other religions into the Zoroastrian religion, which (report) has been printed and published and has been distributed here, and resolves that looking to the present religious, social and other conditions of the Parsi Community, it is improper to admit people of other religions or Communities into the Parsi-Zoroastrian Community for the reason that this act is apt to break the originality and unity of the Community and is injurious to the Community."

The Second Resolution.

" This meeting of the Anjuman (Community) resolves as follows :—

(*a*) That people of other communities or religions claiming in any way to have been admitted into the Parsi-Zoroastrian Community have no manner of right whatever to enjoy the benefits of any of the Dharamnâ Funds (*i.e.*, religious or charity Funds) and places, such as Atash-Behráms, Adariáns or Daremehers (*i.e.*, Fire-temples), Dokhmás (Towers of Silence), Dharamshálás, etc., of the entire Parsi-Zoroastrian Community, at this place and at places up-country and to claim admittance to meetings of the Parsi-Zoroastrians or to take any part whatever therein.

(*b*) That this meeting disapproves the acts, on the part of Parsi priests of any class (? grade) whatever, of their performing the ceremony (of investiture) Sudreh-Kusti (*i.e.*, sacred-shirt and thread) or ceremony of any other kind whatsoever for admitting persons of other Communities or religions into the Parsi-Zoroastrian Community, and that it looks upon the behaviour of such priests with extreme displeasure ; and that this meeting humbly requests all the Mutavalis and Office-holders of the Dharamkhátás (*i.e.*, religious or charity Funds or institutions) and of the Dharamná Makáns (*i.e.*, religious or charitable places), such as Atash-Behráms, Adariáns, Daremehers (Fire-temples), Dokhmás (Towers of Silence), Dharamshálás, etc., of the Parsi-Zoroastrian Community, that they should condemn the acts of such priests and should show (their) extreme displeasure towards them by putting before the public their names and places of residence and that by virtue of their (own) powers they should not give permission to them (to these priests) to perform religious ceremonies of any sort whatever in the aforementioned places (of religion, etc.) under their control and that this meeting requests the Parsi-Zoroastrian Community that the Parsi-Zoroastrians should not get the religious ceremonies relating to their own families performed by such priests nor should the Parsi-Zoroastrians allow the religious ceremonies relating to their own families to be performed in these Dharamná Makáns (places of religion, such as Fire-temples, etc.) where the ceremonies of investing persons of other communities or religions with Sudreh-Kusti (*i.e.*, sacred shirt and thread) are allowed to be performed or where the priests performing such ceremonies are allowed to perform any other religious ceremonies whatever."

The Third Resolution.

"That this meeting resolves and declares that the first two resolutions which this meeting of the entire Anjuman (Community) of the Parsi-Zoroastrians has this day unanimously passed with regard to and in connection with people of other religions or communities, also equally apply to those children and in connection with those children that may be born after this day by (the loins of) Parsi-Zoroastrian fathers and of the wombs of mothers (females) of other religions or communities who claim marriage with them (with such Parsi fathers) or who may not have been married (with them) and that this meeting does not in any way recognise the alleged practice of admitting such children into the Parsi-Zoroastrian Community and of granting them the rights (and) privileges of the Community, holding that practice to be detrimental (? to the interests of the community) but (? and) this meeting further resolves that as a special exceptional case this resolution shall not apply to those of such children to whom the rights (and) privileges of (? enjoyed by) the Parsi-Zoroastrian Community have already been granted be fore this day."

Appearance. The Pársis are one of the fairest, and, especially the village Pársis, one of the most vigorous classes in Gujarát. In most Pársi faces the eyes are large, black, brown or occasionally grey, the nose is long, straight and sometimes hooked and the mouth and chin well cut. On the whole they are better looking and seem better fed than the bulk of their Hindu and Musalmán neighbours. But there is a general complaint that the young men and women, especially in towns, are less robust than their fathers and mothers.(1)

Dress and ornaments.

Neither men nor women ever leave off either the sacred shirt called *sadra* or the girdle called *kusti*. The men always cover the head with a skull cap and the women with a white head cloth called *Máthábána*. Among the men the village Pársi generally shaves the whole head, wears a short white cotton coat reaching to the thighs, loose cotton trousers and native shoes or sandals. At home he lays aside his short coat, and wears a skullcap of coloured cotton or silk. On great occasions he puts on a folded turban in shape like a Surat Vániá's head dress and a long white cotton coat. Town Pársis wear in-doors a skullcap, a waistcoat, fine cotton trousers and slippers without stockings. Out of doors they put on a well-folded turban or a cap-like turban which is known as a *fenta*. They once wholly or partly shaved the head, the old and poorer keeping a topknot and two ear-locks, but now it is more usual to keep the hair. Of face hair they keep whiskers and mustaches or more commonly the latter only, but shave the beard. The old and those who dislike change, both among the rich and the poor, generally wear a white long cloth coat, and sometimes a broad cloth or other woollen coat made in native fashion, and native shaped long cloth trousers. They use light well-made native or English boots. The poor use their heavy native shoes without stockings. Most of the younger men wear coats of cotton, silk or wool cut in European style, use silk or woollen trousers of European make, and stockings and boots of English pattern. The hair is worn short in English fashion. Most have mustaches, but almost all shave the chin. The priests may at once be known from other Pársis by being dressed wholly in white, including the head dress, by wearing a full beard and by not shaving the head.

All orthodox Pársi women wind a white piece of muslin round the head and gather their hair in a Grecian knot at the back of the head. Over the sacred shirt and cord village women wear a tight-fitting sleeveless bodice. The trousers are generally of coloured

(1) *Vide* Bombay Gazetteer, Vol. IX, Part II, Gujarát Population, p. 101. There have been many changes in costume and habits since the date of Campbell's work.

cotton. Over all they wind a silk robe or *sári* round the body and out of doors over the right temple like the higher class Hindu women of Gujarát. On great occasions village women wear trousers of silk instead of cotton and silk robes. Slippers are worn out of doors and occasionally in the house. On high days their ornaments are a gold necklace, gold or silver bracelets, and gold earrings, but except that widows change them for gold or silver their only every-day ornaments are glass bangles *chitals*. The dress of women in cities and large towns does not differ from that of village women. They wear the *sári* hanging in loose folds so as to hide the trousers. Middle class and rich town women always wear silk robes and silk trousers, and in many cases use a sleeved *polka* instead of the bodice. They also wear slippers with stockings in-doors as well as out of doors, and in most cases English shoes. Their ornaments are costly, of diamonds and pearls as well as of gold. Diamond and pearl earrings have almost taken the place of gold earrings, and in very wealthy families pearl necklaces and pearl and diamond studded bangles are also worn.

Language. The home tongue of the Pársis is Gujaráti.

Names. As to the personal names of males they have been mostly taken from the following sources :—

(*a*) The names of the Zoroastrian Yazatas or angels. For example, Hormazji, Bahmanji, Aspandyárji, (Aspandád), A'durji, Khorshedji, Meherji, Behrámji, Dinshawji, Homji.

(*b*) The Iránian names of the Epic of the Shahnameh. For example, Rustamji, Frámji or Frámroz, Sorábji, Burjorji, Tehmulji or Tehmuras or Tehmurasp, Jehángirji, Jehánbux, Narimán, Hoshang, Jamshed, Siávax, Kaikhosru, Kávasji, Nádir (Naodar), Minocher, Erach, Faredun, Kersáspji, Gustáspji or Gustadji, Ardeshir, Shahpur, Sheryár, Hijiárji (Yazadyar), Noshirwánji, Kaikobád, Bejanji, Pestanji (Peshotan), Dárábji Edulji (Adal), Zál, Pahlunji. The last syllable '*ji*' is an honorific which is omitted at times.

(*c*) Some time after their emigration to India the Pársis had some Hindu names as their personal names. In old documents we find several names of this kind, which sound very uncouth now. Most of them have become obsolete. But few have still remained. For example, Ruttanji, Jivanji, Kunverji.

In the case of the personal names of females, they are taken mostly from a few sources :—

(*a*) Some come, as in the case of males, from the Pársi Yazatas or Angels. For example, Bahmanbai, Avanbai, Khorshedbai, Meherbai, Dinbai.

(*b*) Some are taken from the Iranian names of women as given in the epic of Firdousi. For example, Shirinbai, Navazbai, (Arnaváz), Gulbai, Tehmina, Homai.

(*c*) Some come from precious metals and jewels of which ladies are generally fond for ornaments. For example, Soonabái (Gold), Jarbai (Zar, *i.e.*, wealth or gold) Rupábai (Silver), Mánockbai (Ruby), Motibai (Pearl), Hirábai (Diamond) Ratanbai (jewel).

(*d*) Some names come from sweets. For example, Mithibai, Shirinbai, Shakarbai.

(*e*) Some Hindu names have still remained with them as in the case of males. For example, Kuverbai, Dhunbai. Some names of class '(c)' are Hindu names and may be said to belong to this class.

There are no sub-divisions among the Pársis corresponding to sub-castes in other communities. But, since about A.D. 1736, they have been divided into two sects, the Sháhánsháhi and the Kadmi. The ancient Persians observed an intercalation of one month at the end of every 120 years. The ancestors of the original emigrants, who came to India and who seem to have wandered in Persia for some time in the mountainous regions of Khorasan after the downfall of the Sassanian Empire, seem to have held one such intercalation, but the ancestors of the Zoroastrians who remained in Persia, did not hold any. Hence, there arose the difference of one month between the calendar of the Indian Pársis and that of the Persian or the Iráni Pársis. Two Iránian Zoroastrians, Jamasp, who came to India in 1721, and Jamshed who came in 1736, drew the attention of the Indian Pársis to this difference. It is said that one day, Jamasp, while passing through Pársi streets, saw the Pársis closing their shops and places of business earlier than every day. He inquired the reason for the closure and was told that they were that day celebrating the Maidyárem Gáhambár festival for the month of Deh. On hearing this, he was surprised, as, according to his Persian calendar, the month was not the Deh month but the next Aspandád month. On his representation some of the Pársis of Surat, which was then the headquarters of the

Divisions

community, began, under the leadership of Dastur Darab Koomana to observe the Persian Calendar [1] Thus differences arose, and the community was divided into two sects or divisions, the majority holding to the old calendar of the Indian Pársis. Those who stuck to the old calendar made themselves known as Sháhánsháhi, *i.e.*, following the procedure of the Persian Emperors or Kings of Kings. The others called themselves Kadmi (kadimi), *i.e.*, following the old (Kadim) procedure as observed in Persia. In the heat of the preliminary differences when the first schism took place, each sect called the other by a nick-name. The Sháhánsháhis called the Kadmis 'Churigars', *i.e.*, bangle-makers, from the fact, that, among the first few who joined the new movement in Surat, there were several who prepared bangles (Churis). [2] The Kadmis, in turn, called the Sháhánsháhis by the nickname of Rasmis, *i.e.*, followers of a custom (Rasam). In the first heat of the dispute, both the sects stopped intermarriage; but now there are no restrictions of any kind. They observe some difference in the introductory and some other Pazend portions of the prayers and in the ritual. In Bombay and Surat, both sects have their own Fire-temples, Towers of Silence and clergy.

Marriage. Section 3 of the Pársi Marriage and Divorce Act (Act No. XV of 1865 passed on the 7th April 1865), provides for the limits within which marriage is permitted. It says:—

"No marriage contracted after the commencement of this Act shall be valid, if the contracting parties are related to each other in any of the degrees of consanguinity or affinity prohibited among Pársis and set forth in a table which the Governor-General of India in Council shall, after due inquiry, publish in the *Gazette of India*,[3] and unless such marriage shall be solemnized according to the Pársi form of ceremony called "Asirvád" by a Pársi priest in the presence of two witnesses independently of such officiating priest; and unless, in the case of any Pársi who shall not have completed the age of twenty-one years, the consent of his or her father or guardian shall have been previously given to such marriage."

(1) *Vide* my Paper on "Anquetal Du Perron of Paris and Dastur Darab of Surat" in the Journal of the B.B.R.A. Society, Vol. XXIV, pp. 395-396; *vide* also my "Anquetal Du Perron and Dastur Darab," pp. 80-81.

(2) In an old Gujaráti document which lately came to my hand, wherein the first Kadmis bind themselves to be united and to support the first Kadmi Fire-temple, many signatories place before their names the abbreviated word (chu) to signify that they were *churigars* by profession (*vide* the *Jam-i-Jamshed* of 11th June 1919 for the text of the document).

(3) Details of this table are given in Appendix B at the end of this volume.

Up to a few years, there were certain restrictions in the matter of intermarriage, based upon a supposed social or rather professional status. The Athornáns (A'thravans) or the Mobeds, *i.e.*, the priestly class claimed to be endogamous. From times immemorial the ancient Iránians, the ancestors of the modern Pársis, were divided into four classes, based on their profession or occupation. According to the Avesta,(1) the people were at first divided into the following three classes :—

1. A'thravan, *i.e.*, the priests, whose class corresponded to that of the Bráhmans among the Hindus.

2. Rathaéshtár,(2) *i.e.*, the warriors or soldiers, whose class corresponded to that of the Kshatriyas of the Hindus.

3. Váctriya (Váctriya fshuyant) *i.e.*, the Agriculturists, whose class seems to correspond to that of the Hindu Vaishyas.

4. Latterly, as civilization grew, a fourth class—the Huiti. (Pahl. Hutokhsh)—was added. It included the arizans or traders. It may correspond, to some extent, to the Sudras of the Hindus.(3)

According to Firdousi,(4) it was King Jamshed (the Yima Khshaeta of the Avesta, the Yama of the Vedas), who first made this division. Firdousi names the division as follows :—

1. Amuzián	2. Nisáriyan
3. Nasoudi	4. Ahnukhushi

Some manuscripts of the Sháh-námeh, restoring these names to the old Avestaic nomenclature, give them as follows :—

Asurnán	Ratheshtáryán
Vástavars	Ahstukhshi

Ardeshir (Artaxerxes) Bábegán, the founder of the Sassanian dynasty and principal supporter of the Iránian Renaissance, is reported to have made a similar division, with a slight variation in the order of precedence in the case of the last two divisions. His division was as follows :—

1. Achāb-i-Din, *i.e.*, the priests.

2. Mukátel (mardán-i-Kárzár, *i.e.*, the Army).

3. Kuttáb, *i.e.*, the writers. This class included clerks, medical men, literary men, and scientific men.

4. Muhana, *i.e.*, men of the ordinary class of work.

(1) Gah IV, 7 ; Vend. XIII, 45-46, Visparad III, 2.
(2) *Lit.* those who fought standing in *rathas* or chariots.
(3) Yacna XIX, 17, Dibácheh-i-A'fringán.
(4) Le Livre des Rois (Sháh námeh) by M. Mohl., Vol. I., small ed., pp. 34-35. *Vide* the Gujaráti transliteration of the Text in the Shahnámeh of the Kutar brothers, Vol. I, p. 30. *Vide* my translation of the Sháh-Námeh, pp. 25-26.

This class included merchants, agriculturists, workmen, etc.[1]

Ardeshir is said to have made these professions well-nigh heredi tary. Members of one profession or class could not join or pass into another without the sanction of the Government.

From all these three sources,—*viz.*, (*a*) the Avesta, (*b*) the Sháhnámeh and (*c*) the letter of Taosar, the minister of Ardeshir Bábegán —we learn that the priestly class was placed at the top.

In two Silhára grants[2] of the 10th, and 11th, centuries the priestly class of the Pársis is referred to as "*trivagarg*", *i.e.*, of three classes. Dr. Buhler,[3] translates the word as "three castes" and adds the "twice born" in brackets after the word "three"

In the Avesta,[4] the Athrávans—the priestly class corresponding to the Bráhmans—are called *Thráyavan*, *i.e.*, of the three orders. These three orders are said to be those of the three grades of the priests, the Dasturs, the Mobeds and the Herbads. The above grants speak of them as "the holy men". The word *Thráyavan* of the Avesta corresponds to the "*trivagarg*" of the Silhára copper plate grants.

Whatever the precise signification of the word "*trivagarg*" may be, it seems pretty clear, that the priestly class of the Pársis was held to be superior and, as it were, "twice born" like the Bráhmans.

Now, imbued with the idea of preserving this supremacy, the priestly class at one time allowed no free intermarriage with the laymen (Bedhins) who formed the other classes. At times, and that even very rarely, they took the girls of the laymen class in marriage, but never gave the girls of their class to the laymen. This practice at one time led to several internal disputes among the community. About 1727 the Pársi priests of Surat regularly resolved among themselves that they might take in marriage the daughters of laymen, but not give theirs in return.[5] When they sought to put this resolution into force in Bombay, it was resented by the laity, who, at a public meeting convened by the Puncháyat in 1777, resolved that there should be no intermarriages between the clergy and the laity.[6] The priests did not accept this resolution.

(1) The letter of Dastur Tansar or Taosar to the King of Tabaristan (Journal Asiatique, Neuvième Serie, Tome III (1894). p. 214).

(2) *Vide* my article on the subject in the Indian Antiquary. *Vide* J. B. B. R. A. S., Vol. XXI, pp. 4-18.

(3) Indian Antiquary, Vol. V, p. 276.

(4) Athravanái thráyaone (Yt. Khordád, 9; Yt. Behérám, 46; Yt. Abán 86).

(5) Pársi Prakásh by B. B. Patel, Vol. I, p. 56 n. 2.

(6) *Ibid.* The Kholáseh-i-Puncháyat, published by the first Sir Jamsetjee, pp. 43-44.

In 1785, a breach of this resolution occurred, and, at a public meeting of the community convened by the Puncháyat, the offending parties were excommunicated. The point in dispute being represented to Mr. R. H. Bodham, the then Governor of Bombay, he appointed a committee of three European members to inquire into the matter and report. The committee decided, that it was not fair for the priests to take in marriage the daughters of the laymen, and to refuse to give theirs in return.(1) Now-a-days, though the members of the priestly class generally prefer to give their daughters in marriage to the sons of the priestly class only, the former strict prohibition is obsolete, and there are a number of cases of intermarriages.

Looking to the religious books and ancient tradition we find that intermarriages with aliens, *i.e.*, those who followed a religion other than Zoroastrian, were disliked. The Vendidad (XVIII, 62) speaks of prohibition of marriage between the righteous (*dahma*) and the unrighteous (*a-dahma*), between the Mazda-worshipper (*a-daeva-yacna*) and the Dáeva-worshippers (*daeva-yacna*), between the unsinful (*a-tanuperetha*) and the sinful (*tanu-peretha*). This prohibition is generally taken to cover intermarriages with aliens or non-Zoroastrians. History presents some examples of Persian kings marrying princesses of other creeds. But, as a rule, such marriages were disliked. The Dinkard says: "Men who are bound by the precepts of the religion ought, with the object of avoiding sin and strife, to tie the knot of marriage with such believers in the religion, as that strength might accrue to them and to the people of their race for deliverance from hell by means of prayers and devotions to God. The prosperity of the progeny of men is (secured) by marriages entered into with this object of receiving mutual assistance. Khetiodath (*i.e.*, relationship by marriage) is then said to be formed when it is formed within one's own race".(2)

As said above, there were occasional cases of Persians marrying non-Persian women of other religions. But they were very rare and occurred among kings and nobles. According to Herodotus,(3) we have the case of a Persian nobleman Bubares, marrying Gygæa, a Macedonian princess, daughter of the Macedonian King Amyntas. According to Firdousi, we have the instances of King Noshirván (Chosroes I)

---

(1) The decision of this Committee seems strangely inconsistent with caste practice prevailing in many parts of India, particularly in the Punjáb, where many castes take daughters from other castes but will not marry their sons to members of such castes. R. E. E.

(2) Dastur Peshton's Dinkard, Vol. II, p. 91, Bk. III, 80.

(3) Herodotus, Bk. V, 21.

and Khusru Párviz (Chosroes II) marrying Christian princesses. According to the Old Testament, we have the instance of King Ahasuerus marrying a Jewish princess. But these cases were few and far between, and the results of such marriages were, from the Persian or Pársi point of view, disastrous to the country.

As to the marriage of a Persian woman marrying a non-Persian, there has been only one solitary instance recorded by Herodotus, *viz.*, that of Metiochus, the son of the Greek Miltiades, marrying a Persian woman.(1) When Noshirwan the Just (Chosroes I) made peace with the Arabs of the country of Yemen, Arabia Felix, which he had invaded, in the treaty of peace there was a special condition that no Arab was ever to marry a Persian woman, though Persian soldiers might marry Arab women. Thus, when for some special reason as, for example, the long stay of an army in a foreign country, intermarriages were permitted, they took the form of marriages between Persian men and non-Persian women, but Persian women were not allowed to wed non-Persian men. These prohibitions and restrictions derived from the country of their ancestors, the Pársis of India have generally observed, and as a rule, they have avoided intermarriage with non-Pársis, though there have been rare instances of civil marriage here and there. During the last decade or two, meeting in general assemblies, they have more than once affirmed their determination to follow their ancestral custom.(2) The Parsi marriage Act has embodied that determination in legal form.

Pársis have adult marriages at present. No sexual license before marriage is recognized or tolerated. It appears from their marriage service that adult marriage was the rule in old times. The very fact that the officiating senior priest asked, during the marriage service, questions to the marrying couple, whether they chose to enter into marriage till the end of their life with good faith, shows that the marriage was celebrated between adults.(3)

But latterly the community in passing through various vicissitudes of fortunes in India under different Hindu and Muhammadan rulers, had departed from the old custom of adult marriages and allowed

(1) Bk. VI, 41.

(2) The dislike of the Pársis of intermarriage with aliens seems to be of the same kind as that of the ancient Jews of Jerusalem, referred to in the book of Ezra (VII) in the Old Testament and in the Antiquities of Josephus, Bk. XI, Chap. V. (*Vide* my King Solomon's Temple and the Ancient Persians (1908), pp. 54-55. *Vide* my "Glimpse into the Work of the B. B. R. A. Asiatic Society, &c.," pp. 76—79).

(3) For an account of the marriage customs of the Pársis, *vide* my paper in the Journal of the Anthropological Society of Bombay, Vol. V, No. 4, pp. 242—82.

infant marriages. These were common up to about 40 to 50 years ago. But, now, with very rare exceptions, infant marriages are unknown. The few cases of infant marriages that do occur take place in some remote towns.

Polyandry was never known among Pársis in their long history, whether in Iran or India, their mother or adopted country.

Polygamy, in the sense of marrying several wives in the ordinary course, was and is never permitted. But up to about 50 years ago, a man was permitted to take another wife in the life-time of his first wife in exceptional cases, such as continued illness, barrenness, faithlessness or bad conduct, etc., of the wife. In such cases it was necessary to ask the permission of the Pancháyat or the elders of the community, who made inquiries and gave the necessary permission in case of necessity. There have been cases, wherein, the first wife, finding herself incapable of bearing children to her husband, has of her own accord desired the husband to marry a second wife, with whom she lived very peacefully. The elder wife generally managed the household. The Pársi Marriage Act of 1856, given to the community by the British Government at the well-nigh unanimous desire of the community, has now put an end to the practice altogether. But in some of the Native States, where Pársis are not strictly governed by British laws, there still occur occasionally cases of persons having a second wife with the consent of the first wife or on the dissolution of the marriage obtained with the consent of the first wife.

The form of marriage is known as the Ashirvád (lit. blessing) ceremony, which is performed by two priests.

Marriage is taken to be an institution finding favour with God (Ahura Mazda), who prefers a married man to an unmarried man, and one with a family and children to one without them (Vendidád IV, 47). A place where a married man lives feels, as it were, happy (*Ibid* III, 2). **Marriage ceremony.**

After the several vicissitudes of fortune which the community has gone through, it is not possible to say with certainty which of their marriage customs are originally Iránian or Zoroastrian and which Indian or alien. But the strictly solemn or religious part, wherein the priests participate, is Iránian, and is the essential or binding portion. The marriage is celebrated in the presence of an assembly which consists of at least five persons, two of whom are the officiating priests and two witnesses.

The marriage ceremony consists of the following parts :—

I. The Preliminary Ritual.

II. The Ashirvád (the marriage ceremony proper).

I. The Preliminary Ritual consists of the following ceremonies :—

(*a*) The *A'dá antar* or the curtain ceremony, wherein the couple are at first separated by a curtain and made to sit opposite each other.

(*b*) The tying by the senior officiating priest of a marriage knot, wherein the couple are enclosed in a circle by a piece of cloth, the ends of which are tied during the recital of the sacred formula of *Ahunavar*.

(*c*) The Hand-fastening (*Háthevâro*), wherein the priest places the right hand of one in the right hand of the other, and then fastens the hands with raw twist during the recital of the above sacred formula.

(*d*) The encircling of the couple with raw twist passed round them seven times during seven recitals of the above formula.

(*e*) The throwing of the rice, wherein, the couple, who are provided with a few grains of rice in their left hands, at a certain signal given by burning frankincense on fire presented before them in a vase, throw rice upon one another. The one who throws first indicates thereby that he or she will be the foremost in loving and respecting the other.

This preliminary part of the ceremony, not being the solemn and religious part, is now dispensed with by many.

II. The *Ashirvád* recital is the ceremony proper, being the essential or binding part of the marriage ceremony. It consists of the following :—

(*a*) A preliminary blessing, wherein the senior priest blesses the couple, wishing them a healthy and prosperous long life of 150 years and a healthy progeny of sons and grandsons.

(*b*) The asking of consent, wherein the senior priest takes the consent of the couple and their respective witnesses to the marriage.[(1)] This consent is asked thrice.

(1) For a brief account of the marriage ceremony, *vide* my paper on the "Marriage Customs of the Parsees," Journal of the Anthropological Society of Bombay, Vol. V, No. 4, pp. 242—82.

(*c*) A joint address by both the officiating priests, wherein they admonish the marrying couple and say prayers and benedictions. They throw rice over the couple while giving these admonitions and reciting these prayers and benedictions.

Widow re-marriage.

The re-marriage of widows is permitted. The widow may marry, if she likes, her husband's younger or elder brother,[1] but there is no compulsion. As to the limits within which she may marry, there are no particular special limits other than those for a woman marrying for the first time.

The form of marriage and the essential binding portion are the same as in the case of the first marriage. But the affair is a quiet one. The few points of difference are the following :—

(*a*) In the case of first marriages, the ceremony was, at one time, performed twice, once in the evening and again at midnight. But in the case of a re-marriage, it was performed only once, and that even rather quietly at some odd hour between the early part of the night and midnight.

(*b*) In first marriages, rice was thrown by the priests with the palm of the hand lower down, but in the second marriage, with the palm of the hand open above.

(*c*) A change of few words in the preliminary blessing, to say that the lady is not a virgin and that the marriage is a second marriage.

It may be observed that now-a-days the first two differences are not generally observed.

Divorce.

According to the Pársi Marriage Act divorce or dissolution of marriage was permitted in the following cases :—

1. Lunacy or mental unsoundness, at time of marriage, of which one of the contracting parties did not know.

2. Impotence.

3. Continued absence for seven years of either party, without being heard of as alive.

4. Adultery of the wife.

5. Adultery or bigamy with adultery, or adultery with cruelty or adultery with wilful desertion for two years or upwards, or rape or unnatural offence on the part of the husband.

---

(1) It appears from Firdousi's Sháhnámeh that marriage with a brother of the deceased husband was permitted even in old Iran. King Kai Khusro's mother Firangiz married Fariburz, who was a younger brother of her deceased husband Siávakhsh.

Formerly divorce was permitted by the elders for some other reasons besides the above, such as a continued quarrelsome disposition, and when the wife bore no child or was a hopeless invalid.

It appears from old Pahlavi books that in Iran also there was a regular procedure for divorce. In the case of a wife misbehaving, she was sent back to her parents, who had, if aggrieved, the option of sueing the husband before judges who tried the case assisted by some members of the community. It appears that there was some set form of speech whereby the husband declared his intentions to divorce his wife.(1)

It appears from an allusion in Herodotus that barrenness of the wife was held from very ancient times to be a justifiable cause of divorce or for taking a second wife.(2)

The form by which the divorce was formerly effected in India was a written document known as *fárgati* meaning a release (from Persian *fárag* free).

Wives who have been divorced may marry again.

Inheritance. The Pársis follow their own laws of inheritance. The present Pársi Intestate succession Act, No. XXI, of 1865, was framed on their own communal customs. The history of the movement which led to the passing of this Act is interesting and instructive, as it shows how the community tried to rise and to evolve order and a condition of approximate certainty out of old customs which varied at different times and places.(3)

Religion. The Pársis follow the religion of Zoroaster, who was born in the region of Azarbaizán in Persia, and who first promulgated his religion in Balkh or Bactria. Opinions vary as to the time when he flourished, Classical authors(4) refer to him and give as his date, years varying from 7,000 B.C. to 525 B.C. Pársi(5) books well-nigh unanimously give his age as about three centuries before Alexander the Great, *i.e.*, about 700 B.C.

---

(1) Dinkard Book III, Chap. 80 of Dustur Peshotan, Dastur Peshotan's Dinkard, Vol. II, p. 98. S. B. E., Volume XVIII, p. 407.

(2) Herodotus Book, IX, p. 111.

(3) Khán Bahádur Bomanji Behrámji Patel gives a short history of the movement in the Pársi Prakásh, Vol. I, pp. 677—89.

(4) Hermippos, Eudoxus of Cnidus, Aristotle, Pliny, Plutarch, Plato, Diogenes Laertius, Xanthus of Lydia, Lactantius, Suidas, Georgius Syncellus, Ctesias, Diodorus Siculus, Cephalion, Justin, Eusebius, Arnobius, Theon, Paulus Orosius, Aristoxanus, Porphyrius, Agathias. *Vide* Jackson's Zoroaster and Dastur D. P. Sanjana's Zarathushtra in the Gáthas and in the Classics.

(5) Bundehesh, Chap. XXXIV, 7-8; Viráfnámeh, Chap. I, 2-3, Zádsparam XXIII, 9-12 S. B. E., Vol. 47, pp. 165-6.

Ancient Muhammadan authors(1) closely support the Pahlavi authors.

Present European scholars, though not unanimous generally, accept the date given by the Pahlavi works. But, strange to say, the Pársis themselves are disposed to lay aside the testimony of their own books and to accept that of Classical authors.

Their religion is monotheistic, *i.e.*, a belief in one omnipotent, omniscient, omnipresent God Ahura Mazda, whose existence is manifested by the grand and sublime objects of Nature. The harmony, order, law, system, observed in Nature leads the mind from Nature to Nature's God. He is the Creator as well as the preserver of this great universe. He is the ruler of the Physical world as well as the Spiritual world. He is the most Spiritual among the Spiritual ones. His distinguished attributes are Good Mind, Righteousness, Desirable Control, Piety, Perfection and Immortality. He is the Beneficient Spirit from whom emanates all good, all piety. In His moral rule, virtue has its own reward and vice its own punishment. He not only rewards the good but punishes the wicked. All that is created is His work.

The Philosophy of Zoroastrianism supposes "two primeval causes,—the Spenta Mainyu or the Increasing Spirit and Angra Mainyu or the Decreasing Spirit,—which, though different, were united, and produced the world of material things, as well as that of the spirit."(2) The world is the work of these two hostile principles—the Good and the Evil Spirit—both serving under Ahura Mazda. "The history of the world is the history of their conflict...... Man is active in the conflict."(3) In the end, the Evil spirit will be destroyed, and all happiness will prevail in the world. It is incumbent upon man to do actions that would support the cause of the Good principle and destroy that of the Evil Principle.

The moral Philosophy of Zoroaster was moving in the triad of thought, word and action. These three form the ground work upon which the whole edifice of Zoroastrian morality rests. Think of nothing but what is good, speak of nothing but what is true, do nothing but what is proper, and you are saved.

Zoroastrianism believes in the immortality of the soul. On the dawn of the third night, the departed soul is judged by the Spiritual Judge Mithra at a supposed Chinvat bridge between this and

(1) Maçoudi Chap. 69 (B. De Meynard, Vol. IV, p. 107). Albiruni (Chronology of Ancient Nations translated by Sachau, p. 114).
(2) Haug's Essays on the Parsees, 2nd ed., p. 303.
(3) Darmesteter, S. B. E., Vol. IV, Introduction p. LVI.

the next world. If his good actions outweigh his evil ones, he passes to Heaven. If his evil actions outweigh his good ones, he passes to Hell. If the good and the evil deeds are equal, he passes to a middle place called Hamast-gehán.

Fire is venerated as the Symbol of God, the best and the noblest representative of His Divinity. The Sacred Fire is consecrated with several ceremonies and then installed in their Fire-temples, of which there are three grades. The sacred Fire is fed, at least, five times (gáhs) during the day with sandal-wood.

Next to Ahura Mazda are six Amesháspands or Immortal Beings who represent his principal attributes. Ahura Mazda himself is at times spoken of as an Amesháspand standing at the head of all. In that case, there are six Amesháspands. They are :—

1. Bahman (Avesta, Vohumana) *i.e.*, Good Thought or Good Mind.

2. Ardibehest (Avesta, Asha Vahishta) *i.e.*, the Best Piety or Righteousness.

3. Shehrivar (Avesta, Khshathra Vairya) *i.e.*, Desirable control or Independent rule.

4. Spendármad (Avesta, Spenta A'rmaiti) *i.e.*, Holy Humility or Piety.

5. Khordad (Avesta, Haurvatát) *i.e.*, Perfection.

6. Amerdád (Avesta, Ameretát) *i.e.*, Immortality.

These Amesháspands preside over the moral attributes which are represented by the meanings of their names and which belong to Ahura Mazda in perfection. Next to the Amesháspands are the yazads (Avesta Yazatas) who are powerful spiritual existences pervading the whole universe in hundreds and thousands.

Thirty of such Yazatas preside over the thirty days of the month which are, as it were, sacred to them. These 30 days bear the names of these Yazatas. In the religious recitals, the order of the Holy Beings invoked is as follows :—

1. Ahura Mazda, the Great God.

2. The Amesha Spentas, *i.e.*, The Immortal Bountifuls corresponding to the Archangels.

3. The Yazatas, *i.e.*, Those worthy of praise or invocation, corresponding to the Angels.

4. The Asho-Farohars, *i.e.*, The Spirits of the Righteous worthies who have departed from this life.

There are no saints in the sense of the Christian Saints or of the Muhammadan Pirs. But historical personages of ancient Iran, known for performing some great service for the country in their times, are, as it were, canonized. No days are set apart for them. The only way in which they are invoked is that their names are commemorated in the Afringán ceremony performed in honour of the dead. The modern form of commemoration is "*Aidar yád bád anosheh raván raváni, i.e.*, May the soul of the immortal-souled [(1)] be remembered here." For example, the name of Chosroes I (Noshirván Adal or Noshirván the Just), who was an illustrious monarch and who had done a good deal of good to the country of Iran and to its religion, and whose original name was Khosru and whose father's name was Kobád, is commemorated as "*Khosru Kobád aidar yád bád anosheh raván raváni.*" No special offerings are made in their names and no special days are allotted to them. The most that is done is the recital of the Afringan in their honour as done in the case of the near and dear departed ones.

As to the offerings, the Pársis offer sandal wood, frankincense and such fragrant substances to the sacred fires of their Fire-temples, and even to the fire of their houses on special occasions. It is to the Yazad Adar (Atar from which comes Atash, the word for fire), presiding over fire that the offering is made.

An offering of flowers and sugar-candy, and, at times, of a cocoanut, is made to Ardiviçura, Anáhita the female yazata, presiding over water. This offering is thrown into the sea, and now-a-days is made by a few. We learn from Herodotus that the ancient Iranians also gave some offerings to the Yazata presiding over water. For example, Xerxes when he crossed the Hellespont or the Dardenelles made an offering to it.[(2)]

These offerings to the Fire and the Water are mere offerings which may or may not be accompanied by prayers. They can be made by the laymen themselves, except in the case of the Fire-temples of the first two grades, (Atash Behrám and Atash Adarián), where, the laymen hand the sandal wood, etc., to the priest of the temple and it is he who puts it upon the sacred fire. With the sandal wood, they generally give some money, which goes to the officiating priests.

---

(1) Here the name of the person is mentioned.

(2) Herodotus Book VII, Chap. 54.

There is another kind of offering, which may be called strictly religious offering. It is spoken of as the *myazda*.(1) It consists of flowers, fruits, water, Haoma juice, wine and milk. In the liturgical service of the Yaçna, Visparad and the Vendidád, the offerings are of water, milk and Haoma. In the religious service of the Afringán all the above except the Haoma are offered. Fruit and flowers are placed in a tray with water, wine and milk in small vessels or glasses. Fire is kept burning on a vase, and the Afringán prayer is recited with all these things before the reciter.

These prayer offerings are made both on occasions of joy and sorrow. They are made in honour of Ahura Mazda, His Amesha-spentas, His Yazatas and the Asho Farohars. They are generally associated with the names of the dear departed and are made on the occasions of the 4th, 10th, 30th and the anniversary day after death. On such occasions a prayer offering of cooked food is also made, and the prayer known as *satum* (lit. Praise) is recited over these. The eatables in these offerings are eaten by the family, and special care is taken that they do not pass into the hands of non-Zoroastrians.

Both men and women participate in these offerings. But women in an unclean state, *i.e.*, during their sickness and confinement, do not participate.

The Pársis employ priests for religious and ceremonial purposes. It is not all priests who can officiate at all ceremonies. The priests have to go through two kinds of initiation, the *Návar* and the *Martab*. Those who have passed through only the first, the *Návar*, can officiate only at some few religious services, especially the socio-religious services, *e.g.*, (*a*) the *Naojote*, *i.e.*, the investiture of a child with sacred shirt and thread, (*b*) the marriage, (*c*) the preliminary funeral ceremonies at home, (*d*) and the *Afringán*, *Satum* and the like. But, those that have gone through the *Martab* initiation can perform all the services, provided they observe the Bareshnum, which requires passing through a certain special purification for the time being and which requires certain restrictions to be observed.

All the priests receive each other on terms of equality. But they do not all participate in certain ceremonies. The reason is this:—According to the Kisseh-i-Sanján, by the end of the 11th century (about 1090 A.D.), the Pársis had dispersed from Sanjan, their first centre, to different parts of Gujarát. It seems that there arose occasionally some disputes as to which priests should officiate in certain

(1) The same root produces the Zoroastrian word Myazda and the Christian word Mass.

towns or villages. So, in the 13th century (about 1270 A.D.) they amicably settled the question by dividing Gujarát where the Pársis had spread, into five *panthaks* or ecclesiastical divisions. These divisions are referred to above.

Having made this division, the priests of the particular divisions attended to the religious requirements of the laymen of their own districts, and did not officiate in other centres. They also arranged that in certain ceremonies performed within the temple, the priests of one division should not officiate with the priests of another division. In the case of the 2nd division, latterly there arose in Naosári a schism, due to differences between the laity and the clergy. A few of the clergy sided with the laity, and the priests of these two parties or sub-divisions do not officiate together in certain liturgical services. These restrictions apply only to a certain set of strictly liturgical ceremonies. In case of certain socio-religious ceremonies of birth, marriage, death, etc., they all participate freely.

It is the priests who perform all the religious ceremonies. But when death takes place in out of the way places, for example, in Europe, where no Pársi priests can be had, non-priests perform the preliminary religious services required before disposing of the body. In that case also, as far as possible, lay members of the priestly class are generally preferred for the performance of the service.

A Gujaráti document, dated 1631, passed by the laymen of Bulsár in the presence of Government officers to their town-priest, named Shápurji Rána, who seems to have been their first regularly appointed priest, gives us an idea of how their priests were paid formerly for their sacerdotal work. There seemed to be no regular monthly or annual stipends but fees for all religious, social and other functions. The fees were as follow (Pársee Prakâsh, Vol. I, p. 13):—

1. Marriage commencement (*murat*) Re. 1. The custom was and is still, to a certain extent, prevalent, that a certain auspicious day was appointed by an astrologer on which the marriage rites may commence.

2. The commencement of building a house .. Re. 1

3. The laying of the first door while building a new house .. .. Re. 1¼

4. The dismantling of a house for repairs or for building it anew .. .. Re. 1

5. The digging of a new well .. .. Re. 1½

6. The repairs (*Shái*) of a well .. .. Rs. 2

7. The laying of the bottom of (*i.e.*, commencing) a ship .. .. .. Re. 1

8. For a turban on the day of launching a ship .. .. Rs. 3

9. On the Agharni, *i.e.*, the seventh month ceremony of the pregnancy of a daughter .. Re. 1

10. On sending a boy to school .. .. Re. 1

11. On the New Year's day (*Pateti*) .. Re. 1

12. On the Solar Eclipse day, from each Pársi house of the town .. .. .. As. 2

13. Valâvo, the last of the days of Muktád, which, next to the New Year, is considered to be a great Pársi Holiday .. .. .. Rs. 1½

14. Marriage occasion .. .. Re. 1

15. Wheat and cash in honour of Behram Yazad (the angel presiding over, and bringing, success) .. Rs. 2½

16. Silk-cloth (Rejo and Saree)

(These are presents of apparel to the wife of the priest) .. .. Rs. 5

17. On the day of Ashodád (*i.e.*, the day of the gift to the Righteous) according to one's means. (The payment to a Pársi priest is spoken of as Ashodád. The fee is not mentioned, but left to the discretion of the layman to be paid according to his means on grand occasions.)

18. On Gáhambár day, according to the custom. (No special fee is mentioned.)

19. On the investiture of a child with sacred shirt and thread according to the custom. (No special fee is mentioned.)

20. Every five months .. .. .. Annas 4

21. On every festival day .. .. Annas 4.

This list gives us a little insight into the life of the Pársis about three hundred years ago. It also shows that there have been ship-builders from some olden times. The priests at present are paid their fees in money for the sacerdotal functions which they perform on occasions of joy and sorrow and for some social occasions. On certain occasions, they are also paid in kind, *i.e.*, in grain and cloth.

The Pársis expose their dead in round structures known by them as *dokhmás* and ordinarily known as Towers of Silence. In places, where there are no such Towers, they unavoidably bury but never burn. Their practice of exposure is very old. Classical writers like Herodotus (1) and Strabo (2) refer to it. Disposal of the dead.

The Towers of Silence are constructed of solid masonry work on sanitary principles. The bodies are soon devoured by vultures, which are the scavengers of Nature. The Sun, air and rain do the rest of the work to keep the place clean. There are in all seven Towers in Bombay five of which are public Towers and two private. A tower costs from about Rs. 7,000 to Rs. 1,00,000 according to its size. They carry the bodies to the Tower during the day hours only.

In some big centres of Pársi population, there are paid professional carriers. Those who carry the dead body are required to bathe before they mix with others and to change their clothes, which are altogether rejected or used once or twice again for the purpose of carrying the dead bodies of poor Pársis, who cannot afford to furnish suits of clothes to the carriers for such a purpose. The clothes over the dead body are rejected altogether. Even those that attend the funeral are required to wash their faces and other parts of their body that are exposed. The carriers are at least two, and when more are required, they are always in pairs, *i.e.*, in even numbers, never in odd numbers. The mourners who follow the bier also walk in pairs, holding a *paiwand* (lit. connection) between them in the form of a handkerchief.

They perform some ceremonies in honour of the dead during the first three days. They are known as the Sarosh ceremonies. Most of these are performed in their fire-temples. The other principal occasions for the performance of the ceremonies are the fourth (cháhrum), the tenth (dehum), the thirtieth (si-roz), and the anniversary (sál roz) day after death. Those who can afford perform a few ceremonies continuously for the first ten days or for the first month or for the first year. Funeral ceremonies.

In the recital of prayers for the ceremonies, the name of the particular individual, in whose honour they are performed, is mentioned first, and then, the names of the ancestors and other near relatives. Even the names of some great and good Pársis of the past, who have done good to the community, to the city or to the

(1) Bk I, 140. (2) Bk. XV, Chap. III, 20.

country are remembered. For example, the name of Zoroaster, the Prophet, kings like Jamshed, Ardeshir Babegán and Noshirván the Just (Chosroes I), saintly persons of old like Erach, Shiávax and Agriras, national warriors like the great Rustam, Dasturs or Prelates like Ardái Viráf and Aderbád Márespand, all of ancient Persia, learned Dasturs like Neryosang Dhaval and Meherji Rána and benefactors like the first Sir Jamsetjee Jeejeebhoy of Bombay, are still remembered generally during the public, and often during the private recitals in honour of the dead. The modern form of recital is: "May the soul of the pious souled....(here the name of the deceased is mentioned) be remembered here." At the end of the recital of the names of particular deceased persons, as said above, there is a general remembrance of all (hamá) good men of the past, whether priests (áthornán) soldiers (ratheshtárán), agriculturists (váçtrayoçán) and others practising various professions, trades and arts (hutohkshán).

In the performance of these ceremonies, no particular distinction is made in the case of childless persons. The only thing that is done extra, in the case of a childless man, is that if he is of the age of 15 or above, he is given a son in adoption at the *uthamná* ceremony in the afternoon of the third day or at the dawn of the fourth night. It is anounced that such and such a person is selected as the adopted son of the deceased and a *Tandarusti* (a benedictory prayer) is recited for the welfare of that adopted son. His name is also mentioned occasionally in the prayers in honour of the deceased, as one directing the ceremonies to be performed (farmáyashne). A near member of the family, generally a younger brother or a nephew or such near relative, especially from the father's side, is adopted.

There is nothing extra or special in the funeral ceremonies for a person who has met a violent death.

The ceremonies in honour of the dead performed after the third day are generally spoken as the Báj Rojgár ceremonies, and they correspond, to some extent, to the Shráddha of the Hindus, and remind us of the ceremonies in honour of the Lares among the ancient Romans.

Occupation.

Among their early occupations, we find those of agriculture, liquor-selling, toddy-drawing, weaving, ship-building, money-lending, brokerage, etc. The original occupation of most of the Pársis was agriculture. They cultivated land. It is an occupation much recommended by their scriptures, a recommendation spoken of with some approbation by Gibbon [1] and others.

(1) Gibbon's "Decline and Fall of the Roman Empire" (1845), Vol. I, p. 120.

The occupation which they took up next to agriculture in India, in later times, was that of liquor-sellers. Even in Muhammadan Persia, for long after the Arab conquest, the wine-selling trade seems to have been in the hands of the Zoroastrians there. The Pir-i-Moghán (*i.e.*, the old man of the Mágis), often referred to by Háfiz in his Diván, was the Zoroastrian liquor-seller in the country, the orthodox portion of which was ostensibly said to have abstained from wine-drinking.

It appears from some Portuguese documents of the first half of the 18th century that some Pársis did shipping business. They built and owned boats, and carried on the coasting trade. They were also ship-builders and ship-owners. Again, we learn from these documents (1738-39) that the Pársis served the Portuguese as soldiers and were even given ensignship and captainship. On occasions of difficulty, they formed themselves into volunteer campanies commanded by their own officers and fought against the Maráthás on behalf of their Portuguese rulers in the district round Daman and Tarapore.[1] In the village of Jehán (Jehán Bordi) near Golwad, about 90 miles from Bombay, an old Pársi house is still seen, the wall of which is perforated with holes from which bullets can be fired against bandits. This shows that they used arms.

After the advent of Europeans into India, some of the Pársis served them in various capacities. Some well-to-do Pársis were brokers in the factories of the English, the Dutch and other nations. Some served even as domestic servants. Anquetil Du Perron, who was in India from 1755 to 1761, refers to such brokers and domestics. A Pársi family was, up to late, known as Govenders (governors), because the head of the family served a Governor of Bombay. Some served as messmen and chowdries in British Military cantonments. They are no longer seen now in these services.

Of the above-mentioned principal occupations, those of agriculture and liquor-selling still continue, though on a smaller scale and in a different way. Some of the Mofussil Pársis, especially in the Surat district, still own land. They cultivate it, not personally, but through labourers. Up to a few years ago, they had a number of, as it were, hereditary labourers, more like slaves than independent voluntary workers. They were brought up by the Pársi landlords or masters, who fed them and their families, and even got them married, they in turn binding themselves to serve them for life. When

(1) *Vide* my paper "A Glimpse into the work of the B. B. R. A. Society during the last 100 years from a Parsi point of view," p. 18. *Vide* my "A Few Events in the Early History of Parsis", p. 24 n. on the same subject.

the heirs of such a Pársi landlord divided the family property, they even divided among themselves these labourers or semi-slaves.(1)

The liquor-selling trade also continues in the hands of some Mofussil Pársis but not to a great extent as before. Recent Abkari Acts and rules have thrown some of them out of employment in this line.

There are no Pársis serving now in the regular army, but several are members of some Volunteer Corps in Upper India and in some of the Mofussil towns of the Bombay Presidency.

Formerly, when Gujarát, and especially Surat with its surrounding villages, formed their headquarters, they resorted to several arts for their livelihood. The principal among these was that of weaving on primitive looms. Even in the case of those who followed some other profession which did not require their whole time, weaving formed a collateral work. All households had looms on which they worked out *nárás* (laces) *pátis* (broad lace-like ropes for cots) and even cloth. Some worked even in silk. In the well-known silk work of *Kinkháb* for which Surat was then well known, the Pársi weavers had their hand. Both men and women carried on this work of *vankars, i.c.*, weavers.

The only work of weaving which is still carried on by a few, and those few the women of the priestly class, is that of weaving Kustis, *i.e.*, the sacred thread worn by the Pársis as one of the symbols of their faith. This work was considered to be the privilege of women of this priestly class. Some diligent women, who wove very fine Kustis, earned about a Rupee per day. This privilege is, they say, now being encroached upon and even some women of the layman class work at the Kustis. The orthodox still consider it meritorious to put on the Kustis prepared by the women of the priestly class. The Kustis require a kind of consecration, and they think that those stealthily woven by the laywomen are passed on without proper consecration.

The next important occupation of the Pársis at Surat was that of Churis or bangles, from which a class of them was called Churigars, *i.e.*, bangle-makers. The large number of those who joined the new sect of the Kadmis, arising from the above referred to difference of one intercalary month between the Zoroastrians of India and those of Persia, being this class of workers, the new sect had received the

(1) *Vide* my paper on "A Parsi Deed of Partition more than 150 years old: a form of slavery referred to therein." (Journal Anthropological Society, Vol. VI, No. 2, pp. 12-16. *Vide* my "Anthropological Papers," Part I, pp. 167-172.)

nickname or appellation of Churigars. That name forms even now, the surname of some families.

Up to about 60 or 70 years ago, they generally abstained from work, wherein they were required to work with fire, which required blowing with their breath or had to be extinguished. Similarly Pársis have not been known as practical goldsmiths or silversmiths. At one time, they hesitated to take the work of firemen on locomotives or in mills. But that dislike has now died out. An instance in the early part of the last century is recorded, wherein a Pársi requested the Government of the day to kindly direct that all places of work wherein Fire was used may be closed on the festival day of fire. The then Government is said to have complied with his request.(1)

Again, at one time, there was some hesitation to take the medical profession according to the Western methods, though there were several who had taken to the Indian system of medicine and were known as good Unáni Hakims. The reason for this hesitation was that in their study of surgery, etc., they had to deal with corpses which were according to the Vendidád a kind of *Naçu* (decomposing harmful thing), from which they were to abstain. The corpse-bearers (*nasásalárs, i.e.*, experts in dealing with naçá or dead bodies) were treated as a class to be kept apart from others. In a town like Naosári, the headquarters of the Pársi priesthood, they have separate quarters, a little apart from Pársi streets. When invited to public or private dinners, they are provided with meals separate from others. They cannot go to Fire-temples without undergoing a ceremonial purification. Officiating priests, who perform inner liturgical services of the temples, do not touch them. If they accidentally touch them, their officiating qualification for the day being is vitiated and they have to repeat the ceremony for the qualification.

The Pársis, though, at times they owned a large number of ships, and even carried on, as said above, the sea-coast trade in their own boats, were never professional sailors. The reason is this :—Water, like fire, air and earth is held to be one of the best productions of God, useful to mankind. There is a special Yazata or Angel presiding over water. The Pársi scriptures strictly enjoin that water may not be defiled. The injunctions seemed to be chiefly in respect of fresh water of rivers and streams which is used for domestic purposes. That injunction was latterly applied, even in old times of Parthian rule in Iran, to all kinds of water. Tiridates, the Zoroastrian king of Armenia, when required to go to Rome to pay his

(1) *Vide* Appendix C for this letter and the Government Order.

homage to the Roman Emperor Nero, objected on this ground to cross the seas.[1] Valkhash (Volageses), the Parthian king of Iran, also had similar religious scruples to cross the seas. When, in the end, Tiridates did go to Rome, he went by land instead of by sea.

Herodotus, Strabo and other classical authors refer to the sacred respect in which the ancient Iranians held rivers, etc., which supplied drinking water to the people. The restrictions seem to have extended from fresh drinking water to all kinds of water. This seems to be the reason why the Pársis have not taken to sea-faring as a profession.

Food and drink. Orthodox Pársis eat flesh of cloven-footed animals and abstain from beef, pork and the flesh of other unclovenfooted animals. From Herodotus (Bk. I. 126), we learn that the ancient Iranians ate the flesh of horse, camels, oxen, etc., but the Indian Pársis, as a body, abstain from these. As to fish, they eat scaly fish and abstain from unscaly fish. They never eat crocodiles, snakes, and such other creatures. They drink wine.

They do not eat the leavings of others, even if they be of their own co-religionists and relatives, if the leavings are of the food eaten in a way known as *ajithu*, *i.e.*, in a way, wherein the eater has put his fingers into his mouth and then touched the food again. Two persons would not drink from the same glass or cup.

Up to about 40 or 50 years ago, the Pársis did not eat *pakki*, *i.e.*, food cooked by non-Pársis. But that custom is now more honoured in the breach than in the observance among the laity. The priesthood, especially the officiating priesthood, still abstain from food prepared by non-Pársis. Priests, who observe the Bareshnum in order to be qualified to officiate at the liturgical services, eat only food cooked by persons of the priestly class. Up to a few years ago, the Bareshnum-observing priests would not eat at the same table with the laymen. They would not drink from the same glass or cup, until it is washed, if the glass or cup is touched with the lip.

The Pársis as a body do not smoke, but during the last 15 or 20 years—some, and especially those who have travelled in Europe, have commenced to smoke tobacco. Abstinence from smoking was,

(1) " Neither would his (Valkhash's) brother Tiridates refuse coming to Rome to receive the Armenian diadem, but that the obligation of his priesthood withheld him. He would, however, go to the standards and images of Cæsar and there, in presence of the legions, solemnly receive the kingdom. " (The Annals of Tacitus, Bk. XV. Works of Tacitus, Oxford translation, Vol. I. p. 24.)

at one time, one of the distinguishing customs, whereby a Pársi was distinguished from others; but this is no longer generally the case.

PARSOLIA.—A sub-division of Bráhmans.

PARVALE.—A sub-division of Lohárs.

PARVALIA.—A sub-division of Shrigaud Bráhmans.

PARVARI.—A synonym for Mahár.

PASTAGIA.—A synonym for Káchhia.

PASTI.—A sub-division of Gánigs.

PATANE.—A sub-division of Vánis.

PATANE PRABHU.—A synonym for Pátháre Prabhu.

PATANEJE.—A sub-division of Vághris.

PATANI.—A sub-division of Khálpás.

PATANIA.—A sub-division of Parajia Bráhmans and Dhedás.

PATANWADIA.—A sub-division of Kolis.

PATARIHA.—A sub-division of Lodhás.

PATELIA.—A synonym for Talabda.

PATHANS, numbering 170,532 (1901), including 91,300 males and 79,232 females, are found in all parts of the Presidency and in Sind. They are Afgháns who have settled in the Presidency and in many cases intermarried with other classes of Muhammadans. They mostly came originally to serve as mercenaries in the armies of the Musalmán rulers in the Deccan. Regarding the origin of the term Pathán the late Mr. A. M. T. Jackson says:—

"Captain, afterwards Sir Richard, Burton derives Pathán from the Arabic *fathán* victorious. Others trace the word to the Hindustáni *pethna*, to penetrate. Farishtah (1·29, Persian Text) says that though the origin of the name is not certain, yet he thinks that the first Afgháns who came to India settled at Pátna and were hence called Patháns. These are all late Muslim explanations. Afghán tradition derives the name from the title Batán or Patán ('rudder') given by the Prophet himself to their great ancestor Abdur-Rashid. It is, however, now generally agreed that the name Pathán is the Indian form of the name Pushtun (*plural* Pushtánah) now given to themselves by speakers of the Pashtu or Pakhtu language. They inhabit the *koh* or hilly country from Swat and Bajaur in the north to the Siwi and Bhakar in the south and from Hasan Abdál in the east to Kábul and Kandáhár in the west. They are not by any means a pure race, but include Tartar (Ghilzai) Arab (Durrani) and Indian (Swáti) elements, as well as a probably Iránian element, the original speakers of the Paṣhtu language. Darmsteter has shown (Chants Populaires des Afghans, Introd. pages clxxx. ff) that the modern name Pushtun goes back to an earlier form Pashtun, which is derived from the ancient Iránian word *Parshti* " a hill. " These original Patháns are to be identified with the *paktves* of Herodotus (IV. 44) as well as with the *paronetar* of Ptolemy (ch. xviii). The name Afghán does not seem to occur before Varáha-Mihira (A.D. 550) who mentions the race under the name Avagána (Brihat Samhita, ch. xiv). Further discussion of the subject will be found in Bellew's Races of Afghánistan and in the work by Darmsteter already quoted."[1]

Like the representatives of other foreign Musalmáns the Patháns have in most cases by intermarriage with other classes lost their peculiarities of feature and character. The men add *Khán* to their names and the women *Khátun*, *Khátu* or *Bibi*. They marry either among themselves or with any Musalmáns not confined to marriage with their own caste.

They are all Sunnis in religion. They are money lenders[2] horse-dealers, soldiers, constables, messengers and servants. Except some villagers in Belgaum who abstain from the use of beef and offer vows to Hindu gods, their customs do not differ from those of ordinary Musalmáns. (*See* MUSALMAN.)

PATHANTANAS.—A synonym for Shivate.

PATHARVATS, or Stone-cutters, numbering approximately 1,949 Na
(1901), including 968 males and 981 females, are found in small numbers orig
all over the Deccan and Karnátak. They appear to be closely connected with Marátha Kunbis, with whom they eat but do not marry, and are doubtless one in origin. A few are Musalmáns and Lingáyats, possibly by conversion, though information is incomplete regarding these divisions. For the most part, their ceremonies resemble those of the Marátha Kunbis. They are stone masons and also carve and make images, grindstones, etc.

Their exogamous divisions are identical with their surnames, Div
of which the commonest are Ambekar, Bárnáik, Cháphe, Hinge, Holekar, Khage, Lugad, Randeve and Sápe.

---

(1) *Bom. Gaz.*, Vol. IX, Part II, p. 10.

(2) In the Deccan these are known as Dhamdharé meaning " hold your breath ", the explanation being that after making a loan they return to recover it after just as long an interval as the borrower can hold his breath."

Girls are married before they are sixteen, boys before twenty-five. In some places boys are girt with the sacred thread before marriage. Their *devak* consists of an axe and the *pánchpálvi* or leaves of the mango *umbar, shami, jámbhul* and *rui* trees. Polygamy is allowed, but polyandry is unknown. The remarriage of widows is permitted. In Sátára, the widow's intended husband has to give her a robe and bodice and her father a turban and Rs. 25 in cash. On a lucky night the priests visits the widow's house and conducts the ceremony about one hundred yards outside of the house in the presence of five or six men friends of the couple. The couple are seated on low wooden stools in a wheat square marked by the priest, their brows are marked with vermilion, rice grains are stuck on them, and they bow before the priest. The widow puts on toerings or *jodvis*, but she is not allowed to wear the lucky necklace or *mangalsutra*. Married women are not allowed to see her for three days, after which a feast to friends and relations completes the ceremony. In some places, the ceremony consists in tying the hems of the pair's garments and throwing rice grains over their heads. **Marriage.**

Pátharvats are both Shaivas and Vaishnavas. Their family deities are Khandoba, Vithoba, Bahiroba, Devi, Krishna and Ganpati. Their priests either belong to their own caste or are Deshasth Bráhmans. The dead are either burnt or buried. **Religion.**

They eat fish and flesh, except beef, and drink liquor. They eat food cooked by Marátha Kunbis, whom they closely resemble. **Food.**

PATHRAT OD.—A synonym for Dagad Od.

PATIDAR.—A synonym for Kanbi : a sub-division of Leva Kanbis

PATNAVAL.—A sub-division of Devángs.

PATNI.—A sub-division of Ghánchis and Parjia Sonis.

PATRACHANDRI.—A sub-division of Kabbaligars.

PATRAD.—A sub-division of Koravas.

PATRADAVS, a class of Kanarese dancing girls and courtesans, are found mainly in Dhárwár. Their brothers and sons beat drums and play the *sárangi* or fiddle as an accompaniment to their dancing and singing. The girls are married to a drum, and thereafter lead a life of prostitution, but a special position is always assigned to the first lover. The men marry outside the courtesan class, and their daughters either become dancing girls or are given in marriage into other families. In religion and customs they resemble Kalávants.

PAT SALI.—A sub-division of Sális.

PATTANI.—A sub-division of Kunbis.

PATTAR.—A synonym for Sonár.

PATTA SALI.—A sub-division of Sális.

PATWEGAR.—A synonym for Patvekari.

Name and origin. **PATVEKARIS,** or Patvegars, numbering 6,164 (1901), including 2,990 males and 3,174 females, are found in Khándesh, Násik, Poona, Sátára, Belgaum, Bijápur, Dhárwár and Ratnágiri, but chiefly reside in Dhárwár district. In addition to 6,164 Hindus, 415 returned themselves as Muhammadans at the Census of 1901. They are known as Patvegars in the Karnátak. They profess to have come originally from Gujarát about two hundred years ago, in search of work, and this seems probable. Once every two or three years a Bhát or genealogist from near Baroda in Gujarát visits the Bijápur district to record the births and deaths which have taken place in each family since his last visit.

Language. Their home tongue is corrupt Gujaráti. Several Maráthi and Hindustáni words have crept in. In Bijápur they speak a mixture of Gujaráti, Maráthi and Hindustáni. Thus, 'Tell me what is the matter' would be *majkur káy chhe te bolo*; the first two words Maráthi, the second two Gujaráti, and the fifth Hindustáni. Some of their phrases as 'I will come soon,' *Avach sáoni*, can hardly be traced to any of these three languages.

The names in ordinary use among men are Jurása, Kanthisa, Lakshmansa, Mániksa, Mávrasa, Ramkrishnasa and Sakusa; and among women, Ambebai, Anandibai, Krishnabai, Nágubai and Tuljábai. To every proper name of men they add *sa* corresponding to the Maráthi *pant* or *ráv*. The Patvekaris claim to be Kshatriyas, and wear the sacred thread. Their surnames are Kabáde, Kutáre, Povár, Shálgar and Shiralkar.

Divisions. The names of their family stocks are Bháradváj, Gautam, Káshyap, and Náradik, and families of the same surname and stock cannot intermarry. In the Bijápur district their surnames are the names of places and of ancestors. Families bearing a particular surname belong to a particular *shákha* or branch of a *gotra* or family stock. The Bhartárghars belong to the Káthva branch of the Káshyap *gotra*; the Dájis belong to the Daji branch of the Párisva *gotra*; the Jálnapurkars belong to the Gambva branch of the Gokul *gotra*; and the Maljis belong to the Sonekatar branch of the Gautam *gotra*. They marry with the same family stock but not with the same branch of a family stock.

Patvekaris gird their boys with the sacred thread before they are ten years old; the ceremony is not accompanied by prayers, but lasts for two days. Some days before the ceremony a caste feast is given. The boy is invested with the help of the Bráhman family priest, who lights a sacrificial fire or *hom* and retires with his fee. The guests are handed packets of betelnut and leaves, and near relations are feasted. The priest is given two handfuls of wheat, rice, gram pulse, molasses, butter and salt.

Marriage ceremonies.

Their marriages last three days. On the first day a feast is given in honour of the marriage gods, and in the evening the relations and friends of the boy and girl meet in the village temple, and the girl's parents worship the boy. The girl's mother pours water over the boy's feet and the girl's father gently rubs the feet and dries them with the hem of his waist-cloth. Packets of betelnut and leaves are handed round and the guests retire. Next day the marriage is performed at a lucky moment, either in the morning or evening, when the cattle come home. At the time of marriage the bride and bridegroom are made to sit facing each other on a carpet, and a white sheet is held between them. The priests and the guests shower rice on the heads of the pair; and the white curtain with the cross on it is removed. The bride's father performs the girl-giving or *kanyádán*, in which the nine Hindu planets are worshipped, and a burnt offering is made in their honour. The bride's father presents drinking vessels and platters as his daughter's dowry; and the friends and kinsfolk present the bride and bridegroom with half anna to one rupee in cash. The bride and bridegroom are led to the bridegroom's house either on foot or on horseback. The *varát* or married couple's homeward procession brings the ceremony to an end.

Widow remarriage is allowed. In Bijápur district a widow is not allowed to marry a third time.

Religion.

They worship all the usual local and Bráhmanic gods and goddesses. Their chief family goddess is the Jagadamba of Tuljápur, to whom they make vows. They believe her to be an incarnation of their patroness, the goddess Inglaji, who is said to have saved them from the destructive axe of the Kshatriya-slaying Parshurám, the sixth incarnation of Vishnu. They often keep an image of Yellamma also in their houses. They visit the shrine of Ambábái at Tuljápur in the Nizám's country and that of Vithoba at Pandharpur in Sholápur. Milk and molasses—not dressed food—are daily offered to the house deities. They keep almost all Hindu fasts and feasts. *Shivrátra* in *Mágha* or January-February, the eleventh of bright *Ashádh* or June-

July being their chief fast days. Besides Shankaráchárya, the pontiff of all Smárt Hindus, they have a separate *guru* or religious teacher. He is a Bhát by caste, and occasionally visits his disciples and collects money from them. His disciples treat him with great reverence and ask him to dine with them. They do not worship evil spirits but have faith in witchcraft.

Death ceremonies. They burn the dead, but have no *jivkhada* or life-stone as a lodging for the soul of the dead. On the way to the burning ground there is the usual rest and the change of place among the bearers. At the burning ground the heir carries an earthen water vessel round the pyre and lays a quarter-anna piece upon it. Balls of food are laid on the spot where the body was burnt, and on the third day the bones are gathered and thrown into water. On the eleventh a dinner is given to friends. They hold that a death in the family causes ceremonial impurity, and stop work for thirteen days. They give both monthly and yearly mind-feasts.

Occupation. The Patvekaris make silk threads for necklaces, and other head, hand and waist ornaments. They string and fix gems or beads on silk or cotton threads and make fringes, tassels and netted work. They make silk and cotton waistcords called *katdorás* or *kargotás*, by which high caste boys fasten the loincloth a short time after their thread ceremony. In the Bijápur district many of them have taken to weaving. They also work as day labourers and some of them are musicians.

Food. They eat fish and flesh and drink liquor. They do not like to rank themselves with any other caste, and eat no food but what is prepared by their own people.

MUSALMAN PATVEGARS, numbering 415 (1901), including 211 males and 204 females, are found in small numbers in almost all the towns of the Deccan and Karnátak. They marry either among themselves or with any low class Musalmáns. They are Sunnis of the Hanafi school and are seldom religious or careful to say their prayers. They have strong Hindu leanings, eschewing beef, keeping Hindu feasts and offering vows to Hindu gods and goddesses. They respect the *Kázi* and ask him to conduct their ceremonies.

PAVAGADIA.—A sub-division of Chodhrás.

Name and origin. **PAVAYA,** also called Fátadás or Hijdás, that is, eunuchs, numbering 138 (1901) are found in small numbers in Ahmedabad, Panch Mahals, Káthiáwár, Cutch and Khándesh. The caste includes eight females returned in Khándesh Agency; they appear to be prostitutes.

Pavayas are recruited from both Hindus and Musalmáns, who consider themselves the creatures or rather the temples or houses of the goddess Bahucharáji. Except that they do not dine together, Pavayás from Hindu and Musalmán families bear a close resemblance. According to their tradition, a king of Champáner named Bária was unhappy because he had no son. He was a devout worshipper of the goddess Bahucharáji and through her favour a son was born to him and named Jeto. This Jeto was born impotent, and Bária, out of respect to the goddess through whose favour the son was obtained, set him apart for her service. Bahucharáji appeared to Jeto in a dream and told to him to cut off his private parts and dress himself as a woman. Jeto obeyed the goddess and this practice has since been followed by all who join the caste.

Initiation ceremonies

Impotence is an indispensable qualification for admission into the caste. When an impotent man desires to be admitted he applies to one of the Pavayás who breathes into his right ear, bores both ears with the point of a needle, and administers to him a solemn oath never to steal and never to act as a procurator to any woman. The novice is then admitted on probation. He eats coarse sugar, puts on woman's clothes, receives a new name, and gives a feast to the caste. The new names are feminine names generally ending in 'de' such as Dhanade, Jhinide, Ladude and Khimde. The probationary period lasts from six to twelve months, during which the conduct of the novice is carefully watched and the fact of his impotence thoroughly tested. When impotence is established the next ceremony is emasculation. For this purpose the novice bathes, dresses himself in clean clothes and worships the image of the goddess. He prays to her to grant a propitious day for the operation. It is believed that if the operation is performed on a day approved by the goddess the result is seldom fatal. Behind a screen set up for the purpose the cutting is performed with a razor by the person himself without any assistance. This is held to correspond to a birth ceremony which makes the patient a member of the caste. After the operation the patient lies for three days on a cot on his back without moving. During that time 30 pounds sesame oil is continuously poured on the parts affected. For ten days more or till the wound is healed it is washed with a decoction of the *bor* (Zizyphus jujuba) and *bábul* (Acacia arabica) bark. On the 6th day after the operation coarse wheat flour mixed with molasses and clarified butter is distributed among the caste people. The patient remains screened for 40 days, during which he eats light food. Clarified butter is his chief nourishment and he is forbidden the use of red pepper, oil and asafoetida.

In A.D. 1880 the Gáikwár of Baroda forbade castration in his state, to the great sorrow of the Pavayás, who say that by thus remaining in their natural condition they displease the goddess and that during seven future lives they will remain impotent as a punishment for failing to sacrifice the useless member.

Religion. The Pavayás keep images of Bahucharáji in their houses and worship them daily and, when on begging tours, are careful to visit her shrines in the Chuvel. They keep both Hindu and Musalmán holidays.

Death ceremonies. They bury their dead. After death the body is washed and laid on a cot covered with a sheet and perfumed. The body is shrouded in a clean coverlet for burial. As they are neither males nor females they do not touch the coffin which is carried, and the burying performed, by Musalmáns, the companions of the dead standing by, mourning. On the *dasa* or tenth day and on the *chálisa* or fortieth day after a death the dearest companion of the deceased is bound on pain of expulsion to feed the caste people and the Musalmán bier bearers. A tomb is raised over the dead.

Occupation. Pavayás live as beggars, singing the praise of their patron goddess Bahucharáji. In begging they stand in front of some villager, clap their hands and offer the usual blessing 'May mother Bahucharáji do you and your children good' or 'Ado Bhaváni,' that is, Rise, goddess Bhaváni. If any one fails to give them alms they abuse him, and if abuse fails they strip themselves naked, a result which is greatly dreaded as it is believed to bring dire calamity. They beg in bands on certain beats and receive fixed yearly dues in kind or in cash from shopkeepers, carpenters, tailors, shoemakers, goldsmiths, Lohárs, etc. They also receive fees from every Kunbi on the birth of a son and in most parts of Gujarát when a son is born to a barren woman or to a woman who has had no male issue, Pavayás are called in and made to dance in front of the house.

Food. They eat fish and flesh of goats and sheep. They drink liquor.

PAVRA.—A sub-division of Bhils.

PED.—A sub-division of Mángs.

PEDNEKAR.—A sub-division of Gaud Sárasvat Bráhmans.

PEND.—A sub-division of Mángs.

Name and origin. **PENDHARIS** or Pindháris, numbering 3,347 (1901), including 1,734 males and 1,613 females, are found in Násik, Khándesh and the Southern Marátha Country, with a few families in the Poona and

Sholápur districts. It is a noticeable fact that none were recorded in the Bombay Presidency at previous censuses.* They are descendants of the famous free-booters who followed the Marátha armies, and were doubtless recruited originally from numerous sources, including Pathán, Marátha and Ját.† Their religious distribution is as follows :—

		Total.	Males.	Females.
Hindus	..	1,665	905	760
Musalmáns	..	1,682	829	853

The origin of the term is obscure. The word *pendha* in Maráthi means a bundle of rice straw, and *pendhári* would very probably be a common nickname for a body of horsemen looting crops, *i.e.*, the stealers of *pendhás*. This derivation is attributed to Wilson in Hobson-Jobson. Sir John Malcolm traces the name to the habit of drinking *pinda*, an intoxicant, and this derivation seems to have been current among the Pendháris. According to Hobson-Jobson, a better derivation is Mr. Irvine's from Pandhár near Burhánpur on the Nerbudda. It is probable that the correct origin of the term will never be traced.‡

Members of other castes are still admitted to the Pendháris on giving a dinner to the caste.

Hindu Pendháris have five exogamous divisions known as *kuls*. They are Alande, Gháyatalak, Kshiraságar, Ranashing and Thorát. Marriages are prohibited between members of the same *kul*. **Divisions.**

A member of the caste cannot marry his father's sister's or mother's sister's daughter. He may marry his maternal uncle's daughter. A man may marry his deceased wife's sister. Two brothers may marry two sisters. Polygamy is allowed and practised, but polyandry is unknown. Marriage is generally adult. If a girl is seduced by a casteman, he is compelled to marry her. If a girl is seduced by a member of another caste, she may remain in the caste by paying a fine to the caste.

Marriage ceremonies. The offer of marriage comes from the boy's father, who has to pay Rs. 5 to the girl's father. The day for the marriage is fixed by a Brahman, who conducts the service. A respectable member of the caste takes the bridegroom to his house, folds a turban round his head and takes him in procession to the girl's father's house. This is called *simant-pujan*. Idols of wheat flour are made and fried in oil : they are given the names of the deceased ancestors, and are taken to the

* The Mysore census of 1901 shows 2,097 Pindháris.

† "The Pindarra Force * * * was latterly composed of all castes, and all descriptions of people." McNaghten's Nagpore Subsidiary Proce, P. 107.

‡ Hobson-Jobson, 2nd edition, p. 711, *et. seq.*

boy's house to be served to the boy, his sisters, and his friends. This ceremony is known as *rukhvat.* The boy is smeared with oil before he starts for the girl's house. The rest of the marriage ceremony is of the ordinary Marátha type. After a marriage has been performed, idols are brought from a goldsmith's house ; they are taken five steps beyond the village boundary, the ground is worshipped, offerings are made, and the party return home.

The remarriage of widows is permitted. A widow can marry her father's sister's or mother's brother's son. A widow remarriage is always celebrated at night. The caste *panch* are present on the occasion. An elderly member of the caste ties into a knot the hems of the pair's garments, which completes the union. The widow is presented with a robe and a bodice, and bracelets and ornaments, by her new husband. A feast is given to the caste *panch.* A bachelor is not allowed to marry a widow. A husband can divorce a wife if he cannot agree with her. A divorced woman may remarry.

Religion.

The caste follow the Hindu law of inheritance. Hindu Pendháris belong to the Rámdási sect. The chief objects of their veneration are Mariái, Mhasoba, and Khandoba. They do not make pilgrimages. They observe all the Hindu holidays. *Táks* (images of deceased ancestors embossed on silver plates) are made and worshipped with offerings of cooked food. Musalmán *pirs* are also venerated. When an epidemic breaks out, Mariái is propitiated. The religious teacher of the Pendháris is a member of their own caste. They employ Bráhmans to conduct their marriages. The other ceremonies are conducted by the caste elders.

Death ceremonies.

The dead are buried either on the back with the head turned to the west or north, or in a sitting position. On the tenth day after death the faces of the male mourners are shaved. On this day and on the day following flowers are offered on the spot where the death took place and a feast is given to the caste-people. Every year, on the anniversary of the death, the *pitar* is performed, *i.e.*, caste-men are feasted in honour of the deceased. *Pitar* is also performed on *akshatritiya* day and on that day in the dark half of *Bhádrapad* which corresponds to the day of death.

Occupation.

The Pendháris were plunderers and free-booters during the troubled times of the latter days of the Peshwás. On the restoration of peace by the British, they settled down as petty traders and day labourers. They deal in grass, rice, cattle, sheep, etc. Some work as masons.

They eat fish and the flesh of goats, sheep, and fowls, and drink liquor.* Food.

MUSALMAN PENDHARIS are found almost entirely in the districts of the Southern Division. They do not differ from the Musalmáns of Belgaum in their customs and ceremonies. They do not marry with Hindu Pendháris but they will marry with Musalmáns, of other castes, such as Attár, Bágwán, etc., and such marriages have quite recently been performed (1901).

PENTPENT.—A sub-division of Raddis.

PHANSE PARDHI.—A sub-division of Párdis.

PHED.—A synonym for Pend.

PHUDGIS, (1) numbering 1,035 (1901), including 490 males and 545 females, are found only in the Máhim and Bassein *tálukás* of the Thána district. The caste believe that they are descendants from the monkey god Hanumán, whom they hold in great reverence. Once a wandering tribe of thieves and beggars, they have now settled down as peaceful cowherds, cultivators, and labourers, and are only occasionally guilty of petty thefts. There is a strange belief prevalent among the caste that the lilies of the forest and the lotuses of the tank and all fruit-trees of Nature's creation belong to them as of birth-right, they being the favourites of the monkey god Máruti. If a Phudgi is caught in the act of stealing, he protests and wonders why he should be treated so harshly by the Sarkár and the *vádval* (gardener). "Do not," says he, "the monkeys and jackals destroy their plantain trees and their sugarcanes? And, if so, what if a good Phudgi takes away some fruits and vegetables to satisfy his hunger and thirst?" Name and origin.

It has been surmised that the Phudgis are connected with the gypsies of Europe, not only on account of their wandering habits and thieving propensities, but also because they use many words common to the "Romany *chál.*" Instances are as follows :—

Phudgi.	Gypsy.	English.
sáp.	sáp	snake
páni	páni (2)	water
kal	kalli	yesterday
rát	rát	night
kán	kán	ear
dánt	dánt	tooth

* Some interesting information regarding the Pindáris will be found in McNaghten's 'Nagpore Subsidiary Force' and the 'Origin of the Pindáris' John Murray, 1918.

(1) The materials for this article were supplied by Mr. P. B. Joshi.

(2) See Glossary to Borrow's "The Bible in Spain", Vol. II.

Phudgi.	Gypsy.	English.
dud	dud	milk
ischor	chor *	thief
ischib	ischib *	tongue
lál	lál	red
nákh	nákh	nose
ghar	ker *	house.

The vernacular terms, however, are common to all Hindustáni-speaking tribes, and a similar conjecture could be justified of many wandering tribes in India.

Endogamous divisions.

Phudgis consist of two endogamous divisions, *i.e.*, Shinwári Phudgis and Kirpál Phudgis. The Shinwári Phudgis are the Phudgis proper. They are perhaps so named because of the caste observing Shanwár or Saturday as a sacred day, being the birthday of their god Hanumán. The Kirpál Phudgis are the decendants of those Phudgis who were forced by the Portuguese to embrace Christianity, and who on the conquest of Máhim and Bassein by the Maráthás reverted to Hinduism. The caste have no exogamous sub-divisions.

Marriage ceremonies.

Marriage is generally adult. Polygamy and widow re-marriage are allowed, but polyandry is unknown. As soon as a marriage settlement is made, the boy's father pays to the girl's father a sum of not less than Rs. 5, which is spent on feasting relations and caste-men. A marriage booth is erected, to which are tied leaves of five kinds of trees, *viz.*, mango, banyan, *pipal, jámbul* (Eugenia jambolana), and *bel* (Ægle marmelos). As a rule the marriage takes place after sunset. The binding portion consists in tying round the bride's neck a necklace of glass beads by an elderly Phudgi woman, and in throwing sacred grains of rice over the heads of the bride and bridegroom by a Bráhman priest. This is followed by a tumultuous dance, two of the party holding the bride and bridegroom on their shoulders; the lifting of the couple being a common spirit-scaring rite, favoured by numerous tribes in the Presidency. On these occasions much liquor is consumed.

Religion.

Phudgis belong to the Hindu religion. The special deities of their worship are Hanumán, Cheda, and Vira. They observe the usual Hindu fasts and feasts. Their priests are Palshikar Bráhmans.

Death.

The dead are burnt. Those who are too poor to burn, bury their dead. On the third day after death the spirit of the deceased is propitiated by offering cooked food, fowls and liquor on the spot

* See Glossary to Borrow's "The Bible in Spain", Vol. II.

where the corpse was burnt. On the twelfth day after death the caste is feasted.

Phudgis make their living chiefly by working as day-labourers. A few are cowherds, house-servants, and husbandmen. Occupation

In food they resemble Kunbis. Food.

PHUL.—A sub-division of Mális.

PHUL-MALI VAIDU.—A sub-division of Vaidus.

PICHATI.—A synonym for Renukrái Gondhali.

PILLAI.—A synonym for Pille.

PILLES, or PILLAIS, (1) numbering 153 (1901), including 81 males and 72 females, are found in small numbers chiefly in Belgaum, Dhárwár and Bijápur. Pille is a title of the Vellálás, the great cultivating caste of the Tamil country.

PINDHARI.—*See* Pendhári.

PINGLE.—A synonym for Joshi.

PINJARIS, or cotton cleaners, numbering 23,651 (1901), including 11,834 males and 11,817 females, are found all over the Presidency. They have two divisions, Hindu and Musalmán, of whom the latter far outnumber the former, who are found only in Khándesh. They are described below separately under Hindu Pinjáris and Musalmán Pinjáris. Name.

HINDU PINJARIS have six *kuls* or exogamous sections. They are— Exogamous divisions

Barlaskar.	Khairnár.
Jádhav.	Sanoi.
Khanel.	Thákare.

Marriages are prohibited between members of the same *kul*. A man cannot marry his father's sister's or mother's sister's daughter. He may marry his mother's brother's daughter. Marriage with two sisters is allowed and brothers are allowed to marry sisters. Marriage is infant as well as adult. Polygamy is permissible, but polyandry is unknown. The offer of marriage comes from the boy's father, who has to pay a bride-price up to Rs. 100. The day for the marriage is fixed by a Bráhman who conducts the service. The marriage ceremonies of Pinjáris do not differ in any important detail from those observed by local Kunbis. Their *devak* consists of the twigs of the Marriage

(1) Castes and Tribes of Southern India, Vol. VI, p. 198.

Arai (Mimosa rubicaulis) and the *bor* (Zizyphus jujuba) which are brought from Máruti's temple by a married pair as among Kunbis, and tied to the marriage pandal along with a churning stick, a wooden pestle and a stuffed cake. The remarriage of widows is permitted with the sanction of the caste *panch*. A widow cannot marry her father's sister's or mother's sister's son. She may marry a member of her deceased husband's section or her mother's brother's son. The ceremony is attended by the caste *panch*, a Bráhman, a barber, and some married unwidowed women. The essential portion consists in tying a lucky necklace round the widow's neck by one of the widows present. After the ceremony is over the remarried pair go to the village boundary and bury underground a packet of betel leaf and betelnuts. On the first new-moon following the marriage they do not see each other's face. Should a bachelor desire to marry a widow, he is first married to a ring. Divorce is not allowed. A woman taken in adultery can remain in the caste after undergoing a purificatory ceremony and giving a dinner to the castemen

Religion. The caste follow the Hindu law of inheritance and worship by preference Khandoba, Devi and Bahiroba. Their priests are Bráhmans.

Death. The dead are burnt except children under four years of age, who are buried. The standard funeral rites are followed.

Occupation. The hereditary occupation of the caste is cotton-cleaning. Some are husbandmen and day labourers.

Food. In food and drink they follow Kunbis.

MUSALMAN PINJARIS or Pinjárás number 23,351 (1901), including 11,687 males and 11,664 females. They are also called Nadafs and Táis in Gujarát. They are said to represent Hindu Pinjáris who were converted by Aurangzeb. In some places the men take the titles of Shaikh, Sayad or Pathán, after their names. Both men and women dress like Hindus. They eat with other Musalmáns but marry only among themselves. They differ from ordinary Musalmáns in eschewing beef, offering vows to Hindu gods and keeping Hindu festivals. They are Sunnis of the Hanafi school, but are not careful to say their prayers. They respect and obey the *Kázi* and employ him to register their marriages. In many places they have headmen called *mehetars, pátils or chaudharis*, who enquire into and settle their social disputes. They card cotton, cleaning it to stuff matresses, quilts and pillows. Many have left their craft on account of the decline of hand-spinning and found employment as constables, messengers and servants.

PIPAVASI.—A synonym for Darji.

PIRANA MATIA.—A sub-division of Matia Kanbis.

POKHARNA.—A synonym for Pushkarna.

POMLA.—A sub-division of Vághris.

POMLAS, numbering 131 (1901), including 70 males and 61 females, are chiefly found in Ahmedabad, Broach and Surat. Their home tongue, which resembles Telugu, seems to show that they originally belonged to Southern India. They are a primitive tribe and practise the *couvade.* They are great devotees of the goddess Lakshmi Máta. They were formerly tumblers, but now make their living by weaving baskets.

PORNALA.—A sub-division of Vághris.

PORVAD.—A sub-division of Bráhmans and Vániás.

PORVAL.—A synonym for Porvád.

POTACHOR.—A sub-division of Udámbar Bráhmans.

POTRAJA.—A sub-division of Holayás.

POTRE.—A synonym for Dukre.

PRABHUS, sometimes incorrectly called Parbhus, numbering 26,060 (1901) including 13,202 males and 12,858 females, are found in Ṭhána, Kolába, and Bombay city. Name.

They consist of the following divisions :— Endogamous divisions.

1. Chándraseniya Káyasth.
2. Davne.
3. Dhruv.
4. Páthare or Pátáne.

The Davne division, formerly separated from the Chándraseniya, now intermarries freely with the latter. On the other hand, the Dhruv, which separated from the Páthare division, remains distinct to this day, being regarded as socially inferior. Chándraseniyas and Páthares do not intermarry or interdine. They appear to have little in common beyond the name Prabhu, and are described separately below. It is to be noted that Páthare Prabhus seem once to have been closely connected with Pánch Kalshis.

CHANDRASENIYA KAYASTH PRABHUS [1] numbered (1901) 21,941 (males 11,159 females 10,782) of whom 5,162 were found in

(1) The following account has been compiled from materials received from the Thána Chándra Seniya Káyasth Prabhu Club, Baroda Chándra Seniya Káyasth Prabhu community assembled in a public meeting, Devás public meeting of the caste, Rai Saheb B. A. Gupte of Indore, Messrs. Narayan Raghunath Deshpande of Urawada in Mával, Balkrishna Vithal Potnis, Kashinath Malhar Karnik, and Ramchandra Nilkantha Inamdar, by T. V. Gupte of Poona, and adopted by the Chándra Seniya Prabhus assembled in a public gathering of the caste under the auspices of the Chándra Seniya Kayasth Prabhu Social Club, Poona. The materials were examined by Dr. Sir R. G. Bhandarkar.

Thána, 5,782 in Kolába and 2,922 in Bombay city. These numbers include the Davne division. It is usual to refer to both simply as Prabhus or Parbhus.

Chándraseniyas claim to rank as Kshatriya and to be one of the three twice-born castes of the historic divisions of which the members are authorized to perform the *upanayana* ceremony. The custom of not allowing marriage in the same *gotras*, therefore, is obeyed out of reverence for the *rishis*, whose guidance was required in early times as teachers for the performance of the *upanayana* ceremony by the ancestors of this community.

Formerly Davne Prabhus fed with Chándraseniyas but did not intermarry. But after satisfying themselves that the Davne Prabhus were simply thus named on account of their residence in the district of Daman, Davne being a form of Damane, and that they were originally Chandra Seniya Káyastha Prabhus who had gone to Daman to reside, the Chándra Seniya branch resumed marriage connections with this division. They are now treated on an entirely equal footing. The re-union of the branches is of comparatively recent date, and may be taken to exemplify an interesting tendency in certain societies towards the removal of barriers due to geographical causes, barriers which improved means of communication are likely, in many instances, to undermine. Chandra Seniyas must marry with Chandra Seniyas or Davnes and outside the *gotra* or exogamous sub-division. Intermarriage is forbidden between those who are related as *sapindas*. This relationship extends to six degrees when the common ancestor is a male, and four degrees when the common ancestor is a female. In reckoning degrees of relationship, the person under consideration is excluded. Thus, beginning from the bride or bridegroom, six or four degrees exclusive of the couple, *i.e.*, six for the male ancestor and four in case of a female, must be counted without encountering a common progenitor, if marriage between the parties is to be permitted.

Origin and traditions. Popular tradition regarding the origin of the Chándraseniya Káyasth Prabhu caste is in accord with the legendary accounts given in the Mahábhárata and the Puráns of the conflict in early ages between Bráhmans and Kshatriyas. These legends abound in tales of the repeated exterminations of the Kshatriyas by the warlike Bráhman Parashurám. It is related that Vishnu, for the purpose of exterminating the Kshatriya or warrior caste, then guilty of repeated attempts to assert its authority over the Bráhmans, became incarnate as Parashurám. Twenty-one times Parashurám rid the earth of these rebels against Bráhman ascendancy; yet there remained in the end a few to perpetuate the race, and save the caste from extinction. Parashurám was the son of a Bráhman, Jamadagni, and a Kshatriya woman, Renuka, a daughter of Renu of the family of Ikshváku. Parashurám killed Arjuna Sahasrabáhu, according to the Vishnu Puran. Arjuna was of the race of Yadu, and ninth in descent from Haihaya, the great-grandson of that prince. It is believed that Chandrasena was one of the hundred sons of Arjuna.

The caste claims descent from Chandrasena, a Kshatriya king of Oudh. According to the Renuka Máhátmya of the Padma (? Skandha) Purán it is alleged that after Parashurám, in fulfilment of his vow to destroy all Kshatriyas, had killed Arjuna and King Chandrasena, he discovered that Chandrasena's wife had taken refuge with Dálabhya, one of the *rishis*, and that she was with child. To carry out his vow Parashurám went to the sage, who asked him to name the object of his visit, assuring him that, his wish would be fulfilled. Parashurám replied that he wanted Chandrasena's wife. The sage without any hesitation brought the lady, and Parashurám, delighted with the success of his scheme, promised to grant the sage anything he might ask. The sage asked for the unborn child, and Parashurám agreed to give him the child, on the sage engaging that it and its offspring should be trained as clerks, not as soldiers. The child was name Som Rája and his sons Vishwánáth, Mahádev, Bhánu, and Laxumidhar, and their descendants were called Prabhus. They were called Parbhus by Shudras as they could not pronounce the word Prabhu. Bráhmans, taking advantage of this mispronunciation, declared that their true name was Parbhu, that is, bastard or people of irregular birth, but the word is spelt Prabhu in letters and deeds granted to those of the community who served the Sátára and Peshwa governments; and it must be noted that the claims of the Prabhus to the position and rites of Kshatriyas were admitted as recently as the days of the Peshwás.

Mr. Rámrao Narayan Pradhán [1] says that descendants of Chandrasena ruled over Oudh and parts of the North; and that about ninety-five generations had gone by when Mahápadmánand began his rule over Hastinápur, *i.e.*, Delhi. A great reformation had taken place in religion during the days of this Mahápadmánand and his successors, who were known as Navanandas. These Navanandas were succeeded by kings of the Maurya dynasty, among whom Chandragupta and Asoka were strong supporters of the Buddhist religion.

(1) Chandra Seniya Káyastha Prabhuncha Itihas, p. 5.

Mahápadmánand is described in the Bhavishya Purán as a great persecutor of the Kshatriyas, who were strong adherents of the old religion. Many Kshatriya families had to quit their homes and seek shelter with their brother kings. In these days of trouble the descendants of Chandrasena and their followers appear to have left Oudh. An old Maráthi *bakhar*, published by B. A. Gupte in Materials for the History of the Káyastha Prabhus, says that an account of this caste is to be found in Sahyádri Khand, that is, the description of the mountain Sahyádri, in the Abud Khand, that is, the description of the mountain Abu, and Prabhás Khand, that is, the description of Prabhás (*i.e.* Somnáth). Prabhus are found in Nepal. The Prabhu Ratnamála [(1)] informs us that nearly eighty families left Oudh and went to reside at or near about Tal Bhopal. From these various accounts we are led to believe that the migration of these Kshatriyas from Oudh must have taken place in the troublesome time of Mahápadmánand and his successors. All old documents agree in placing the original home of this caste in Oudh. There is further evidence on this point of origin in the admitted fact that the original sanctuary of the goddess Vinzai or Vindhyáchalavásini worshipped by some families of the community is situated on a hill known as Vindhyáchal near Mirzapur in the North-West Provinces.[(2)] In this same province the celebrated hermitage of the sage Dálabhya, who was the proverbial protector of the caste from the persecution of Parashurám, in memory of which fact the caste has adopted a common *gotra* Dálabhya in addition to the special one, is situated on the banks of the Ganges 16 miles from Raibareli and 14 miles to the north of Fatehpur. From Oudh some Prabhus seem to have gone to Nepal and Kashmir, while some took refuge in the Abu mountains. Others again settled near Tal Bhopal, and a few settled in Prabhás. Although the Prabhus found in Nepal and elsewhere have no social intercourse with the Káyasth Prabhus on this side of India, it seems probable from the foregoing account that they are all come from one stock. They all claim a Kshatriya origin. Those who sought an asylum in Kashmir established their position there, and acquired estates for the service they rendered to the State. Romesh Chandra Dutt in his history of India, remarks that the ministers of Kashmir were almost all Káyasths. He does not explain whether the Káyasth ministers of Kashmir were Brahma Káyasth or Chitragupta Káyasth, or whether they were Kshatriya or Chándraseniya Káyasth or even

---

(1) Prabhu Ratnamála, published by the Historical Society of the Chándra Seniya Prabhus of Baroda and Poona, p. 12.

(2) See note on the Vindhiáchalavásini in Appendix II.

Sankarja Káyasth. He is, however, of opinion that they were all Kshatriyas.(1) From the following piece of evidence there is further ground for inferring that they were Kshatriyas. The author of Rájatarangini, which narrates the history of Shriharsha and other Kashmir kings, was the son of a Prabhu minister Mahámátya Champak Prabhu. This suggests that the ministers of Kashmir were styled Prabhu, *i.e.*, lord a synonym for Kshatriya. It has already been stated that nearly eighty families are said to have come from Oudh to Tal Bhopal about the time of Mahápadmánanda, *i.e.*, 724 years before the Sháka era,(2) and there acquired great influence. These were hard days, not only for these Kshatriyas, but for all Hindus who followed the old Vedic religion, as the Buddhist religion had taken root and was fast spreading throughout India. These Kshatriyas had thus to struggle for their own caste privileges. The history of the religious controversy at this period, which was chiefly conducted by Baladev Prabhu and Harlal Prabhu, is given below. The author of the Prabhu Ratnamála and some antiquarians are of opinion that the Gupta dynasty which ruled over Central India for more than eight centuries sprung from these eighty families. The surnames of some families such as Gupte, Ráje, Prádhán, Chaturbal *alias* Chaubal, Ranadip *alias* Randive, Dalapati *alias* Dalavi, Thákur *alias* Thákare, and others seem to have been adopted by those families from the positions they held in the Gupta period, just as the surnames of Chitnis, Fadnis, Potnis, Kárkhánis, Sabnis, Jamenis, and others seem to have been accepted by some families from the occupation or office they held under Marátha rule. The Guptas had established their power in 319 A.D. and made their capitals at various places. That their rule spread over a great part of the country is proved by the stone inscriptions and coins and copper-plates found at various places. That this Gupta dynasty had connection with this branch of the Haihaya Kshatriyas is suggested by the fact that their coins bear the mark of the goddess Sarasvati riding on a peacock with a *trisul* or trident in her hand, a goddess held in great reverence by the caste to this day. Cunningham says that the Gupta kings of Mahákosal were Haihaya kings of the Lunar Dynasty. He is successful in tracing a family which, though calling itself Thákur, claimed to be Kshatriyas of the Haihaya branch of the Lunar Kshatriya race which ruled over Mahákosala. Instances of names such as Guptas or Gupte and Thákurs *alias* Thákare are common. A Haihaya prince of the Lunar Kshatriya race is considered

---

(1) History of Civilization in Ancient India by Romesh Chandra Dutt, Vol. III, pp. 347-350.

(2) Prabhu Ratnamála, p. 170.

an ancestor of the caste, giving fresh ground for the belief that the caste may originally have been connected with the Gupta dynasty. The Silhar and other kings in the Deccan and southern parts of India once admitted the suzerainty of the Guptas. Many Prabhus held high posts at the courts of the Silhar princes, and controlled the civil and military administration of the country. In a stone-inscription found at Chaul, dated 1088 A.D., the name of one Velji Prabhu is found.[1] In the same way, in a stone-inscription of the time of a Silhar prince Aparáditya, dated 1182 A.D., it is mentioned that Anantaráya Prabhu was the officer who governed the Sahásashti, now Salsette, *pargana*; and the Prabhus have a Sáshtikar family among them. The inscription is said to have been written by a Káyasth by name Válig Pandit. Pandit in those days meant a writer. The Prabhus who settled about this time in the Konkan, Mával and Maháráshtra controlled the civil administration of the country. These were the people who kept the accounts of the land revenue and were entitled Deshapandits. The word Deshapandit was afterwards changed into Deshpánde. These Deshapandits, now known as Deshpándes, had to colonise the waste lands in the country, and were also held responsible for the civil administration and the revenues of the land. It was their right to write the documents concerning rights in the land as is the practice even now. It is therefore not unnatural that the stone-inscription above referred to should have been written by Válig Pandit of the Káyasth Prabhu caste. Almost all Deshapandits or Deshpándes in the Mával and Konkan are Káyasth Prabhus. The history of their *vatans* also shows that they were acquired by the families before the Muhammadan power was introduced and established in the Konkan and the Deccan. The fact that the Sahyádri Khand, which is said to have been written about the 10th century, makes mention of the Chándraseniya Prabhus as Káyasths to signify their new profession is also corroborative evidence of the fact that the Chándraseniya Káyasth Prabhus had settled on the slopes of Sahyádri mountains at or about this period. There is another inscription of the time of the Silhar princes. It is a grant made by a Silhar king Hirapál to a Bráhman, and the name of his minister Lakshman Prabhu is mentioned in it. From the genealogies of some of the families in this community we learn that the ancestors of some of them served the kings of Chitor and other Rajput dynasties. The name of Shripat Prabhu, one of the ancestors of the Sátára Chitnis family, is inscribed upon the pillar at Chitor in connection with a victory gained by Rána Lakshman Sinha. This information is also given in a genealogy in

(1) Journal, Bom. Branch R. A. S., Vol. I, p. 135.

the possession of the family. There is an endorsement on it that the genealogy is embodied with the genealogies of forty other families in the *Vanshavriksha* which is in the records of the Rája of Sátára. The Konkan, that is, the Thána and Kolába districts, the old northern boundary of Ratnágiri, the Mával, *i.e.*, the slopes of the Sahyádri including Poona, Sátára, Kolhápur Daman and Baroda State, are the chief centres of this community, and it is generally believed that these places, with the exception of Baroda, were the first settlements of the caste when they came from the north. The representatives of the caste in the Baroda State are so numerous that, were it not for the history of the Maráthás which does not support such a conclusion, it might be inferred that this caste settled there during their progress from north to south. It would be interesting to discover which of the places already mentioned were first selected by the community when they came from the north, and at what period the immigrants arrived. It is a common saying among the old men of the community that their ancestors arrived in numbers from Chitor and the vicinity to settle in the Konkan and Mával, and joined those who had already settled there when Mándavgad was sacked by Ala-uddin in 1295. Reference must be made to the history of Mándavgad with a view to noting the connection between it and this community. In the year 313, when the Gupta emperors took Málwa from the Sháka kings and there established their rule, the fort of Mandu must have passed into their hands; though evidence on the point is wanting, there is ample proof that the Guptas had full sway over the country up to the borders of Khándesh. Various branches of the Guptas were established in this tract of country. The Guptas of Mahákosal are well known to be one of them. This house was connected with the kings of Vakatak or Vindhya Shakti. In the same way there may have been some connection between the kings of Mándavgad and the Guptas. From an inscription found at the Ajanta Caves and Toran-Mal, it appears that Pravarsen, son of Prabhávati Gupta, the daughter of Shridev Gupta, was lord of the fortress Toran-Mal. The mention of the maternal ancestors of a king in an inscription about his estates naturally suggests that it must have been inherited by him from his maternal relations. Whether the descendants of this Pravarsen ruled over Mándavgad and the territories under it is not known, but the point should form an interesting subject for enquiry. The Vindhya Shakti princess, of whom this Pravarsen was born, subsequently became very powerful, and extended her rule over Málwa as far as the confines of Khándesh. Rája Malkadev, from whom the fort was taken, may have some connection with the Guptas through these Vakatak kings. In spite of heroic efforts on the part of Rája Malkadev of Mándavgad to save the fort and the kingdom, eighteen thousand Kshatriyas were slain on the battlefield, and he was forced to fly from the fort to take shelter with his kinsmen residing in the Sahyádri hills.

There is further evidence to show that this community had once connection with Mándavgad. A letter addressed to them in the year 1703 by Shri Chhatrapati Shahumaháráj of Sátára in favour of Rámchandra Mahádev Mándavgadkar proves that they once resided at Mándavgad. From the two inscriptions found at Chaul and other places mentioned above it seems that the Prabhus had begun to settle in the Konkan when the Silhar princes were the rulers of that country. The history of the *vatans* of Deshpándes shows that they were obtained before the kings of the Bahmani dynasty had established their power in the Deccan. Thus the conclusion is again suggested that the Konkan and Mával were inhabited by the caste progenitors in the tenth or eleventh century, and it may thus be shown that since then they have remained stationary and formed an important element in the Marátha confederacy which afterwards embraced those regions. It must next be seen whether these people penetrated elsewhere in the Deccan in search of a home. It has been observed above that many went to the Karnátak and there represented the paramount power. The surname of a family now known as Karnik is given as Karnátakas in a list of surnames which was probably compiled when the people first settled, or at least within a period when they could recollect the history of the ancestors of those families. The Karnátak would seem to have been the early home of the Karnátakas. There are instances of families who even now say that they formerly inhabited Hyderabad in the Deccan and came to this side after the establishment of Marátha rule. The Támhanes and Fanases originally served the Muhammadan kings at Bedar and Bijápur. They subsequently entered the service of the Nizám and then came over to the Maráthás. *Sanads* in their possession prove this. There are families living in the Nizám's territory who claim to be Kshatriya Káyasth and follow the Vedic religion. They allege that they came from the north and took service with the Musalmáns. Some Prabhus in the Karnátak have adopted the Jain religion, but they still style themselves Prabhu and are the holders of estates such as Deshmukh or Deshpánde Vatans. They are known as Desáis. From this it may fairly be concluded that the Kshatriya Prabhus, nicknamed Káyasths, who were able to maintain communication with their caste-fellows in the Konkan or Mával. formed one caste known as Chándra Seniya Káyasth Prabhus.

The history of this caste is readily traceable since the introduction of Muhammadan rule in the Deccan. They served that government with an unsparing zeal in civil and military service. Peace was secured in the country by the Muhammadan rulers by renewing the *vatans* of the Deshmukhs and Deshpandits or Deshpándes in ratifying their grants. After the great famine in 1396, very signal service to the country was rendered by these Deshmukhs and Deshpándes by re-colonising it and by helping in the restoration of peace. At this time they had to perform military service in order to quell the rebellious mountainous tribes. The King of Bidar sent Mulk-ultijar in 1429 with an army to help these Deshmukhs and Deshpándes in the settlement of the country. Titles were bestowed upon some of the Deshmukhs which are enjoyed by those families to this day. The title Abhangrao of the Prabhu Deshmukh at Atawne, and the title of Sarjerao of the Deshmukh of Náte, as well as the title Adarrao of the Prabhu Deshpándes of Mával are well-known. In this way they helped the Muhammadan rulers in maintaining civil order and protecting the fortresses from foreign aggression. The *vatans* continued to the Chaubals of Chaul, Nádkars of Mahád, Deshmukhs of Náte and Nizámpur in the Konkan, and Vaidyas and Dighes of the Mávals, and many other Deshpándes and Kulkarnis bear ample historical testimony to the fact. We find the name of Parashram Prabhu Karnik in a *sanad* as far back as about 1426 granted by the King of Bidar to the Vajaseniya Bráhmans. He was a courtier of the king and was appointed to settle the disputes of the Bráhmans.

The caste exhibited remarkable bravery, statesmanship, loyalty and intelligence during Marátha rule, virtues for which it was justly famed. It was one of the chief sources of the strength of Shiváji and his successors. Murár Báji Deshpánde of Mahád,(1) Vishvasrao Nánáji, Bábáji Boaji, (2) Dádji Raghunáth and others were eminent military and civil Prabhu officers of Shiváji. Báláji Aoji Chitnis was his chief adviser and secretary. Shiváji was favourably disposed to the caste. (3) On one occasion he dismissed all the Bráhmans who held high posts and engaged Káyasth Prabhus in

(1) Grant Duff, p. 92, J. Ranado's History, pp. 104, 78

(2) Prabhu Ratnamala, pp. 36, 42.

(3) Grant Duff, p. 62.

their places; and in reply to complaints he remarked that while all the Musalmán places of trust held by Bráhmans had been given up without a struggle, those held by Prabhus had been most difficult to take, and that one of them, Rájpuri, had not yet been taken. [1]

The brothers Lingo Shankar and Vasaji Shankar helped Rájárám in safely conveying his family to Jinji. Khando Ballál played an unparalled part in Marátha history in the reorganization of the Marátha power. Prayágji Anant, the ancestor of the famous Raoji Apaji of later Marátha history, defended the fort of Sátára, and Mahádaji Báji, brother of the illustrious Murár Báji Prabhu and ancestor of the Sardár Potnis family, recovered Sinhgad and other places from the Musalmáns when Rájarám was at Jinji. These and others were the chief supporters of the new Hindu dynasty that was established in Mahárásbtra. The *sanads* granted by the Nizám—Asuffja Bahádur Nizám-ul-Mulk Sipa Sálar—to Vyankat Prabhu Támhane testify to the gallant service he rendered to the State with five thousand horse in several campaigns. Vyankat Prabhu was granted in his old age the Faujdári Mahál *jáyhir* of the districts of Fatiábád (now Dharur) and Khujista Buniad (now Aurangabad). His sons Lakshman, Mahádeva and Govind succeeded to the *jaghir*. Of these sons Lakshman Prabhu was afterwards very useful to the Bhonsles of Nagpur and Akalkot in the establishment of their power. Even during the rule of the Peshwás, persons of this community, like the warlike brothers Sakhárám Hari and Báburao Hari Gupte, of whose unswerving loyalty to their master Nána Fadnavis was extremely jealous, and Nilkanthra Page played a conspicuous part in the maintenance of Marátha rule. Murár Rao Daulat rendered gallant service to Sindia in capturing Gulám Kádir of Delhi, upon which the well-known Diwáni Mutalki *sanad* was obtained from the Emperor of Delhi; Ráji Appáji made the Gáekwár's rule secure in Gujarát; Vithalrao Devaji's name is still held in great reverence and respect in Káthiáwár; Bapuji Raghunath Dighe was a popular Diván at Dhár.

This caste has maintained its character for loyalty and trustworthiness to the present day. Members of it hold places of trust both in Native States and under the British Government, to whom they have always exhibited conspicuous loyalty.

---

(1) Bombay Gazetteer, Thána Volume, p. 88.

They have the following exogamous divisions or *gotras* :— Exo-gamous divisions.

1.	Agashi.	14.	Krip.
2.	Atri.	15.	Maitrayan.
3.	Bhagur.	16.	Paingya.
4.	Bhardvaya.	17.	Pulaha.
5.	Bhargawa.	18.	Raibha.
6.	Bhrigu.	19.	Samir.
7.	Dewal.	20.	Sandilya.
8.	Gandhamadan.	21.	Sankhyayan.
9.	Garga	22.	Vaidhruva.
10.	Gautama.	23.	Vasishta.
11.	Jamdagni.	24.	Visvamitra.
12.	Kapit.	25.	Vyaghra.
13.	Kashapa.		

These *gotras*, unlike those of the Bráhmans, do not indicate that a family included in any one of them is a descendant of the particular eponymous *rishi*, but the members merely claim to be disciples.

As a rule girls must be married after the completion of the eighth year and before attaining puberty, the boys generally being four or six years older. Thus child marriage and not infant marriage is allowed. No cohabitation or even familiarity or introduction is recognised or tolerated before marriage. Polygamy is allowed, but it is resorted to mainly in cases of failure of male issue. It is highly unpopular, and has very largely died out. Polyandry is strictly prohibited. The first of the eight forms of marriage, *viz.*, the Bráhma form, is followed by this community, and the procedure is according to the Rig Prayoga. This Bráhma form consists in the gift of the daughter clothed only with a single robe to a man presumably learned in the Vedas whom her father voluntarily invites and respectfully receives. In the actual marriage ceremony there are numerous forms; the following are the principal :— Marriage.

(1) *Vágdán*, *i.e.*, gift by word.

(2) *Simántpujan*, *i.e.*, reception and adoration of the bridegroom at the entrance of the town.

(3) *Vadhugrihagaman*, *i.e.*, going to the place of the bride.

(4) *Madhuparka*, *i.e.*, a respectful offering made to a guest or the bridegroom on his arrival at the door of the father of the bride.

(5) *Parasparanirikshan*, *i.e.*, the ceremony of gazing at each other through the screen called "Antarpat" and of garlanding the bridegroom by the bride.

(6) *Kanyádán*, i.e., the ceremony of giving away the girl in marriage.

(7) *Viváhahoma*, i.e., offering of oblation by throwing *ghi* into the consecrated fire in honour of the marriage.

(*a*) *Pánigrahana*, i.e., ceremony of taking by the hand.

(*b*) *Lájáhoma*, i.e., throwing parched grains into the consecrated fire.

(*c*) *Saptapadi*, i.e., the ceremony of bride and bridegroom walking together seven steps after which the marriage becomes irrevocable.

The *Viváhahoma* ending in *Saptapadi* is the operative and essential portion of the ceremony. On completion of the last step the actual marriage is considered to be complete. While performing the ceremony under the Bráhma form as used by the Bráhmans this caste has retained up to date certain special customary observances which go to prove or rather remind the community of their Kshatriya origin. Some of them may be briefly noted here :—

(1) The marriage of the Prabhus must necessarily be in a *mandap* (pendal) and in the presence of all relations and friends like the *Swayamwar* in a *Sabha* of the olden Kshatriya period, whereas the Bráhmans perform their marriages in the inner part of the house.

(2) Holding unsheathed swords over the head of the couple behind.

The remarriage of widows is not permitted. Divorce is not permitted. A woman may be abandoned by her husband on the ground of misconduct or of a change of religion, etc. ; a wife so renounced cannot marry again. A man can be divorced by his wife for a change of religion, but she cannot marry again in such a case.

Religon. The Hindu Law of inheritance is followed by the caste. The members of the caste follow the Vedic form of religion, and are Shaivas. They worship the god Shiva in preference to other members of the Hindu Trinity, a usage based on immemorial custom and the assumed superior potency of this deity. They are followers of the Advaita school of Shankarácharya, but also worship Vishnu, Ganpati, and other gods. Such of the minor gods as are admittedly manifestations of the supreme spirit are recognized by the Prabhus. Khanduba and Bhairav are regarded as incarnation of Shiva and the goddesses such as Ekavira, Vinzai, Vyághrámbari are manifestations of Párvati the wife of Shiva. Bráhmans are employed for religious and ceremonial purposes and for the recital of *mantras* but the actual ceremony is performed by the members of the community. These priests are received on terms of equality by other Bráhmans. No other class of Hindus can sérve them as priests.

Death ceremonies.

Prabhus burn their dead, but infants who have not cut their teeth as well as persons dying of small-pox are buried. The ashes, whenever possible, are finally disposed of in holy waters, and a few bones at least are invariably set aside from the ashes and consigned to holy waters. In the case of burial the head is placed facing the south. The *shráddhas* and funeral obsequies are the only ceremonies performed for the salvation of ancestors. No particular ceremonies are prescribed for the propitiation of childless ancestors or persons who have died a violent death. The funeral obsequies are performed during the first thirteen days after death. Oblations of rice are offered every day, in consequence of which the soul of the deceased attains a spiritual body limb by limb till on the thirteenth day it is enabled to start on its journey. During the first year after death the offering is repeated every month as the soul accomplishes each portion of its journey. In twelve months the journey ends, and a *shráddha* ceremony is performed on an extensive scale on the anniversary of the death. This ceremony is repeated on each successive anniversary. In the dark half of *Bhádrapada* a *shráddha* ceremony technically called *paksha* or *mahálaya shráddha* is performed for the salvation of the *manes* on the same day of the month as the death took place. If the *mahálaya shráddha* is not performed on the proper date within the fortnight it may be postponed till any day before the sun enters Capricorn. The *mahálaya shráddha* of a person dying a violent death is performed on the thirteenth of the fortnight which is called *Gháyál Trayodashi*, *i.e.*, the thirteenth day for a violent death. Besides this, daily oblations of water are offered to the dead after *Sandhya* adoration. The leading rite in the *shráddha* is the offering of the funeral ball made of rice. Three such balls are offered to the three paternal ancestors, three to the three maternal ancestors, the rest of the ancestors receive a smaller ball, while the remote relations only receive oblations of water.

The caste is not named after any animal, plant, weapon, or implement. Arms are now worshipped at the *Dasara*, which is the commencement of the military year, an apparent survival of a worship appropriate to warlike times. On the 5th day after the birth of a child, sword and pen, paper and ink are worshipped, the sword being the symbol of the Kshatriya origin, and the pen, paper and ink that of the present occupation of a writer. The cow is regarded as sacred and is worshipped. A cow is not killed or eaten or cut or burnt or yoked to the plough. It is not used for labour of any kind, and is universally regarded as a symbol of the deity Gáyatri. The only other animal worshipped by the Prabhus, like other Hindus, is the serpent. This serpent worship has a legendary justification in the ancient myth that the earth rests on the hood of a thousand headed cobra called Shesh, whose mighty coils form also the resting place of the great Lord of the Universe. In honour of this Indian Atlas, the divine cobra, cobras are worshipped once every year on Nágpanchami day; and in some families a golden image of a cobra is chosen as object of special worship, along with the Shivlingamban.

The *tulsi, pipal,* banyan, *shami* and *umbar* are considered sacred trees and are worshipped generally on particular days assigned for the worship of each of them.

Occupation. The original occupation of a Prabhu was that of a soldier until by force of circumstances he became a writer. Between these extreme traditions of war and peace they continually worked in politics and rose to be great generals, ministers, politicians and secretaries. They have not given up these occupations up to the present time and they either serve in the army in high capacities in the Native States, or are Government servants. The only new professions which they hitherto have been induced to take up are those of lawyers, doctors, and engineers. A great number hold responsible posts under the British Government and in the Native States, or are eminent professional men. Some of them are *jághirdhárs, inámdárs* and land-owners, and some are agriculturists.

Food. The caste does not eat the leavings of any people, not even their own. The Prabhus of the present day are, as a rule, vegetarians and in public dinners of the caste animal food of every kind is strictly excluded. But in private dinners mutton and fish are admitted to the table. Prabhus living up-country very rarely eat fish. As regards wine and other alcoholic drinks, many of the caste allow them but only in private. The caste does not eat *kachi, pakki,* drink or smoke with any lower caste. No Prabhu would smoke a pipe used by his caste fellow, much less by a man of any other caste. The Bráhmans generally do not object to *pakki* at the hands of Prabhus. Except from vegetarian Bráhmans of Mahárashtra, the Chándra Seniya Káyasth Prabhus will not take *kachi, pakki,* or water from any other caste.

Gujaráti Bráhmans are sometimes employed at some places by local custom as water-bearers, but not as cooks.

PATHARE PRABHUS also called Pátáne or Paithane Prabhus, numbering 4,119 (1901), including 2,043 males and 2,076 females, are found chiefly in the Town and Island of Bombay, a few having settled on the Thána coast and in Poona. The latter, they say, came to Poona from Bombay about a hundred years ago as clerks in Government offices, and after retiring from service settled there with their families. The rest appear to have also come from Bombay as clerks within the last fifty years, and are not permanently settled in Poona.

According to Bráhman accounts, the term Pátáne is properly Patit or Fallen, because the Prabhus have fallen from being warriors to writers. The Konkan traditions and to some extent the evidence of their home speech suggest that the Pátáne Prabhus are descended from Rajputs of Anhilváda Pattan in North Gujarát, and may take their name from that town.(1) According to Rao Bahádur P. B. Joshi, the term Pátháre is a tribal name derived from Pratihára.(2)

Pátháre Prabhus also claim to be Kshatriyas. Their claim, which is supported by their appearance and by their history, has been admitted by the Shankaráchárya of the Shringeri *Math*.

According to the Sahyádrikhand (chapter 28), on one occasion king Ashvapati of the solar race, a supposed patron or ancestor of the Pátháre Prabhus, happened to go to the holy city of Paithan. While he was staying in that city, the sage Bhrigu also happened to arrive. Owing to his other engagements, the king was not able to receive him with the honours due to his high and sacred position. Bhrigu took offence, and being greatly enraged, he cursed the king saying that from that day he would lose his sovereign power and that his race would become extinct. Thereupon the king fell at the feet of the sage and implored his forgiveness. To this the sage replied that his words were bound to take their effect, but as a favour, he granted that, in future, the king's descendants should be required to maintain themsleves, not by the power of the sword, but by the power of the pen. And he further ordained that their family name Pátháre Prabhu should be changed to Paithan-Pattan or Pattan Prabhu in memory of this event.

---

(1) Bom. Gaz., Vol. XIV, p. 90. (2) Pátháre Prabhus, p. 10.

From historical evidence [(1)] it appears probable that the Páthàre Prabhus belong to the race of the Pratihára kings of Kanauj and Rájputána. From their original home which, in all probability, was in Sauráshtra and the United Provinces, the Páthàre Prabhus migrated between the 11th and 12th centuries of the Christian era to Paithan on the Godávari, and from Paithan, at the close of the 13th century they came to the Northern Konkan along with their *gurus* or spiritual guides, the Shukla Yajurvediya, otherwise called Palshikar, Bráhmans.

Language. In their houses Prabhus talk Maráthi. Besides by the Gujaráti element their home talk differs from the speech of others by the large number of Hindustáni, Portuguese and English words in every day use. The names in common use among men are Dwárkánáth, Moreshvar, Moroba, Sadánand and Vishvanáth ; and among women, Hirábái, Nánibái, Sokarábái and Sundarábái.

Divisions. Páthàre Prabhus do not eat together nor intermarry with Dhruv Prabhus. They have several *gotras* or exogamous sections, the chief of which are, Bharadwáj, Brahma Janárdan, Gárgya, Gautam, Jamadagni, Mudgal and Vashishtha. They say that formerly they had no surnames and that the fashion of using surnames has been introduced within the last sixty years.

Marriage. Marriages are prohibited between members of the same *gotra*, as also between the children of sisters. Marriage between a sister's daughter and brother's son is not allowed. The old restriction of marrying girls before they come of age is not now followed. They do not allow widow marriage and divorce. Their customs come under the six heads of marriage, pregnancy, birth, infancy, thread-girding and death.

Except that a sword is worshipped in the *Sathi* or fifth day birth ceremony and in the *devapratishtha* (installation of the marriage deity), that a drawn sword is held by one of the two persons who hold the marriage curtain, and that the bridegroom carries during the marriage ceremony a weapon—now a penknife—their religious ceremonies do not differ from those of Bráhmans.[(2)]

Religion. Most Páthàre Prabhus are followers of the Smárt sect. Their spiritual head is the Shankaráchárya of the Shringeri monastery.

---

(1) Pathare Prabhus—Rao Bahadur P. B. Joshi, p. 17.

(2) For a detailed description of these ceremonies, *see* Bom. Gaz., Vol. XVIII, Part I, pp. 194—235.

Formerly their chief goddess was Prabhávati. to whom they dedicated their earliest shrine at Mahim. Originally the priests of the caste were Shukla Yajurvediya or Palshikar Brahmans, but now they are mostly Rigvedi Deshasths Karhádás and Chitpávans, their high priest being a Deshasth. Few Prabhus became ascetics or religious beggars.

Páthúre Parbhus are mostly writers. They have played a conspicuous part in the early settlement and developmet of Bombay; and under the Hindu and Muhammadan rulers as well as under the British Government, the members of this community have held positions of trust and responsibility. At one time their monopoly of clerkships was so general that their caste name became a synonym for English writer, and was used as such in the office records. Their monopoly has broken down, but they are pushing and successful as doctors, lawyers, engineers, and in the higher branches of Government service. Occupation.

Patháre Prabhus eat fish and the flesh of goats, sheep, wild pig, deer, hare, the wood-pigeon, quail and water fowl. The use of liquor is prohibited. They will eat cooked food at the hands of Bráhmans only. Food.

DHRUV PRABHUS, literally Lords descended from Dhruv, are found only in the city of Poona. According to tradition, Dhruv, from whom they claim descent, was the son of Uttánpát, a Kshatriya king of Oudh, whose name Uttánpát, according to their story was the origin of the name Pátáne Prabhus. Dhruvs are said to be descended from some Páth áres who, about 240 years ago, were put out of caste for a breach of caste rules. But the Dhruvs claim to be the same as Páthares. In about 1881 A.D. they applied to be readmitted into caste; but the Páthares refused on the ground that the two classes had been so long separate. The Dhruvs have many written statements from the Poona Páthare Prabhus stating that their ancestors admitted that the two classes were the same. The Dhruvs say that they came as writers from Bombay and Thána to Poona during the time of the Peshwás, and have since settled in the district. They have no sub-divisions. Among their surnames are Kotkar and Mánkar. They resemble the Páthare Prabhus in appearance and customs. They are either Smárts or Bhágvats, and have house images of Ganpati, Mahádev, Vishnu, Rám, Krishna and Annapurna. Their family deities are Indráyani at Alandi, Ekvira at Kárli in Poona, Khandoba of Jejuri and Bhaváni of Tuljápur. Their priests are Deshasth Bráhmans, whom they greatly respect. They keep the usual Bráhmanic fasts and feasts, and make pilgrimages to Benares, Pandharpur, Jejuri, and Vajreshvari in Thána.

PRADHAN.—A sub-division of Mahárs.

PRANTHALIA.—A sub-division of Ahirs.

PRASHNORA.—A sub-division of Nágar Bráhmans.

PRETWAL.—A sub-division of Bráhmans.

PUJARI.—A synonym for Shaiva Gurav; a sub-division of Jangams.

PULAR.—A sub-division of Mahárs.

PUNDWAL.—A sub-division of Bráhmans.

PURBHAYYA.—United Provinces men coming into the Deccan and Gujarát.

PUSHKARNA.—A sub-division of Bráhmans.

PUSHKARVAL.—A sub-division of Vániás.

RABADIA.—A sub-division of Karád Vániás.

Name and origin.

RABARIS,[1] numbering 108,715 (1901), including 56,680 males, and 52,035 females, are chiefly found in Cutch, Káthiáwar, Pálanpur and Ahmedabad, and a few in other Gujarát districts and Native States. They are an immigrant tribe of herdsmen who were formerly resident in Márwár and Sind and perhaps at a remote date in Baluchistán. They still worship the goddess Hingláj and make pilgrimages to her shrine in Baluchistán. The chief seat of their tribal goddess Sikotra is at Jodhpur.

Rabáris are also known as Bhopás,[2] Moghás, Ráikás, Vishotars and Sinais in Cutch. The term Bhopa is applied to them because many of them serve in the temples of the *mátás* or local mother goddesses, distinguished from others by wearing red instead of white woollen turbans and a *dhoti* instead of trousers. Mogha means 'mute, confused' and bears reference to Sámbal, their traditional ancestor, who is said to have been prevented from exchanging words with his celestial wives, on pain of separation. Rabáris are called Ráikás after one of the celestial wives of this Sámbal. According to the Bombay Gazetteer the term Vishotar is applied to them because at the time of Parshurám's persecution one of them saved the lives of twenty, *viz.*, Kshatriyas. But another account states that Vishotar, more correctly Vinshottar (twenty more than hundred) is applied to

(1) The information contained in this article is taken largely from notes supplied by Mr. M. K. Mehta.

(2) Bhope or Bhute is similarly a caste of servants of goddesses in the Deccan.

a gathering of hundred and twenty families. The headman of the Rabáris is known as Sinái, and hence any Rabári is called Sinái.

Rabáris are unanimous in naming Sámbal as their common ancestor; the first Rabári (Ad Rabári) as they call him, whom they believe to have been created by god Shiva to take charge of a dromedary, also of celestial origin. Tradition relates that Shiva gave him three of his *apsarás*, celestial damsels, as wives, Ráyaka, Kunan, and Renuka. In course of time, Sámbal had children, a son and four daughters. Shiva, the ascetic god, asked Sámbal, now that he had a large family, to leave his celestial abode and live outside, and from that time forward, Sámbal was known as Rahabári, *i.e.*, he who lives outside. It is further related that Sámbal was not permitted to exchange a word with his celestial wives on pain of separation from them. He thus became mute which, it is said, conferred on him the appellation of Mogha or mute to the Rabáris. When the four daughters of Sámbal, Námal, Kámal, Premal and Uma, all very beautiful, grew up, they were wooed and won by four Rajput youths of Ráthod, Padiár, Parmar and Yádav stocks, and these and their descendants, became Rabáris. Further, at the time of Parshurám's persecution the Rabári tribe was strengthened by the joining of other tribes, who hid their Rajput origin and betook themselves to a Rabári life. Whatever discrepancies there may be in details, it is certain that, with the exception of that of Sámbal, all the exogamous divisions of Rabáris have Rajput names. This fact gives some support to their claim to a Rajput strain in their blood or at least to their being closely allied to Rajputs. Traditions.

According to another tradition, the Rabáris were originally Rajputs, who, instead of marrying Rajput women, married celestial damsels, *apsarás*, as stated above. According to this account they were called Rahábáris, that is, goers out of the path, because they did not marry Rajput wives. It is possible that Rahábári refers to their nomad habits as dwellers in pasture land, but the derivation is more probably a pun on the name of the tribe.

The original home of Rabáris was Márwár. According to one account, the Rabáris of Cutch had their home in Jhálra Pátan, in the time of Alla-ud-din Khilji. In one of his expeditions to Rájputána, Alla-ud-din heard of the extraordinary beauty of a Rabári girl of that place and wanted to marry her. The Rabáris craved a short respite to consider the matter, giving their bards as hostages. They then secretly left the place, and wandering west came to Nagar Summa in Sind, where a Sumra prince was ruling. He gave them shelter. Soon after, about the year 1315 A.D. the Sumra power in Sind was crushed by the Muhammadans. The Rabáris then took refuge with the Sammas and went with them to Cutch, supplying them with milk from their herds of camels and cows. But they never forgot their former patrons, the Sumrás, and to this day, their women do not colour their ivory bangles but wear them white as a sign of mourning.

The earliest settlement of Rabáris in Cutch was Morchimána, a village near Mátáno Madha in Lakhapat district. Vágham Chávda Gadha and Ghunthali, the two villages with which the first advent of Sammas in Cutch is associated, were also situated in or near the same district—a circumstance which lends support to their belief that they came to Cutch with the Sammas about the year 1320 A.D. The Rabáris further attribute the easy terms on which they hold land in Cutch to their devotion to the present ruling tribe of Cutch. So complete was their exodus from Sind that not a single family was left. The present Rabári families in Sind are immigrants from Cutch. Some of the Rabári families, especially those in Anjár and Vághad, appear to have come from Márwár.

Appearance, dress and ornaments.

Rabáris are strong, tall and well-made, with high features, large eyes and oval faces. In South Gujarát, the men's dress mostly resembles that of poor Rajput cultivators. In Central Gujarát, they wear a loose headcloth, a jacket and a waistcloth. In South Gujarát, a woman's dress consists of a petticoat, a long-sleeved bodice reaching to the waist, and a piece of cloth or a black woollen blanket thrown over the head. In Central Gujarát, the bodice is short and short-sleeved and no blanket is worn on the head. Except that the women wear a red and black worsted thread round the left anklet, the ornaments of Rabári women do not differ much from those of Kanbis. Both men and women are fond of tattooing their bodies, the men their arms, and the women their cheeks, chin, lower lip, breast and arms.

The Rabáris have a headman but he has little authority, and most disputes are settled at meetings of the men of the caste.

Language.

The home speech of almost all is Gujaráti, with Márvádi inflections in Cutch, where a few speak Brij. The names in use among men are Jiwan, Khengár, Gova, Mándan, Paba, Amar ; and among women Devi, Láchhu, Ráju, Jasi, Surtáni, etc. There is no superstition as to the naming of children but opprobrious names, such as Kachra (refuge), Ukarda (dunghill), etc., are given to a son whose elder brother has died.

The Rabáris live in small hamlets of huts with mud walls and thatched or tiled roofs. In Káthiáwár, they are termed *rus* and in Cutch *vándhas*. They wander with their flocks, cattle and camels in search of pasture, and when it fails, move as far as Thána, North Gujarát and Márwár.

In Káthiáwár, the Rabáris have six divisions, the Sorathiás, the Vadhiárás of the Bhádar bank, the Aligiás living near Kodinár, the Vinviás of the Venu river, the Gujarátis of Hálár, and the Honás of Porbandar whose goddess is at Sangaváda in Junágadh. These six divisions eat together but do not intermarry. Some of the surnames of Rabáris are the same as Rajput surnames. Their surnames are Aga, Ajána, Al, Amla, Badh, Barád, Bhadka, Bhangla, Bhárin, Bhátcha, Bhuka, Bhubhalia, Bhungalia, Bhungar, Chadka, Chároneta, Chávda, Cheláns, Chohán, Daichal, Damál, Dev, Dia, Dharbutia, Dedia, Gángoda, Gohel, Gotána, Jhor, Jádhav, Jihor, Kachila, Kond, Kalar, Kalotra, Kambhlia, Karchod, Karmata, Kataria, Khár, Kharod, Kodiatar, Langhar, Lavituka, Lodha, Luni, Makvána, Mangra, Mari, Markata, Moida, Muku, Nagal, Padhár, Pahuvála, Pankuta, Parmár, Parmáta, Patwádi, Puchhalia, Ráthod, Rojia, Samod, Sávdhar, Selana, Sheval, Ur, Vangal, Varana, Varmái, Varchar, Vasa, Vatma and Vava. In Cutch they are divided into thirteen clans or sub-divisions as under :— Endogamous divisions.

1. Avalpura :—Kramta.
2. Bhatti :—Kálar, Gángar, Ghatti, Ratti.
3. Chávda :—Bhunbadia, Ajána, Kalbhána, Katária.
4. Chohán :—Bostar, Rojia, Luni, Káchhela, Bhángra, Sábdhara, Bhádka, Bárad, Bukan, Muriya, Bujbhukan, Sadtar.
5. Dábhi :—Gurchhar, Ulva, Karbata, Dhagal.
6. Padiar :—Khámbla, Pasuára.
7. Parmár :—Motan, Sukel, Sábadharia, Bheet, Gihad, Kola, Vána, Máru, etc.
8. Ráthod :—Nángasa, Shekha, Gujar, Daiya, Khekha, Vákhán, Shevár.
9. Sambal.
10. Sisodiá :—Mori, Mordáv, Dhumbal, Merán.
11. Solanki :—Chelána, Khátána, Mahesh, Motman.
12. Tunvar :—Bhima, Makavána, Traváya, Ráváya, Tadtána.
13. Yádav :—Al, Vághel, Siwádia, Pandit, Langhat, Kadva.

Marriage is allowed with a maternal uncle's daughter, but is prohibited with a father's sister's daughter or mother's sister's Marriage rules.

daughter. Marriage with a wife's sister is allowed during the wife's lifetime or after her death. Two brothers may marry two sisters. Girls are married from nine to sixteen and boys from twelve to twenty. Sexual license before marriage is not allowed. If a girl commits sexual indiscretions with a man of her caste before marriage and becomes pregnant, the slip is condoned by her marriage with the man involved. The man is also heavily fined. Polygamy is permitted, but polyandry is unknown.

Birth Ceremonies.

No ceremonies are performed on the day of birth. On the sixth day after a birth Rabáris worship the goddess Chhatti After childbirth the mother remains impure for twelve to twenty-five days. Children are named on the fifteenth day after birth. Very few perform any ceremony on the first giving of cooked food to a child.

Marriage Ceremonies.

Among Rabáris all marriages take place on the same day. The Rabáris of one village or of two or three villages who wish to have their daughters married meet in a temple. A Bráhman is called and he fixes the marriage day. Four days before the day fixed a booth is set up in front of each girl's house. On the evening of the marriage day the bridegrooms go to the brides' houses and seat themselves in the booth beside the bride. A Bráhman recites verses, the hands of the bride and bridegroom are joined, and they walk seven times round a fire which is lighted in the centre of the booth. This is the binding portion of the ceremony. The father of the bridegroom pays the bride's father Rs. 25 to Rs. 150, and also feasts the bridegroom's relations.

Widows generally re-marry, except in Surat, where the caste levy a prohibitory tax on widows' marriage. In most cases the widow marries the younger brother of her deceased husband. In Káthiáwár and Cutch the younger brother of her deceased husband or a more distant younger male relation of the family has the first choice.

The rule regarding divorce varies in different parts of the Province. In some places both husband and wife are free to break the marriage bond ; in other places the wife cannot divorce the husband ; and in others the husband cannot divorce his wife without the sanction of the head of the caste. A divorced woman is allowed to marry a second time, her marriage being conducted in the form of a widow re-marriage.

Religion.

Rabáris follow the Hindu law of inheritance. They are generally worshippers of mothers or *mátás*, though a few among them belong to the Bijmárgi, Rámánandi and Shaiva sect. In Cutch many of them serve as priests in *máta* temples. The commonest forms under which the *máta* is worshipped are a peacock's feather and a conch-shell. They worship the cobra on the *Kálichaudas* or dark fourteenth in October-November and offer the cobra milk and cocoa kernel. They also worship minor deities like Pábu, Yakshas, Kshetrapáls, etc., and make offerings to them on days sacred to them. The offerings are partaken of by the offerers themselves. They keep the ordinary Hindu holidays, but among the Bijmárgis their great day is the second of every Hindu month, especially the second of *Mágh* in January-Feburary. On the second of every Hindu month they drink the whole day's supply of milk or give it to Bráhmans or other religious beggars. Few believe in sorcery or witchraft but they trust to the ordinary Hindu omens. Only a few visit places of Hindu pilgrimage. Their priests are Audich, Sompará and Rájgor Bráhmans.

Death ceremonies.

They burn their dead. The dead body is tied to a bamboo bier and is taken out of the house feet foremost. The corpse-bearers do not halt on the way, do not offer rice-balls, and do not change the position of the body. After reaching the burning ground, the mourners raise a pile of wood and carry the corpse four times round the pile and lay the wood upon it. The chief-mourner, with fire in his hand, walks four times round the pile and sets light to it. After the body is burnt the mourners bathe and return to the house of the deceased. On the third day the chief mourner goes to the burning ground and there sets an earthen pot filled with water. On the eleventh day with the help of a Káyatia Bráhman they perform the *shráddha* ceremony. Caste people are feasted on the eleventh and twelfth days.

Occupation.

Rabáris rear cows, buffaloes, goats and sheep, and camels in Káthiáwár and Cutch. In Káthiáwár they are particularly fond of camels, which they tend in the large salt marshes which fringe a great part of the peninsula.* They make their living chiefly from the sale of clarified butter and the wool of sheep. A few among them work as husbandmen and messengers. In Central Gujarát, like the Bharváds, they make money by penning their flocks in unsown fields. The men are dull and stupid, but the women are shrewd and intelligent. In

* Colonel Tod notices the cattle-stealing habits of the desert Rabáris. He says the word Rabári is (A.D. 1820) used throughout Hindustán to denote persons employed in rearing and tending camels, who are always Moslems. In Rájputána they are a distinct tribe employed entirely in rearing camels or in stealing them, in which they evince a peculiar dexterity, competing with the Bháts in the practice. When they come upon a herd of camels, the boldest and most experienced strikes his lance into the first he reaches, then dips a cloth in the blood which at the end of his lance he thrusts close to the nose of the next, and, wheeling about, sets off at speed followed by the whole herd lured by the scent of blood and the example of their leader—Annals of Rájasthán, II, 293.

South Gujarát the women sell wool and clarified butter and manage all money matters, and are much more trusted by the wool and butter merchants than their husbands. In south-west Káthiáwár a class of Rabáris has attached itself from time immemorial to the Jethvás, and, like the Mers, can be called on for military service when required. In return they have to pay fewer taxes than other people; and a gift of Rs. 100 is given to the heir of any one who is killed in the chief's service.

Food. Most of them take flesh and spirits, and in Káthiáwár they do not scruple to eat with Musalmáns. In Cutch they live for days almost solely on camel's milk.

In Cutch the Rabáris will eat kachhi, pakki, drink and smoke with Ahirs, Chárans, Bharváds, Rávals, Parjiyas, Sutárs, Kunbis, Kumbhárs, Valands, and Sáis. Rajputs will eat pakki, kachhi, drink and smoke with Rabáris.

RACHEVARS numbering 959 (1901), including 535 males and 424 females, are found in small numbers in Ahmednagar, Khándesh and Dhárwár. They are tumblers and acrobats and come from Mysore.(1)

Name and origin. **RADDIS,** numbering 82,858 (1901), including 41,798 males and 41,060 females, are a large cultivating caste who appear to have immigrated from Mysore and Madras at a remote period. They are most numerous in Bijápur (31,000) but are also found in considerable numbers in Dhárwár and Belgaum districts and in the States of the Southern Marátha Country. A small number (390) have penetrated as far north as the Sátára Agency, while the Gazetteer reports a few following the profession of water-carriers in the Poona district. They are partly Hindu, partly Lingáyat, the divisions in 1901 being nearly equal :—

Hindu	40,000
Lingáyat	42,000

The Raddis are a well known and largely represented caste in Mysore, where they are included in Vakkaligs or cultivators with eight endogamous divisions, of which one, the Páknáts, is found in this Presidency. They seem in some way connected with the Ráshtrakuta or Ratta dynasty, and it is held by some authorities that the Rattas were Raddis (Kan. *Radderu*). It is certain that they still claim descent from Hem Ratti, who, in their tradition, was the son of Kudavakkal and brother of Kurupi, the eponymous ancestor of the

(1) Census of India, 1911, Vol. XXI, Part I, p. 174.

Kurubas. If this tradition is worth anything, it tends to show a former close connection with the Kudavakkal and Kuruba castes. Another tradition is that the caste is descended from a woman Hemraddi Mallava, who was a devoted worshipper of Venkataráma, and the god, pleased with her devotion, transformed a dungheap into gold for her. Raddis profess to have come from Venkatgiri in Madras. They still worship Shri Venktesh. Their former connection with the tribes of Mysore is also suggested by the fact that the worship of the milk-post forms part of their marriage ceremony. This is an equally important ceremony with the Kurubas, Holeyas, Bedars and Agasas in Mysore.

Endogamous divisions.

Raddis consist of seven endogamous divisions :—

1. Námada
2. Chitmit
3. Lalgond
4. Nirval
5. Páknák
6. Pentpent
7. Vithála

Of these, the Námadas are Hindu and the rest Lingáyat. Their former close connection is proved by the practice that still prevails of the Lingáyat divisions taking brides from the Námadas, who may not marry Lingáyat girls. The Lingáyat divisions are non-Panchamsális with the *ashtavarna* rites (see LINGAYAT). Before they take a Námada girl in marriage they invest her with the *linga*. It is clear from this that the Raddis considered themselves raised socially by their conversion to the religion of Basava. Námada Raddis who become Lingáyat are said to be admitted to the Chitmit division. A certain number of the Páknák division formed in the time of Abbé Dubois a wandering tribe, having broken away from the rest of the caste owing to some grievance.(1)

The Raddis speak Kanarese, but some use Telugu as their home tongue. The names in common use among men are, Bálappa, Govindappa, Krishnappa, Bharmappa, Chundappa, Fakirappa, Gurappa and Ramappa, and among women Bálava, Krishnavva, Laxmava, Irrakka, Somakka, Jyankavva, and Yellamma.

Exogamous divisions.

The Námad Raddis are divided into thirty-six exogamous divisions known as *bedagus*, of which the most important are :—

Bhimalvále	Durmandalvále
Chalvále	Gadgivále
Dadigalvále	Galvále

(1) Abbé Dubois, "Hindu Manners and Customs," p. 71.

Guggulvále	Mulivále
Jákvále	Padgalvále
Jhyanghivále	Raddikonevále
Kadalevále	Ragtivále
Kathárvále	Sangtivále (1)
Kondraddivále	

Marriages are prohibited between members of the same *bedagu.* A member of the caste may marry his father's sister's or mother's brother's daughter. Marriage with a mother's sister's daughter is not allowed. According to some, descendants of sisters may intermarry if their *bedagus* be different. Marriage with a wife's sister is permitted. Two brothers are allowed to marry two sisters. Polygamy is allowed and practised, but polyandry is unknown. Girls are married before they come of age. There is no restriction on the marriageable age of boys.

Marriage ceremonies. The offer of marriage comes from either side. If the girl's parents are well-to-do they pay a dowry to the boy. If the boy's parents are poor they have to pay a *teru* or bride-price to the girl's parents. The day for the marriage is fixed by a Bráhman who conducts the service. A few days before the marriage the *velye* or betrothal ceremony is performed at the girl's house. The boy's father goes to the girl's house with a robe, a bodice cloth, and a silver neck ornament, or some gold or silver ornaments if he is rich. A Bráhman priest and relations and friends are invited by the girl's father to be present on the occasion. The girl is brought before the boy's father, who gives her the robe, bodice cloth, and ornaments he has brought, marks her brow with vermilion, fills her lap with two-thirds of a pound of dry dates, two-thirds of a pound of betelnuts, 100 betel leaves, one-sixth of a pound of turmeric roots, and five plantains, and puts a little sugar into her mouth. The girl's father rises and taking betel in his hand says to the boy's father, "My daughter is betrothed to your son," and ties the betel to the skirt of his shoulder-cloth. The boy's father then rises and says to the girl's father, "My son is betrothed to your daughter," and ties the betel to the skirt of the girl's father's shoulder-cloth. Sugar and betel are distributed to the party assembled, and money and uncooked articles of food are given to Bráhmans. The girl's father treats the boy's father and his relations to sugar rollypolies, which ends the ceremony.

---

(1) In Dhárwár the following are found:—Amadla, Araval, Battal, Bengla, Boode Chitmal, Chuchal, Gangla, Kasige, Páde, Sátpule, Utamal and Yersal.

On a lucky day two or three days before the wedding, the ceremony of *devákárya* is performed at the houses of both the boy and the girl, when Ganpati is worshipped, money and uncooked articles of food are given to Bráhmans, and kinsmen are feasted. On the following day the boy is rubbed with turmeric paste and oil, and the ceremony of *airane* is performed, in which the boy is seated with his parents and two unwidowed women in a square with a water pot at each corner and a thread passed several times round the necks of the jars. These jars are filled with water, turmeric powder, and vermilion, and the persons seated in the square are bathed in hot water by unwidowed women. When the pouring of water is over, the persons in the square are told to bend down, and a brass or copper dish is held over them with its bottom up. On the bottom is placed a gold nose-ring and water is poured on the ring. The thread passed round the jars is unwound and tied to a post of the marriage booth. Afterwards unwidowed women go to the girl's house in procession accompanied with music. They carry turmeric powder, vermilion, turmeric paste, a white robe and a bodice for the girl; and a cocoanut, rice, and betelnuts to fill the girl's lap. When they reach the girl's house, the girl's mother or some other unwidowed woman rubs her with the turmeric paste, and the girl is bathed in the same way in which the boy was bathed.

On the night before the wedding day the boy and his party go to a temple, and after they are seated they are joined by the girl's father and a band of his friends and relations. When the men and women of the two parties meet, they throw *abir* or frankincense on one another. The girl's father washes the boy's feet, marks his brow with sandal paste, and presents him with a dress. Afterwards the boy is led on a horse in procession to his house.

On the morning of the marriage day the *hálakamb* (milk post) ceremony is performed at the houses of both the boy and the girl. A branch of *rui* (Calotropis gigantea) or *pipri* (Ficus tsiela) is brought and placed in the temple of the family god of the party concerned. Next, a party of males and females go to the temple, worship the branch, bring it home in procession and tie it to a post of the marriage booth.

An hour or two before the time fixed for the marriage, the girl's sister takes vermicilli or *shevaya* cooked in milk with molasses, and gives the dish to the boy to eat. The boy is then taken in procession to the girl's house, the girl is brought and made to stand facing him, a curtain with a central turmeric cross is held between them, marriage verses are repeated, and grains of rice coloured red are thrown over the pair by all assembled. At the end the curtain is drawn on one side, and the boy with his two hands throws rice grains on the girl's head and fastens the lucky necklace round her neck, this being the binding portion of the ceremony. Next, the pair are taken to bow before the house gods, uncooked articles of food and money are given to Bráhmans and betel is distributed amongst the guests. In the evening the girl's father gives a feast to the caste people, in which the pair eat out of the same dish. After the feast the pair are taken on horse-back to bow before the village Máruti and thence to the boy's house. Here the pair are made to worship Ganpati, and the girl is seated on the laps of the chief of the boy's male and female relations. Next, a feast is given to the girl's party by the boy's father. On the following day the girl's father treats the boy and his leading relations to a feast and presents them with clothes, which ends the marriage ceremonies.

The remarriage of widows is permitted. A widow may marry her father's sister's or mother's brother's son. She cannot marry her mother's sister's son or a member of her late husbund's section. A widow remarriage can be celebrated on any lucky day except a Tuesday. The widow and her new husband are rubbed with oil and bathed in hot water. The latter then presents the former with articles of dress and ornaments and fills her lap with a cocoanut and rice. Next, the pair throw garlands of flowers round each other's necks and an elderly kinswoman of either party knots together the hems of their garments. The widow's new husband then fastens a lucky necklace round her neck, which is the binding portion of the ceremony. A feast to the caste people ends the ceremony. The widow's face should not be seen by unwidowed women till she bathes in the following morning; but of late the rule is losing its rigidity. A bachelor is not allowed to marry a widow. Divorce is allowed on the ground of disagreement between husband and wife, the wife's infidelity, or the husband's impotency. A divorced woman can marry again after the widow remarriage ritual, except in the case of adultery, which is punished with excommunication. The caste follow the Hindu law of inheritance.

Religion.

Námada Raddis are Hindus of the Shri Vaishnava sect. They claim to keep, and some of the well-to-do keep, nine of the sixteen Bráhmanic *sanskars* or sacraments. The special deity of their worship is Shri Venkatesh, who is their family god and to whom offerings of *kadabus* or sugar dumplings and *khichdi* or rice and pulse boiled and strained are made on Fridays. The *dásás* or servants of the god are easted on Fridays and holidays. The Námada Raddis also worship Yellamma, Máruti, Dyámavva, Kerevva, and Mallayya. They observe the leading Hindu holidays and the full-moons of *Ashádh*, *Ashvin*, *Kártik*, and *Márgashirsha*. On the full-moon days of *Ashádh* small earthen bullocks are made and worshipped with offerings of cooked food. They make pilgrimages to the shrine of Venkataráma of Tirupati. They believe in soothsaying, astrology, lucky and unlucky days, and witchcraft. Their great spirit-scaring god is Máruti. When a person is possessed by a spirit, he or she is seated before the god, and ashes from the censer are rubbed on the sufferer's forehead. When an epidemic breaks out, village gods are propitiated with offerings of water and cooked food. The priests of the Námada Raddis are the local Bráhmans.

Death ceremonies. The married dead are burnt, the unmarried being buried in a sitting position. The deceased is bathed, dressed in his daily clothes, and placed in a sitting position. When the chief mourner has bathed and taken the fire to be set to the funeral pyre, the corpse is laid on the bier, and red powder or *gulál* and betel leaves are thrown on the corpse. At the burning place the chief mourner buries five pice on the spot where the body is to be burnt, and other mourners build the pyre, strip the clothes off the body, and lay it on the pyre. The chief and other mourners lay *durva* grass on the corpse, the chief mourner sets fire to the pyre, and all the party clap their hands, and say "The deceased has gone to the highest heaven." When the body is consumed all bathe and return to the deceased's house and disperse. In the evening millet is boiled with split pulse and spices and the corpse-bearers are feasted. On the third day the bones and ashes are collected and thrown into water. A mud image of the deceased is made on the spot where the corpse was burnt, and articles of food liked by the deceased are offered to the image and given to crows. On the sixth, ninth, or eleventh day the clothes and ornaments of the deceased are washed and laid before the house gods along with an offering of boiled rice and sugar rollypolies. Within the first month a brass or silver plate made with a ruddy embossed figure is placed with the house gods in the name of the deceased, and is worshipped. Every month for twelve months on the lunar day corresponding to the death-day cooked food is offered to the ghost. The ceremony of *shráddha* is not performed.

Occupation. The hereditary occupation of the caste is agriculture, and almost all follow it, though a few have taken to trade in grain and to money-lending. The Raddis are among the best of the dry-crop cultivators;

they seldom attempt garden tillage. Most of them till their own land, and others hire fields, paying the owner one-third or one-half of the produce. Those who own no land live by field labour which lasts almost throughout the year. Their women help them in the field. They cut off millet ears in harvest time, pick and gin cotton, weed, and scare birds. Many Raddis are substantial farmers, though most of them suffered in the 1876 famine.

Agricultural ceremonies.

Like other husbandmen they have many field rites. The beginning of each of the leading field processes is marked by one of these rites. The leading rites are the *kurgi-puja* or drill-plough worhsip, *charags* or Lakshmi's feasts, and the *dáng* or a feast in which the *dáng* or field song is sung. The *kurgi-puja* or drill-plough worship is held on the day, or the day before, sowing is begun, in late May or June in the beginning of the south-west monsoon. The day for worshipping the plough and beginning other field works is fixed either by the *joshi* or village Bráhman astrologer, or, where there is no Bráhman astrologer, by the village Máruti. In consulting Máruti *yes* is written on one piece of paper and *no* on another. The two papers are rolled into small balls and thrown before the god, and a boy of three or four is told to pick one of the two. If the boy picks the *yes* paper, the rite is begun on the proposed day. If he chooses the *no* paper, the rite is put off, and the oracle is again consulted. The drill-plough worship is held in the house, in the front yard, or in the field which is to be sown. When the plough is worshipped in the house or in the front yard, the spot on which the plough is to be worshipped is cow-dunged, a cocoanut is broken, and the pieces are thrown to the right and left as an offering to the place spirits that they may leave it and make room for Lakshmi, who is to be worshipped in the form of the plough. The plough is made ready and complete in every part. It is washed in fresh water, wrapped in a robe, part of it is clad in a bodice, and it is set on the cow-dunged spot. It is marked with sandal paste and turmeric powder, vermilion, and flowers are thrown on it. Glass bangles and women's gold and silver ornaments are hung from different parts of the plough, frankincense is burnt before it, and sweet food is offered to it. Sometimes the old silver or brass mask (*mukhavata*) of the village Lakshmi is fastened to the plough as its face-plate. Afterwards, when the plough is taken to the field, a cocoanut is broken and the pieces are thrown to the right and left of the path along which the plough is taken to appease the spirits, and prevent them doing mischief to the plough, for if they are not pleased the spirits will break the plough. When the worship takes place in the field it is performed on the day on which sowing is begun. It is done in the same way as in the house or front yard without much show, as the plough is to be used soon after the worship. Before beginning to plough, the field-guardian is worshipped. The field-guardian lives in a small stone generally under a *shami* tree (Prosopis spicigera), which was set there for it when the field was first ploughed and has since been regularly smeared with red lead. A pot of water is poured over the stone, it is daubed with sandal-paste and dressed food is laid before it. Before the bullocks are yoked to the plough their heads are rubbed with cow-dung ashes and the owner bows before them. They are given a sweet dish to eat and some dressed food is waved about them and thrown to the spirits. The first of the *charags* or Lakshmi's feasts falls on the *Bhádrapad* or August-September new-moon which is called *Yellámási* or the sesame new-moon, from *yell* sesame and *ámási* no-moon. Dressed food is taken to the field and some of the dressed food is thrown to the four quarters of heaven and the rest is eaten by the house-people. The next feast comes on the *Ashvin* or September-October full-moon which is called *Sigi hunnavi*, that is, the earth-cone full-moon. Five days before the full-moon, on *Dasara* or the bright tenth, married unwidowed women take a copper dish filled with millet, go to a potter's, give him the millet and bring from him in the dish two cones of earth of unequal height six to eight inches high, and five to eight smaller earthen cones about a couple of inches high. The large cone is supposed to represent the father, the slightly smaller one the mother, and the tiny cones the children of the family. Besides the millet the potter is given a betel-nut and a copper coin, and all the cones are daubed with *kunku* or vermilion. They are set in a niche in the house, rubbed with sandal-paste, and rice and flowers are put on them and dressed food is laid before them. On the full-moon day the cones are marked with alternate stripes of lime and red lead and worshipped in the same way as on *Dasara*. At noon all cultivators except Bráhmans take dressed food to the fields. At the time of going to the fields they take with them four of the tiny cones, set them in the middle of the field, and offer them food. Afterwards some food is thrown in the middle and into the four corners of the field. The food offered to spirits includes a sweet dish and generally boiled rice mixed with curds, a favourite dish with almost all spirits. The people then sit down to eat. Before eating they throw pinches of food round their dishes as an offering to the spirits of the place on which they sit, that the spirits may not distrub them. In the evening they return, and next day unwidowed women dressed in new clothes and singing songs as they go, take the remaining cones and throw them into a river or pond. In cotton fields boiled rice and curds are thrown into different parts of the field before the cotton-picking begins. The *khanda-charag* or thrashing-floor Lakshmi's feast is held when the thrashing floor is prepared; it does not differ from the *Yellámási charag*. When the thrashing-floor is ready, a post is driven into the ground in the centre of the floor and the floor is cow-dunged. The root is rubbed with sandal-paste and frankincense is burnt before it. Some ears of grain are thrashed by a wooden pestle, and the grains are boiled whole in an earthen vessel and are offered to the post. When the place is consecrated no one with shoes on is allowed to step on the floor, though persons with sandals may walk freely across it. In the evening the ears of grain that are to be trampled are heaped round the post and four to eight bullocks are made to go round the post. As they drive the bullocks they sing songs which are called *dángors*, and hence the rite is called *dángor*. In driving the bullocks they are not allowed to use the whip. On the day after the grain has been winnowed, a cocoanut is broken, and pieces of it are thrown to the right and to the left of the grain-heap as an offering to spirits, frankincense is burnt before the heap, and turmeric powder and vermilion are thrown on the heap. Most local husbandmen, sometimes even Lingáyats and Bráhmans, sacrifice a goat. The Lingáyat or Bráhman does not kill the goat himself but pays the price of the goat, and a Marátha, Rajput, or some flesh-eating Hindu kills the goat before the heap of grain, and sprinkles its blood about the thrashing floor. If the owner of the field is a flesh-eater he dresses the flesh, offers it to the heap, throws it to the spirits, and eats it with his family and friends. Before measuring the grain, the grain-heap, the measure-basket, and the broom are worshipped in the following manner. On the top of the heap is set a small cone of bullock-dung which was dropped by bullocks as they left the thrashing-floor; and on the cone some hair of the bullocks' tails are stuck as a top-knot. Before the heap, the basket, and the broom, frankincense is burnt, and four lemons and ten plantains are laid. A cocoanut is broken and its pieces are thrown to the left and to he right. As a rule the new grain is measured either in the first part of the day or in the first part of the night, never after midday or midnight. When waste land is brought under tillage the day on which the clearing is to begin is fixed either by the Bráhman astrologer or *joshi* or by asking the village Máruti. Before beginning to clear the field the owner breaks a cocoanut and throws the pieces about the field as an offering to the place spirits. When the field is cleared and made fit for ploughing the *kurgi* or plough is worshipped as has been described, with this difference that it is worshipped either in the house or house-yard and never in the field. When the plough has been worshipped a stone is picked up in the field, washed with fresh water, smeared with vermilion paste, and set under a tree, generally a *shami* (Prosopis spicigera) as the field guardian or *kshetrapál*.

The Námada Raddis neither eat flesh nor drink liquor. Though classed by Bráhmans among Shudras they rank with Lingáyats, hold a high position, and will not eat from the hands of Bráhmans. **Food.**

LINGAYAT RADDIS differ little from Námada Raddis in form, speech, food, or dress. Among them the men's names in common use are Basappa, Mallappa, Malkappa, and Shankarappa, and the women's Gangava, Párvaleva, and Shankarva. Like Námada Raddis, husbandry is their hereditary calling, and they have the same beliefs and observe the same field rites. Shiva is their great god, and *Shivarátri* their great feast day. As they are Lingáyats they use cow-dung ashes instead of sandal-paste, and in their field rites mark the object of worship first with ashes and then by sprinkling it with scented powder. Though old converts to Lingáyatism, they have not abandoned all their former customs. To a stranger their marriage ceremonies seem to differ little from those of Námada Raddis. Though they are married and buried by Jangams, they show as much honour to Bráhmans as they show to Jangams. Like the Panchamsáli Lingáyats, rich Raddis carry their dead in a canopied chair or *vimán*, bury them, close the grave with a stone slab, and wash the feet of the beadle or *mathpati* on the top of the grave. Like Námada Raddis, they carry food to the grave, deify the ancestral spirits, and worship them as house gods.

RAFAI.—*See* under Minor Musalmán Castes.

RAFUGAR.—*See* under Minor Musalmán Castes.

RAHDURI.—A sub-division of Meváda Bráhmans.

RAHTADKAR.—A sub-division of Kolis.

RAIKA.—A synonym for Rabári.

RAIKARIS, or grovesmen, numbering 78 (1901), including 47 males and 31 females, are found only in the Bhiwandi *táluka* of the Thána district. They are also called Gal Bhois, because they fish with the *gal*, hook, and not with the *jále*, net. The term Ráikari comes from *rái* a grove which in inland Thána is used for mango or jack groves, and sometimes along the coast of palm gardens. The Gal Bhois or Ráikaris seem to be of the same origin, and to hold much the same social position as the Várlis do, to whom they have a much **Name and origin.**

closer likeness than to the coarse and sturdy coast fisherman. Their customs seem to show that, like the Várlis, they are among the oldest inhabitants of the north Konkan. Though a few are settled as field workers, most live by fishing and by raising vegetables. Their household gods are Vághamári, Cheda, Hirva, Gira and Savári, who are demons rather than gods. Gira and Savári are said to be husband and wife, and to live in, or rather rule over, the pools where the Ráikari fishes. When a Ráikari is drowned, the favour of the demon of the pool is sought by daubing some big rock close by with red lead. They call in a Bráhman to name their children, but for no other purpose. They believe that a Bráhman-married couple never live long.

Marriage Ceremonies

Their marriage ceremony is conducted by an elderly woman of the caste who is called *davleri*. The day before the marriage two mediums, *bhagats*, are brought one to the bride's, the other to the bridegroom's house. The spirits of departed ancestors enter into their bodies and foretell the happiness of the married pair and bless their union, while the bride's mother fasts, and the bride and bridegroom are rubbed with turmeric by two married women. On the marriage day the boy goes towards the girl's house on horseback, a cocoanut being broken on the road in front of him. The bride's relations come to meet his party, give them tobacco and water, and present the boy with one of the bride's marriage ornaments, *báshings*, taking one of his in return. All then move to the booth, the girl is brought in, and the ceremony begins. The pair stand facing each other with the tips of the fingers of their joined hands touching, and the *davleri*, helped by two or three brides-maids, *karavlis*, generally sisters of the boy and girl, chants verses. When the chanting ceases the bride and bridegroom change places, and one end of a thread is tied round each of their necks. The husband's end is then unfastened, and both ends are bound round the wife's neck. Then they sit on stools, and the *davleri*, lighting the sacred fire, feeds it with clarified butter and rice. The day after the marriage the husband pretends to go off in a rage, and the bride follows him, soothes him by the promise of a cow or some other gift, and when she has overcome his anger he takes her on his hip and carries her back to the booth. Here they rub turmeric on one another's mouths and bite leaf cigarettes from between one another's teeth. This closes the ceremony. They wash and go to the husband's house and take off the marriage ornaments, *báshings*. The girl stays for five days and then returns to her parents, whence after another five days she is again fetched home for good by her brother-in-law.

Ráikaris either bury or burn their dead. A man who dies of cholera, or who is drowned or who dies suddenly without any apparent cause, is buried; while one who has died from a lingering disease is burnt. If the decased is unmarried, turmeric is not sprinkled on the body. On the way to the burning ground the bier is set down, and the two front bearers change places with those behind, a copper coin and a stone *jivkhada* are placed over the deceased's chest, and then hid in the ground close by, and the party moves on. In the corpse's mouth is placed a rupee, and in his waistcloth five copper coins and some rice. Every year in *Bhádrapad* (August-September) the Ráikaris lay cooked food on the roofs of their houses for the spirits of their relations to come and eat. Death ceremonies.

RAIKULA.—A sub-division of Bráhmans.

RAIPURA.—A sub-division of Bráhmans.

RAISTHALA.—A sub-division of Bráhmans.

RAJ.—A synonym for Mahádev Koli.

RAJBHOI.—A sub-division of Bhois.

RAJGOR.—A sub-division of Audich Bráhmans.

RAJKALI.—A sub-division of Darjis.

RAJPURKAR.—A sub-division of Gaud Sárasvat Bráhmans.

RAJPUT.—A sub-division of Khárvás, Gaolis and Kumbhárs.

RAJPUTS, numbering 386,896 (males 201,555, females 185,341) at the census of 1901 and 455,605 (males 241,880, females 213,725) at the census of 1911, are found all over Gujarát and in the Presidency generally, but mostly in Káthiáwar and in the north of the province, where imitation of Rajput customs and a claim to Rajput descent are recognised alternative roads to social advancement for castes which in other areas would probably endeavour to establish their position by a close adherence to Bráhmanical ceremonial. They claim to be modern representatives of the Kshatriya race. The bulk of the tribe have however lost their original purity by marrying for a long time past into land-holding and ruling families of other tribes such as Kolis and Bhils, and it is not uncommon even now for members of lower castes to set the seal to their social and material prosperity by claiming a Rajput status and forming marriage connections with the lower classes of Rajputs. At the census of 1911 an examination of certain entries in Sind disclosed the fact that even the humble

Dhed from Gujarát made a bid for social advancement by this ladder.

Rajputs are hereditary soldiers and landlords, but the demand for soldiers is limited and few Rajputs have any occupation except as land-holders. Exclusive of the large classes of Garásiás and Tálukdárs who merely hold estates of varying sizes on favourable terms, the Rajputs of Gujarát are still a dominant race, holding sway over nearly half of the area of Gujarát and over nearly one-third of its people. Statistics in the Bombay Gazetteer showed that in 1891 the clans to which the ruling chiefs belonged were as follows :—

1. Chávada	6. Jádeja	11. Rehvar
2. Chohán	7. Jethva	12. Sarvaiyya
3. Daima	8. Jhála	13. Sisodia
4. Gohil	9. Parmár	14. Solanki
5. Gori	10. Ráthod	15. Vághela

Out of these the area ruled by No. 1, 3, 5 and 11 was very small, and the area ruled by No. 6 by far the largest. Besides these tribes or clans, to which the ruling chiefs belong, there are to be found the Chudásama, who like the Jádeja belong to the great Yádav stock, and the Vádhels or Vájás who are of Ráthod stock. Other clans such as the Ghelots and Makvánás are represented, but only by poor persons such as servants and tenants. A full list of clans is given below.

Not included in the clans are the lower class Dángs, Karádiás and Pádhrás, who allow widow-marriage and let their women appear in public. With these the higher class Rajputs eat, and, in places, through the intermediate class of Gámetia Rajputs, have marriage connections with Karádiás. Karádia girls are married by Gámetiás and Rajput land-holders and Tálukdárs marry Gámetia girls. Thus Gámetiás serve as a connecting link between Karádiás and high class Rajputs. The Dángs are of the same stock as the Jádejás and are confined to Cutch. The Karádiás are scattered in small numbers all over Gujarát and Káthiáwar. The Pádhrás are found solely in the Surat district.

The chief social peculiarity of the Rajput race is its division into clans. All clans eat together and intermarry ; but the clan as such is exogamous. The dread of marriage among relations is sometimes carried to a strange extreme. As all Jádavs are in theory of the same stock, members of that great clan, whether Jádejás, Chudásamás or Bhátis, ought not to intermarry. A Jádeja should not marry a

Chudásama, although the tribes separated in very early times; and instances have occured of marriages being annulled in such cases. The origin of the smaller clans seems to have been that when the members of a clan became very numerous and spread over a large extent of country, the practice of naming groups of families after a distinguished common ancestor or, less commonly, after the place of residence came into vogue. Sometimes clan names are taken from a calling, as in the case of *vethiás* or carriers of Government property; at other times a mere change in dress is sufficient to create a new clan name. The Kachhotiás are so called because their women adopted the practice of passing the robe back between the feet and tucking the end into the waistband. As far as was known at the time of the Gazetteer, Gujarát Rajputs have one hundred and three clans. They are as follows:—

Ada, Avera, Baláter, Bárod, Bháti, Bihola Solanki, Biya, Bodáv, Chamarpa, Chandavrat, Chávada, Chávad, Chochu, Choid, Chobán, Chudávat, Dábhi, Dágh, Daima, Dairja, Devchand, Devda, Dhándhu, Dod, Dodiya, Duval, Ed, Galecha, Ghelot, Gohel, Golter, Gor, Gujjar, Hadial, Harashi, Hátha, Humad, Jádav, Jádeja, Jhála, Jiriya, Jodha, Ráthod, Joja, Jut, Kaba, Kachhotia, Kalam, Karodia, Kher, Khod, Khula, Kukan, Lakam, Mahida, Makvána, Mál, Masáni, Mer, Mohal, Mori, Narwán, Padhár, Padhiár, Palonia, Parmár, Pesrau, Puravia, Chohán, Ráua, Ranráthod, Ráthod, Rával, Rávar-Solanki, Rehevar, Revod, Sedhál, Sisodia, Sodha, Sodria or Sádria, Sojatria, Solanki, Songad, Surcha, Suvar, Tank, Tantol, Thokiya, Tuar, Vádhel, Vadvásia, Vághela, Vaish, Vája, Vála, Vámla, Vanol, Vantia, Varam, Vejola Vehtia, Vezánia, Virpura-Solanki, Udvat and Uma.

The Gujarát Rajput as a rule is tall and well built, fair-featured and with a manly and pleasing expression and address. The nose is straight or hooked, the eye large and lustrous, the iris usually black but not uncommonly brown or gray almost to blackness, the mouth small, the face oval. Like the men the women are well-formed and fair. They are famous for their good looks and for the care they take to preserve their beauty in advanced years. Appearance.

The dress worn by Rajput men in mainland Gujarát differs considerably from that worn in Káthiáwár. In Cutch the men's headdress, is a common silk *masru* cap and over it a large loosely-rolled turban red in the case of the young and white in the case of the old; a double-fronted waistcoat with sleeves varying in length from three to eight cubits Dress.

and the strings about a foot long; a long coat with wide sleeves; a scarf, dark in the case of the young and white in the case of the old, wound round the loins, the ends falling to the knees, and fastened at the waist by a variety of waistcloths; a pair of loose trousers with a tight button at the ankle and pointed shoes. The Káthiáwár dress does not differ much from the Cutch dress except among the cultivating Rajput women of south Gujarát, who, like Kanbi women, wear the long robe instead of the petticoat, passing back the skirt between the feet. The dress of Rajput women all over Gujarát consists of the same three articles, the petticoat, the backless bodice and the head-scarf, all differing in fashion according to the locality and in material according to the means of the wearer.

Language. As a rule the home tongue of Rajputs is Gujaráti. In Cutch the home tongue of the Jádeja Rajput is Cutchi, which closely resembles the dialect in use in lower Sind. Most Gujarát Rajputs also understand Hindustáni; and the home speech of those who come from Márwár is Márwári.

Birth. In the seventh month of her first pregnancy the girl generally goes to her father's house for her delivery. With the first signs of labour a midwife of the barber or some other caste is called in. An astrologer is present to mark the moment of birth and to cast the horoscope. As soon as the child is born the midwife beats a metal platter if it is a boy and an earthen pot if it is a girl. If the child is a boy, musicians come and perform at the house, and if the father's means allow, packets of sugar are distributed to every house in the village. A messenger is sent to carry the *vadhámni* or joyful news to the child's father with a paper marked with the boy's footprint in vermilion. The boy's father rewards the messenger with a dress or cash and distributes sugarcandy among friends and relations. If the father is poor he feeds the messenger and presents him with a rupee. As soon as the child is born the midwife cuts its navel cord and buries it in a corner of the compound in front of the house. The father's sister feeds the child wth a few drops of honey mixed with clarified butter and water. It is believed that the child takes to the nature of the woman who first feeds it. The midwife receives fifty pounds of wheat, one rupee in cash, a cocoa-nut, $1\frac{1}{4}$ to $5\frac{1}{4}$ pounds of molasses, and if the child is a boy a robe. Even poor Rajputs have to pay the midwife grain and 4 to 8 annas in cash. On the sixth night after the birth the child's and the mother's foreheads are marked with vermilion. A piece of cloth long enough to make a jacket for the child is begged from a friend or relation, a jacket is made and the child is dressed in it. A space on the floor near the mother's bed is cleansed with cowdung and in the space is set a wooden stool covered with green silk or brocade called *chattio* with an earthen pot on either side. The child is laid in a *má ki* or small cradle near the stool. According as the child is a boy or a girl, a boy or a girl is seated at each of the four corners of the stool who beat metal dishes and are rewarded with *suvah vadás* or birth-cakes made of wheat flour and molasses fried in butter. Near the stool the wall is marked with seven vermilion spots and over the spots clarified butter is rubbed. On the stool are laid a piece of paper, a reed-pen, and a mixture of vermilion and water in the belief that *Chhathi* or Mother Sixth comes on that night and writes the future of the child. A sword covered with a robe called *pámri* and a lamp fed with clarified butter are placed near the writing materials, and all the people, except the mother and child, leave the room for a short time to give the goddess an opportunity to do her work. Cooked rice and *kansár* or wheat flour boiled in clarified butter and molasses are eaten in the house. The ceremonial impurity on account of child birth lasts ten to forty days. During this period the mother bathes four times. Her bath on the tenth day is called *dasuthán*, and that on the twentieth, *visuthán*, after which she is allowed to touch the members of the family. Her third bath is on the thirtieth day and her fourth on the fortieth. On the fortieth day the mother goes with the child in her arms to a neighbouring well and offers sandal paste, vermilion, rice and flowers to the *jal-devtás* or water nymphs. A Bráhman priest attends and is rewarded with money. The mother then fills a small vessel with water and fetches it home. *Kansár* or wheat flour cooked in clarified butter and sugar is eaten on that day in the house, and friends and relations are asked to dine. After this ceremony the mother is held to be clean.

Sun worship.

On the morning of the child's twelfth day, if the child is a boy, the mother takes it in her lap and sits on a low stool before the door of the house with a wooden pestle in her hand. Five to seven children are made to sit on her back one after the other and she is asked to walk a few steps. She worships the sun, a Bráhman priest officiating and receiving money. The children are fed with cocoa kernel and the ceremony is complete.

Naming

The child is named on the twelfth day. As a rule the name-giver is the father's sister, and in her absence, the mother's sister; and in the absence of both, some elderly woman of the family. Several names are suggested by the astrologer, who is guided in his choice by the position of the moon in the heavens at the time of the child's birth. The child is bathed by his *phoi* or paternal aunt, or, in her absence, by some husband-owning woman of the house, and dressed in a coat of green silk or brocade. He is then laid in a handkerchief marked in the middle with a lucky cross or *svástik* and held by the four corners by four children, boys in the case of a boy and girls in the case of a girl. This handkerchief serves as a temporary cradle which is swung to and fro by the four children. The child's aunt, who names the child, lays with the child in the handkerchief a betelnut, a *pipal* leaf, and a coin either of gold or silver or copper. She then, with the consent of the elderly members of the house, chooses one of the names suggested by the astrologer, swings the handkerchief-cradle, and repeats the name four times in a couplet. The children who have swung the cradle are treated to boiled wheat sweetened with molasses; and sugar is distributed to the women friends and relations who have been asked to the house. Among the Gohils wet millet mixed with *suva* or dill-seed is distributed to children. During the third, fifth or seventh month after the birth of the child, the mother is presented with a new dress and the child with ornaments which are sent to the father's house.

Mango blossom. Next comes the *mohorpán* or mango-blossom drinking. On the first *Holi* (February-March) holiday after the birth, a low stool is set on the ground and covered with green silk or brocade. On the stool is set a cup of milk mixed with sugar and mango blossoms. The child is laid on the low stool and children are asked to the house. A Bráhman priest attends and kindles the *holi* fire. The Bráhman then dips a silver piece into the milk in the cup on the low stool and four times lets a few drops fall into the child's mouth. Sweetmeats are distributed to children and the Bráhman priest is rewarded with money.

First feeding *Botan*. The first feeding or *botan* takes place in the case of a girl either in the fifth or seventh, and in the case of a boy, in the sixth or eighth, month. On a lucky day rice is cooked in milk and mixed with sugar, and friends and relations are asked to dine at the house. Besides the dinner the only observance is that the father's sister or in her absence some elderly woman of the house takes out a little milk on a gold or silver coin and drops it five times into the child's mouth.

Hair-clipping. When a boy is three to five years old, on a lucky day fixed by a Bráhman astrologer, his hair is clipped. Five days before the clipping a betelnut Ganpati and the family goddess are installed and worshipped in the house, the boy is rubbed with turmeric paste mixed with oil, and women friends and neighbours meet at the house and sing songs. Five measures of unhusked rice are laid in five wooden mortars and five husband-owning women are asked to pound the rice five times, each singing songs. A week or ten days before the hair-clipping at a neighbour's house in a clay pot filled with earth a few grains of wheat are sown and watered so that the seedlings may be two or three inches high before the hair-clipping day. On the third day the worship of *Rándal* the female-faced cocoanut is performed with the same details as at the time of marriage. The women of the house bring from the potter's the earthen pots required for the ceremony. A booth is erected before the house on or before the day of hair-clipping, which should have five posts covered with *asopálo* (Polyalthia longifolia) leaves. The women sing songs and rub the boy with turmeric and perfumed oil. In the booth a small canopy is spread and under it a raised earthen seat and on the seat two low stools. The father and the mother of the boy are seated on the low stools and perform the planet-humouring ceremony called *grahashánti*. A Bráhman officiates and the boy's hair is clipped. Friends and relations are fed, and at night the boy is dressed in rich clothes and taken on horse-back with music and a company of friends through the village.

Rajputs claim the right to wear the sacred thread with the same formalities as Bráhmans, but only a few are careful to invest their boys at the usual Bráhman age. If a Rajput boy is separately invested with the sacred thread the ceremony takes place when he is between ten and twelve. But in most cases the investiture is made one of the marriage ceremonies. On the day of the thread-girding, after he has been invested, the boy runs off to the local temple, feigning to be angry. His maternal uncle goes to the temple and, by promising him his daughter in marriage, pretends to soothe and dissuade the boy from persisting in taking a vow of celibacy or *brahmacharya*. The boy consents, and the uncle presents him with a suit of clothes and carries him on his shoulder to his father's house with music and a company of friends and relations. Only a few of the Choháns, Parmárs, Solankis, and Vághelás, and the religious-minded of other clans, always wear the sacred thread. Other Rajputs put it on only on the occasions of *grahashánti* or planet-pleasing and of *shráddha* or mind-rites for their forefathers. On one other occasion every Rajput must wear his thread; when he is either chief mourner or one of the four bearers of a bier to the burning ground.

Marriage.

As the tribe is sprung from one ancestor, any marriage in the tribe is incestuous and forbidden. Poverty does not lower a Rajput's social position. But his position is injured if he marries a woman who is not a Rajput. He also lowers himself if he marries his daughter to some one who is socially his own inferior. The daughter of a Chudásama Rajput is considered fit for the hand of a ruling chief, and a

Chávada maiden may marry a Mevád Sisodiya. The names of daughters given in marriage to a husband of lower rank are not entered by the genealogist in the list of the women of the family. Daughters married into a family of inferior birth are not entitled to any special honour at any family gathering or feast. A peculiarity of the Jádejás is the extent to which they practised female infanticide. The probable explanation is that, on attempting to return to Hinduism, though they could get wives for their sons, no one of proper position would take their daughters in marriage. The story is that a chief of the Samma tribe had a beautiful and accomplished daughter for whom he wished to find a suitable match. He accordingly sent his family priest to travel in search of a young chief who should be her equal not only in rank and age but also in beauty and accomplishments. The Bráhman travelled in vain and finally returned unsuccessful, reporting to his master that such a paragon was not to be found. The chief in despair asked the Bráhman what to do and was advised to put his daughter to death. This he did and other Jádejás followed the chief's example. In Káthiáwár the marriageable age among girls is between fifteen and twenty, while among Pálanpur Thákors the marriageable age is between eight and ten. Rajputs are never careful about the age of the husband, who is sometimes two or three years older or younger than the girl. Betrothals take place either immediately before or some years before marriage. Betrothals are always verbal and never written.

Betrothal. On a lucky day the relations of the girl go to the boy's house taking with them a small gold cocoanut and some ornaments and dresses and a horse, if the gift of a horse has been previously agreed to. When they reach the boy's village the boy's father receives them with friends and music. Before leaving the house the boy's priest hands to some husband-owing woman of the house a gold or silver spouted vessel called *jhári* filled with water, with a cocoanut stopper in its mouth. When the boy's father meets the girl's party he welcomes them. The girl's father puts some cash into the vessel and makes money presents to the priest and musicians, and distributes dry dates to the women who sing marriage songs and accompany the woman who holds the spouted vessel. The woman who holds the vessel with the spout leads the procession to a house specially furnished for the girl's party, and here the boy's father feeds the bride's party with rice cooked with sugar and clarified butter, acid and pungent articles being scrupulously avoided. A lucky day is fixed for the acceptance of the gold cocoanut of betrothal, when the girl's party go with music and friends to the boy's house carrying a brass platter containing the gold cocoanut and the presents for the boy with packets of sugar, red powder *gulál,* cloves, cardamoms and raisins, vermilion, rice and flowers. If a horse is among the presents it is led in front of the party. Women sing songs and men throw red powder. The boy's relations and friends meet at his house. The boy is richly dressed and seated on a raised seat. On reaching the boy's house the girl's priest marks the boy's brow with vermilion and presents him with the gold cocoanut and other articles brought from the girl's house. He then asks the mother of the boy to accept the brass salver containing the presents. A servant girl of the house comes and takes the salver and daubs the forehead of the boy with the vermilion from the dish, and sticks grains of rice on the spots of vermilion. If there be more servant girls in the house, each of them in turn daubs the boy's brow with vermilion and rice, and the boy drops the gold cocoanut in the lap of the last of them. The boy's father then removes the presents and fills the dish with dry dates and money. He opens the sugar packets and takes a little sugar into his hollow hands and offers it to four men of each party. Sugar is then distributed to friends and relations met at the house and the girl's party is treated to opium-water *kusumba* On the next day the girl's party ask the boy's party to their lodgings to sip *kusumba* and distribute sugar to the guests. The boy's father afterwards presents the girl's party with dresses and feeds them so long as they stay in his village. After this, on a lucky day fixed by the astrologer, the boy's party goes to the girl's village to make her a present of ornaments and dresses. The girl's father receives the boy in the same manner as his own party was received. The girl is seated on a low stool and presented with ornaments and a petticoat, bodice and headscarf, which she puts on. The other presents consisting of packets of sugar, rice, flowers, cloves, cardamoms and dry dates are received by a woman of the family who marks the girl's forehead with vermilion. The boy's father presents the girl with a cocoanut and a rupee. The girl's father is required to treat the boy's party in the same way and for the same number of days as his party was treated at the boy's village. The boy's party asks the girl's party to a *kusumba* entertainment and distributes sugar to all who are present. The boy's relations are presented with dresses before they leave. and the ceremony is complete.

Afterwards, when the father of the girl wants to marry his daughter, he sends for an astrologer, who, consulting the birth papers of the boy and girl, finds out a lucky day for the wedding ceremony. If the birth papers are not available, the astrologer is guided by the names of the boy and the girl. He takes a slip of Ahmedabad-made paper and writes an invitation or *lagan patrika* to the boy's father, naming the day and the time. On this paper a silver coin, some rice and five dry dates are laid and it is marked with saffron and vermilion, and the whole is formed into a conical packet and wound round with a *náda chhadi* or yellow and red cotton thread. The girl's priest takes this invitation packet called *laganno pado* with four conical shaped packets of 1¼ pounds of sugarcandy, 1¼ pounds of sugar, 1¼ pounds of raisins and 1¼ pounds of vermilion and five cocoanuts to the boy's house, where the boy's father welcomes him to some place in his neighbourhood and asks him to his house at some lucky time of the day. Friends and relations meet at the house, music plays, and the women sing marriage songs.

The boy's priest then asks the girl's priest to seat himself on a low stool. An unmarried girl of the boy's family marks the forehead of the girl's priest with vermilion and on the vermilion sticks grains of rice. She then throws four pinches of vermilion and rice on the invitation packet and takes it into her hand. The boy's priest offers the girl's priest four handfuls of sugar, and, dipping his open right hand in the vermilion and water, marks the chest and back of the girl's priest with the lucky red right hand. The girl's priest then leaves the stool and the boy takes his place. The boy's priest daubs the boy's forehead with vermilion, and four unmarried girls one by one drop on him pinches of vermilion and rice. The boy's priest reads the invitation. A local astrologer is consulted, and if the moon at the time proposed for the wedding is favourable to the boy, the invitation is accepted and the day for the girl to put on the bangles and for the marriage are fixed. Sugar or molasses are distributed to the guests and they are treated to opium-water. The girl's priest is told whether the boy is to come personally to the girl's house for the marriage or is to send his *khándu* or sword. He then leaves the boy's house with the present of some article of dress or cash or both. As by sending the sword the bridegroom escapes expensive presents to bards and singers, the practice has become common. From the day the bride's priest leaves the bridegroom's village the bride and bridegroom are dressed in rich clothes and ornaments and at both houses a party of women sing marriage songs morning and evening. At the house both of the bride and of the bridegroom on the third, fifth or seventh day before the marriage day booths are erected. On the same day at both houses takes place the ceremony of fixing the *mánakstambh* or ruby pillar. The wooden post is made by a carpenter. It is about a foot long and is handed to the women of the house, who give the carpenter five measures of wheat and a cocoanut. A hole is dug either on the right side of the main door of the house or in a place specially chosen by the astrologer. In front of this hole the parents of the bride or of the bridegroom, as the case may be, are made to sit on low stools facing east, their foreheads are marked with vermilion, and the ends of their garments are knotted together by the family priest. They throw in the hole a few drops of water mixed with vermilion, curds and milk, a copper, and a betelnut. Their garments are then untied. To the wooden post are bound with cotton thread and *pipal* leaf a betelnut, a copper, a bamboo rod and a branch of the *khijda* (Prosopis spicigera) tree, and the post is planted in the hole. While the post is being planted, music plays and women neighbours and friends sing songs. On the same day the bride's and bridegroom's mother and father, each at their village, go with music and a party of male and female relations to the potter's to worship his wheel and to bring earthen vessels. The Bráhman priest walks in front with a brass platter filled with rice, a cocoanut, molasses and turmeric powder. The women follow him singing songs. The bride's and bridegroom's mother and father throw rice and turmeric powder over the wheel and present the potter with the cocoanut, rice and molasses. The women then sing *phatánás* or jest songs and return in procession with the earthen vessels required for the wedding. When they reach home, dry dates are distributed to the guests and the ceremony of *chák vadhávani* or wheel-inviting is over. On the same day, at both houses follows the installation of Ganpati and of Gotraj, the family goddess. Inside the house a portion of the northern or eastern wall is whitewashed with *khadi* or white clay and daubed with vermilion. Near the wall is set a low wooden stool covered with a piece of white or red cloth a cubit and a quarter square. On this cloth are laid five measures of rice or wheat and a cocoanut and a lamp fed with clarified butter. The boy or the girl sits on a bed before the low stool. A betelnut Ganpati is laid in a brass salver and washed in milk and afterwards placed on the stool. Sandal-paste, rice and flowers are offered to the god, incense is burned before him, and round him is waved a light fed with clarified butter, *kansár* or wheat-flour cooked in clarified butter and sugar is laid before him, and a lamp fed with clarified butter is again waved round him. The boy or girl is made to repeat verses in praise of the god. On the same day the boy's and the girl's father, each at his house, invokes the family goddess. A portion of the wall is whitewashed, and on the white part a picture of the family goddess is drawn with vermilion water. Rice, flowers and turmeric paste are stuck upon the picture, incense is burned before it, a light fed with clarified butter is waved round it, and sugar is offered to it. The members of the house eat *kansár* on that day and the family priest is feasted. After the invocation of Ganpati and the family goddess, both at the boy's and the girl's house, comes the *rándal* ceremony. A small ornamental booth is erected in the house, and in it is placed a stool covered with white or red cloth a cubit and a quarter long. On the cloth are laid five measures of rice or wheat, and on the rice or wheat is set a jar with its mouth covered by a green silk cloth. On the jar is laid a cocoanut draped in a woman's robe so as to represent a female face. Near the jar a lamp fed with clarified butter is kept burning day and night. Another ceremony, that of *gotardo bharvo* or pot-filling, takes place at both the houses. The father and mother or a brother and his wife have the ends of their garments tied together and go with a party of men and women and music to buy a new *bedu*, that is, a pair of earthen pots. With these pots they visit a well, pond or river and bring water to bathe the bride and the bridegroom. The pair, that is, either the father and mother or the brother and his wife, first worship the river, well or pond and then the earthen pots. The earthen pots are filled and carried by the mother or the brother's wife. A day or two before the marriage the bride and bridegroom are rubbed with turmeric paste and scented oil, and *mindhals* or marriage-nuts are tied round their right wrists.

Sword marriage. In the case of a sword-marriage, when the *khándu* or sword is to be sent to the girl's house, the boy sits in a litter with a sword and a cocoanut and passes with music and a company of friends and relations as far as the boundary of his village. There he alights, leaving the sword and a cocoanut in charge of a maid-servant who takes his place in the litter. The procession marches to the bride's village and is welcomed at the boundary by the girl's party, who take the guests to a house specially furnished for them and feast them. After the feast is over, at a lucky moment for the girl to put on the marriage bangles, the boy's Bráhman takes to the girl's house a robe and a pair of bangles. The girl is seated on a low stool before the family goddess who has been previously installed in the house; the Bráhman repeats verses and the girl bows before the goddess and puts on the robe and the bangles and again bows before the goddess. The bridegroom's party then carries the sword in procession to the bride's house, where, under an arch or *toran*, the maid in charge of the sword waits till a *varmáchi* or bridegroom's chair is brought for her to stand upon. The bride's mother comes, wearing on her head a *mod* or three-cornered tiara of gold set with pearls, and over it a *chundadi* or female robe and stands before the maid. The girl's priest holds a cloth between them. He then sends for the *dhoshru* or miniature yoke, marks it with vermilion, covers it with one end of a robe, and, after waving it over the handle of the sword, passes it to a man standing behind. He repeats the same process with the miniature *sâmbela* or pestle, the *ravai* or churning stick, and the *trák* or ladle. The girl's priest waves over the handle of the sword four balls, two made of rice or wheat-flour and two made of ashes. Of the two flour balls, one is thrown to the north, the other to the east, and of the two ash balls one is thrown to the south, the other to the west. Two *kodiás* or earthen lamp saucers filled with rice put brim to brim and bound together with cotton thread are waved over the sword and placed on the ground. The maidservant breaks them with her foot and enters the booth. In the booth are placed a *varmáchi* or chair and a stool opposite to it. The maidservant with the sword sits on the chair and the girl sits on the low stool opposite to her. At the lucky moment the right hands of the girl and the maidservant are joined together. At each corner of the booth a brass jar is placed and in the north-east a stone daubed with redlead is set to represent the *khetrapál* or field-guardian. Near the field-guardian is laid a copper pot containing rice and pulse with a cocoanut laid on its mouth. The girl's father performs the ceremony of *kanyádán* or girl-giving by taking a little water in the hollow of his joined hands and pouring it on the ground. The priest repeats verses and the *kanyádán* is complete when the water is poured on the ground.

In the centre of the booth a *chori* or square is made. At each corner of the square a pillar of nine metal or earthen vessels, piled one above the other, is kept upright by bamboo supports. In the centre of the *chori* a heap of cowdung cakes is piled. The bride's priest kindles the pile of cakes and feeds the fire with clarified butter, barley and sesame. He then makes the bride and the maidservant go round the fire twice in such a way as to make their right feet touch the *khetrapál* or field-guardian. Then the boy's party presents the girl with rich robes and bodices, ornaments and cash, and the girl's father pays the boy the sum of money or gold agreed upon, first laying it on a brass platter and showing the amount of money to the boy's party. The chief of the boy's party accepts the amount on behalf of the boy and returns the salver after laying some cash upon it. The girl bows to the family goddess ; and after the girl's father has presented dresses to the boy's party and cash to the assembled Bháts and Chárans, the boy's party are allowed to leave in good time to reach their village before the arrival of the bride. **Marriage.**

Two or three days after the sword-marriage the bride is sent to the bridegroom's house seated in a carriage with the maid who brought the sword. Before starting, the bride's mother worships the wheel of the carriage and lays a cocoanut and copper coins under the wheel. As the carriage starts, the cocoanut is crushed and the pieces are laid in the bride's lap to be kept during her journey to the bridegroom's house. When the bride's party reaches the village boundary the bridegroom marches on houreback with his friends and relations and music to receive the bride. The march turns into a race among the bridegroom's friends for the honour of being first to reach the bride, and the winner is rewarded with a cocoanut and a silver coin and the others with sweets. When he reaches the bride's carriage the bridegroom asks the maidservant to give him her place. She refuses and he offers her money. When she is satisfied she leaves the carriage and the bridegroom takes her place. When they reach the bridegroom's house the pair leave the carriage and enter the booth, where, under a silk canopy, at each corner of a square, is placed an earthen pot freshly brought from the potter, and, in the middle, two low stools for the pair. Under the arch of the booth the bridegroom's mother waves round the pair a miniature pestle and mortar, a ladle, a plough-yoke, and a roller, and the pair are then led to their seats in the canopy. A sacred fire is kindled by the bridegroom's priest. The hands of the couple are joined and they are made to move round the fire. The pair are then taken inside to worship the *gotraj* or family goddess. Next they play the game of *eki beki* odds or evens with betelnuts, dry dates and coins. The women affirm that the mastery in wedded life falls to the victor in this game. After the game the priest unties the *mindhals* or wedding nut-bracelets and the marriage is complete.

On the next day presents are made to Bháts and Chárans. When the bridegroom goes personally to the bride's house he takes the place of the maidservant and performs all the necessary rites at the bride's house. When this is done, the rites of hand-joining and going round the sacred fire are not repeated at his house.

After marriage Rajput women as a rule remain within the *zenána* or private apartments. As, among the rich, polygamy is usual, the inmates of the *zenána* always enjoy the interest of rivalry or affection. Among Tálukdárs and Garásiás widow marriage is not allowed, and the Rajput cultivators who permit the practice are held to forfeit their position as true Rajputs.

eg- ncy. In the fifth month of a Rajput woman's first pregnancy the husband's sister ties a guardian-thread called *rákhdi* or keeper round the right wrist of the pregnant woman, and during the seventh or ninth month performs the lap-filling ceremony. A lucky day for the lap-filling is named by a Bráhman priest, and the husband's father sends a *kankotri* or invitation marked with turmeric or vermilion to the woman's father, who sends by a Bráhman dresses and ornaments to be presented to his daughter. On the day of the lap-filling, her female friends and relations take the pregnant woman for a bath to a neighbour's house. Into the bathing-place a cocoanut is thrown, and the pregnant woman is bathed and dressed in green clothes sent by her father. Her brow is marked with vermilion, her head is decked with a *mod* or three-cornered diadem which contains an iron needle or *trák* and her lap is filled with four pounds of wheat and a cocoanut. She then leaves for her house attended by a band of musicians and by her women friends and neighbours singing songs. On her way home she is made to walk on cloth spread for the purpose by the women of her ftaher's house who come to attend the ceremony. At her first step a silver coin is laid on the cloth, at the second a cocoanut, and at each of the succeeding steps a betelnut. In rich families silver coins take the place of the cocoanut and betelnuts. The cloth, the silver coins, and the cocoanut and betelnuts are supplied by the father of the pregnant woman and are given to her husband's sister. When she reaches her home, in the *oshri* or apartment next to the veranda, her husband's brother marks her cheeks with turmeric or vermilion water and receives for his trouble up to Rs. 5 in cash. The pregnant woman then goes inside the house to worship the family goddess, who is painted in turmeric on the wall. She sits before the goddess and lays sandal-paste, turmeric, vermilion, rice and flowers, and bows, before her. While she sits before the goddess her lap is filled with unhusked rice and a cocoanut, silver coins and a robe and bodice, and her cheeks are rubbed with turmeric powder. She joins her hands and bows and stands before the goddess. Molasses are distributed to such friends and relations as have been asked to the house. The pregnant woman then empties the contents of her lap into the lap of some woman whose husband and all of whose children are alive. With the same articles the matron refills the pregnant woman's lap and the process is repeated three times. The pregnant woman then leaves for her father's and carries with her the unhusked rice with which her lap was filled. This rice is kept at her father's till the sixth day after delivery, when it is husked, boiled and eaten.

Death.

A short time before death, according to his means, a Rajput gives a cow, a horse, grain and gold to Bráhmans, and a Bráhman priest reads the Bhagvatgita to the dying person. On the near approach of death, the dying-person is laid on his back with his feet to the south on a portion of the floor which has been freshwashed with cowdung, sprinkled with water from some holy river, and strewn with sacred *durbha* grass. On the left of the dying person is set a zinc cup with a ball of wheat flour and ashes, and a lamp fed with clarified butter is kept burning near the zinc cup. In the dying mouth are laid five jewels, that is, clarified butter, curds, basil leaves, holy water, and gold. The relations sit near and repeat *Rám Rám* till life is gone. The deceased, if a male, is shaved and bathed and dressed in five garments, a waist-cloth, a shouldercloth, a coat, a waistcoat and a turban. A bamboo bier is prepared and furnished with a mattress and cushions and a white sheet. The body is laid on the bier and covered with a silk or brocade cloth according to the means of the dead. A cocoanut is tied to each of the four corners of the bier. In the case of chiefs and the members of chiefs' families a *sinhásan* or lion seat is made to carry the dead to the burning ground. To carry the bier five persons bathe and put on the sacred thread. Four of them bear the bier, and the fifth walks in front carrying fire in an earthen pot set in a bamboo frame hanging from his hand. The widow dresses in a holiday robe and bodice and ornaments. When the bier is carried out of the house she goes to some river or pond with women neighbours and friends crying bitterly, she breaks her ivory bangles and puts off her gay clothes and ornaments, bathes in the pond or river, and, dressed in plain dark garments, returns home weeping. At a short distance from the burning ground the bearers halt and lay a ball of rice flour and a silver coin in the right hand of the dead. The bier is again lifted and taken to the burning ground, which is generally near a pond or river. A pile of wood and cowdung cakes is prepared and the body is again bathed and laid on the pile. On the body are dropped sacred basil leaves, pieces of sandalwood, *gugal* or incense, and cocoanuts. The hands and feet of the dead are rubbed with clarified butter. The Bráhman priest repeats the sacred verses; the chief mourner moves five times round the pile with a burning brand in his hand and touches the mouth of the dead with the brand, repeating the words *Nás práni Ag ávi*, that is, Flee Oh soul, fire has come. The pile is then kindled; when it is completely burnt, water is poured over it and the embers extinguished. Then they go to a neighbouring river or pond, bathe, and return home crying aloud. On that day no food is prepared in the house of the dead. The inmates are fed with cooked rice, pulse and clarified butter prepared at the house of the father of the chief mourner's wife or at the house of some near relations or neighbours. For nine days cooked rice with pulse called *kadváni khichadi* is eaten in the house. For the first ten days a Bráhman priest pours sugar, water, milk and opium-water into leaf cups and the cups are placed on the roof of the house. On the third day letters bearing the sad news are sent to relations and friends who do not live in the same village, stating the time of death and the time when the death rites are to be performed. On the same day the chief mourner with relations and friends goes to the burning ground taking a new earthen vessel covered with a new earthen saucer called *Rámvátra* or Rám's saucor and a little milk in a brass or copper vessel also covered with a metal saucer and flowers. He pours the milk over the cold embers, gathers the ashes and, except a few bones which are preserved to be sent to some holy place or river, such as Benares, Gaya or Sidhpur, removes them to some neighbouring tank or river. In the place of the ashes he lays the earthen vessel filled with water and on the vessel's mouth Rám's saucer with a wheat-flour ball in it. He then bathes and returns home. For the first ten days after a death the inmates of the house are considered impure and keep apart even when visitors come to console them. For these comforters the chief mourner keeps dry opium and water and a smoking pipe ready. Every morning from the first to the ninth balls of rice flour are offered to the dead. On the tenth day the chief mourner, who is generally the eldest son, shaves his face, the eyebrows and the head except the topknot, and performs the tenth day *shráddha* or mind-feast. For the other men of the family, the rule is that only those younger than the dead shave the moustache. On the eleventh day all members of the mourning family bathe and put on fresh washed clothes. On the mornirg of the eleventh the waistcloths, bamboo baskets, metal idols, rice and other grains and flour, turmeric, sandal paste, flowers, earthen vessels, sesame and molasses required for the eleventh-day rites are taken to the village river or pond, and during the course of the day a *shráddha* or mind-rite is performed. A young bull and a heifer are wedded, balls of rice-flour are offered to the spirit of the dead, and the chief mourner returns weeping aloud. A caste feast is given to the relations of the dead. On the twelfth, as on the eleventh, the mourners go to the village river or pond and perform the twelfth day rites. When they return, the priest lays before the house twelve balls of wheat-flour each in an earthen saucer covered with a rim-down cup, of brass, copper or, in the case of a chief, of silver. Each cup and saucer is tied togeher with cotton-thread. On the thirteenth day the village potter comes and removes the thread and receives an earthen vessel and a cup for his trouble. Of the remaining vessels half go to the Bráhman and half to the daughter's or sister's sons of the dead. Castepeople and servants as well as ascetics and beggars are then fed with sweetmeats and *mori biranj*, that is, pounded rice and pulse cooked in clarified butter and condiments, or *lápsi* wheat flour cooked with molasses and mixed with clarified butter, pulse and *khichdi*, that is, cooked rice and pulse, or *shiro*, that is, wheat flour cooked in clarified butter and molasses. If the deceased is a woman thirteen shallow bamboo baskets called *chhábdis*, each containing a petticoat, a bodice and a robe, are presented in the name of the dead person to near relations. If the deceased is a man, thirteen deep baskets are filled each with a headscarf, a waiscoat, a shouldercloth and a waistcloth, and are given to near relations. At night a cot is laid out furnished with a mattress, pillows and cushions and a pair of shoes. A metal lamp, five garments, a waistcloth a shouldercloth a headscarf, a coat and a waistcoat, wheat, rice, *juvár* molasses and clarified butter, dice and playing cards, betelnuts, brass salvers, jars, cups, and smoking pipes are also placed on the cot. A cow is brought in, the wife of the dead comes and holds the tail of the cow with both hands, and over her hands the priest pours water. The bedding or *sejja* with the rest of the articles are presented to a Bráhman, who is generally called *Káyatiya*, that is, funeral Bráhman. The Bráhman is laid on the bedding, and the cot is lifted by four men and carried out of the house to the village boundary. The men and women of the house follow for a short distance crying bitterly, and burning cowdung cakes are thrown after the *Káyatiya*. They then return home. If the family is well-to-do, two sets of bed presents or *sejjás* are given one to the *Káyatiya* the other to the family-priest.

On the thirteenth day, the thirteenth-day rites are performed and the family priest is given a milch cow, a cot with mattresses, pillows and cushions, a cup, a lampstand, waistcloths, robes, bodices and packets of sugar. Friends and relations are asked to dine at the house and Bráhmans are feasted and presented with money. The chief mourner is given a turban or cash by his father-in-law or maternal uncle, and such friends and relations as are present are entertained with *kusumba* and betel-leaves and nuts. The sister or daughter of the dead distributes sweet balls of wheat flour to relations and friends in the village. On the fifteenth day a dinner is given to Bráhmans and castepeople ; and till another month is over, that is for six weeks in all, the members of the family do not join in marriage or other feasts nor do they eat the special dishes which are taken on festive occasions. At the same time as the seclusion of the mourning family ceases, that is a month and a half after the death, the third fortnightly *shráddha* is performed ; and four and a half months later the sixth-monthly *shráddha* follows

On the bright fifth of *Bhádrapad* (Sep.-Oct.) grain is cooked and served to Bráhmans. On the next day the members of the house feed on sweet balls. Three days later, on the bright eighth of *Bhádrapad* (Sep.-Oct.), balls of rice or Indian millet flour mixed with molasses or sugar and clarified butter are made and given to Bráhmans with cash. A bamboo lantern is made and in it are put a headscarf, a waistcloth, a shouldercloth, a coat and a jacket, with copper-pots, ornaments, a looking glass, a silk waistcord and articles used in playing games. All of these, including the bamboo lantern, are presented to Bráhmans in the presence of the relations who add gifth of cash. On the bright tenth of *Aso* (Oct.-Nov.) Bráhmans are fed. And on the *Diváli* a wheat-flour lamp in a leaf cup is launched on the nearest river. On the *Sankránt* (Jany. 12) Bráhmans are fed with balls of *mag* Phaseolus radiatus flour mixed with sugar and clarified butter and are presented with earthen vessels and cash. On the *Akhátrij* or bright third of *Vaishákh* (May-June) earthen vessels filled with water are presented with cash to Bráhmans. A little less than twelve months after the death the first year feast is held, when bamboo baskets and earthen and metal vessels and a cot with bedding, waistcloths and metal vessels are given to the Bráhman priest, and Bráhmans and castepeople are feasted. From this day to the actual anniversary counting by months, a Bráhman and an ascetic are fed daily, and, on the twelfth month death-day they are presented with dresses and cash. On the twelfth month death-day Bráhmans are presented with money. The widow and the sons of the dead leave off mourning and the widow goes to her father's house. On each anniversary a *shráddha* or mind rite is performed and Bráhmans are fed.

Religion.

Except their clan and local peculiarities, Rajputs do not differ from other Hindus in their religious observances and practices.(1) Though many are followers of the special forms of Vaishnavism preached by Vallabhácharya and by Rámánuja, and though the modern sect of Sváminaráyan still gathers adherents, Rajputs from remote ages have been partial to the worship of Shiva. At the same time they worship all Hindu gods and goddesses, and their house-shrines contain the images of Shiva, Vishnu, Ganpati, and of the tutelary goddess of the clan. The Jádejás worship the northern Ashápuri, the

(1) Before A.D. 1818 Cutch Jádejás were half Hindu half Musalmán. They visited mosques and gave their daughters in marriage to Musalmáns. Since A.D. 1818 the example of several strictly Hindu Rávs, the decline of infanticide, the division of land and the spread of poverty have combined to make the Jádejás give up several of their un-Hindu ways. Of their former Musalmán beliefs and practices nothing remains but the reverence for certain Musalmán saints and the occasional marriage into Musalmán families.

hope-fulfiller, whose principal shrine is in Cutch. The Jhálás adore a goddess named Adya whose shrine is at Halvad. The Gohils worship the Khodiád Máta whose chief shrine is at Rájapara near Sihor. The goddess of the Jethvás is Vindhyavásini whose original shrine is on the Nágmáta river close to Navánagar and whose chief temple is at Chháya near Porbandar. The Parmárs worship the goddess Mandavri whose temple is at Muli. Chávadás and Vághelás worship Chámunda. Rich Rajputs have Bráhman priests to do the daily worship of their household gods. After his marriage a Rajput visits the principal shrines of his *máta* or tutelary goddess in company with his bride. Part of the marriage ceremony consists in knotting the end of the bridegroom's shouldercloth or waistcloth to the bride's veil or *chundri*, and these knots are always loosened in front of the family goddess. Among the Cutch Jádejás the most gorgeous festival in the year is the Ráv's procession to the snake temple in the Bhuj fort. Jádejás show great respect to their priests, who are Bráhmans of the Rájgor sub-division, and to Bháts and Chárans, their family bards and chroniclers. Except a few who are disciples of Sváminaráyan, the Parmárs of Muli are as a rule worshippers of the sun. Sun-worshippers fast on Sundays. Bardái Bráhmans, called after the district at the foot of the Barda hills in south Káthiáwár, are the priests of Jethvás. These Bráhmans worship Shiva and Shakti, and visit the local temples of these deities morning and evening.

As a rule the Vághela chiefs are worshippers of Shakti. Náthanji, the first Vághela, who came to Sánand in A.D. 1315, built a temple to his family goddess Hajari Máta which is still known by the name of Adya Máta the family goddess of the Jhálás. Among the cultivating Vághelás, both the Vallabhác ya and the Rámánuja forms of Vaishnavism have found a large following. Except a few who keep a conch shell or *shankh* and the image of the *máta* in their house, Vághelás as a rule have no household images. On Dasara Day in September-October, they mark the brow of the horse with vermilion and rice and tie a seven-knotted thread marked with vermilion round his right pastern. The girls meet at the house and paint on a wooden board a tree with a *koyel* or Indian cuckoo perched on it. They then take the board to the river and bathe in the river with the board, lay vermilion flowers and rice on it, go to a neighbouring garden and call the bird, imitating its voice till he answers. When there is danger from floods, Vághelás go to the river or seashore or to a pond and worship water. The chief throws a woman's robe and a cocoanut into the sea to pacify the flood spirits and save his people. Vála

Rajputs, though not Muhammadans, visit *tájiás* or Muharram biers and the tombs of Muhammadan saints and offer them cocoanuts and make them vows. This leaning to Muhammadanism is not peculiar to Válás. Vow-making to the Muharram *tájiás* or biers and to the tombs of Muhammadan saints is common among lower Hindus and is often met with among the higher castes. Besides their own special days the different clans of Rajputs keep all Hindu fasts and feasts.

In manners Rajputs are courteous and polite but somewhat touchy and ready to take offence. They are fond of children and respectful to women. A Rajput of good family, if reduced to be a cultivator, would rather himself fetch water in the dark than allow his wife to bring it. Their sensitiveness to female honour is so keen that a man, however distantly related to a woman who has dishonoured herself, considers it his duty to destroy her and her seducer. They have a good name for honesty and they have given such brilliant examples of *swámi-bhakti* or master-worship that ready self-sacrifice is considered the typical feature of the Rajput character. The Rajput is hospitable and loves to entertain strangers. The Rajput woman is faultlessly neat and careful of her looks, she is enterprising and high-spirited, according to the proverb "the wise mother of fools" She is intriguing, jealous, ambitious, thrifty and fond of show, as the proverb says, "She marries the land, not the man". Character.

Followers of Swámi-Náráyan, Vallabhácharya and Rámánuja eschew fish, flesh, garlic and liquor. All other Rajputs eat animal food, drink liquor, smoke tobacco, and eat opium. Except the Válás and a few other divisions, most Rajputs eat fish, partridge, duck, goat, sheep and hare.(1) Of animals which split the hoof they eat only the *chikaru* or gazelle. In Rewa Kantha they eat the wild boar, but no Rajput will touch the flesh either of the horse or of the ass. Strict Rajputs have a strong feeling against the flesh of the domestic fowl. But in south Gujarát the feeling on this point is lax. Food and drink.

All the different divisions of Rajputs eat together in the same row but not from the same dish. The majority of the Rajputs neither

(1) In A.D. 1818 many Jádejás of Cutch, though nominally Hindus, continued in matters of food Muhammadans, employing Musalmán cooks, taking flesh and refusing to eat things forbidden in the Kurán. Now, except about five per cent., they live as Hindus, most of them on simple fare, respecting the Rajput feeling against eating the domestic fowl and seldom using animal food. Some among them of the Vaishnav sect are strict vegetarians. When meat is used, it is duly killed by a Musalmán and cooked at a distance from the usual kitchen. The custom of asking a Musalmán to kill an animal is not necessarily a remnant of the former leaning to Islam. Like the Jádejás many Deccan Maráthás object to eat meat which has not been duly killed by a Musalmán.

eat from the same dish nor smoke the pipe of those who allow widow-marriage, who marry with Kolis and Musalmáns, and who are of low social position. Rajputs eat food cooked by all classes of Hindus, except Kolis, Vághris, and the depressed castes.

A brief description of the chief of the Rajput clans is given below.

Chávadás. CHA'VADA'S, the founders of Anahilaváda (A.D. 746) and once (A.D. 720—956) lords of Gujarát, now possess only the two small chiefships of Mánsa and Varsoda in the Mahi Kántha and the two estates of Bhilodia and Rámpura in the Rewa Kántha. In Káthiáwár where, so far back as the late fifth and sixth centuries, they ruled at various places on the coast, notably at Dwárka, Somnáth-Patan and Diu, their political power has long passed away, and they are now found only here and there as *garásiás* or upper landholders. Most of the Cutch Chávadás have fallen to be servants. Recent census and inscription details seem to establish the fact that the Chávadás belong to the great Gurjara or White Huna race who conquered northern India during the fifth century A.D.[1]

Chudásamás. CHUDA'SAMA'S are an offshoot of the Samma tribe, probably of Turk origin, which entered India during the seventh or eighth century and ruled at Nagar Thatha in Sind. The Chudásamás appear to have established themselves in Cutch during the early tenth century. From Cutch they pushed on to Káthiáwár and settled at Vanthali about nine miles south-west of Junágadh, from which they held Girnár until, in A.D. 1427, Junágadh was taken by Mahmudsháh Begada of Ahmedábád and the last of the local rulers, Ra Mandlik, surrendered to the conqueror and forsook the faith of his fathers. Soráth became Moslim territory, and on his death Ra Mandlik was raised to the rank of a saint under the title of Khán Jehán. The Chudásamás are now found in Dholera as *garásiás* or upper landholders. As Yádavs and descendants of Shrikrishna they claim superiority over all other Gujarát Rajputs, and though only a few of them are left, the daughters of the clan are held to be fit brides even for ruling houses.

Dáimás. DA'IMA'S, who have no historical importance in Gujarát, hold a few small estates in the Sankheda Mehvás in the Rewa Kántha.

Chohána. CHOHA'NS, the representatives of the imperial family of Delhi (A.D. 1191), have possessions in the Pálanpur and Rewa Kántha Agencies only. The chiefs of Suigám and Váv in Pálanpur and of Báriya and Chhota-Udaipur in the Rewa Kántha are Chohâns as also are the

(1) Compare Bombay Gazetteer, Vol. I, Part I, pp. 127, note 2, and 465.

owners of eight states in the Sankheda and of one in the Pándu Mehvás. Chohâns are also found scattered in small numbers over other parts of Gujarát and Káthiáwár, where they live in poor circumstances as servants or as small peasant proprietors.

Goris. GORIS, like the Dáimás, have a solitary settlement in the Sankheda Mehvás in the Rewa Kántha Agency, where they hold three small estates.

Gohils. GOHILS, also called Gehlots and Sisodiyás, whose head is the Rána of Udaipur in Rajputána, the premier Hindu house in India, are one of the four great divisions of the Rajput race, which still hold sway in Káthiáwár and give their name to Gohilvád, the eastern section of the peninsula. They claim descent from the Válás of Valabhipur (A.D. 509—750) who, though formerly supposed to be descended from Shálivâhan or Kanaksena, that is the house of the great Kushan emperor Kanishka (A.D. 78), are now believed to belong to the White Huna or Mihira hordes by whom Valabhi was conquered about A.D. 490. On the ruin of Valabhi by Arabs from Sind about A.D. 770 a branch of the ruling family retreated to Mevád. There they gained possession of the fort of Chitor and ruled to the thirteenth century when a portion of them withdrew to Kichli in south Márwár. From Kichli they were driven by the Ráthods about A.D. 1290 and forced their way into Káthiáwár. According to the local tradition their leader Sejak married his daughter to the eldest son of Ra Kavát, the Chudásama chief of Sorath, who gave him a few villages in the east of his territory. Sejak had three sons Ránoji, Sárangji, and Shaháji. Ránoji is the direct ancestor of the houses of Bhávnagar and Rájpipla, Sárangji of Láthi in east central Káthiáwár, and Shaháji of Pálitana about twenty-seven miles south-east of Láthi. Many small estates in Gohilvád are offshoots from the house of Bhávnagar. Under Sorath the Ain-i-Akbari (A.D. 1590) notices a population of 25,000 Gehlots. These people, who are known as Asil Gehlots, are said to be descendants of Báppa who migrated from Valabhi to Chitor in the eighth century. They are said to have returned to Káthiáwár before a generation had passed. They now form the Gehlot subdivision of Mers found in Porbandar and along the coast. In spite of their high standing in Káthiáwár, the few Gohils, in Cutch, with the exception of two houses, have sunk to the position of family servants.

Jádejás. JA'DEJA'S are the most numerous and at the same time the most powerful Rajput clan in Gujarát. Besides Cutch, they own nearly one-third of Káthiáwár, the two chiefships of Santalpur and Chádchat in the Pálanpur Agency, and a small estate in the Pándu Mehvás in the

Rewa Kántha. In Káthiáwár, besides minor offshoots, the important states are Navánagar, Gondal, Morvi, Dhrol, Rájkot, and Mália which were founded between A.D. 1540 and A.D. 1720. The Jádejás are the leading Hindu representatives of the tribe of Samma Rajputs who ruled Sind from A.D. 1351 to 1521. The Jádejás claim to belong to the great Yádav stock whose pedigree goes back to Sámb, son of Krishna, but there seems little reason to doubt that they are among the latest immigrant Turks who preceded the Arab conquest of Sind in A.D. 713. Under the Sumra rulers of Sind (A.D. 1053—1351), the Sammás probably maintained a half-independent position in the south of Sind and seem at several times between the eleventh and the fourteenth centuries to have moved south to Cutch to avoid Sumra tyranny. About A.D. 1351 the Sammás overthrew the Sumrás, and with their head-quarters at Samai near Thatha, became the rulers of south Sind. During the spread of Muhammadan power, the Sammás, before the close of the fourteenth century, had adopted Islám and since their conversion, though it is still borne by several large pastoral tribes, the name Samma is less known than Sameja and Jádeja, the Hindu branches of the tribe. According to the latest accounts, the name Jádeja was taken by the Cutch branch about A.D. 1350, when they called in as their chief Lákha, a son of Jám Jáda of Thatha. From Cutch they entered Káthiáwár. It is said that about A.D. 1313, Bahmani Samma led a band as far as Ghumli in the Barda hills, then the capital of the Jethvás, and destroyed it, but did not gain a permanent footing in the country. Santalpur and Chádchat were taken by Ráo Khengárji of Cutch (A.D. 1548—1586) from Sarkháji, the son of Lunáji Vághela.

Jethvás. JETVA'S probably came from the north, and first established themselves near Morvi. Thence they spread westward along the coast, captured Dwárka from the Chávadás, and moving to the south-west, established themselves in the strip of land between the Barda hills and the sea. They never passed far inland. Their first capital was at Ghumli in the Barda hills about forty miles north-east of Porbandar. From Ghumli they moved to Chháya on the coast about two miles south-east of Porbandar, and about A.D. 1785 in the decline of Musalmán power, established themselves at Porbandar which has since been their capital. The tribe, which is comparatively small, is united under one head, his Highness the Maharána of Porbandar. Makardhvaj, the founder of their clan, was, they say, the son of Hanumán, the monkey god, and of a female alligator, and, until recently, it was said and believed that as a mark of their descent the Jethvás were born with taile. It is established that the Jethvás are Mers, the representatives of the great Mihira hordes who in A.D. 490 captured Valabhi and overran Káthiáwár. The name Jethva, which is locally taken to mean either Elder or Born under the constellation *Jyestha* may be a trace of Yeta, one of the names by which the Mihiras or White Huns were known.[1]

JHA'LAS, though well known in Rajputána, are in Gujarát confined to east Káthiáwár. Their ancestor Hirpál is said to have belonged to a Makvána family of Cutch, who, in the thirteenth century, moved to Gujarát and took service with Karan Ghelo, the last (A.D. 1296--1304) Vághela prince of Anahilaváda Pátan. That chieftain probably gave Hirpál a grant of territory to the east of the Ran of Cutch and he established his residence at Patdi. The next capital of the clan was at Kuva, whence being driven by Mahmud Begada of Gujarát in A.D. 1488 they established themselves at Halvad, and in A.D. 1800 moved their head-quarters to Dhrángadra. The common derivation of the name Jhála is that Hirpál's sons were in danger of being trampled by an elephant, when their witch-mother, stretching her arm from an upper window, snatched them up and carried them to a place of safety. From this they were called Jhála or 'caught up'. The fancifulness of this derivation, together with the facts of their history which associate them closely with the Mihira or White Huna conquerors of the fifth century, suggest that the name is Jauvla, the stock title of the great White Huna leaders Toramána (A.D. 450--500) and Mihirakula[2] (A.D. 500—540). From the parent stem of Dhrángadra, besides other small estates, have sprung the independent chiefships of Chuda, Lakhtar, Limbdi, Sáela, Vadhván, and Vánkáner. Jhálas.

PARMA'RS who own chiefships in north Gujarát and Káthiáwár appear to have come from Sind. According to the Rás Mála, at some remote period 2,000 Sodha Parmárs came from Párkar during a famine and established themselves near Sáela in Káthiáwár. The Vághela, who then ruled at Vadhván, employed Mujo their head, to attack the Bhil chiefs Aho and Pháto who lived on the banks of the Sábarmati, hoping that the attempt would end in disaster. But the Sodhás were successful, and the Vadhván chief gave them the four districts of Muli, Thán, Chotila, and Chobári. Of these the estate of Muli is now alone held by Parmárs. To the Mahi Kántha, where they hold the two chiefships of Dánta and Sudásna, the Parmárs came from Nagar Thatha, whence they were driven by the Muhammadans about Parmárs

(1) Compare Bombay Gazetteer, Vol. I, Part I, p. 127.

(2) Compare Bombay Gazetteer, Vol. I, Part I, p. 146.

A.D. 1050. Tharád in the Pálanpur Agency is said to have originally belonged to Parmár Rajputs, and to this day many Parmárs of the Suvar and Kalva sub-clans are found in subordinate positions in Tharád villages. In the Rewa Kántha they hold only one estate in the Pándu Mehvás. Like the Káthiáwár Parmárs, the Cutch Parmárs belong to the Sodha sub-clan of the Parmárs and appear to have come from Sind. At the beginning of the present century these Sodha Parmárs were in a wretched condition, living chiefly as bandits, and, for several years after the beginning of the British connection with Cutch (A.D. 1819—1822), their raids caused the greatest ruin and distress in the east of the province. They are settled in small numbers in the north of Cutch and in some of the Ran islands, and except a few cultivators are herdsmen, most of them in poor condition. Their chief connection with Cutch is through the marriage of their daughters with the leading Jádeja and Musalmán families. These Sodha women are of great natural abilities and much personal beauty. In A.D. 1819 Capt. MacMurdo described them as so ambitious and intriguing as not to scruple to make away with their husbands that their sons might obtain the estate.(1)

olankis. SOLANKIS, the once (A.D. 961—1242) powerful successors of the Chávadás in the sovereignty of Gujárat, have their possessions confined to the wilds of the Rewa Kántha and Bánsda. In the Rewa Kántha they hold the state of Lunáváda and an estate in each of the two Mehváses Sankheda and Pándu. In A.D. 1225 Virbhadra Solanki killed Viro Báriya, chief of Virpur, and established himself at that town eight or nine miles west of Lunáváda. From this town the Lunáváda Solankis are called Virpura Solankis. The town of Lunáváda was founded by Bhimsingh, a descendant of Virbhadra. Of the early history of the Bánsda Solankis, no details are available. Recent information leaves little doubt that, like the Chávadás, the Solankis belong to the great tribe of Gurjjaras or Gujars who apparently represent the main body of the great fifth century conquerors, the White Hunas.(2)

áthods. RA'THODS own chiefships in the Mahi Kántha. The Ráthods were driven south from Kanauj by the Muhammadans about the end of the twelfth century, and under the guidance of Siyoji, the son or nephew of Jaychand Dale Pánglo of Kanauj, established themselves in the sandy deserts of Márwár. Siyoji's second son Sonangji repaired to the court of Anahiladáda, whose sovereign, probably Bhim Dev

(1) Transactions, Bombay Literary Society, II, p. 253.

(2) Compare Bombay Gazett ., Vol. I, Part I, p. 468.

II (A.D. 1179—1242), assigned him the fief of Sámetra in the district of Kadi. Not many years later, the Ráthods won the fort and lands of Idar. Besides Idar, Ráthod chiefs hold Pol, Málpur, Magodi, Valásna, and Vásna in the Mahi Kántha. Idar is not now held by the old Ráthods but by the Ráthods of Jodhpur. Of the succession of the Jodhpur chiefs two stories are told ; one that they were called in by the Idar ministers, the other that they had been in revolt against their brother, the Maháraja Abheysingh, viceroy of Gujarát (A.D. 1730-1733), and were pacified by the grant of Idar. Ráthods also own seven estates in the Sankheda Mehvás and two estates in the Pándu Mehvás in the Rewa Kántha. In the Pálanpur Agency they are landowners, village-sharers and holders of service lands, but in Káthiáwár, where their number is small, most of them have fallen to be servants.

REHVAR Rajputs [1] are confined to the Mahi Kántha, where they hold the minor estates of Bolandra, Mohanpur, Ranásan, Rupál, and Vadagám. Jaspál Rehvar emigrated from Chandrávati near Mount Abu to Hadol in the Mahi Kántha in A.D. 1227 and thence in the thirteenth generation Thákor Pruthuráj moved to Ghodváda, having obtained a grant of that and the neighbouring districts, which in course of time were divided among the present chiefships. Rehvars are also found in small numbers in poor circumstances in Káthiáwár and in other parts of Gujarát. **Rehvars.**

SARVAIYA'S, who are probably Chudásamás, are found only in Gohilvád, where they are landowners. **Sarvayás.**

SISODIYA'S, the representatives of the Mevád house of Udaipur and the same in origin as the Gohils, own the state of Dharampur in the Surat district and the chiefships of Dadhália in the Mahi Kántha. According to their own traditions, the Dharampur Sisodiyás, about 700 years ago, under a certain Rám Rája conquered from the Bhils this portion of the hill lands of south Gujarát. About the middle of the seventeenth century, Vaháji, the first Thákor of Dadhália, with a body of horse entered the service of Kaliánmal, the Ráo of Idar. **Sisodiyás.**

---

(1) Of the origin of the Rehvar Patávats the following account is given. The Rehvar Rajputs are Parmárs who came originally from Ujjain and settled at Chandravati. They afterwards moved to Parkar, to Mount Abu, and lastly to Táringa from all of which places they seem to have been expelled. They took possession of Taringa in A.D. 1226 (S. 1282). Their deeds or *pattás* are derived from the former Ráos of Idar, and their dependence on the present Rája is limited to the payment of *khichdi* in cash. Of the origin of the name Rehvár the story goes that one of their Abu ancestors, on his way to win his bride, stopped to pay his devotions at a temple of Devi. As she knew his future father-in-law intended to kill him, the goddess said *Rehvar* Bridegroom go no further. In obedience to the goddess' warning the bridegroom remained and all who went on were murdered. (Bom. Gov. Sel., XII, 120.)

Vádhels and Vajas.

VA'DHELS and VAJAS who are branches of the great Ráthod clan are found in Káthiáwár. They entered the peninsula about the thirteenth century from Rajputána. The Vádhels treacherously drove out the Chávadás from Dwárka and Bet, and established themselves there, while the Vájás settled on the south coast, their leader Vejo founding Vejalkot on the Rával river in the south of the Gir. From Vejalkot they conquered Una and spread their rule east to Jhánjhmer and the Mánári river. Later, as they were much harassed by the *garásiás*, they sought the protection of Bhávnagar, where they are now found as small landholders.

Vaghelas.

VAGHELAS, who after the Solankis ruled over Gujarát (A.D. 1242—1304), now hold the three chiefships of Tharád, Morváda, and Diodar in the Pálanpur Agency and the one chiefship of Pethápur in the Mahi Kántha.

In addition to these clans, members may be found of all the great Rajput tribes and sub-tribes Bhátis, Dábhis, Ghelots, Jádavs, Makvánás, Moris, Pádhiárs, and Válás. These miscellaneous Rajputs have fallen to be servants and peasant proprietors. In most cases they hold scarcely land enough to support their families.

The Rajputs of the Deccan and Southern Marátha Country form a distinct community from those of Káthiáwár and Gujarát. They are known as Suratváls in Bijápur. They are also known as Pardeshi, a term generally applied to men coming from the United Provinces and also to illegitimate children of Upper India men and local women. They are the descendants of those Rajputs who came to the south in search of military service. These Rajputs kept or married Marátha, Dhangar or other low caste women, and the offspring of such unions came to be called Rajputs. In Kanara, the home of several prostitute castes, such children generally joined one of the prostitute classes. It is said that the issue of some of these marriages formed the clans of Chaváns, Pavárs and Jádhavs, who afterwards became heads of powerful Marátha families. These Rajputs claim, and to a certain extent are given, a higher social position than Maráthás. Traces of their Rajput descent are to be found in the customs among most of them of not allowing widow re-marriage, not eating the domestic fowl, and employing Upper India Bráhmans where available to conduct their ceremonies. They have such Rajput clan names as Chaván, Pavár, Tavar, Solanki, Ráthod in addition to surnames adopted from local tribes such as Ajmode, Bagale, Dikshit, etc. Some of them also claim to have *gotras* such as Bháradwája, Mahirão, Káshyap, Garga. But marriages are generally regulated by surnames, persons bearing the same surname not being allowed to intermarry. Their birth, marriage and other ceremonies resemble those followed by the Maráthás though in some places their marriages are performed in North India fashion. Like true Rajputs they are followers of the Smart sect, the chief object of their worship being Shiva. Their hereditary calling is soldiering or *sipáigiri*, but they are now mostly labourers, husbandmen, house servants and petty dealers. In food and drink they resemble Maráthás, but as stated above, many object to the use of domestic fowls, like true Rajputs.

RAJVAL.—A sub-division of Bráhmans.

RAKHIA.—A synonym for Meghvál.

RAMABHAKTA.—A synonym for Rámoshi.

RAMDESHI.—A sub-division of Bhávsárs and Darjis.

RAMOSHI.—A sub-division of Berads.

RAMOSHIS, numbering 60,555 (1901), including 31,444 males and 29,111 females, are found throughout the Presidency except Gujarát but mainly in Poona, Sátára and Ahmednagar. The word Rámoshi is said to be a corruption of Rámavanshi, *i.e.*, the descendants of Ráma. An alternative origin for the word given by Campbell (1) is Ránavási or forest-dweller as the Rámoshis mainly live on the outskirts of villages. They are also called Náiks or Náiklok. Those of them who do not eat flesh are styled Rámabhakts or devotees of Ráma. The Rámoshis appear to be the outlying northern section of the great Kanarese or Telugu tribe or group of tribes which go by the general name of Bedars, with whom they may once have been more intimately connected than is now the case. The Rámoshis of Belgaum still state that they are of the same caste as the Bedars, with whom they eat but do not intermarry. The existence of a Bedar division of the tribe, the use of Kanarese names for their men, the traces of Telugu words in their language, their title of Náiks and their traditional occupation of committing robberies, for which the Bedars are also notorious, lend much support to the theory of their Bedar origin. It appears that the tribe has been recruited from other castes such as Kunbis and Mángs. Many of them once married Kunbi women, and some keep Kunbi women to this day. The result of their connection with the Mángs has been the formation of an endogamous group of the tribe known as the Máng Rámoshis. Regarding the theory of the connection of their name with Ráma, tradition relates that

Name and origin.

(1) Bombay Gazetteer, Vol. XIII, Part I, p. 409.

Ráma, the hero of the Rámáyan, when driven from his kingdom by his step-mother Kaikayi, went to the forest land south of the Narmada. His brother Bharat, who had been raised to the throne by Kaikayi, followed Ráma to the forest, began to do penance, and made friends with a rough but kindly forest tribe. After Ráma's restoration, Bharat took the foresters with him to Ayodhya and brought them to the notice of Ráma, who appointed them village watchmen and allowed them to be called Rámavanshi or children of Ráma.

Rámoshis speak Maráthi. They have also a special language which they use when they are engaged in crime. The names in common use among men are Dhondi, Itu, Khandu, Lakshman, Náráyan, Narsu, Pándu, Pángya, Tátya, Tukárám, Tulsirám, Nágappa, Shivappa, and Yellappa; and among women, Aija, Begu, Chaitra, Dhondi, Kondi, Lakshmi and Rakhma.

Endogamous divisions. There are five endogamous divisions of the caste—

1. Bandate
2. Berad
3. Halge
4. Kadu
5. Máng

Bandates are superior in status to Halges. Máng Rámoshis are the offspring of intermarriages between Mángs and Rámoshis, whose touch is defiling and who live beyond the outskirts of villages. Halges are also found as a division of the Bedars. Each of these divisions have two clans, Chaváns and Jádhavs, of whom the former are the social superiors of the latter. On ceremonial occasions one of the leaders or Náiks of the Chaváns, without whose presence no ceremony can be performed, takes precedence.

The Kadu or bastard division is the result of the practice, still in favour, of Rámoshis keeping Marátha and Kunbi women. The offspring of such unions are looked on as inferior in social status to the other members of the tribe. It is however open to a Rámoshi to admit a son by such a union to the full status of a Rámoshi by giving a dinner to the tribe and seating the boy in the lap of one of the members. Such recruits then enter the *kul* of the father. Girls by such unions remain in the Kadu division, and marry with boys of the same.

Exogamous divisions. The exogamous sub-divisions of the tribe are identical with surnames, though in some cases marriages can take place between persons bearing the same surname. The common surnames are, Ajgire, Berje, Bhosale, Chaván, Chukati, Phokne, Gergal, Ghodgar, Gopne, Gudgul, Jádhav, Jhávle, Jháparde, Kshiraságar, Konde, Lándge,

Madne, Rode, Saparde, Shelár, Shinde, Shirke, Vaghmare and Yelmar. Marriages are prohibited between members having the same *devak*. Every section has a seperate *devak*. The chief *devaks* are, *pánchpálvi*, the *pánkanis* (reed-mace), *vásanvel* (Cocculus villosus), the *suryaphul* (sunflower), the *umbar* (Ficus glomerata), the *jámbhul* (Eugenia jambolana), the *kadamba* (Anthocephalus cadamba) and the *shami* (Prosopis spicigera). These *devaks* appear to be totemistic, as a member will not eat the fruit of, or otherwise use or injure, the tree which represents his *devak*. A member of the caste may marry his father's sister's, mother's sister's or mother's brother's daughter. He cannot marry his mother's sister's daughter. A man may marry two sisters and brothers may marry sisters. Polygamy is allowed and practised, but polyandry is unknown.

Rámoshis have four chiefs or *náiks* and a head chief or *sarnáik*. The head chief, according to Campbell,[1] is a Marátha of the Chaván clan, who marries with Maráthás but comes to Rámoshi weddings. The *náiks* settle caste disputes and hear charges of breaches of caste rules at meetings of the castemen. Of late the power of the heads is declining, but they are still asked to settle disputes about the *devaks* of different families, and at marriage dinners they distribute the liquor.

Boys are generally married from five to thirty, girls even after puberty. A maiden committing sexual indiscretions is, as a rule, turned out of the caste. But if the man involved be a casteman of a different section and *devak* from that of the girl, and if the girl is not pregnant, he is fined and made to give a dinner to the caste people, and compelled to marry the girl.

Marriage ceremonies.

The offer of marriage comes from the boy's father, who has to pay a bride-price of from Rs. 25 to Rs. 150 to the girl's father. The settlement of the marriage day and the ceremony itself are entrusted to a Jangam, or in his absence, to a Bráhman priest. The betrothal, which is known as *kunku lávane* or *sákharpuda,* is celebrated after the fashion of the Kunbis. It takes place one to four years before marriage, the boy's father giving the girl a yearly present of clothes. The other ceremonies also resemble those of the Kunbis with the following peculiarities.

Halad or rubbing the boy and the girl with turmeric paste :—After this ceremony is performed, five ear-bearing plants of Indian millet or *jovári* are dug out of the ground, bound together by a thread,

(1) Bombay Gazetteer, Vol. XVIII, Part I, p. 425.

and with the roots covered with earth are set upright near the family gods and daily sprinkled with water. Next, the family gods are worshipped. Four betelnuts representing the gods Khandoba and Bahiroba and the goddesses Bhaváni and Navalái are rubbed with turmeric powder or *bhandár* and red powder or *kunku*; and enough sheep are slaughtered in front of the booth to feast the guests. The *devak* is then brought and installed in the same way as amongst the Kunbis. In the evening the party feast on the sheep that were sacrificed and drink liquor. This is followed by a *gondhal* dance. All these ceremonies are performed at the houses of both the boy and the girl.

On the afternoon of the wedding day, the boy, dressed in rich clothes, with a dagger in his hand and a marriage coronet on his head, starts in procession for the girl's village. When he reaches the village boundary, a Mahár waves a lighted lamp before his face and is presented with clothes. The bridegroom then proceeds to Máruti's temple and thence to the girl's house, the ceremonies observed during the interval being the same as those amongst the Kunbis. Two heaps of rice-grains are made near the altar and a curtain called Ganga-Jamna is held between the heaps. The bridegroom stands on one of the heaps facing the west, with a dagger in one hand and a cocoanut in the other, and a relation stands close by holding a naked sword over the boy's head. The girl is brought and made to stand opposite the bridegroom, facing east; marriage verses are repeated and yellow grains of rice are thrown over the boy and the girl: the details being the same as amongst the Kunbis. *Kankans* or marriage wristlets are then tied round the wrists of the boy and the girl, a lucky necklace is fastened round the girl's neck by the boy, and the ceremony of *kanyádán* is performed. Next some stalks of *surti* Citysus cajan, of *sonkari* Crotolaria juncea, or of *jovári* are lighted on the altar, the marriage sacrifice is performed and the boy and the girl walk five times round the sacrificial fire. This ceremony is known as *panchapadi* and is the operative portion of the marriage service. Next, the pair go into the house and prostrate themselves before the house gods. While bowing to the gods, the bridegroom hides one of the gods under his robe. The girl's father demands the god, and the boy returns it after receiving some money from him. A feast to the party assembled and the performance of the ceremony of *shesa* end the day's festivities.

Next morning the bride and bridegroom, with music and guests, go to the village *chávadi*, where presents are made to the headman of the village by the bridegroom. In the evening a dinner of mutton and liquor is given to the caste people by the boy's father, presents of articles of dress are made to both parties by relations and friends, and the day's festivities end. On the third, fifth or any other odd day of the wedding, the bridegroom returns to his house in procession with his bride, which terminates the marriage.

The remarriage of widows is permitted. A widow may marry her father's sister's or mother's brother's son or a member of her late husband's section. A widow remarriage is celebrated on a dark night. The service is conducted by a Lingáyat priest, who reads in a low tone. The widow's new husband has to give her toe-rings, a nose-ring, four bracelets and an outfit of clothes. Only men attend the ceremony. As it is considered unlucky for married unwidowed women to hear the service, the ceremony is celebrated in a deserted place. A dinner is given to the caste people. The widow and her new husband separate after the ceremony has been performed, and do not see each other or any of the caste for a day. If a woman has lost three husbands and wishes to marry a fourth, she holds a cock under her left arm when the ceremony is being performed. The priest reads the service first in the name of the cock, and then of the man, the object evidently being that, in case the spirits of the woman's former husbands, or rather the spirit of the first husband who killed the next two for meddling with his property, be inclined to do any harm, it may fall on the cock and not on the man. A bachelor is not allowed to marry a widow.

Divorce is allowed with the sanction of relations and the caste *panch* if the husband and wife do not agree, the wife's conduct is bad, or the wife is desirous of marrying another man. A divorced woman may remarry by the widow remarriage form. A woman taken in adultery is excommunicated. The caste follow the Hindu law of inheritance.

Religion.

Rámoshis belong to the Hindu religion. Some of them are followers of the Várkari sect. They state that they were once Lingáyats, which appears probable from their custom of still employing Jangams to conduct their ceremonies and the fact that there are some Rámoshis (Rámabhakts) who abstain from flesh. Some of them say that Mahádeva is their great god, and that the *ling* is the proper object of worship. Since they have taken to eating flesh they worship the *ling* through Khandoba, who, they say, was a Lingáyat Váni before he became a god. The chief object of their worship is Ráma. They also worship Mahádeva and Vishnu. Of the minor gods they worship Vetál, Bahiroba, Ambábái, Jánái, Kálái, Fringái,

Návalái, Tukái, Vághya, etc. Goats and fowls are offered to these gods, which are eaten by the offerers themselves. Musalmám saints are reverenced.

Rámoshis observe all the leading Hindu holidays, worship all the plants and animals held sacred by the Hindus, and make pilgrimages to the holy places in their vicinity. When an epidemic breaks out, Mariái, Mahálakshmi, or Shitaládevi is propitiated with offerings of goats, and caste dinners are held. When the epidemic abates a little, a Máng woman is dressed in a robe and bodice and becomes possessed by the goddess. The woman is then styled *devi* or goddess and is taken in procession beyond the village boundary.

The spiritual teachers of Rámoshis are Gosávis. After a man is married he becomes a disciple of one of the Gosávis, generally of his father's teacher, or if he is dead, of his successor or disciple. Their priests are Jangams or Deshasth Bráhmans.

Death ceremonies.

The dead are buried with head to the north. The married dead are carried on a bamboo bier, the unmarried are tied to a bamboo. The ceremonies from the moment of death up to when the corpse is carried to the burial ground are the same as amongst the Kunbis, with this peculiarity, that the son or chief mourner of the deceased puts on the turban of the deceased when the corpse is lifted to be carried to the burial ground. When the grave is ready, the chief mourner loosens the body from the bier, goes to a neighbouring stream and bathes with his turban on. He then goes to the grave and squeezes one end of the wet turban so that the water drops into the dead mouth. Next, he breaks the corpse's waist-string, beats his mouth with his hand, and, crying aloud, comes out of the grave and throws earth over the body. Large stones and thorns are laid over the grave. The funeral party then bathe or wash their feet and return to the house of the deceased, each carrying in his hand a few blades of *durva* grass. On reaching the house, a lamp is shown to them and they sit down and throw the grass on the house top. Next day all go to the grave taking cowdung and cow's urine. The cowdung is spread on the grave, the urine is sprinkled over it, and the grave made clean. The son bathes and fills with water the pot which held fire on the previous day, sets it on his shoulder, and piercing it with five holes, lets the water trickle on the ground as he walks round the grave. He dashes the pot on the ground at the head of the grave and calls aloud, beating his mouth with his hand. He shaves his head except the top-knot and his face except his eyebrows. Rice is boiled and each person present lays small balls and a little butter on leaves near the grave. They watch till a crow eats from one of the leaves. Next they return home each carrying a few blades of grass. On the third day after death the funeral party with a Jangam go to the spot where the corpse is buried. A small raised seat is made on the spot and it is cowdunged. On this seat the Jangam makes mud idols of the phallus of Mahádev and his bull. They are worshipped by the chief mourner, and the Jangam declares that the deceased has ascended to *Shivaloka* (Shiva's abode). Next, the party bathe and go to the Jangam's house. The Jangam purifies them by applying ashes to their persons, which ends the mourning. On the seventh day after death a goat is killed in the name of the deceased and castemen are feasted, when the four corpsebearers and the chief mourner eat from the same dish. The Jangam is given uncooked articles of food including some fruit or vegetable, from which the chief mourner has determined to abstain during the year, in honour of the deceased. The guests give the chief mourner a few rupees and a new turban. This ends the death ceremonies. Some Rámoshis make tombs over the graves of the deceased, on which are carved images or horses or men with weapons in their hands.

For the propitiation of the deceased ancestors uncooked articles of food are given to Bráhmans and Jangams on that day of the latter half of *Bhádrapad* which corresponds to the day of death, and four castemen, whose wives are alive and who have not married widows, are worshipped, and water off their feet is sprinkled over the heads of the family members. Next, rice balls are offered to crows on the roof of the house and castemen are feasted. On every anniversary of the deceased uncooked articles of food are given to Bráhmans and their feet are worshipped.

Occupation.

The hereditary occupation of the tribe is stealing. Formerly, under the Marátha Government, Rámoshis and Mángs were in charge of the hill-forts, and their depredations were winked at. Under British rule, Rámoshis and Mángs are mustered every night, all except those who have been convicted being permitted to rest at home. Rámoshis are included among the criminal tribes of the Presidency. The chief occupation of the tribe is now Government or private service as watchmen, and husbandry. When out of work they live by stealing. They are very honest among themselves, and do not betray their comrades even at the risk of their lives. They are treacherous with others, but those who have entered Government service have a great regard for their masters and are true to their salt. Many are landholders. Some hold *inám* lands for serving as village watchmen.

Some are field-labourers and are paid either in cash or in corn. Those who are well-to-do lend money.

Food. They eat the flesh of goats, sheep, fowls, wild pigs, deer, hares and fish, and drink liquor. The devotees of the goddess Bolái do not eat the goat. They say that they do not eat from the hands of Buruds, Ghadshis, Parits, Sonárs, Sutárs, Telis and Musalmáns. Kunbis smoke with them from the same pipe.

RAMREHA.—A sub-division of Bhárgav Bráhmans.

RANA.—A synonym for Gola.

RANDESANTAN.—A sub-division of Mogers.

RANGADA.—Men from United Provinces and Central India.

RANGARI.—A synonym for Nilári ; a sub-division of Shimpis.

RANGWAL.—A synonym for Rajwál.

RANIMANGA.—A sub-division of Bháts.

RAO.—A title applied to Bháts ; this name is assumed as a caste name by the old Marátha settlers in the Thána district, such as the Ráos of Murbád.

RASANIA.—A sub-division of Mochis.

RASULSHAHI.—*See* under Minor Musalmán castes.

RATHOD.—A sub-division of Telis.

RATHODIA.—A sub-division of Dublás.

RATHOR.—*See* under Minor Musalmán castes.

RATI.—A sub-division of Mahárs.

RAUL.—A synonym for Rával.

RAUT.—A sub-division of Mális.

RAVAL.—A sub-division of Vaidus.

Name and origin. **RAVALS, RAVALIAS** or **RAULS** numbering 39,916 (1901), including 20,217 males and 19,699 females, are found chiefly in Gujarát and in small numbers in the Deccan, Konkan and Karnátak. The latter appear to have formerly emigrated from Gujarát but have lost all connection with the Gujarát Rávals, who will not intermarry with them and who speak a different language. They are bards, beggars, carriers, and weavers of tape, and some are agriculturists. They are sometimes known as Jogis.

Endogamous divisions

The endogamous divisions of the caste are as follows :—

In Gujarát—

1. Baria
2. Bhalia
3. Bhorria
4. Makvania
5. Palái or Máru
6. Sakhia and Vahaba
7. Udlia

In the Deccan, Konkan and Karnátak—

1. Akaramashe or bastard
2. Padamroti
3. Rával or Gosávi proper

The Gujarát Rávals admit into their caste, Kolis, Kunbis and Rajputs, who have to first give a dinner to the castemen. The following particulars apply to the Rávals of Gujarát.

Exogamous divisions.

Their surnames are Parmár, Chohán, Vánia, Patalia, Gadhediya, Bhálya, Kalsariya, Horanchi, etc. Of these the Horanchi and Parmári Rávals in Panch Mahâls are considered to be socially superior to the others. The Horanchi and Parmári Rávals may marry a girl of the Gadhediyas or Bhályas, but would not give their daughters in marriage to the latter. The Rávals have formed groups of ten or twelve villages, and marriages must be performed within those groups. Marriage with mother's sister's daughter, father's sister's daughter and maternal uncle's daughter is not allowed. Two brothers may marry two sisters. Boys and girls are married between five and twenty.

Marriage ceremonies.

The offer of marriage comes from the bride's father. The boy's father pays to the father of the girl a sum of about forty rupees. The auspicious day is fixed by an astrologer. The service is conducted by a Bráhman priest. 3, 5, 7 or 9 days before the celebration of marriage, at the houses of the bride and bridegroom, Ganpati is installed and women sing songs at night. On the marriage day the ceremony of *ukardi noturvi* (inviting a dunghill) is performed, and the marriage booth is erected. The planet soothing ceremony is preformed by the family priest. At night the bridegroom goes through his village in a procession, *fuleku*, and starts for the marriage. When the party arrive at the bride's village they are welcomed by the bride's father, *samayya karyu.* The bride's mother leads the bridegroom to the marriage hall. The bride's right hand is then joined with the bridegroom's right hand, the marriage garlands are put on, and the hems of their garments are tied together. The leaves of the mango, *aso* Polyathea lorgifolia, *pipal*, etc., are used for the ceremony The bride and bridegroom take five turns round the sacred fire, feed each other with five morsels of *kansár*, and are welcomed by five women who throw rice grains over their heads. Their brows are also marked with red powder by friends and relatives. The cermonies of joining of hands, turning round the *chori* and the eating of *kansár* are supposed to be the binding portions of the ceremony.

Widow remarriage is allowed. A widow cannot marry her mother's sister's son or father's sister's son. She may marry her maternal uncle's son, the younger brother of her deceased husband or any other member of his family. They consider it desirable that a widow should marry a person of her deceased husband's family or at least some resident of her village. The ceremony does not differ from the ordinary widow remarriage ceremony in Gujarát. A bachelor wishing to marry a widow is first married to a *shami* tree.

Divorce is allowed, and the husband is at liberty to leave his wife at any time ; but the wife cannot leave the husband without his consent. The divorce is effected on account of incompatibility of temper, when the husband is unable to maintain his wife or when the husband and wife dislike each other. When a woman enters the house of another person and lives with him as his wife without the knowledge of her husband and headman of the caste, the man has to pay a sum of eighty rupees as damages. A divorce is known as *chhuta cheda karva*. A divorced woman is allowed to marry a second time, when her marriage is effected on the form of widow remarriage.

Religion. They follow the Hindu law of inheritance and belong to the Hindu religion, worshipping Hingláj Máta. They have a special liking for the worship of goddesses. They visit the sacred shrines of Mahákáli, Ambáji, Bahucharáji and other goddesses. They hold the *pipal*, *shami* and sweet basil trees in great reverence. Their principal holidays are *Diváli*, *Dasara* and *Holi*. Their priests are ascetic *sádhus* of their own caste who officiate at all their ceremonies except at marriages, when they call in a Tapodhan Bráhman.

Death ceremonies. The Rávals commonly bury their dead. The dead are buried in a sitting position facing the south. On the evening of the twelfth day after a death they set a low stool before a lamp made of rice flour paste fed with clarified butter, and on the stool lay rice, wheat, vermilion, flowers, fruit and cocoa-kernel and sit near it all night.

Food. Except in Kaira and Ahmedábád, where they are said to eschew fish and flesh, Rávals eat fish, mutton and fowl and drink liquor.

They drink water and eat *pakki* at the hands of Bhils and Náikdás. Kolis, Kunbis, etc., eat *pakki* and drink water at the hands of men of this caste.

The surnames of the Marátha Rávals are Chaván, Chhatrabuj, Gadade, Lake, Powár, Abdule, Gáikwád, Jádhav, Kavad, Naikjaole, Saluke, etc. In Sholápur district the Abdules and Jádhavs do not marry with the rest. Persons of the same surname cannot intermarry. They marry their girls between six and twelve and their boys between twelve and twenty-four. Betrothal takes place a fortnight to a couple of years before marriage, when the girl is presented with a packet of sugar and a robe and bodice. Two to four days before the wedding, the boy is rubbed with turmeric at his house, and what remains is sent to the girl with a green robe and bodice and a chaplet of flowers or *mundávlis*. Her body is rubbed with turmeric. She is dressed in the robe and bodice, and the flower chaplet is bound on her brow. Next day a goat is killed and a feast held in honour of the family guardian or *devak*, which consists of mango, *rui* Calotropis gigantea, and *shami* Prosopis spicigera leaves. On the marriage day the boy is dressed in new clothes, seated on horseback, and carried in procession to Máruti's temple, and is there presented with a new turban and sash. From the temple he is taken to the girl's house and a marriage ornament is bound to his brow. At the girl's house, before he dismounts, a married woman waves a piece of bread round his face and throws it on one side. The boy is led into the house by the girl's father or some other near relation of the girl's and is made to stand on a low wooden stool in front of the girl, a cloth is held between them, and while Bráhmans repeat the marriage verses or *mangaláshtaks*, the musicians play. The cloth is then drawn aside, and the boy and the girl are husband and wife. They are seated near each other on the altar, the sacrificial fire is lit, the hems of their garments are knotted together and they bow before the house gods. A feast is held in the evening. Next day, after the exchange of clothes between the two houses and the handing over of the girl to the boy's parents with prayers to treat the girl with kindness, the boy walks in procession with the girl to his house, and a caste feast ends the marriage.

Marátha Rávals.

They are religious and worship Mahádev, Mahádev's trident or *trishul*, the *ling*, the dry gourd or *patár*, and silver *táks* or masks of Bahiroba, Devi, and Khandoba. They have house images of Bahiroba, Bhaváni of Tuljápur and Chatarshingi, Gorakhnáth, Khandoba, and Machhandranáth, and of the Náth of Sonári in Sholápur. They had formerly priests of their own caste, but they now employ ordinary Deshasth Bráhmans at their marriages, births and deaths. They go on pilgrimage to Pandharpur, Tuljápur, and Parli-Vaijánáth in the Nizám's country. They fast on *Mahá-shivrátra* in February, *Rám-navmi* in April, *Ashádi-ekádashis* or July lunar elevenths, on *Shrávan* or August Mondays, on *Gokal-ashtami* in August, and on *Kártiki-ekádashis* or November elevenths. Their holidays are *Holi* in March, *Gudi-pádva* in April, *Nág-panchmi* in August, *Ganesh-chaturthi* in September, *Dasara* in October, and *Diváli* in November. Their spiritual teachers or *gurus* are Emnábáva of Parali in the Nizám's country and Bhivánáthságar of Wái in Sátára.

When a Rával is on the point of death a few drops of Ganges water and cow's urine are poured into his mouth. When he dies he is placed in a bamboo frame or *makhar* and carried on the shoulders of four men, with a Rával blowing a conch-shell in front. In some places the body is seated in a *jholi* or cloth caught up at the corners and carried by four men to the funeral ground. At the burial ground an arched three-cornered hole is dug four feet in diameter and four feet deep and the body is placed in the hole with its face to the east. The chief mourner pours a little water from a conch-shell into its mouth. Salt is heaped over the body and the grave is filled with earth and a mound raised over it. An elder stands over the mound and repeats verses.* While he is repeating these verses the rest of the mourners stand with handfuls of dust, and as soon as the last word is repeated throw the dust on the mound. They return home, rub ashes on their brows, and are pure. They observe no mourning. On the morning of the third day, they go to the burial ground and offer the dead cooked rice and cakes. On the eleventh night a flower garland is hung from a beam of the house and under the garland is placed a water pot or *támbya*, a dough lamp with butter in it is set close by, and a goat is offered. The spirit of the deceased comes into one of his kinsmen, and tells what his wishes are, and how he came by his death. After the spirit has left him the possessed person lies senseless on the ground and the house-people say the deceased has reached the gates of heaven. The ceremony ends with a feast. They give dinners on the anniversaries or mind-days of their deceased ancestors, or *Nág-panchmi* in August, and on *Dasara* in October.

* The Maráthi runs :—*Dhartari mai pindaku rahk, Brahma Vishnu saksh om namas shivayanamo charampuja padukaku adesh.*

The hold themselves higher than any caste except Gujarát Vánis, Lingáyats, and Bráhmans. Still they eat from the hands of Maráthás and dine in their company, and are considered equal to or lower than Maráthás.

The West Khandesh Rávals are said to have migrated into the district about 800 years ago from Abu and Chitor. According to them the term Rával is a title representing the head of the family. They appear to be an offshoot of the Rajputs from the facts that their sons are designated "*kunvar*," a title generally given to youths of royal blood, that they prohibit widow marriage, that some of their clans perform the thread ceremony, that their women do not appear in the public, and that the names of their clans are identical with Rajput clan names. It is not known why they left their original home and came and settled into West Khándesh, and how they became separated from the parent stock. They are said to have ninety-six clans, of which only the following are met with in West Khándesh :—

Chaván	Jádhav	Pawár
Chita	Kumbhe	Solanki
Dhawal	Lamle	Shishudhe
Dorik	Marale	Thákar
Gohar	Parmár	Wágh

Marriage is allowed with a mother's brother's daughter, but not with a father's sister's or mother's sister's daughter. Girls are generally married between seven and twelve, boys between fifteen and twenty. The betrothal takes place some days before the marriage, when a ceremony called *phadki* is performed, in which the girl is presented with a packet of sugar. Except that from the day of the installation of the *devak* till the marriage is over no animal is killed, that both the hands of the bride are put into the hands of the bridegroom when the cloth held between them is drawn aside, and that the bridal pair feed each other with five morsels of *kansár* (a sweet preparation of wheat flour and *ghi*), their marriage ceremonies do not differ from those of the Marátha Ráuls. Members of the Chita and Dorik clans do not wear the *báshing* or marriage garland. Their chief objects of worship are Mahádev, Ganpati, Vithoba, Krishna, Trishul, Devi and Khandoba. They observe the leading Hindu fasts and feasts and visit the principal places of Hindu pilgrimage. Their priests are either Gujaráti or Deccani Bráhmans. Their religious teachers are Gosávis. Of late some have become disciples of Bráhman saints. Members of the Chita and Dorik clans perform the thread ceremony. The dead are either burnt or buried. A little water is dropped into the mouth of the deceased with a *pipal* (Ficus religiosa) or *vad* (banyan) leaf. On the 11th day after death a hole is dug on the ground where the deceased breathed his last. In this hole a live fish is buried and rice grains are spread thereon in a circular shape. Eleven lighted lamps and eleven cakes are placed on the circle and the whole is worshipped. *Shráddha* and *mahálaya* are performed for the propitiation of deceased ancestors. The West Khándesh Rávals are mainly agriculturists. Some of them hold big *inám* lands. Some are labourers. They eat flesh and drink liquor. They eat cooked food at the hands of Phul Mális, Kunbis, Maráthás and Chaudharis.

RAVALIA.—A synonym for Rával.

RAVJIN.—A sub-division of Vanjáris.

RAWAL.—A sub-division of Meváda Bráhmans.

RAWATS, numbering 360 (1901), including 203 males and 157 females, are chiefly found in Ahmedábád and Káthiáwár. They are said to have immigrated from a village (Sabli) in the Idar State. They are also called Thákor and bear Rajput clan names. They marry Tunwár girls, but do not give their girls to Tunwárs. They are horse-breeders and coachmen and also decorate horses with ornaments for marriage and other processions. Marriages are prohibited within seven degrees of relationship. Marriage with a father's sister's, mother's sister's or mother's brother's daughter is not allowed. Marriage with a wife's sister is allowed, and brothers are allowed to marry sisters. The remarriage of widows is permitted. Divorce is allowed. Their chief object of worship is the goddess Takhta. Their priests are Bráhmans. They burn their dead and perform *shráddha*. They are said not to eat fish and flesh and drink liquor.

RAYAKWAL.—A sub-division of Bráhmans.

REDA LONARI.—A synonym for Lonári.

RENUKRAI.—A sub-division of Gondhalis.

REVA.—A sub-division of Gujar Kanbis.

REWAKANTHIA.—A sub-division of Bhávsárs.

RIGVEDI.—A sub-division of Deshasth Bráhmans.

RIKHIA.—A synonym for Meghvál.

RISHIA.—A synonym for Meghvál.

RODHWAL.—A sub-division of Bráhmans.

ROHIDAS.—A synonym for Chámbhár Vanjari.

ROMABAN.—A sub-division of Ahirs.

ROTWAL.—A synonym for Rodhwál.

SACHORA.—A sub-division of Bráhmans.

SADA.—A sub-division of Sonárs and Lingáyats.

SADHU.—A sub-division of Bháts.

SAGARS,* numbering 11,305 (1901), including 5,703 males and 5,602 females, are found principally in Káthiáwár, Mahi Kántha, Ahmedábád and Broach, a few emigrants being recorded in the Deccan. They claim descent from Sagar, a king of the solar race. Sagar was a son of Báhu, and tradition relates that he was called Sagar (*sa* with and *gar* poison), born with poison, on account of his mother being poisoned by another wife of his father. By his wife Sumati Sagar had 60,000 sons. He aspired to dethrone Indra by the performance of 100 sacrifices. He successfully performed 99, but when he commenced the hundredth, his sacrificial horse was stolen by Indra and carried down to *pátála* (the lower region) where the sage Kapil was practising penances. Sagar, thereupon, commanded his 60,000 sons to search for it. Finding no trace of the animal on earth, they began to dig downwards and in so doing naturally increased the boundaries of the ocean, which thus came to be called *ságar*. Meeting with the sage Kapil they rashly accused him of having stolen the horse, as a punishment for which, the sage who could not control himself, reduced them all to ashes. These ashes remained unpurified and consequently the souls of the dead could not find absolution, until Bhagirath, the great grandson of Sagar, practised penances of the greatest austerity for a dozen years, and as a reward the celestial river Ganges was allowed to flow from heaven to earth and from the earth to the lower regions to purify the ashes of his 60,000 ancestors. From the Gangetic valley the Ságar descendants came down to Bhilwáda, where a quarrel arose between them and the Chief of Jeypur. From Bhilwáda they came to Gujarát and then to Mángrol, the seat of the Governor of Gujarát being at Kusukwáda. About 360 families went to Daliadri (under Bhávnagar) near Verával and settled there as cultivators and labourers. **Name and origin.**

* Contributed by Mr. K. G. Pandit, B.A., LL.B.

Divisions.

There are two main divisions of the caste, Gujaráti Ságars and Sorathia Ságars, evidently territorial. The principal exogamous sub-divisions are :—

Bhumbáda	Gundhli	Kanhel	Nánera
Bhesánia	Kálhena	Kodavda	Parmár
Gájnotar	Kalthia	Máru	Pathár

Shilha.

Most of these names refer to the profession followed by the caste. For instance, Patbárs (from *pathro* stone) are stonecutters; Bhesánia (from *bhens* buffalo) are keepers of cattle; Bhumbáda (from *bhumbhaki* a water-pot) probably made earthen pots; Kalthia (*kalthi*), Gájnotar (*gágar*), Gundhli (*gundhli* grain for cattle), Kanhel (*kanher*) point to the holders of these surnames being agriculturists. The other names are curious, *e.g.*, Kodavda means gourmands; Máru means hospitable; Nánera means those who refused to accept anything or denied everything; Kálhena means of a dark complexion; and Shilha means well-bred.

Marriages are prohibited between members of the same sub-division. A member of the caste cannot marry his father's sister's mother's sister's or mother's brother's daughter. He can marry his wife's sister during the life-time or after the death of the wife. Two brothers may marry two sisters. There is no objection to intermarriages on the score of pecuniary circumstances, or territorial limits, or religious beliefs, or difference in occupation. But it seems that Sorathia Ságars would as a matter of convenience not naturally marry among the Gujarát Ságars.

Girls are generally married before they are twelve, boys before they are twenty. Sometimes, owing to the poor circumstances of the affianced, a girl may remain single till she is twenty, but she is never allowed to remain unmarried longer. Sexual intercourse before marriage is strictly prohibited. If it takes place, either the marriage of the couple is enforced, or a fine varying from 300 to 500 *koris* is levied, until payment of which the girl's family is put out of caste. Polygamy is permitted on the ground of idiocy, physical deformity, quarrelsome temper, etc., on the part of the wife. Polyandry is unknown.

Marriage ceremonies.

The negotiations for marriage are opened by the girl's father through five elderly members of the caste. These negotiations are known as *sayái*. The boy's father has to pay a *des* or bride price of 500 *koris* (a *kori* being worth about annas $3\frac{1}{4}$). On an auspicious day clothes and ornaments are presented to the girl by the boy's father after the receipt of a marriage note sent through a *gor* (priest). The writing and despatching of the note are called *lagna lakhavun*. The priest who carries the note is welcomed by the boy's people (*lagna vadhávavun*), is seated on a wooden seat, a spot is made on his forehead with red powder, and a cocoanut is presented to him. On the eve of the marriage day a fruit called *bhindol* is tied to the wrist of the couple and turmeric powder mixed with water is applied to their cheeks and foreheads (*haldhar chadávvi*). On the marriage day the bridegroom and his party (called *ján*) proceed to the house of the bride. This is known as *Sámaiyyun*. The bridegroom is presented with a cocoanut, when the priest makes a red spot on his forehead and applies rice grains. The *ján* or marriage party are then taken to a suitable residence in the village, where dry dates are presented to those present, and necklaces including a *Mangalsutra* are given to the bride. In the marriage booth, the four corners of which are decked with columns of earthen pots, seven in each, the bride, bridegroom and others gather. The pair go four times round the altar dedicated to the field-god (kshetrapál), and this constitutes the binding portion of the ceremony. The bridegroom then returns home with his bride, where the *bhindols* are removed from their wrists and the turmeric washed off. This concludes the marriage.

Widow remarriage is allowed. A widow cannot marry the three prohibited degrees or her late husband's brother. The caste panch must be consulted before a widow remarriage can be contracted. An auspicious occasion is chosen for the marriage, at which some respectable members of the same caste or of another caste must be present. The following ceremony is followed. In the yard attached to the widow's father's house the bride and bridegroom are seated opposite one another. Between them a dry earthen pot containing a cocoanut oil lamp is put. Between the two, again, but overhead, a cocoanut is held by the bride's sister. The bridegroom's father and the bride's father pass and repass to each other two *koris* four times; which done, the bride and bridegroom touch the opposite sides of the cocoanut held between them. This is the binding portion of the ceremony. Molasses are then distributed among those present and the ceremony is over.

Discord, misconduct on the part of the wife, etc. justify a divorce by the husband, who alone can exercise the right after satisfying the caste *panch* or some five respectable residents of the village. The emblem of divorce is the tearing off a piece of his turban cloth,

A divorced woman of the caste may live with another man of the same caste. But in this case no special ceremony is required. Adultery is punished by a fine of from 300 to 500 *koris* or by excommunication in default. The caste follow the Hindu law of inheritance.

Religion.

Ságars are Hindus of the Rámasnehi sect. They believe in all Hindu gods. Each sub-division or a group of sub-divisions have a separate family deity. The chief family deities are as follows :—

Family deity.		Sub-divisions.
1. Avad	..	Nanera, Bhesánia.
2. Chámunda	..	Kalthia.
3. Dagái	..	Kodávda, Parmár, Kanhel.
4. Haradatta	..	Gájnotar.
5. Khodiyar	..	Gundhli, Kalhena.
6. Mahámáya	..	Páthar, Máru, Shilha, Bhumbáda.

Their special saint is Rámdepir. Their religious teachers or *gurus* are Gondhalis. Their religious head lives at Sháhápur in Márwár. They visit the ordinary places of Hindu pilgrimage, and believe in exorcism, sorcery and the ordinary omens. A Ságar from each family must visit the Ganges at least once in twelve years. They observe all the Hindu holidays. The cow is treated with veneration. Weapons are worshipped on *Dasara* and agricultural tools on sowing days. The offerings which consist mainly of grain, cocoanuts and molasses are taken by temple servants called *bhuvos*. The Islámpir is treated with great respect, and cocoanuts given in offering to him are broken and distributed among the members of the family. Whenever an epidemic breaks out, Khodiyár is pacified with offerings of the nature above mentioned. The priests of the caste are Báj Khedawál Bráhmans.

Death ceremonies.

The dead are generally burnt. The caste saints and children up to six years old are buried, as also those who have suffered from small-pox, leprosy or cholera. Those who die from snakebite are burnt on the village common, the belief being that if not so burnt, they would fail to get absolution. Saints are buried in a sitting posture facing the north, the rest in a lying posture with head to the north. On the third day the ashes are put in an earthen pot, on the lid of which is placed a ball of cooked rice, and the pot is then immersed in a river close by. The bones, if any remain, are carried to the Girnár hills and thrown into the Dáma pool. The *shráddha* is performed for the propitiation of ancestors in general, but ancestors dying without issue or of accidents are pacified more commonly by the marriage of a male and female calf.

The Ságars believe that they were once *girássias* land-holders, but most of them are now cultivators. Some are stone-cutters. A few are day-labourers and are paid either in cash or in kind.

The caste do not eat fish or flesh of any kind. They have no objection to eating *pakki* at the hands of men of inferior castes, nor to eating cooked food if the vessel in which the same is cooked is fresh, unused and made of earth. Water is by itself pure and cannot carry any polution with it. The *hookah* also can be passed, but would be used with a fresh bowlpipe. **Food.**

Hátis, Káthis, Bábriás and tribes of similar standing would not object to eating with Ságars.

SAGHODIA.—A synonym for Sajodra.

SAGUNA SALI.—A sub-division of Sális.

SAHADEV JOSHIS, or Hussaini Bráhmans, not recorded at the Census of 1901, are found only in Poona and Ahmednagar. They claim descent from Sahadev, the son of a Bráhman astrologer by a Kunbi woman. It is not known why they are called Hussaini Bráhmans. They are beggars and astrologers. They allow widow marriage and eat the flesh of goats and sheep and drink liquor once a year in October on *Dasara* day after offering it to the goddess Bhavâni. Except that they bury their dead, their ceremonies and customs resemble those observed by local Marátha Kunbis.

SAHAKUL SALI.—A sub-division of Sális.

SAHASRA.—A sub-division of Audich Bráhmans.

SAHASRARJUNA.—A sub-division of Khatris.

SAHASRAVADI.—A synonym for Sahasra.

SAHAVASI.—A sub-division of Bráhmans.

SAI.—A synonym for Darji.

SAIB.—A sub-division of Lingáyats.

SAIGOR.—A sub-division of Audich Bráhmans.

SAIKALGAR.—*See* under Minor Musalmán Castes.

SAI SUTAR.—A synonym for Darji.

SAJJAN.—A sub-division of Gánigs.

SAJODRA.—A sub-division of Anávla Bráhmans.

SAKHAYAT.—A sub-division of Káthis.

SAKHIA.—A sub-division of Rávals.

SAKLAPURI.—A sub-division of Havik Bráhmans.

SAKUL SALI.—A sub-division of Sális.

SAKUNA SALI.—A sub-division of Sális.

SALADE.—A synonym for Saládi.

SALADI.—A sub-division of Mahárs.

SALAT.—A sub-division of Vághris.

Name and origin. **SALATS** or stone-workers, from *salya* a stone, numbering 4,227 (1901), including 2,114 males and 2,113 females, are found only in cities and in some large towns in the Gujarát districts and States.

Endogamous divisions. They have three endogamous divisions :—

(1) Sompara Salát.

(2) Kumbhár Salat.

(3) Talabda Koli Salát.

These divisions neither eat together nor intermarry. The Somparás form the bulk of the caste and are found in North Gujarát, Káthiáwár and Cutch. Kumbhár Saláts are an offshoot of Kumbhárs or potters who have taken to masonry. They are found mainly in Cutch. Similarly Talabda Koli Kumbhárs are those Talabda Kolis who have adopted the occupation of storecutting. Except that they do not eat or marry with the parent castes, Kumbhárs Saláts and Talabda Koli Saláts do not differ from Kumbhárs and Talabda Kolis respectively in any of their social or religious customs.

Sompara Saláts, according to their story, were originally Bráhmans. At the desire of Somnáth Mahádev, whose temple is at Prabhás on the south coast of Káthiáwár, half of the Bráhman disciples of a sage took to stone-cutting. The other half of the disciples remained Bráhmans, and were ordered to act as priests to those who had became Saláts. After this division, though they never intermarried, Sompara Bráhmans and Saláts are said for a time to have continued to dine with each other. According to another account, the Sompara Saláts lost their Bráhmanic purity under the following circumstances. A Jain merchant of Navánagar named Vardhmán, in building some Jain temples, employed a large number of Sompara Saláts. When all the temples were finished the idea struck Vardhmán that if one of his descendants turned out a miscreant, his religious labours for the glory of Jainism would be fruitless. He wished therefore to be without a child. Childlessness could be secured only by provoking Bráhmans to curse him. To secure the wished-for curse Vardhmán invited all his Sompara Saláts to a dinner prepared by Bráhman cooks. Before they had finished dining, Vardhmán went into the dining hall and, as is done to fellow-castemen in all feasts, presented the guests with betel-leaves. When the Bráhman Saláts saw Vardhmán, a Vaishya, in their midst, distributing betel-leaves, they considered themselves defiled, and in their fury called down the curse of childlessness on Vardhmán. Vardhmán thanked the Bráhmans, accepted their curse in good grace, and was satisfied. Thus the Sompara Saláts ceased to be Bráhmans. In support of this story they say that a stone or *paliya* near Vardhmán's Jain temples records this event, and that even to this day Somparás do not drink water at Navánagar, the place of their defilement.

Sompara Saláts wear the Bráhmanic thread, the thread ceremony being performed either immediately before marriage or in connection with some other family rite. Their ceremonies do not differ materially from those performed by Bráhmans. Marriage between near relations is avoided. Girls are married at from one to thirteen. They do not allow divorce ; but their widows marry, the widow of a man sometimes marrying his younger brother.

Religion. They are Swáminaráyans and Shaivas, worshipping Mahádev but respecting other Hindu gods. In Cutch some of them are Vallabhácháryas. They believe in witchcraft, exorcism, the evil eye and the ordinary omens. They keep the regular Hindu fasts and feasts and visit the usual places of pilgrimage. Their priests are Audich and Sompara Bráhmans.

Occupation. They live by stone-cutting, the working in the oolitic limestone or Porbandar and the sandstone of Jhálávád affording employment to a large number of masons. Besides being used for house building, the stones are worked into articles of domestic use and ornaments such as images, filters and water-bottles. Some of them, especially in Navánagar, have a talent for portrait painting.

Food. Sompara Saláts do not eat fish or flesh or drink liquor.

SALI.—*See* Devang.

SALIMALI.—A sub-division of Bharádis.

SALTANGAR.—*See* under Minor Musalmán castes.

SALTANKAR.—A synonym for Saltángar.

SAMANYA.—A sub-division of Jangams.

SAMAYA SALI.—A sub-division of Sális.

SAMGAR.—A synonym for Chámbhár.

SAMVEDI.—A sub-division of Bráhmans.

SANADI.—A sub-division of Koravas.

SANADI MANG.—A synonym for Vájantri Máng.

SANAOLA.—A synonym for Sanodia.

SANATH.—A synonym for Sanodia.

SANGAMESHVARI.—A sub-division of Vánis.

SANGAR.—A sub-division of Dhangars.

Name and origin. **SANGARS** or wool weavers, numbering 7,118 (1901), including 3,579 males and 3,539 females, are found chiefly in Sátára, Sholápur, Ahmednagar, Poona, Kolhápur and the Southern Marátha Country. In their customs they have much in common with Marátha Kunbis. They seem to have been formerly under the influence of the Lingáyat religion and to have been degraded because they took to fish and flesh eating and to drinking liquor. They still call in Jangams for their marriage and death ceremonies; and they preserve certain Lingáyat customs such as burial and the *tirth* (*see* LINGAYAT). The term 'Sangar' signifies a wool weaver. It is applied also to Dhangars and Mahárs who weave wool, but these have no connection with the Sangars proper.

Divisions. There are no endogamous divisions of the caste. The commonest surnames are Dhoble, Gonjáre, Kárande, Palshánde, Rául, Hingshe, Gavre, Tergune, Cholshe, Limbar, etc. The following are some of the exogamous divisions :—

Yavge	Hingshe	Tergune	Limbkar
Panchande	Gavre	Cholshe	

Marriage ceremonies. Girls are married even after they attain the age of puberty. The boy's father finds a bride for his son, and then both the boy's and girl's fathers ascertain from the village astrologer whether the stars are in favour of the match. If the astrologer says the stars are favourable, the boy's father presents the girl with a new green robe and bodice, a rupee, and a cocoanut, and rubs her brow with red powder. A dinner to caste-men is given at the joint expense of both the fathers. Within three years the marriage takes place. Booths are built in front of both houses, and the boy and girl are rubbed with turmeric at their homes. Their marriage guardian or *devak* consists of the five-tree leaves or *pánch pálvis, i.e.*, the mango, *umbar*, *shami*, *jámbhul* and *rui*. On the marriage day, while on his way to the girl's, the boy goes to the village temple, lays his dagger before the god, and swears that he may forsake his dagger but never his wife. He lays a packet of betel before the god, and taking back the dagger goes in procession to the girl's home, and takes his stand before the door of the booth. One of the girl's kinsmen waves a lemon and a cocoanut round the boy's head, and the boy dismounts and walks into the booth. The boy and girl are then bathed, and, dressing in new clothes, stand facing each other. Behind them stand their maternal uncles with knives, daggers or other weapons in their hands. The Bráhman priest repeats marriage verses, and, at the end, with the guests, throws rice over the boy's and girl's heads. The hems of their garments are knotted together, and the boy and girl are taken before the house gods. While bowing before the gods, the boy removes an image of a god and hides it about his person, and does not give it back until his mother-in-law gives him a new waist-coat. The boy and girl dine in front of the house gods, and take their seats on an earthen altar raised in a corner of the booth. The brows of both are rubbed with red powder and turmeric on which rice grains are stuck; and in the evening, the proceedings end with a feast. A day or two after, the boy goes back in procession to his house with his bride, musicians, and relatives and friends, and after a feast, the guests retire.

Widow remarriage is allowed.

Religion.

The Sangars worship the usual local and Bráhmanic gods and goddesses, and their family deities are Bhaváni of Tuljápur, Khandoba of Jejuri, and Pali and Janái and Jotiba of Ratnágiri. They make pilgrimages to Alandi, Jejuri, Pandharpur and Ratnágiri and their fasts and feasts are the same as those of Maráthás. They believe in sorcery, witchcraft, soothsaying. omens and lucky and unlucky days, and consult oracles. Their religious guides are Jangams and Bráhmans.

Death ceremonies. They either bury or burn their dead; but a pregnant woman who dies within fifteen days of child-birth is burnt. Their funeral priests are Jangams. They hold the family of the deceased impure for three days and on the morning of the fourth they sip cow's urine and are pure. They are sometimes purified on the first day of mourning by drinking water in which a Jangam's feet have been washed, known as *tirth*, a common Lingáyat ceremony.

Occupation. They weave blankets and sell them. They also serve as day labourers. They buy wool from Dhangars. A family earns about four annas a day. The women and children assist in the work.

Food. They eat fish and flesh and drink liquor.

SANGARIA.—A sub-division of Kachhias.

SANGHADIA.—A sub-division of Gandharias; a synonym for Kharádi.

SANKHI BARADI.—A sub-division of Girnára Bráhmans.

SANMUKH.—A synonym for Nhávi.

SANODIA.—A sub-division of Bráhmans.

SANOTHIA.—A sub-division of Bráhmans.

SANTALA.—A sub-division of Chodhrás.

SARANIA.—A sub-division of Vághris.

SARANIAS are found in small numbers throughout Káthiáwár and the adjacent districts. The name covers two distinct groups, one settled and the other of wandering habits. Both follow the same occupation of sharpening swords. Both branches allow widow marriage and divorce, marriage with a younger brother of the deceased husband being compulsory among the former. The latter practise *khandálio*, that is winning their brides by service of the parents.

SARASVAT.—A sub-division of Bráhmans.

SARAVIA.—A synonym for Sarvia.

SARBAN.—*See* under Minor Musalmán Castes.

SAREKARIS, numbering 56 (1901), including 28 males and 28 females, are found in small numbers in the Mángáon and Mahád *tálukás* in the Kolába district. They were originally palm-juice drawers, but have now become labourers.

SARIA.—A sub-division of Khálpás.

SARODIS or Dakojis, numbering 36 (1901), including 22 males and 14 females, are found only in Kolába. They are immigrants from the Berárs and are fortune-tellers by profession.

SARVADES, also called Sarvade Joshis or fortune-tellers, numbering 989 (1901), including 477 males and 512 females, are found entirely in the Ratnágiri district. They are a class of wandering beggars, and move all over the district with their families from November to May. Before starting on their begging tours, they make a low bow to their drum or *hudki*, the bread-winner. When begging they carry the *hudki* (a small drum) slung on their back, and an old almanac in their pocket which they do not know how to read. They are astrologers and fortune-tellers, and tell fortunes with great solemnity. But their prophesies are not believed, and they are frequently driven from the door. They occasionally obtain old clothes or money, and grain is given to them in small quantities. They relate that in the *Satya Yug* they told the gods their fortunes, and what they now get is in reward for this and is not given in charity. They do rot admit that they beg. Name and origin.

The exogamous divisions of the caste are identical with surnames. The common surnames are, Bhosle, Chaván, More, Sinde, and Sálunke. The names indicate a Marátha origin. They marry their children, whether boys or girls, at any age. Divisions.

They are Shaivas in religion and have house-images of Janái Jokhái, Yellama and Khandoba. Their fasts and feasts are the same as those of the Marátha Kunbis. They do not hold a mother unclean after child-birth or a girl after coming of age, which indicates that they are without the pale of regular Hinduism. Their priests are Deshasth Bráhmans, to whom they show great respect. Religion.

They bury their dead and allow the dying to breathe their last on their beds. The chief mourner does not shave his moustache, but on the third day near relations go to the burying ground and lay some pinches of earth on the grave of the deceased and return home. They mourn seven days and end the mourning with a feast to the four corpse-bearers. On the deceased's death-day a dinner is given to a few near relations and crows, and the Bráhman priest is presented with uncooked food or *sidha*. Death ceremonies.

The Sarvades eat anything that is given them in alms, and have no objection to fish and the flesh of goats, sheep, hare and deer. They seldom drink liquor. Food.

SARVADE JOSHI.—A synonym for Sarvade.

SARVARIA.—A sub-division of Bráhmans.

SARVIA.—A sub-division of Dublás.

SARVIRJA.—A synonym for Sarviyai.

SARVIYAI.—A sub-division of Vániás.

SASASHTIKAR.—A sub-division of Gaud Sárasvat Bráhmans.

SASHTIKAR.—A sub-division of Pánchkalshis.

Name and origin. **SATARKARS**, numbering 101 (1901), including 55 males and 46 females, are found only in the Kanara district. The decrease in numbers between 1891 and 1901 seems to show that many returned themselves as Kunbis. They appear to be a division of Konkani Kunbis who have immigrated from Sátári, a village in Goa near the British frontier; and they still marry and eat with the Goa Sátárkars. They have no stock-names, surnames, or badges. Their family goddesses are *Shaktis* or powers called Ramanimáya, Sávitrimáya, Kelvaimáya and Náyakimáya. Persons who have the same family goddess are held to belong to one clan, between the members of which marriages are forbidden.

Girls are generally married before 12, but there is no rule against their remaining unmarried till they come of age. Widow marriage is allowed, polygamy is rare, and polyandry is unknown.

Religion. They daily worship their family gods, whose images they keep in their houses. They offer blood sacrifices to the village gods and never go on pilgrimages. They observe the leading Hindu holidays. They have a strong faith in sooth-saying and ghosts. Their spiritual teacher is the head of the Smárt monastery at Shringeri in Mysore. They pay him tithes and receive from him flowers offered to the god of the shrine or *prasád* through his representative the *párupatyagár*, who makes yearly tours and settles social disputes. Their priests are Karháda Bráhmans.

Death ceremonies. They either burn or bury their dead, mourning three days and then cleansing themselves by drinking water brought from the house of the priest. On every new moon crows are fed to please the family spirits. They are husbandmen and field labourers. Some are house servants.

They eat flesh except beef, tame pork, and bison, and drink liquor. They rank next to Maráthás and along with the Konkan Kunbis.

SATHODRA.—A sub-division of Nágar Bráhmans.

Name and origin. **SATHWARAS**, numbering 39,588 (1901), including 19,981 males and 19,607 females, are found chiefly in Káthiáwár, Gujarát and

Cutch. Their surnames Chávda, Dábhi, Kachetia, Maghadia, Parmár and Ráthod seem to indicate a Rajput origin.

They have no recognized divisions though Ahmedábád Sathwárás do not marry with the Sathwárás of Káthiáwár. They speak Gujaráti.

Marriages are forbidden between the descendants of collateral males within seven degrees. Girls must be married before they are fourteen, and in some cases boys and girls are married when not more than a month old. Marriages are held on a day fixed by an astrologer. Five or six days before the marriage, Ganpati is worshipped, and the bride and bridegroom are rubbed with turmeric. On the evening of the marriage day the planet-pleasing ceremony is performed at the house of the bride, and presents in clothes and ornaments are sent to the bride by her mother's brother, and to the bridegroom by his mother's brother. At midnight the bridegroom richly dressed goes to the bride's house with music and a company of friends. At the door he is received by the bride's mother, who shows him a miniature plough, an arrow and a churning staff. The bridegroom is then led to the marriage booth and seated near the bride. The ends of the bride's and bridegroom's clothes are tied by the priest who joins their hands. The bride and the bridegroom move four times round the fire and feed each other with coarse wheat flour mixed with clarified butter and sugar. The friends and relations make presents to the bride and the bridegroom, who bow to Ganpati, to the pole star, and to their parents. The fathers of the bride and bridegroom make presents in money and grain to the priest. Caste dinners are given, and the bridegroom's friends and relations are feasted for three days by the bride's father. Marriage ceremonies.

Widow remarriage and divorce is allowed. Younger brothers may marry the elder brother's widow. Both husband or wife can seek a divorce.

In religion the Sathwárás are Shaivas and Vaishnavas of the Vallabhácharya, Rámánandi, Swáminaráyan and Bijmárgi sects. They often visit Hindu temples, and in their houses worship the images of Vishnu, Mahádeo and Máta. The only bird they worship is the *nilkanth* or jay on *Dasara* day in October. Sathwárás make pilgrimages to Dákor, Dwárka, Sidhpur, Benares, Gokul, Mathura and Allahábád. They observe all Hindu holidays. Their priests are Audich, Shrimáli or Modh Bráhmans. Religion.

When a member of the caste is on the point of death he is bathed, laid on a freshly cowdunged part of the floor, and his brow marked Death ceremonies.

with yellow pigment. Leaves of the basil plant, curds, sugarcandy and silver coin are placed in his mouth. When life is extinct, the body is tied to the bier and is carried to the burning ground. When the body is half burnt, the mourners bathe and return to their homes. On the third day the chief mourner, accompanied by the priest, goes to the burning ground with two earthen pots, the larger filled with water, the smaller with milk. The water and the milk are poured over the ashes of the deceased. The small pieces of bone are collected in the smaller pot and the larger pot is placed over the heap of ashes. The bones are thrown into a river. The chief mourner bathes and returns to his house. The nearest relations remain impure from five to nine days. They perform the regular *shráddha*. Caste people are feasted on the twelfth day after a death and on the death day at the end of one month, of six months, and of a year.

Occupation. Sathwárás are husbandmen, field-labourers and bricklayers. Those who are cultivators work in the fields throughout the year, and are helped by their wives and children. In Káthiáwár they rear rich garden crops.

Food. The Káthiáwár Sathwárás eat the flesh of goats and sheep after sacrificing the animal to their goddess. They do not eat the flesh of any bird, but eat fish except in the evening. They drink liquor.

SAUDAGAR.—A synonym for Naváyat.

SAV.—A sub-division of Láds.

SAYADS, Pirzádahs, or Mashaiks, not returned separately at the Census of 1901, are found in all parts of the Presidency. They claim descent from Fatimah and Ali, the daughter and son-in-law of the Prophet, and are the representatives of the Sayads who, during the Musalmán supremacy, as religious teachers, soldiers and adventurers, flocked to India from Turkey, Arabia and Central Asia. To mark their high birth the men place the title *Sayad* or *Mir* before or *Sháh* after, and the women the title *Begum* or *Bibi* after their names. The term is very loosely used.

As a rule a Sayad's daughter marries only a Sayad, and among some exclusive classes of Sayads, family trees are examined, and every care taken that the accepted suitor is a Sayad both on the father's and mother's side. But many take wives from any of the four chief Musalmán classes, and sometimes, though rarely, from among the higher of the local or irregular Muslim communities.

Sayads are Sunnis in religion. But in North Gujarát many are Shiáhs at heart, though all profess to be Sunnis. The Shiáh Sayads form a distinct community, their chief bond of union being the secret celebration of Shiáh religious rites. As a class, Sayads are by their profession obliged to show that they are religious and careful to observe all the rites enjoined by the *Kurán.*

Sayads follow many callings. They are landlords, religious teachers, soldiers, constables and servants. In Gujarát, there is a class of Sayad beggars belonging to the Bukhári stock. They wander over Gujarát in bands of two to five, chiefly during the month of *Ramzán,* and are famous for their skill in inventing tales of distress.

SEVAK.—A sub-division of Bráhmans.

SHAIKH.—A sub-division of Bhangis.

SHAIKHS, numbering 967,857 (1901), including 496,521 males and 471,336 females, are found in all parts of the Presidency. The word Shaikh, meaning an elder, is a general term of courtesy which is freely applied in the Presidency to the descendants of local converts. But it belongs strictly only to three branches of the Kuraish family; the Siddikis who claim descent from Umar Al Faruk; and the Abbásis from Abbas, one of the Prophet's nine uncles.

The Farukis include two branches, the Chishtis and the Faridis; the former descendants of Shaikh Nizám-ud-din Chishti, the latter of Shaikh Farid-ud-din Shakarganj. Many of both these families owing to their forefathers' name for holiness, are spiritual guides, *pirzádáhs*, and have large numbers of followers. In Rádhanpur a class of unknown origin call themselves "Telia" Shaikhs. They wet their *kafni* or shroud-like shirt in oil, and drink quantities of oil pretending that their bowels are proof against its aperient action. They go about villages begging.

Of the Shaikhs the *Mirát-i-Ahmedi* mentions (1) the Siddiks, (2) the Farukis, (3) the Chishtis, (4) the Abbásis and (5) the Kuraishis. Of these, the Siddikis, the Farukis, the greater part of the Chishtis and the Abbásis are generally of pure foreign descent, being descendants of Arab settlers. Many of the Chishtis and the Kuraishis, though they may include descendants of foreign Musalmáns, are the children of converted Hindus. Chisht being the name of the Sufi or mystic school founded by Maulána Muin-ud-din Chishti of Ajmere, all the followers of that school, though descendants of converted Hindus, call themselves Chishtis. Kuraish is the name of the Arab tribe to which the Prophet belonged. On the strength of the Prophet's tradition (*hadith*) that "all converts to my faith are of me and my tribe," the descendants of all Hindu and other converts to Islám occasionally call themselves Kuraíshis. Of Abbásis there are few in India. The *Mirát-i-Ahmedi* (II. 85) notices the Kuraishis of Thásra in the Kaira district and the Jindaráns, vulgarly called Jhadráns (a class of foreign Patháns), settled in the neighbourhood of Pálanpur and the Gáikwár districts of Unjha, to be two classes of foreign settlers who were assigned lands by the Sultáns of Gujarát in military tenure in those districts. The Jindaráns, who believe themselves to be descendants of settlers who came from Mazindarán in Persia are still handsome and fair-skinned, robust and well-formed, tall and hairy. They are given to opium. They are generally cultivators and landholders, but some have entered the service of the native states of Pálanpur and Baroda as *sawárs*, troopers and policemen. They intermarry with the Khokhars, Gakhars and other foreign Patháns of Pattan.

As the Shaikhs include many classes of Musalmáns, they present a great variety in appearance, and as a whole they are not easily distinguished from Sayads. The men have the title *Shaikh* or Muhammad placed before their names and the women *Bibi* after theirs. Except by the tie of a common faith, Shaikhs are in no way bound together as a community. Many of them are devout. Musalmáns. They follow many callings and are found in every grade of life.

SHAIKHDA.—*See* under Minor Musalmán Castes.

SHAIVA GURAV.—A sub-division of Guravs.

SHAKUNA SALI.—A sub-division of Sális.

SHANAIPAIKI.—A sub-division of Gaud Sárasvat Bráhmans.

SHANVAR TELI.—A synonym for Bene Isráel.

SHASRA GOLLA.—A sub-division of Gollas.

SHEGAR.—A sub-division of Gavandis.

SHENVA.—A synonym for Sindhava.

SHENVI.—A synonym for Gaud Sárasvat.

SHEROGAR.—A sub-dvision of Láds.

SHEROGARS, or messengers, are found only in the Kanara district. They are also called Konkan Válegárs from the Kanarese *vale*, the palm-leaf, on which messages were formerly written. They are said to have come from Goa and to be a branch of the Konkani Maráṭhás. They were formerly soldiers, but most are now husbandmen. Some serve as messengers in public offices. Girls are married between eight and eleven, and boys between fourteen and eighteen. Widow remarriage is forbidden. Their family gods are Raulnáth, Nirankár, Kálbhairav and Mahámái, whose shrines are in Goa. Their priests are Havik Bráhmans. They burn their dead except infants, who are buried. They perform *shráddha.* They eat fowls and mutton when they sacrifice to the village gods, and game whenever they can get it. They do not drink liquor.

SHETVAL.—A sub-division of Jains and Shimpis.

SHEVTE.—A synonym for Shivate.

SHIKARI.—A synonym for Párdhi.

SHILOTYA.—A sub-division of Dhangars.

SHILVANT.—A sub-division of Sonárs and Bánjigs.

Name and origin.

SHIMPIS, or Tailors, numbering 77,025 (1901), including 38,539 males and 38,486 females, are found all over the Deccan, Konkan and Karnátak. Of this number, 7,725 were returned as Lingáyats, 1,663 as Jains and 109 as Musalmáns at the 1901 census.

Like many other castes, Shimpis claim a Kshatriya origin, and have a legend describing how they became tailors at the time of Parshurám's persecution of the Kshatriyas. They are evidently an occupational caste evolved from numerous castes and tribes, as are other occupational castes of the Deccan. Originally Shimpis were both tailors and dyers, but in time, probably from its unpleasantness, dyeing came to be looked down upon, and is now the calling of a distinct caste, Rangáris. There is still a Rangári division of Shimpis, who are considered lower in status than the other divisions of the caste.

Most Shimpis claim Námdev, a great Shimpi saint who flourished in the fourteenth century, as the founder of their caste. If this were the fact, the caste of Shimpis could not have been in existence before the fourteenth century, which is improbable. There is an endogamous division of the Shimpis called Námdev Shimpis, who may be descendants of Námdev, as the Eknáthi Bráhmans, an endogamous division of the Deshasth Bráhmans, are the descendants of Eknáth. The present tendency among all the Shimpi divisions is either to call themselves Námdev Shimpis or to prefix the name Námdev to their sub-divisional name, *e.g.*, Námdev Konkani Shimpis, Námdev Marátha Shimpis, etc.

Endogamous divisions.

Shimpis have the following endogamous divisions :—

1. Ahir
2. Bhavsár
3. Chatur
4. Konkani
5. Marátha
6. Náglik
7. Námdev
8. Rangári or Gopál Káli
9. Pancham
10. Shetvál
11. Shrávak or Jain
12. Yaktáte
13. Lingáyat or Shivashimpigár
14. Musalmán

In the Ahmednagar district are found Námdevs and Jains only. In Khándesh, there are Ahir, Jain, Námdev and Pardeshi divisions. The Shimpis of the Násik district are Ahirs, Jains, Námdevs and Bhavsárs, who neither eat together nor intermarry. The Poona Shimpis have seven divisions, Chatur, Konkani, Marátha, Námdev, Pancham, Shrávak and Shetvál, who neither eat together nor intermarry. In Sátára are Jains and Námdevs. The divisions found in Sholápur are Bhavsár, Jain, Námdev and Rangári. Rangáris eat from Jains and Námdevs, and Námdevs eat from Jains. Jains neither eat from Rangáris nor from Námdevs. The Belgaum and Dhárwár Shimpis have four divisions, Námdevs, Yaktátes or diners from separate dishes, Shivashimpigárs and Rangáris who are called Gopál Kális as they dine from the same dish. None of these divisions eat together or intermarry. In Bijápur are found Námdevs and Nágliks. The Kanara Shimpis are divided into Konkanis and Rangáris who eat together but do not intermarry. The Shimpis of Ratnágiri and Thána districts are divided into Konkani and Marátha who neither eat together nor intermarry. The latter are more generally called Deshis or Ghátis as they have come from the Desh or the Gháts. Both divisions also style themselves Námdevs. The Konkani and Gháti or Marátha divisions have been formed by the barrier of the Sahyádri Gháts. The same surnames are found amongst both, and their ceremonies and customs are also the same, except that divorce is not allowed among the Konkanis. The Námdev Shimpis of the Násik district have evolved a separate division. These do not eat cooked food at the hands of Kunbis and Maráthás like the bulk of the Námdevs, but have formed a group of about 155 villages, and marry only among themselves. Many of the Shimpi divisions have an Akarmáshe or bastard division for irregular progeny.

Exogamous divisions. Shimpis have numerous surnames which are exogamous. The commonest surnames are as follows:—

Avasare	Kalas	Nirgude
Bagáde	Kalaskar	Pádalkar
Bakhre	Kále	Párpate
Bárber	Kámble	Phutáne
Bártake	Kárangkar	Pise
Basále	Karmuse	Pote
Bhárságle	Kavitkar	Sarode
Bhosale	Khedkar	Sarolkar
Chandan	Khol ale	Shárangdhar
Choke	Kolhe	Shendi

Dambe	**Korde**	**Sindekar**
Dare	**Kumthekar**	**Suband**
Denthe	**Kshiraságar**	**Sulákhe**
Dhekne	**Lachake**	**Tikar**
Ganchare	**Litake**	**Tirmule**
Gite	**Lokhande**	**Upare**
Gote	**Málvade**	**Uredkar**
Gujar	**Mete**	**Vachrane**
Indre	**Mándre**	**Vade**
Jálhav	**Neváskar**	**Váhatre**
Javalkar	**Nikhal**	**Velhál**
Kadáre		**Vinchu**

The Konkani Shimpis profess to belong to the Paulasti, Valmik and Káshyap *gotras*; but marriages are not regulated by these *gotras*, showing that they have been adopted in imitation of the Bráhman practice, with a view to rise in the social scale. The Námdev Shimpis of Bijápur and the Ahir Shimpis of Khándesh, Sholápur and Ahmednagar appear to be more advanced in this respect as they do not allow marriages between members of the same *gotra*. The *gotras*, found amongst the Námdev Shimpis of Bijápur are Atma Rishi, Pimpal Rishi, and Shring Rishi; those found amongst the Ahirs are, Agasti, Atri, Bhringiráj, Paulasti, Vámdev and Vibhándak.

Marriage.

Marriages are prohibited between members having the same surname. A Shimpi can marry his mother's brother's daughter. He cannot marry his mother's sister's daughter. Marriage with a father's sister's daughter is allowed in some places; in others it is prohibited. A man may marry his wife's sister but brothers are not allowed to marry sisters; polygamy is allowed and practised, but polyandry is unknown. Divorce is allowed among all divisions except the Konkanis. A divorced woman can marry again by the widow remarriage form. Adultery is punished by expulsion from the caste. A woman expelled for adultery generally joins the Akarmáshe or Kadu division.

Boys are generally married from the age of five to twenty-five, girls from three to twelve. The offer of marriage comes from the boy's father. The marriage ceremonies of Shimpis do not differ from those of local Kunbis, except that Shimpi girls do not always get a new name from their husbands, but in many places keep the name which was given them at birth. In the Belgaum district, among the Gopálkális, after the marriage ceremony is over, the bridegroom goes to the bride's, steals one of the house gods and goes home. The bride, putting on man's clothes, goes to the bridegroom's house, beats him on the back with a light rattan, and persuades him to go with her to her house. The *devaks* of the Shimpis worshipped at the time of marriage are, in the Deccan and Karnátak

(1) A pair of scissors, some needles, and the measuring rod or *gaj* ;

(2) *Pánchpálvi* or leaves of five trees, *viz.*, mango, *umbar* (Ficus glomerata), *jámbhul* (Eugenia jambolana), *palas* (Butea frondosa), and *ság* (Tectona grandis) ;

and in the Konkan

(1) Mango leaves and *umbar* (Ficus glomerata) sticks ;

(2) *Pipal* (Ficus religiosa) leaves.

The *devak* of the Ahir Shimpis consists of a winnowing fan, an earthen pot and mango leaves. In the Deccan, the *devak* is brought from Máruti's temple and tied to a post of the marriage booth. In the Konkan, it is kept in a winnowing fan near the house gods.

The remarriage of widows is permitted. A widow cannot marry her father's sister's or mother's sister's son, or a member of her deceased husband's section. A widow remarriage is celebrated at night when the moon is not shining, in any month of the year except *Paush*, *Ashádh* and *Bhádrapad*. In some places, it is also not allowed in the months of *Chaitra* and *Shrávan*. The ceremony is attended by the caste headman, a Bráhman priest and relations on both sides. The widow bride is bathed by another widow, and dressed in a new robe, bodice and ornaments. Next, the couple are led to a secluded spot by the priest, where Ganpati and Varuna are worshipped, the widow's brow is marked with red powder, her lap is filled with rice grains, turmeric roots, cocoanuts, betelnuts, etc., and the ends of the pair's garments are tied into a knot. They then go and make a bow to the house gods and elders. Early next morning, the pair visit the temple of Máruti unseen by anybody. A feast to the castemen ends the ceremony. In Thána, the widow is married to a piece of white cloth on which red and yellow patches are drawn. The cloth is then handed over to the bridegroom, the widow's lap is filled, and the ends of the pair's garments are tied into a knot. It is considered unlucky to see the faces of the remarried pair for three days after the marriage. In the southern part of the Ratnágiri district, a cock is waved off the widow before the marriage takes place. In Násik, the essential portion of the ceremony lies in bringing together the heads of the couple and in tying into a knot the hems of their garments. In the Konkan and in many of the Deccan districts, a bachelor is not allowed to marry a widow. In some places, he is allowed to do so after marrying a *shami* bush (Prosopis spicigera) or a ring.

Shimpis follow the Hindu law of inheritance and belong to the Hindu religion. Most of them are followers of the Várkari sect. In Khándesh, a few have joined the Sváminaráyan and Kabirpanthi sects. They worship the ordinary Bráhmanic gods and goddesses and in places Musalmán Pirs. Their chief objects of worship are Bahiroba, Báláji of Giri, Bhaváni, Janái, Jotiba, Khandoba, Satvái and Vithoba. Their family deities are Devi of Tuljápur in the Nizám's country and of Saptashring in Násik, Khandoba of Jejuri in Poona, and Vithoba of Pandharpur in Sholápur. They visit the ordinary places of Hindu pilgrimage, especially Pandharpur and Alandi, and observe all the Hindu holidays. They believe in witchcraft, soothsaying and evil spirits. Their priests are the ordinary local Bráhmans. They have two spiritual teachers, Bodhalábáva and Tuljáharanbáva. The former lives at Dhamangaon in Sholápur, the latter at Tuljápur in the Nizám's country. Religion.

The dead are burnt. The death ceremonies of Shimpis do not differ from those of Kunbis. The *shráddha* and *mahálaya* ceremonies are performed annually for the propitiation of the deceased ancestors. It is to be noted that members of the Marátha and Kunbi caste are allowed to represent the deceased at the *shráddha* and *mahálaya* feasts. This suggests that the three castes were originally one, which in course of time separated into three distinct castes, on account of their taking to different occupations. Death ceremonies.

The hereditary and chief occupation of Shimpis is needlework. They are also cloth dealers, writers, money-changers, cultivators and labourers. The women help the men in their needlework. Occupation.

In food and drink they resemble Kunbis. They eat food cooked by Kunbis, Mális and Maráthás, who eat food cooked by Shimpis. Food.

SHINDE.—A synonym for Lenkávale; a sub-division of Bhandáris.

SHINDIGAR.—A synonym for Iliger.

SHINGADYA.—A synonym for Mahár Vanjári.

SHINGTOKI.—A sub-division of Kolis.

SHINWARI.—A sub-division of Phudgis.

SHISHGAR.—A synonym for Manyár.

SHIVABHAKTA.—A synonym for Lingáyat.

SHIVACHARI.—A sub-division of Devángs.

SHIVALI.—A sub-division of Havik Bráhmans.

SHIVA-SHIMPIG.—A sub-division of Lingáyats.

SHIVATE.—A sub-division of Mángs.

SHRAVAGI.—A synonym for Alkari.

SHRAVAK.—Religious distinction, generally returned as a caste name by Jain Vániás in contradistinction to Meshri Vániás.

SHRI BASTAM KAYASTH.—A synonym for Bhadbhunja.

SHRIGAUD.—A sub-division of Bráhmans.

SHRIMALI.—A sub-division of Bráhmans, Vániás and Sonis.

SHUBHRA SALI.—A sub-division of Sális.

SHUDDHA SALI.—A sub-division of Sális.

SHUKRAVARI.—A sub-division of Telis.

SIDHI.—A sub-division of Kátkaris.

Name and origin. **SIDIS,** or Habshis, literally Masters, numbering 12,848 (1901), including 6,767 males and 6,081 females, are found in small numbers in all parts of Gujarát districts and States and in the Janjira State and the Kanara district. They are both Musalmán and Hindu, the latter being known as Marátha Sidis, the two divisions having nothing in common except the fact that they originally belonged to the same stock. In parts of Kanara a few Christian converts are found.

Divisions. Musalmán Sidis have two divisions—Wiláitis, that is, newcomers, and Muwallads or countrymen. They marry only among themselves, but the country-born Sidis, looking on the newcomers as their betters, and fearing that their daughters will not rest contented in a country-born Sidi's house, never ask them in marriage. They are Sunnis in faith but are not religious, few of them knowing the *Kurán* or being careful to say their prayers. Their chief object of worship is Bába Ghor, an Abyssinian saint and great merchant, whose tomb stands on a hill just above the Ratanpur carnelian mines in Western Rájpipla. Many were originally imported to work in these mines. Musalmán Sidis live mostly by house service and begging. Still, Indian history is not wanting in instances of Sidis raising themselves to position and power. The favourite equery of Sultánah Raziah (A.D. 1239), for whom the Sultánah lost her crown was a Sidi. Malik

Ambar of Ahmednagar. whose successful arms won from the Mughals the epithet 'The Hatetul,' was a Sidi. So was Jhujhár Khán, the Gujarát noble who slew Changiz Khán (A.D. 1568), the powerful leader who had nearly usurped the sultanate of Gujarát, and who was in turn slain by Akbar on his conquest of Gujarát in A.D. 1573-1574. The Sidis have given rulers to Janjira and Sachin, and, as late as A.D. 1820, Sidi Ismáil, a native of Cambay, was long powerful in North Gujarát as minister to the Bábis of Rádhanpur. The Sidi eunuch nobles of Delhi and Lucknow up to as late as the 1857 mutinies are well known.

Sidis are fond of singing and dancing. On marriage and other high days men and women dance together in circles to the sound of the drum (*dhol*) and a rough rattle (*jhunjhuna*). In begging they go about in bands of ten to fifteen, playing the drum and singing in praise of Bába Ghor. They hold their musical instruments in great veneration, never touching them unless they are ceremonially pure. They call the *jhunjhuna* or rattle the instrument of Máma of Mother Misrah, and their big drum that of the leading male saint. If a Sidi is careless in touching the instruments when sexually impure Mother Misrah or Father Ghor is sure to punish the offender.

Marátha Sidis are found chiefly in Kanara, in Supa, Yellápur, and Ankola. They are said to have come to Kanara from Goa, where they were brought from East Africa by the Portuguese as slaves. Some were formerly Christians, and changed their religion after settling in Kanara. They eat with the Goa Sidis but do not marry. Their parent stock is said to be found in Mozambique. The names in common use among men are partly Christian, as Mannia for Manoel and Bastia for Sebastiáo; and partly Kanarese, as Pootia, Sanna, Ganpa and Lookda. The women's names are said to be all Kanarese, as Jetu, Puti, Laxmi, Gampi, Somi, Sukri and Nagu. The Christian names in use among men and the absence of Christian names among the women supports their tradition that, when they fled from Goa, they left their wives behind, and took up with Kanara women, some of whom are said to have been Bráhman outcastes. Their surnames are Musen, Matua, Muzua, Yambani and Marai. Sameness of surname is no bar to intermarriage.

Boys are generally married between sixteen and twenty-five, and girls before they are twenty. Widow marriage is allowed and practised; polyandry is unknown. Proposals for marriage come from the bridegroom's house. When the parents of a boy think of proposing a marriage, the father asks a Havig Bráhman, who is generally his creditor, whether the match will prove happy. If the answer is favourable, he goes with a few friends and relations to the girl's house with flowers, betel leaves, plantains and betelnuts. They tell the girl's parents that they have come to ask the girl in marriage, and drop into their hands a couple of betelnuts folded in betel leaves. The acceptance of these offerings implies consent. Then all sit on mats spread on the ground, the bride is brought out, and, after the men have settled the price of the girl, which varies from Rs. 16 to Rs. 40, the women from the bridegroom's house ornament her head with flowers and distribute plantains and betelnuts and leaves. A meal of rice, curry, liquor and sweet gruel is then served. After this, on a convenient day, the heads of the bridegroom's and bride's houses go together to a Havig astrologer and get a day fixed for the wedding, for which they pay the priest 2 annas.

Marriage ceremonies. The marriage ceremonies last three days. In the evening before the beginning of the rejoicings two or more men from the bride's and bridegroom's houses go to the house of the headman or *budvant*, then to the house of the orderly or *kolkár*, and afterwards to the houses of all other caste people, and ask them to the wedding. On the first morning in each of the houses women sing songs and rub the bridegroom and bride with turmeric paste and bathe them in warm water. The bridegroom has a best-man with him and the bride a bridesmaid. After this, the cocoanut-god is worshipped and guests are feasted with liquor, rice, curry and sweet gruel. The clothes worn by the bride and bridegroom at the time of bathing are given to the bridesmaid and the best-man. The next evening the bridegroom, wearing a waistcloth, a shouldercloth, a headscarf, and a pair of sandals, and carrying in his hands a knife, a cocoanut and a couple of betelnuts and leaves, and wearing the marriage coronet or *báshing*, goes in procession with his guests to the bride's, where they are seated on mats. The women sing songs, but there is no music. The headman or *budvant* and the orderly or *kolkár* and the bridegroom and his best-man sit on separate mats. When all are seated the head of the bridegroom's house hands to the parents of the bride a tray containing a robe, the price of the girl, flowers, and any other ornament he intends to give the girl, with betelnuts and leaves. These things are taken into the house, and the bride is dressed in the new robe and decked with flowers. She is then brought into the booth, where she stands before the bridegroom, separated by a cloth curtain held by two men. The headman calls aloud *sávadhán* or take care, the curtain is withdrawn, and the parents join the hands of the couple and pour water on them from a small pot. A dinner is then given to all the guests. The newly married couple remain in the bride's house till the evening of the next day, when the bridegroom, wearing the marriage coronet, comes in procession to his house. He remains at home one day and one night, and goes back to the bride's, where he stays five days. He then returns to his own house, leaving his wife with her parents. He again goes to the bride's house on the first holiday and returns to his own house after one day's stay, taking his wife with him. They perform no ceremony either in honour of a girl coming of age or of her first pregnancy.

Marátha Sidis are firm believers in soothsaying and in ghosts. **Religion.** They consult professional mediums who are called *devlis*, employ no Bráhmans to perform their ceremonies, and have no spiritual guide. They worship an unhusked cocoanut in which they believe the spirits of their ancestors live. This cocoanut is changed every year on the last of the *Pitrupaksha Mahál* or ancestor's days in September. The flesh of the cocoanut is used for making oil which is burnt before the cocoanut-god during the *Dasara* holiday in October. On *Dasara* day a new cocoanut is installed and the old one taken away. Cooked flesh and liquor are offered and caste people are feasted. The daily worship of the cocoanut consists in offering it flowers, waving a lighted lamp in front of it, and laying before it all the cooked food in the house. They have a great regard for village gods and for local spirits, among whom Sidi or Káphri spirits are most reverenced. To these they offer fowls and sheep and feast on their flesh. In villages where the local spirit is a Sidi the priest is a Sidi. The land owners, who are generally Havik Bráhmans, propitiate these spirits through Sidi priests, whose office is hereditary, by offering them animal sacrifices, cooked food, fruit, flowers and scents. The propitiatory ceremonies are performed once a year, just before the sowing season. They do not perform any worship on Hindu holidays except on the last day of *Mahápaksha* or All Souls' Day, and on the day of the yearly fair at the shrine of the nearest mother or *Durgi* when they offer blood sacrifices.

They bury the dead, and, after mourning three days, purify them- **Death cere-** selves with ashes and soda brought from the house of the village **monies.** washerman. On the third day, after undergoing purification, as is done on the occasion of a birth, they go with cooked rice, fowl, curry, and liquor to the grave, and asking the spirit of the dead to strengthen himself by feeding on the offerings, ask him to come home and live with the ancestors in the cocoanut. They then return home to feed the crows and caste people. A person of the sex and age of the deceased is presented with a suit of clothes. A similar feast is given to the community, and the present of a suit of clothes is made on the first anniversary of the death.

Occupation. Marátha Sidis are hardworking and robust, but cruel and given to robbery, and are regarded by their neighbours with fear and distrust. They work either as field labourers or on public works.

Food. They drink liquor, and have no scruples about eating any flesh except beef, from which they abstain.

They rank next to Arers, Kunbis, and fishermen, above Mahárs and other impure classes.

SIDHPURIA.—A sub-division of Ghánchis.

SIHORA.—A sub-division of Kansárás.

SIHORI.—A sub-division of Audich Bráhmans.

SIKALGAR.—A synonym for Saikalgar.

SIKLIGAR.—A synonym for Saikalgar.

SILVAN.—A sub-division of Mahárs.

SINAI.—A synonym for Rabári.

SINDHAVA.—A sub-division of Gujarát Sárasvat Bráhmans.

Nome and origin. **SINDHAVAS,** or Shenvás, numbering 2,170 (1901), including 1,165 males and 1,005 females, are found in the Kaira district and Pálanpur State, and a few families in Rewa Kántha. The caste has decreased rapidly since 1881 when the number was returned at 5,956, and 1891 when it was 4,628. In Pálanpur they are known as Shenvás, elsewhere as Sindhavás. Their main occupation is plaiting wild date leaves into mats, the name Sindhava being derived from *shendi*, the wild date palm.

Divisions. The caste has no endogamous divisions or exogamous sub-divisions The families are known by the names of the places in which they reside, *e.g.*, Anandaria : from Anand ; Pálanpuri : from Pálanpur, etc.

Marriage. Marriage is prohibited within four degrees of relationship. A man may marry two sisters, and two brothers may marry two sisters. In theory a member from a higher caste may be admitted into this caste, but the only instance known is that of a Dhed who was admitted on his giving a dinner to the caste people. Marriage is generally infant. Polygamy is allowed, but polyandry is unknown. The offer of betrothal is made by the girl's father. The boy's father usually pays to the girl's father a sum of Rs. 30. The day for the marriage is fixed by a Gáruda priest, who conducts the ceremony. The marriage commences with the installation of Ganpati. Then follow *kulenkás*, in which feasts are given to relations and friends by the parties to the match, who in their turn feast the bride and bridegroom. The marriage booth is next erected and turmeric paste is applied to the bride and the bridegroom (*Pithi*). The bridegroom then goes in procession to the girl's house with a *khumpa* (marriage garland) fixed on his head and a knife or a dagger and a cocoanut in his hand. He is made to sit on a low wooden stool in the marriage booth and the girl is seated by his side. Then follows the ceremony of *hastameláp*, *i.e.*, the joining of the right hands of the bride and bridegroom, marriage garlands being fastened round their necks. The *mangalphero*, in which the bride and bridegroom go five times round the sacred fire, is the binding portion of the ceremony.

The remarriage of widows is permitted. A widow generally marries her late husband's younger brother. She cannot marry her father's sister's, mother's sister's, or mother's brother's son; but she may marry a member of her late husband's family. A widow's marriage is celebrated on a Sunday, Tuesday or Thursday Unwidowed women are not allowed to be present on the occasion. The ceremony consists in tying a *nádu* cotton thread round the right wrist of the man and the left wrist of the woman. Should a bachelor desire to marry a widow, he must first be married to a *shami* or *jhingi* bush. Divorce is allowed. The caste follow the Hindu law of inheritance.

Sindhavás are Bijmárgis, Rámánujas and devotees of Rámdi Pir and Bhildi Máta. Except the devotees of Bhildi Máta, they have no household gods. Bhildi Máta is represented by a cocoanut, and is only worshipped when an enemy is to be worried. They observe the ordinary Hindu fasts and feasts, but the followers of Rámdi Pir fast on new-moon days and do not work on Fridays. Most of them believe in sorcery, witchcraft, omens, and the evil eye. When an epidemic breaks out, Shitalámáta (small-pox goddess) is worshipped, lamps fed with ghi are lighted, and cocoanuts are offered. The *shami* and *jhingi* trees are worshipped on the tenth day of the bright half of *Aso* with offerings of molasses. Their religious head, who resides at Dákor, occasionally visits them and receives two to eight annas from each house. Some of them go on fair days to Amba, Bahuchra, Dákor, and Dwárka. They do not enter the temple, but worship standing near the door. Their priests are Gárudás. Religion.

Death. The dead are buried with head to the north. No ceremonies are performed for the propitiation of ancestors.

Occupation. Most of the Sindhavás earn their living by plaiting wild date leaves into matting or making brooms or ropes of *bhindi* Hibiscus esculentus fibre. The rest are letter-carriers, messengers, barbers, and village servants. As village servants they enjoy a yearly cash allowance of Rs. 12 and hold and till small plots of land. In their leaf plaiting and field work they are helped by their wives and children.

Food. They eat fish and the flesh of goats, sheep, cows, fowls, and ducks, and drink liquor. They rank between Dheds and Bhangis.

SINDHWAL.—A sub-division of Bráhmans.

SIPAHI.—*See* under Minor Musalmán Castes.

SIPRIA.—A sub-division of Dublás.

SIROHIA.—A sub-division of Lohárs.

SIRSATKAR.—A sub-division of Mahárs.

SOLANKI.—A sub-division of Machhis; also *see* under Minor Musalmán Castes.

SOLESI.—A sub-division of Kolis.

SOMA.—A sub-division of Mahárs.

SOMA KAMBLE.—A sub-division of Mahárs.

SOMA SALI.—A sub-division of Sális.

SOMAVANSHI.—A synonym for Soma Mahár.

SOMAVANSHI KSHATRIYA PATHARE.—A synonym for Pánchkalshi.

SOMPARA.—A sub-division of Saláts.

SOMPURA.—A synonym for Sonpura.

SOMVAR TELI.—A synonym for Tilvan Teli.

SON.—A sub-division of Kátkaris.

SON-AGLE.—A synonym for Sudh Agri.

SONAIBALKAMBLE.—A sub-division of Mahárs.

SONAR.—A sub-division of Vanjáris; a synonym for Soni.

Name and origin. **SONARS** or goldsmiths, from the Sanskrit *suvarnakár* worker in gold, numbering 116,478 (1901) including 59,704 males and 56,774 females, are found all over the Deccan, Konkan, Karnátak and Kanara. In Kanara they are also called Aksális, Agsális or Pattárs. Like the other artisan castes such as Sutárs, Lohárs, Támbats, etc., they claim descent from Vishvakarma, the divine architect, and occasionally call themselves Páncháls. Some divisions of them claim to be Bráhmans. The highest in social status are probably the Devángas, who call themselves Daivadnya Bráhmans. Vaishya Sonars are sometimes grouped with the above and in some localities even the Ahir Sonárs have set up similar claims. Lád Sonárs occupy a lower position. Ahir, Lád and Marátha Sonárs worship the *pánchpálvi* as a *devak*, which may be taken as an indication of a non-Bráhmanical origin. Shilvant and other Sonárs stand lower still. It may be safely asserted that the occupational group of Sonárs has received so many recruits of varying social status that the title Sonár ceased to be respected, and those of good birth refused to be classed by the name with more recent recruits. It is clear at least that the former in their standards of cleanliness and ceremonial ritual closely approximate to the Bráhmans whom they resemble so closely.

Naturally such dangerous rivals as wealthy Sonárs were not regarded with favour by orthodox Bráhmans. According to certain historical evidence, during the time of the Peshwás they were not allowed to wear the sacred thread, and they were forbidden to hold their marriages publicly, as it was unlucky to see a Sonár bridegroom. Sonár bridegrooms were not allowed to use the state umbrella or to ride in a palanquin, and had to be married at night and in remote places. In Kanara this dislike for Sonárs was carried so far that orthodox and superstitious persons would not even utter the word 'Sonár' at night, and did their best to avoid the sound of their implements at the time of offering prayers and worshipping the gods. Even to this day, in Kanara, members of the lowest castes will not take their meals in the house of a Sonár or sleep under his roof. This attitude towards the Sonár is said to be due to his *penchant* for stealing gold.

Endogamous divisions.

Sonárs have twelve endogamous divisions, as follows :—

1. Ahir or Khándeshi.
2. Ajhra.
3. Devángan or Devágni—
   (1) Deshi,
   (2) Konkani.
4. Kadu, Dásiputra or Vidur.
5. Kanade or Aksáli.
6. Lád.
7. Málwi.
8. Marátha or Deshi.
9. Pardeshi.
10. Sáda.
11. Shilvant.
12. Vaishya or Jain.

Of the above divisions, the Devángans appear to form a distinct group, having little in common with the other divisions except their occupation of working in gold. They are described separately at the end of this article.

The others are mostly of the territorial type. Kadus are bastards. Ahirs are an off-shoot of the great tribe of Ahirs. Vaishyas or Jains are followers of the Jain faith. None of the above divisions eat together or intermarry.

Exogamous divisions.

Those sub-divisions of Sonárs which claim to be Bráhmans follow the Bráhmanical system of *gotras*. The common *gotras* are :—

Ahabhuvan.*	Káshyap.	Sánkhyáyan.
Angiras.	Kaundinya.	Savita.
Atri.	Kaustubh.	Shándilya.
Bháradwáj.	Párásar.	Suparna.*
Bhárgav.	Pratna.*	Vashishtha.
Dadhich.	Sánag.*	Vasta.
Gautam.	Sanakasya.	Vishvámitra.
Jamadagni.	Sanátan.*	

The exogamous divisions of the others are represented by surnames.

Marriage rules.

A man is allowed to marry his mother's brother's daughter but not his father's sister's or mother's sister's daughter. Marriage with a wife's sister is allowed and brothers are allowed to marry sisters. The *devak* of the Maráthás, Ahirs, Málwis, Láds, and Kadus consists of the *pánchpálvi* and includes their pincers or *sándas* and their blow-pipe or *phunkani*. Boys are girt with the sacred thread before marriage. Girls are married before they come of age. Widow re-marriage is allowed among Maráthás, Málwis, Ahirs, Láds and Kadus. The other divisions shave their widows' heads and do not allow their remarriage. Divorce is allowed except among those who claim to be Bráhmans.

Religion.

Sonárs are followers both of the Smárt and Vaishnava sects. Those in Kanara are exclusively Vaishnavas of the Mádhva school. They worship all the ordinary Hindu gods and goddesses. Their family deities are Narsoba, Rámeshwar, Jogeshvari, Khandoba, Mulvir, Ekvira, Shántádurga, Mahámáya, etc. Those who claim Bráhman rank observe the Bráhmanic *sanskárs*. In some places, notably in Bombay, they have priests of their own caste, but many

* These are the wellknown *gotras* of the Pánchàls (*see* PANCHALS).

employ local Bráhmans also. The Kanara Sonárs have three temples of their own at Bád, Sunkeri and Kadwad, the ministrants at which are Sonárs. The spiritual head of the Kanara Sonárs is the Swámi of Sonda, one of the eight *maths* or monasteries of Udapi.

Ceremonies.

The birth, marriage and death ceremonies of the higher sections of the caste resemble those of Bráhmans. In other cases they are similar to those of local Kunbis. The marriage ceremonies of the Kanara Sonárs differ in some details from the standard type obtaining in the district. They are as follows :—

Marriage ceremonies of the Kanara Sonars.

The proposal of marriage comes from the father of the bride. He seeks a match for his daughter, and when her horoscope is found to agree with that of a boy, he addresses the father of the boy. On a certain day he sends for the boy's father and gathers some friends; music is brought, and the formal betrothal takes place. The boy's father brings with him a cocoanut, plantains, betel leaves and nuts, and 500 offerings of boiled treacle poured into a mould and thus made into small sticks; and flowers and an ornament, the last two for the bride-elect. The boy's mother is not present on this occasion. The bride's mother adorns the bride with the flowers and ornament referred to. The boy's father and others present are then treated to rice mixed with *jágari*, and *pán supári* is distributed. At night the boy's father and his friends stay with the girl's father for supper, and return home next morning.

Next, on an auspicious day the lucky pole is planted at the bride's house with the assistance of the family priest. The pole to be planted must be cut from the mango tree and be five-forked. When planting, a hole is first dug and the pole is worshipped with incense, lamp-waving and the offering of a cocoanut and plantains. *Five* balls of earth are placed at the foot of the pole. *Five* more balls for the hearth are placed by the bride in the kitchen.

On the morning of the day fixed for the marriage, the ceremony of grinding black gram is performed at the bride's *pandal*. Turmeric powder mixed with oil is brought by married women and is applied to the body of the bride by one whose lucky star is the same as hers. The auspicious string with black glass beads is tied round her neck. In the marriage procession the mother of the boy, or some married woman, carries a wicker basket in which an earthen vessel is placed full of oil and containing a wick burning. This is called *shakundivo*, and every care is taken that it does not go out, for this would be a bad omen. The sister of the boy holds a *kalash kannadi* or brass plate containing rice, leaf dishes, cocoanuts and a mirror. For this service she afterwards receives a *sári* as a present. Another man carries a bundle of the new clothes which consist of four *sáris* and one bodice cloth for the bride, the rule being that the *sáris* may be of any bright colour but not dark in hue. The bundle contains another *sári* for the bride's mother. When the bridegroom reaches the *pandal* of the bride, he is received by her father, who offers him a hanging lamp and a cocoanut, and is led to the *mandap* where he is seated. After worshipping the family *nandi*, the girl is brought and seated on the right lap of her would-be father-in-law, and the ceremony called *hat-vido* is performed. This is the same as *salo* or *sado, i.e.,* the actual contract of the marriage. It is this :—The fathers of the bride and bridegroom exchange a piece of turmeric, *five* sticks of *jágari*, one packet consisting of *five* betel leaves, *five* betelnuts, and *five* plantains, the bride's father promising to give his daughter and the boy's father accepting the offer. The girl is then decked with flowers and ornaments by the boy's mother. She is then brought by her maternal uncle to the *mandap*, and the bride and bridegroom exchange garlands. The ceremony known as *dháre* is next performed. Then comes the time for *sádyagoda*, i.e., *jágari* contract. The father of the bridegroom and other castemen assembled demand the pieces of the *jágari* which were brought by the boy's father on the day of the betrothal. They are produced and distributed. The number must be at least nine times twenty ; if by chance they fall short of this number, serious quarrels arise. Another cause of dispute at the time of the marriage is in connection with the *vade, i.e.,* small cakes prepared with rice powder and fried in oil. These must be of the same size and shape when served ; so many disputes arise in consequence that the following has become a proverb : "*Sonárágharche vade,*" *i.e.,* like the squabbles among the Sonárs. The bridegroom is given *jodo*, silk-cloth, a turban, silver zone, a ring, etc., according to the circumstances of the party. The village Joshi receives his dues as such, and presents are given to other Bráhmans.

On the fourth day the *chavtandán* is performed, when the actual ceremony of making over the girl is carried out. This ends the marriage.

Occupation. The hereditary occupation of Sonárs is making gold and silver ornaments and setting precious stones. Some of them are agriculturists, and others are in Government service. Some, especially in Bombay, have become followers of the learned professions. Formerly, in return for testing the village coin, the village Sonár was styled *potdár* was ranked among the village office-bearers, and was given grants of grain by the landlords.

All Sonárs except Kanades and Vaishyas eat fish and flesh. Sonárs eat food at the hands of Bráhmans only, except the Kanade section, who will not eat with Bráhmans even. Maráthás, Mális, Kunbis, Kumbhárs, Nhávis, Dhangars, etc., will eat food cooked by Sonárs. The Sonárs of Kanara do not eat with any other caste, and no caste, however low, will eat food cooked by them. Food.

DEVANGANS, also known as Devágnis, are chiefly found in Thána, Kolába, Ratnágiri, Kanara, Poona and Sátára districts and in the Kolhápur State and Goa. They are split up into two territorial divisions, Deshi and Konkani.

The Konkanis in Ratnágiri are divided into

(1) Tánksále (2) Angsále

of whom the former are socially superior as having been originally employed in minting coins under the Maráthás, whereas the latter only tested them. They claim to be Bráhmans and style themselves Daivadnya Bráhmans, claiming descent from the Vedic Bráhman artisans such as Vishvakarma or Twashti and the Ribhus. They derive the term Daivadnya from *daiva* pertaining to god, and *dnya* knower, the term Daivadnya, according to them, meaning "one who knows (the work) relating to gods, *viz.*, that of making idols, *raths* (cars) and *devárás* (shrines for idols) of gold and silver and ornaments, etc., required for idols. They state that in ancient times many individuals practised more than one craft, and the Rathakárs, *i.e.*, car-makers, who were Bráhmans and with whom they identify themselves, worked in gold, iron, wood and stone. In support of this they give quotations from the Rigveda describing Vishvakarma as the maker of iron *vajra* (weapon) and also gold *vajra* and of *rath* (car); and the Ribhus as workers in wood and metal. Later, members of the other divisions, Kshatriyas, Vaishyas and Shudras, took to these crafts; and as society became more complex, these crafts became differentiated and hereditary. The Páncháls or Vishva Bráhmans, who form one community, still follow these five crafts, and their claims to Vedic rites have been admitted by the religious heads whenever disputes between them and Bráhmans of the orthodox type have been referred to them for decision. The admission of the Páncháls' claim to Bráhmanical rank has naturally led the artisan castes following the Páncháls' crafts, *viz.*, Sonárs, Sutárs, Lohárs, Támbats or Kásárs and Pátharvats, to advance similar claims, and the fact that the Devángan Sonárs have, like the Pánchháls, their own priests and that their right to employ priests of their own caste was upheld by the Peshwás against the opposition of the Poona Joshis,(1) to some extent supports their claim to Bráhmanical status. Their religious ceremonies do not differ in any important detail from those of Bráhmans and are performed according to Vedic rites, which is permissible only in the case of the three twice-born castes. Many of them, especially in Bombay, have taken to higher education and have become followers of the learned professions.

In connection with the Sonár claims to Bráhman rank it is worthy of notice that their functions as makers of idols and of ornaments and other requisites for the gods, involving access to the inner sanctuary of the temples has undoubtedly led to their being assigned a special status in the past. They appear to have been allowed in early Hindu times to reside in the quarter of the city allotted to Bráhmans for residence.(2)

SONARO.—A synonym for Soni.

Name and origin.

SONIS or Goldsmiths, from *sonu* gold, numbering 79,016 (1901), including 40,371 males and 38,645 females, are found in all towns, cities and large villages in Gujarát, Káthiáwár and Cutch. They are also called Sonárs or Sonáros and Soni Mahájans. They are an occupational caste evolved from many sources such as Vániás, Gujars, Kansárás, etc. The term Soni connotes an occupation which is followed by many other castes besides Sonis, such as Luhárs, Sutárs, Kansárás, Mochis, etc., who are called Luhárs Sonis, Sutár Sonis, and so on. Out of these, the Kansára Sonis have already evolved an endogamous group in Márwár, and the others perhaps may, at a not distant date, do the same, as the occupation of a Soni is more respectable than that of a Luhár, Sutár, Mochi, etc. Many of the Mochis have already formed distinct groups by taking to cleaner callings and severing all connection with the parent caste. (*See* MOCHI.)

In appearance Sonis do not differ from Vániás. Their women are generally fair, and some of them remarkably beautiful. Except that some Gujar Sonis wear the Bhátia turban and that some

(1) The late Mr. Justice M. G. Ranade's Introduction to the Sátára Rájás and the Peishwa's Diaries, 1902, p. 29.

(2) History of Aryan Rule in India, by Havell, pp. 19-70.

Parjiás wear tight-fitting kneebreeches, the Soni does not differ from the Vánia in dress.

Language. The home tongue of all Sonis, except Pátnis, is Gujaráti. The Pátnis speak Cutchi. The names in common use among men are Chutarbhuj, Devaji, Hansráj, Kunvarji, Meghji, Mulji, Prágji, Purushottam and Velji ; and among women, Dáhibái, Gangábái, Kesharbái, Manibái, Párvati, Premábái, Rámbái and Sákarbái. There is little superstition as to the naming of children, though such names as Ladho (foundling), Kacharo (refuse), Nathu (one whose nose is bored), etc., are often given to boys whose elder brothers have died in infancy. The first born is called Jetho or Jethi.

Endogamous divisions. Sonis have twelve endogamous divisions as follows :--

1. Gujar.
2. Kansára.
3. Marátha.
4. Máru.
5. Mel.
6. Mevádá.
7. Mostan.
8. Mulehari.
9. Parjiá.
10. Shrimáli or Vánia, also called Gujar in Cutch.
11. Trágad.
12. Vohora.

The Gujars belong to the great Gujar or Gurjar tribe, who gave their name first to Rájputána and then to modern Gujarát. Kansára Sonis are found in Cutch. They are Kansárás by caste, who have taken to the goldsmith's calling, and in several villages in Cutch they alone are the village goldsmiths. At Bhuj they have a separate headman from that of the other Kansárás who work in copper and brass, but they dine and marry with them. They appear to be in process of forming a separate caste, and in Márwár they have already done so by adopting the name Bráhmaniya Soni. Marátha Sonárs are found in very small numbers here and there. They are said to have settled in Gujarát during Marátha [rule], between 1711 and 1727 A.D. They have not mixed with Gujarát Sonis. Their home speech is Maráthi and their dress, habits and customs are the same as Marátha Sonárs. Mel Sonis are found in Káthiáwár. They claim to be the first *Ad* Sonis and to have been created by Párvati from the dirt *mel* of her body. Márus or Márwáris as their name shows, are immigrants from Márwár. Mevádás are supposed to be an offshoot of the Meváda Vániás. Parjiás, called after the village of Parjar about twenty-four miles south of Junágadh, claim to be Rajputs. They are supposed by some to have come from Persia, on account of the reverence they show to fire, but this theory is difficult to accept as there is no other evidence in support of it, fire being worshipped more or less by all Hindus. Their character and physique support their claim to a Rajput descent, and it is conjectured by some that they belonged to the Palhavas mentioned in Sah or Sinha inscriptions. They have two branches (1) Garána and (2) Pátni. The first branch was founded by Gango, the second by Nando, a Songhad Rajput. Nando is said to have gone to Pátan during the reign of Sidhráj Jaysing (A.D. 1094—1143) and so astonished the king by his skill that he promised Nando to give him whatever he asked. Nando asked to be allowed to reign in Pátan for three and a half days. During these days he remitted all taxes and set free all prisoners, and for these charitable actions his descendants claim immunity from giving alms to beggars. The Garánás are found in Halár, Sorath and Bhávnagar in Káthiáwár, the Pátnis in Cutch and Káthiáwár. The Pátnis of Cutch do not like to be called Parjiás. They consider Garána Sonis to be inferior to them, alleging that though, originally of one stock, the Garánás adopted certain customs from castes of lower status, such as marrying a maternal uncle's daughter. The two do not intermarry. Shrimáli Sonis or Soni Vániás originally belonged to the Vánia community of the same name. They have a tradition that they are descended from a Bráhman. They are the most respectable of all Sonis, and enjoy more confidence of the people than any other Soni division. They have two divisions (1) Ahmedábádis and (2) Charotariás. These two eat together. The Ahmedábádis used to take Charotaria wives but not give their daughters to Charotaria men. The Shrimáli Sonis of the Charotar have now formed *gols* or marriage groups and keep their girls within the villages forming the *gol*. Cambay is one such *gol*, and Mehmadábád, Kaira, Vaso, Sojitra, Petlád and Borsad form another. Trágads claim descent from a Vánia father and Bráhman mother. In token of their past Bráhman origin they wear the Bráhman thread and do not eat food cooked by anyone other than a Bráhman. They have two divisions—Motu or large and Nánu or small. Vohora Sonis are found in Cambay. They are Daudi Bohorás and are so called because they do goldsmith's work.

Exogamous divisions. Each of the Soni divisions proper have several exogamous sections, some of local origin such as Kadikalolia, Khadsaria, Kondhia, Mandlia and Raidhanpuria, some named after Rajput clans, *e.g.*, Budha Bhatti, Chhatrálu Bhatti, Ghelot, Komal or Pomal, Parmár, Solanki, Trambela, and some after their occupation, as

Panchigor, Luhár, Jataria, etc. In Cutch the Shrimális have the following divisions:—Kondhia, Asambiac, Patania, Godhaya, and the Patnis have Dhakan, Sunsánia, Jakhia, Hanjha, Satpokhya, Dhoeda and Khimani divisions.

Marriages are prohibited within five or six degrees of relationship. Marriage with a father's sister's, mother's sister's or mother's brother's daughter is not allowed. A man may marry his deceased wife's sister. Boys are generally married before twenty, girls from ten to twelve. The exchange of daughters is not allowed. The Márus, Parjiás and Charotaria Shrimáli Sonis practise polygamy and allow widow-marriage. A widow cannot marry a younger or elder brother of her deceased husband or even a member of his section. Among Charotaria Shrimális alone the wife is free to divorce her husband. The Trágad Sonis do not permit divorce.

Sonis are Hindus of the Shaiva, Vallabhácharya and Swáminárayan sects. All have their family goddesses. The commonest family goddesses are Vágheshvari, Mahálakshmi, Hingláj, Momái and Asir. Vágheshvari is believed to have created two men, both of them Vániás. The elder took to making ornaments and was called *Soni*, and the younger, taking to trade, was called *Vepári*. The Parjiás worship fire morning and evening, and offer incense (*dhup*) to the fire. In Cutch some of the Parjiás have as their guardian spirit Khetrapál, the god of boundaries, or a Musalmán saint. The family goddess, especially Vágheshvari, is represented by a trident painted with *kanku* or red powder in one of the niches in the shop. A lamp fed with clarified butter is placed near the goddess, who is worshipped, especially on Sundays, before setting to work. Sonis keep the ordinary Hindu fasts and feasts and visit places of Hindu pilgrimage. Their family priests are Audich, Sárasvat or Shrimáli Bráhmans. **Religion.**

On the sixth day after a birth the goddess Chhathi is worshipped. Among the Parjiás the worship of the sixth day has the peculiarity that a tool is wrapped in red cloth, set upright in the lying-in room, and worshipped by the women of the family with *kanku* (red powder) and flowers. On the twelfth day after birth the child is named by the father's sister. Of all the divisions of Sonis the Tragads and Parjiás alone wear the Bráhman thread. Among the Trágads the thread ceremony is performed when the boy is from seven to nine years old with full Bráhman rites. Among the Parjiás the boy is girt with the sacred thread at marriage if he is **Ceremonies.**

married before he is fifteen, or at fifteen if he is not married before that time. The boy is girt with the thread without any ceremonies either by a family priest or by a Vaishnav Maháráj. Like Vániás, the other divisions wear the Bráhmanic thread only when performing *shráddha* or death ceremonies. Except that the women sing coarse or lucky songs, the Soni marriage does not differ from the Vánia marriage. Among Trágads the bridegroom's relations start the betrothal negotiations, and among Shrimális, the bride's. In the case of other divisions either side may make advances. Except among some Parjiás the lap-filling ceremony takes place in the course of the seventh month after a woman's first conception. Sonis burn their dead; Parjiás who reverence Musalmán saints alone bury. The death ceremonies of those who burn do not differ from Vánia ceremonies.

Occupation. The hereditary occupation of Sonis is to work in gold and silver, though some solid plain silver bracelets, silver anklets and silver pots and vessels are prepared by Luhárs. According to their work, Sonis are gold smelters and workers of gold ornaments, *jadiás* or tracers of designs on ornaments, and *páchchigárs* or diamond or precious stone setters. The famous ornamental Cutch work in gold and silver is mostly turned out by Pátni Sonis. Formerly the art of coating sword handles was also in the hands of the Pátnis and gave them the name of Muthithárás: but this work is now-a-days done only by a few. The women do not as a rule assist the men in their work, but some are trained to make necklaces, armlets and bracelets. Sonis have a bad name for filching gold and for mixing metal. The saying is: "A Soni takes gold even out of his own daughter's ornaments." Except a few Parjiás in Cutch, who are stone masons, carpenters and husbandmen, Sonis stick to their hereditary calling and are averse to new pursuits.

Food. Sonis are strict vegetarians and abstain from liquor. The Shrimális are particularly fond of parched rice. Socially they hold a high position, ranking next to Vániás, who, with few exceptions, will smoke from a Soni's pipe. Like Vániás they enjoy the title of Mahájan or great man. Though they rank next to Vániás, in south Gujarát village Dhedás will not eat food cooked by a Soni, because like Khálpás or tanners, Sonis in their work use a shallow earthen jar (*kundi*) and because the Dhedás will not eat food cooked by a Khálpa.

SONI LOHAR.—A sub-division of Khojáhs.

SONI MAHAJAN.—A synonym for Soni.

SONI VANIA.—A synonym for Shrimáli Soni.

SONKAMBLE.—A sub-division of Mahárs.

SON KOLI.—A sub-division of Kolis.

SONPURA.—A sub-division of Bráhmans.

SORATHIA.—A sub-division of Ahirs, Sagars, Rabáris, Chárans, Vániás, Kumbhárs, Lohárs, Bráhmans.

STHAVARA.—A sub-division of Jangams.

SUCHIA.—A sub-division of Chárans.

SUDH AGRI.—A sub-division of Agri.

SUDIRS (1) or Shudras numbering 1,626 (1901), including 1,179 males and 447 females, are found mostly in Kanara in Yellápur and Haliyál *tálukás*, in Supa and Mundgod *pethas* and in some villages of the Kárwár *táluka*. The term Shudra is the name of one of Manu's fourfold divisions, and is used extensively for castes below the *dvija* or twice-born. It is not clear how it came to be applied to this caste, whose original home according to their popular tradition is Kolhápur. From Kolhápur they went and settled in Goa, why and when is not known, whence they fled to Kanara during the Portuguese inquisition. The fact that the shrine of the family god of one of their sub-divisions is in Kolhápur and of most of the rest in Goa, supports the belief that they originally belonged to those parts. **Name and origin.**

There are twenty-two exogamous divisions of the caste which are as follows :— **Exogamous divisions.**

	Name of Division.	Family god.	Locality.
1.	Asnotkár	Virambasti	Kárwár *táluka.*
2.	Bmaniyekár	Chandeshvar	Goa.
3.	Bandodkár	Durga	Do.
4.	Belálkár	Betál	Do.
5.	Betkár	Yellamma	Belgaum *táluka.*
6.	Bhármaikár	Sateri	Supa.
7.	Borkár	Mhálsa	Goa.
8.	Gunjikár	Yellamma	Belgaum *táluka.*

(1) A community of what is called Sudirs as a distinct caste is found in Goa. They are peasants and tenants of lands as a rule, but poor. It is said that the oldest known land owners in Goa were Kurumbis (Kunbis), who regarded themselves as a high caste, the Vaishya class. They were the original Gávkars (villagers) enjoying all the rights of landlordship and village administration. To help them in their cultivation, they admitted a lower caste into the village, who were Shudras. The Kurumbis in their turn were overrun by Maráthás and Bráhmans (Gaud Sárasvats), and reduced to the status of tenants. Their original auxiliaries the Shudras continued to be called Shudras or Sudirs. A large portion of these Shudras emigrated to North Kanara where they are still called Sudirs.

	Name of Division.	Family god.	Locality.
9.	Kalsurkár	Yellamma	Belgaum *táluka.*
10.	Kolelár	Mahálakshmi	Kolhápur.
11.	Kudtarkár	Chavándridevi	Goa.
12.	Kulgadkár	Márimhámai	Do.
13.	Mainolkár	Yellamma	Belgaum *táluka.*
14.	Mhálsaikár	Mhálsa	Goa.
15.	Mhápsekár	Do.	Do.
16.	Moráskár	Mori	Do.
17.	Mulekár	Chandreshvar	Do.
18.	Ráikár	Kámákshi	Do.
19.	Shelvankár	Chavándáidevi	Do.
20.	Shibkár	Nágesh	Do.
21.	Shirodkár	Kámákshi	Dc.
22.	Ulgekár	Mháridevi	Kárwár *táluka.*
23.	Vujkár	Ramling	Supa.

Marriages are prohibited between members bearing the same surname. A maternal uncle's daughter is preferred to any other alliance. Marriage between children of brothers and sisters is not allowed; but a man is allowed to marry his mother's brother's or father's sister's daughter. Marriage with a wife's sister can be effected during the life-time of the wife, as well as after her death. Polygamy is allowed, but rarely practised, unless the first wife is sickly or barren. Polyandry is unknown. There is no limit as regards marriagable age. Girls are married even after they attain puberty. Sexual license before marriage is neither recognised nor tolerated.

Marriage ceremonies. The offer of marriage comes from the boy's father. If the girl's father is poor the boy's father pays him a sum of Rs. 20 for expenses. This amount is spent by him in presenting a waistcloth, a turban, a ring, etc., to the bridegroom. The day for the marriage is fixed by the family priest. A marriage booth is erected both at the house of the boy and the girl, the chief part of which is made of the Ficus glomerata tree. The boy and the girl are rubbed with turmeric powder and oil. If a party has to go to another village for the marriage they worship their *devak*, which consists either of the twigs of the *kalamb* (Anthocephalus cadamba) and banyan tree or of peacock feathers. If the marriage ceremony is to be performed at home, two cocoanuts are worshipped in place of the *devak*. The *budvant* (headman) and the *miráshi* (temple officiator) each fills a pot with water, places a cocoanut over it and worships it, which completes the ceremony of the *devak* installation. The *devakárya* or god honouring is next performed by both the parties in honour of their family gods. The bridegroom goes to the girl's house for the marriage, wearing a *báshing* or marriage garland, which is sometimes made of pieces of cocoa kernel, when one of the usual kind is not procurable. When the lucky moment arrives, the bride and bridegroom put garlands of the *goinchampe* (Plumeria acutifolia) round each other's neck, this being the binding portion of the marriage. The *dháre* ceremony (pouring water or milk over their clasped hands) and the marriage sacrifice are then performed and a dinner is given to the caste people. On the second day the ceremony of *shes* (throwing rice grains over the heads of the newly married pair) and the *opni* (the ceremony of giving over the bride) are performed. On the third day the *gharbharan* or house-entering ceremony is performed at the bridegroom's house. On the fourth the bridegroom's party return to the bride's, and a dinner is given to the caste people, which brings the marriage festivities to an end.

Widows are allowed to remarry. A widow cannot marry any member of her deceased husband's family. Widow remarriages are held at night time only. Widows, remarried widows and male members of the caste are present on the occasion. The widow and her intended husband bathe and the widow dresses herself in the dress brought for her by her intended husband. Next, the head of the family of the widow's deceased husband takes from her all the clothes, ornaments, etc., given to her by her late husband, and applies grains of rice to her forehead and makes her over to her intended husband, for which he receives a sum of rupees six. Then the *miráshi* ties a lucky necklace round the widow's neck, and the remarried widows and castemen present throw rice grains over the pair, which completes the ceremony. Should a bachelor desire to marry a widow, he is first married to a *rui* tree, which is cut to pieces before his marriage with the widow takes place. Divorce is not allowed. The caste follow the Hindu law of inheritance.

Sudirs are Hindus of the Smárt sect. They worship all Bráhman Religion. gods as well as local village gods and goddesses. They observe all the Hindu holidays and make pilgrimages to Benares, Pandharpur, Gokarn and Rámeshwar. On the first day of *Kártik* they worship all their agricultural implements and cattle. On the *Dasara* day they worship all their tools and implements of husbandry with an offering of a cock, which is eaten by the members of the household only. Gold or silver images are made in the name of men who die in advanced old age and they are installed among the household gods. Special worship is offered to these idols on all festive occasions. During epidemics, special prayers are offered to the village deities and vows made to avert the evil. The spiritual head of the Sudirs is the Shankarácharya of Shringeri in Mysore, to whose representative at Gokarn they pay contributions. Bráhmans are employed only to conduct marriages and *mahálayas*. The priests employed are Haviks in Yellápur, Karhádás in Supa, and Karnátaks, Karhádás or Chitpávans in Kárwár.

Death ceremonies. The dead are burnt. Persons dying of small-pox and cholera and children under the age of twelve are buried in a recumbent position with head to the south. The bones and ashes of the burnt are collected and thrown into water. Mourning is observed for ten days. On the third, eleventh and twelfth days obsequies are performed alike in all cases of death, ordinary or violent. No *shráddha* is performed, but only the annual *mahálaya* in propitiation of all deceased ancestors.

Occupation. The hereditary occupation of Sudirs is husbandry. Besides doing field-work the men serve as messengers and domestic servants, and men, women and children work as unskilled labourers. As husbandmen they rent lands from the holders, generally paying the rent in kind.

Food. They eat the flesh of goats, sheep, fowls, wildboars, hares, venison and fish, and drink liquor. They eat cooked food from the hands of Bráhmans, Vánis, and Maráthás only.

SUGANDHI.—A sub-division of Láds.

SUI.—A synonym for Darji.

SUKHA SALI.—A sub-division of Sális.

SUKLIAR.—A synonym for Vanjári.

SULAIMANI.—A sub-division of Bohorás.

SULERS are a caste of courtesans found mainly in the Dhárwár district. They marry their girls when ten years old to the god Parashurám, and with this ceremony their life of prostitution begins. The chief objects of their worship are the goddesses Dyámavva, Durgavva and Yellavva. They eat flesh and are excessively fond of intoxicating drinks.

SULI.—A sub-division of Koravas.

SULTANI.—A synonym for Musalmán Kasái.

SULTANKAR.—A synonym for Alitkar.

SUNGAR.—A sub-division of Gavandis and Lingáyats; a synonym for Kabbaligar.

SUNNAKALLU BESTHA.—A synonym for Kabbaligar.

SUNNI BOHORA.—A sub-division of Bohorás.

SUNTA SALI.—A sub-division of Sális.

SUPPALIG or Devadig numbering 796 (1901), including 386 males and 410 females, is a caste found in the Honávar, Siddápur, Kumta, Ankola, and Sirsi *tálukás* and in the Mundgod *petha* of the Kanara district. It is not found in any other district of the Presidency. Suppalig means 'noise-maker' from the Kanarese *suppal* noise, while Devadig is god's musician from *dev* god and *vadig* music. Some of the Suppaligs bear the surname of Padial, a Telugu word for a temple servant, which suggests that the caste were once temple servants like the Devlis, Pátális, and Padiárs. Name and origin.

The Suppaligs are divided into two endogamous divisions known as *Makkalsantán* and *Aliyasantán*, so named after the law of succession followed by each. The former are found entirely in North Kanara, while the latter in small numbers in North Kanara and in greater numbers near Bednur in Mysore. The two divisions neither eat together nor intermarry. Endogamous divisions.

The caste contains twelve exogamous sub-divisions or *balis* which are as follows:— Exogamous divisions.

1. Ajjan bali .. Ajja = the fruit of the *ekke* tree.
2. Ane bali .. Ane = the elephant.
3. Báler bali .. Balai = a fruit tree *Diospyros Melanoxylon*, or Bála, the plantain.
4. Chendi bali .. Chendi = a tree *Cerbera odollam.*
5. Gangar bali .. Ganga = the river Gangávali.
6. Hole bali .. Hole = a field.
7. Honne balli .. Honne = a tree *Calophyllum inophyllum.*
8. Sályan bali .. Saler = a porcupine.
9. Shetti bali .. Shetti = a fish.
10. Shirin bali .. Shire = a tree *Gynandropsis pentaphylla.*
11. Shivin bali. .. Shivani = a tree *Gmelina asiatica.*
12. Tolan bali .. Tola = a wolf.

The eponymous animal or tree of each *bali* is worshipped by the members of the sub-division, who are careful to refrain from injuring it at all times.

Marriages are prohibited between members of the same *bali*. A member of the caste can marry his father's sister's daughter, and may marry his deceased wife's sister. Outsiders are not admitted into the caste. Girls are married between the ages of eight and twelve and boys at any age. A girl who is not married by the age of twelve is considered to have lost caste, and commonly lives by prostitution. Polygamy is allowed if the first wife is barren. Polyandry is unknown. Widow remarriage is permitted if the widow is childless.

Marriage ceremonies. The first ceremony in a marriage is that of rubbing the boy and the girl with turmeric and oil. A Havig Bráhman is asked to fix a lucky day for binding the *báshing* or marriage ccronet round the bridegroom's head. The essential and binding portion of the marriage ceremony is the *dháre* or pouring of milk on the joined hands of the bride and bridegroom. This is done by the bride's father. The remarriage of widows is not permitted. Divorce is allowed with the sanction of the *Shetti* or headman of the caste. A divorced woman is not allowed to marry again. The main body of the caste follow the *Makkalu-santán* or practice of succession through males. The *Aliya-santán* or succession through females is only practised by a minority.

Religion. The Suppaligs belong to the Hindu religion. Their chief object of worship is Venkatráma of Tirupati. They also reverence the leading Bráhman gods and respect the local village deities such as Chavdi, Jatga, Eru and Mhasti. Offerings of fowls, ghi, oil, rice and *khichri* (rice and pulse mixed together) are made to the village gods on Tuesdays, Thursdays, on *Dasara* day, and on the *Bhánds* or hook-swinging festivals, which are always held in May before the sowing season. Offerings to Venkatráma are made on Saturdays only. The caste observes the leading Hindu holidays and believes in sooth-saying witchcraft and sorcery. Havig Bráhmans are employed to conduct marriage and death ceremonies. Those who can afford it burn the dead ; the rest bury. The well-to-do collect the ashes of the burnt, carry them to Gokarn, and throw them into the river Támbragauri. The ceremony of *shráddha* is performed for the propitiation of ancestors.

Occupation. The hereditary occupation of the caste is music. Their instruments are the bass-horn or *shriti*, the clarionet or *movri* the double drum or *sammelu*, the drum or *dholu*, cymbals or *tál* and the small drum or *gidbidki*. Like Bhandári Vájantris, they perform in temples and in private houses on high days and during street processions. Some of them own lands and till them themselves. Some are *chalgani* tenants, that is, tenants-at-will, and some *mulgani* or permanent tenants. They also work in the fields. Before the salt works in Bhatkal were closed they were employed in making salt.

They eat fish, fowls, mutton and the flesh of wild animals, and some drink liquor. They will smoke the *gudgudi* or hubble-bubble pipe after any other caste not inferior to them in the social scale. Food.

SURTI.—A sub-division of Khárvás, Dhedas, Dasa Desával Vániás, Khatris, Ghánchis, Lohárs, Mochis.

SURYAVANSHI.—A sub-division of Láds, Kolis, Khatris.

SUTAD.—A sub-division of Mahárs.

SUTAR.—A synonym for Pánchkalshi.

SUTARS (Suthars) or Carpenters, numbering 211,183 (1901), including 107,918 males and 103,265 females, are found in all parts of the Presidency. They have the following divisions :— Name and origin.

1	Ahir.	6	Márwári.
2	Bádig.	7	Meváda.
3	Deshi.	8	Pánchál.
4	Gujar.	9	Pancholi.
5	Konkani, Thavi or Vadve.	10	Vaishya.

They are described below separately, under Márátha, Gujarát and Kanarese Sutárs. The caste is known as Sutár in the Maráthi-speaking districts, as Sutár or Suthár in Gujarát, and as Bádig in Kanarese districts. The name Sutár or Suthár appears to be a corruption of the Sanskrit *Sutradhár*, meaning a holder of string, referring to the strings used either in joining planks or in planning and measuring. Though the Marátha and Gujarát Sutárs follow the same occupation, they are two distinct castes speaking a different language and neither eating nor marrying with one another. The Kanarese Sutárs appear to be an offshoot of the Marátha Sutárs, the term Bádig, in Kanarese, meaning a carpenter. Carpenters belonging to the Mahár and Máng castes are known as Mahár and Máng Sutárs, while the Jingars who do carpentry are adopting the title of Arya Kshatri (*see* JINGAR); but these groups are entirely distinct from the main Sutár castes.

Sutárs are hereditary carpenters and make and mend carts, ploughs and other agricultural implements. They form part of the village staff, and are paid in grain at harvest time by the villagers, or, as in parts of Gujarát, hold land at a light quit-rent in return for the services they render to the village community. The town carpenters build houses and shops and make various articles of furniture.

MARATHA SUTARS sometimes call themselves Pánchâls and claim to be descendants of Twashta, the divine architect. They are apparently closely allied to Marátha Kunbis, and seem to have a common origin. The prevalence of *devaks*, notably among the Konkani Sutárs, tends to confirm this theory of their origin. In Khándesh they admit descent from Marátha Kunbis. There is a movement in progress amongst them to claim to rank as Bráhmans. With this object they have, in some places, trained members of their caste to be priests, and stopped eating and drinking with members of other castes.

Marátha Sutárs are fairer than the Marátha Kunbis, but less robust. They rank above them. The men dress in the Deshasth Bráhman or Marátha Kunbi fashion. The dress and ornaments of women are similar to those of Marátha Kunbi women.

The Deshi Sutárs in the Deccan speak a corrupt Maráthi, both at home and abroad. The Konkani Sutárs in Ratnágiri and Kanara speak Konkani like local castes of similar standing. The names in common use among men and women are the same as among Marátha Kunbis. The men add *mistri* or *mest* that is, foreman, to their names.

Marátha Sutárs have three endogamous divisions, (1) Deshi, (2) Konkani, (3) Pánchál, and the usual half caste division known as Vidur, Kadu, Dásiputra, Ákarmáse or Shinde. Of the above, the first two are territorial in origin. The Pánchâls are those who claim a higher social status as already explained above (*see* PANCHAL).

Deshi Sutárs have no exogamous divisions above families bearing the same surname. The most common surnames are :—

Bhálerái	Gore	Khare	Pipale
Chandane	Jagtáp	Kothale	Rávat
Chánkar	Jhende	Máne	Sasáne
Chaván	Kále	More	Sinde
Dolas	Kangle	Musale	Sonavane
Dorkle	Kedár	Pagár	Vághmáre.
Gháytal	Khánkar	Palkhe	

Lately, in some places they have adopted Bráhmanical *gotras*, but their marriages are still regulated by surnames.

Marriage with a mother's brother's daughter is allowed, but not with a mother's sister's daughter. A man may marry two sisters. Polygamy is allowed, but polyandry is unknown. Divorce even where locally permissible is seldom practised. Girls are generally married from five to twelve, boys from ten to twenty. Boys are girt with the sacred thread before marriage.

The birth, death and marriage ceremonies of Deshi Sutárs resemble those of Marátha Kunbis. Their *devak* consists of the *pânchpálvi* or leaves of five kinds of trees.

In some places, widows are allowed to remarry, in others not. A widow cannot marry her mother's sister's or mother's brother's son or a member of her deceased husband's section. She may marry her father's sister's son. A widow remarriage is generally celebrated on a dark night in a secluded spot in the months of *Ashádh*, *Bhádrapad* and *Pausha*. The caste priest, the caste head-man, some widows of the caste, and the widow and her intended husband are present on the occasion. The widow is bathed and dressed in a white robe and new bangles by widowed women. The priest then makes the pair worship Ganpati and Varuna, marks the widow's brow with red powder, fills her lap with rice grains, betelnuts, turmeric roots, cocoakernels and five kinds of fruit, and ties together the hems of the couple's garments, the last being the binding portion of the ceremony. Next, the newly married pair proceed to bow to the house gods and elders. On the following morning, before daybreak, the pair bathe and go to Máruti's temple, thus completing the ceremony.

Deshi Sutárs follow the Hindu law of inheritance and belong to the Hindu religion. They are mostly Smárts. They worship all Bráhmanic and local gods and goddesses, observe all Hindu fasts and feasts and visit all the sacred places of Hindu pilgrimage. Their family deities are Bhaváni, Khandoba, Vithoba and Kálamma. Their priests either belong to their own caste or are local Bráhmans.

The practice regarding food is not the same in all places. Some eat fish and flesh and indulge in drink. Others profess to be vegetarians. They eat cooked food at the hands of Bráhmans only. They rank above Maráthás and below the trading castes.

KONKANI SUTARS, also known as Thavis and Vádves in some parts of the Ratnágiri district, have a division called Dhávad Sutárs or Dábholes, who are found in the Dápoli *táluka* of Ratnágiri. During the Portuguese insurrection, some of them settled in the Sholápur district and are known there as Shiva Bráhma Sutárs. They still marry with their castemen in Goa and Ratnágiri. In the Ratnágiri district, families residing in one village form an exogamous group; in Sávantvádi also exogamous groups of families are found. Their *devaks* or *kuls* consist of the *kalamb* (Anthocephalus cadumba) *kocha*, *jámbhul* (Eugenia jambolana) mango, *palas* (Butea frondosa), *umbar* (Ficus glomerata), *vad* (banyan tree), etc., for which they show their reverence by not cutting these trees and by not using their wood or leaves for any purpose. Members having the same *devak* may inter-marry. Except in some parts of the Ratnágiri district, widows are not allowed to remarry. Divorce is not permitted. In food, drink, religion and customs they follow Maráthás.

GUJARAT SUTARS are also called Mistris and Gaidhars in Cutch. Mistri means a foreman and Gaidhar appears to mean the holder of a *gaj*, a foot measure. They have six endogamous divisions, (1) Ahir, (2) Gujar, (3) Márwári, (4) Meváda, (5) Pancholi and (6) Vaisha. Of these the Pancholis and Vaishas are found only in Gujarát proper, the Gujars and Márwáris in Gujarát, Káthiáwár and Cutch, and the Ahirs in Khándesh and Cutch. The Gujars, Mevádás, Pancholis and Vaishas claim descent from Vishvakarma, the divine architect. The Vaishas are supposed by some to be the descendants of a courtesan or *veshya*, but their high position seems to show that they may be a trace of the old Hindu division of Vaishya or traders. Similarly, the low position of the Pancholis supports the view that the word is Panchuli or Panchkuli, the same as Panchas, that is, the half of the Dasás or only one quarter pure blood. The Márwáris, Mevádás and Gujars, as their names suggest, appear to be territorial in origin. Except that the other five divisions eat food cooked by Vaishas, none of the six divisions eat together or intermarry. The cause of the Vaishas being superior to the rest appears to be that they wear the sacred thread and do not allow their widows to remarry. The Panchas rank lowest because they alone prepare oil presses, build ships and do other work in wood involving loss of animal life. Each division has several exogamous sections which either resemble Rajput clan names or are derived from names of villages. Marriage is generally prohibited within four or five degrees from the common ancestor on the mother's side. Marriage with a father's sister's, mother's sister's or mother's brother's daughter is not allowed. Marriage with two sisters is allowed and brothers are allowed to marry sisters. Girls are generally married before eleven and boys before sixteen. Among Vaishas and Mevádás in North Gujarát, widow remarriage and divorce are not allowed; among the rest, widows are allowed to remarry and divorce is permitted. A bachelor is not allowed to marry a widow.

Gujarát Sutárs follow the Hindu law of inheritance and belong to the Parnámi, Rámánandi, Shaiva, Swáminaráyan and Vallabhách-árya sects. In Káthiáwár and Cutch they chiefly worship goddesses, their family goddesses being Bhaniban, Chamunda, Dhrangad, Mahá-máya, Mátag, Solánki, Verai and Vachran. The Vaishas and Mevádás in

North Gujarát invest their boys with the sacred thread with full Bráhmanic rites. All believe in sorcery, witchcraft and the ordinary omens, keep the usual Hindu holidays and visit places of Hindu pilgrimage. Except the Márwári Sutárs, who employ the degraded Parjia Bráhmans, their priests are the Audich and Modh Bráhmans.

Except a few in the wilder parts of Surat who drink liquor and privately eat fish and the flesh of goats, they live on vegetable food and abstain from liquor.

KANARESE SUTARS or Bádigs, as stated above, are an offshoot of the Deshi Sutárs, whom they resemble in many respects; but the following particulars may be noted.

The Bádigs in Belgaum and Kanara allow widow marriage and divorce, though they are not much resorted to. Divorced women are allowed to remarry. The Dhárwár Bádigs do not allow their widows to remarry. The family deities of Bádigs are Kálamma, Dyámavva, Ravalnáth and Malhár. In Belgaum, they employ local Bráhmans as priests. In other places, all their ceremonies are conducted by priests of their own caste. The Bádigs of Dhárwár observe the Bráhmanic *sanskárs* or sacraments. Their spiritual teacher lives at Yatgiri in the Nizam's country. The spiritual teacher of the Kanara Bádigs is a man of their own caste, who lives in celibacy in his monastery at Hubli in Dhárwár and receives tithes. The dead are generally burnt, but in the Belgaum district those who cannot afford the expense bury their dead. Except those in Dhárwár, all eat fish and flesh, and except in Kanara and Dhárwár, all drink liquor. The Kanara Bádigs do not eat with members of other castes. Breach of this rule is punished by excommunication.

SUT SALI.—A sub-division of Salis.

SUVARS numbering 74 (1901), including 39 males and 35 females, are a small caste of water-carriers found chiefly in Ahmedábád and Káthiáwár.

SWAKUL SALI.—A sub-division of Sális.

TADDODI.—A sub-division of Kudavakkals.

TADVI.—A sub-division of Bhils.

TAI.—*See* under Minor Musalmán Castes; a synonym for Pinjári.

TAKARI.—A synonym for Bhámta.

TAKARIS or hand-mill makers, numbering 652 (1901), including 344 males and 308 females, are found chiefly in Khándesh, Násik, Ahmednagar and Sholápur. They are also called Vághris and **Name and origin.**

Párdhis. They seem to have come from Telangan, and they still speak Telugu at home. They are considered by some to be a branch of the Bhámtás. They admit into their caste members of higher castes. These facts taken with the synonyms Párdhi and Vághri would seem to show that they have been recruited from time to time by outcastes from other castes.

Divisions. They have an endogamous division in Khándesh called Ghátole. The Takáris of Khándesh marry girls from the Takáris of the other parts of the Deccan, but do not give their daughters in marriage to the latter. They have six *kuls* or exogamous sections each with a separate family goddess as follows :—

	Kul.		Family goddess.
1.	Chaván	.. ..	Unknown.
2.	Dabháre	.. ..	Chatarshingi.
3.	Mavale	.. ..	Unknown.
4.	Pavár	.. ..	Kálika.
5.	Sh[illegible]e	.. ..	Unknown.
6.	Solanki	.. ..	Devi of Junágad.

Marriages are prohibited between members of the same *kul* and those having the same family goddess. Marriages are also prohibited within four or five degrees of relationship. Marriage with a father's sister's or mother's sister's daughter is not allowed.

A man may marry his maternal uncle's daughter. Marriage with two sisters is allowed, and brothers are allowed to marry sisters. Marriage is both infant as well as adult. If a girl is found to have misbehaved before marriage, her father has to give a dinner to the castemen, and she has to undergo a penance. If the man involved be a casteman, his head is shaved and he is made to give a dinner to the caste, or he is married to the girl. If he belong to a lower caste, the girl is excommunicated.

Marriage ceremonies. The offer of marriage comes from the boy's father who has to pay a sum of Rs. 24 to the girl's father. The whole caste has the same *devak*, *viz.*, the *pánchpálvi*, which is tied to a post of the marriage booth. The remarriage of widows is permitted. The widow must marry the younger or elder brother of her deceased husband. If he has none, she may marry a member of his or of any other *kul*. Should a bachelor desire to marry a widow, he is first married to a *rui* bush. Divorce is allowed on the ground of the wife's unchastity or the husband's impotency. A divorced woman can marry again by the widow remarriage form.

Religion.

Takáris follow the Hindu law of inheritance and chiefly worship such minor gods as Khandoba, Devi, etc., whose images they keep in their houses. They also worship all local gods and keep the usual fasts and feasts. They employ Bráhmans to conduct their marriages. The other ceremonies are conducted by the caste elders. The dead are generally buried.

Occupation.

The chief occupation of the caste is to chisel and rechisel grinding stones. A few of them work as day labourers and some are husbandmen.

Food.

They eat fish and the flesh of goats, sheep, fowls, hares, deer, pigs, peacocks, etc., and drink liquor.

MUSALMAN TAKARIS, also known as Takárás or Dhondphodás, numbering 94 (1901), including 41 males and 53 females, are found all over the Deccan. They are said to have been descended from Hindu Takáris and ascribe their conversion to Aurangzeb. They marry among themselves only, but have no special caste union and no head. They honour and obey the Kázi, who settles social disputes and registers marriages. They are Sunnis of the Hanafi school with strong Hindu leanings, eschewing beef, offering vows to the Hindu deities Satvái and Mariái and keeping Hindu festivals.

Many of them have given up their hereditary occupation of stone carving and have taken to new pursuits, some serving as messengers and servants and others as labourers and carriers.

TAKARIA.—A sub-division of Chodhrás.

TALABDA.—A sub-division of Bhávsárs, Vághris and Kolis.

TALABDA KOLI SALAT.—A sub-division of Saláts.

TALAVIA.—A sub-division of Dublás.

TALHERI KUNBI.—A sub-division of Kunbis.

TALVAR.—A synonym for Berad.

Name and origin.

TAMBATS or Coppersmiths, from the Sanskrit *támrapat*, numbering approximately 22,755 (1901), including 11,601 males and 11,154 females, are found throughout the Deccan and Konkan and in the City of Bombay. They are also known as Kásárs or Kánsárs; but they do not like to be called by either of these names. They style themselves Twashta Kásárs after Twashti, one of the five sons of Vishvakarma, the architect of the gods; and those of them who claim to be Páñchâls, Vishvakarma Vanshasth Pánchál Bráhman, that is, Pánchál Bráhmans of the stock of Vishvakarma. As these names indicate, all profess to trace their origin to Vishvakarma. As a matter of fact, little is known of the origin of the caste beyond the fact that it appears to have come from the Karnátak and Telangan over a thousand years ago. Támbats present the interesting aspect of a Bráhman caste in embryo. They style themselves Bráhmans, wear the sacred thread, possess Bráhmanistic *gotras* and have made several efforts to train their own castemen as priests, which so far have met with little success on account of the occupation of a copper-smith being more lucrative than that of a priest.

Divisions. In contrast to these efforts to rise in the social scale, they have still traces of a totemistic organization in the survival of the *devak* or god of the exogamous section. They have also *kuls* or family stocks like the Maráthás. Marriage between members of the same *kul* is not allowed. The *kuls* have different *devaks*, and no marriage can take place between persons worshipping the same *devak*. In the Deccan, however, this prohibition has become obsolete, and is replaced by a rule forbidding intermarriage between members of the same *gotra*. The chief *gotras* are :—(1) Angrias, (2) Atri, (3) Bháradwáj, (4) Bhrigu, (5) Gautam, (6) Jamadagni and (7) Káshyap. Marriage within four degrees on the side of the boy and three degrees on the side of the girl is forbidden ; marriage with two sisters is allowed ; and two brothers are allowed to marry two sisters. In the case of the Deccan Támbats boys are usually girt with the sacred thread at the age of eight. The Konkan Kásárs have not yet adopted this mark of a second birth.

Marriage ceremonies. Polygamy is permissible. The offer of marriage is made by the parent of the boy or girl, whichever is of inferior social position ; and the offer is followed by payment of dowry, varying from Rs. 100 to Rs. 300 according to the means of the parties concerned. Both the settlement of the marriage day and the ceremony itself are entrusted to a Bráhman priest. The marriage ceremonies are modelled on the lines of those in use among the Deshasth Bráhmans, which are described elsewhere. The most important are :—(1) *Kunku lávane*, applying red powder to the bride's forehead ; (2) *Gadagner*, dining the relatives of the parties ; (3) *Simantapuja*, the worship of Ganpati and presentation to the bridegroom of a turban and shoulder-cloth by the bride's father ; (4) *Ghána*, the waving of lamps and singing of auspicious songs ; (5) *Devakapratishtha*, the worship of the *devaks* ; (6) *Vágnischaya*, the oral settlement of the marriage in the presence of relatives, and accompanied by the presentation of gifts to the bride; (7) *Rukhavat*, the giving of sweetmeats to the bridegroom; (8) *Saptapadi*, the seven steps round the sacred fire. The last of these is the binding portion of the ceremony. The fifth or *Devakapratishtha* is of special interest. Betel nuts, *palas* (Butea frondosa) sticks, and mango leaves are placed in a winnowing fan and worshipped. It is to be noted that special days are fixed for the worship of the banyan, the *pipal*, the *umbar*, the *ávali* and the *tulsi*. These facts suggest that the common Marátha *devaks* may once have been of equal importance in regulating the marriage restrictions in the caste. The Konkani Támbats have *devaks* consisting of the mango, *pipal*, banyan, *payari*, (Ficus rumphii) and *jámbhul* (Eugenia jambolana) leaves. It seems reasonable to assume that the *gotras* are a modern innovation which has displaced an original totemistic formation. On the last day of *Phálgun* the implements of work are worshipped. It is of interest to note that the banyan, *pipal*, *ávali* and *tulsi* are special objects of worship among the women of the caste.

In the Deccan and among the more advanced of the Konkani Támbats, widow remarriage is forbidden. In the backward sections a widow may remarry provided she avoids a member of her late husband's *kul*, the son of an aunt, and the maternal uncle's son. An unmarried man may not marry a widow. The ordinary *pát* ceremony is followed. Divorce is not allowed.

Religion.

Támbats worship the ordinary Hindu gods and goddesses, and are chiefly Smárts. The special object of their devotion is Kálika. Besides Kálika, their other family deities are Bahirichandika, Ekvira, Kumárika, Khandoba and Mahálakshmi. They observe the usual Hindu holidays, make pilgrimages to the sacred places of the Hindus, worship the sacred plants and animals and believe in witchcraft, evil spirits and the ordinary omens. They employ local Bráhmans to officiate at their ceremonies.

Death ceremonies.

They burn their dead. Children without teeth, and those who have died from small-pox, are buried on their backs, facing the south. The death ceremonies are modelled closely on those in vogue among Deshasth Bráhmans. If a member of the caste dies a violent death, the ordinary ceremonies are performed; but if the body is not found, it is usual to prepare a figure of the deceased in wheat flour and to burn it with sticks of the *palasa* tree, the ceremonies being performed at the same time. When a woman dies in childbirth her head is pierced with needles and *pami* seed is thrown after the corpse as it is conveyed to the burial ground.

The spirit of the deceased is greatly feared ; but it is believed that it cannot return over the *pami* seed.

Occupation. The original occupation of the caste was the manufacture of copper and brass vessels and the tinning of metal utensils. A few of the caste have been educated to be doctors, clerks and pleaders. Their characteristic mark is the signature of a lever of a weighing balance.

They eat fish and flesh, and drink liquor. They profess not to eat *pakki* or *kachhi* at the hands of any other caste except the Bráhmans, but they will smoke with any but the castes whose touch defiles, such as Mahárs and Mángs.

TAMBOLI.—A sub-division of Shrigaud Bráhmans.

Name and origin. **TAMBOLIS** or betel-leaf sellers, numbering 3,807 (1901), including 1,927 males and 1,880 females, are found scattered in small numbers all over the Deccan but especially in Khándesh and Sátára. They derive their name from the Sanskrit *támbul*, a betel-leaf packet. They are sometimes called Bári, but incorrectly, as the Báris form a distinct community, their occupation being the growing and not the selling of betel-leaves. The Támbolis in Poona state that they came into the district from Sátára and Ahmednagar during the time of the Peshwás. They eat and marry with Marátha Kunbis. They look and dress like Maráthás and resemble them in religion and customs, and settle social disputes at meetings of the caste-men.

Divisions. There are three endogamous divisions of Támbolis—Hindu, Lingáyat, and Musalmán—who neither eat together nor intermarry. Their exogamous sub-divisions, which are identical with surnames, are Chaván, Lone, Kápase, Sagure, and Asyákul. Persons bearing the same surname cannot intermarry. The caste has only one *gotra*, that of Káshyap, the first to be adopted by social climbers. A member of the caste cannot marry his father's sister's or mother's sister's daughter. He may marry a daughter of a younger brother of his mother. Marriages between descendants of brothers and sisters are prohibited for two or three generations. A man may marry his wife's younger sister during her lifetime or after her death. Two brothers may marry two sisters. The habit of the caste is settled. Outsiders are not admitted into this caste. Polygamy is allowed and practised, but polyandry is unknown.

Girls are married from five to twelve, but they may remain unmarried till after the age of puberty. Boys are married from eight to twenty-five. Sexual license before marriage is not tolerated. If a girl commits sexual indiscretions with a caste-man, both are fined and made to give a dinner to the caste-people, and are re-admitted into the caste only after being purified by a Bráhman. If the man involved belong to a higher or lower caste the girl is excommunicated.

Marriage ceremonies. The offer of marriage comes from the boy's father. The day for the marriage is fixed by a Bráhman who conducts the service. The *mágni*, *sáyakhada* or *kunku-lávane* is first celebrated, in which the boy's father goes to the girl's house with relations and friends, applies red powder to her forehead, and presents her with ornaments and articles of dress. The party are treated to a dinner by the girl's father, after which they retire. Next, the boy and the girl are rubbed with turmeric paste at their houses by unwidowed women. On the same day a marriage card is taken to the girl's house by the boy's father, on which are written the lucky moments for the marriage, the turmeric ceremony, and the marriage sacrifice. Five betel-nuts, five turmeric roots, and five pice are folded into this paper and it is woven into a string which is used as the marriage garland. The boy's father ties a lucky necklace round the girl's neck and returns home. Then follows the *grahashánti*, or propitiation of planets, which is performed at the boy's house on the day previous to the marriage, and at the girl's house on the marriage day. Feasts are then given in the marriage booth both at the boy's and the girl's house, and they are made to look into a cup of *ghi* known as *telvan*. Then some unwidowed women from the girl's house go to a potter's, and worshipping his wheel bring home four earthen pots, which ceremony is known as *kumbhakár-chakra-puja* or the worship of the potter's wheel. The bridegroom then starts in procession for the bride's village. He halts in a temple of Máruti, where he is received by the bride's party. He is seated on a low wooden stool and his feet are washed by a barber from the girl's party, who also folds a turban on his head. The bride's father presents him with articles of dress and other things and he is taken to his house. He is seated under the *muhurtatáli*, auspicious arc of the marriage booth, the girl is seated in front of him, their hands are joined, the marriage garland is placed thereon, and the girl's father pours water over them (the *dháre* ceremony) and worships the bridegroom. Then the garland is put round the neck of the boy and the girl successively by an unwidowed woman, and is allowed to remain on the neck of the latter. On the second day the ends of the garments of the bride and bridegroom are tied into a knot, the marriage sacrifice is performed, and the bride and bridegroom walk five times round the fire. Next, Ganpati and Varuna are worshipped by the pair in the middle of a square of the four earthen pots brought from the potter's, placed on four sides. This is known as *chavari*, which is followed by *saptapadi*, in which heaps are made of unhusked rice mixed with betel-nuts, over each of which is placed one betel-nut. The pair worships the heap, and the bridegroom, seizing the great toe of the bride's foot with his right hand, pushes aside the betel-nuts placed on the heaps. A dinner is then held, and presents are made by persons on both sides to the bride and bridegroom.

On the third day a feast of rice and milk is given to the boy's party by the girl's father, and the boy returns to his house with his bride, which terminates the marriage. The essential portion consists in the tying of the knots of the garments at the time of performing the marriage sacrifice.

The remarriage of widows is permitted. A widow cannot marry her father's sister's or mother's sister's son or a member of her late husband's section. She may marry her mother's elder brother's son. A widow remarriage can be celebrated on any dark night in the dark fortnight of a month, but the eighth day of that fortnight and the new-moon day are considered to be the best days. The widow and her new husband are seated side by side, red powder is applied to their foreheads, the hems of their garments are tied into a knot by a Bráhman priest, and the widow's lap is filled, and this completes the ceremony. The remarried pair are not then seen till the following morning. Should a bachelor desire to marry a widow he is first married to a *shami* bush. Divorce is allowed. The caste follow the Hindu law of inheritance.

Religion. They belong to the Hindu religion. Some of them are followers of the Rámdás and Várkari sects. The special deities of their worship are Shiva and Ganpati. They worship all minor gods, especially Bahiroba, who is supposed to be the deity of the betel-leaf gardens. Goats and fowls are offered to the minor gods, which are received by the temple ministrants, or in their absence by the offerers themselves. Támbolis worship all the plants and animals held sacred by the Hindus and observe all the Hindu holidays. They go on pilgrimages, chiefly to Pandharpur and Benares. They reverence the Musalmán saints. When an epidemic breaks out, goats and fowls are offered to the goddess supposed to preside over the disease. Their priests are Bráhmans. According to some accounts the death ceremonies are conducted by the caste elders.

The dead are generally burnt. Those who cannot afford to burn, bury their dead. Children who have not cut their teeth and unmarried persons up to twenty or twenty-two years old, must be buried. At burial the corpse is laid with head to the south. The bones and ashes of the burnt are consigned to water. The ordinary funeral rites are observed. For the propitiation of deceased ancestors, cooked food is offered to crows on the roof of the house on the anniversary of the deceased and on the corresponding death day in the latter half of *Bhádrapad*. For the propitiation of childless ancestors and of persons who have died a violent death, such ceremonies are performed as their spirits request through mediums employed to ascertain their wishes. Death ceremonies

The main occupation of the caste is selling betel-leaves in retail. They also sell betel-nuts, cement, tobacco, and the spices used in chewing betel leaves, such as cardamoms, cloves, and catechu; and also cigarettes of the *ápta* (Bauhinia racemosa) and *temburni* (Diospyros melanoxylon) leaves. They are not agriculturists. Some work as day labourers on fields and are paid either in cash or in corn. Occupation.

They eat the flesh of goats, sheep, fowls, and fish, and drink liquor. Food.

LINGAYAT TAMBOLIS number 360 (1901), including 204 males and 156 females. They are chiefly found in the Sátára district. They are non-Panchamsáli Lingáyats entitled to the *ashtavarna* rites (*see* LINGAYAT) of which they perform only one. that of tying the *linga* round the child's neck after it is born. They have no endogamous divisions.

They have the usual five *gotras*, *viz.*, Nandi, Bhringi, Vir, Vrishabha, and Skandha; but these *gotras* do not stand in the way of inter-marriage as amongst the Bráhmans. The exogamous sub-divisions of the caste are identical with the surnames. The commonest surnames are, Todkar, Gáde, Ambole, Kharáde, Bhise, Bhoite, Jeble, Hagavane, Dalave, Dhavane, Shinde, Kadam, Ranashing, and Paránde. Persons bearing the same surname cannot intermarry. A member of the caste can marry his father's sister's or mother's brother's daughter. He cannot marry his mother's sister's daughter. A man may marry two sisters, and two brothers may marry two sisters. Girls are married up to the age of twelve before attaining puberty; boys a little later. If a girl remains unmarried till after she attains puberty, she becomes a Basavi, or prostitute. Polygamy is allowed and practised, but polyandry is unknown. The offer of marriage generally comes from the boy's father. If the girl's parents are poor the boy's father has to pay them from Rs. 50 to Rs. 100 for the marriage expenses. The day for the marriage is fixed by a Jangam who conducts the service. Their marriage god is the branch of a *jámbhul* tree which they tie to the marriage hall along with a betel-nut folded in a piece of yellow cloth. The marriage ceremonies of the Lingáyat Támbolis are partly Bráhmanical, partly Lingáyat. Their *devak* or marriage guardian consists of a conch-shell which is brought in procession from a Jangam who sits in a temple. The *devak* is installed amongst the household gods. The operative portion of the marriage service is the *kanyádán*, or handing over of the bride to the bridegroom.

The remarriage of widows is permitted. It is celebrated on any dark night during the marriage season or in the month of *Shrávan*. The widow and her new husband are made to worship Ganpati and Varuna by the Jangam ; red powder is applied to the widow's forehead, her lap is filled, and the hems of the pair's garments are tied into a knot, the last being the binding portion of the ceremony. A bachelor is not allowed to marry a widow. Divorce is allowed. A woman taken in adultery with a member of a lower caste is excommunicated. A divorced woman is allowed to remarry after the fashion of the widow remarriage ceremony. The caste follow the Hindu law of inheritance.

Though Lingáyats by religion, they worship all Hindu gods and goddesses and observe all the Hindu holidays. Some of them are followers of the Várkari sect. They go on pilgrimages, chiefly to the shrine of Shiva at Singnapur, and also to distant holy places of Shiva, if means permit. They believe in witchcraft and spirits, and consult oracles, and although they believe that simple besmearing of the brow with ashes removes ceremonial impurity, they hold a mother impure for four days after a child-birth and the chief mourner for five days after a death. When a girl comes of age she is also considered unclean for five days. Their priests are Jangams. In their absence Bráhmans of the Shaiva sect are also employed.

The dead are buried. Their death ceremonies resemble those of other Lingáyats. For the propitiation of deceased ancestors a Jangam is worshipped and presented with uncooked articles of food on every anniversary of the deceased, and castemen are feasted.

The Jangam blows a conch-shell and applies cow-dung ashes to the forehead of the heir of the deceased, which ends the ceremony. They abstain from both flesh and liquor.

MUSALMAN TAMBOLIS, converts from the Hindu Támboli caste, numbering 1,184 (1901), including 593 males and 591 females, are found all over the Deccan. They ascribe their conversion to Aurangzeb. They form a separate community marrying only among themselves and have well organised class unions under local headmen called *chaudharis* or *pátils*. They are Sunnis of the Hanafi school, but they are not religious or careful to say their prayers. Many, especially women, have strong Hindu leanings, privately worshipping and paying vows to Hindu gods, keeping Hindu festivals and eschewing beef. They, however, respect the Kázi and ask him to conduct their marriage and funeral services.

TAMBURI.—A sub-division of Vanjáris.

TANDALYA.—A sub-division of Modh Bráhmans.

TANDEL.—A title applied to the sea-faring castes of Thána, Kolába and Ratnágiri.

TANGALIA.—A sub-division of Modh Bráhmans.

TANGMODIA.—A sub-division of Bráhmans.

TANKRI.—A sub-division of Kolis.

TAPODHAN.—A sub-division of Bráhmans.

TARAL.—A synonym for Mahár.

TARGALA.—A synonym for Bhávaiya.

TARUS, numbering 1,288 (1901), including 617 males and 671 females, are chiefly found in the Ahmednagar and Násik districts and the Sávantvádi State. They take their name from the Maráthi *tárun* a ship, their occupation being ferrying. They state that they were originally Maráthás and became isolated on their taking to ferrying. This appears probable from their customs and social organization. It is not known when the separation from the general body of Marátha Kunbis occurred. Name and origin.

There are no endogamous divisions of the caste, nor have they exogamous sub-divisions above families bearing the same surname. The commonest surnames are, Jagadale, Nawale, Gavli, Vákchaure, Desái, Pawár, Vágh, Nátkar, Jagtáp, Jágadhane, Vábare, Ghogare, Dhotre, Lokhande, and Shikare. Persons bearing the same surname cannot intermarry. Sameness of *devak* or marriage guardian is a bar to intermarriage. Every section has a separate *devak*, Divisions.

the chief *devaks* being the peacock's feather, the *pánchpálvi* (leaves of five kinds of trees), the sun-flower, and the *maryádvel* (Ipomœa biloba).

Marriage. A member of the caste cannot marry his father's sister's or mother's sister's daughter. He may marry his mother's brother's daughter. A man may marry two sisters and two brothers may marry two sisters. Boys are generally married from twelve to twenty, girls from seven to twelve. Polygamy is allowed and practised, but polyandry is unknown. The offer of marriage comes from the boy's father. The day for the marriage is fixed by a Bráhman, who conducts the service. The principal ceremonies of marriage are: *kanku lávane*, or applying red powder to the girl's forehead, and presenting her with articles of dress and ornaments; *halad*, or applying turmeric paste to the persons of the bride and the bridegroom; the installation of the *devak*, which is done after the fashion of the Kunbis; *simant-pujan*, or reception of the bridegroom in a temple of Máruti at the village boundary; *lagna*, in which a cloth is held between the bride and bridegroom, marriage verses are repeated and rice grains are thrown over the pair; *kanyádán*, in which the girl's father makes the gift of the girl to the boy by joining her hand with his; *lájáhom*, or the marriage sacrifice; and *saptapadi*, or walking seven times round the sacrificial fire, in which the bride crushes under her right foot seven heaps of rice grains, the bridegroom touching the foot with his right hand, the last being the essential portion. On the second or third day after the marriage a ceremony known as *phal-bharane* is performed, in which a square of wheat grains is formed and the bride and bridegroom are seated over it. Next, one of the boy's relations worships Ganpati and Varuna and applies red powder to the girl's forehead, a lucky necklace is tied round her neck by the bridegroom, her lap is filled, and ornaments and articles of dress are presented to her.

The remarriage of widows is permitted. It can be celebrated on any dark night. The ceremony consists in seating the widow and her new husband side by side, applying red powder to the widow's forehead, filling her lap, and tying into a knot the hems of the pair's garments. A bachelor is not allowed to marry a widow. A husband can divorce a wife on the ground of her misconduct or incompatibility of temper. The divorce is effected by performing funeral rites in the name of the divorced woman. A woman divorced on account of disagreement can marry again after the fashion of the widow remarriage ceremony.

Religion. The caste follow the Hindu law of inheritance and belong to the Hindu religion. Some of them are followers of the Várkari and Mánbháv sects. They worship all the Bráhmanic and village gods and offer blood sacrifices to the latter. *Táks* or images of deceased ancestors embossed on metal plates are installed amongst the household gods. Musalmán saints are reverenced. The caste observe all the Hindu holidays. Their priests are Deshasth Bráhmans.

Death ceremonies.

The dead are either burnt or buried. The bones and ashes are consigned to water. On the tenth day after death rice balls are offered to the deceased and crows are fed. On the eleventh day various kinds of gifts are made to Bráhmans, and castemen are feasted. For the propitiation of the deceased ancestors *paksha* is performed every year in the latter half of the month of *Bhádrapad* and *shráddha* on the anniversaries of the deceased.

Occupation.

The original occupation of the caste was ferrying boats across rivers. Improvements in communications have very greatly decreased the demand for their services. They are now mostly husbandmen and petty traders. Some hold land under the *rayatwári* system, while others are labourers and are paid either in cash or in kind.

Food.

They eat the flesh of goats, sheep, fowls, and fish, and are said not to drink liquor.

TARVADI.—A sub-division of Mewáda Bráhmans.

TAYADE.—A sub-division of Kolis.

Name and origin.

TELIS, *i.e.*, oilmen, from *tel* oil, numbering approximately 90,160 (1901), including 45,486 males and 44,674 females are found all over the Deccan and Konkan. They claim descent from Saturn or Shani. According to a tradition current in Sátára, Telis were created by Shiva to destroy the five demons Kardásur, Ambádásur, Karalásur, Javasásur and Tilásur, who were troubling the world. The Telis crushed them in their mill and extracted oil from their bodies. It is to be noted in this tradition that the names of the five demons are the names of five kinds of seed from which oil is extracted by Telis(1). The origin of the myth is therefore to be traced to the daily occupation of the caste. From their appearance, ceremonies and customs, and the survival of totemism in the form of *devaks* to be found amongst them, it seems that they are an occupational caste chiefly recruited from the Maráthás, like many others. The greater number are still known as Marátha, Tilvan or Somvár Telis.

Endogamous divisions.

Telis have fourteen endogamous divisions, which neither eat together nor intermarry. They are as follows :—

1. Ayar.
2. Bhute.
3. Gandhi.
4. Gujar.

(1) The five kinds of seed are :—*Karda* = safflower, *Ambáda* = the hogplum niger seed, *Javasa* = linseed, and *til* = sesamum.

5. Kadu or Akarmáse (that is, bastards).
6. Kanade.
7. Kandhi.
8. Lád.
9. Pancham or Lingáyat.
10. Pardeshi.
11. Ráthod.
12. Shanvar or Saturday, *i.e.*, Bene Isráel.
13. Shukravári.
14. Tilvan, Somvár or Marátha.

Shanvár or Saturday-keeping Telis are described under BENE ISRAEL.

The Telis of the Ratnágiri district have certain local groups, marriage outside the area of the group being prohibited.

Of the above divisions, Tilvans, Somvárs or Maráthás are most numerous. They are called Somvár because they do not work on Monday (*Somvár*). The following particulars apply to them.

Exogamous divisions.

The *kuls* or exogamous divisions of the Tilvan or Marátha Telis are identical with surnames. The commonest surnames are as follows:—

Amle.	Ghodke.	Rájmáne.
Bedre.	Hadke.	Ráne.
Bhágvat.	Karpe.	Ráut.
Bhise.	Kasture.	Saijandar.
Bhoj.	Kátekar.	Shelár.
Chaván.	Kerulkar.	Thombre.
Chichkar.	Korde.	Tilekar.
Dalve.	Lokhande.	Ubále.
Deshmáne.	Mahále.	Vákchavade.
Divkar.	Mahádik.	Valmunjkar.
Dolse.	Mangar.	Vibhute.
Gáikvád.	Raháte.	Zagade.

In the southern part of the Ratnágiri district persons living in one village are supposed to belong to one family stock, and marriage between them is prohibited. The *devak* of the Telis of the Poona district consists of an iron bar *pahár* and the stone oil mill or *ghána*. In Sátára traces of every *kul* having once had a separate *devak* are still noticeable. Instances of these are :—

Name of kul.	*Devak.*
1. Chaván	*Vásanvel* (Cocculus villosus).
2. Vákchavade	Do.

Name of kul.	*Devak*
3. Vibhute	..*Pánchpálvi, i.e.*, the leaves of the five trees, mango, *rui* (Calotropis gigantea), *vad* (banyan), *jámbhul* (Eugenia jambolana), *shami* (Prosopis spicigera).
4. Chichkar	Do.

The Nasik Telis have the *pánchpálvi*, that is the leaves of the mango, *umbar* (Ficus glomerata), *shami*, *jámbhul* and *rui*. In the Ratnágiri district the common *devaks* are the *kalamb* (Anthocephalus cadumba), *umbar* (Ficus glomerata), *apta* (Bauhinia racemosa) and *anjan* (Hardwickia binata). Except near Chiplun in the Ratnágiri district, sameness of *devak* is no bar to intermarriage. In this district the *devak* is also held in great reverence, and it is neither cut nor burnt nor used for any other purpose.

In the Násik district the boughs of the five *devak* trees are placed in a temple of Máruti by a Gurav at the time of a marriage. A married couple are sent to fetch them, to the accompaniment of music. The boughs are then tied to a post of the marriage booth. Similarly, on the fifth day after the birth of a child the boughs of these trees are worshipped.

Marriages are prohibited between members of the same surname Marriage. or *kul*. Members of the Bhágvat, Hadke and Chichkar *kuls* are considered to belong to one family stock, and intermarriage between them is forbidden. So also Bhises and Dalves form one exogamous group. Marriage with a mother's brother's daughter is allowed, but not with a mother's sister's daughter. Except in some places in the Sátára district, marriage with a father's sister's daughter is not allowed. Marriage with a wife's sister is allowed and brothers are allowed to marry sisters. Girls are generally married between five and fourteen, boys between seven and twenty-five. Polygamy is allowed but polyandry is unknown. Divorce is not allowed except in Sátára. A woman taken in adultery with a member of a higher or lower caste is excommunicated. In other cases, a divorced woman may marry again by the widow remarriage form.

The remarriage of widows is permitted. In the Deccan, a widow may marry her mother's brother's or father's sister's son. In the Konkan, she is not allowed to do so. Marriage with a member of the deceased husband's section is prohibited in all places.

In the Sátára district the ceremony is conducted by a Jangam in Lingáyat fashion. (*See* LINGAYAT.) In other places in the Deccan the ordinary *pát* ceremony is followed. In the Ratnágiri district, before the marriage takes place a bundle of cloth containing a rupee, a cocoanut and a betelnut is sent to the widow's deceased husband's house, and a cocoanut and a cock are waved off her face to free her from molestation by her deceased husband's spirit. The marriage is then performed, in which the widow wears a new robe and ornaments presented by her intended husband, and her brow is marked by red powder by another widow. A bachelor is not allowed to marry a widow except in the southern part of the Ratnágiri district, where he can do so after marrying a *rui* bush (Calotropis gigantea).

Religion. Telis follow the Hindu law of inheritance and, except the Shanvár division, belong to the Hindu religion. Their family deities are Bahiroba of Sonári in Ahmednagar, Devi of Tuljápur in the Nizám's territory, Khandoba of Jejuri in Poona, Mahádev of Singnápur in Sátára, etc. Their priests are the local Bráhmans. The dead are generally burnt, though in some places in the Ratnágiri district some bury their dead as enjoined by family usage. Except in the Sátára district where they have largely copied Lingáyat customs, the birth, death and marriage ceremonies and religious beliefs of Telis do not differ from those of Kunbis.

Occupation. The hereditary occupation of Telis is to extract oil from cocoanut, *kárla* or Niger seed, *kardi* (Carthamus tinctorious), ground-nuts, the fruit of the oilnut tree or *undi* (Calophyllum inophyllum), linseed, sesamum seed and the hogplum or *ambáda*. Some are husbandmen, labourers, cartdrivers, messengers and oilcake sellers.

Food. Telis eat flesh and drink liquor. In some places they eat food cooked by Marátha Kunbis, who do not eat food cooked by Telis. In Násik, they are said to eat only at the hands of Bráhmans.

TELUGU.—A synonym for Kámáthi.

TENGINA DIVAR.—A sub-division of Halepaiks.

TENGINA MAKKALU.—A synonym for Tengina Divar.

Name and origin. **THAKARS,** not recorded separately at the Census of 1901, and perhaps confounded with Thákurs, are found chiefly in the Ratnágiri district and the Sávantvadi State. They are also known as Bágde Thákars, which suggests a connection with the Bágdi caste of Kolhápur, both being fishermen and weavers, occasionally repairing blankets. The main occupation of Thákars is a kind of puppet show exhibition given at nights, especially before temples. During the fair weather they wander from place to place as far as Kanara and Belgaum with their shows and beg for alms. The puppets they show are generally made of wood and represent heroes from the Mahábhárat and Rámáyan, the two great epics of the Hindus. Some, like Nandiváles, exhibit performing bullocks; while others, like Gondhalis, sing ballads and dance to the accompaniment of drums. Some make and sell *gangávans, i.e.*, braids of false hair. During the rainy season they work as agricultural labourers.

Divisions.

Thákars have no endogamous divisions. They have several surnames which are exogamous in some places, while in others marriages are prohibited between members having the same *devak*. The principal surnames are :—

Atak.	Páchinge.	Sásnik.
Gangávane.	Pálve.	Tárápure.
Garud.	Pángul.	Tomre.
Ghogare.	Ranshing.	Vánkade.
Ketkar.	Rasál.	
Maráthe.	Rasulkute.	

The *devaks* discovered so far are (1) the *kalamb* (Anthocephalus cadumba), (2) *umbar* (Ficus glomerata), (3) *sávari* (Bombax malabaricum), (4) *vad* (Banyan), (5) *surya kántache phul, i.e.*, the sunflower. The *devaks* are held in great reverence. Marriage with a father's sister's or mother's sister's daughter is not allowed. In some places, marriage with a maternal uncle's daughter is allowed. A man may marry his wife's sister and two brothers may marry two sisters. Marriage is infant as well as adult. If a girl commits sexual indiscretions with a casteman she is allowed to remain in the caste after the payment of a fine fixed by the caste *panch*. If the man involved belong to another caste, she is excommunicated. Polygamy is permissible, but polyandry is unknown.

Marriage ceremonies.

The offer of marriage comes from the boy's father, who has to pay a bride-price up to Rs. 50. The marriage ceremonies are in most respects similar to those of Maráthás without the *homa* or marriage sacrifice. The remarriage of widows is permitted. A widow cannot marry her father's sister's, mother's sister's or mother's brother's son, or a member of her deceased husband's section. The widow remarriage ceremony is similar to that followed by Bhandáris. A bachelor desiring to marry a widow is first married to a branch of the *rui* bush. A husband can divorce a wife for adultery or for any other serious offence. A man seeking divorce has to give a caste feast or pay annas eight or more according to his means. A woman divorced for any other cause except adultery can marry again by the widow remarriage form.

Religion. Thákars follow the Hindu law of inheritance and are Hindus by religion. They worship the ordinary Hindu gods and goddesses, observe the chief Hindu holidays and make pilgrimages to the sacred places of the Hindus. Their family deities are Kesharling, Bhaváni. Rasaye, Khandoba, Sidoba, etc. In every household a cocoanut is installed in the name of the first ancestor of the family and is called Talkhámba. It is worshipped daily and is renewed every year. The priests of Thákars are the local Bráhmans.

Death ceremonies. The dead are either burnt or buried according as means permit. The ordinary funeral rites are observed. The *shráddha* and *mahálaya* are performed for the propitiation of the deceased ancestors.

Food. Thákars eat the flesh of goats, sheep, wild boars, fowls and fish and drink liquor. They do not eat food cooked by Sutárs, Sonárs, Parits, Nhávis, etc. They are looked down upon as a very low caste by Maráthás and Bhandáris, the chief cultivating castes of Ratnágiri and Sávantvádi.

THAKARDA.—A sub-division of Kolis.

THAKKAR.—A synonym for Bhátia.

THAKOR.—A synonym for Rávat.

Name. **THAKURS** (1) or Chiefs, numbering 122,019 (1901), including 63,347 males and 58,672 females, are found principally in the Thána, Kolába and Násik districts. In Násik the term Thákur is also applied to Brahmakshatri writers, and to a class of carpenters from Gujarát. There is another caste known as Thákurs, who are found mainly in Sátára and are closely connected with the Marátha Bháts. This latter is a very small community and will be described briefly at the end of this article.

Origin. Thákurs are an early tribe living in or near forests, but always choosing a level spot for their hamlet. They hold aloof from other castes, and live by themselves. The term Thákur or Thákor is found among Rajput chiefs, and it is supposed by some on this account that the tribe contains a strain of Rajput blood. This is supported by a copper plate inscription found in possession of a Thákur at Igatpuri

(1) Thákur or Thákor, like the terms Náik, Gauda, and in a sense Rajput, seems to be a title, and to have been applied in the past to tribes of very different origin.

in Násik from which it seems that the word Thákur has been used since A.D. 650. The Rajput element in the tribe is said to be due to certain fugitives from Gujarát having taken refuge among them during the reign of Mahmud Begada (1459—1511).

Appearance, dress and ornaments.

Thákurs are a small squat people, many of them, especially the women, disfigured by swollen bellies, most of them with hard irregular features in some degrees redeemed by an honest kindly expression. The men wear a loin-cloth and occasionally a waist-cloth and a blanket and a piece of cloth tied round the head. On his upper arm a Thákur often has one or more brass rings, and at his waist hangs a small leather bag, *tostán*, with two pouches containing betelnuts and leaves, tobacco, a small hollow bamboo called *sokta*, filled with cotton from the silk cotton tree, and a piece of flint *gár* and steel *tikha*. The women wear a robe very tightly wound round the waist so as to leave almost the whole leg bare. The end of the robe is always tucked in at the waist and never drawn over the head. The only covering of the upper part of body is a very scanty bodice and a heavy necklace of several rounds of white and blue glass beads.

Language

The home tongue of Thákurs is Maráthi, spoken with a long drawl. The names in common use among men are Bángo, Bhádya, Budhya, Dhavlu, Goma, Hema, Ján, Kamb, Maidya, Mángya, Nan, Padu, Posha, Sakroo, Soma, and Válu; and among women, Ahili, Báli, Dháni, Gomi, Hemi, Kánhi, Nági, Námi, Pádi, Páli and Tháni.

Endogamous divisions.

Thákurs have two main endogamous divisions, Ka-Thákurs and Ma-Thákurs, of which the origin is obscure. According to some, Ka-Thákurs is short for Koli-Thákurs and Ma-Thákurs for Marátha Thákurs. Others maintain that Ka stands for Kadu or bastard and Ma for Marátha. Against the probability of the former of these two explanations it is to be noted that the Várli Thákurs who are found in some places are not known as Va-Thákurs, but are called by the full name Várli-Thákurs. The Ma-Thákurs claim descent from the sun, and are the social superiors of the Ka-Thákurs. The two divisions neither eat together nor intermarry.

Exogamous divisions.

Thákurs had originally three surnames, each with a separate *devak* as follows :—

Surname.	Devak.
Jádhav	Gold.
Nargude	Sunflower.
Pavár	Sword-blade.

These surnames were exogamous. In course of time new surnames were adopted by many families, all of which have the common *devák* consisting of the twigs of the mango, *umbar* (Ficus glomerata), *jámbhul* (Eugenia jambolana) and the teak (Tectona grandis).

They have a number of exogamous divisions called *kuls*, each consisting of a group of families bearing different surnames. Such groups are as follows :—

1.	2.	3.
Sotok.	Soldár.	Nirgude.
Vágh.	Sidh.	Mengála.
Pavár.	Lachke.	Sarái.
Zugarya.	Khoke.	Hindola.
Vákh.	Kámdi.	Kevára.
Bhurbade.	Sávat.	Pingla.
Lotya.		Phasle.
		Thombra.

4.	5.	6.
Dhobi.	Telam.	Rera.
Bhamgára.	Agivla.	Madya.
Ughadya.	Kavatya.	Hindola.
Sávlya.	Bhasmya.	
	Zangya.	
	Jádhav.	
	Vára.	
	Gira.	

Marriage rules.

Marriage with a maternal uncle's daughter is allowed, but not with a father's sister's or mother's sister's daughter. Marriage with a wife's sister is allowed, and brothers are allowed to marry sisters. Marriage is generally adult. A curious custom prevails among the Thákurs. Sometimes young women live with men as their wives without going through the marriage ceremony. Such couples are then married with full marriage rites at the time when their children are to be married, as otherwise such children are considered illegitimate. If an unmarried girl misbehaves herself with a casteman she is married to him if the caste rules permit, or to some other man. A girl accused of misconduct with a man of another caste is excommunicated. Polygamy is permissible, but polyandry is unknown.

Birth ceremonies.

Among Thákurs the midwife, who is of their own caste, stays for five days after a birth. On the fifth day the women of the house bring the midwife some red and scented powder, and she covers her hand with the red stuff mixed in water. She then slaps it against the wall, leaving the mark of her palm and fingers thereon. *Yekhand* (orris-root) is then tied round the child's neck, and the mother's purification is over. On any suitable day the child's father goes to a Bráhman, tells him the day and hour of the child's birth, and asks him for a name. The Bráhman gives two, and the father coming home consults the members of the family and chooses one of the two names. No name feast is held and no horoscope is drawn up. Nor is it necessary or even usual for the husband's people to give the girl a fresh name after marriage.

Marriage ceremonies. The offer of marriage comes from the boy's father, who has to pay a *dej* or bride-price of Rs. 16½ and a quantity of rice grains and peas to the girl's father. The day for the marriage is fixed by a Bráhman priest, and the service is also conducted by him, or, in his absence, by a Thákur priest known as Kamdi. After the offer of marriage or *mágni* comes the *supári phádane* or the ceremony of breaking betelnuts. This is attended by kinsmen on both sides and the headman of the tribe. A leading member of the party takes *five* betelnuts and breaks them with the consent of the fathers of the boy and the girl. Next the party is treated to liquor. A marriage contract cannot be broken after this ceremony has been performed. Three days before the marriage the marriage booth is erected, one post of which must be of the *umbar* (Ficus glomerata) tree. To this post are tied two cocoanuts and some rice grains, and below it are planted twigs of the trees representing the *devak*. The *devak* is worshipped with red and turmeric powder. Next the bride and bridegroom are rubbed with turmeric paste at their own houses. The bridegroom is then dressed in a white robe, a dagger or knife is put into his hand (with which he must not part till the end of the marriage), a *báshing* or marriage garland and a *mundával* or chaplet of *rui* (Calotropis gigantea) flowers are tied to his brow, and he is taken in procession to the girl's house. The boy's father first enters the marriage booth, and is welcomed by the girl's father. Next, two married women known as *dudis* approach the bridegroom at the entrance of the booth with two empty earthen pitchers on their heads. The bridegroom puts into each of the pitchers a betelnut and a pice and they retire. The mother of the bride then waves a lighted lamp round his face and applies red and turmeric powder to his forehead. She receives a present of annas eight. Next, the bridegroom is led into the booth and seated on a *páta* or stone slab. The bride stands opposite to him in a basket filled with rice husk. A curtain is held between them and their *báshings* are joined by a cotton thread. Marriage verses are recited by the priest, and grains of rice are thrown over the heads of the pair by the guests. When the lucky moment arrives the curtain is removed and the cotton thread joining the *báshings* of the pair is tied round the bride's neck. The bride and bridegroom then exchange seats and the ceremony of *kanyádán* is performed, in the course of which the bride's parents pour water over the hands of the bride and bridegroom (*dháre*) and present the latter with some cash and utensils. This is followed by the marriage sacrifice, and the bridal pair then walk *five* times round the sacrificial fire. The ceremonies which follow are similar to those observed by Kunbis. The throwing of rice grains over the heads of the bride and bridegroom is considered to be the binding portion of the ceremony.

The remarriage of widows is permitted. A widow cannot marry her mother's sister's or mother's brother's son or a member of her deceased husband's family. She may marry her father's sister's son. The widow's intended husband presents her with a new robe and bodice and ornaments. The widow puts these on, applies red powder to the bridegroom's forehead, and waves a lighted lamp round his face, thus completing the ceremony. A bachelor desiring to marry a widow is first married to a *rui* bush (Calotropis gigantea). A widow who has lost two husbands and marries a third, tramples to death a cock with her foot while entering the house of the third husband. This is supposed to prevent the third husband dying a premature death, the misfortune having been accomplished in the death of the cock. Divorce is allowed. Divorced women may marry again by the widow remarriage form. Widows divorced for adultery are not allowed to remarry during the life-time of their husbands.

Religion. Thákurs worship the leading Hindu gods, but the chief objects of their devotion are Cheda, Vághya, Bahiri, Bhaváni, Supli, Khandoba, Kánhoba, Vetál, and the spirits of several mountains in Mokháda and Násik. Images of these, embossed on silver plates, are kept by them in their houses. Their chief holidays are *Akshatritiyá*, *Dasara*, *Diváli* and *Shimga*. They have a strong faith in ghosts and are often possessed by Vághya. Their priests are men of their own tribe, who are known as Kamdis. Of late many have taken to engaging Bráhman priests for their ceremonies, who are not thereby degraded in the estimation of other Bráhmans.

Death ceremonies. Thákurs bury their dead. The corpse is washed, rubbed with turmeric, and covered with a new cloth. On the way to the grave the bearers stop, the body is lowered and a copper coin is laid under a stone. At the burying ground the face cloth is rent and some rice and a silver coin are dropped into the mouth. While the grave is being filled, the chief-mourner breaks an earthen pot over the grave, which is then covered with branches of the thorny *karvand* (Carissa carandas). Next day some Thákurs go and take the copper coin from under the stone, and put it under another stone, on which they generally pour some milk and lay some bread. Milk and bread are also laid at the head and foot of the grave. On the twelfth day, a Bráhman is called, and, on performing the *hom* sacrifice, is given a copper coin. The chief-mourner lays down nine heaps of meal, and then gathering them into one, throws it into a pond or river. Then five children are feasted. On the first of *Ashvin* food is laid on the roof for the souls of the dead, and crows are called to come and eat it.

The main occupation of Thákurs is husbandry. They work in the fields during the hot, rainy and early cold weather months. At other times they find stray jobs, gathering firewood for sale and wild fruits and roots for their own eating. In the rainy season most of them till upland fields, *varkas*, raising crops of *náchni* and rice. They do not take the land on a regular lease, but occasionally sublet it from government tenants, to whom they pay a share of the produce. Most of their tillage is done by the hand and hoe. Occupation.

They eat fish and fowls and the flesh of goats, sheep, hare, deer and the wild pig, and drink liquor. Food.

The Thákurs of Sátára state that the founder of their tribe was Gangáram Bhát. Their surnames are Chaván, Gáikvád, More, Povár and Sinde, which suggest a Marátha origin. Their family gods are Bahiroba and Khandoba. They do not employ Bráhman priests, all their ceremonies being conducted by the elders of the tribe. They allow widow marriage and burn their dead. They are husbandmen, labourers and messengers. They are among the village staff of *balutedárs* or servants. Sátára Thákurs.

THALAVADI.—A synonym for Darji.

THALE.—A sub-division of Bhandáris.

THANKAR.—A sub-division of Kolis.

THAVI.—A synonym for Konkani Sutár.

THILARI.—A synonym for Khilári Dhangar.

THORCHAKE.—A synonym for Lád Kumbhár.

Name and origin.

THORIS a wandering tribe, numbering 328 (1901), including 205 males and 123 females, are found chiefly in Panch Mahála and Rewa Kántha. Thirteen are recorded in Poona district. They are divided into Garásiás and Makvánás, who differ in no way except that intermarriage is not allowed. Though apparently partly at least of Rajput descent, Thoris are one of the classes whose touch is held to pollute. Of the cause of their degradation no tradition remains. They travel in bands of ten to fifteen, making small reed or *sárkát* huts where they halt and carrying the reed baskets and bedsteads on asses when they move. They form two bands, one settled in Kapadvanj who travel in Dholka, Kaira and the Panch Mahála, the other, whose head-quarters are at Mándva close to Chándod on the Narbada, seldom pass beyond Rewa Kántha limits. When at their head-quarters during the rains, their only work is the tending of goats, which they place in charge of Rabáris or shepherds when they start on their tour. In moving from place to place the well-to-do show much kindness to the poorer families, supplying them with asses to carry their kit. Their home tongue is a rough Gujaráti and they understand Hindustáni.

Marriage.

They do not marry their girls till they are old enough to live with their husbands. Before the wedding the father of the bridegroom pays thirty rupees to the bride's father, five of which are given to the committee to be spent in liquor. On the marriage day a cloth booth or tent is raised in front of the house of the bride's father. All marriage ceremonies are performed by a committee or *panch*, not by a Bráhman. The committee sit in the booth and in front of them two heaps of rice are piled. On one of these heaps is set a lighted lamp of *ghi* or clarified butter. The bride is carried in by her sister's husband and seated on the open side of the tent facing the piles of rice. The bridegroom is carried in by his sister's husband, who pays the bride's maternal uncle a rupee and a half and is seated on the bride's right. The bride and bridegroom stretch out their right hands, the bridegroom's hand resting on the bride's. Two members of the committee tie round the right wrists of the couple a string to which is fastened a wedding-nut or *midhal*, and wind cotton thread round the two wrists. A ball of cooked rice is dropped into the right hand of each of the couple, which they smell and throw behind them. The ceremony ends with the bride giving the bridegroom cooked rice to eat. In the latter part of the day the father of the bride entertains the caste with cooked rice and *ghi* accompanied, in the case of the men, by a draught of liquor. In the evening with singing the bride is taken to the bridegroom's. She remains five days, returns for five days to her father, and after five days more is led with singing to her husband. The bride's father presents the bride with a goat and a knife. Relations also give both bride and bridegroom many small presents in cash.

A widow may marry her husband's brother or, if there is no brother, one of his relations on the father's side. The only rite in connection with remarriage is that the castemen are given liquor and the castewomen molasses, and that the father of the bridegroom makes the bride a small money present as dowry.

Bechra is the only deity worshipped by Thoris. They make a cloth shaped image of a woman, burn a *ghi*-fed lamp in front of the image, and call it Bechra Máta. On *Dasara* in October they sacrifice and eat a buffalo or a goat in Bechra's honour. When threatened with cholera, they also eat buffalo or goat's flesh mixed with that of a fowl or of some other animal, but pork and beef are prohibited. Religion.

Any one dying of small-pox or any one who dies without having ever had small-pox is buried. All others are burnt. On the third day after death, relations make millet balls mixed with *ghi* and molasses and throw them to dogs to eat. On the twelfth day after the death of a man and on the eleventh day after the death of a woman, the castemen are feasted on cooked rice and *ghi*. Children are feasted on the fifth day after the death of a child. Death ceremonies.

The Thoris support themselves by making and selling bedsteads called *kathrots* or *chatvas* with frames of wood and mattresses of coarse tape. Their women sell or barter for grain plaited reed baskets. They used to carry salt. They neither labour nor beg. They sometimes earn a little by singing and playing on a lute. They are reputed to be cattle-lifters and pilferers. Occupation.

THORLEGHARCHE.—A synonym for Mahár.

TIGALAS also known as Tilgar or Tilvai, numbering 1,144 (1901), including 451 males and 693 females, are found in Belgaum, Bijápur, Dhárwár and Kanara. They are a branch of the Mysore Tigalás, who numbered 64,847 in Mysore at the Census of 1901, and were found chiefly in the city and district of Bangalore. The resemblance to the parent caste is still close. The word Tigala is a synonym for the Tamil Raddi or Palli, the Mysore Tigalás being Palli emigrants from the Madras Presidency. The Tigalás of Bombay have now formed themselves into a separate caste. Both Name and origin.

the Pallis and Tigalás claim a Kshatriya origin, and are taking to wearing the sacred thread; but their hereditary occupation is agriculture. The Pallis of Madras form an important element in the local population. They numbered 2,554,316 at the Census of 1901. The Tigalás of Bombay speak at home a corrupt Tamil known as Ebbár indicative of their origin. They also wear the sacred thread, and bury their dead. They do not eat or marry with the parent stock, whom they call Hale or old Tigalás. They have no sub-divisions.

Marriage. Marriages are prohibited between descendants of a common ancestor. A member of the caste may marry his father's sister's or mother's brother's daughter. He cannot marry his mother's sister's daughter. A man may marry two sisters and two brothers may marry two sisters. Girls are married even after they come of age. Sexual license before marriage is not tolerated. If a girl is seduced by a casteman, he is compelled to marry the girl. If a girl commits sexual indiscretions with a member of another cast, she is excommunicated. Polygamy is allowed and practised, but polyandry is unknown.

The offer of marriage comes from the boy's father, who has to pay a *teru* or bride-price to the girl's father. The day for the marriage is fixed by a Karnátak Bráhman who conducts the service. The marriage consists of the following ceremonies:—

Hasaru Ville or the betrothal ceremony, in which castemen assemble at the girl's father's house, the girl is made to put on a robe and bodice presented by the boy's father, *pánsupári* and sugar are distributed, and the party are treated to a dinner.

Devakárya.—A man and wife bathe and go to a pond or well with two earthern jars containing milk and *ghi*. The contents of the jars are poured into the pond or well, and the jars are filled with water. Next, three balls of earth are made and placed before the jars and worshipped. The couple then return home with the jars. On the threshold of the house, water is poured on the feet of the couple by a woman in the house, rice grains are thrown over the jars, and frankincense is burnt before them. The jars are then taken into the house and placed near the gods. The jar brought by the male is covered with a male garment, that brought by the female with a female garment. Next, the jars are worshipped with offerings of a dish of sweets and a dish of flesh, and relations and friends are feasted.

Arishinakárya or the turmeric ceremony:—A blanket is spread on the ground, rice grains are strewn over it, the girl is seated thereon, and she is rubbed with turmeric paste by unwidowed women. On this day or the day following the boy is taken in procession to the girl's village and seated in a temple. He is received there by the girl's father and taken to his house, where he and his party are treated to a dinner. The boy remains here till the end of the marriage ceremonies. On the next day the girl is again rubbed with turmeric paste, the marriage booth is erected, two branches of the Indian fig tree, which have first been placed in a tank, are brought and tied to the door of the booth and are worshipped. On the same day, a marriage coronet, which has been kept in the temple of the family god, is brought in procession, placed near the household gods, and worshipped.

Suraginiru.—Five unwidowed women go to a pond or well, each taking a jar. Then, as described in the *Devakárya* ceremony, they fill the jars with water and bring them home. Four of the jars are placed at four corners of a square, and one in the middle. The boy and his female relations are seated near the jar in the middle, the boy is made to touch a five-threaded string, and the string is passed round the four jars. Next, they are all bathed with hot water, and come out of the string enclosure without touching it. The marriage coronet is then put on the boy's head, and he is taken on a horse or a bullock to a neighbouring house.

Hireville.—The five women mentioned above bring from the boy's father a robe, eleven plantains and two cocoanuts. The *Suraginiru* ceremony is then performed on the girl, she is taken into the house, and a marriage coronet is fixed on her head.

Dháremuhurta.—The boy is then brought from the neighbouring house and seated on a cot in the marriage booth. The girl is brought and both are made to stand facing each other. *Kankans* or marriage wristlets made of the string passed round the jars of the *Suraginiru* are tied round the right wrists of the boy and the girl, a cloth is held between them, they are made to take mutual oaths of fidelity, and the cloth is removed. Next, the boy fastens a lucky necklace round the girl's neck. Both the boy and the girl then take in their hands rice grains and a cocoanut. The girl's maternal uncle then takes an earthen jar containing *ghi* and milk. walks thrice round them, and at the end of each round pours the contents of the jar over the cocoanuts held by them. Next, the Bráhman priest takes the cocoanuts from the boy and the girl, and the pair throw the rice grains over each other thrice. Rice grains are similarly thrown at them by the Bráhman priest and the party assembled. Next, the hems of the pair's garments are knotted, they are made to utter each other's name, taken near the house gods, and the marriage coronets on their heads are removed. A feast to the party assembled ends the ceremony. On the following day the boy and girl are made to play certain games, and on the next day the boy returns to his house in procession with his bride. The binding portion of the marriage is the *dháremuhurta* ceremony.

The remarriage of widows is permitted. A widow cannot marry a relation of her deceased husband or her mother's sister's son. A widow remarriage always takes place at night on any day. Widows and remarried widows only attend the ceremony. The widow to be married is taken into a dark room, bangles are put on her wrists, a lucky necklace is tied round her neck, and she is made to put on a new robe and bodice. A light is then set in the room and the intended husband of the widow comes in, leads her out, and takes her to his house, thus completing the ceremony. A bachelor is not allowed to marry a widow. A husband can divorce a wife on the ground of her unchastity. The divorce is effected by tearing off the end of the woman's robe and by removing the lucky necklace round her neck. A woman divorced on account of adultery with a casteman or a member of a higher caste, can marry again by the widow remarriage form. If the offence is committed with a member of a lower caste, she is put out of the caste. The Hindu law of inheritance is followed.

Religion.

Tigalás are Hindus of the Vaishnava sect. They chiefly worship Ráma, Hanumán, Rangnáth, and Bhairava. Their family goddess is Gurunáthamma who has shrines in Mysore and Kárkal in South Kanara. Dyámavva, Durgavva, Kariyavva, Marevva and other minor gods are also worshipped. Tigalás go on pilgrimage to Tirupati in *Ashvin* and to Udapi in *Chaitra*. They observe all the Hindu holidays. Offerings of goats are made to all minor gods at the time of their fairs, and are eaten by the offerers themselves. Musalmán saints are venerated. When an epidemic breaks out, a jar filled with water and covered with leaves of the *nim* (Melia azadirachta) is worshipped. The religious teacher of the Tigalás is a Bráhman Swámi of Anegundi. They employ Bráhmans to conduct their marriages. The widow remarriages are conducted by widows of the caste.

Death ceremonies.

The dead are either burnt or buried with head to the south. Persons who have worn *mudrás* are burnt. The ashes of the burnt are collected on the fifth day and consigned to water. The corpse to be burnt is carried on a bier, that to be buried, in a blanket.

Before it is lifted, it is dressed in old clothes, seated, and worshipped. When the party reach the burial ground, the old clothes are removed and it is covered with a new piece of cloth, to one end of which is tied a pice. After the corpse is burnt or buried, the party bathe and return home, bringing with them the old clothes in which the corpse was dressed. The house of the deceased is cowdunged, and a jar filled with water and a light are kept on the spot where the death took place. The party look at the light and disperse. The son of the deceased is made to wear the head-dress put on the corpse's head. A sweet basil plant is planted on the spot where the corpse was burnt or buried. This plant is worshipped on the fifth day after death with an offering of cooked food. The mourning ends on the seventh day, when a jar filled with water is worshipped with offerings of dishes of sweets and flesh, and the caste is feasted. For the propitiation of the deceased ancestors, a jar filled with water is worshipped on the new-moon day of *Bhádrapad* and a man and wife of the caste are feasted. They do not perform the *shráddha*.

Occupation. The hereditary occupation of the caste is agriculture and gardening. Some hold land under the *Rayatvári* system. Some are tenants of superior holders. Some are labourers and are paid either in cash or in kind.

Food. They eat the flesh of goats, sheep, hares, deer, fowl, and fish, and drink liquor.

TIKALE.—A sub-division of Devángs.

TILARI.—A sub-division of Lingáyats.

TILGAR.—A synonym for Tigala.

TILOLE KUNBI.—A sub-division of Khándesh Kunbis.

TILORI KUNBI.—A sub-division of Khándesh Kunbis.

TILVAI.—A synonym for Tigala.

TILVAN.—A sub-division of Telis, Gánigs and Mahárs.

TIMALIYAS are a small caste of smiths found in Surat.

TINGARE.—A sub-division of Lohárs.

TIPRA.—A sub-division of Khálpás.

TIRALI.—A synonym for Tilári.

Name and origin. **TIRGARS,** numbering 1,417 (1901), including 752 males and 665 females, are found in Ahmedabad, Kaira, Panch Maháls, Mahi Kántha, Pálanpur and Rewa Kántha. They take their name from *tir* an arrow, having formerly dealt in arrows. But there being no demand for arrows now, they have given up this occupation and taken to husbandry.

Divisions. They are divided into eight clans, *viz.*, Chuván. Ghánek, Makwána, Parmár, Ráthod, Rávalia, Solanki and Wángar.

Marriage. Members of the same clan cannot intermarry. Marriages are also prohibited within seven degrees of relationship. A member of the caste cannot marry his father's sister's, mother's sister's or mother's brother's daughter. A man may marry two sisters, and two brothers may marry two sisters. Polygamy is permitted. A man can marry a second wife after the age of thirty, if the first wife is barren, or is suffering from an incurable disease, or he cannot live with her. Polyandry is unknown. Girls are generally married from the age of seven to twelve. In the case of poor people, they sometimes remain unmarried till after they come of age. If a girl commits sexual indiscretions with a casteman or a member of a higher caste, she may remain in the caste by paying a fine or giving a dinner to the caste people. If the man involved belong to a lower caste, she is excommunicated.

Marriage ceremonies. The offer of marriage comes from the girl's father. The boy's father has to pay a sum of Rs. 18 to the girl's father. The day for the marriage is fixed by the caste priest who is a Gáruda, who also conducts the service. The Gáruda goes to the boy's father's house and asks him on behalf of the girl's father if he is willing to accept his girl. On his agreeing, the priest takes from him annas twelve, and buys cocoanuts worth annas eight and molasses worth annas four. He then calls the relations of both the boy and the girl one by one, and asks them if they can stand security to the match. On their assenting he distributes the cocoanuts and molasses among them. This ceremony is called *Vágnischaya.*

A day or two before marriage, Ganpati is installed, and the boy and the girl are bathed and rubbed with turmeric paste and oil. On the marriage day the boy starts for the girl's house and stands at the entrance of the street in which the girl resides. Here he is received by the girl's parents and taken to the marriage booth. He is seated in the booth, and the girl is brought and seated by his side. Figures are then drawn on the marriage altar with red powder, flour and turmeric paste. Next, the priest repeats sacred verses and reads the *astári* (a sacred book). When half the portion of the book is read, two *mangals* are said to be completed, and the ends of the couple's garments are tied into a knot. When the book is read to the end, the couple are made to eat rice and curds. Next they are made to walk round the *chori*, marriage altar, which is the last and also the binding portion of the marriage ceremony.

The remarriage of widows is permitted. A widow cannot marry her father's sister's, mother's sister's or mother's brother's son. She may marry a member of her late husband's clan or his younger brother. A widow remarriage is brought about by the caste priest. The ceremony is very simple. The widow is seated inside the house where the ceremony is to be performed, and her intended husband is seated outside the house. The priest fastens a cotton thread round the wrist of each, and the widow puts on the garments brought by her intended husband, which completes the ceremony. Should a bachelor desire to marry a widow he is first married to a *bor* (jujube tree) or a *shami* tree (*Prosopis spicigera*).

A husband can divorce a wife with the sanction of the caste *panch*, who take from each a fine of Rs. 10. A divorced woman can marry again according to the first marriage ceremony if the cause of divorce be not adultery on her part, in which case she is excommunicated and again admitted into the caste after two years on exacting a fine or dinner from her. The caste follow the Hindu law of inheritance.

Religion.

Tirgars are Hindus of the Bijpanthi sect. They chiefly worship Krishna. Their family goddess is Chámunda Devi. Every day they light a lamp in her name. The cow, the *pipal* and the sweet basil plant are worshipped. They make pilgrimages to Gangáji, Dwárka, Reváji, Dákor, etc., and observe all the Hindu holidays. Their religious teachers are Dheda saints. Images of deceased ancestors are worshipped. When an epidemic breaks out, Mátáji is propitiated, Gárudás are feasted, and caste feasts are held. Their priests are Gárudás who are the priests of all depressed classes in Gujarát including even Bhangiás.

Death ceremonies.

The dead are either burnt or buried. Bachelors and maidens must be buried. At burial the corpse is laid with head to the north. The bones and ashes of the burnt are thrown into the river. Where there is no river, the bones and ashes are made into a heap after the corpse has been burnt, and water is poured over the heap from a jar. Funeral rites are performed on the tenth, eleventh and thirteenth days after death. On the last-mentioned day a feast is given to the caste people. For the propitiation of the deceased ancestors, *sapindi* is performed once before the year ends, and three, five or seven Gárudás are feasted in the month of *Kártik*. The *shráddha* is also said to be performed.

Occupation. The original occupation of the caste was making *tirs* or arrows. When the demand for arrows ceased, they took to working as field labourers. All of them now work on fields as day labourers and are paid in cash.

Food. They eat the flesh of goats, sheep, cows, buffaloes, domestic fowls, hare and fish and drink liquor.

TIRGUL.—A sub-division of Bráhmans.

TIRMALA.—A sub-division of Dásas.

Name and origin. **TIRMALIS** or bullock showmen, also called Káshikápdis, numbering 2,126 (1901), including 1,079 males and 1,047 females, are found in Khándesh, with a few families in Ahmednagar, Násik and Sholápur. They are a class of wandering beggars and petty dealers, of Telugu extraction. They speak Telugu at home and use Telugu names of males and females. They live in tents or *Páls* outside of villages.

Divisions. They have no exogamous sub-divisions above families having the same surname. The commonest surnames are Gadu, Kadam, Kánere, Kánehkemodu, Mayakalla, Medur, Nandále, Patar, Rasoti, Sanku, Shebul, and Wasardi. They all belong to one *gotra*—Káshyape which is frequently adopted by those anxious to rise in the social scale.

Marriage. Marriages are prohibited between persons having the same surname. Polygamy and widow remarriage are allowed and practised, but polyandry is unknown. Girls are generally married before they are ten and boys before they are twenty. Their marriages are generally performed in the month of *Shrávan,* when all castemen return home from their tours. The couple are rubbed with turmeric two or three days before the marriage and *udid* pulse is worshipped as the marriage guardian or *devak.* The Bráhman priest visits the booth and joins the hands of the couple, while musicians of their own caste play, and the pair are then husband and wife.

Religion. They are Hindus of the Shaiva sect. Their family deities are Ambábái, Chartalaji of Tuljiápur, Durga, Bhaváni, and Báláji and Ganpati in Telangan. They also worship the local gods and goddesses and observe all the Hindu holidays. They believe in soothsaying, witchcraft and evil spirits, and make pilgrimages to Alandi and Dehu in Poona, and Pandharpur in Sholápur. Their priests are Telang Bráhmans, but in their absence Deshasth Bráhmans are also employed.

The dead are either burnt or buried. The body is laid on the bier, and without a rest on the way is taken to the burning or burial ground by four kinsmen. At burial the body is at once laid in the grave, water is squeezed into its mouth and it is covered with earth. Crows and Bráhmans are fed on the 10th or 11th day after death, and caste-people are feasted on the 13th or any day before the end of the fifth month. They remember the dead on their anniversary and on the day in the *Mahálaya Paksha* or all souls' fortnight in dark *Bhádrapad* corresponding to the death day. Death ceremonies.

Their hereditary calling is begging from door to door. They keep a bull decked with brass ornaments and bells and cover his back with a patched quilt of various colours. The driver dresses in a red turban and throws a scarf round his neck while a follower beats a drum or *dholki*. They also sell sacred threads or *jánvas*, holy *rudráksha* berries (Elæocarpus lanceolapus or ganitrus), whetstones, pieces of sandalwood, and sweet basil rosaries. They deal in sandalwood dolls and offer their wares in exchange either for cash or clothes. The women darn secondhand clothes and mind the shop when the men are away. Occupation.

They eat flesh, except beef and pork, and drink liquor. Food.

TIROLE.—A synonym for Tilole.

TIWARI.—A synonym for Tarvádi.

TOGATI.—A sub-division of Devángs.

TOKARPHODE.—A sub-division of Mángs.

TOKRE.—A synonym for Dhor Koli.

TOLAKIA.—A sub-division of Audich Bráhmans.

TORI.—A sub-division of Vághris.

TORKE NADOR.—A sub-division of Nádors.

TOTIGAR.—A synonym for Hugar.

TRAGADA.—A sub-division of Sonis.

TRAVADI.—A synonym for Tarvádi.

TRIGARTH.—A synonym for Tirgul.

TRIPALA.—A sub-division of Modh Bráhmans.

TRIVADI.—A synonym for Tarvádi.

TRIVEDI.—A sub-division of Modh and Shrigaud Bráhmans.

TUDUG WADAR.—A synonym for Bhámta.

TUHLIA.—A sub-division of Kaikádis.

TUMBEL.—A synonym for Tumer.

TUMER.—A sub-division of Chárans.

Name and origin. **TURIS** or Drummers, numbering 3,195 (1901), including 1,565 males and 1,630 females, are found chiefly in Ahmedabad, Kaira, Káthiáwár, Mahi Kántha, Pálanpur and Rewa Kántha. Nearly half the number recorded in 1901 were resident in the Pálanpur State. They take their name from the *tur*, drum. According to their own story, the Turis are the descendants of a Bhát. In the reign of Siddharája (A. D. 1100) a Dhed named Mahid offered himself as a sacrifice to stop the leakage of the Sahasralingh lake in Patan. At that time Dhedás were forced to go bareheaded, to carry a spittoon hung round their necks, and to drag branches of the *shami* (Prosopis spicigera) tree to wipe out their footmarks. They were forbidden to rear cows and buffaloes or to worship the *pipal* tree or the basil plant. As a return for his self-sacrifice, Mahid begged Siddharája to free his caste people from these degrading rules and to give them a priest and a bard. Siddharája agreed.

Another account is that Turis are descended from a Bhangia and a Musalmán dancing girl. In appearance, house, dress and language Turis do not differ from Dhedás. In position they rank between Dhedás and Bhangiás. Dhedás will not dine with Turis, and Turis will not dine with Bhangiás.

Marriage. Boys and girls are married between seven and ten. Marriage between relations, whether on the father's or the mother's side, is forbidden. A Gáruda or Dheda Bráhman acts as a priest. Ganpati and a *shami* twig are worshipped, the pair pass four times round the central square, and the parents and relations of the bridegroom are feasted. At the bridegroom's the bride and bridegroom worship the goddess Umia, play a game of chance, and struggle for a rupee and a silver ring in a jar of water.

Widow marriage is allowed, the younger brother of the deceased husband having the first claim on the wife. Divorce is granted on the ground of adultery or of disagreement. A divorced woman receives nothing from her husband, lives at her father's, and has no claim over her children.

Religion. They are followers of the goddess Umia, whose shrine is at Unja, fifty-five miles north of Ahmedabad, and of the goddess Harshid, whose shrine is at Ujjain. To these shrines they go on pilgrimage. The goddess Umia is represented in every house by an iron trident.

Near the goddess they keep a lamp, and burn incense and offer a goat during the *Navrátra* or Nine Night Festival. They bow to the rising sun and to the full-moon. After building a new house the earth is propitiated by burying a goat. Their teacher is a Dheda saint at Dákor, who receives a yearly contribution of Re. 1, and one day's provisions from each house. Their chief holidays are *Holi* in February-March, *Nágpanchmi* or the Cobra's fifth in August, and the fifteenths and the seconds of every Hindu month.

Death ceremonies.

The dead are buried. The dead body is carried to the burial ground on a bamboo bier with a cocoanut hanging from each of the four corners. Before laying the body in the grave, the eyes, mouth, hands and feet are bathed in cocoanut milk. On the third day a pot filled with water, a sweet ball, and a lamp fed with clarified butter, are placed near the burial ground. Death ceremonies are performed for nine days and unmarried children are feasted on rice. On the tenth day the male relations shave their upper lip.

Occupation.

Turis cultivate during the rains. In the fair season they wander about, playing the drum called *tur*, and reciting tales half prose half verse to the accompaniment of a guitar, *sáranji*. Owing to the competition of the Rávalias, their income has, of late years, greatly decreased, and they are now a poor class.

Food.

Turis eat the flesh of goats, sheep, fowls, deer, bears, hares, and porcupines. They drink liquor and eat opium.

TURKAR.—A sub-division of Lingáyats.

TWASHTA KASAR.—A synonym for Kásár.

UCHLIA.—A synonym for Bhámta.

UDA.—A sub-division of Kanbis.

UDAMBAR.—A sub-division of Bráhmans.

UDLIA.—A sub-division of Rávals.

UKHARIA.—A sub-division of Dublás.

UMMAD.—A sub-division of Vániás.

UMRIA.—A sub-division of Dublás.

UNDE.—A sub-division of Mális.

UNNIKANKAN.—A sub-division of Kurubás.

UPADHYA.—A sub-division of Jains.

Name and origin.

UPPARS numbering 29,351 (1901), including 14,838 males and 14,513 females, are found in the Belgaum, Bijápur, and Kanara districts. The occupation of the caste was formerly salt-making, the name Uppár being derived from *uppu* salt. Now they are chiefly stone-cutters, lime-makers, and masons. It is stated that the original home of the caste was Mysore, where they are found in large numbers (45,405 in 1901). Mr. Rice (Mysore I, 337) notices two divisions of Uppárs: Karnátaks who make salt, and Telugus who make bricks. Buchanan (Mysore I, 304) described the Telugu Uppárs as mud wall builders, husbandmen, and carriers. They were Vaishnavas, worshipping Dharmarája and the mothers or *Shaktis*. The caste tradition regarding their origin is that they were created by Shiva to make salt.

Endogamous divisions.

The caste is split up into three endogamous divisions: Námada Uppár, Katani or Koli Uppár, and Lingáyat Uppár, who neither eat together nor intermarry. The Námada Uppárs wear the sacred thread and abstain from flesh; the Katani Uppárs form the main body of the caste; while the Lingáyat Uppárs are those Uppárs who have embraced Lingáyatism and joined the followers of Basaveshwar*.

The Uppárs speak Kanarese. The names in common use among men are, Bhima, Hanma, Phakiri, Bala, Mhásti, Durga, Honnappa, and Manja; and among women, Mári, Kanne, Mhásti, Durgi, Lakshmi, Márki and Nágu.

Exogamous divisions.

The caste contains nine exogamous sub-divisions known as *bedagus*. These are named after the nine sons of one Námagopál, believed to be the common ancestor of the caste. Members of the same *bedagu* cannot intermarry. In Kanara they have the following *balis*, members of which cannot intermarry:—

1. Dyavana .. Tortoise.
2. Ganga .. Gangávali River.
3. Hole .. A tree (Terminalia arjuna).
4. Shetti .. A fish.
5. Tolana .. Wolf.
6. Nága .. The Champa tree.
7. Ammana .. The goddess Amma.

A member of the caste can marry his father's sister's or mother's brother's daughter. He cannot marry his mother's sister's daughter. A man may marry two sisters, and brothers may marry sisters.

---

* For further information regarding Lingáyat Uppárs *see* "Lingáyat".

Girls are generally married before they attain puberty. Polygamy is allowed and practised, but polyandry is unknown. The offer of betrothal comes from the boy's father, who has to pay a *teru* or bride-price to the girl's father. The day for the marriage is fixed by a Bráhman, who conducts the service. The marriage consists of the following ceremonies:—*Halad*, or rubbing the boy and the girl with turmeric paste; *Devakárya*, in which a party of males and females goes in procession to a *Pipri* (*Ficus tsiela*) tree or a *Shami* (*Prosopis spicigera*) bush, which is worshipped by five unwidowed women; a bough is then cut off and brought home and tied to the chief post, known as *hálagamb*, of the marriage booth; *Airáni*, or bringing in procession seven earthen jars from a potter's, filling them with water from a well, and worshipping them; and *Pánigrahan*, in which the right hands of the boy and the girl are joined and a lucky necklace is tied round the girl's neck by the Bráhman priest, this being the binding portion of the ceremony. On the fourth day after marriage the ceremony of *Merawanige* takes place, when the boy and the girl are taken on a bullock's back to a temple and thence to the bridegroom's house. Amongst the Kanara Uppárs, the marriage ceremony is conducted by a *budvant* or headman of the caste, and the ceremony of *dháre*, or pouring milk over the joined hands of the bride and the bridegroom, is performed. **Marriage ceremonies.**

The re-marriage of widows is permitted. A widow can marry her father's sister's or mother's brother's son. She cannot marry her mother's sister's son or a member belonging to her late husband's section. The ceremony takes place on a dark night. It consists in tying a lucky necklace round the widow's neck, after which a dinner is given. A bachelor is not allowed to marry a widow. Divorce is allowed. The caste follow the Hindu law of inheritance.

Uppárs belong to the Hindu religion. The special deities of their worship are Yellamma, Hulideva, Hanumán, Venkataráma and Virabhadra. The *Shami* (*Prosopis spicigera*), the *Bel* (*Aegle marmelos*) the *Pipal*, the sweet basil plant, and the cow are worshipped. They have great faith in soothsaying, witchcraft, ghosts, and the power of evil spirits. They observe almost all the Hindu holidays, and make pilgrimages to Gokarn, Pandharpur, Tuljápur, and Tirupati. Silver busts of deceased ancestors are made and installed amongst the household gods. When an epidemic breaks out, the goddess supposed to preside over the disease is propitiated with offerings of water, cooked food, goats, and fowls. Their priests are either Deshasth or Karnátak Bráhmans. **Religion.**

Death ceremonies. The Námada Uppárs burn their dead; but children who have not cut their teeth are buried. The Katani Uppárs bury the dead, except those who have died of leprosy. At burial, the unmarried dead are seated, the married are laid with head to the north. On the eleventh day after death, a feast is given to the caste people. For the propitiation of the deceased ancestors, their busts are worshipped with offerings of articles of dress on a day between the third day of *Vaishákh* and the ninth day of *Ashvin*.

Occupation. The original occupation of the caste was making salt. When salt-making became a Government monopoly, they took to masonry work, stone-cutting, and making shell-lime. Formerly they also made images of Hindu gods and saints and sold them at considerable profit. Some of them hold land under the *rayatwári* system. A few hold *watan* lands as *pátils*. They also work as day labourers and are paid either in cash or in kind.

Food. The Katani Uppárs eat the flesh of goats, sheep, fowls, and fish, and drink liquor.

UPPU NADOR.—A sub-division of Nádors.

URAP AGRI.—A sub-division of Agris.

UR KAIKADI.—A sub-division of Kaikádis.

UR KORAVA.—A sub-division of Koravas.

UR OD.—A sub-division of Ods.

UTEGAR.—A sub-division of Dhangars.

VADADRA.—A sub-divisin of Bráhmans.

VADAR.—A synonym for Od.

VADARI.—A synonym for Bhámta.

VADHIARA.—A sub-division of Rabáris.

VADI.—A synonym for Lád Vanjári.

VADIS, numbering 734 (1901), including 396 males and 338 females, are found chiefly in Káthiáwár. They are a wandering tribe of jugglers and snake-charmers. They also sell stone hand-mills, winnowing fans and the straw pads on which the women balance their earthen pots. They allow widow marriage.

VADNAGRA.—A sub-division of Nágar Bráhmans.

VADVAL.—A sub-division of Pánchkalshis.

VADVE.—A synonym for Sutár.

VAGHE.—*See* Murli.

VAGHERS [1], numbering 2,198 (1901), including 1,092 males and 1,106 females, are found chiefly in Okhamandal in the north-west of Káthiáwár. They claim to be the earliest settlers in the peninsula, but have now spread along the south coast of the Gulf of Cutch, and are found in Okhamandal and most of the coast villages and towns of Hálár in the Navánagar State. There are several villages entirely peopled by them, in which they hold *girás* lands granted to them by the Vádhel Chiefs of Arnala near Dwárka. **Name and origin.**

"The name Vágher is popularly derived from *va* without and *gher* smell, meaning a tiger who is devoid of the sense of smell. In time the term was applied to the Kála tribe, who were as cruel and sanguinary as tigers. Another fantastic legend is that the Vághers were so called because they cooled the gods on a visit to hot Okhamandal by *gher* (or enclosing) of *vá* (or wind), and thus refreshed them [2]." A third derivation is from *vágh* wearing apparel and ornaments and *har* carrying away, meaning robbers of costly clothes and ornaments, which is suggestive of the thieving propensities of the tribe.

Vághers are a turbulent and warlike race, and for a long period caused great trouble by their piracies and dacoities. They were reduced to order in 1867 by the combined British and Gáikwári forces. Even now they have retained predatory tendencies and are under special political control. They claim to be Kshatriyas, and state that in the eleventh century Okhamandal was divided between the Herol and Chávda Rajputs, who were treacherously murdered by some Rathods, invited to settle their feuds. The Herols took refuge with the Vághers and became merged in them. Later, Hemirji, a Vádhel prince of Cutch, married a Herol girl, and their issue, called Vághers, took the title of Máneks and became the rulers of Dwárka and Okhamandal.

"Another tradition is that the original inhabitants of Okhamandal were divided into three tribes Kába, Moda and Kála. The Kábás were known in the days of Krishna as the savage people of Sauráshtra, the modern Káthiáwár, but the race is said to be now (A. D. 1900) extinct. The Modás also have disappeared. Traces of the Kálás are still to be found, and it is from this tribe that the present Vághers are said to be descended. Krishna is believed to

---

(1) Compiled from the Bombay Gazetteer, Vol. IX, and materials supplied by Mr. K. G. Pandit.

(2) Bombay Gazetteer, Vol. VIII, p. 587.

have subjugated Okhamandal after a struggle with the Kálás[1]." It seems most probable that Vághers were in origin Kolis, and contain an admixture of degraded Rajputs.

Vághers have two main divisions, Hindus and Musalmáns. Hindu Vághers do not eat food cooked by Musalmán Vághers, but give their daughters in marriage to the latter if they can pay for them Marriages, however, do not take place between the Musalmán Vághers on the southern coast of Cutch and the sea-coast villages in the Hálár Division of Káthiáwár. The two divisions are described below separately :—

HINDU VAGHERS have several *Shákhás* or exogamous sections resembling Rajput clan names. The chief of them are—

Bathad.	Bhagya.	Gigla.	Jagatia.	Ker.	Solanki.
Bathia.	Chámadia.	Hathal.	Kala.	Makwána.	Vagha.
Bhagád.	Gál.	Jáda.	Karja.	Mánek.	

Marriage with a father's sister's and mother's brother's daughter is allowed. Marriage with two sisters is allowed and brothers are allowed to marry sisters. Girls are generally married between thirteen and eighteen, and boys between eighteen and twenty-five. The remarriage of widows is permitted. Except in the family of the headman of the tribe (the Mánek family) *dervatun* or marriage with the deceased husband's younger brother is permitted but is not very common, though where a widow remarries outside her late husband's family, she has to recompense her brother-in-law for his loss of the bride due to him. Divorce is allowed.

The marriage ceremonies of Vághers are of the standard type obtaining in Gujarát, the essential and binding portion being the *phera pharvun* or the bridal pair's walking four times round the sacrificial fire.

Vághers follow the Hindu law of inheritance, and are followers mostly of Shiva, though in and near Dwárka they hold Vishnu and Ranchhodji in great reverence. Some among them are followers of Rámde Pir Their family deities are Ashpura, Vachhdo, Mohamaya, Khodyár, Kálika, Vijwasan, Bela and Balvi. All Vághers go to Dwárka on the *Bhim Agiaras* holiday, the eleventh of the bright half of *Jeth*, when they bathe in the Gomti and worship Ranchhodji. Their priests are Rájgor Bráhmans, but their religious ceremonies are mostly conducted by the Vaida sub-division of Gugli Bráhmans.

(1) Bombay Gazetteer, Vol VIII, p. 587.

Vaghris

The dead are generally burnt. Infants and children up to six years old and persons dying of small-pox and leprosy are buried with head to the north. The ashes of the burnt are thrown into the sea at Dwárka or Beyt. The unburnt bones are thrown into the river Gomti. On the eleventh day after death an image of the deceased is made of wheat flour and worshipped on a river bank. During the first year, each month, alms are given to a Bráhman with a cash present of annas four. Propitiative ceremonies for the deceased are performed every year on the ninth day of the dark half of *Bhádrapad*.

Vághers, who appear to have been originally fishers, have indulged freely in piracy in the past; they are now landholders, fishermen and sailors. The Okhamandal Vághers still hold their *girás* lands, but the soil is poor, and from A.D. 1860 they pay a tax of one rupee a family to the Gáikwár. Some are labourers and a few are police patels.

Vághers eat food cooked by Khárvás, Kumbhárs, Rabáris, Bharváds, Ghedia Kolis and Khavásas. Rajputs, Mers, Válands, Ahirs, Chárans and Káthis eat food cooked by Vághers.

MUSALMAN VAGHERS include the Bellas, Máliás, and Vavániás, as also the Bhádelas. They have such surnames as Chámadia, Chávda, Dal, Jam, Mának and Subáni, which indicate their Hindu origin. They are Sunnis by religion and follow the general Musalmán customs. They are hardy long voyage sailors and sail to Calcutta, Ceylon, Karachi, Madras, the Malabár Coast, Maskat, the Persian Gulf and Zanzibar, also to south-east African ports. They go in their own vessels commanded by Vágher captains or *nákhudás*.

VAGHRI.—A sub-division of Párdhis; a synonym for Takári.

VAGHRIS, numbering 59,856 (1901), including 31,190 males and 28,666 females, are found in all parts of Gujarát, but chiefly in Ahmedabad, Kaira and Káthiáwár. According to their own priests or Bhuvás, the name Vághri means tiger-like, but a more likely derivation is from the *vagads* or sand-hills of the Rajputána desert. It may however, be derived from *vagurs* or *vaghars* meaning net, in which case Vághris would mean a tribe of netters. The Vághris of Gujarát probably belong to the Bágri tribe inhabiting the Bágar country, a tract between the south-western border of Hariana and the Shara in the United Provinces.[1] They are said to have

Name and origin.

(1) Bombay Gazetteer, Vol. IX, Part I, p. 510.

sprung from the Sansyas or Sansis, a well known race of plunderers in the Punjab and other countries. Sansis say they were Rajputs but they have degenerated to a very low social position. The progenitor of the Sansi family was Sans Mull, from whom sprang the Bágris, Budhuks, Gidias, Haburias, Kichacks, Kunjars, Moghias, and others, their clan names varying with the country they inhabited. The children of Mullania, the younger brother of Sans Mull, are the Beriabs, Kolhatis and Doms, who are also variously named according to the territory in which they mostly reside. As the Sansi tribe multiplied and their means of subsistence diminished, they migrated and divided into clans which were variously called, but those who stayed in Márwár obtained the name Bágoras or Bágris. Whether they were so called from the country of Bágar, which they chiefly occupied before their dispersion, or whether that country obtained its name from them is not clear. Their name, which seems to connect them with the *vagads* or sand-hills of the North Rájputána desert, and their cringing gipsy-like ways suggest both their descent from some tribe of Jats and their origin from some invading Scythians or northern conquerors, who, on the defeat of their masters by Hindu kings, mingled with Bhils, Kolis and other low tribes and sank to a degraded position. Though the variety in features is very great, a resemblance is often traceable to a Negrito-Mongolian type. Both among men and women the high cheek bones and narrow eyes are often observable, combined with thick lips, massive jaws and flat noses. The black hair, though not woolly, is mostly wavy. Vághris are superior to Dhedás but inferior to Kolis. In appearance and occupation they seem associated with the fowlers and bird-catchers known as Párdhis or Phánse-Párdhis. According to their own account they are Chohan Rajputs whom Vihát claimed as her own and made Vághris. Their surnames do not favour a separate tribal origin. The names Bráhman, Chaván, Cháran, Koli, Kumbhár, Pinjáro and Vánio suggest a mixed people, descendants of men of higher classes, who, either in times of famine, or from a passion for a girl of the tribe, or for some breach of caste rule, sank to be Vághris. It is at the same time more likely that Vághris took these higher class names because they formerly held service under Rajput and other high class families. That the Vághri community contains an element of higher caste outsiders seems beyond doubt.

Divisions. Vághris are divided into Chunarias or lime-burners, who are also cultivators and fowlers, Dátanias who sell twig tooth brushes, Vedus who grow and sell the *aria*, a species of gourd, and live in cities,

Pátánejis who trade in wood and bamboos and sell chickens, Salats who work in stone, Mori, Bagania, Kakodia, Bamcha and Pomla, all endogamous divisions. They are also sub-divided into Talabda, Por nála, Márwári, Kánkoria, Sáránia, Badia, Dhandari, Tori, Chawta, Chunara and others. The Talabdás and Pornalás neither eat nor drink with other divisions. The other divisions are of a lower grade and eat and drink together but do not intermarry. The Talabdás marry only among themselves. In Vánkáner, there are two main divisions of Vághris, one of which is again sub-divided into forty-four sections, *e.g.*, Sorankhia, Charolia, Kedval, Shrikáni, Lohia, Kuthia, Vaghelia, Bhesjalia, and others. All these were originally Rajput Garásias but degenerated afterwards. None of these intermarry. The second main division is that of the Vedvás, who are mostly found in Márwár. These two main divisions neither eat nor drink together nor intermarry. In the Panch Maháls there are many sub-divisions, the chief among them being Phatia, Kankodia, Chuvalia, Dandachor, Dhandaria, Vahola, Márwári, Verula, Dátania, Vedna, Chunária and Vasla. Their surnames are Vaghela, Parmár, Solanki, Chohán, Rathod, Sodha, Dangerathia, Vehuna, Maknigia, Kochdia, Baralia, Keplia, Jotania, Kanjia. In Surat, their sub-divisions are Ughád-pagia, Metrai, Khoblávála and Buchia. In Dhanduka, there are three divisions of Vághris, Lakadias or wood cutters, Vedarias or graziers, and Gámadiás or villagers. The habits of some of the Vághris are settled. According to some, Vághris admit high caste men into their caste by receiving a dinner from the convert.

Marriage rules.

Marriage with a maternal uncle's daughter, father's sister's daughter, and mother's sister's daughter is not allowed. Some Vághris marrying their daughters in a particular village take objection to marrying their sons with the girls of that village. A man can marry his wife's sister during the wife's life-time or after her death and two brothers may marry two sisters. Boys and girls are married after they are twelve years old. If a girl commits sexual indiscretions with a man of her caste or with a man of a superior caste before marriage, the girl is fined up to twenty rupees. But if she has cohabited with a man of a lower caste, she is turned out of her caste. A girl guilty of bad conduct is sometimes tried by ordeal, *i.e.*, her hand is dipped in boiling oil, or she is made to hold a burning charcoal. Polygamy is permitted, but polyandry is unknown.

Marriag ceremonies.

The offer of marriage either comes from the bride's or bridegroom's father. Twenty rupees are given to the bride's father together with a set of clothes for the bride. A Bráhman priest fixes the date of marriage and either he or a casteman, who acts as a priest, conducts the service of marriage. At the time of the betrothal the bridegroom and his parents come to the bride's house, where dinner is served, after which they go back. A few days before the marriage, a booth is erected before the houses of the bride and bridegroom. The boy is asked to dine at the girl's house, and when he is approaching the house a light is waved round his head. He is then taken to the marriage altar or *chauri*, a raised clay platform about five inches thick and about two feet square. On the platform are placed betelnuts and eight coppers. A Bráhman priest officiates in some cases, while in others one of themselves acts as a priest. The bride and bridegroom are made to bow to Ganesh, and afterwards, when their clothes are tied together, they take four turns round the *chauri* and sit on a quilt. A fire sacrifice or *hom* is performed, and a member of their caste joins the hands of the bride and bridegroom. A dinner is given to the caste in honour of the occasion.

Among Vághris of the Panch Mahals, the family goddess is first installed in the house before and during the marriage. No Bráhman priest officiates at the marriage. The younger brothers of the bride and bridegroom are marked with vermilion. Marriage wristlets of the *midhal* (Vangueria spinosa) nut are tied round the wrists of both the bride and bridegroom, and the skirts of their garments knotted together. They are made to bow before the goddess, and their hands are joined together. The wristlets as well as the knots are untied by the men who first tied them, and they are rewarded in cash or kind by the parents of the bride and bridegroom. The bride and bridegroom are then fed with *kansár*, that is, wheat-flour mixed with clarified butter and sugar, and the marriage is complete.

Widow marriage is allowed. A widow is allowed to marry the younger brother of her deceased husband or any other member of his family. A widow remarriage is celebrated on Sunday, Tuesday or Thursday. The new husband of a widow gives her a pair of *sáris*. The widow puts these on, and they both sit near each other. A saucer containing a lighted lamp and molasses is placed near them. Then the hands of the widow and the bridegroom are filled with grains of rice five times, and their brows are marked with red powder. A cotton thread is passed round them, they are fed with molasses, and they are husband and wife. The widow's new husband pays to her father from twelve to twenty rupees, and if he be a bachelor the sum exceeds this amount by one to five rupees.

Divorce is allowed, and is effected with the consent and in the presence of the headman of the caste, in cases of incompatibility of temper or when a husband or his wife is suffering from some incurable disease. The act of divorce consists in tearing a piece of cloth from the husband's and wife's garments. The wife, in addition to this, takes off the bangles from her right arm and gives them to her husband. A deed of divorce is then passed on a stamped paper. A woman divorced for adultery with a man of her caste or with a man of a higher caste is allowed to remain in her caste on paying a fine of five rupees. But when she has committed adultery with a man of a lower caste, she is turned out of her caste.

Vághris follow the Hindu law of inheritance and believe in spirits and lucky and unlucky days and omens. In the Panch Mahals many of them are called spirit-slayers. They believe that all diseases are caused by spirit-possession. The Bhuvás are the only Vághris into whose bodies Vihátmáta enters. Except these Bhuvás, men of the Vághri caste are seldom possessed. Among the women, cases of possession are not uncommon. They believe that their *daklo* or hourglass-shaped drum has power to force the possessing spirit to give its name and state on what terms it will leave the possessed.

Vághris are Hindus by religion and worship gods and goddesses, Religion chief amongst whom are Dagaiya, Hanumán, Kálika, Khodáir, Maháráj Meladi, Thákor, Varbhani, Hadki, Sámal, Vishotri, Shakti, Rupni and Vihát; they also worship planets and elements. Some of them are followers of the Bijpanthi sect. They make sacrifices of animals for the propitiation of the goddesses on Sundays and Tuesdays. The worshippers of goddess Vishotri make an offering of a calf, while those of Sámal Máta make an offering of a goat. Occasionally an offering of 1¼ seers of *sukdi* (wheat flour) mixed with sugar and *ghi* is made for the propitiation of their dead ancestors in the month of *Chaitra* (March-April). They go on pilgrimages to Benaras, Dwárka, Girnár, etc. Their principal holidays are *Holi* in *Fálgun* (March-April) fullmoon, *Gokal Ashtami* or Krishna's birth-night, the dark eighth of *Shrávan* (August-September), *Navarátra*, the Máta's nine nights, the *Diváli* or lamp feast in October-November and *Amli Agiáras* in March-April. On the *Gokal Ashtami* day in August-September they make a clay Krishna. The women sing and dance before him, and next morning throw him into the sea. On *Navarátra* or Máta's nine nights they fast, and some of them keep images of the goddess in their huts. On the *Ambli Agiáras* day they eat uncooked food and plant a tamarind tree in front of their house and worship it with red powder.

flowers, frankincense, etc. They have religious preceptors of their own. They need no Bráhman priests for betrothals, marriages or deaths, but sometimes give small presents of a copper or two to a Bráhman if he visits their houses and makes a *chándla* or red powder mark on the forehead. The *gor* of the Vághris is an Audich Bráhman. The Bhuvás or priest-mediums play an important part in many Vághri ceremonies. A Bhuva is a male child born after the mother has made a vow that, should Vihát grant her a son, she will devote him to Vihát's service. No Bhuva may cut or shave his hair on pain of a fine of ten rupees, and no Bhuva may eat carrion or food cooked by a Musalmán.

Vághris pride themselves on the chastity of their women. When a family returns home after a money-making tour to Bombay or some other city, the women are taken before Vihát, and with the women is brought a buffalo or a sheep, which is tethered in front of Vihát's shrine. They must confess all, even their slightest short comings. "Two weeks ago when begging in Pársi Bazár Street a drunken sailor caught me by the hand. Another day a Miya or Musalmán ogled me, and forgive me, Devi, my looks encouraged him." If the Devi is satisfied the sheep or buffalo shivers. The Bhuvás cut off its head and after offering a few tit-bits in the goddess' fire the tribe holds a feast on its flesh. If the woman fails to make a clean breast of her shortcomings, Vihát refuses her offerings, and, in her wrath, sickens or slays some member of the family. If a Vághri woman's chastity is suspected, her husband asks a Bhuva to attend at Vihát's shrine. He brings his wife along with a buffalo and sheep before the Mother. The sheep and the buffalo are tethered in front of the shrine. The husband asks the woman swear to tell the truth. The woman swears her innocence. The Bhuva addresses the Mother: "Mother, if this woman has committed no sin, be pleased to take the sheep." If the trembling of acceptance seizes the sheep the woman's innocence is half established. The Bhuva again turns to the Mother and says: "If this woman is guiltless be pleased to take this buffalo." If the buffalo trembles and falls, the woman is guiltless; and the Bhuvás attack the buffalo and sheep with their swords and slay them. Another ordeal is for the suspected woman to spread a cloth in front of the Mother. On this cloth the woman drops a handful of grain, generally wheat. The woman says either odd or even. If for eighteen continuous times the woman is right she is innocent. When in the first form of ordeal the victim is not accepted, or if in the second form the woman's choice proves wrong, the Bhuvás sit in judgment and fine the suspected woman, who has to suffer alone. The woman lives with her husband as if nothing had happened, only a little lowered in the estimation of her neighbours.

Generally Vághris bury the dead, burning being too expensive. Those who have visited Benares or some such holy place are occasionally burnt, and the ashes and bones of the dead are thrown into a river or are sent to a holy place for immersion. While burying, the head of the dead is turned towards the north. On the occasion of the death of a grown up member of a family a caste-dinner, consisting of rice, *mug* and *ghi*, is given, and about a hundred rupees spent. In the Panch Maháls the mourners bury the dead, then bathe, and return home. They eat *nim* or Indian lilac leaves, and wash their mouth with water and are considered pure. The son in-law of the deceased brings cooked *juvár* from his house and feeds the mourners with it. On the third day the chief mourner shaves his face clean and bathes and takes a ball of wheat from the house of the deceased and places it on the spot under which the body is buried. On the twelfth or some other day a caste feast is given if the means of the deceased permit. At Gogha on the twelfth day cooked rice, pulse and oil are given to the sister's son and to dogs. In Cutch every year or every alternate year a Bráhman priest is called, a new sacred thread is put on, a sacred fire is kindled, and the tail of a cow is bathed in water. **Death ceremonies.**

Vághris earn their livelihood by various means. They go to work in the fields when there is work to be had. At other times they tend *mahuda* (Bassia latifolia) and *rayán* (Mimusops hexandra) trees. They pay a lump sum to the owner of the trees, and sell the produce. They grow vegetable and fruit for sale. They generally keep fowls and sell eggs, catch birds, and go as *shikáris* or hunters. At other seasons they move from village to village, repair grind stones, rear sheep, goats and cattle and sell them. Some are labourers. The Vághris of Nadiád earn their livelihood by painting. Some keep pack bullocks and work as carriers. They closely imitate the call and voice of game and wild animals; they catch birds and make Hindus pay for letting them go. They supply the twigs used in the tooth-cleaning and they fish in rivers. They chiefly depend on begging. They beg also under the disguise of *Jogis* or astrologers. They traffic in green parrots which they buy from Bhils and sell for profit. They have a bad reputation for stealing. A few Vághris are said to have benefited in Ahmedabad by the introduction of steam factories, and a few have laid out their money in ornaments **Occupation.**

and in building houses. They trade in young bullocks, which they take in droves to all parts of Gujarát, from Sirohi in Rajputána to Bulsár; and sell to cultivators, giving their customers a year's credit

Food. Excepting the cow and jackal, they eat all animals, including the pig. They do not eat carrion nor, as they say, other than Hindu food. Their favourite food is the flesh of the iguana or *gho* and *sandha*, a reptile of the lizard species but darker and faster, living in the sand. They eat the leavings of other people and drink liquor. They do not eat at the hands of lower castes such as Mochis, Bhangis, etc., or of Musalmáns.

VAGMUDI VAIDU.—A sub-division of Dádhichevála Vidus.

VAHIVANCHA.—A sub-division of Bháts.

VAIBASE.—A sub-division of Kaikádis.

VAIDESHI.—A sub-division of Nhávis.

Name and origin. **VAIDUS,** or sellers of drugs, from *vaid* a drug, numbering 1,103 (1901), including 586 males and 517 females, are mendicant physicians and beggars. They are an interesting instance of a caste recruited from numerous other castes, such as Bhois, Dhangars, Kolis, Mális, and Phul-mális. Probably the census figures are inaccurate as many would have returned themselves by their original caste-name. Nearly half were recorded in the Poona district, and the rest almost entirely in the Khándesh, Násik and Ahmednagar districts. They allege that they originally came from Hyderabad territory, and this seems probable from the fact that they still worship as spiritual teacher a Dhangar of Kudermatti near Hyderabad, and their god is Venkoba of Tirupati. It would appear that the bulk of the caste were originally Dhangars, and that a new element has been introduced since they came to the west Deccan by recruitment from Maráthi-speaking castes. Many Vaidus still speak Telugu at home.

Endogamous divisions. Vaidus consist of three main endogamous divisions, namely *Jholiwálás* or bagmen, *Dádhichewálás* or bearded men, and *Chataiwálás* or mat-weavers. Among the Dádhichewálas are the following divisions which eat together but will not intermarry :—

(1) Bhoi	(6) Mirju-máli.*
(2) Dhangar	(7) Phul-máli.
(3) Khutekar.	(8) Rával.
(4) Koli.	(9) Vágmundi.
(5) Máli.	(10) Zinga.

* Probably named after the Mirya hill near Ratnágiri, famous for its herbs — Bombay Gazetteer, Vol. XVI, p. 65.

Vaidus

Dádhichewálá Vaidus wear the beard. The other two divisions do not allow the beard to grow. Vaidus are known as Gols, Gandgirs, and Pandits in Miraj, Dhárwár, and Sirsi respectively.

All divisions of the Vaidus wander all over the Deccan and Konkan throughout the year, selling drugs and begging alms. They generally camp outside of towns and villages in cloth tents or *páls* which they carry with them on donkeys. They pretend to cure any disease from a simple cough or headache to hopeless dropsy or consumption. They also bleed both by cupping and by applying leeches. Besides drugs they also use mineral medicines and poisons. On halting at a village or town the men and women walk through the streets and lanes with one or two ochre-coloured cloth bags hung across their shoulders tied to both ends or to one end of a stick. These bags contain drugs, the skins of lizards, porcupine-quills, tiger claws, bear's hair and teeth, foxes' heads, and deadly poisons. As they move along they shout *Nádiparaksha Vaid* (pulse-feeling doctor), *Mandur Vaid* (medicine selling doctor), *Garmi Vaid* (heat-curing doctor), *Vaila okhád* (a cure for wind), *Sardila okhád* (a cure for cold), and so on. The women of the Chataiwálás also plait date-mats as they walk. The women of the Dádhichewálás grind quartz into the powder called *rángoli*. No Vaidu is allowed to work as a labourer. Any one found working for hire is put out of the caste and not allowed back until he feasts the whole caste. A few own lands which they cultivate themselves.

The Jholiwála Vaidus are also known as Marátha Vaidus. The exogamous sub-divisions, which are identical with surnames, are Ambile, Chitkal, Kolyanti, Mánpáti, Metkal, Farkanti, Shingade, More, Shitole, Pawár, Jádhav, and Shinde. The Dádhichewálás have the following surnames: Máli, Pavár, Koli, Parit, Ambile, Chitkal, Matkal, Shingádi, Mánpáti, Chanchivále. Persons bearing the same surname cannot intermarry. Marriages are prohibited within two degrees of relationship between descendants of brothers and sisters. According to some, the Jholiwálás have no *devaks* or marriage guardians. According to others, every section has a separate *devak*, and sameness of *devak* is a bar to intermarriage. But the information collected regarding the *devaks* shows that only those sections which bear the Marátha surnames have *devaks*, a fact which suggests the probability of the Maráthás who have joined this caste having retained their *devaks*. Instances of such *devaks* are the *pánchpálvi* of the Jádhavs, the axe of the Mores and Shitoles, and so on.

Exogamous divisions

Members from Kunbis and Dhangars are still admitted by the Jholiwála Vaidus. The novice is made to worship a cloth bag of their medicines, which is presented to him in the presence of the caste *panch*, and he is initiated into their art of healing. Next, a feast is given to the caste-people by the new comer, which completes the admission ceremony.

Girls are married after they come of age; boys after sixteen. Sexual license before marriage is not tolerated. Girls committing sexual indiscretions with caste-men or members from higher castes are retained in the caste on their paying a fine and giving a dinner to the caste-people. In some cases they are branded on the tongue with a red hot gold wire, or beaten with sticks of tamarind, while the man is scalded with hot water and branded with a copper pice. A curious practice of the Dádhichewálás is that a man guilty of such indiscretion is relegated to the Kadu or inferior division of the caste and only allowed to marry a girl who has been unchaste. If the man involved belong to such a low caste as Mahár or Máng, they are excommunicated. Polygamy is allowed and practised, but polyandry is unknown.

Marriage ceremonies.

The offer of marriage comes from the boy's father, who has to pay a *dej* or bride-price of Rs. 15 to the girl's father. The day for the marriage is fixed by the village astrologer. The service is conducted partly by a caste-elder and partly by a barber; but the Marátha sub-divisions employ a Bráhman also, while the Dhangar Vaidus or Telugu speakers call in a washerman. The marriage ceremonies of the Vaidus vary in minor details in different localities, and also in the different sub-divisions, in which can be traced the original castes from which this caste has been recruited. But the marriage ceremony common to all can be briefly described as follows:—

First, the bride and bridegroom are rubbed with turmeric paste and oil at their respective houses. Next, the boy is taken in procession to the girl's house and seated on a square of wheat grains formed on a piece of cloth spread on the floor. The girl is brought and seated to his left. Next, five unwidowed women, three from the boy's side and two from the girl's, apply cow-dung ashes or *bhasma* to their foreheads, and the day ends with a feast. Next day a *garsoli* or marriage string is tied round the girl's neck, *kankans* or marriage wristlets are tied round the right wrist of the boy and the left wrist of the girl by a barber, and the skirts of their garments are tied into a knot. The pair are then made to utter each other's name, and they are taken to the boy's house, where the knot is untied and the marriage ceremony ends. The essential portion is the tying of the *kankans*. Among the Marátha Vaidus, *i.e.,* those recruited after the caste came from Hyderabad, the *devak* is carried in a dish to Máruti's temple, placed before the image, and then brought back to be installed among the household gods of the newly married couple.

The remarriage of widows is permitted. A widow cannot marry a member of her late husband's section. A widow remarriage can be celebrated on any dark night except a new-moon day, during any month of the year except *Bhádrapad*. The ceremony consists in seating the pair side by side, applying red powder to the widow's forehead, filling her lap by another widow, and tying into a knot the ends of the pair's garments. Next, the pair are made to utter each other's name, which ends the ceremony. The widow and her new husband must hide themselves in a lonely place for three days after the marriage. On their return on the fourth day a feast is given to the caste-people.

A husband can divorce a wife if he cannot agree with her, her conduct is bad, or if she passes a single night away from home without the company of a relation. The sanction of the caste *panch* is required, to whom the wife's parents have to pay a fine of from Re. 1 to Rs. 3. A divorced woman can marry again after the fashion of the widow remarriage ceremony.

Religion

The caste follow the Hindu law of inheritance and belong to the Hindu religion. They worship all Bráhmanic and village gods, the special deities of their devotion being Venkoba, Mariamma and Máruti. They seldom go on pilgrimages. They observe only the *Dasara* and *Shimga* holidays. On the *Dasara* day they offer a goat to their gods and eat its flesh. Goats and fowls are also offered to gods on Sundays, Tuesdays and Fridays. Musalmán saints are reverenced. They have great faith in sorcery, witchcraft, soothsaying, omens, and lucky and unlucky days, and they consult oracles. In the Khándesh district, after the *Dasara* holidays they go to the Saptashringi hill, and, offering a goat to the goddess on the hill collect herbs, which they use in healing diseases. They consult Bráhmans only in fixing the marriage day, their marriage ceremony being conducted by a barber. All the other ceremonies are conducted by the caste elders.

Death ceremonies. The dead are either burnt or buried. All the Dádhichewálá divisions bury their dead. The married dead are buried in a sitting position ; the unmarried on their back. The corpse is placed in a sling hung from the middle of a pole, which is carried to the burial ground on the shoulders of two men. The corpse to be burnt is carried on a bamboo bier. On the third day after death the ashes of the burnt are thrown into water and an earthen jar filled with water and cooked rice are placed on the spot where the corpse was burnt or buried. On the eleventh day after death the chief mourner goes to a river with a Jangam and caste-men. He stands in the river, throws behind his back a winnowing fan containing three rice balls, and throws himself into the river, when the Jangam blows a conch shell and says that the deceased has gone to Kailás (the god Shivá's abode, meaning heaven). Eleven pice are paid to the Jangam and the party returns home. Within a month or two after death a feast is given to the caste-people. They do not perform the *shráddha* or any other ceremony to propitiate the deceased ancestors.

Food. They eat the flesh of goats, sheep, hogs, deer, jackals, rats and squirrels, and drink liquor.

The Dádhichewálá Vaidus do not differ much from the Jholiwálás but the following peculiarities may be noted. They do not limit the age of marriage, but betroth the couple a few days after birth. They worship Venkoba of Tirupati in North Arcot, and eat the flesh of crocodiles.

Chataiwálás resemble the Marátha or Jholiwálas in all respects.

VAINSH VADHRA.—A sub-division of Bráhmans.

VAISHE.—A synonym for Lohána.

VAISHYA.—A sub-division of Sonárs and Sutárs.

Name and origin. **VAITIS** numbering 2,766 (1901), including 1,516 males and 1,450 females, are found only in the Thána district, a few being recorded in the adjacent district of Surat and in the State of Jawhár. They appear to be a degraded section of the Son Koli tribe, though they are socially inferior to them. Some of them state that the founder of their caste was Válhya Koli, others assert that his name was Kaivartaka. They trace their original home to Chaul in Kolába district.

Divisions. They have neither endogamous nor exogamous divisions.

Vaidu woman

Marriages are prohibited between persons related as brothers and sisters. A member of the caste is allowed to marry his wife's younger sister. Two brothers are not allowed to marry two sisters. Polygamy is allowed and practised, but polyandry is unknown. Girls are married either before or after they come of age. If a girl commits sexual indiscretions with a casteman, she may remain in the caste by paying a fine to the caste *panch*, and is free to marry her seducer. If the offence is committed with a member of another caste, the girl is excommunicated. Marriage.

The offer of marriage comes from the boy's father. When a match is settled, liquor is served to the party assembled. The boy's father has to pay a sum of money to the girl's father for the marriage expenses. The day for the marriage is fixed by a Bráhman who conducts the service. The *devak* of Vaitis consists of the *pánch-pálvi*. The marriage ceremony is the same as amongst local Kunbis.

The re-marriage of widows is permitted. A widow cannot marry a member of the family of her deceased's husband. A widow remarriage is celebrated in the months of *Chaitra*, *Jeshtha*, *Bhádrapad*, *Ashvin* and *Kártik*. A Bráhman priest and the caste *panch* attend the ceremony. Ganpati is worshipped, and a lucky necklace is tied round the widow's neck, which completes the ceremony. A bachelor is not allowed to marry a widow. Divorce is not allowed. A woman taken in adultery with a casteman can remain in the caste by paying a fine to the caste *panch*. If the offence is committed with a member of another caste, she is excommunicated. The caste follow the Hindu law of inheritance.

Vaitis belong to the Hindu religion. They chiefly worship Rám and the sea. They have no images in their houses excepting a cocoanut which they occasionally worship. They observe all the Hindu holidays and make pilgrimages to the sacred places of the Hindus. Images of deceased ancestors are worshipped with offerings of goats and fowls. When an epidemic breaks out, Jarimari is worshipped with offerings of goats, which are set at liberty in the name of the goddess. Their priests are Palshikar Bráhmans, but the death ceremonies are conducted by the caste elders. Religion.

The dead are burnt. Persons died of leprosy and small-pox and children up to a year old are buried with head to the south. On returning from the burning ground they go to their houses, bathe, and bringing their dinners to the mourner's houses, dine with them. Death ceremonies.

The bones and ashes of the burnt are thrown into water on the third or fifth day after death. On the 11th day rice balls are offered to the deceased and castemen are feasted.

Occupation. They are fishers, sailors, cultivators and day-labourers, and a few deal in timber and hay. They do not catch crocodiles or tortoises.

Food. They eat the flesh of goats, sheep, hares, deer, antelopes, swine, fowls and fish, and drink liquor.

VAJANTRI.—A sub-division of Nhávis and Mángs.

VAJARKAR.—A sub-division of Gavlis.

VAJIR.—A synonym for Khavás.

VALAM.—A synonym for Balam.

VALAND.—A synonym for Nhávi

VALANDRA.—A synonym for Vadádra.

VALAR.—A synonym for Shivate.

VALE.—A sub-division of Kolhátis.

VALEGAR.—A synonym for Sherogár.

VALER.—A synonym for Holaya.

VALGE.—A synonym for Halge Berad.

VALHARS numbering 985 (1901), including 523 males and 462 females, are found chiefly in the States of the Southern Marátha Country, a few being recorded in Poona and Dhárwár. In food, dress, religion and customs they do not differ from Kunbis, of whom they seem to be a division. They play on flutes and drums and beg. Some are husbandmen, some make horse whips, and some are day-labourers.

VALIAR.—A synonym for Vale.

VALMIK.—A sub-division of Káyasths; a synonym for Berad.

VALVAI.—A sub-division of Chodhrás.

VANIA.—A synonym for Lohána.

Name and origin. **VANIAS** or Vánis, numbering 352,138 (1901), including 183,742 males and 168,396 females, form the bulk of the trading castes of the Presidency excepting in the Karnátak and Southern Marátha Country, where they are represented by Lingáyat Bánjigs. Vánia, Váni or Bánjig is a functional term meaning a trader and is applied to members of other castes also who are traders by occupation. All the three terms are derived from the Sanskrit *vanij* a trader, Vánia being Gujaráti, Váni Maráthi and Bánjig a Kánarese term. Vániás are also called Baniyás and sometimes Vánis.

The Gujarát Vániás and Marátha Vánis are two distinct groups neither interdining nor intermarrying with one another. They are described below separately. Lingáyat Bánjigs are described under LINGAYAT.

GUJARAT VANIAS claim to be Vaishyas, the third of the fourfold division of Manu, although they do not perform the thread ceremony, which is compulsory in the case of the first three divisions. Possibly the caste may have evolved from members of many castes engaged in trade, who later, when they rose in social position on account of their wealth, claimed to be Vaishyas, as many castes claim to be Kshatriyas although there is nothing in their ceremonies and customs to support their claim. The fact, however, that the Vániás have still *mahájans* or trade guilds referred to in ancient Sanskrit literature, seems to indicate that they are connected by descent with the ancient Vaishya class.

Endogamous divisions.

Gujarát Vániás consist of forty sub-castes. They are as follows :—

1. Agarvál.
2. Agarya.
3. Bagaria (Bagada).
4. Báj.
5. Chhebroda.
6. Dasara.
7. DesháváI (Disával).
8. Dindu (Didu).
9. Govalvál (Goyalvál).
10. Gurjar (Gujar).
11. Harsola (Harsora).
12. Jelvál (Jailvál.)
13. Jhárola (Jhárora).
14. Kapol (Kapola).
15. Karad.
16. Katrivál (Kadharvál).
17. Khadáyata.
18. Khandevál.
19. Lád.
20. Ládsakka.
21. Mad.
22. Medora (Medera).
23. Meváda.*
24. Modh.
25. Modia.
26. Nágar.
27. Nágori (Nághori, Nágri).
28. Nandora (Nandodra).
29. Narsipura*
30. Nema* (Nima).
31. Osvál.
32. Palivál (Palilevál).
33. Porvád* (Porvál).
34. Pushkarvál
35. Sarviya (Sarvirja).
36. Shrimáli.*
37. Sorathia.
38. Ummad (Humad, Humbad).
39. Váyada.
40. Yerola.

Of the above the following have corresponding **Bráhman** sub-castes :—

Desháválí.	Modh.	Shrimáli.
Harsola.	Nágar.	Sorathiya.
Jhárola.	Nandora.	Váyada.
Khadáyata	Palivál.	
Meváda.	Pushkarvál.	

For an explanation of this similarity of names see **BRAHMAN.**

Those of the above divisions which have been marked with asterisks have Jain sections. The Hindu sections are commonly known as Meshri and the Jain as Shrávak. The Jain element predominates in the Porváds and Shrimális, while the Ummads and Osváls are wholly Jains. Most of the sub-castes are split into Visás or 'twenties' and Dasás or 'tens'. The Visa sections were probably so called because they represented pure descent than the Dasás can claim. In support of this theory it is to be noted that in some sub-castes still smaller sections are described as Panchás or fives, who are regarded as degraded and with whom other Vániás do not dine. All the main divisions with their Visa and Dasa sub-divisions and local sections generally eat together but do not intermarry. The close connection between the Meshri and Shrávak sections of these various Vánia groups is a good instance of the greater strength of the social than the religious nexus in Gujarát. In North Gujarát, Cutch and Káthiáwár, Shrávaks and Meshris eat together, and until the recent revival of sectarianism, used not infrequently to intermarry. But in Gujarát restrictions on marriage do not stop at the caste or sub-caste. The process of fission still continues, and each sub-caste is broken up into marriage groups (*ekadás* or *gols*) of villages or towns within which all girls are reserved as brides for the young men living in the circle. Originally these *gols* were a practical protest against the hypergamy of the town families. The latter naturally did not care to give their girls who were used to the luxury of a city life to husbands who lived in the country, but they had no objection to brides taken from rural surroundings, and for a time the attractions of a city home made all families established in cities truly hypergamous to those who retained a rural domicile. But it was soon found that brides were scarce for rural husbands, and the revolt led to the formation of these marriage groups which are now general in many castes throughout Gujarát. These groups are liable to change. Villages drop out or are added ; and it is stated that if a man cannot get a bride from within his own *gol*, he may marry a girl from another *gol* with the sanction of the *gol panchāyat*, sometimes on payment of a prescribed fine or fee. Thus these *gols* are not impassable barriers, and if a man is turned out of his own *gol* for giving a daughter outside the magic circle, he can find an asylum in the new group which he has thus benefited. He probably has also to feast the members of the new *gol* to obtain admission, but he almost certainly receives a handsome remuneration in the gift—no longer a free one as prescribed by the *shástra*—of a daughter.

All the Vánia sub-castes mentioned above resemble one another in most details in religion, ceremonies and customs. The points common to them all are described below, the peculiarities to each being described separately, under each of the important groups, at the end of this description. The Meshri and Shrávak groups differ from one another only in the performance of their ceremonies and in religion. They have been described below separately, the points common to them both being described first.

The different divisions of Vániás differ little in colour, but their appearance and dress varies according to locality. The main divisions in the matter of looks and of dress are into North Gujarát, Káthiáwár and Surat. The North Gujarát and Káthiáwár men and women are strongly and actively made, while the South Gujarát men and women are slightly made and of poor physique. Some Káthiáwár and North Gujarát Vániás wear whiskers, and most Surat Vániás wear the head hair shaven at the crown and in a line down the back of the head. South Gujarát Vániás always keep the moustache trimmed (1). Appearance.

The outdoor dress of Vánia men includes a turban, a waist cloth, a jacket *badan*, a longsleeved cotton coat *angarkha* reaching to the knees, and a shoulder cloth *pichodi*. The Vánia turban varies in different parts of Gujarát, partly in accordance with local customs, partly as a mark of special calling or profession. In Cutch and Káthiáwár Vániás employed in state service wear the loose scarf or *phenta*, probably a trace of the practice of their former Musalmán rulers. Vániás following other callings wear a large Rájput-like turban. The North and Central Gujarát Vánia wears a small tightly-folded cylinder-shaped turban with numerous folds in front and several coils behind. The Broach Vánia turbans are of two kinds, a small tightly-folded low caplike turban known as the Mughalái turban worn by Government servants, and the larger looser and higher North Gujarát turban worn by traders. The Surat Vánia turban Dress.

(1) *Bombay Gazetteer*, Vol. IX, Part I, pp. 74-75.

is round with folds in front, a projection at the crown, and a smaller horn on the right corner; the rightside back and top are covered with gold lace. The outdoor dress of a Vánia woman includes a robe *sádi*, a bodice *choli* or *canchli* and a petticoat *ghághra* worn under the robe. Almost all Vánia women have rich and gay clothes, some of silk with gold borders. [1]

Ornaments. Both men and women are fond of ornaments. If well to do, a man's every-day ornaments are a silver girdle and a gold armlet worn above the elbow; if he is rich, he wears besides these a pearl earring, a gold or pearl necklace, and finger rings; if he is very rich, he adds wristlets of solid gold. Costlier and more showy ornaments are worn at caste dinners and on other special occasions. A Vánia woman wears a goldplated hair ornament called *chák*, gold or pearl earrings, a gold and pearl nosering, gold necklaces, a gold armlet worn above the left elbow, glass or gold bangles or wooden or ivory wristlets plated with gold *chudás*, silver anklets, and silver toe and finger rings. Indoors a Vánia woman wears earrings, a necklace, bangles or wristlets *chudás* and anklets. [2]

Marriage rules. Many of the Vánia sub-castes claim to have *gotras* such as Aupamanya, Bháradwája, Chandrás, Gautam, Kapinjal, Káshyap, Kaushik, Páráshar, Sanakas, Sándil, Vatsa, etc., but few can tell to which *gotra* they belong, which shows that the *gotra* form of exogamy is still in the process of formation; and its absence indicates, as stated above, the evolution of the caste from divergent elements. Marriages are generally prohibited between near relatives. Marriage with a father's sister's, mother's sister's or mother's brother's daughter is not allowed. In theory there is no objection to two brothers marrying two sisters, but no instances of the kind are to be found in actual life. A Vánia may marry his deceased wife's sister. Polygamy is permissible with this restriction that the consent of the first wife is necessary. Polyandry is unknown. Except the Cutch section of Oswáls known as Letás and some Panchás, none allow widow marriage. Divorce is forbidden. Girls are generally married between seven and eleven. Among Kapol Vániás this limit is sometimes extended to sixteen, and among Ummads and Oswáls to twenty or even twenty-five.

Birth. MESHRI VANIAS:—A Vania woman generally goes to her father's house for her confinement. On the birth of a child the family astrologer is asked to note the time and the news is sent to the child's

(1) *Bombay Gazetteer*, Vol. IX, Part I, pp. 75-76.
(2) Do. do. p. 76.

father and his relations. The father and his relations go to see the child and give it money. The mother's father adds something to the gift and returns it. For ten days after the birth the husband's people and friends and relations of the mother daily send clarified butter, molasses and spices. On the sixth day the *Chhathi pujan* or sixth-day worship is performed. In the evening, on a footstool near the mother's bed are laid a piece of paper, an inkstand, a reed-pen, red powder, rice, flowers, six coppers, a lamp burning with clarified butter, a piece of a man's coat, molasses, and cocoakernel. These things are taken away on the following morning. On the morning of the tenth day the mother bathes, but continues to be considered impure for thirty days more. On the twelfth day the *báran balians* (twelve sacreds) are worshipped. Twelve small heaps of rice are laid on a footstool, and near them twelve betel-nuts, twelve betel-leaves and twelve copper coins. Red powder or *kanku* and flowers are dropped over them, and all are given to the family-priest. The mother worships the well, the door-post, and the house privy or *khál*. Generally on the twelfth day, but sometimes on some other suitable day, the child is named by the father's sister, who receives a robe (*sári*) worth about Rs. 4. In the third month after the birth, the mother is sent to her husband's house with a child's cap, petticoat, cradle, a silver anklet (*kalli*), and a girdle (*kandoro*).[1]

Betrothal

Children are betrothed sometimes immediately before and sometimes many years before marriage. Generally the parents of the boy and sometimes the parents of the girl make the offer of betrothal. If the other parents approve, the horoscopes of the boy and the girl are compared and, if the comparison is favourable, betrothal takes place. To complete the contract the girl's father, on a lucky day, pays Re. 1 to the caste fund. After this present has been made, the betrothal is in most cases not broken except when either of the contracting parties is found to be incurably diseased. In ordinary cases, after the present has been made to the caste fund, the boy's father, accompanied by four relations, goes to the girl's father and gives him Rs. 2 or 3 and the girl's father presents the boy's relations with cocoanuts and coppers. Then the boy and the girl are in turn asked to the father-in-law's house and get a money present varying from Rs. 5 to Rs. 10 according to the means of the giver. On the occasion of their first visit to the girl's house, the boy's parents also get from the girl's parents a money present according to the means of the girl's parents. Every year on *Diváli*

(1) *Bombay Gazetteer*, Vol. IX. Part I. p. 89.

(October-November), *Holi* (February-March), *Balev* (August), and *Dasara* (October), from the time of betrothal to the time of marriage, the girl gets new clothes and the boy a money present from their parents-in-law. Besides this, every year in *Ashád* or July, when the girl observes a five days' fast, dry and fresh fruit are sent to her by the boy's parents. In the first year after betrothal these presents are carried by the boy's female relations, the mother and sisters receiving a present of silver and the other women of copper coins.[1]

Marriage ceremonies.

Girls are married when they are seven, nine or eleven years old. Among Kapol Vániás some girls remain unmarried till they are fourteen or sixteen. The fixing of the marriage-day, which must fall between the eleventh of *Kártak Sud* (October-November) and the eleventh of *Ashád Sud* (June-July) rests with the girl's parents. Some days before the marriage the girl's father calls friends and relations and an astrologer who fixes a lucky day for the ceremony and is presented with husked rice and a rupee. The marriage-day is written on a roll of paper which is sent by the girl's family-priest to the boy's father, who feasts the priest and gives him a handsome present. Three or five days before the marriage, at both houses, Ganpati is worshipped, the family-deity is installed, and a booth (*mándva*) is erected. At each of the houses the *mándva*-making ceremony is performed. A hole about six inches deep is dug in a corner of the booth. The parents of the boy and of the girl with friends and relations sit near the hole and throw into it red powder, milk, curds, betel-nuts and a copper coin. A *khichda* (*Prosopis spicigera*) log about a foot long is dressed by a carpenter and while music is played it is set up in the hole. The women of the boy's and of the girl's families go separately to a potter's house with music, throw sandal-dust and flowers on the potter's wheel, and bring home earthen pots to be used in the marriage ceremonies. The bride and bridegroom, each at their houses, are then rubbed with turmeric and are given sweetmeats by friends and relations. The rubbing of the mixture is repeated till the marriage-day, and women relations sing songs in the mornings and evenings. One or two days before the marriage-day a ceremony in honour of ancestors and to propitiate the planets is performed at the house of the bride and bridegroom.

On the marriage-day at the bride's house a space generally in front of the entrance door of the house, about four feet square, is enclosed by four bamboo posts, one at each of the four corners. At each of

---

(1) *Bombay Gazetteer*, Vol. IX, Part I, pp. 89-90.

the four corners three bamboos are set in the ground, leaving between them a space of about eight inches, and round the three bamboos a red string is tied. In the space between the three bamboos seven plain empty earthen pots are piled, the largest at the foot, the smallest at the top. In the square, between the four piles of pots, which is called the *chori*, the bride and bridegroom sit and the marriage ceremonies are performed. On the marriage-day the brother of the bride's mother and the brother of the bridegroom's mother bring presents to the bride and bridegroom accompanied by musicians. The brother of the boy's mother gives the boy a pair of embroidered shoes, a cocoanut, a garland of flowers, and a waistcloth ; the brother of the girl's mother gives the girl a robe, a white satin bodice, ivory bracelets plated with gold, a gold nackless, a pearl nose-ring, silver anklets, and silver toe and finger rings. After the presents have been made the female relations of the bride go to the bridegroom's house, taking with them seven wheat cakes, a leaf-pot full of sugar, brass cups containing milk and curds, a pair of wooden sandals, and a silk and a cotton waistcloth. The mother of the bride offers these presents to the bridegroom, who eats, a piece of one of the wheat cakes, and the bride's party return to the bride's house. The bride is bathed at her house and the bridegroom at his house by four unwidowed women. They are dressed in the clothes and ornaments presented by their mother's brother and worship the family-deity. Then his mother's brother sets the bridegroom on a horse, the bridegroom holding seven leaves, seven betel-nuts, a cocoanut and a rupee in his hollow hands. To ward off the influence of the evil eye the sister of the bridegroom waves a pot of water over his head and pours it on the ground. The procession then starts between six and nine in the evening with music, the men walking in front of the bridegroom and the women behind singing songs, and the mother of the bridegroom holding a flaming lamp fed with clarified butter. At the bride's house, where in some cases the spiritual head or Mahárája has been invited to bring the blessing of his presence, the procession stops, the bridegroom alights from his horse, and stands on a wooden stool just outside of the doorway. Here he is met by the bride's mother, who makes a red mark on his brow, pulls his nose, and shows the bridegroom a miniature plough, a grinding pestle, a churning stick, and an arrow. A ball of cowdung ashes is then thrown towards each of the four quarters of heaven. Two small earthen pots full of curds are held mouth to mouth, waved seven times round the bridegroom's body, and set on the ground ; the bridegroom puts his right foot on the pots, breaks them to pieces, and enters the marriage-hall (*mándva*). He is then led to the square (*chori*) where he sits on a wooden stool, and, with the help of the family-priests, worships Ganpati. The parents of the bride then wash the bridegroom's great toes with milk, curds, honey, sugar and clarified butter. After the worship is over, the bride dressed in ornaments and clothes presented to her by her mother's brother is brought in and placed by her mother's brother on another stool opposite the bridegroom. A piece of cloth is stretched between the bride and the bridegroom. The Bráhmans recite luck-bringing verses, and the family-priests watch the water-clock or time-keeper, shouting at intervals of a minute or two "*Sávadhán* (Take care, the time is near)." When the lucky moment comes, the hands of the bride and bridegroom are joined, the cloth between them is snatched to one side, the hems of their robes are tied together, the marriage garland of cotton threads is thrown over their necks, and the musicians strike up music. Then the relations and friends make presents to the bride and bridegroom. In the middle of the square (*chori*) a sacrificial fire is lighted. The brother of the bride then comes to where the fire is lighted, holding a winnowing fan with barley and sesame, and drops into the hands of the bride and bridegroom four pinches of barley and sesame. Then the bride and bridegroom, along with clarified butter, throw the barley and sesame into the fire, walk once round the fire, throw some more barley and sesame into the fire, and again walk round. This is repeated four times. Then the bride and bridegroom seat themselves on the stools, the bride on the bridegroom's left, and feed each other with four morsels of coarse wheat-flour mixed with clarified butter and sugar prepared by the bride's mother. The bridegroom and bride then worship the constellation of the Great Bear. Then the bride and bridegroom, in front of the family-deity inside the house, play at odd and evens, each in turn holding some coins in a closed hand and the other guessing whether the number of coins is odd or even. Luck in this game is an omen of luck in the game of life. The winner of the game will be the ruler of the house. Sometimes instead of the coins a deep brass plate or dish is laid near the house-hold god, filled with water, and into the water are dropped seven betel-nuts, seven copper coins, seven dry dates and a silver finger ring. The bride and bridegroom then dip their right hands into the dish and feel among the nuts and coins, each trying to be the first to come across the ring, for luck or cleverness in this is again a sign who will be the luckier and cleverer in after-life. The married couple then come back to the marriage-hall and the bride's father-in-law presents her with ornaments and the bride's parents make return presents to the parents of the bridegroom. The bride's male relations smear the chins and cheeks of the bridegroom's elder male relations with red powder or *kanku*, and dipping their hands into wet pink powder, mark with their palms the back and front of their guests' white calico coats. The same is done by the bridegroom's relations to the bride's relations. Then sweetmeats are served to the male and female relations of the bridegroom. When the refreshments are over, the bridegroom's carriage is brought, and with a great show of sorrow, generally with much real sorrow, even with tears, the bride's family bid her goodbye. Her mother worships the carriage, sprinkling sandal-dust and flowers on one of the wheels and laying a cocoanut in front of it as an offering to the carriage that it may bear them safely. When the carriage moves, the mother gathers the pieces of the cocoanut and lays them in her daughters lap. No one from the bride's house goes with the party. It consists wholly of the bridegroom's friends and relations, the men walking in front of the carriage and the women walking behind, singing songs. The bridegroom is given a couch, a mattress, a plate, and a jar by the bride's father, besides other articles of value. When the procession reaches the bridegroom's house the bride and bridegroom, with the ends of their clothes tied together, step out of the carriage and stand in front of the doorway on a wooden stool. The bridegroom's sister keeps the doors closed until she receives money presents from the bridegroom. They are then led into the house by the bridegroom's mother and taken to bow before the family-deity, and again before the god they play at odd and evens to see which of them is the luckier. This ends the marriage ceremony. Caste dinners are given at the house both of the bride and of the bridegroom on the marriage-day or on some day before or after the marriage. The relations of the bridegroom have a right to dine at the bride's house, but the relations of the bride do not dine at the bridegroom's house [1].

Two ceremonies are performed at the husband's house in honour of a woman's first pregnancy. One called *Panchmási* takes place generally at the beginning of the fifth, and the other called *Simant* generally in the seventh month. In the beginning of the fifth month the family astrologer fixes the lucky days for the *Panchmási* and *Simant* ceremonies. As a rule the *Panchmási* ceremony is performed in the fifth month, but when this is difficult or inconvenient it is performed on the *Simant* ceremony **Pregnancy.**

(1) *Bombay Gazetteer*. Vol. IX. Part I. pp. 90-93.

day. In the morning of the lucky day in the fifth month the lap-filling or *kholo bharvo* ceremony is performed. The pregnant woman, wearing a white cotton robe and an embroidered bodice, accompanied by her mother-in-law and other elderly women of the family, comes in front of the house-god or *gotraj* and after bowing to the god, is seated on a low stool ; her mother-in-law, sister-in-law or some other unwidowed woman or *saubhágyavanti* lays in her lap five and a quarter pounds of rice, a cocoanut, betel-nuts and leaves, a rupee, a flower garland, and a robe bodice and petticoat, all of them supplied by the husband. Then the family-priest binds round the woman's right wrist a red thread or *nádáchhádi*, a piece of black silk cloth, an iron ring, five grains of Indian millet, some red lead and oil from an image of Hanumán, and the dust from the place where four streets meet. When the ceremony is over, the woman bows at the feet of her mother-in-law and the other elderly women. After the ceremony a dinner is given, generally to friends and relations, and in the case of the rich to the whole caste. In some sub-divisions of Vániás, at the end of the fifth month the pregnant woman goes to her father's house, and, after passing a night there, returns to her husband's house, on her return bowing low at her mother-in-law's feet.

The *Simant* ceremony is performed generally in the seventh or eighth and sometimes in the ninth month. For four days before the ceremony the woman is rubbed with turmeric powder, richly dressed, and decked with ornaments, and every evening seated on a raised seat among a crowd of women friends and relations who sing songs for two or three hours. When the singers leave they are presented with betel-nuts or coppers. On the fourth day the woman goes to her father's house and bathes. On coming back she stands at a short distance from her husband's house when her sister-in-law comes out with red powder and a white cloth which she lays on the ground for the woman to tread on, the parents dropping coppers and betel-nuts at every step the woman takes. Before she crosses the threshold her mother-in-law waves round the woman's head a miniature plough and other articles as at a marriage. She is then allowed to enter the house, care being taken that she steps over the threshold without touching it. Here she is met by her husband and they walk together followed by his mother, the Bráhman priest, and the women of his family, in front of the house-god or *gotraj*. After bowing to the house-god the husband and wife sit on two wooden stools holding each other's right hands, the wife on the left and worship the deity. At the close of the ceremony a party of *mosálu* including the woman's father, mother and brother all richly dressed and ornamented, come from the wife's family with presents of a wooden stool, a red earthen pot, a brass pot, a brass box, sweetmeats, and rich clothes in a basket. The woman's father gives her husband and his parents and other members of the family presents of garments or money or both. The same evening, and in some sub-divisions on the next evening also, the husband's father gives a caste dinner. After this ceremony is over the woman is asked to dinner by her friends and relations in turn. She attends wearing rich clothes and ornaments, and is given presents of clothes or of money. Fifteen or twenty days after the *Simant* ceremony the woman goes to her father's house where she stays till the child is three or four months old.[1]

Religion

Vániás are staunch adherents of the Vallabhácharya sect, to which they are said to have been converted about four hundred years ago. To the Mahárája or religious head of their sect they show extreme respect, though of late owing to the spread of education it has been slowly declining. Instead of the sacred thread, both men and women wear a basil bead necklace or *kanthi*. Only the Agarvál and Bam Nágar Vániás wear the sacred thread. They worship daily at the Vallabhácharya temples and in their houses, and of late they have in a great measure emancipated themselves from religious control by deciding that home worship or *seva* can take the place of public worship or *darshan*. This refusal of *darshan* was the Mahárája's great weapon of control over the community in former times; and nothing exhibits more clearly the weakening of religious control and the increasing power of wealth in Gujarát than this evasion of their spiritual authority's punishments. Their priests are Bráhmans who belong to the corresponding sub-division of the Bráhman community. Practically a plutocracy has arisen in Gujarát and the Vánia is often socially more important than the Bráhman.

Death ceremonies.

A Vánia on his deathbed gives a Bráhman the *gaudán*, that is, the gift of a cow or of a cow's worth not less than one rupee and four annas. He is then made to pour some water on the ground, saying 'So much (naming a sum) will be be given in charity after my death.' When the end draws near, he is bathed, and, with his head to the north is laid on a part of the entrance-room on the ground-floor, which has been cleaned with fresh cowdung wash. While he lies on the ground

(1) *Bombay Gazetteer*. Vol. IX. Part I. pp. 93-94.

he is told to remember Rám, and drops of *charanámrit*, that is, water in which the feet of the Mahárája have been dipped, and Ganges water and basil or *tulsi* leaves are laid in his mouth, a sweetmeat ball is laid on his mouth, and a lamp is lighted. If the dying person is a man, sandal-dust marks are made on the brow; if a woman, vermilion marks are made on her brow, temples and cheeks and lamp-black is applied to her eyes. When life is gone the body is covered with a sheet, and the relations raise a loud cry. A bier of simple bamboo poles is brought and the body is clothed in a waistcloth if a man, and in a silk robe if a woman, and bound on the bier and borne head first out of the house. The bier is carried on the shoulders of four near male relations who are called *dágus*, the chief mourner, going a little in front carrying, slung in a string, an earthen jar holding lighted cowdung-cakes. The widow of the deceased and other women of the family follow the party for some distance and then go back to the house. About halfway to the burning-ground the bier is turned round and set on the ground, and rice, betel-nuts and coppers are laid on the spot where the bier was rested. From this spot to the burning ground the body is carried feet first instead of head first. On the way the bearers chant to each other 'Call Rám, brother, call Rám' *Rám bolo bhái Rám*. At the burning-ground the body is unbound, bathed, and laid on the funeral pile. When all is ready the chief mourner takes out the lighted cowdung-cake from the earthen jar, and after dipping it in clarified butter lays the cake on the mouth of the corpse. He fills the jar with water, standing at the head of the corpse. He next walks round the pile and lights it at the head. When the body is being burnt all withdraw to a little distance. When the body is consumed, the fire is put out and the ashes are taken in a cloth and thrown into the sea or into a river. The place where the body was burnt is washed with water. Then an earthen pot of water is set on the spot and broken by a stone thrown by the chief mourner through his legs. A cow is brought and milked so that the milk may fall on the spot where the body was burned. The cloth which was drawn over the bier and the robe or waistcloth which were wrapped round the body are given to the Bhangia or sweeper. The carriers raise a loud cry, leave the burning-ground, bathe, and go home.

When the women who have followed the bier for some distance return to the house they break the widow's glass, ivory or wooden bangles, and, leaving her in the house, go and bathe in a river or pond, and return to the house before the funeral party come back from the burning-ground. On their return to the house of mourning the strangers go to their own houses. Soon after this, the father-in-law of the chief mourner sends rice, pulse and butter to the house of mourning. If the deceased was elderly it is cooked and eaten, and if the deceased was young the food is given to dogs. At the house of mourning, for ten days, female relations and friends come and weep morning and evening. Either on the day of the death or on the next day men also come to mourn. At this time milk and water are set on the *tolla* or wooden peg of the house on the first day by a Bráhman and on the succeeding three days by some member of the household. When the deceased has left a widow, on the tenth day caste-women come and weep. The widow's hair is cut off and the heads of the male members of the family are shaved, and, if the deceased was old, the men also shave their moustaches. On the tenth, eleventh, twelfth and thirteenth days the chief mourner performs death ceremonies. The leading rite on the eleventh day is marrying a steer to a heifer, on the twelfth day it is giving cooked food to crows, and on the thirteenth day it is giving a bedstead, bed-clothes and some money to a Bráhman. If the deceased was an old man, the chief mourner, when he makes gifts to the Bráhman, receives from his friends and relatives money presents to buy himself a turban. Caste dinners are given on the twelfth and thirteenth. At the end of each month for a year after death the *másiso* or monthly death ceremony is performed, when a few friends and relations are asked to dinner. At the end of the year a caste dinner is given. In the case of a rich old man caste dinners are given two or three times in the year, and in memory of the deceased presents of a copper or brass pot with some sweetmeats in it are made to the caste people.[1]

Occupation.

Of Gujarát Vániás a few are landholders and some are in Government or private service, but the bulk are traders and shop-keepers. Most Vánia landholders have invested in land money made in trade or as pleaders. The rest are mortgagees or holders of lands granted for services rendered as district revenue superintendents *desáis* and as district accountants *majmundárs*. Of those in service the greater number are in native firms, some in posts of trust well paid and with chances of private trade and profit; others simple clerks poorly paid and badly off. Of the rest, some are in Government employ, many as clerks and a few in high positions. Some, especially among the Modhs, are clerks and administrators in the Native States of Káthiáwár and in Cutch, some are in European merchants' offices and in railway and spinning companies in Bombay. A few earn

(1) *Bombay Gazetteer*, Vol. IX, Part I, pp. 94-95.

their living as lawyers, medical practitioners and engineers and still fewer as mechanics, manufacturers and craftsmen.

Food. Vániás are strict vegetarians and the use of liquor is forbidden. They eat food cooked by Bráhmans only.

AGARVALS are found chiefly in North Gujarát and take their name from the ancient Indian midland town of Agar about forty miles north-east of Ujjain. The Agarváls are said to have come from Rájputána, where they occur in large numbers. They are divided into Visás or twenties and Dasás or tens. Their family-priests are Agarvál Bráhmans. They wear the sacred thread. The Agarváls are proverbial for their impatience of caste control and for disregard of caste distinctions. The Hindi proverb illustrative of their character runs : *Agarvále sab Thakrále*, that is, Among Agarváls each individual constitutes himself chief.[1]

CHITRODAS are found in Broach and Baroda. They take their name from Chitrod in Rájputána. Their family-priests are Chitroda Bráhmans.[1]

DESAVALS are found chiefly in North Gujarát. They take their name from Deesa, an ancient town near the military station of the same name about eighty-nine miles north-west of Ahmedábád. They are divided into Visás, Dasás and Panchás. The Dasás are further sub-divided into Ahmedábádis, Suratis and Ghoghtáris Both Visás and Dasás eat together but do not intermarry. The Panchás form a separate community. The Suratis and Ahmedábádis sometimes intermarry but not without a fine as penalty. At marriages the bride and bridegroom go round the *chori* or square eight times instead of four times as is the case among other Vániás, and the *kansar* with which the pair feed each other is composed of curds and molasses instead of wheat flour, sugar and clarified butter. Their family-priests are Desávál Bráhmans.[1]

DIDUS are found chiefly in Surat. They are said to have come to Surat from Márwár about three hundred years ago when Surat was the great centre of trade. They take their name from Dindvána, a small town in Márwár. They are not divided into Visás and Dasás, but have two divisions Didus and Nághoris who obtain their name from Nághor in Márwár. They are an offshoot of the Meshri Vániás of Márwár. Both dine together and intermarry. Their family-priests are Shrimáli Bráhmans.[2]

(1) *Bombay Gazetteer*. Vol. IX. Part I. p. 70.

(2) *Bombay Gazetteer*. Vol. IX. Part I. p. 71.

GUJARS are found chiefly in Ahmedábád, Broach and South Gujarát. They are said to have settled in Gujarát before the other Vániás. Most of them work as clerks and traders but some hold rent-free lands which they are said to have received in reward for bringing the land under tillage. There seems little reason to doubt that these Vániás were originally Rajputs, some of whom have continued Rajputs under the name of Chávadás, Parmárs and Solankis, and represent the seventh century Gurjara rulers of North Gujarát and of Broach. Formerly the Gujars were divided into Visás and Dasás. Lately the Visás finding themselves diminishing joined the Dasás. Their family-priests are Shrimáli Bráhman. (1)

HARSOLAS are found chiefly in North Gujarát. They take their name from Harsol about thirty miles nort-west of Ahmedábád. Their family-priests are Harsola Bráhmans. (1)

JHAROLAS, commonly called Jhálorás, are found chiefly in Baroda and East Gujarát. They take their name from the well-known fort and trade centre of Jhálor in Márwár, the seventeenth century northern limit of Gujarát about halfway between Jodhpur and Shrimál. They are divided into Visás, Dasás and Panchás. The Visás and Dasás dine together but do not intermarry. The Panchás form a separate community. Their family-priests are Jhálora Bráhmans.(1)

KAPOLS are found chiefly in Káthiáwár and trace their origin to Junágadh or Girnár. They are not divided into Visás and Dasás. They are chiefly found in Amreli, Delvára, Mahuva, Bhávnagar, and Sihor in East Káthiáwár. Their family-priests are Kandolia Bráhmans, who take their name from Kandola near Thán in Káthiáwár. Their family-goddess is Samudri Máta, whose chief shrine is at Sundri, a Dhrángadhra village twenty miles from Thán. The Kapols hold a high place in Bombay, where some of their families are said to have been settled for about 150 years. (1)

KARAD VANIAS are found principally in Cutch. They are supposed to be an offshoot of the Meshri Vániás, and are said to have migrated to Gujarát, Káthiáwár and Cutch from Márwár, their original home. They trace their descent to two Meshri (2) Vániás, Aja and Angore, who gave shelter to a prince named Ful when his father, a chief of Kanthikot in Cutch, was assassinated by his brother-in-law Dharan, chief of Ghedia. When Ful came of age, he invited Aja, Angore and their sister Boládi to his court, and in recog-

(1) *Bombay Gazetteer*, Vol. IX. Part I, p. 71.

(2) There is a sub-caste of Vániás in Márwár known as Mahešri or Meshri.

nition of the shelter given to him by the two brothers named two of his forts after them. This is said to have happened about the year A.D. 900. Later Aja and Angore had a dispute with their caste-fellows, from whom they separated breaking an agreement *karár*, and formed a separate caste. Karád is thus supposed to be derived from *karár*.

Karád Vániás have several sub-divisions. The chief of them are :—

Badad.	Kurva.	Rabadia.
Dhrona.	Mándan.	Vitária.
Khombhadia.		

Owing to the decrease in the numerical strength of the caste they are not allowed to marry into their own caste, but must marry girls of the Dasa Oswál Vániás. They are mainly followers of the Hindu religion, but some, on account of their intercourse with Dasa Oswál Vániás, have taken to the Svetámbari and Derávási sects of Jainism. Still they have all a leaning for the worship of Shiva. In other respects they resemble the general Vánia community.

KHADAYATAS, found all over Gujarát, take their name from Khadát, a village near Parántij about thirty-five miles north-east of Ahmedábád. They are divided into Visás and Dasás. Their family-priests are Khadáyata Bráhmans and their family-deity is Kotyarkeshvar of Khadát Mahudi near Vijápur in Baroda territory. They are said to be an offshoot of the Nágar Vániás. Among Khadáyatás large sums of money are frequently paid for marriageable girls.

LADS are found chiefly in Baroda, Broach, Dabhoi and Surat. They take their name from Lát-desh, the old name of South Gujarát. They are divided into Visás and Dasás. Their family-priests are Khedávál Bráhmans, and their family-deity is Ashápuri of Ashnai near Petlád. Lád women, especially those of Baroda, are noted for their taste in dress. Their old surnames are Khata, Khichadia, Patári and Rokadia, and their old names ended with *rai* and *pál* instead of *dás* as Kalánrái and Dhanpál.(1)

MEVADAS are found cheifly in Baroda, Kaira and Surat. They are said to have come from Mewár. They are divided into Visás and Dasás. Their family-priests are Meváda Bráhmans. They are partly Vallabhácharya Vaishnavs and partly Jains.(1)

(1) *Bombay Gazetteer*. Vol. IX. Part I, p. 72.

MODHS are found all over Gujarát but chiefly in North Gujarát and in Káthiáwár. They take their name from Modhera on the banks of the Vátrak about eighteen miles north-east of Ahmedábád. They form an important element in the Vánia community, including three subdivisions, Adálaja from the village of Adálaja about ten miles north of Ahmedábád; Ghoghva from Gogha in East Káthiáwár; and Mándaliya from Mándal, formerly a place of consequence, about forty-eight miles north-west of Ahmedábád. None of the three sub-divisions intermarry in Gujarát proper, though the Goghvás and Adálajás intermarry in Káthiáwár and Cutch. They are divided into Visás and Dasás. At the wedding of Modh Vániás a sword and a flywhisk are used. The sword suggests a Rajput origin, but no trace of tribal surnames remains. The family-priests of Modh Vániás are Modh Bráhmans and their family-deity is at Modhera. Besides engaging in trade, Modh Vániás have proved able and successful administrators in Native States. The large class of oilmen known in Gujarát as Modh Ghánchis were originally Modh Vániás who, by taking to making and selling oil, lost their position as Vániás.(1)

NANDORAS are found in Surat and Rewa Kántha. They take their name from Nándod, the capital of Rájpipla. Their family-priests are Nándora Bráhmans and their family-deity is Nandikeshvar Mahádev of Nándod.(2)

NAGARS are found all over Gujarát, Baroda and Kaira. Like Nágar Bráhmans, they claim Vadnagar as their original seat. They are divided into Visás and Dasás. Their family-priests are Nágar Bráhmans, and their family-deity is Hatkeshvar of Vadnagar. A small sub-division known as Bam Nágars pride themselves on being strict observers of religious ceremonials and do not eat with other Vániás. They wear the sacred thread and are mostly Shaivs.(3)

NARSIPURAS are found chiefly in Baroda. They are said to take their name from Narsipur in Pálanpur. Their family-priests belong to different divisions of Gujarát Bráhmans. They are partly Vaishnavs, partly Jains.(3)

NIMAS are found chiefly in Panch Mahál. They are said to have entered Gujarát from Márwár about two hundred years ago. They are divided into Visás and Dasás who neither eat

(1) *Bombay Gazetteer*, Vol. IX, Part I, p. 72.
(2) Do. do. pp. 72-73.
(3) Do. do. p. 73.

together nor intermarry. The Visás are both Vaishnavs and Jains and the Dasás are followers of the Vallabhácharya sect. Their family-priests are Udambara Bráhmans, and their family-deity is Shámláji near Idar. Marriages among Dasás take place in alternate years on a day fixed by the caste.(1)

PORVADS are found all over Gujarát. They are said to take their name from Porvád, a suburb of Shrimál, the old capital of south Márwár. They are divided into Visás and Dasás. Their family-priests are Shrimáli Bráhmans, and their family-deity is the Shri or Mahálakshmi of Shrimál. They are partly Vaishnavas partly Jains.(1)

RAYAKVALS are found chiefly in Ahmedábád. They take their name from Ráika near Dhandhuka. Their family-priests are Ráyakvál Bráhmans.(1)

SHRIMALIS are found all over Gujarát but chiefly in Ahmedábád and Kaira. They take their name from Shrimál, now Bhinmál, in Márwár, about fifty miles west of Mount Abu. Like Osvál Vániás, they were formerly Solanki Rajputs and originally Gurjars. They are divided into Visás and Dasás, who eat together but do not intermarry. Their family-priests are Shrimáli Bráhmans and their family-goddess is Vágheshvari of Shrimál. The Visa Shrimális are exclusively Jains. The Gujarát Shrimáli Sonis or goldsmiths originally belonged to the Shrimáli Vánia class.(1)

SORATHIYAS are found chiefly in south Káthiáwár. They take their name from Soráth, the south coast of Káthiáwár. They are divided into Visás and Dasás. The Sorathiyás of the sea-coast towns, chiefly Porbandar, Mángrol, Verával, Jáfarábád, and Diu, are remarkable for their commercial enterprise. From ancient times they have been in the habit of making voyages to Arabia and Zanzibar, going in their youth and returning to their native land after nine or ten years, when they generally marry. The Bombay brokers and trade agents known as Chháparias are chiefly Sorathiya Vániás. Their family-priests are Kandolia Bráhmans, and their family-deity is Sámudri, whose chief shrine is at Sundri in Dhrángadra.(2)

UMMADS are found chiefly in north Gujarát. They are said to have entered Gujarát from Márwár about two centuries ago. They are divided into Visás and Dasás. Their family-priests are Audichya and other Gujarát Bráhmans. They are partly Vaishnavs, partly Jains.(2)

---

(1) *Bombay Gazetteer*, Vol. IX, Part I, p. 73.
(2) Do. do. p. 74.

VAYADAS are found chiefly in north Gujarát. They are said to take their name from Váyad, a village near Pátan, about fifty-four miles north-west of Ahmedábád. They are divided into Visás and Dasás, who eat together but do not intermarry. The Visás are further divided into Ahmedábádis and Suratis, who eat together and intermarry. Their priests are Váyada Bráhmans. Most of them are Vaishnavas of the Vallabhácharya sect, and a few are Shaivs. Unlike other Vániás, the bridegroom goes to the bride's house in an open bullock cart with his face masked in cloth, and the marriage ceremony takes place at or after midnight. On his way to the bride's house the bridegroom performs the *chakla* or cross-roads worship. In the middle of the square a sweet ball is placed on a fried cake, and at each corner an earthern pot with a sweet ball and a copper in it. During the worship, to conceal the bridegroom from public gaze, a strip of cloth is held round him by his friends and relations. After the worship is over, the corner pots are given to four unmarried boys as a lucky present to ensure a speedy marriage. A sweet ball is then set on the ground and on it a waistcloth is spread. On the waist cloth a sword is placed and the bridegroom's cart is made to pass over the sword. If the edge of the sword is broken it is considered a bad omen. The bride also performs the cross-roads worship in company of her friends and relations.(1)

SHRAVAK VANIAS :—Immediately before the birth of a child a midwife is called. If a male child is born, a brass plate is beaten and a Bráhman astrologer is asked to note the hour of birth. The news of the birth is carried to the child's father, and the door-posts of his house are festooned with the leaves of the *asopálo* (Polyalthia longifolia). molasses and coriander seeds are distributed among friends and relations, and if the father of the child is rich, music is played at his house. On the sixth day Mother Sixth or Chathi is worshipped with all the ceremonies observed by Meshris. In Pálanpur and other parts of north Gujarát the child is laid on a silk handkerchief and is rocked by four unmarried girls. On the tenth day the mother bathes, but remains unclean for thirty days more. The child is named on the twelfth, the fortieth, or some other day after the third month. Before naming the child they worship the family goddess or *gotraj*. The goddess is represented by a gold or silver plate, engraved with footprints, or by a leaf of the banyan (Ficus indica) tree, or by a dried mango stone. With the help of a Bráhman priest the representation of the goddess is laid

Ceremonies.

(1) *Bombay Gazetteer*, Vol. IX, Part I, p. 74.

with betel leaves and nuts on a heap of rice or wheat and vermilion powder, and flowers are thrown over them by the father's sister. The child's father feasts his friends and relations, and his sister names the child. The names of Shrávak women do not differ from those of other high caste Hindu women; but the names of men generally end in *chand* and sometimes in *ji*. Except among the well-to-do the full naming ceremonies are performed only in the case of the first boy; girls are named by the mother without any ceremony. On the fortieth day after childbirth the mother bathes and worships a well. No ceremony is performed at the first giving of cooked food to the child. When the child is three, five or seven years old, the boy's head is completely shaved, and a tuft of hair is cut from the back of the girl's head. Except that the boy is sent to school with music, and that friends and relations are feasted, no ceremonies are performed at the time of hair-cutting. The Shrávaks do not wear the sacred shoulder-cord At the time of worshipping their idols they were a silken tape or a piece of cloth or a gold chain across their shoulders in the way in which Bráhmans wear their thread. With few exceptions the Shrávak Vánia marriage ceremony is the same as that performed by Meshri Vániás. Boys and girls are betrothed sometimes immediately before and sometimes many years before the marriage. The marriage day is fixed by a Bráhman astrologer. Five days before the marriage the parents of both the bride and bridegroom worship an image of Ganpati which is painted with vermilion on the house wall. The women of the bride and bridegroom's families go separately with music to the potter's house, worship his wheel, and carry away a store of earthen jars. At the bride's house a marriage booth is made, one of the posts of which among the Nimás is of *gugal* Balsamodendron wood. A square or *chori* is made in the centre of the booth. No planet-pleasing or *grahashánti* ceremony is performed. On the day before the marriage the family goddess is invoked and worshipped. Among the Ládva Shrimális a razor made of wet wheat flour or of sugar is laid near the goddess. In the evening of the marriage day the bridegroom, dressed in rich clothes, with a cocoanut and a rupee in his hands and with a black silk thread tied to his right ankle to ward off the evil eye, goes on horseback with music to the bride's house, the men of his party walking in front, and the women, except for a few paces, among the Visa Shrimális in the rear. Among the Osváls the bridegroom wears a wedding coronet *mugat* and in other divisions a turban. In all he holds a sword in his hand. When he reaches the bride's house the bridegroom dismounts and is received at the entrance by the bride's mother. She shows him a miniature plough, an arrow, and a churning handle, pinches his nose, and leads him to the marriage booth. He sits on a wooden stool, and on his left on another stool sits the bride, who has been brought there by her maternal uncle. The bride's parents then formally offer the bride in marriage to the bridegroom. The maternal uncle lifts the bride and carries her four times round the husband. The Bráhmans recite texts or *mantras* : a piece of cloth is held between the bride and the bridegroom, and at the favourable moment, regarding which the Shrávaks are very particular, their hands are joined. The hems of the bride's and bridegroom's clothes are tied together and they walk four times round a fire which is lit in the middle of the central square. They then feed each other with coarse wheat flour and worship Ganpati and the family goddess. The bridegroom and bride then go with his friends and relations to his house, where they worship Ganpati and play at odd and evens. On the second or third day after the marriage the bride's father makes presents of money and clothes to the bridegroom and his near relations. In some villages bordering on Márwár the marriage consummation takes place on the marriage night. Before consummation the bridegroom presents the bride with ornaments worth from Rs. 25 to Rs. 100. On the second day the bridegroom and his friends are feasted by the bride's father with sweetmeats or with whey and millet. During the seventh month of a woman's first pregnancy, lapfilling *kholbharvo* and wristlet-tying *rákhdi* are performed. These ceremonies do not differ from the corresponding ceremonies among Meshri Vániás.[1]

Shravaks follow Jainism and are divided into two leading sects, Digambarás or air-clad and Svetámbars or white-robed. The Digambarás are also called Ummad and the Svetámbars Tappás. Among Digambarás the image has no eyes and no loincloth. Among the Svetámbars the image has gold eyes fixed with glass and a piece of linen carved round the loins. Again, the Digambara priests are naked and keep to their monasteries, and the Svetámbar priests are clothed. Of the two sects, the Svetámbar sect has by far the largest number of adherents in Gujarát. The Svetámbars are sub-divided into eighty-four sub-sects or *gachhas*, of which about fifteen to twenty only now remain. Of the existing *gachhas*, the Lonka *gachha* is more careful not to destroy animal life than the other *gachhas*. They believe in *arhats* or saints but are opposed to idol-worship and Religion.

(1) *Bombay Gazetteer*. Vol. IX, Part I, pp. 99—102.

ridicule the idea of an idol granting a prayer. The Shripujya or spiritual head of the *gachha* resides at Baroda and has *thivars* or deputies at Delhi, Ajmere and Jálar. The Shripujya goes every year on tour, visiting his disciples. About 500 years ago a schism arose in the Lonka sect. A priest disputed the authority of his Shripujya and was expelled the congregation. He practised severe austerities, and gaining a large following, founded a new *gachha*, which is called Dhundia. Like the parent *gachha*, the Dhundiás are opposed to idol-worship and building temples, and accept only thirty-two *sutras* or aphorisms of the Jain faith. Their priests do not beg, but live on such offerings of food and clothes as are freely made by the congregation and own no property. They are clad in white, and mask their mouths with linen to prevent their breath from killing insect-life. They never stir out in the rain lest they should kill some animal, and always brush the ground before they sit. Some go even to the length of brushing the ground in front as they walk. They neither wash their clothes nor any part of their body. The Dhundiás are mostly found in Káthiáwár. Their opposition to idol-worship has alienated most of their adherents in Gujarát proper.[1]

Though idol-worship is prohibited by Jainism, Shrávaks worship the images of the twenty-four Jain Tirthankars--or patron saints. In their temples or *dehrás* are also placed images of Hindu gods and goddesses below the idol of the principal Tirthankar in the temple or in other niches or shrines or upper storeys. The ministrants at the temples are mostly Shirmáli Bráhmans, sometimes Tapodhans, Mális and Kanbis. These ministrants, except when on duty, are allowed to act according to their own religion. Any Hindu who is not a flesh-eater or spirit-drinker is considered a fit temple servant. The principal holidays of Shrávaks are the *Pachusan* or *Paryusan* that is, the sacred season, and the *Siddhachakra Puja* or saint wheel worship. Among the Svetámbars, the *Pachusan* begins with the twelfth of the dark half of *Shrávan* and ends with the fifth of the bright half of *Bhádrapad*. Among the Digambaras the *Pachusan* lasts for fifteen days beginning from the fifth of the bright half and ending on the fifth of the dark half of *Bhádrapad*. The whole *Pachusan* period must be observed as a fast period, but, except a few devotees, almost all fast on the last day only. The *Siddhachakra Puja* is performed twice a year in *Chaitra* and *Ashvin* and lasts for nine days beginning on the seventh and ending on fullmoon day.

(1) *Bombay Gazetteer*, Vol. IX, Part I, pp. 105-106.

When a Shrávak Vánia is at the point of death a text from the Punya Prakásh is read to him by a religious-minded Shrávak, and an image of one of the Tirthankars is brought from the temple and shown him. The dying person makes presents to Bráhmans in grain and in cash. Among the Osváls and Shrimális the dying are dressed in their full dress; if a man, in a waistcloth, a long cotton tunic and a turban, and if a woman, in a bodice, a petticoat and a robe. After this robing they are laid on a mattress with a coverlet spread over it. Among other Shrávak Vániás a dying man is dressed in a waistcloth and a dying woman in a petticoat and bodice. The dying person is then laid with the head towards the north on a part of the floor which has been freshly cowdunged, but no *darbha* Poa cynosuroides, barely and sesame seed are strewn over it. When life is gone some sweetmeat balls are thrown to street dogs. Without washing or again changing the clothes the body is tied to a ladder-shaped bamboo bier and carried to the burning ground. The relations and castefellows follow, calling upon Rám. When the burning ground is reached the body is carried three times round the pile, the clothes are stripped off and the body is laid on the pyre. Except when the grandfather is alive, the eldest son of the deceased sets the pile on fire. After the body is burnt the mourners bathe and return to the house of the deceased. They then separate but meet again at the house, where they peep into the house well and wash their hands with earth and water. The near relations of the deceased remain unclean five to ten days. During these days of uncleanliness among the Osváls, the chief-mourner feeds bull-buffaloes. On the last day of mourning the near male relations of the deceased have their head and chin shaved. The practice of shaving the upper lip which was common fifty years ago is falling into disuse as it is contrary to the Jain religion. The widow of the deceased, if an elderly woman, has her wristlets broken but her head is not shaven. She wears an ochre-coloured robe and, like a Meshri widow, wears no ornaments, makes no brow-mark, and does not anoint her head. If the widow is a young woman, the only change that is made in her dress is that she is not allowed to wear jingling anklets and earrings and to make the brow-mark. Between the end of the mourning and the thirteenth day the Gorji is daily feasted. Except among the Bhawsárs, Sálvis and other artisan classes who have adopted Jainism, no memorial or *shráddha* ceremony is performed between the tenth and the thirteenth, but presents of grain, clarified butter, molasses and coppers are made to Bráhmans. On the thirteenth day the chief-mourner goes to the temple, worships the idols with the help of

Death ceremonies.

Bhojaks, and makes offerings of safflower, frankincense and sandalwood, and if his means permit, ornaments and clothes. In honour of the deceased the chief-mourner feasts his friends and relations or his castepeople, or, if he is well off, the whole village. Shrávak Vániás do not keep monthly or yearly memorial days.[1]

Shrávaks are strict vegetarians and are more careful than Meshris not to take animal or vegetable life.

MEVADAS are found chiefly in Baroda and north Gujarát. Meváda Shrávaks were originally Ummad Shrávaks. Within the past sixty years many have adopted the Vaishnava religion and are called Meváda Meshris. Their family-priests are Meváda Bráhmans.[2]

NARSIPURAS are found chiefly in Baroda. They take their name from Narsipur in Pálanpur.[2]

NIMAS are of two divisions, Visás and Dasás. The Visás are both Vaishnavas and Jains, and the Dasás are Vaishnavs. The Visa Vaishnavas and Jains used to intermarry but the custom has ceased since A. D. 1850. Their family deity is Shámláji near Idar. They differ from other Gujarát Shrávaks in holding a caste feast in honour of king Harischandra on the 7th of *Mágsar sud* (November-December). Their family priests are mostly Udambara Bráhmans.[2]

OSVALS are found all over Gujarát. They are divided into Visás, Dasás, and Pánchás or Letás. The story of their origin is that the Shrimál king Desal allowed none but millionaires to live inside his city walls. One of the lucky citizens, a Shrimáli Vánia named Ruád, had a brother named Sáad, whose fortune did not come up to the chief's standard of wealth. Sáad asked his brother to help him to make up the required million, but as he met with no encouragement he and Jaychand, a discontented son of the king of Shrimál, and many Shrimális, Rajputs and others left Shrimál and, settling in the town of Mandovad, called it *Osa* or the frontier. Among the settlers were Shrimáli Vániás, Bhatti, Chohán, Ghelot, God, Gohil, Hada, Jádav Mákvána, Parmár, Ráthod and Thar Rajputs, all devout worshippers of Shiva. Ratnasuri, a Jain priest, by working miracles, converted Jaychand their king and all the settlers, and calling them Osváls, formed them into one caste. This is said to have happened on the 8th *Shrávan vad* (August) A. D. 166. That there is some truth in the story appears from the fact that some of the Osváls have as

(1) *Bombay Gazetteer*, Vol. IX, Part I, pp. 101-102.
(2) Do. do. p. 96.

surnames Chaudhri, Dhonsa, Gola, Jhála, Johán, Kanayia, Madári and Oza. Of the three divisions, Visás, Dasás and Pánchás, the Pánchás or Letás rank lowest. They allow their widows to marry, and few Shrávaks or Meshri Vániás eat with them. The family goddess of all Osváls is Osia in Márwár. Dasa Osváls marry Dasa Shrimális and Dasa Porváds, but Dasa and Visa Osváls, though they eat together, do not intermarry. The family-priests of Osváls are mostly Audichya Bráhmans.[1]

PORVADS are found all over Gujarát. They and the Shrimális seem to have originally been one community. The family goddess of both is Mahálakshmi and their yearly feast in her honour is held on the same day. Porváds have two divisions, Visás and Dasás, who are found chiefly in Ahmedábád, Kaira and other parts of north Gujarát. Visa and Dasa Porváds eat together but do not intermarry. Dasa Porváds have begun to marry with Dasa Shrimális, but the old practice of intermarriage between Visa and Dasa Porvád Shrávaks and Visa and Dasa Porvád Vániás has of late fallen into disuse. The family-priests of Porvád Shrávaks are Shrimáli Bráhmans.[2]

SHRIMALIS are found all over Gujarát. They are divided into Visás, Dasás and Ládvás. The Dasás and Visás are found all over the province including Cutch; Káthiáwár, Baroda and other Native States, and the Ládvás are found only in Surat and Broach. According to their caste story, at Bhinmál in Márwár 90,000 families were created by Sri or Mahálakshmi, the daughter of the sage Bhrigu, out of her flower garland according to one account, and out of her thigh according to another, to maintain 90,000 Shrimáli Bráhmans. About the origin of the Dasás and Visás, three stories are told. According to one, those Shrimális who had first settled in Gujarát after wandering through the four quarters of heaven or *disha* were called Dasás, and those who had settled in the four corners of *vidish* were called Vidishás or Visás. According to another story, those Shrimális who sprang from the right side of Mahálakshmi's garland were called Visás and those from the left Dasás. According to a third, the Visás or twenties came to be so called because they are twice as high as Dasás or tens. The Ládva Shrimális were so called because they lived in the old Látdesh or south Gujarát, the neighbourhood of Cambay, Broach and Surat. Visa Shrimális do not dine with Ládva Shrimális. Among the Visa Shrimális there are seven minor divisions, Ahmedábádis,

(1) *Bombay Gazetteer*, Vol. IX, Part I, pp. 96-97.
(2) Do. do. p. 97.

Kathoriás, Pálhanpuriás, Patanis, Sorathiás, Talabdás, and Thará-diás, and among the Dasa Shrimális there are three, Horásáth, Chanápahua and Idadia. The Ládva Shrimális have no minor divisions. The three main divisions with their sub-divisions eat together but do not intermarry. In north Gujarát Dasa Shrimáli Shrávaks marry Dasa Shrimáli Vániás or Meshris. The family-priests of all Shrimáli Shrávaks are Shrimáli Bráhmans. The family-deity of Dasa and Ládva Shrimális is Mahálakshmi, and of Visás, Mahálakshmi and Sachai.[1]

UMMADS are found chiefly in north Gujarát. The two divisions Visás and Dasás eat together but do not intermarry. They are said to take their name from Humda, the *guru* or spiritual head who established the class. They are also called Vágadiya, from the Vágad or wild country including Dungarpur, Partápghad and Ságváda where considerable numbers are still settled. The head-quarters of the caste are at Ságváda near Dungarpur.[2]

MARATHA VANIS fall under eight heads. They are as follows :-

Bávkule.	Kulum, Kunbi or Marátha.
Kathar.	Neve.
Kharote.	Pátane.
Kudále.	Sangameshvari.

The only nexus between these groups is a common occupation and they neither eat together nor intermarry. They are described below separately.

BAVKULE VANIS are found only in Kárwár in the Kanara district. They seem to have come from Goa, their home tongue being Konkani. They have no surnames, and persons belonging to the same stock do not intermarry. Girls are generally married between seven and twelve, and boys between fourteen and eighteen. A boy is girt with the sacred thread on his wedding day. The bridegroom's father has to pay a bride-price of from Rs. 20 to Rs. 200 to the bride's father. Widows' heads are shaved and they are not allowed to marry. Their family deities are Shivnáth of Angdi in Kárwár and Mhálsa of Maddol in Goa. They are Smárts and consider the head of the Shringeri monastery their spiritual teacher. Their priests are Chitpávan, Karháda or Karnátak Bráhmans.

(1) *Bombay Gazetteer*, Vol. IX, Part I, pp. 97-98.
(2) *Bombay Gazetteer*, Vol. IX, Part I, p. 98.

They burn their dead. Their hereditary calling is trade. Most of them go hawking, carrying headloads of rice, cocoanuts, fruit, spices, betel leaf and cheap sweetmeats. They also own and till land. They eat fish and flesh but do not drink liquor. In ceremonies and customs they resemble Kudále Vánis.

KATHAR VANIS are found in small numbers in Jalgáon and Nasirábád in East Khándesh. They have such *gotras* as Bháradwája, Káshyap, Kaundinya, and Vashishtha, which are exogamous. Marriage with a father's sister's, mother's sister's or mother's brother's daughter is not allowed. Marriage with a deceased wife's sister is allowed and brothers are allowed to marry sisters. Widow remarriage and divorce are permitted. The *devaks* of Kathar Vánis consist of the *pánchpálvi* or the leaves of the mango, *jámbhul* (Eugenia jambolana), *aráti* or *shami* (Prosopis spicigera) and *boráti* or *bor* (Zizyphus jujuba). In ceremonies and customs they do not differ from the surrounding Kunbi castes.

KHAROTE VANIS are found mainly in the *Jámner táluka* of East Khándesh. They call themselves Lád Vánis as the name Kharote signifies a bastard. They have such *gotras* as Bháradwája, Gautam, Shándilya and Vashishtha. They allow widow marriage and divorce. Their *devak* consists of the *pánchpálvi* like that of Kathar Vánis. in addition to which it includes *hariáli* (Cynodon dactylon) and the *nim* (Melia azadirachta). In ceremonies and customs they resemble Kathar Vánis.

KULUM, KUNBI or MARATHA VANIS appear to have been evolved from those Marátha Kunbis who took to trade. They do not differ from Marátha Kunbis in their ceremonies and customs.

KUDALE VANIS, also known as Bándekar Vánis, are found mainly in the southern part of the Ratnágiri district, the Sávantvádi State, Kanara and Goa. They call themselves Arya Vaishya or Arya Dakshini Vaishya, but are popularly known simply as Vánis. They are called Kudáles and Bándekars after the *pethas* of Kudal and Bánda in the Sávantvádi State, where they are found in large numbers. Their original home appears to be Goa, where they were both cultivators and traders, but on migrating to the Sávantvádi State they gave up cultivation and continued only to trade, which is their present occupation. They claim to be Vaishyas, but the facts that till 1850 thay dined with Maráthás on the occasion of the Darbári *shráddha* ceremony at Sávantvádi, and that they occasionally married Marátha girls, seem to show that they originally belonged to the same stock as the Maráthás. It is, however, to be noted that although they took to wife Marátha girls, they never gave their daughters in marriage to Maráthás.

They have eighteen *gotras* which are exogamous. They are as follows :—

Bábhrava	Káshyap	Saunalya
Bháradwája	Kaundinya	Shándilya
Chanakash	Kaushik	Vishnuvardha
Harit	Nánábhaya	Vatsa
Jamadagni	Nitundan	Vishvámitra
Kapi	Purish	Vriddhavishnu.

Marriages are prohibited between members of the same *gotra*. Marriage with a father's sister's or mother's brother's daughter is allowed, but not with a mother's sister's daughter. A man may marry his wife's sister, and brothers may marry sisters. Polygamy is permissible, but polyandry is unknown. Girls are generally married by the age of twelve, boys between eighteen and twenty. Widows are not allowed to remarry and sometimes their heads are shaved as among Bráhmans. Divorce is forbidden.

The offer of marriage comes from the girl's father, who pays a dowry of from Rs. 50 to Rs. 1,000 to the boy's father according to his means. The marriage ceremonies of Kudále Vánis do not differ from those obtaining among the higher castes in the locality, the principal ceremonies being (1) Mandapsthápan, (2) Fulsádi, (3) Telsádi, (4) Kunku, lávane, (5) Vágnischaya, (6) Simantpujan, (7) Rukhvat, (8) Madhupark, (9) Muhurta-puja, (10) Lagna or marriage, (11) Kanyádán (12) Lájáhom or the marriage sacrifice, (13) Saptapadi, which is the binding portion of the ceremony, (14) Sáde and (15) Kankan Sodane or untying the marriage wristlets.

Kudále Vánis worship all the Bráhmanic as well as the local gods and goddesses, and observe the regular Hindu fasts and feasts. Although they claim to be Vaishyas, they do not perform the thread ceremony, the sacred thread being worn without any ceremony at the time of marriage. Their priests are Karháda or Chitpávan Bráhmans in Ratnágiri and Sávantvádi and Haviks in Kanara. They burn their dead. Their death ceremonies are of the standard type and they perform the *shráddha*.

They eat fish and flesh, but do not drink liquor. They have no objection to taking *pakki* from Maráthás.

NEVE VANIS are found in small numbers in Khándesh and Násik. They have twelve *gotras* which are as follows :—

Bháradwája	Gauriáyan	Káshyap
Champáyan	Gural	Kaundinya
Chittáyan	Kadaváyan	Manyán
Dattátraya	Kadyán	Shándilya.

Except that they also prohibit marriage between members whose maternal uncles' *gotras* are the same, they do not differ from Kathar Vánis in ceremonies and customs.

PATANE VANIS appear to be a local branch of the Kulum Vánis named after Pátan in the Sátára district where they are mainly found. They do not differ from the Kulums in their ceremonies and customs.

SANGAMESHVARI VANIS, named after Sangameshvar in the Ratnágiri district, are chiefly found in that district. They have several surnames, but they do not regulate intermarriage. Marriages are prohibited between members having the same *devak*, which suggests an original totemistic social organization and a Marátha origin for the caste. The principal surnames with their *devaks* are as follows :—

	Surname.	*Devak.*
1.	Bendkhale	.. Peacock's feather.
2.	Chaudhri	.. Coral.
3.	Chingle	. Conch shell.
4.	Gandhi	.. *Tulsi* (sweet basil).
5.	Gángan	.. *Iswogar* (Rhazya stricta).
6.	Khedekar	.. Cobra.
7.	Lugamkar	.. *Umbar* (Ficus glomerata).
8.	Redij	.. *Kalamb* (Anthocephalus cadumba).
9.	Sadvilkar	.. Kocha (Turmeric bulb).
10.	Shete	.. *Karanj* (Pongamia glabra).
11.	Takle	.. *Shindi* (Wild date palm).

Marriage with a mother's brother's daughter is allowed, but not with a father's sister's or mother's sister's daughter. A man may marry a deceased wife's sister if the former dies childless. Brothers are not allowed to marry sisters. Girls are generally married from ten to thirteen, boys from fifteen to twenty-five. Polygamy is permissible, but polyandry is unknown. Widows are allowed to remarry, but a bachelor cannot marry a widow. Divorce is prohibited. The marriage ceremonies of Sangameshvari Vánis do not differ from those of Kudáles except that they do not perform the *Saptapadi*. In other respects they resemble Kudále Vánis.

VANIA BHATIA.—A synonym for Bhátia.

VANIA SONI.—A synonym for Shrimáli Soni.

Name and origin.

VANJHAS * numbering 3,884 (1901), including 2,037 males and 1,847 females, are found principally in Káthiáwár, and in small numbers in Pálanpur, Rewa Kántha, Surat Agency and Jawhár. Seven males were recorded at Aden. In Káthiáwár they are to be found mostly in Bagasra, Jámnagar, Amroli, Dhoráji, Porebunder and Junágadh. The Bárots of the caste have a common saying that a man is a Vánjha either by residence in a village, or by profession, or by descent. Regarding their origin, tradition asserts that, when Parashurám decimated the Kshatriyas, some of them, to save themselves, surrendered to Hingláj Mátá, who promised to preserve them, provided they gave up the profession of fighting and took to weaving. They agreed and repaired to the Vindhyáchal mountain. A sage named Tantupál (*tantu* thread and *pál* protector) taught them the art of weaving. Having become Vindhyáchalis, they assumed the shorter denomination Vánjhás. They say their *gotra* is Márkand and their *shákha* Mádhyandin. They further claim to be of the same social rank as the Brahmakshtriyas. The names in common use among them, such as Keshav, Karsan, Jerám, Bhovan, Bechar, Purushottam, Rághav, etc., suggest that they were originally Vaishyas, while their section names and surnames lead to the inference that they were connected with Rajputs.

Divisions.

The following are the principal sections, those with a common ancestor being grouped together :—

1. Bárakhda, Chávda.
2. Chuván, Chocha, Sonagra, Mahávadia, Vegda, Nadha.
3. Gohel, Báberia.
4. Hingu.
5. Jádhav.

---

* From materials supplied by Mr. K. G. Pandit, B.A., LL.B,

6. Jethwa, Gadhia, Gerwala, Gomalia.
7. Kámoti, Mándalia, Khencha.
8. Mákwána.
9. Parmár, Sindhwa, Supeda.
10. Ráthod, Bhadresda, Amalchheda.
11. Silodra.
12. Surviya.
13. Seta.
14. Wádhel, Borkhatria, Wája.
15. Wághela, Solanki.

There are three territorial sub-divisions, *viz.*, Gadhia (from *gadh* or fort of Junágadh), Nagaria (from Nagar, *i.e.*, Jámnagar), and Wadhwáni (from Wadhwán).

Marriages are prohibited between members of the same or allied section. A Vánjha cannot marry his mother's sister's, father's sister's or mother's brother's daughter. Two sisters can be married to the same man, before or after the death of the elder. Two brothers may marry two sisters. A Vánjha of Káthiáwár cannot marry among any Vánjhás outside that province. The reason appears to be that the Káthiáwár Vánjhás do not eat flesh, whereas those outside mostly do. Boys and girls are generally married between twelve and fourteen. Consequently sexual indiscretions before marriage are rare. Should a marriage be delayed beyond fourteen, the cause would generally be poverty. If any indiscretion takes place, the girl's father is fined Rs. 50 and the boy's father Rs. 101. The caste is then entertained at a dinner and the young people taken back into the caste. Polygamy is allowed. Failure of issue, want of harmony, or misconduct on the part of the wife, are reasons justifying marriage with another woman. In theory there is no limit to the number of wives. In actual life instances are not known of men having more than two wives. Polyandry is unknown.

The offer of marriage comes from the boy's father through a mediator who is generally an elderly member of the community. If the offer is accepted, he is given Rs. 2-8-0 known as money for *chándlo*. The betrothal is called *sagái* or *veswál*. When it is arranged, molasses are distributed among those present. About Rs. 140 is the usual expenditure on a marriage. On an auspicious day a Bráhman Marriage ceremonies.

writes a marriage-note announcing the lucky day for the marriage, and carries the note on behalf of the girl's father to the boy's father (*lagan lakhi mokalavun*). The messenger on arrival is seated on a low stool, a mark (*chándlo*) being made on his forehead with red powder, and a present of a cocoanut and silver coin being made to him (*lagan vadhávavun*). Two days before the marriage, booths are erected, columns of six earthen pots are constructed at each corner, and a *toran* of five kinds of leaves is woven and hung at the entrance. Ganpati is worshipped, the presiding deity of the marriage booth being Kshetrapál. On the day previous to the marriage, a fruit *mindhol* is tied to the right wrist of both the bride and bridegroom, and turmeric powder mixed with water is applied to their forehead and cheeks (*mindhol bándhva* and *pithi chadhávavi*). On the marriage day the bridegroom and party (*ján*) leave for the bride's village in a procession (*fulenkun*). The bride's party come forward to meet them (*sámaiyun*). The bridegroom is taken to the marriage booth, where the bride's mother waves over him a miniature yoke, a churinng pestle, a spindle, etc. (*poukhavun*). The bridegroom is then seated on a low wooden stool, and the bride is brought out and seated opposite to him. A garland is passed round both. The sacrificial fire being kindled and fed with parched rice, *ghi*, etc., the couple go four times round the fire (*fera farwa*), this being the binding portion of the marriage service. Next the pair bow to the family deity of the bride and the marriage is concluded.

Widow remarriage is allowed. The levirate is not permitted. The widow's intended husband has to pay her Rs. 3 for *kamkha* (bodice cloth) and Rs. 80 as *des* or dowry. The marriage is celebrated by hanging garlands on the necks of the pair, giving *annas* eight in charity and distributing molasses among those present. Rs. 20 are spent by the widow's new husband on a caste dinner. A husband can divorce a wife if he cannot agree with her or if her conduct is bad. A divorced woman does not lose caste. She is allowed to remarry. The Hindu law of inheritance is followed with slight modifications. During the father's lifetime the son cannot claim a partition of the ancestral property. The daughter cannot claim her mother's *stridhan* on the latter's death, unless it has been promised to her during her lifetime.

Religion.

Vánjhás belong to the Hindu religion. Some are followers of Kabir, others are Rámánandis, and a few are Rámdásis. Their chief god is Vishnu. Their family deities are Chámunda, Pothad, Harshad, Jagrái, Varnai, Chorwád, Ghugarmal, Kankai, Ganga

Bhováni, Ashápuri and Wáchhdo (calf). Their spiritual guide is the Gosaiji Maháráj of Gokul. The red *pipal* (ficus religiosa), mango and *nim* (Melia azadirachta) are venerated, and their leaves and flowers are not plucked. Offerings of grain are made to the gods, and are received by the caste priests, who are Audich Bráhmans. On every new-moon day *lápsi* (wheat flour cooked into a thick paste and sweetened with molasses) is offered to Hingláj Máta in memory of her having protected the caste from Parshurám.

Death ceremonies. The dead are burnt. Children under eighteen months, lepers, and *sádhus* (saints) are buried. At burial the latter are seated with face to the north. The ashes are thrown into a river. The unburnt bones, if any, are thrown into the Dáma pool in the Girnár, if circumstances permit; otherwise into a pit close by a rivulet so as to be carried away in the rains.

Occupation. Vánjhás are hereditary weavers. Some have taken to carpentry, while others are husbandmen.

Food. The Vánjhás living in Káthiáwár do not eat flesh. They eat at the hands of Sonis and Sutárs. Lohárs, Hajáms and Rajputs eat at their hands.

VANJHAGOR.—A sub-division of Audich Bráhmans.

VANKAR.—A sub-division of Dhedás.

VANTIYAT.—A sub-division of Ganigs.

VARADHI.—A sub-division of Bhois.

VARAP.—A sub-division of Agris and Kátkaris.

VARIA.—A sub-division of Kumbhárs.

VARIK.—A synonym for Nhávi.

VARLI.—A sub-division of Bhils.

Name and origin. **VARLIS**, numbering 151,693 (1901), including 76,656 males and 75,037 females, are found in large numbers in the Thána district, Jawhár, Surat Agency, Násik, and the Khándesh Agency, a few emigrants being recorded in the adjoining districts. Their head-quarters are in Dáhánu in Thána. In Násik they are found in Peint and on the Sahyádris. In Khándesh, like the Bhils, they live in the mountainous tract that stretches about thirty miles west of Akráni.

The term Várli, according to Dr. Wilson,* is come from *varál* a small patch of cultivated land and means an uplander. It is connected by some with Varalát, the sixth of the ancient seven Konkans. But neither of these derivations appears convincing. Regarding

* Aboriginal Tribes II.

their origin nothing is known. The fact that they possess merely a vague notion of a supreme being, that they have no priests, that their ceremonies and customs differ from those followed by orthodox Hindus, that they attribute all diseases and misfortunes to the influence of evil spirits, etc., show them to be an aboriginal tribe only slightly influenced by Bráhmanism.

Appearance, dress and ornaments. The Várlis of Thána are darker and slimmer than Thákurs, with whom they are connected, Thákurs containing a Várli division who do not marry with other Thákurs. They are generally fairer and better made than Káthkaris, and differ little from Kunbis in appearance and feature. Few of those who live in Umbargaon shave either the beard or the head. The rest almost always shave the head except the top-knot. The Khándesh Várlis are tall and dark, very slim but well made, with features somewhat negroid in type. In Thána, the men go with their heads bare, and on their bodies have nothing but a loincloth. The women, except a few of the well-to-do, wear nothing but a robe, one end of which is drawn over the shoulder and chest. In Khándesh also the men wear no head-dress but part their hair in the middle and let it flow loosely over their shoulders. Their women usually go naked to the waist. The Gujarát Várlis appear to be more refined. The men wear a waist-band and a tattered head-cloth. The women wear a cloth over the head, a bodice, and a cloth round the waist. The women of the Khándesh Várlis wear on both legs, from the ankle half way up the calf, tiers of massive brass rings fitted so tight as to cause the flesh to shrink. These rings are never taken off, and are buried with the wearers. In Gujarát the ornaments of men are silver or tin ear-rings, silver or brass bracelets, and a brass finger-ring; those of women are: a silver chain worn on the head, brass ear-rings, coils of glass beads round the neck, and brass bracelets.

Language. The home tongue of Várlis differs little from that of local Kunbis. In Thána they always speak Maráthi except those in the extreme north, who speak Gujaráti. Besides the common tendency of the wilder tribes to clip their words, *kot jás*, for example, standing for *kothe játos*, they use several non-Maráthi words such as *nánge* to see, *át* here, *tat* there, *davar* an old man, *jhinguor* a blanket, *kámara* a servant and *gáytel* clarified butter. The names in common use among men are, Badga, Deváji, Dival, Gopáji, Hindis, Holis, Kákava, Láshis, Rupáji, and Shámji, and among women Harkhu, Kahwa, Rupai, Sonái, and Thakali.*

* Dr. Wilson (J. R. A. S. VII, 18).

The habit of Várlis is to some extent both settled and wandering. They live in small communities, often under their own headman and seem to avoid neighbours, except Kolis, Káthkaris and Thákurs, with the last of whom they have some affinity. For the greater part of the year they are settled in villages or *padas* (hamlets) of villages. But a certain number of them wander considerable distances in the dry weather in search of labour, especially if they have experienced a scarcity. A death in a family—especially if due to cholera or small-pox—is sufficient to cause the whole family to abandon the village, and to go elsewhere to reside, like the Kolis, Thákurs, Káthkaris and other forest tribes. The houses of the well-to-do are much like Kunbi houses. The dwellings of the poor are small huts, generally square, on a stone and cowdung or simple cowdung foundation, with a frame-work and rafters of wood, walls of reed or *karvi*, and roofs thatched with grass, rice-straw or palm-leaves.

Endogamous divisions.

The Várlis have four endogamous divisions, Shuddha or pure Várlis, Murdes, Dávars and Nihirs. Murdes and Dávars, who are found in the north of the Thána district, eat and drink together and intermarry, but they neither eat, drink nor marry with the Nihirs, who belong to South Máhim, Bassein, Jawhár and Váda.

Exogamous divisions.

The tribe is divided into a number of clans or *kuls*, the chief of which are as follows :—

Bantria.	Jádháre.	Nikhade.	Shanvár.
Bhángara.	Karbat.	Nimbore.	Sumbháte.
Bhávar.	Kirkire.	Pagi.	Tabále.
Bhendár.	Kondária.	Pileyána.	Thode.
Gabhále.	Meria.	Rávatia.	Thakaria.
Jádhav.	Miske.	Sankar.	Vángad.

Marriage rules.

Marriages are prohibited between members of the same *kul*. A Várli cannot marry within the degree of cousinship. A man may marry two sisters, the first married being the chief wife. A Várli will seldom look for a wife beyond the limits of the *táluka* in which he lives. It is said that marriages are not contracted between families whose occupations are different. Polygamy is allowed, but a man has not generally more than two wives, the first married being the chief. Polyandry is unknown. Marriage is infant as well as adult, the latter being more common. Sexual immorality before marriage is said by some to be connived at unless the girl becomes pregnant. According to others, a fine is imposed upon the guilty person.

Birth ceremonies.

On the fourth or fifth day after the birth of a child the mother's room is painted with red lead, and the midwife, who belongs to their own tribe, rings a peal on a pewter pot. The mother's purification is performed by the midwife laying on the ground some little heaps of red lead, repeating the name of some god as she touches them one after another, and tying a piece of thread round the child's neck. The neighbours and relations are treated to a cup of liquor, and if the husband can afford it, are feasted. The father must wait to name the child until a marriage is performed in the neighbourhood. He then goes and gets the name from the medium, *bhagat*, who, as noticed later on, always plays a leading part at weddings.

Among Gujarát Várlis, on the sixth day after a birth the goddess Chhatti is worshipped. The wall of the house is spotted with red powder, rice is thrown at the marks, a lamp is lighted before them and a dinner is given to women. The father names the child.

Marriage ceremonies.

The offer of marriage comes from the boy's father. When a match is settled, the boy's father gives to the girl's father liquor worth Re. 1-8-0, and if well-to-do, spends Rs. 2 more on liquor at his own house. Várlis require no lucky hour, day or month for their marriages. The service is conducted by an old lady of the tribe who is called *davleri*. The marriage ceremonies last three days. On the first day, a marriage booth is erected and offerings of liquor and cocoanuts are made to the tribal god Hirva. A day before the marriage the boy is rubbed with turmeric at his own house by his women relations, and in the evening a man is called, into whose body Vághyádev or the tiger spirit enters. When Vághya has entered the medium, oil is thrown on the fire to make it burn brightly and some rice is put into a water pot, *támbya*. In this water pot the medium reads the bridegroom's fortune and is consulted by fathers as to the best names for their children. Next day the bridegroom comes from his house and sits a little way from the marriage hall in front of the bride's house. On this several of the bride's relations come out and carry him into the marriage hall, and taking him on the shoulders, dance to the music of the pipe, *sanai*, and drum, *dholki* and *timki*. When they set him down the bridegroom walks into the house where the bride is sitting waiting for him and presents her with a green robe and a red bodice. She puts them on, and then, on the brows of both, marriage coronets and flower wreaths are tied. On the morning of the third day the marriage priestess, or *davleri*, ties the hems of the bride's and bridegroom's robes. Then, followed by the bride's and bridegroom's sisters carrying water pots and by the bride and bridegroom, she walks from the house to the marriage hall, sprinkling water as she goes. The party walk five times round the marriage hall, ending in the centre. On reaching the centre the priestess gives the bridegroom a knife or spear to hold in his hand. The bride and bridegroom are set facing each other, the bride looking east, and a cloth is drawn between them. Then the priestess, with a lamp in her hand, begins chanting the words of the marriage service.

When the priestess has finished her chant the cloth held between the couple is drawn aside, and she takes a water pot and, repeating some mystic words, sprinkles the couple with water. Then the pair are raised on the shoulders of two of their relations, and the guests, both men and women, headed by the priestess, form a ring and dance round them. The bride and bridegroom are then seated on a blanket, on which their sisters have placed a copper coin and sprinkled rice grains in lines and cross lines. The priestess sits in front of them singing amusing songs. The guests are then feasted and, after the feast is over, the bride, bridegroom, priestess, and guests go to the bridegroom's house. Here the bridegroom is rubbed with oil, turmeric and red lead, and a copper coin and a few grains of rice are laid on the ground and the bride and bridegroom are seated on them and fed. Then four earthen water pots full of water are brought and they are bathed. After they are dressed the priestess retires, and the bride leaves for her parents' house, where she stays for five days, and is then taken to her husband's house by her husband and his sister.

The marriage ceremonies of the Gujarát Várlis differ materially from the above. They are as follows :—

When a marriage has been settled the boy's father feasts the village on liquor spending Rs. 2 to Rs. 5 and fixes the marriage day. For two days before the marriage the bride and bridegroom are rubbed with turmeric powder. On the marriage day, to the sound of the *tur* drum, played by a Náik, and accompanied by a party of friends, the bridegroom goes to the girl's house. Here under a booth of bamboo roofed with grass the bridegroom is seated on a blanket. The father of the bridegroom pays the bride's father Rs. 5 as dowry, and gives the bride two clothes and a bodice, worth in all about Rs. 2-8-0. Either a Náik or a woman ties the hems of the bride's and bridegroom's clothes and joins their hands. The bride's friends tell her not to quarrel with her husband and from her earnings make good the money he has spent on her marriage. The bride and bridegroom then feed each other with cooked rice. A dinner follows. When the dinner is over the bridegroom leaves, taking with him the bride, who is accompanied by her relatives. During their stay for a day and night at his house, the bridegroom's father entertains the bride's relatives with rice, pulse and *tádi* palm beer. After five days the bride comes back to her father's house, and again after five days more goes to her husband. Among the Gujarát Várlis the practice of serving for a wife *khandádio* prevails.

Widow remarriage. Widow remarriage is allowed. A widow cannot marry a brother of her deceased husband or a member of his clan. The ceremony takes place at night, and is conducted by an old woman of the tribe. The couple are seated together and tied together by the necks, and released when the marriage is over. The bridegroom gives a black glass bead necklace to the bride. Members of the tribe are feasted. There is no form of divorce beyond the simple separation of husband and wife on the ground of infidelity on the latter's part, or by mutual consent. A divorced woman can marry again by the widow remarriage form. But if she leaves her first husband without his consent, the second has to pay the expenses of the first marriage as well as of his own. The tribe follows the Hindu law of inheritance.

Religion. In 1859, Mr. Boswell, the then Assistant Collector of Thána, described the religion of Várlis as follows :—

> Their religion consists chiefly in spirit worship. They think that every place is under the care of some spirit who lives in a tree or in a stone. Some they think unfriendly and spiteful, others friendly, and others indifferent, friendly or unfriendly according as they are propitiated or not. They seldom have recourse to these spirits except to escape from evil. They stand in great awe of them. They are much given to the use of charms to turn aside evil caused by ill-natured spirits or neighbours. If any one falls sick they suppose the illness to be the work of an unfriendly spirit or neighbour, and send for some charmer, who either performs certain rites by which he divines the cause of the sickness, and what particular spirit has sent it, or he is himself seized with a shaking fit, and being thus, as they suppose, possessed by a spirit, tells the cause of the sickness and the means of recovery. In such cases medicine is seldom used. The usual cure is the sacrifice of a goat, a fowl, or a cocoanut. The sacrifice is performed by a medium cutting the animal's throat, and then cooking and sharing it with the sick man's friends. At other times a sick person remembers that some one has lately abused him, and imagines his sickness to be the result of his abuse, and counter charms have to be used.

The Várlis seem to have made little progress in their religious conceptions since 1859. They do not employ a Bráhman at birth, marriage or death. They have no sacred books and no religious guides except mediums, who are augurs and oracles rather than religious guides. They are unacquainted with the Bráhman gods and have no idea of a Creator, or Supreme Governor, though they believe in a future state. The god whom they chiefly worship is Vághya or Vághoba in the form of a roughly carved tiger or a piece of wood covered with red lead. The favourite place for Vághya's image is on the village boundary or under a large banyan tree. They say that the tiger is Vághya's dog, and that he comes about once a month to Vághya's image to pay his respects, and lies there for some time. Every year in the month of *Kártik*, all Várlis go to Vághya and have a grand ceremony in his honour, daubing him with red lead and offering sacrifices. Their household god is Hirva, who is represented either as a bundle of peacock's feathers, as a hunter with a gun, a warrior on horse-back, or a five-headed monster riding a tiger. He is worshipped at intervals all the year round, but his great day is in *Márgashirsh*. They also worship the god Nárayan and the goddess Humai * who is represented either by a ball made from the brains of a cow or by little brass figures of cows. At the *Diváli* the childern put peacock's feathers into a brass pot and dance round it. Like the Káthkaris, they sometimes set up Cheda the devil-god in their houses, but unlike Káthkaris, they are not on good terms with Cheda and hang up his image only to appease him. They never worship Bhiri, Bhaváni, or Supli as household gods. They are said to worship Bahiroba and Khandoba. The only festivals they have in common with the Kunbis are *Shimga* and *Diváli*. Their gods and goddesses are not found in every house but in the houses of the well-to-do, where the rest come and worship, especially in *Mágh*. The mango and young rice are worshipped before their produce is eaten by the offering of a small portion thereof. The *tulas* sweet basil is worshipped fasting in *Bhádrapad*. The usual offerings are cocoanuts and liquor, sometimes fowls. In April two fairs take place which are largely attended by Várlis. One of these is at Mahálakshmi in Dáhánu and the other at Nagar close to Fattehpur in the Dharampur State, at a temple of Bhairu or Bhairav. At the Nagar fair a Várli Bhagat of Ráipur in Dáhánu called Pariar, in whose family the right is hereditary, hooks a couple of Várlis and swings them. After the swinging the Várlis gather in gangs of from 100 to 150 and forming shooting parties march to Asheri in Máhim, and Takmak and Tungar in Bassein, and burning and driving the forests for fifteen days, kill all the game they come across.

*** Humai perhaps the Dravidian *ammai* or *ummai* mother. Caldwell's Grammer (2nd Ed.), 492, 499.**

Death ceremonies.

Várlis bury corpses that have sores on them; other bodies they burn with music and noise. Those who have not the means bury the dead in all cases. At burial the corpse is laid with head to the south. The body is washed in warm water and wrapped in the best available garments, and a few rice grains are tied to the hem of its clothes and taken to be burnt either on the same, or if the death happened during the night, on the next day. A little way from the house the deceased's old clothes are thrown away and an earthen water pot is set down. When the body is laid on the pile the face cloth is torn, some rice and a copper coin are put into the mouth and two copper coins are put in the hands. When the pile has been lighted the chief mourner takes an earthen pot, makes a hole in it, and pouring water in an unbroken line, walks round the pile five times and dashes the pitcher on the ground, breaking it to pieces. When the burning is over, the ashes are put out and the bones are gathered and thrown away. They then go home, bathe, and drink. This bath is thought to take away all impurity from the mourning household. On the fifth day after death a medium, *bhagat*, is called, and while he chants mysterious words, the chief mourner lays cooked rice on a leaf on the top of his house and calls to the crows *káv, káv*. On the twelfth day the nearest relations are asked to a dinner. After the dinner an earthen pot is given to one of the guests, and a cocoanut is cut into small pieces by the medium and a piece handed to each of the relations. They then go on singing and drumming till morning. During the night the spirit of the dead enters one of his relations, who entertains the rest with the story of some event in the dead man's life, and after daylight, all go together to the village watering place and wash, and returning home, close the ceremony with a second drink. They perform the fifth and twelfth day ceremonies at any suitable time, and have a yearly service for the dead when the mediums repeat verses, kindle lights, and strew flowers at the place where the ashes of the dead have been scattered. Every year at *Shimga, Diváli* and when the new grain is ready, before any of the living have tasted it, the Várlis lay some cooked rice on the roofs of their houses for their departed relations. Among Gujarát Várlis, when a death takes place, the body is bathed, rubbed with red lead, and carried to the burning ground on a bier. The pyre is kindled by a son or other near relation, and when it is half burnt the mourners bathe and return to the deceased's house and drink toddy. On the fourth day the mourners go to the burning ground, gather the ashes, and sprinkle toddy over them. Balls of cooked rice or *pindas* are also placed in front of the ashes. They then bathe and return home, where they are entertained by the deceased's heir. In the case of a well-to-do Várli a dinner is given at the end of the year.

Occupation. Várlis follow no regular craft or calling. None of them are in the army, in the police, or in any branch of Government service, except the forest department. Their love for the forests is so great that, though there may be plenty of waste land ten or twelve miles from a forest and though they may be very anxious to get land, they cannot be induced to go so far from their woods. The daily life of those who own land and have not pledged it, and of those who till other people's land is much the same as the Kunbi's daily life. Those who have pledged their land, and whose assessment is not paid by a money-lender, are employed during the rains in tillage, and during the fine weather, in gathering and selling grass and fire-wood to pay their assessment, themselves meanwhile living on wild roots and fruits. A large number hold no land and are the tenants of Bráhmans and other large landholders. A third class are the servants, often the born servants, of some rich money-lender or Kunbi, to whom they have pledged their labour, or have been pledged by their fathers for twelve or fifteen years in consideration of having their marriage expenses paid. The daily life and occupation of the rest are the same as those of the Káthkaris. They are passionately fond of sport and will take their guns into the forest and stay there for days together, shooting *sámbhar*, *bhekri*, peacocks, and jungle and spur fowls over the forest pools and springs.

The Várlis of Khándesh lead a pastoral life, growing little corn and having large herds of cattle, the milking of which is the women's chief occupation. They are unwilling to part with their cows, but freely dispose of their bullocks as they seldom use the plough, doing most of their tillage with hand tools. The Gujarát Várlis, besides the produce of their small patches of hill-side cultivation and rice land, earn something from the sale of fowls, numbers of which they rear. They also act as woodcutters and gather firewood.

Food. The Várlis eat rice and other grains and all kinds of meat except beef, bison and *nilgai*. They are fond of fowls, and always cook them for their wedding and other feasts. They also eat land crabs of several kinds, the roots of the wild plantain and those of another wild plant which is very unwholesome unless boiled, tender bamboo sprouts, and some leaves and vegetables. The bamboo is eaten largely for some months before the rains set in. The

Várlis are stated to accept leavings from meals of the higher castes. They are immoderately fond of drinking, which by many of the poor is often preferred to food. If he has a palm tree or two, a Várli is content to drink toddy morning and evening without trying to earn anything until forced by hunger.

The Várlis can accept food from Agris, but not from Bhandáris, Vádvals or Kunbis. They can drink with Agris and Kolis but not with Bhandáris, Vádvals or Thákurs. They can smoke with any one except Thákurs, Káthkaris, Mahárs and the degraded castes. Members of no other caste or tribe eat with them. Agris and Kolis will drink and smoke with them. Kunbis will smoke with them.

VARSALIYAVARU.—A sub-division of Kurubás.

VASAVA.—A sub-division of Dublás and Bhils.

VASAVDA.—A synonym for Vasáva Dublás.

VASTRADAVARU.—A sub-division of Jangams.

Name and origin.

VASUDEVS, numbering 571 (1901), including 334 males and 237 females, are a class of wandering religious beggars. At the time of the 1901 Census they were recorded all over the Deccan districts except Poona, and in the Southern Marátha Country. They claim descent from Sahadev, the son of a Bráhman astrologer by a Kunbi woman. They are said to have come into the Deccan from Dwárka in west Káthiáwár about a hundred years ago, but there is nothing in their customs and ceremonies which can justify this statement. They look like Marátha Kunbis and resemble them in their religious and social customs. They wander from village to village begging alms, halting in temples and rest houses. Sometimes they lodge at Kumbhárs' houses, whom they call their paternal uncles or *kákás*, and present the house owner with two halves of a cocoanut.

Endogamous divisions.

There are two endogamous divisions of the caste, Proper, and Kadus or bastards for those who have infringed the caste rules. The two divisions eat together, but do not intermarry.

Exogamous divisions.

Their exogamous sub-divisions are identical with surnames. The common surnames are Hande, Kolavane, Konhere, Paigvede, Sumalkar, Watsar, Dhurve, Gavli, Peke, and Sálunke. Persons bearing the same surname may not intermarry. Polygamy and widow re-marriage are allowed and practised, but polyandry is unknown.

Religion.

Vásudevs are Hindus of the Smárt sect. A few are followers of the Vaishnava sect. Their family gods are Bahiroba of Sonári in Ahmednagar, Devi of Tuljápur in the Nizam's territory, Khandoba of Jejuri in Poona, and Fringái in the town of Poona. They also worship Vishnu, Vithoba and the local Márutis. They observe all the Hindu holidays and make pilgrimages to Alandi, Pandharpur and Tuljápur. They believe in sooth-saying, witchcraft and evil spirits. Their teachers are Gosávis. Their priests are Deshasth Bráhmans, but the death ceremonies are conducted by Kumbhárs.

The dead are buried. On the second day after death the chief mourner visits the burying ground, makes ten balls in the name of the deceased, and offers them flowers and vermilion. On the 13th day castemen are feasted. The *shráddha* and *mahálaya* are performed for the propitiation of the deceased ancestors. **Death ceremonies.**

Vásudevs are hereditary beggars. When a boy is old enough to beg, he is invested with his begging robes. On the initiation day a Bráhman priest dresses the boy in a long hat and coat, repeating verses and marking his brow with sandal paste. He is given five pice and a packet of betelnut and leaves. A feast to the caste fellows ends the ceremony. Vásudevs rise early in the morning, wash their hands and feet, put on a long hat adorned with peacock feathers and a brass top, and a long full-skirted coat. They take with them two metal cups or *táls*, two wooden pincers or *chiplyas*, brass bells, jingling rings, and a wooden whistle. They move about the streets begging from door to door, singing to the accompaniment of the *táls*. Sometimes, while begging, three or four dance in a circle, striking together their *táls* and *chiplyas*. They return home at about noon. A few of the Vásudevs are husbandmen. **Occupation.**

They eat the flesh of goats, sheep, fowls, hares, deer and fish and drink liquor. **Food.**

VATALIA.—A sub-division of Kumbhárs.

VAVANIYA.—A synonym for Musalmán Vágher.

VAVDICHASKI.—A synonym for Hajám.

VAYADA.—A sub-division of Bráhmans and Vániás.

VAZAGOHEREN.—A synonym for Bhátia.

VEDU.—A sub-division of Vághris.

VEGAO.—A synonym for Bhansáli.

VEGU.—A synonym for Bhansáli.

VELLALAS,[1] numbering 22 (1901), including 12 males and 10 females, are found in small numbers only in Poona. They are immigrants from Madras. Most of them are writers.

---

(1) Castes and Tribes of Southern India, Volume VII, pages 301—388.

VERAVADA.—A sub-division of Memans.

VEROLA.—A sub-division of Shrimáli Bráhmans.

VESKAR.—A synonym for Mahár.

VINVIA.—A sub-division of Rabáris.

VIR.—A sub-division of Gopáls ; a synonym for Bid Korava.

Name. **VIRS,** numbering 119 (1901), including 59 males and 60 females, are found only in Poona. They are a class of beggars devoted to the Khandoba of Jejuri, and as such many of them must have been confounded with Vághes, a class of devotees dedicated to Khandoba.

Divisions. There are two divisions of Virs, Proper and Dungat, who eat together and intermarry.

Marriage. Early marriage, widow marriage and polygamy are allowed, and polyandry is unknown.

Religion. The family god of the Virs is Khandoba. They go on pilgrimage to his shrine only, and to no other place. They observe all the Hindu holidays, worship local or village deities, and boundary gods and spirits, and offer them rice and pulse or meat. Their chief holiday is the bright sixth of *Magh* known as *Champa-Shashthi*, on which the silver image of Khandoba is dressed and worshipped with great pomp. Their religious teacher is a Gosávi, who belongs either to the Giri, Puri, or Bhárati sect. Their priest is a Bráhman. Their ceremonies and customs do not differ from those of the Marátha Kunbis.

Occupation. Their hereditary and only calling is begging. Men, women, and children of ten and over beg either at their own village or in neighbouring towns, and earn enough to keep them in fair comfort. They take their seats at Khandoba's temple at Jejuri and beg alms from pilgrims visiting the place, offering them the god's turmeric or *bhandára*.

Food. They eat the flesh of goats, sheep, fowls, and fish, and drink liquor. They rank themselves with Maráthás, but Maráthás look down on them.

VIRAKTA.—A sub-division of Jangams.

VIRSHAIVA.—A synonym for Lingáyat.

VIRSHAIVA KSHATRIYA.—A synonym for Mallava.

VISA.—A sub-division of many Bráhman and Váni castes.[1]

VISHOTAR.—A synonym for Rabári.

VISHUTI.—A sub-division of Jangams.

(1) For the full significance of the term *see* "Dasa"

VISNAGRA.—A sub-division of Nágar Bráhmans and Kansárás.

VITARIA.—A sub-division of Karád Vániás.

VITHALA.—A sub-division of Raddis.

VITOLANAS, also known as Kotwália of the Ghánch caste, Wánsphoda, Pálvada Kotwália, Vitolia and Vitoria, numbering 413 (1901), including 206 males and 207 females, are found only in the Surat Agency. The term Wánsphoda is used by outsiders and indicates the occupation of the caste, who appear to be a collection of outcastes earning their living, like the Buruds, by making bamboo baskets, mats, etc. They will admit into the caste Chodhrás, Dublás, Gámits and others of similar standing, and probably originated from these low castes. Name and origin.

There are no endogamous or exogamous divisions of the caste. Divisions.

Marriages are prohibited within four degrees of relationship. Marriage. Marriage with a father's sister's daughter and maternal uncle's daughter is allowed. A man may marry his wife's sister after the wife's death. Two brothers may marry two sisters. The habits of the caste are settled. There is no limit of age for the marriage of boys and girls. Girls are married even after they attain puberty. If a girl commits sexual indiscretions with a man of her caste it is condoned. But when the girl is pregnant, the man involved is forced to marry her. When the man happens to be of a lower caste, the girl is fined five rupees or so, and is at once married to a casteman. The money is spent in drinking liquor. Polygamy is permitted but polyandry is unknown. The offer of marriage is made by the bride's father when he wishes that his son-in-law should live at his house. Otherwise it is made by the boy's father. The bridegroom's father pays from ten to thirty rupees to the bride's father. The day for marriage is fixed by the castemen themselves. It is celebrated on any day of the week, except Saturday or Sunday, but usually on Monday. At the time of betrothal an old man on the girl's side says to the assembly on the bridegroom's side: "I offer this girl to you", to which one of the latter replies: "We accept the girl". On the morning of the marriage day the bridegroom and his relations start in procession with music for the bride's house. There they are met by the bride's friends, and the bridegroom is seated in the marriage booth, which is built in front of the house. The bride is brought in, and both bride and bridegroom are rubbed with turmeric powder and bathed. After bathing, they are dressed in their best clothes, and the bride's brother, receiving one anna for his trouble, ties the skirts of their clothes together. This and the joining of hands completes the ceremony. Then the party begin a dance which they keep up till the early morning. While dancing, the bride's brother or cousin takes the boy on his shoulder and the bridegroom's brother or cousin takes the girl on his shoulder. For two days the bridegroom and his party stay at the bride's house. Then, leaving the bride with her father, he goes home. His bride joins him after five days, and spending five days with him, returns to her father, coming finally to her husband's house after five days more. During marriage they worship the god "Pandar". A small shrine is prepared and an earthen image is brought from a potter's house and placed beneath it. Toddy, liquor and goat's flesh are offered to the image.

Widow remarriage is allowed. A widow can marry her father's sister's son or maternal uncle's son or any member of her deceased husband's family who is not older than she is. A widow can also marry the younger brother of her deceased husband. But when the widow has children by the deceased husband and when the younger brother of her deceased husband is a bachelor, it is obligatory for her to marry him. Widow remarriage is brought about generally by courtship. The widow has to obtain the permission of her parents-in-law by paying a sum of five to ten rupees. A widow remarriage can be performed on any day; but Wednesday is generally selected for it. No ceremony is performed on this occasion. A widow is generally consigned to the care of the new husband. A bachelor is allowed to marry a widow. Divorce is allowed. Either the husband or the wife can secure divorce by paying a fine of five rupees. The sum is paid by the party who seeks to be divorced. A divorced woman is allowed to remarry, and her marriage is performed in the fashion of widow remarriage. They follow the Hindu law of inheritance.

Religion. Vitolánás are Hindus and worship Dewáli of Songadh, Pandar Dev, Simario and Kákábalia the small-pox goddess. The most popular deity of their reverence is Dewáli. They take oaths in her name and offer goats, hens, etc., to her. They observe the *Diváli*, *Holi* and *Balev* holidays. To goddesses offerings of liquor, flesh, goats, hens and cocoanuts are made either on Sundays or Tuesdays. They worship their dead ancestors, images being prepared of them and placed in shrines made by potters. The images are painted with vermilion, and flags of pieces of cloth are erected before them

Offerings of fowls, goats, cocoanuts, etc., are made to them when their children fall sick or when they have taken vows. They do not revere Muhammadan saints. When epidemics break out they worship the god Pandar and make an offering of a clay image of a horse. They do not employ Bráhmans for religious and ceremonial purposes.

Death ceremonies

They bury or burn their dead. Small children are buried. Persons dying of cholera, small-pox and leprosy are buried, the belief being that by burning the disease spreads. While burying, the dead body is laid on its back, and the head is turned towards the south. The ashes and bones are either thrown into a river or left where they be if there is no river near. When life is extinct the body is bathed, rubbed with turmeric, tied on a bamboo bier, and carried by four men to the burning ground. The funeral pile is lighted on all four sides. On the second or third day, rice and pulse cooked together is placed on the spot where the body is burnt or buried, for the deceased to eat. A dinner is given to castemen. After two months, with the same ceremonies as those observed by the Náiks, a stone smeared with red lead *sindur* is placed below a tree as a memorial stone or *khatran.*

Occupation.

The hereditary occupation of this caste is to make baskets, winnowing fans, and mats of bamboo. Some are husbandmen and abourers.

They eat the flesh of sheep, goats, cows, bulls, hogs, fowls, ducks, parrots, ringed-turtle, cocksparrow, fish, rats, mice and squirrels. They drink liquor. They eat the leavings of other people.

No higher caste will eat at the hands of this caste. Only Bhangis eat at their hands.

VITOLIA.—A synonym for Vitolána.

VITORIA.—A synonym for Vitolána.

VOHORA SONI.—A sub-division of Sonis.

VOHRIA.—A sub-division of Dublás.

VRISHNIVANSHI.—A synonym for Bhátia.

VYAS.—A sub-division of Bhávaiyás.

WADDAR.—A synonym for Od.

WADHWANI.—A sub-division of Vánjhás.

WALI.—A sub-division of Kolis.

WANSFODA.—A synonym for Burud.

WARRAK.—*See* under minor Musalmán Castes.

WILAITI.—A sub-division of Musalmán Sidis.

WODDE.—A synonym for Od.

YADAO.—A synonym for Bhátia.

YADAV GOLLA.—A synonym for Krishna Golla.

YAHUDI.—A synonym for Bene Isráel.

YAJNIKVAL.—A sub-division of Bráhmans.

YAJURVEDI.—A sub-division of Deshasth Bráhmans.

YAKLARS, numbering 120 (1901), including 69 males and 51 females, are found in small numbers in Belgaum and Dhárwár. They are immigrants from Madras and are cultivators by profession.(1)

YATTIRAK.—A sub-division of Kudavakkals.

YELMAR.—A sub-division of Nhávis.

ZARE.—A sub-division of Mángs.

ZAREKARIS, numbering 34 (1901), including 14 males and 20 females, are found in some parts of the Deccan and Gujarát. In Gujarát they are known as Dhuldhoyás or Jalgárs. They buy the ashes and sweepings of gold-smiths' shops and try them by washing for gold and silver.

ZENDEVALE.—A synonym for Hatkar Dhangar.

ZINGA VAIDU.—A sub-division of Dádhichevála Vaidus.

(1) Castes and Tribes of Southern India, Volume II, page 203 (*vide* Ekán).

APPENDIX A.

1640. The first Pársi who came to, and settled in, Bombay was Dorabji Nanabhoy Patel. He came with his family from Suvali (near Surat) in 1640 A.D. and served under the Portuguese. When Bombay passed, in 1661, into the hands of the English, this Pársi transferred his services to the British.

1667. When the fortifications were being built, a Pársi, Mr. Kharshedji Pochaji Panday was the contractor who supplied materials.

1673. The first Tower of Silence—the Modi Tower—was built by Modi Hirji Wacha.

1673. The first Pársi Fire-temple founded by the same Modi, at Modikhana in the Fort. This Fire-temple no longer exists. It is said to have been destroyed in the great fire of 1803.

1690. Banaji Limji, the founder of the Banaji family, came to Bombay from Bhagvádándy at Surat, and settled here as a servant of the East India Company.

1692. Yakut Khan, the Sidi of Janjira, invaded Bombay, whereupon Dorabji Nanabhoy, the son of Dorabji Nanabhoy Patel (vide *supra*) collected an army of Kolis in Bombay and drove off the Sidi. In return for these services he was given the Patelship of Bombay.

1709. The second Fire-temple, the Banaji Fire-temple in Cama Street, founded.

1720. Jamshedji Bhimjibhoy Patel, the founder of the Patel family of Framji Sands & Co., came to Bombay from Tána near Surat, and opened in the Pársi Bazár the first shop for the sale of English and country liquors.

1721. The arrival of Jamasp Velayati from Persia, who originated the controversy about intercalation that led to the schism, which divided the community into two sects—the Sháhansháhis and the Kadmis.

1723. The Pársi Puncháyet formed about this time. Bomanji Rustamji, the son of Rustam Manock, broker of the English Factory at Surat, on his way to England to lay before the Directors of the East India Company his differences with the Chief of the Factory at Surat, stayed in Bombay for some time, and, with his brother Naoroji, founded the Pársi Puncháyet.

The first members of the Puncháyet, besides these two brothers, were the following :—

1. Banaji Limji (died 1734, aged 80), founder of the Banaji family of Bombay, who founded the Banaji Fire-temple in the Banaji Pore near Cama Street, Fort.

2. Jejeebhoy Jamshedji Modi (died 1738,) the grandson of Hirji Wacha Modi, who founded the first Tower of Silence in Bombay. Jejeebhoy was a contractor who supplied stores to the East India Company. Jejeebhoy's three sons carried on the work of the contract after him, and were leaders of the community. The eldest of these, Hirjeebhoy, died in 1754, the second Bogabhoy in 1771, and the third Manockji in 1773. On the third day (Uthamna) ceremony of this third son, there arose the question of adopting a daughter's son. The Pársis assembled on the occasion, resolved that the sons adopted must be from the male line of an ancestor and not from the female line, because daughters after marriage pass to their husband's families. In those days many a communal question was decided by the Anjuman (*i.e.*, the Communal gathering) at the third day Uthamna gathering of a leading Pársi, where a large part of the community, especially the elders who formed the members of the Puncháyet, were expected to meet. This question of adoption in the Modi family was taken into Court and the decision of the Anjuman upheld. The lady who adopted and the adopted son carried the question to the Privy Council, who, in 1795, threw over the decision of the Bombay Court and decided in favour of the lady and her adopted son.[1]

1730. The arrival of Manockji Seth from Surat. He settled in Bombay and founded Manockji Seth's Fire-temple in the Bazar Gate Street in 1733 and an oart or Wadi, still known as Manockji Seth's Wadi in Gunbow Lane. The Fire-temple is the head-quarters of the Pársi priests coming from Naosári. He founded a Tower of Silence at Naosári in 1747, and left in his will a large donation for a Tower in Bombay, which was wholly built from his money in about 1751 or 1752, after his death in 1748. It still bears the name of Manockji Seth's Dokhma (Tower of Silence).

1735. The arrival from Surat of Lovji Nusserwanji Wadia, who founded the Wadia family of the Master-builders of the Govern-

(1) For a history of the Parsi Punchayet, *vide* Dr. Modi's contribution to the Gazetteer of Bombay by Mr. S. M. Edwardes, C.S.I.

ment Dock. With him came a Mr. Dudley, the Master-Attendant. He had begun his life in Surat as a Mistri, serving under Dhanjibhoy, who was the Master-builder at Surat and whose ancestor Sorabji had served as Master-builder there. The same year saw the arrival of Camaji Kooverji, the founder of the Cama family of Bombay.

1740. The arrival from Naosári of a priest. Before this, other priests may have come; but this is the date of the first appointment under a formal agreement.

1749. The recorded date of the first Samast Anjuman, *i.e.*, the first public meeting of the Community in Bombay (16th April 1749). The occasion was the consideration at a public meeting of a letter from Naosári, saying that, from a religious point of view, the feet of the dead must be kept stretched and not left folded. This question had become a highly controversial one in the community. Even now, some, including the whole Naosári priestly community, keep the feet stretched and others keep them folded.(1) The public meeting resolved, that no one particular method may be prescribed, but that it may be left to the choice of the people.

1750. The Bombay Pársis wrote to the Naosári Anjuman, asking them to send two qualified (Bareshnumwála) priests to perform the Tána ceremony for laying the foundation of a Tower of Silence. This showed, that Bombay was then, under the ecclesiastical jurisdiction of Naosári. A fact worth noting in this letter is that it was signed, among other leading Pársis, by two Pársi ladies, wives of the above-mentioned Manockji Nowroji Seth, who had provided in his Will that these two ladies should be given an annuity of Rs. 2,000. These ladies did not sign their individual names but signed as "the two wives (Sethanis) of Andhiaroo (priest) Manockji Naoroji." They were interested in the matter, as their husband had made a liberal provision for the expenses of the proposed Tower.

1754. The Naosári Anjuman sent two more priests to Bombay under formal agreements. It seems that possibly these two priests were sent to replace two previously sent, who were

(1) *Vide* Khan Bahadur Bomanji Byramji Patel's article in the K. R. Cama Memorial Volume, entitled "A Brief Outline of some controversial questions that led to the advancement of the study of Religious literature among the Pársis" (pp. 172—82).

quarrelling among themselves, because a note had been found of the same year, saying that Khursedji Desai, a leading member of the Pársi priestly families of Naosári, had to write to Bombay, asking the two contending priests to cease their sacerdotal functions. In 1755, seventy-seven Pársis jointly sent a memorial to the Naosári Anjuman, complaining about the four Naosári priests who worked here, saying that they did not give Braeshnum (purificatory ceremony) to other priests and laymen here.

1754. In this year Rustomji Dorabji, a son of the first comer was exempted from the forced service of supplying carts to Government. He died in 1763 aged 96. His son Cowasji was appointed the head of the Market establishment of Bombay in 1763.

1756. A Pársi, Hirji Jivanji Readymoney, the founder of the Readymoney family, of which the present Sir Cowasji Jehangir, Bart., is a representative, went to China. He was the first Pársi to undertake the voyage. He died in 1794 aged 81.

1757. Behramji Homji (Behli Homji) rewarded by Government for his good services by a grant of a piece of land named Monotho at Parel.

1760. A second dry dock was built by Lovji Wadia for Government. In 1772 this Lovji was presented with a silver foot-measure with a proper inscription by the East India Company. Lovji died in 1774 aged 64. Manockji and Bomanji, the sons of Lovji, also received a presentation of a silver ruler and a shawl in 1776.

1775. Cowasji Patel, who, as his father before him had carried on successfully the Patelship of Bombay, in succession to his grandfather the first Pársi settler in Bombay, was, in recognition of his services, presented with a Dress of Honour by the East India Company. This Patel built in 1776 the great tank at Khetwadi, which is partly filled up now, but which is still known as Cowasji Patel tank.

1776. The Bombay Pársis wrote to the Naosári Anjuman, and complained that though the *Varasio* (a sacred and consecrated white bull, whose hair and urine were used for religious purposes, and on whose death another had to be consecrated for the use of his hair and urine) had died at Naosári about a year previously, nothing had been done in the matter of sending the *vars*, *i.e.*, the hair of a new bull, the consequence being, that as, owing to the prevalent cholera many deaths occurred, difficulties were found in performing funeral ceremonies for want of fresh *vars*. We find that, to meet such exigencies, a *varasio* was consecrated in Bombay itself by the Naosári priests for the first time in 1791. The next year the Bombay Pársis consulted the Naosári Anjuman as to the way in which a temporary Tower of Silence might be put up, to meet the immediate demand for an additional tower due to the spread of cholera in the city.

1777. There began in this year the disputes about inter-marriages referred to in the monograph. The Pársi priests took the daughters of the laity in marriage, but did not give theirs in return. Hence the laity, assembled at a meeting, resolved that thenceforward they would not give their daughters in marriage to the priests. In 1785 a layman, notwithstanding this resolution, gave his daughter in marriage to a member of the priestly community. The disputes increased and the matter went to Government, who, in 1786, appointed a Committee of Inquiry. The Committee decided in favour of the Laity. Government in 1786 appointed the Board of the Punchayet consisting of six members of the laity and six of the priestly class.

1779. A third Tower of Silence was built.

1783. The first Kadmi Atash Behram founded by Dady Nusserwanji (Dady Seth).

1787. It seems that in these times, those who wanted to drive in a phaeton had to ask for permission from the Government. Such a permission was given to Pestonji Bomanji Wadia in this year. It was this Pestonji who, in 1790, built at his own expense (Rs. 1,300) the Siri road leading from Gamdevi to the Tower of Silence. In 1790, during the great famine, known as "*Sadtalo*" he and his cousin helped many poor Pársis from Gujarát. This help was continued till 1791. Sorabji Manockji Seth, who died in 1798 aged 62, was another Pársi who helped people in this famine. He kept and maintained them in his family's *wádi* referred to above as Manockji Seth's *wádi*.

1793. It has been noted above that ship-building and sea-trading were occupations of the Pársis. In this year there were 27 Pársis who owned ships.

1796. The first regular Pársi school for teaching the Zend Avesta to children was founded in 1796 by Dadabhoy Nusserwanji (Dady Seth). He also founded, in the same year, a house or

Dharamsala to accommodate the Iráni Zoroastrians who migrated from Persia. In 1798 he founded for family use a private Tower of Silence in his own extensive compound at the foot of Malabár Hill, on the left of Siri Road, leading from the Sea Face to the Ridge on Malabár Hill.

The attempt to help the Zoroastrians from Persia was preceded by an attempt to help them in their own country. Nusserwanji Koyajee, who died in 1797, aged 80 had been to Persia for trade purposes. On return he arranged measures for sending help to Persia. He is said to have founded an Atash Behrám at Yazd.

APPENDIX B.

A Man shall not marry his

1. Paternal grand-father's mother.
2. Paternal grand-mother's mother.
3. Maternal grand-father's mother.
4. Maternal grand-mother's mother.
5. Paternal grand-mother.
6. Paternal grand-father's wife.
7. Maternal grand-mother.
8. Maternal grand-father's wife.
9. Mother or step-mother.
10. Father's sister or step-sister.
11. Mother's sister or step-sister.
12. Sister or step-sister.
13. Brother's daughter or step-brother's daughter, or any direct lineal descendant of a brother or step-brother.
14. Sister's daughter or step-sister's daughter, or any direct lineal descendant of a sister or step-sister.
15. Daughter or step-daughter, or any direct lineal descendant of either.
16. Son's daughter or step-son's daughter, or any direct lineal descendant of a son or step-son.
17. Wife of son or of step-son, or of any direct lineal descendant of a son or step-son.
18. Wife of daughter's son or of step-daughter's son, or of any direct lineal descendant of a daughter or step-daughter.
19. Mother of daughter's husband.
20. Mother of son's wife.
21. Mother of wife's paternal grand-father.
22. Mother of wife's paternal grand-mother.
23. Mother of wife's maternal grand-father.
24. Mother of wife's maternal grand-mother.
25. Wife's paternal grand-mother.
26. Wife's maternal grand-mother.

27. Wife's mother or step-mother.
28. Wife's father's sister.
29. Wife's mother's sister.
30. Father's brother's wife.
31. Mother's brother's wife.
32. Brother's son's wife.
33. Sister's son's wife.

A Woman shall not marry her

1. Paternal grand-father's father.
2. Paternal grand-mother's father.
3. Maternal grand-father's father.
4. Maternal grand-mother's father.
5. Paternal grand-father.
6. Paternal grand-mother's husband.
7. Maternal grand-father.
8. Maternal grand-mother's husband.
9. Father or step-father.
10. Father's brother or step-brother.
11. Mother's brother or step-brother.
12. Brother or step-brother.
13. Brother's son or step-brother's son, or any direct lineal descendant of a brother or step-brother.
14. Sister's son or step-sister's son, or any direct lineal descendant of a sister or step-sister.
15. Son or step-son, or any direct lineal descendant of either
16. Daughter's son or step-daughter's son or any direct lineal descendant of a daughter or step-daughter.
17. Husband of daughter or of step-daughter, or of any direct lineal descendant of a daughter or step-daughter.
18. Husband of son's daughter or of step-son's daughter, or of any direct lineal descendant of a son or step-son.
19. Father of daughter's husband.
20. Father of son's wife.

21. Father of husband's paternal grand-father.
22. Father of husband's paternal grand-mother.
23. Father of husband's maternal grand-father.
24. Father of husband's maternal grand-mother.
25. Husband's paternal grand-father.
26. Husband's maternal grand-father.
27. Husband's father or step-father.
28. Brother of husband's father.
29. Brother of husband's mother.
30. Husband's brother's son, or his direct lineal descendant.
31. Husband's sister's son, or his direct lineal descendant.
32. Brother's daughter's husband.
33. Sister's daughter's husband.

Note.—In the above table the words "Brother" and "Sister" denote brother and sister of the whole as well as half blood. Relationship by step means relation ship by marriage.

(*Gazette of India*, 9th September 1865, pages 981-982.)

APPENDIX C.

May it please Your Honour,

On the 24th instant we want to perform the ceremony of Fire. I therefore beg the favour that Your Honour will be pleased to order the smiths, silver-smiths, copper-smiths, sweetmeat-makers, Bhuttariahs, not to work by Fire, both day and night for private and public offices, as usual, which will oblige me.

I am with respect Honourable Sir,

Your most obliged and obedient servant,

(JAMSHEDJI BHOGABHOY MOODY.)

Bombay, 11th June 1802.

The Superintendent of Police will take care that this ceremony is performed.

(Signed) JAMES RIVET CARNAC.

APPENDIX II.

The Vindhiachalvásini.

The Vindhiachalvásini is a goddess believed to be the manifestation of Sarasvati or the goddess of learning. She is distinguished by the local worshippers from Mahákáli and Mahálakshmi, and is styled Mahá-Sarasvati.

The first half of the name, Vindhia, is the well known Vindhia or Vindya mountains, and the local offshoot where the shrine is found is taken as their eastern "beginning." It is a small hill about 500 feet above the plains. The temple is situated in a natural cave formed by the slipping of soft earth or layers of *trap* in a landslip caused by perennial springs or floods of water from a neighbouring waterfall. As the hill is formed of sedimentary rocks in horizontal layers like slate, it looks in its exposed parts like a "split up" mountain and hence the name (*viz.*, *Vindya* = split up, *achala* = mountain). The cave faces the north, and so does the image, which is carved out of the southern facade. There is nothing very special about the shape or the general outlines of the goddess. She has the usual eight hands and the beheaded giant lies in front in the shape of a buffalo. It is rough work and there is no attempt at artistic delineation. To the right of the figure is a male figure in a separate niche seated in the crossed legged attitude generally found in Buddhist temples. It is said to represent Márkandeya, the saint of immortality or eternal longevity on earth. On the eastern rock there is another niche occupied by the representation of Annapurna, the goddess of plenty, with her ladle and tongs. She has four hands. The door-frame is formed by, or supported in, a stone-wall to the south. To the west, the natural cave is left open a little beyond the termination of the chief rock which forms the roof and is then closed by the addition of a room, built, it is said, by one Suryabhatt, who performed a *tap* or long series of austerities on an adjoining square solid seat still preserved as a memento. To the southeast of this chief temple, which is approached by a broad flight of over 200 steps, another temple dedicated to Mahákáli is found. It is rock cut, underground, and possesses eight or nine secret ill-ventilated chambers. Tradition attributes it to one Bhavánand Swámi, a Shákta. It contains no rock-cut idol, but an idol is shown as the original deity, placed in an idol-stand and worshipped by the present occupier, which represents the cult of Bacchus. The image is of foreign manufacture, being carved out of a black basalt stone not found in the locality. There are grounds for thinking that the worshipper and the image have both come from Bengal. The chambers he occupies were possibly the habitation of those who originally carved the chief goddess out of rock, or the residence of the chief of the tribe.

Outside the original temple is carved the image of Bharat, the proverbially loyal brother of Rám of Oudh, and of Hanumán, his equally faithful monkey-general. A figure of Káli, in black basalt, and a couple of Lingams have been added subsequently. In front of the cave is a small temple built over the figure of a lion, supposed to represent the charger of the goddess, but curiously modern in appearance.

At present the goddess is specially propitiated on the 8th of Cháitra (Shuddha), the 8th of Ashvin (Shuddha) and the Diváli days.

Between the original rock-formed temple and the artificially carved cave of nine chambers, is a waterfall, nearly dry at the beginning of December, the moisture being supplied by a few fresh water springs. Near one of these springs is a naturally formed "hollow" about a foot deep, which contains clear fresh water. Another receptacle for spring water, said to be an old one, is formed by placing upright three of the local flat slabs to form a triangle fitted into a rock-cut groove, but the water leaks through. The triangular shape of this receptacle, called *Kund*, represents the *yoni* while its artificial construction suggests a modern origin, and this is rendered probable by the presence of the black Káli in the cave. The natural receptacle is called Bhairav *Kund* and there is a Kálbhairav carved near it. The triangular or modern receptacle has near it a fresh water spring which is apparently drying up.

On one side of the waterfall is engraved in the rock the following legend :—*Rudra deva Padma Sadáshiva.*

Rudra-dev means Mahádev or Shiva, and Bhairav is said to be his manifestation, and, therefore, the legend would mean

"*Sadáshiv, the devotee of Shiva.*"

The interesting feature of this inscription lies in the name Sadáshiv, which is not common in the North-West Provinces where the temple is situated, nor in Bengal, but is in use in the Bombay Presidency. The local priests, who are settlers from the banks of the

Sharayu, that is, from Oudh, declare that the hill was formerly inhabited by people who went to the Deccan and that Sadáshiv is not a local name. This tradition is in harmony with the tradition of the Prabhus, who believe they came to the Deccan from this part of the country after their migration from Oudh. The presence of the Sharayupade Bráhmans shows that people from the Oudh province did follow the course of the river of that name and did settle in this tract in pre-historic times.

The corroboration to the tradition of the Prabhus may be said, therefore, to be in (1) the fact that the goddess is called Maha-Saraswati, which is their chief deity, representing the power of "learning"; (2) the Annapurna or the Grecian goddess-of-plenty which is always given to the bridegroom at marriage as a gift from the father-in-law; (3) the name Vinzayi, that is *Vindhiai*, the mother of the Vindhia mountains. This is perhaps the original or primitive name of the goddess, latterly transformed by the Bráhmans into Vindhiachalvásini, a new grandiloquent Sanskrit form; (4) The Márkandeya Muni or the saint of eternal longevity, which is significant of a small band of people struggling for existence, whose sole desire was centered in the longevity of the life of their Chief Chandrasen's posthumous child, Prince (Prabhu) Somraj; (5) The presence of Bharat and Hanumán in the temple of a goddess, which is unusual unless it is explained by the theory that their loyalty to their master was the pre-eminent model for imitation by this band of devoted tribesmen who were determined to save their race from extinction at the hands of their Bráhman enemies headed by Parashurám; (6) The name Sadáshiv, which is very common among the Prabhus. Bráhmans of the Deccan also use the name, and this would be unconvincing without additional evidence as to who this Sadáshiv really was.

But the facts remain that Vinzai is not the only goddess of the Prabhus, and that all families do not accept her as their chief goddess; hence it may be that one only of the tribal sections passed through the Vindhiachal near Mirzapur.